To Charlotte Anderson, Anita Duffy, Charlotte Gerlach,
Ava Gipe, and Elsie Rasmussen—
special women, special memories;
and to two important "Charlies" in my life,
Charlie Duffy and Charles Gerlach.

As always, to Mom and Dad.

And my favorite work companion, Tillie.

Fifth Edition

Multiple Paths to Literacy

Classroom Techniques for Struggling Readers

Joan P. Gipe

Professor Emerita, University of New Orleans
Lecturer, California State University–Sacramento

Merrill
Prentice Hall

Upper Saddle River, New Jersey
Columbus, Ohio

Library of Congress Cataloging-in-Publication Data

Gipe, Joan P.
   Multiple paths to literacy: classroom techniques for struggling readers/Joan P.
     Gipe–5th ed. p. cm.
   Includes bibliographical references and index.
   ISBN 0-13-030899-4
     1. Reading–Remedial teaching I. Title.

   LB1050.5. G545 2002
   428.4'2–dc21   2001030404

Vice President and Publisher: Jeffery W. Johnston
Editor: Linda Ashe Montgomery
Production Editor: Mary M. Irvin
Production Coordination and Text Design: WordCrafters Editorial Services, Inc.
Design Coordinator: Diane C. Lorenzo
Photo Coordinator: Valerie Schultz
Cover Designer: Galen Ludwig
Cover Art: Courtesy of Joan Gipe
Production Manager: Pamela D. Bennett
Director of Marketing: Kevin Flanagan
Marketing Manager: Krista Groshong
Marketing Coordinator: Barbara Koontz

This book was set in Garamond by The Clarinda Company. It was printed and bound by Courier Kendallville, Inc. The cover was printed by The Lehigh Press, Inc.

Earlier editions © 1987, 1991, 1995 by Gorsuch Scarisbrick, Publishers.

Photo Credits: pp. 3, 65, 217, 276, 315, Anne Vega/Merrill; pp. 21, 50, 92, 107, 149, 290, Scott Cunningham/Merrill; pp. 178, 252, 355, Anthony Magnacca/Merrill.

Pearson Education Ltd., *London*
Pearson Education Australia Pty. Limited, *Sydney*
Pearson Education Singapore Pte. Ltd.
Pearson Education North Asia Ltd., *Hong Kong*
Pearson Education Canada, Ltd., *Toronto*
Pearson Educación de Mexico, S.A. de C.V.
Pearson Education—Japan, *Tokyo*
Pearson Education Malaysia Pte. Ltd.
Pearson Education, *Upper Saddle River, New Jersey*

Merrill
Prentice Hall

10   9   8   7   6   5   4   3   2   1
ISBN 0-13-030899-4

Preface

I would like to begin this preface by saying that this text, in particular this fifth edition, embodies a profound respect for teachers as knowledgeable, thinking professionals. I feel there is a need for such a statement when state legislatures around the country are mandating curriculum and program "police" are monitoring classrooms to ensure that teachers be technicians of a particular program rather than be trusted to teach as the professional educators that they are. Teaching is very hard work. It requires a view of oneself as a life-long learner. Teachers also view themselves as researchers, constantly questioning their methods and trying new ideas that might help them to meet the needs of all the students entrusted to them.

Just as classroom teachers are continually developing as professionals, so am I, as the author of this text. Between editions I regularly read professional literature, attend conferences, work with students of all ages, and discuss ideas with colleagues for the express purpose of identifying the methods and theories related to literacy assessment and instruction that represent the best of what is known in the field of literacy education. Therefore, as I have done for prior editions, I offer, in this edition, information based on the most current research in the field and the best thinking of literacy experts representative of a variety of viewpoints to present a balanced look at what we educators can do to help all learners achieve literacy. A continuing goal is also to provide teacher education students, classroom teachers, and reading teachers with a guide and a resource for meeting the needs of readers experiencing difficulty, including second-language learners, found in most classrooms throughout the United States. The use of quality children's literature as a starting point for literacy instruction remains a major focus.

This edition also strongly supports a view of literacy development that includes multiple forms of literacy. From text-based forms to technology-related literacy to visual literacy and the performing arts, incorporating a variety of forms is essential to meeting the needs of learners in today's world. The conceptual framework that best illuminates this view is Gardner's (1983, 1999) multiple intelligences (MI) theory, which is greatly expanded upon in this edition.

In addition, a conscious effort has been made to present techniques appropriate to, or easily modified for, any grade level from primary through secondary school. Students can experience difficulty at any point in their literacy development. Difficulty is often first noticed when students are asked to read material such as expository text that requires strategic reading behaviors different from those for reading narrative text.

WHAT IS NEW IN THIS EDITION?

- Expanded coverage of Gardner's multiple intelligences theory throughout the text. Included are margin notes that make explicit connections between a particular strategy and the specific intelligence it represents as an entry to literacy development.

- Expanded coverage of literacy development for second-language learners (SLL), including a major revision and earlier placement in the text of a foundational chapter on language diversity, and highlighting within chapter boxes particularly effective SLL strategies for each domain chapter.

- A new chapter on integrating the arts and literacy instruction. This chapter contains actual examples that describe specific activities for linking literacy with the visual arts, drama, music, and dance.

- A more logical arrangement and increased coverage of comprehension topics. There is now a separate chapter on meaning vocabulary, with chapters on general comprehension strategies, strategic reading for both narrative and expository material, and study skills, for a total of five chapters that deal specifically with comprehension issues.

- More integration of technology throughout the text with updated websites throughout as well as within an extensive appendix. There is also a Companion Website for the fifth edition offering opportunities for self-assessment, special information for teachers, and assistance for instructors, such as a Syllabus Manager.

- Expanded treatment of phonemic awareness and spelling instruction.

- Updates throughout the text for lessons, websites, suggested readings, and multi-ethnic children's literature.

HOW IS THIS EDITION ORGANIZED?

This edition continues to provide teachers with an analytic approach and techniques for (1) recognizing readers with difficulties, (2) identifying readers' specific strengths and needs, and (3) planning instruction that takes into account the special talents and multiple intelligences of their students.

The new edition maintains the two major sections: Part I, "Foundations," and Part II, "The Major Domains." Part I reviews the fundamentals of the reading process and introduces the nature of corrective reading; describes analytic teaching and the analytic process; presents foundations of language diversity; discusses reading-related factors such as physical, psychological, and environmental correlates; and describes ways to assess and evaluate literacy performance. Part II provides specific information on instructional techniques for the major literacy domains of oral and written language, word recognition, reading comprehension, meaning vocabulary, strategic reading for narrative text, strategic reading for expository text, and study skills, as well as for the special topic of integrating literacy instruction and the arts. The extensive coverage of instructional techniques for all literacy domains and for all grade levels is a strength of this text.

The chapters in Part I are best studied in the order presented, while the chapters in Part II are independent of one another and can be studied in any order. The text organization corresponds especially well to a course organization that includes a field experience or a practicum or clinic experience. While the basis of the text is supported by reasearch and theory, the overall flavor of the text remains more applied and practical than theoretical.

SPECIAL FEATURES

Certain format features aid learning from the text. Each chapter begins with a list of learning objectives, important vocabulary words, and an extended study outline. The terms listed as important vocabulary for each chapter are also boldfaced within the text for quick location. An annotated list of suggested readings at the end of each chapter helps the reader gain further understanding of the concepts discussed. These features aid the reader in preparing to read each chapter and in studying the material and aid the instructor in anticipating topics that may need additional explanation or hands-on experience. Within each domain chapter, margin notes make explicit connections between strategies and the multiple intelligences. Also within each domain chapter is an SLL box that highlights a particularly effective strategy for second-language learners.

The appendixes provide specific aids for readers and include materials for: communicating student progress to parents, locating relevant Internet sites, reviewing national Standards for the English Language Arts, identifying appropriate multiethnic children's literature, determining readability of written material, assessing instructional environments, reviewing the steps in the analytic process, examining readers' attitudes toward reading and self-concept, determining spelling development, analyzing writing samples, viewing creative books by young learners, and reviewing phonics generalizations. A glossary is also available for quick reference to a term's meaning. Finally, supplementary material is available; a Companion Website supports this book. The URL is http://www.prenhall.com/gipe

ACKNOWLEDGMENTS

Thanks to colleagues and students across the country, and to the staff at Prentice Hall, this text is now in its fifth edition. While its primary focus on the analytic process and the view that there are many ways to help a learner achieve literacy has not changed, this edition contains an expanded treatment of multiple intelligences theory, more ideas for second-language learners, and an even greater number of instructional techniques appropriate for, or easily modified for, older students. Suggestions for instruction continue to focus on the use of whole text through children's literature and include writing, and now the arts, whenever possible. In addition, teachers are encouraged and helped throughout the text, to accommodate their students' many and varied natural talents.

The feedback from my own students and from other instructors and students who used the previous editions provided the impetus for the changes in this edition. I sincerely thank all who offered suggestions for this new edition. Special thanks to Cherie Clodfelter, University of Dallas; Margaret M. Dermody, Loyola University; Mary Ann Dzama, George Mason University; Sandra Lettrich, Seton Hill College; and Julie Roth, California State University–Chico, for their thorough and thoughtful readings and reviews of the fifth edition. I hope all of you will find this edition even more appealing and helpful than the previous ones.

Joan P. Gipe

Discover the Companion Website
Accompanying This Book

THE PRENTICE HALL COMPANION WEBSITE:
A VIRTUAL LEARNING ENVIRONMENT

Technology is a constantly growing and changing aspect of our field that is creating a need for content and resources. To address this emerging need, Prentice Hall has developed an online learning environment for students and professors alike—Companion Websites—to support our textbooks.

In creating a Companion Website, our goal is to build on and enhance what the textbook already offers. For this reason, the content for each user-friendly website is organized by topic and provides the professor and student with a variety of meaningful resources. Common features of a Companion Website include:

FOR THE PROFESSOR

Every Companion Website integrates **Syllabus Manager**™, an online syllabus creation and management utility.

- **Syllabus Manager**™ provides you, the instructor, with an easy, step-by-step process to create and revise syllabi, with direct links into Companion Website and other online content without having to learn HTML.
- Students may log on to your syllabus during any study session. All they need to know is the web address for the Companion Website and the password you've assigned to your syllabus.
- After you have created a syllabus using **Syllabus Manager**™, students may enter the syllabus for their course section from any point in the Companion Website.
- Clicking on a date, the student is shown the list of activities for the assignment. The activities for each assignment are linked directly to actual content, saving time for students.
- Adding assignments consists of clicking on the desired due date, then filling in the details of the assignment—name of the assignment, instructions, and whether or not it is a one-time or repeating assignment.
- In addition, links to other activities can be created easily. If the activity is online, a URL can be entered in the space provided, and it will be linked automatically in the final syllabus.
- Your completed syllabus is hosted on our servers, allowing convenient updates from any computer on the Internet. Changes you make to your syllabus are immediately available to your students at their next logon.

FOR THE STUDENT

Topic Overviews—outline key concepts in topic areas

Strategies—these websites provide suggestions and information on how to implement instructional strategies and activities for each topic

Web Links—a wide range of websites that allow the students to access current information on everything from rationales for specific types of instruction, to research on related topics, to compilations of useful articles and more

Electronic Bluebook—send homework or essays directly to your instructor's email with this paperless form

Message Board—serves as a virtual bulletin board to post—or respond to—questions or comments to/from a national audience

Chat—real-time chat with anyone who is using the text anywhere in the country—ideal for discussion and study groups, class projects, etc.

To take advantage of these and other resources, please visit the *Multiple Paths to Literacy* Companion Website at

www.prenhall.com/gipe

Brief Contents

Contents

Chapter 3   **Language Diversity Foundations for Literacy Instruction   50**

Chapter 4   **Reading-Related Factors   65**

Chapter 5   **Reading Assessment: Indirect Measures   92**

Chapter 6   **Reading Assessment: Direct Measures   107**

I Foundations

CHAPTER 1

Fundamental Aspects of the Reading Process and Corrective Reading

Objectives

After you have read this chapter, you should be able to:
1. identify dimensions of the reading process;
2. explain the importance of teachers developing a set of beliefs about reading;
3. describe several characteristics of your own philosophy about literacy learning;
4. explain the nature of corrective reading instruction;
5. describe possible characteristics of corrective readers.

Key Concepts and Terms

academic reading	graphophonic cue system	pragmatic cue system
aliterates	holistic view	proficient reader
balanced reading	interactive view	recreational reading
best practices	language	schematic cue system
corrective reading	language comprehension	semantics
early reader	language production	skills-based view
emergent literacy	morphology	syntax
emergent reader	multiple intelligences	viewing
fluent reader	phonology	visually representing

3

As teachers, we continuously seek better ways to facilitate the learning of *all* our students. My years of experience as a classroom teacher and as a teacher educator have led me to believe strongly in certain principles of learning that I try to model in my own teaching. I also view these learning principles as universal; that is, they apply to all learners of all ages and stages of development. Learning principles that I try to put into practice and that are equally applicable to literacy development are:

- All learners are capable and can be trusted to take responsibility for their own learning.
- Learning is a social process—all learners share a need to communicate and learn from each other.
- Learning is a building process, and so learning occurs over time.
- What is learned is unique for each learner, as what you already know affects new learning.
- Reflection and self-monitoring are necessary to learning.
- Learning occurs in the context of use; that is, we learn by doing, by being actively involved. Thus written language (reading and writing), like oral language, is learned "in the context of its use" (Whitmore & Goodman, 1996, p. 3).

When I teach a university course that is intended to help preservice teachers learn techniques for assessing and instructing readers having difficulty, I am careful to include my university students in the planning of the curriculum that will be implemented in accompanying tutoring sessions. My students work with learners of all ages, from kindergarten through high school. I provide opportunities for small- and whole-group sharing and discussions, and expect students to read professionally and reflect on that reading, plan instruction specific to a particular learner, monitor that learner's progress, and construct a portfolio of their own learning.

The vignette that follows is intended not only to provide a view of their experiences, but also to help others visualize how they might design their classroom environments to support literacy growth for all learners, especially those identified as having difficulty in reading and language arts. The activities and procedures used in this clinic-type setting also apply to a classroom setting. Classrooms can be organized to accommodate all of the ideas presented here. In this vignette the children being tutored are referred to as *learners* and *pupils*. The term *students* refers to university students.

Vignette	The twenty-two university students enter the large classroom with their young charges, ranging in age from 4 to 14. Some head for the message board to check for important information or relevant newspaper articles; others sign in on the Attendance Sheet and then get materials from the book cart. Most start the tutoring session by going first to a table or desk to talk about an overview of the day's work. Several move quickly to one of the centers located throughout the room (art, writing, publishing, math, science), or check the schedule for the computer lab. CD-ROMs are signed out and carried off to the lab, where pupils will also read and answer their e-mail and visit sites on the World Wide Web. Groups of learners are working together on different projects. One interesting project is a Blindfolded Treasure Hunt to accompany the story *The Cay* (Taylor, 1969) in which one of the main characters goes blind. Others are working in the science center on answering the question posted there, "How many different kinds of seashells are there?" Later, a new question appears, along with the skin of a water snake: "How are water snakes and sea snakes alike and how are they different?" (Questions are posted by any member of this learning community, but whoever posts a question must also provide materials that assist other visitors to the center in getting started on finding an answer to the question.) One young pupil chooses a book on tape to listen to while he follows along in the book. Another listens to a tape of whale songs as a follow-up to reading about the sounds that whales make. Yet another learner creates a song about sea life and records her sung version on tape. Pupils add new and interesting words to the Word Wall, and examine them later for similar characteristics, or for categorizing. Invitations are created and sent for others to come and celebrate the accomplishment of a learner, or to participate in the newly developed Blindfolded Treasure Hunt. Since it is the end of the week, during the last five to ten minutes of the session university students and their pupils sit together and complete a weekly progress report that presents a self-evaluation of the week's work by the learner, an evaluation by the tutor/teacher, and a place for parent comments (see Appendix A). All three parties provide their signature on the form. As the semester progresses, both students and pupils work on their respective literacy portfolios that will demonstrate areas of growth, new knowledge, and other relevant information.

This is the flavor of the multi-age, inquiry-based, thematic curriculum that the university students and I have designed together. The theme, "At the Beach," lends itself to a wide variety of topics to be explored, as well as use of a wealth of quality children's literature (e.g., *The Sign of the Seahorse* by Graeme Base; *A House for Hermit Crab* by Eric Carle; *The Magic School Bus on the Ocean Floor* by Joanna Cole; *Swimmy* by Leo Lionni; *Sukey and the Mermaid* by Robert San Souci; and *The Whale's Song* by Dyan Sheldon) and CD-ROMs (e.g., Microsoft's *Explorapedia, Oceans,* and *The Magic School Bus Explores the Ocean;* the Discovery Channel's *Seaside Adventure* and *Ocean Planet;* and Living Books' *Just Grandma and Me* by Random House/Broderbund).

As course instructor I often model instructional strategies, so I began the first session by modeling the K–W–L strategy (see Chapter 12) and at the same time introduced our theme by brainstorming "At the Beach" with the new pupils. Thus began the Word Wall of words related to this theme (see Chapter 8). I also presented the first inquiry activity by showing a sand dollar and asking the young learners to look at it, touch it, and listen to its interior pieces when shaken. Questions like "What is this?," "Where would you find one of these?," and "What do you think is inside?" lead to further K–W–L-type activities between the university students and their pupils. This inquiry activity is also the lead-in for an introduction to the World Wide Web and the concept of bookmarking sites of interest to which pupils will want to return (see Appendix B for some relevant Web sites). Through these activities the tone for the semester was set, and these learners began to explore, read about, and write about a variety of topics of interest to them such as sea life, oceans, beaches, and travel in general. For example, one 14-year-old, who stated quite emphatically on the first day that he was only interested in sports and not at all happy about coming to this summer program, became quite enthralled with traveling across the ocean to lands where there are castles. By visiting various locations on the Internet he was able to find many castles that one may tour and stay in, along with pricing information. And since the currency listed needed to be translated into U.S. currency, a meaningful math lesson ensued.

These thematic activities also provided a wealth of information to be used in assessing learners' literacy needs and planning appropriate instruction. Pupils were motivated because they were pursuing topics of interest to them from among a variety of venues, and could choose the nature of their reading and writing tasks.

As this brief scenario suggests, students of *all* ages sometimes need assistance in learning to read or in extending their literacy development. Such assistance is one of the most important tasks facing classroom teachers at all levels. It is also a challenging task because paths to literacy development are often unique and distinct. Use of hands-on activities, computer technology, music, art, drama, group work, and self-evaluation, as well as creative writing and reading material of one's choice, provides a context that allows pupils to cultivate their linguistic intelligence even when their strengths may lie elsewhere (Gardner, 1983, 1999).

DIMENSIONS OF READING

It is important to note that while the term *reading* is being used, it has become more and more apparent that *literacy* learning involves writing, speaking, listening, viewing, visually representing, and thinking, as well as reading. Thus, the *process* of reading is complex. How it all actually works is not clear, but some aspects that usually interact during the process have been identified.

Reading Is a Language Process

The sophisticated system through which meaning is expressed is **language.** Language enables individuals to communicate—that is, to give and receive information, thoughts, and ideas; it can be oral, written, or visual. Communication does not exist in a vacuum. A message has both a sender and a receiver. The sender has specific intentions and produces a message that is reconstructed by the receiver. The sender uses this language system for particular functions, such as sharing a personal experience, asking a question, or complaining. The sender can also use language to persuade, inspire, comfort, or encourage others.

Sending a message is called **language production,** which can be oral, written, or visual; receiving or decoding the message is **language comprehension.** Speaking, therefore, is the production of oral language, while listening is the comprehension of oral language. Similarly, writing and reading are the production and comprehension, respectively, of written language. As young children learn to read and write, they are already giving and receiving information by speaking and listening. We know that a strong oral language base facilitates reading and writing development. Likewise, **visually representing** and **viewing** are the production and comprehension of visual language. Young children also have a background of producing and comprehending visual language (or meaning in images) that can be built upon in learning to read and write.

Some components of language important to the reading process are phonology, syntax, morphology, and semantics. Briefly, **phonology** refers to the system of speech sounds, **syntax** to word order and the way words are combined into phrases and sentences, **morphology** to the internal structure of words and meaningful word parts (prefixes, suffixes, word endings and inflections, compound words), and **semantics** to word meanings or to understanding the concepts represented by the language.

While reading is basically an act of communication between an author and a reader, it is only one aspect of the communication process. Reading, writing, speaking, listening, viewing, and visually representing are mutually supportive and must be seen as interrelated and developing concurrently. Reading, listening, and viewing share common receptive and constructive processes, while writing, speaking, and visually representing share common expressive processes. As Fox and Allen (1983) state:

> Writing [and visually representing] suggests the reading [and viewing] of one's compositions by others and the input that reading experiences can give to written language. In addition, speaking will be drawn out with writing because it is the other expressive skill. Since oral language initially precedes written language, experiences in oral composition influence success in written composition. Listening, the remaining segment, is firmly attached to speaking and reading . . . because the language that one hears, especially the "story language" one hears [or views] when books are read aloud or when stories are told, is another source of written expression. (p. 12)

A firm language base, resulting from many hours spent experiencing oral, written, and visual language through activities such as book sharings, is crucial to success in reading. Fortunately, all students bring to school a wealth of language and cultural experiences upon which teachers can build literacy. K. S. Goodman (1968, 1973, 1994, 1996) has helped us understand the language cue systems so important for reading growth by analyzing the oral reading behaviors of students and demonstrating how they use specific language cues to recognize words and predict meaning in the reading process. He terms these language cues the *graphophonic, syntactic*, and *semantic* cue systems. As users of language, students bring to the reading task expectations about language that are basic to their ability to make sense of printed text. For example, assume a student encounters the unknown word *sidewalk* in the sentence "The dog ran down the _____." The reader may rely on one or all of the following: (1) the syntactic cue system, which indicates the unknown word is a noun, (2) the semantic cue system, which indicates the possible words that would make sense (e.g., street, alley, path, stairs, hill, sidewalk, and so on) in the context of the sentence, and (3) the **graphophonic cue system,** which provides sound and symbol clues, in this case, an initial sound of *s,* a final sound of *k,* and a possible long *i* because of the vowel–consonant–silent *e* pattern.

Additionally, language is only really meaningful "when functioning in some environment" (Halliday, 1978, p. 28). Therefore, language users also develop a **pragmatic**

cue system—that is, rules related to the use of language in social or cultural contexts. For example, the sentence *This is cool* can be interpreted several ways depending on the context of the situation. Consider the two different meanings of the sentence if it were spoken by a person tasting some coffee that has just been poured for them in a restaurant or by two teenagers enjoying a rock concert. Similarly, one might say in an informal conversational setting, "Nice to meet ya"; in a more formal context, such as an academic gathering, this statement might become, "It is a pleasure to meet you." The **schematic cue system** is viewed by some as separate from the semantic system, and is defined as information from a reader's prior knowledge or personal associations with both the content and the structure of the text. Thus, reading about a familiar topic or within a familiar format (e.g., narratives) allows readers to use their schematic cue system (see next section). Because language is so critical as an underlying process for success in reading, students who are linguistically diverse require special attention. This topic is discussed in more depth in Chapter 3.

Reading Is a Cognitive Process

Cognition refers to the nature of knowing, or the ways of organizing and understanding our experiences. The system of cognitive structures that represent knowledge about events, objects, and relationships in the world is called a *schema* (pl. *schemata*). Thus, the formation of concepts is basic to cognition. The more experience learners have with their environment, and the richer that environment, the more concepts they develop. A limited conceptual development affects reading. Even if a reader correctly pronounces the words, understanding is hindered unless those words represent familiar concepts. Active involvement with their world provides students with the necessary background for concept development and, ultimately, for literacy development. Schema theory and cognitive development are crucial to reading comprehension, and are discussed in more detail in Chapter 9.

Reading Is a Psychological or Affective Process

The student's self-concept, attitudes in general, attitudes toward reading, interests, and motivation for reading affect the reading process. Each of these factors is closely related to the student's experiential background in home, school, and community. Frank Smith (1986) contends that learning is never separated from feeling. He states, "Even if we succeed in learning under conditions that are threatening, embarrassing, or punitive, then we will experience the same miserable feelings whenever we try to practice whatever we learned" (p. 60).

Psychological factors are crucial both in helping students learn to read and to improve their reading. The desire to learn or improve reading must be present; unless success is experienced, the tendency is to avoid the reading situation. This is only human nature; all of us avoid the things we do poorly, or associate with negative feelings.

Developing positive self-concepts and attitudes is often the most important part of a student's reading program. This important dimension of the reading process is discussed in more detail in Chapters 4 and 6.

Reading Is a Social Process

Readers are influenced by the social culture of which they are a part. If reading is a valued act in the home or in the classroom, then it is likely to be valued by the reader. Sharing what has been read quite obviously requires a social interaction with at least one other person. Even past social experiences can influence present reading. An adult reader fondly recalls being read to by a parent at bedtime, and now carries on that tradition with his or her own child. In addition, the meaning readers bring to text reflects the knowledge, attitudes, concerns, and social issues of their particular communities at a particular point in time. Thus, the possibility exists that books read several years prior might now be reread with completely different understandings or appreciations.

Probably the most common application of reading as a social process is discussion, or dialogue, as it relates to reading comprehension and learning from text. Dialogue "is a natural way for people to learn and construct meaning" (Peterson & Eeds, 1990, p. 21). There is increasing evidence that as students participate in small-group discussions such as literature circles, book clubs, or reader response groups, they acquire deeper understanding of text, increased higher-level thinking and problem-solving ability, and communication skills (Palincsar, 1987; Morrow & Smith, 1990; Eeds & Wells, 1989; Almasi, 1996; Villaume & Hopkins, 1995; McMahon & Raphael, 1997). Almasi (1996) concludes that "students who talk about what they read are more likely to engage in reading" (p. 19) and "as students participate in discussions of literature, there are many opportunities for cognitive, social, emotional, and affective growth" (p. 21).

Reading Is a Physiological Process

Anticipating the reading act in turn activates the language and cognitive processes (i.e., nonvisual information). However, for reading to proceed, printed stimuli (i.e., visual information) must be received by the brain. These stimuli normally enter through a visual process. If a reader is blind, the stimuli may enter through a tactile process, as in using braille, or through auditory means, as in listening to a taped reading. Under normal circumstances the reader must be able to focus on the printed stimuli, move the eyes from left to right, make return sweeps, discriminate likenesses and differences, and discriminate figure-ground relationships. In addition to visual acuity, physiological factors include good health, auditory acuity, and neurological functioning. Physiological (to include neurological) and other reading-related factors, such as psychological and environmental factors, are discussed in Chapter 4.

Reading Is an Emerging Process

Emergent literacy is a term describing the transformation that occurs when young children, having been exposed to printed material, actively attempt to discover how oral and written language are created. Viewed from the child's perspective, early literacy learning is as much a social activity as it is a cognitive one. Studies (Doake, 1988; Henderson & Beers, 1980; Kastler, Roser, & Hoffman, 1987; Taylor & Dorsey-Gaines, 1988; Teale & Sulzby, 1986) observing children in their homes and communities provide the basis for the following conclusions (modified from Teale & Sulzby, 1989, pp. 3–4):

1. Literacy begins at birth as children are placed in contact with print in their environment (e.g., alphabet books, being read to, labels, signs, and logos). Experimentation with writing begins as scribbles.
2. Children view literacy as a functional activity. Their experiences show literacy events as ways to get things done (e.g., reading a recipe to bake cookies, writing checks to pay bills, viewing a city map to find a particular street).

3. Aspects of literacy development occur simultaneously in young children and in relationship to oral language development. As reading or viewing experiences influence oral language, writing and drawing (i.e., visually representing) experiences influence reading, and developing reading ability influences writing. Thus each of these areas provides support for the development of the others.

4. Children learn through active involvement, constructing for themselves an understanding of written language. Through a process of trial and error, of forming and testing hypotheses about the symbols used in written language and the sounds used in oral language, children learn how written language works. Their emerging knowledge is revealed by their attempts at spelling.

These insights strongly imply a need to connect reading and writing instruction more closely than has been done in the past. This important component of effective literacy instruction is discussed in Chapter 7.

Emergent literacy also supports the view that literacy develops continuously and over time when children are helped to explore and interact with written language. This development proceeds from what many refer to as **emergent readers,** or readers who engage in pretend reading and who are just beginning to understand the nature and meaning of print, to **early readers** who are learning strategies for word recognition and comprehension, to **proficient readers** who demonstrate skills, strategies, and reading achievement appropriate to their age and grade level, and finally to **fluent readers** who read comfortably with both accuracy and comprehension at levels beyond normal expectations. Roller (1998) describes the development of readers and writers, and refers to developing readers as emergent, beginning, and transition. Roller also provides specific developmental characteristics related to word identification and recognition, comprehension, fluency, and writing for each of these levels (see p. 48 in her text).

Reading Represents a Linguistic Intelligence

Fortunately, beliefs are shifting about how people learn, with a growing recognition that we are "smart" in different ways. There is not one way to learn or to demonstrate ability.

> [Children labeled] "disabled" and "handicapped" students were able to learn to speak and otherwise communicate their thoughts, needs, feelings, and ideas. . . . These children were able to acquire reading and writing behaviors as they "read" environmental print, scribble-wrote their names in coloring books, and talked about all they planned to read and write about once they got to school. When they arrived at school, however, everything changed. . . . These children learned that they were different [not that they only learned differently], and they were taught that they could not learn. . . . Programs in many schools attempt to make all children the same instead of celebrating and building upon their strengths and differences. (Strickland, 1995, p. xi)

In 1983 Howard Gardner published *Frames of Mind,* proposing a theory of **multiple intelligences,** or an expanded framework for thinking about intelligence. In his book *Intelligence Reframed: Multiple Intelligences for the 21st Century* (1999), Gardner has continued to refine and expand this theory of multiple intelligences (MI theory), and to clarify implications for its use. He now defines an intelligence as "a biopsychological potential to process information that can be activated in a cultural setting to solve problems or create products that are of value in a culture" (pp. 33–34). In other words, these potentials are essentially neural in nature and every member of the species has them. These intelligences are, however, only realized as a consequence of experiential, cultural, and motivational factors. A person is, therefore, not "smart" or "stupid" across the board. Depending on the values of a person's culture, opportunities, and/or personal decisions by the individual, his or her family and teachers, and others, these biopsychological potentials will or will not be activated. For example, the ability to use language and explore mathematical concepts is especially valued in our society, while spatial intelligence is valued in Eskimo cultures "because noticing subtle differences in snow and ice surfaces is critical to survival" (Cecil & Lauritzen, 1994, p. 5).

Gardner has proposed eight intelligences, leaving open the possibility of others; for example, he is currently exploring the parameters of a ninth intelligence, one with the core ability of pondering "ultimate" issues and referred to as an existential intelligence (Gardner, 1999). In order to determine the intelligences, Gardner established eight criteria for judging whether a "candidate" could be considered as a separate intelligence. He believes the establishment of these criteria[1] to be one of the enduring contributions of multiple intelligences theory. Briefly, the eight current intelligences are described as follows:

- *linguistic:* language competence, using words effectively, orally or in writing
- *musical:* competence in perceiving, discriminating, transforming, and expressing musical forms, and having a strong sensitivity to rhythm, melody, and tone
- *logical-mathematical:* competence in using numbers, inductive and deductive reasoning, and abstract patterns
- *spatial:* three-dimensional thinking, and ability to form mental images and perceive the visual world accurately
- *bodily-kinesthetic:* competence in using one's whole body in skilled ways for expressive or for goal-directed purposes
- *interpersonal:* social understanding of other people's moods, intentions, motivations, and feelings
- *intrapersonal:* self-understanding and awareness of one's own strengths and limitations, and the capacity for self-discipline
- *naturalist:* competence in the recognition and classification of the many species of flora and fauna in the environment

MI theory is especially relevant to a text on helping learners having difficulty in reading because it provides teachers a way of revaluing learners and a way for learners to revalue themselves. Too often our perception of students having difficulties in literacy leads us to view these students as slow, as individuals with problems, or even as lazy. However, all learners are unique individuals, each with their own natural strengths and preferences for learning. By looking for diverse ways in which learners demonstrate what

---

[1]Gardner's Eight Criteria for Considering an Intelligence:
1. The potential of isolation by brain damage
2. An evolutionary history and evolutionary plausibility
3. An identifiable core operation or set of operations
4. Susceptibility to encoding in a symbol system
5. A distinct developmental history, along with a definable set of expert "end-state" performances
6. The existence of idiot savants, prodigies, and other exceptional people
7. Support from experimental psychological tasks
8. Support from psychometric findings

they know and how they think best, educators will begin to appreciate each learner's individual cognitive profile. MI theory encourages us to perceive the best in learners, and to appreciate that there are several ways to reach a common goal. As Gardner (1999) states, "a commitment to some common knowledge does not mean that everyone must study these things in the same way and be assessed in the same way" (p. 152).

Many learners who experience difficulty with literacy tasks begin to feel insecure about themselves as learners, period! They describe themselves as "dumb" and will be quick to say, "I can't do it," rather than take a risk and try. They have failed too often to believe in themselves as learners. However, if learners are made aware of the various ways to know something and to problem-solve, then they can rebuild their self-esteem. With an improved self-image and varied opportunities to demonstrate knowledge will come a greater likelihood that the learner will take more risks and accept more responsibility for his or her own learning.

The goal of this text is literacy development. We can also think of this as cultivating linguistic intelligence. "Linguistic intelligence is activated when people encounter the sounds of language or when they wish to communicate something verbally to others. However, linguistic intelligence is not dedicated only to sound. It can be mobilized as well by visual information, when an individual decodes written text; and in deaf individuals, linguistic intelligence is mobilized by signs (including syntactically arranged sets of signs) that are seen or felt" (Gardner, 1999, pp. 94–95). Reading, as a discipline or domain in and of itself, can be realized through the use of several intelligences. By recognizing which intelligences represent strengths in our students, especially those students experiencing difficulty with linguistic tasks, we can then capitalize on their demonstrated intelligences in our efforts to enhance the underdeveloped linguistic intelligence. This is done by integrating linguistic activities with those that represent a student's demonstrated intelligences. In other words, for students with an underdeveloped linguistic intelligence, we must provide *more* experiences with books, stories, and print, not fewer (Allington, 1994). But these experiences can be embedded within the context of a student's intelligences profile. For example, the student who demonstrates a propensity toward the logical-mathematical intelligence could be asked to write triangle poems.[2] Or, the student with a strong interpersonal intelligence could be group leader for a literature circle discussion (Campbell, Campbell, & Dickinson, 1996; 1999).

Several checklists are available for observing multiple intelligences (see Figure 6.14 in this text; Armstrong, 2000, pp. 24–27). However, a word of caution is in order at this point. It is NOT appropriate to use these observation checklists to then label a learner according to particular intelligences—recall that all humans possess all of the intelligences but may not have had opportunity to develop them all. It is also NOT appropriate to distort the multiple intelligences by simplifying them. For example, having students stand up and move around or do stretching exercises may be helpful in terms of getting blood to flow to the brain, but does not enhance or use the bodily-kinesthetic intelligence. Likewise, having a student sing a list in order to remember it is only a mnemonic device and does not enhance or use musical intelligence. MI theory may help us most by reminding us of these three key principles: "we are not all the same; we do not all have the same kinds of minds . . . ; and education works most effectively if these differences are taken into account rather than denied or ignored" (Gardner, 1999, p. 91).

---

[2]Triangle poems consist of three lines, each line is one side of the triangle, and each line leads into the next. Thus, there is no predetermined starting or ending point. Any line can be the first or last.

BELIEFS ABOUT READING

Clearly, reading is a complex human endeavor. Edmund Huey (1908/1977) believed that developing a complete description of the reading process would be psychology's greatest achievement, equivalent to explaining the intricate workings of the human mind. Regardless of how complex reading is, teachers are expected to help students learn to read and, therefore, must have some insight into the reading process. To be effective facilitators of reading growth, teachers must develop their own personal philosophy about reading.

A teacher's beliefs or theoretical orientation about reading can make a significant difference in the approach (i.e., basal, intensive phonics, language experience, literature-based), materials (i.e., basal readers, skill sheets, workbooks, children's literature), and techniques or methods (i.e., directed reading-thinking activity, cloze procedure, book sharings, creative bookmaking, reading response logs) chosen to help students read (Richards, 1985). Teachers who believe that the reading process basically involves learning a sequential set of subskills will undoubtedly stress those in their instruction. Those who believe that reading is primarily the act of processing language in print will approach its teaching quite differently. Authors of reading materials reflect their own beliefs about reading, and perhaps those of the marketplace, in the materials they produce. Thus a teacher's beliefs, approach, and techniques may or may not be in harmony with the materials available, although knowledgeable teachers with firm beliefs can easily manipulate most materials in ways consistent with their beliefs. As Gambrell and Mazzoni (1999) state, "Teachers are ultimately the instructional designers who develop practice in relevant, meaningful ways for their particular community of learners" (p. 13).

Prevalent Views

Knowledge about the ways in which humans learn, along with increasing knowledge about the emergence and development of literacy, will influence one's beliefs about literacy instruction. For example, proponents of a **holistic view** of literacy growth (also referred to as "top-down") claim that students should be exposed to a form of reading and writing instruction more like the process of learning to talk, in which experimentation and approximation are accepted and encouraged. Learning activities are based on students' interests and needs and are placed in meaningful contexts. Students are encouraged to integrate new information with what they have already learned. Fragmenting and fractionalizing areas of literacy learning are avoided, so not only are reading, writing, listening, speaking, viewing, and visually representing integrated *within* language arts, they are often integrated *across* the curriculum. In other words, learning is not subdivided into artificial subject area time periods. Such classrooms generally encourage students to take an active part in their own learning, with much cooperation and collaboration among students and teachers. Harste, Woodward, and Burke (1984, p. 43) describe these classroom environments as "littered with literacy," including professionally published as well as student-authored works. Evaluation focuses on what learners *can* do, not on what they cannot do.

Proponents of a **skills-based view** of literacy growth (also referred to as "bottom-up") focus on the products of reading and writing. They believe there are important subskills related to reading and writing that students must learn before becoming adept in the area of literacy (e.g., recognizing long and short vowel sounds, stating main ideas, drawing conclusions, comparing and contrasting, identifying pronouns, writing adverbial clauses, using guide words). They emphasize that learning the code for written language is a key subskill in learning to read. Teaching subskills and then assessing student mastery of subskills are common activities found in such programs. Advocates of a skills-oriented reading program believe that a carefully controlled reading program, in which behaviors are examined one by one, will lead more students to maturity in reading, and that without specific and direct subskills instruction, many students may not become proficient readers.

Many educators find something of value in both these views, and talk about balance in reading instruction. But **balanced reading** instruction is not just a blending of different views. Routman (2000), who prefers the term *comprehensive view,* talks about the teacher providing "the balance of skills, strategies, materials, and social and emotional support [learners] need" (p. 15). Blair-Larsen and Williams (1999) define a balanced approach as "a decision-making approach through which a teacher makes thoughtful decisions each day about the best way to help each child become a better reader and writer" (p. 13). This particular definition is consistent with an **interactive view,** which says that "reading is a cognitive process, meaning results from the interaction between reader and text, [and] processing proceeds from whole to part and part to whole. . . . [As a result,] different emphases in instruction are appropriate at different times" (Lipson & Wixson, 1991, p. 12). Cantrell's (1998/1999) research further indicates that skills instruction provided within meaningful contexts according to students' needs is most effective in primary classrooms. Jill Fitzgerald (1999) views balanced reading *not* as an approach but rather as a philosophical perspective based on a set of beliefs about the kind of knowledge, who has the knowledge, and how the knowledge can be learned. "Local knowledge about reading is important, such as being able to read words at sight, knowing how to use various strategies to figure out unknown words, and knowing word meanings. Global knowledge about reading is important, such as understanding, interpreting, and responding to reading. Love of reading is important. There are equally effective multiple knowledge sources, including the teacher, parents, and other children. There are equally important multiple ways of learning through which children can attain the varied sorts of knowledge about reading. . . . As a result, a teacher who holds a balanced philosophical view of the reading process values multiple ways of learning and arranges her or his reading program to incorporate diverse instructional techniques and settings" (p. 103).

Each of these viewpoints has merit. It is clear that there is no one best way to teach reading. But in order for all of us as teachers to be able to meet the literacy learning needs of all our students, we must continuously seek greater knowledge about literacy development. Fortunately, the research on literacy development has provided a strong knowledge base for the improvement of literacy instruction. Recent insights from this research are readily shared in the form of scholarly works, conference presentations, and reports available online (Gambrell, Morrow, Neuman, & Pressley, 1999; National Reading Panel Report, 2000 at http://www.nationalreadingpanel.org/Documents). This knowledge base has led to the use of the term **best practices** in literacy instruction. Gambrell and Mazzoni (1999) have compiled a list of ten research-based practices that are descriptive of the methods and techniques described throughout this text:

- Teach reading for authentic meaning-making literacy experiences: for pleasure, to be informed, and to perform a task.
- Use high-quality literature.
- Integrate a comprehensive word study-phonics program into reading/writing instruction.
- Use multiple texts that link and expand concepts.
- Balance teacher- and student-led discussions.

- Build a whole class community that emphasizes important concepts and builds background knowledge.
- Work with students in small groups while other students read and write about what they have read.
- Give students plenty of time to read in class.
- Give students direct instruction in decoding and comprehension strategies that promote independent reading. Balance direct instruction, guided instruction, and independent learning.
- Use a variety of assessment techniques to inform instruction. (p. 14)

We also need to regularly reexamine our beliefs and knowledge about literacy instruction. Dixie Spiegel (1999) poses several questions that are relevant for teachers to regularly ask themselves: "Do I have a comprehensive view of literacy?," "Do I have a clear understanding of a broad range of options for promoting literacy development?," and "Can I match children with strategies?" (pp. 20–21). One of my goals for this text is to help you better match children with strategies by providing a wide variety of options and attempting to identify a strategy's relationship with the multiple intelligences beyond the Linguistic Intelligence (see the "Multiple Intelligences" margin notes in every domain chapter, Chapters 7–14). Through continued professional reading and teaching experience, belief systems and knowledge about learning change; as belief systems change and knowledge increases, instruction will change accordingly. These changes are never easy and they take time. Routman (1991, p. 27) shares the stages for her own change process:

1. I can't do this. It's too hard, and I don't know enough.
2. Maybe if I find out about it, it's possible.
3. I'll do exactly what the experts say.
4. I'll adapt the experts' work to my own contexts.
5. I trust myself as an observer-teacher-learner-evaluator.

Personal Beliefs

As I have continued to learn more about myself as a teacher and a learner, I have rediscovered some previously held beliefs. More accurately, I can now identify theories that formally describe and define those beliefs. Howard Gardner's multiple intelligences theory is one example. When I was teaching elementary school students as a classroom teacher, I believed that every child had strengths. These were not necessarily academic strengths, what I would now think of as the linguistic and logical-mathematical intelligences, but strengths nonetheless, to be nurtured and celebrated. In fact, my fifth-grade students and I would search out these strengths and celebrate them within our classroom community. Several children were so proficient in art that they were designated the classroom artists in charge of designing monthly door displays and classroom bulletin boards; another child was well-known as the fastest runner; several were especially adept at mathematics, so when we needed to calculate what time we would need to leave school to travel to the museum in a nearby city and arrive there by ten A.M., these students were in charge. What were, at the time, "gut feeling" beliefs have become firm beliefs supported by theories that are advanced in the professional educational literature.

I have also found the social and the integrated cognitive/motivation perspectives that describe learning as a collaborative, conversational, and self-directed process to be two theoretical views that closely align with my own views of learning (Menges, 1994). Likewise, Cambourne's (1988, 1995) "conditions of [literacy] learning" theory supports my own belief in the notion of engagement as the key to learning. These personally constructed views, or theories, have been the impetus for all of my teaching, including the university level. I use collaborative learning groups, plan for meaningful engagements with literacy development concepts, and provide opportunities for students to exercise choice in their learning by pursuing, through reading and writing, inquiry topics of interest to them. There is much social interaction in my classes that helps all of us clarify concepts, make connections between theory and practice, and construct knowledge about the teaching and learning of literacy. I strongly agree with something Carol Edelsky (personal communication, April 26, 2000) said recently, that it is "easier to theorize from practice than it is to imagine practice from theory."

Every teacher has to focus on identifying his or her own set of beliefs, or personal theories, and teach in order to test those theories. Each teacher also needs to define what he or she means by the term *reading*. For me, reading is a transaction that takes place between a reader and a text in a particular situation. The reader constructs meaning by actively processing graphic, syntactic, and semantic cues representing language, and by actively using memories of past experiences to aid in building new thoughts and/or revising, reinforcing, or expanding current thoughts. Along with my personal definition of reading, my views about the assessment and evaluation of reading growth are also changing, for I too am a "teacher in process." For example, at this point in my professional development, the lines between instruction, assessment, and evaluation are blurred. It seems to me that good instruction and good assessment involve the same activities. It follows that the key to helping readers grow is good instruction. I have become less concerned with *my* evaluation of students' growth, but more concerned with students' own evaluation of their growth.

I encourage you to formulate your own beliefs about reading so that you can better evaluate suggestions in this and other texts and in materials such as basal reader manuals. Your beliefs will help you make decisions about what to teach and how best to teach it. Don't be afraid to change your beliefs or your instructional practices as you read more and gain experience working with students. Practice informs theory, and a continuous cycle of interaction between practice and theory begins. Every teaching experience helps us construct knowledge about teaching and learning.

TWO MAJOR GOALS OF EVERY READING PROGRAM

When planning a reading program, a teacher is responsible for addressing long-term goals for student literacy achievement. These goals generally fall into two categories:

1. Academic or instructional reading
2. Recreational or independent reading

Academic Reading

Good instructional programs usually have well-specified goals. Major objectives for **academic reading** include increasing proficiency in strategies for comprehending what one reads, expanding sight vocabulary, and improving ability to decode words, as well as learning to locate and organize information and understanding the special and technical vocabularies of the various content subjects. The International Reading Association (IRA) and the National Council of Teachers of English (NCTE), two major organizations devoted to furthering understanding of literacy development, together developed Standards for the English Language Arts (International Reading Association & National Council of Teachers of English, 1996). These standards only provide guidance toward developing curriculum and instruction and are *not* prescriptions for particular approaches. The twelve IRA/NCTE standards are listed in Appendix C. For further information, visit http://www.ncte.org/standards/.

Most states or school districts also publish content standards for language arts, as well as other content areas. These content standards further specify and define goals for what students should know and be able to do as a result of being educated in their particular schools. However, as with the IRA/NCTE standards, the means teachers choose to achieve these goals will reflect their individual philosophies about reading, and the way teachers combine theory and practice will determine the effectiveness of the reading program. The teacher is the key to the success of any reading program.

Recreational Reading

Recreational reading or independent reading, deals primarily with affective dimensions: fostering positive interests, attitudes, and habits concerning reading. If teachers and others fail to encourage the desire to read in children and young adults, many students will become **aliterates:** people who can read but choose not to. Building positive attitudes toward reading is of particular concern when working with students who have difficulty reading.

Frustration, failure, and overemphasis on skills and drills may kill the desire to learn to read. When this happens, teachers' jobs become much more demanding. They must not only handle the instructional facets of reading but try to overcome the negative attitudes of the student as well.

As Goodman and Marek (1996) state so beautifully:

> It will not be enough merely to turn troubled readers into reluctant readers. Schools have already produced too many people who can read but do not choose to do so. Reading for troubled readers has been difficult, tedious, and nonproductive, and its development has been associated with much embarrassment and pain. Teachers must patiently help such students to find reading materials that give them personal satisfaction and pleasure. They must help them realize that reading is something they can do when traveling, when waiting, when there is some time available for a quiet, personal activity, or when there is nothing interesting on television or nobody to talk to. Students must reach the point where they choose to read when there is nobody to make them do it before educators can really claim success. (p. 20)

Major objectives for recreational reading include (1) providing students with the opportunity to practice reading in a relaxed atmosphere, (2) sharing good literature with students, and (3) making provisions for students to share books with one another. Appendix D provides a wealth of suggestions for quality children's literature that is grouped according to a variety of ethnic groups (i.e., African, Asian-Pacific, Latin, Mexican, and Native American). "Multicultural affirmations are especially important for students from divergent cultures" (Hoover & Fabian, 2000, p. 475). Students achieve better when given materials and themes relevant to their cultures (Freire, 1992). For teachers working in today's increasingly diverse classrooms, providing and sharing children's literature that reflects their students' own cultures is imperative for effective communication (Diller, 1999).

The two goals of the reading program should be maintained and balanced at least throughout the elementary school years, although emphasis may change according to the needs of the students. Both goals are equally important for student reading programs at all levels of education. Suggestions to help teachers expand their repertoire of methods, materials, and techniques occur throughout the remainder of this text.

WHAT IS CORRECTIVE READING?

As used in this text, **corrective reading** refers to supplemental and enhanced reading instruction conducted within the classroom context and intended to foster continuous and *accelerated* growth in literacy development for students who find reading difficult. The term *corrective* is used only in a descriptive sense, to suggest that for a student experiencing difficulty with some aspect of literacy, the situation can be ameliorated in some way and growth in literacy can continue. Supplemental instruction means more than is usually provided—instruction *in addition* to what might be expected. Enhanced instruction requires that teachers recognize and accommodate each student's individual strengths and needs, as well as receive support from special program teachers or other adults, time to provide the needed supplemental instruction, and adequate instructional materials.

Not only do we want growth to occur, but we want it to occur quickly. For too long we have designed instruction for students having difficulty in ways that restrict their opportunities to actually engage in reading and writing. These students typically receive instruction in isolated and fragmented subskills of reading or writing, and at a slower pace than classmates not experiencing difficulty (Allington, 1994, 1995). A memorable *Simpsons* episode vividly points out the flaw in this approach, when Bart inquires in the context of a remedial class, "Let me get this straight—we're going to *catch up* by going *slower* than everyone else?" Corrective instruction means more experiences, more often, in reading and writing whole text, as well as direct instruction in areas of specific need. Allington (1994) supports this conclusion when he states, "sheer quantity of reading experience is an important factor in children's literacy development" (p. 16).

Thus the term *corrective reading* maintains a positive view of the learner and looks at ways to adjust the learning environment to better meet students' needs. All of us have been in need of corrective instruction at some time or another: when we haven't quite grasped a new concept, after an extended illness or absence causing us to miss certain information, or even as a result of a poorly planned and/or presented learning experience. The need for corrective reading instruction is only a temporary condition brought on by a particular set of circumstances.

Materials used for corrective reading instruction range from basal readers, magazines, and newspapers to games for motivation and practice, multimedia resources, language experience stories, trade books, and children's literature. Teachers may use any instructional materials available or they may design their own, but instruction should focus on specific areas identified through careful observation and analysis. Teachers use interviews, checklists, surveys, anecdotal records, story retellings, informal reading inventories, and miscue analysis, as well as standardized measures such as diagnostic tests if they are available and appropriate to the teacher's needs. These and other assessment procedures and tools are discussed at length in Chapters 5 and 6. In addition, the teacher's role in implementing corrective reading instruction in the classroom setting is introduced in Chapter 2.

WHO IS THE CORRECTIVE READER?

No set of characteristics describes the "corrective" reader. Initial identification may be based on observation of a student who consistently struggles with grade-level textbooks. Or, once the teacher has listened to a student read aloud, the teacher may notice a lack of fluency or an inability to use flexible strategies for decoding words. A student may appear to be reading a passage as if it were a list of unconnected words. Or there may seem to be little monitoring of reading (comprehension) occurring.

For the most part, though, corrective readers are making progress in their literacy development, although it may be at a slower rate than many of their classmates. More often than not this slower development is a result of lack of experience with books, stories, and print (Allington, 1994). This view is supported by a two-year longitudinal study indicating that exposure to print is a contributor to cognitive growth in the verbal domain (Echols, West, & Stanovich, 1996). Similarly, Fisher, Gallego, Lapp, and Flood (2000) report on the positive effects of increased access to print through the use of community libraries on word identification, attitudes toward reading, and overall academic performance.

Often corrective readers are able to recall and discuss selections read to them better than they can recall and discuss selections they read themselves. While they may seem to learn from nonprint media more easily than from printed material, corrective readers do demonstrate some independence in reading. They are able to engage in recreational reading without direct assistance and should be provided more opportunities to do so. Additionally, corrective readers' attitudes toward improving their reading are for the most part positive, and they do not need constant and sophisticated motivational encouragement. These readers may simply need to be involved in literacy activities that exploit their strong intelligences. For example, if a student has a well-developed spatial intelligence, then reading activities should include the use of pictures and diagrams, or drawing.

Ken Goodman (1986) provides a more socio-emotional description of the corrective reader:

> There are lots of ineffective and troubled readers and writers. You easily recognize them. They are often in conflict with themselves and usually their own worst enemies. . . . They try to read and write by busily attacking words and looking up spellings. They mistrust their own language strategies and become dependent on teachers to tell them what to do as they read and write. They are reluctant to take the necessary risks, with the result that their reading and writing looks far less competent than it actually is. They believe that everyone knows they are literacy failures, and they act the part. . . . [They] do have strengths . . . but through lack of self-confidence and overkill on isolated skills, they don't recognize their own strengths. (pp. 55–56)

It is important to remember that decisions about individual students' reading abilities should reflect the multidimensional nature of the reading process. The total reader must be considered, not just achievement test scores or other standardized measures. The best advice I can give teachers is to build upon what their students already know and what they bring to the learning setting. "Teachers need to develop the attitude that all students have talents and strengths upon which to build their learning. . . . Building on students' strengths means, first, acknowledging that students have significant experiences, insights, and talents to bring to their learning, and second, finding ways to use them in the classroom" (Nieto, 1999, p. 109).

The remainder of this text focuses on helping teachers identify readers who need support as literacy learners; analyze their specific strengths, intelligences, and needs; and provide appropriate instruction. What it means to consider the total reader is addressed in a discussion of the analytic process, analytic teaching, and the analytic teacher (Chapter 2). Topics range from the gathering and interpretation of relevant information (Chapters 2 through 6) to the implementation of effective instructional techniques for the major domains of reading (Chapters 7 through 13). Many useful assessment and instructional procedures for language development, word recognition, comprehension, study skills, and strategic reading are provided. Chapter 14 presents ideas for addressing students' multiple intelligences related to the arts and demonstrates through examples how literacy instructional strategies, multiple intelligences, and the arts can be interwoven.

SUMMARY

In order to provide effective reading instruction for the wide range of abilities and talents found in the classroom, teachers must be able to recognize in readers signs of needing assistance and support in their efforts. This chapter reviews the reading process and discusses the importance of teachers developing a personal philosophy about reading. Two major goals of any reading program are identified. Individual teachers can achieve these goals in a variety of ways, depending on their individual beliefs about reading. The concept of corrective reading instruction is introduced, and characteristics of corrective readers presented.

Suggested Readings

Armstrong, T. (2000). *Multiple intelligences in the classroom* (2nd ed.). Alexandria, VA: Association for Supervision and Curriculum Development.

Presenting the theory of multiple intelligences in an easily understandable style, this book also serves as a guide for identifying, nurturing, and supporting the unique strengths of every student. Includes many helpful charts and checklists.

Cambourne, B. (1995). Toward an educationally relevant theory of literacy learning: Twenty years of inquiry. *The Reading Teacher, 49* (3), 182–190.

A classroom teacher shares the results of his journey of constructing a theory of literacy learning over many years of teaching.

Fitzgerald, J. (1999). What is this thing called "balance"? *The Reading Teacher, 53* (2), 100–107.

This article looks at balance as a philosophical stance. A set of beliefs and guiding principles for a classroom reading program are discussed.

Morrow, L., Tracey, D., Woo, D., & Pressley, M. (1999). Characteristics of exemplary first-grade literacy instruction. *The Reading Teacher, 52,* 462–476.

This article provides a rich description of what is meant by exemplary balanced reading instruction at a first grade level. Characteristics of this instruction are presented through examples, charts, tables, and photographs.

2 The Analytic Process
Its Nature and Value

After you have read this chapter, you should be able to:
1. define the analytic process;
2. justify the analytic process and contrast it with assumptive teaching;
3. describe analytic teaching;
4. explain the importance of ongoing teacher observation as a function of the analytic teacher;
5. describe the steps in the paradigm for the analytic process;
6. compare and contrast the teaching models of nondirective and direct instruction;
7. describe teacher objectives and correlated student-learning objectives;
8. discuss the difference between didactic and discovery teaching;
9. contrast problem-solving questions and facilitating questions.

Key Concepts and Terms

analytic process	evaluation activity	problem-solving
analytic teaching	facilitating questions	questions
assumptive teaching	guided practice	reflective thinking
deductive teaching	independent practice	structured practice
diagnosis	inductive teaching	teachable units
didactic teaching	learning centers	teaching hypothesis
direct instruction	learning style	transactive
discovery teaching	nondirective teaching	transfer of training
entry point	paradigm	

Study Outline

I. Justification for the analytic process
   A. Problems associated with assumptive teaching
   B. The analytic process paradigm

II. Analytic teaching: Supporting all literacy learners
   A. The analytic teacher
      1. Classroom organization: Groupings
      2. Classroom organization: Learning centers
      3. Classroom organization: Student-teacher conferences
   B. The analytic process and multiple intelligences theory

III. Analyzing components of the reading process
   A. Levels of analysis and correlative diagnostic questions
      1. Level 1: Determining lack of success in reading
      2. Level 2: Determining the domain(s) in which difficulty occurs
      3. Level 3: Determining the area(s) within the domain(s)
         a. Oral and written language ability
         b. Word recognition
         c. Reading comprehension and strategic reading for narrative text
         d. Strategic reading for expository text and study skills
   B. Components outside the major domains: Reading-related factors

IV. Basic steps in the analytic process
   A. Analysis of reading behaviors
      1. Step 1: Gathering information
      2. Step 2: Evaluating the information
   B. Generation of possible teaching hypotheses
      1. Step 1: Determining alternatives
      2. Step 2: Selecting a tentative hypothesis
   C. Teaching
      1. Nondirective teaching
         a. Phase 1: Defining the helping situation
         b. Phase 2: Exploring the problem
         c. Phase 3: Insight
         d. Phase 4: Planning and decision making
         e. Phase 5: Integration
      2. Direct instruction
         a. Step 1: Orientation or overview
         b. Step 2: Direct instruction/modeling
         c. Step 3: Structured practice
         d. Step 4: Guided practice
         e. Step 5: Independent practice
         f. Step 6: Evaluation activity
   D. Reexamination of reading behaviors
      1. Step 1: Gathering information
      2. Step 2: Evaluating the information
      3. Step 3: Generating possible teaching hypotheses
      4. Step 4: Selecting a teaching hypothesis

V. From teaching hypotheses to lesson plans
   A. Objectives

"Teachers are increasingly expected to take the crucial and primary role of accelerating the reading growth of . . . struggling readers . . . , a shift from the previous reliance upon compensatory and special education teachers to teach children with reading difficulties" (Duffy-Hester, 1999, p. 480). Teachers must become not only more analytical and better observers of their students, but also more knowledgeable about the reading process and various methods for literacy instruction. The analytic process can be used by any classroom teacher in any curricular area to meet this new demand. The **analytic process** is defined here as a systematic way to help teachers observe and assess aspects of the reading process in their students, identify areas of strength and need for individual students, and provide instruction for specific reading domains regardless of the curricular area or the teaching methods used.

Our current understanding of the reading process recognizes the importance of the reader, the text, and the context of the reading task. As Barr suggests (cited in Berglund, 1987), teachers must "look with new eyes" at students while they are reading. Rather than depend on test instruments, even nonstandardized ones such as informal reading inventories, teachers should initially gain insights into students' reading ability by observing their individual competence in areas such as oral reading, story retellings, written summaries, answers to key questions, and background knowledge. The analytic process described in this chapter recognizes the **transactive** nature of reading, which in turn requires assessment procedures that are also transactive; that is, allowing learners to "use active strategies for constructing meaning as they interact with print" (Rhodes & Dudley-Marling, 1988, p. 29). Katherine Au (1993b) has referred to this view of assessment as classroom-based assessment.

JUSTIFICATION FOR THE ANALYTIC PROCESS

Problems Associated with Assumptive Teaching

Sometimes teachers make inappropriate assumptions about the reading status of their pupils. Herber (1970) calls the resulting instruction **assumptive teaching.** While teachers make many unfortunate specific assumptions, most fall into two general categories.

First, teachers often assume their pupils need to learn something when, in fact, they already have learned it. When this assumption is made, those pupils are in a *minimal-growth* instructional setting. The teacher may spend a great deal of time and energy teaching something that is of little use to those receiving instruction. This type of assumptive teaching leads to student boredom, inattentiveness, and disruptive behavior. Second, and perhaps of vital significance to all concerned with corrective reading, teachers may assume their pupils have learned something when, in fact, they have not. If this occurs with some regularity, reading deficits will accrue and students will slip into a *no-growth* instructional setting. Teaching a lesson well will not guarantee that pupils learn. Figure 2.1 lists common assumptions that teachers should try to avoid.

Assuming too much about students can lead to a mismatch between the learner and the instructional program. For example, if a sixth-grade teacher gives everyone in the class a sixth-grade text at the beginning of the school year, the teacher has assumed that all the students are reading at the level of the text and will profit from instruction at this level. This is a dangerous assumption to make. Teachers must verify that each student in the class can respond appropriately to assigned reading materials.

Similarly, faulty assumptions about individual students can lead to inappropriate teaching. Consider the following example: A fifth-grade teacher accurately determines each student's *instructional reading level* (grade level of material that is challenging but not frustrating for the student to read successfully with normal classroom instruction). Two boys, according to test results, are reading at third-grade level. The teacher gives both of them appropriate reading materials, assuming that instruction can proceed in a manner similar to that of a typical basal reading program, in this case, reading and reviewing stories and workbook exercises at the third-grade level. This teacher has done well in finding each boy's proper instructional reading level but has failed to pursue the *reasons* that each boy is unsuccessful with age-appropriate material. One boy may be reading at third-grade level because he is having difficulty with the word meanings and comprehension, while

Figure 2.1 Common Assumptions Classroom Teachers Should Avoid

1. Assuming that a child has attained readiness for a particular learning
2. Assuming that a report card grade reflects the instructional level of a child
3. Assuming that a report card grade from one teacher means the same as that from another teacher
4. Assuming that all teachers develop independent reading habits in all pupils in the primary grades
5. Assuming that all teachers use instructional material diversified in difficulty and content in each grade
6. Assuming that readers having difficulty are able to use material on a frustration level of difficulty
7. Assuming that group instruction is the best method to meet the reading needs of all pupils
8. Assuming that a basal reader series constitutes an entire reading program
9. Assuming that children can learn a new skill without direct instruction
10. Assuming that children who read well will read widely
11. Assuming that teacher-pupil relationships are unimportant to reading growth
12. Assuming that mastery of reading skills and mastery of reading are identical
13. Assuming that instruction for "different" children is identical to instruction for "normal" children
14. Assuming that all children have the same capacity for learning
15. Assuming that reading deficiencies are nonexistent when the class average on standardized reading tests reaches or exceeds the norm
16. Assuming that the child's reading abilities remained unchanged over the summer
17. Assuming that individual difficulties in word analysis in the intermediate grades will correct themselves
18. Assuming that all materials are adequate and appropriate as corrective materials
19. Assuming that teachers make only fortunate assumptions

the other boy may be having difficulty recognizing the printed form of the words. Each needs a corrective program designed for his particular reading needs. After the learner is given appropriate materials (see Appendix E for methods to determine difficulty levels of materials), deeper analyses of strengths and weaknesses within that level are essential to avoid inappropriate teaching assumptions.

Assumptions have features similar to hypotheses. Both terms connote the involvement of a hunch or a notion about something. They differ in that the word *assumption* implies that the hunch is accepted or taken for granted, while the word *hypothesis* always implies tentativeness and the need for verification, after which acceptance or rejection occurs.

The Analytic Process Paradigm

A loose and unstructured corrective reading program, based on unverified assumptions, often perpetuates reading problems in the classroom. Employing the analytic process alleviates many of the unfortunate results of faulty teacher assumptions. The reason is that the analytic process follows a **paradigm,** or pattern. The teacher (1) analyzes reading behaviors, (2) forms teaching hypotheses, (3) teaches, and (4) reexamines reading behaviors. This paradigm can be expanded to allow for necessary specificity in terms of individual strengths and difficulties, and also to allow for *teacher* self-assessment. The process is simple in that it parallels a natural instructional progression; as you will see later in this chapter, however, it can become quite intricate when put to use, and requires a knowledgeable teacher—one who knows what to look for and how to interpret behaviors observed. Figure 2.2 presents a graphic representation of the analytic process cycle.

ANALYTIC TEACHING: SUPPORTING ALL LITERACY LEARNERS

Analytic teaching is teaching that supports all literacy learners by recognizing their unique strengths, interests, and competencies and meeting their specific instructional needs. Analytic teaching offers ways of observing and assessing students' literacy development that respect students as naturally creative persons who possess a broad range of human aptitudes and who learn in different ways (Kornhaber & Gardner, 1993). Irrespective of one's beliefs about reading instruction, analytic teaching begins with a teacher's firm convictions that (1) all students can learn and have the capabilities to become

Figure 2.2   The Analytic Process Cycle

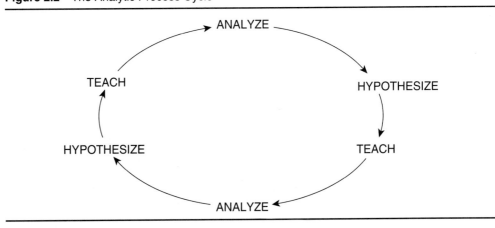

successful readers and writers, (2) diversity "has special value within the classroom community because it provides challenges that lead students and teachers to new learning" (Au, 1993a, p. 74), (3) all students deserve opportunities to develop their unique competencies and strengths, and (4) students who are afforded diverse ways of interrelating new information and concepts with previously acquired background knowledge, or schemata, will have greater opportunities to reach their fullest potential.

Analytic teaching consists of activities that foster student-teacher communication, student choice, student discovery, student self-expression, and student engagement. This type of teaching encourages students to construct meaning from authentic tasks, set goals for achievement, acquire new literacy concepts, and enhance problem-solving abilities using students' preferred combinations of aptitudes or intelligences (e.g., through linguistic, musical, spatial, or bodily-kinesthetic activities), and assume some responsibility for evaluating their own achievements and instructional needs. I agree with Sonia Nieto (1999) when she states, "Learning begins when students begin to see themselves as competent, capable and worthy of learning" (p. 123).

The Analytic Teacher

Analytic teachers work hard to ensure that they and their students work together as a community of learners, sharing their individual talents and unique ways of solving problems. Analytic teachers are good listeners; they listen to their students' ideas and encourage them to share opinions. They often use whole-class meetings in which students and teacher face one another in a seated circle to foster group communication and facilitate student-teacher communication (Glasser, 1969, 1975).

Analytic teachers are also reflective practitioners. It is well documented that **reflective thinking** (i.e., questioning and trying to solve educational problems in a thoughtful and deliberate manner) helps teachers make quality decisions about students and their instruction (Dewey, 1933; Grossman, 1992). For example, analytic teachers determine what their students already know about reading and writing and they figure out what concepts and cognitive tasks are causing confusion for students (Greene, 1995).

Another aspect of being a reflective practitioner is constant examination of one's own teaching and learning. For example, effective analytic teachers need to know how to tap resources in all the multiple intelligences in order to meet the needs of all their students. Therefore, analytic teachers would do well to examine their own profile of multiple intelligences so they can develop those that are underdeveloped and thus expand their teaching repertoires (see Armstrong, 2000, Figure 2.1). For instance, a teacher with a strong interpersonal intelligence might readily use cooperative learning strategies, but having an underdeveloped spatial intelligence might avoid using visuals or graphic materials. While we cannot be masterful in all the intelligences, awareness of our own profiles will encourage us to ask for the help of colleagues, students, or parents in certain areas, or to know when to use available technology (e.g., music CDs, videotapes, calculators).

Analytic teachers are most concerned with teaching all students effectively—not with covering a specified amount of reading material or teaching a predetermined number of writing lessons. Thus, analytic teachers are decision makers—teachers who adapt programs to their students' needs. As Duffy (1997) states, "the best literacy instruction is provided by independent, enterprising, entrepreneurial teachers who view instructional models as ideas to be adapted rather than as tenets to be followed" (p. 351). Therefore, analytic teachers constantly observe their students to determine how their students learn best, to recognize what their students are ready to learn next, and to watch for the emergence of reading and writing patterns and achievements. Teacher observation is never wasted time. Observation also helps the teacher assemble instructional materials. In fact, materials for literacy instruction (e.g., basal readers, developmentally appropriate litera- ture, content-area texts, pictures, art and creative bookmaking supplies, and magazines) should *not* be assembled before students' literacy instructional strengths, needs, and in- terests are determined (see Chapter 6 for more on observation).

Because analytic teachers are effective observers of students and reflective practi- tioners, they feel confident in their abilities to formulate literacy instructional plans and long-range goals for individuals and groups of students. Professional decisions are made before, during, and after instruction. In the course of one school day, a teacher might ask the following questions while reflecting on various students. The remainder of this text should help prepare you to answer these questions.

1. Is this student reading as well as he can? If not, why? What reading or writing in- structional technique might help? Will an individual conference help? Will peer tutoring help? What are this student's unique talents and aptitudes? How can I build on this student's personal interests and particular talents and strengths to enhance his reading and writing abilities?

2. Should this student remain in the reading group that is exploring poetry? If so, what additional instructional techniques may enable this student to grasp the ideas and concepts represented (e.g., artwork, writing, peer discussions, drama- tization, composing a melody, researching the lives of some poets)?

3. How can I motivate this student to become an avid, wide reader and/or an en- thusiastic writer?

4. How can I plan literacy activities that will stimulate my passive learners?

5. How can I structure the classroom environment to provide a blend of learning experiences that promote all students' growth in reading and writing?

Classroom Organization: Groupings

Most teachers group students in some way for literacy instruction. Reading and writing groups need to be flexible because students' instructional needs change daily. Therefore, analytic teachers do not lock students into a particular group.

Analytic teachers communicate to students the reasons for group flexibility. Students receive direct instruction in what they need at a particular time. Analytic teachers think of individual students and their literacy needs. They are not bound by practices such as comparing one student against another or grouping by test scores.

The analytic teacher continually thinks, "Who is ready to learn what now?" or "Who needs a little extra help in understanding this concept?" Ad hoc (temporary) groups are easily formed to meet several students' instructional needs or interests and are disbanded when students' needs have been met. Occasionally, more advanced students enjoy tutor- ing their peers in ad hoc groups. Partner grouping is also effective when two students want to research a topic of mutual interest (e.g., collecting statistics about the destruction of rain forests) conduct a science experiment.

Some analytic teachers place a chart adjacent to their reading-group space on which students may sign up for reading-group participation according to topic (Figure 2.3). Stu- dents may sign up for any of three interest reading groups, which provides choice and encourages them to accept some responsibility for their own learning. For example, if one group is reading about a particular topic such as "African Americans of Achieve- ment," the analytic teacher encourages students who are particularly interested in that topic to sit in on that reading group, regardless of their reading ability. Perhaps on an- other day, a lesson covers a word identification strategy. The analytic teacher knows

Figure 2.3　Example of a Student Sign-up Sheet

Options for students include (1) previewing and voting for the literature selection they particularly wish to read; (2) offering suggestions for additional literature selections to be included under a listed topic; (3) brainstorming ideas for further extensions of topics that encompass art, music, dance, drama, and computer research activities; and (4) offering suggestions for future reading topics.

GROUP 1	GROUP 2	GROUP 3
Topic: *Dinosaurs*	**Topic:** *African Americans of Achievement*	**Topic:** *All Sorts of Survivors*
Literature:	**Literature:**	**Literature:**
1. *A Dozen Dinosaurs*	1. *Sounder*	1. *The True Confessions of Charlotte Doyle*
2. *Dinosaurs, Dinosaurs*	2. *Nat Turner: Slave Revolt Leader*	2. *Dear Mr. Henshaw*
3. *100 Dinosaurs from A to Z*	3. *James Weldon Johnson: Author*	3. *Sarah, Plain and Tall*
Extensions:	**Extensions:**	**Extensions:**
1. Create papier maché dinosaurs	1. Readers' Theater	1. Create a play about survivors
2. Graph sizes of different dinosaurs	2. Interview and write about a friend or relative who is a person of achievement	2. Write about a time when you "survived"
3. Visit kindergarten to give short talks on dinosaurs	3. Create a chart, song, dance, or book depicting the lives of persons of achievement	3. Create a chart depicting the personal traits of the survivors portrayed in the books listed above
4. Use the internet to research facts about dinosaurs		

GROUP 1: 1.____ 2.____ 3.____ 4.____ 5.____
GROUP 2: 1.____ 2.____ 3.____ 4.____ 5.____
GROUP 3: 1.____ 2.____ 3.____ 4.____ 5.____

The author wishes to thank Kathy Babin, Millie Breun, and Rosa Porter, graduate students at The University of Southern Mississippi, for contributing suggestions for the reading topics and literature listed above.

Armour, R. (1967). *A Dozen Dinosaurs*. New York: McGraw Hill.
Armstrong, W. (1969). *Sounder*. New York: Harper and Row.
Avi [Wortis]. (1990). *The True Confessions of Charlotte Doyle*. New York: Avon.
Bison, T. (1988). *Nat Turner: Slave Revolt Leader*. Danbury, CT: Grolier.
Cleary, B. (1983). *Dear Mr. Henshaw*. New York: Dell.
Craig, M. (1968). *Dinosaurs, Dinosaurs*. New York: Four Winds Press.
MacLachlan, P. (1985). *Sarah, Plain and Tall*. New York: Harper and Row.
Tolbert-Rouchaleau, J. (1988). *James Weldon Johnson: Author*. Danbury, CT: Grolier.
Wilson, R. (1986). *100 Dinosaurs from A to Z*. New York: Grosset and Dunlap.

which students would benefit from a preview or review of this particular reading strategy and groups accordingly.

Classroom Organization: Learning Centers

Analytic teachers organize their classroom to provide space for learning centers. Learning centers can be permanent or temporarily arranged areas in which students can work individually, in pairs, or in small groups, or they can be a set of activities organized into binders, boxes, or manila folders and stored on shelves. **Learning centers** provide opportunities for students to meet informally for a designated amount of time each day or for scheduled time throughout the week in order to engage in activities such as exchanging ideas, rehearsing a play, reading, writing, conducting research, or practicing a newly learned skill. Analytic teachers plan appropriate tasks for their students to complete in learning centers. In addition, they provide specific guidelines so that their students know the purpose of the centers and understand their roles as center participants.

Classroom Organization: Student-Teacher Conferences

Students are quite capable of helping the teacher formulate plans concerning their literacy instruction. The analytic teacher conducts daily informal conferences and also schedules weekly student conferences to discuss an individual student's literacy progress, strengths, problems, interests, and goals. At this time the teacher can also suggest some literature selections a student may enjoy reading, or perhaps teach a mini-lesson on a reading-comprehension or writing strategy that may benefit the student. Students look forward to student-teacher conferences when teachers are nonjudgmental, empathic, fair, and honest and show that they are learners along with their students.

Beginning teachers who are eager to use the analytic approach to literacy instruction may find it difficult initially to implement the preceding reflective-thinking, problem-solving, and decision-making cycles because of a lack of experience, time, understanding of reading and writing processes, or confidence in professional judgment. *Do not worry!* If you sincerely believe in the benefits of analytic teaching, you will become increasingly knowledgeable about these processes. You will consider students' self-esteem, interests, background knowledge, and special talents, and you will gain confidence and grow in your abilities as a reflective decision maker.

The Analytic Process and Multiple Intelligences Theory

Even though enhancing reading ability is the focus of this text, it is important to observe during the analytic process that students can, and likely do, excel in other areas. As Armstrong (2000) states, "MI theory emphasizes the rich diversity of ways in which people show their gifts *within* intelligences as well as *between* intelligences" (p. 9). So while corrective readers may demonstrate an underdeveloped linguistic intelligence, they may demonstrate strength in at least one aspect of linguistic intelligence and likely do demonstrate strength in at least one of the other intelligences (see Figure 6.14). For example, a student who has difficulty *reading* a story may very well be able to *tell* a wonderful story (both linguistic), and is also observed to be very popular with classmates (interpersonal). This information will assist the analytic teacher in instructional planning. MI theory would describe this approach to planning as using the concept of the **entry point,** or finding ways to *engage* learners and *at the same time* place them centrally within the desired literacy task. See Table 2.1 for a description of Gardner's seven entry points and an example activity for each (Gardner, 1999). Also be aware that any of the intelligences can serve as entry points to another intelligence. It is important to recall that each person possesses all eight intelligences, but they function in ways unique to each person depending on his or her biology, personal life history, and cultural background. Thus, the analytic process helps teachers focus on appreciating and welcoming diversity within the classroom, and ultimately helps students revalue themselves as learners.

The following example suggests how one student who demonstrates spatial, bodily-kinesthetic, and intrapersonal intelligences can be helped to develop his linguistic intelligence (IRI/Skylight Publishing, 1995).

> Trevor [12 years old] is a seventh grader who is just as proud of his collection of doodles and pictures as he is of his good grades [in math]. Many of his drawings are done during school in classes that are lecture-based or "just plain boring," as Trevor puts it. Others are a result of long hours of detailed work on sketches and designs.

Table 2.1   Gardner's Seven Entry Points

Entry Point	Description	Example Literacy Activities
Narrational (can align with linguistic, spatial, and interpersonal intelligences)	For students who enjoy learning through stories, in either linguistic or film form	"Tell the story of what you saw (or heard)." "Work with a partner to create a story for the pictures you drew."
Quantitative/Numerical (closely aligns with logical mathematical intelligence)	For students motivated by numbers and their patterns and operations	Creation of triangle poems, or some of the "formula" poems (e.g., haiku)
Logical (closely aligns with logical-mathematical intelligence)	For deductive thinkers	Syllogisms (e.g., teacher covers the *th* in the word *that* and points to the *at,* and says, "If this word is /at/, and if this word starts like the *t-h* in /the/, then the word is /th/+ /at/, or /that/.")
Foundational/Existential (can align with intrapersonal intelligence and the "potential" ninth intelligence, existential)	For learners attracted to the "larger" questions	"Why is reading important?" "How can it affect your life?" "How does reading make you feel?"
Aesthetic (aligns with spatial, musical, and naturalist intelligences)	For learners drawn to works of art or features in nature that represent symmetry, balance, and harmony	"Describe the shapes of the letters/ words. How are they alike/different?" "Choose some music that could accompany this story."
Hands-On (aligns with bodily-kinesthetic intelligence)	For students who learn when active and fully engaged	Manipulating letter cubes to form words: "How many words can you make out of the word *student*?" "Design a dance that shows the meaning of the word *swarm*."
Social (aligns with interpersonal intelligence)	For learners who function best in a group setting	Participating in literature circle discussions with a variety of job roles over time

While his classmates make simple book covers, Trevor creates covers with intricate and complex geometrical designs or cartoon characters.

Trevor is drawn to classrooms that are picture rich. Slides, mobiles, photos, overhead transparencies, and other visuals that reinforce the lesson make all the difference in his motivation and understanding. He is easily frustrated by an overdose of words, whether he's reading, writing, or listening to them. His frustration about long writing assignments quickly changes to excitement, however, when he is encouraged to include visuals. . . . Trevor's teacher can identify Trevor's reports without his name because they always have one picture on the front, one on the back, and several throughout.

Trevor spends most of his free time putting together and painting models. . . . He loves math class this year because, as he says, the teacher "keeps us really busy when we learn. We move around to different centers and use manipulatives."

Trevor is definitely not a social butterfly. . . . He has a small group of close friends and is happy to spend time alone. His mental and physical well-being are very important to him, as is his academic achievement. (pp. 45–46)

These representative behaviors reveal Trevor's strengths and propensities for learning as well as show the linguistic intelligence as an area in need of further cultivation. In order to develop his linguistic intelligence, Trevor's teacher provides opportunities that allow Trevor to use his strong intelligences when engaged in tasks involving his underdeveloped linguistic intelligence. For example, when asked to read a book, Trevor is encouraged to draw a picture that shows how the book made him feel, or what it meant to him. This instructional technique, appropriately implemented with seventh-graders, is called *sketch-to-stretch* (Whitin, 1996). Sketch-to-stretch readily combines two of Trevor's strong intelligences—spatial and intrapersonal—to nurture the linguistic task of reading a book. Analytic teachers provide opportunities for students to use their particular combinations of intelligences to support and enhance students' literacy efforts and development.

It should be noted that MI theory is not the same concept as **learning style.** Proponents of learning styles suggest that the learner approaches different contents (e.g., language, numbers, music) in the same way (e.g., global, analytical, impulsive, reflective). (See http://www.geocities.com/~educationplace/ls.html for more on learning styles.) MI theory supports the possibility that a learner may have more than one learning style. For example, a learner might respond reflectively in the music realm, but analytically while working a jigsaw puzzle (spatial realm). With such complexity, it is not possible for teachers to completely individualize their teaching to match each of their students' learning styles, nor is it necessarily appropriate. However, it *is* possible for teachers to expand their instructional methods in order to provide a variety of activities within their literacy curriculum that link learning to as many intelligences as possible. Armstrong (2000, p. 41) provides instructional strategies that link MI theory and the learning of information:

- Listen to it, talk, read, or write about it (linguistic)
- Draw, sketch, color, or visualize it (spatial)
- Dance it, act it out, build a model of it, or find some other hands-on activity related to it (bodily-kinesthetic)
- Create a song or chant about it, find music that illustrates it, or put on background music while learning it (musical)
- Relate it to a personal feeling or inner experience, reflect on it (intrapersonal)
- Conceptualize it, quantify it, or think critically about it (logical-mathematical)
- Teach it, work on it with another person or group of people (interpersonal)
- Connect it to living things and natural phenomena (naturalist)

ANALYZING COMPONENTS OF THE READING PROCESS

Reading is recognized as a total dynamic and transactive process; representing its components in isolation and in static form is a distortion of the process itself. Some distortion is acceptable, however, if it helps the teacher attain the level of specificity needed for direct instruction. Additionally, the kinds of materials students read and the nature of the methods, materials, and tasks used in the classroom, as well as the social and cultural environment of the classroom, must also be examined (see Appendix F for an instructional environment survey). This latter analysis can lead to *changes* in the teacher's methods, materials, tasks, and approach.

Levels of Analysis and Correlative Diagnostic Questions

Following observation of reading behaviors, three levels of analysis help answer the question, "What strategies and lessons should I plan to help this student?" Each level has a correlative diagnostic question, and some questions have important related subquestions. A summary of the levels of analysis and correlative diagnostic questions can be seen in Appendix G. Because the reading process is complex, teachers should always approach analysis of reading difficulties with the knowledge that the resulting hypotheses may be imprecise or only partially correct. During the teaching phase, hypotheses and instructional practices can be verified, modified, and further adapted to the needs of the corrective reader. This again points out the integrated nature of instruction and assessment.

It is very important to determine what strategies the reader *does* use, in order to build upon those areas, and assist further development. The strengths a learner brings to reading determines the point at which instruction can begin. Thus the attitude of instruction becomes one of "moving forward" as opposed to "catching up" (Jewell & Zintz, 1986).

Level 1: Determining Lack of Success in Reading

At this level of analysis, only one diagnostic question needs to be answered:

- Is the learner experiencing a lack of success in reading?[1]

A teacher may find the answer to this question several ways. The most obvious way would be by listening to the student read. Teachers are strongly advised to collect information about each of their students' reading abilities, using the trade books, textbooks, readers, and skill development books available in the classroom. Informal reading inventories and use of running records are also common means of analyzing reading behaviors (see Chapter 6).

Another indication of reading ability may be the student's score on a standardized reading achievement test, usually readily available in the student's cumulative folder. But be careful not to let one test score identify the student's level of success. Reading achievement tests probably do a good job of identifying good readers, so by comparison teachers can identify students who have been unsuccessful. On the other hand, teachers must be careful not to assume that students who score high have the reading abilities necessary for any reading tasks not represented on the test (Farr & Carey, 1986).

The teacher may notice a discrepancy between a student's reading achievement test scores and mathematics achievement test scores. Reading difficulties *may* be indicated if the mathematics scores are higher. A reading achievement test score alone may also suggest further analysis if, for example, the scores on the vocabulary and comprehension subtests vary significantly.

Using a student's achievement records, the teacher may expect to find one of three basic patterns (Kennedy, 1977):

1. From the beginning of formal reading instruction, the student failed to achieve as rapidly as average intellectual ability would warrant (i.e., one year's growth for each year in school).

---

[1] It should be noted that for this question, as with *all* the diagnostic questions that follow, a follow-up question needs to be asked: "Under what conditions or in what situations?"

2. The student had a successful beginning, but progress gradually slowed.

3. The student had a successful beginning, but progress suddenly dropped.

The first pattern may reveal students whose test results are unduly influenced by some reading-related factor (see Chapter 4). Aspects of emergent literacy might also be examined.

The second pattern may not be recognized until a student has already experienced difficulty. Teachers must be alert to the proportionate gains that a student makes through the years, as in the following example: Six-year-old Jody makes good progress through first grade and her end-of-the-year test shows an average level of achievement. By the end of second grade, Jody's achievement is slightly below average. At that point Jody's teacher might feel concern about her progress or decide that her score merely reflects the imprecise nature of tests. When the third-grade test reveals that Jody is further below average, however, this teacher should recognize the pattern and decide that Jody needs assistance.

The third pattern, good progress followed by a sudden drop, may have a number of causes. It may indicate an omission of instruction; an emotional factor interfering with the student's learning rate, such as a recent divorce or a death in the family; or something as simple as the student not feeling well on the day of the test. In any case, the teacher should continue with the analytic process to pinpoint possible learning gaps.

Level 2: Determining the Domain(s) in Which Difficulty Occurs

Once teachers have identified students displaying difficulty with reading, they must begin to determine where the difficulty lies. The reading process can be characterized by certain universals, or reading-related factors, and the four major domains: *oral and written language ability, word recognition, comprehension and strategic reading for narrative text,* and *strategic reading for expository text and study skills* (this last domain is often referred to as "reading to learn," or content-area reading). Usually, a student exhibits difficulty within one or more of these domains and demonstrates strengths in others. The four primary diagnostic questions to be answered are as follows:

- Does the learner demonstrate underdeveloped oral and/or written language ability?
- Does the learner have difficulty with word recognition?
- Does the learner have difficulty with comprehension of narrative text?
- Does the learner have difficulty with strategic reading of expository text or with study skills?

When the answer to a question in Level 2 is no, analysis in that domain ends. When the answer to a question is yes, that domain is analyzed further to define the difficulty more precisely. If the answer to *all* the questions in Level 2 is no, the teacher must consider reading-related factors and may require the help of a specialist to meet the student's needs. If the answer to several of the questions is yes, the teacher should consider whether difficulty in one domain is influencing another and, if so, provide instruction in the dominant domain. Reading-related factors may also be involved.

Level 3: Determining the Area(s) within the Domain(s)

Experts disagree about dividing the domains into smaller segments. Some label the segments differently, and others resist the separation process even for the purpose of analysis. Thus, neither empirical data nor the consensus of experts directly supports the manner in which the domains will be segmented here for analytical purposes.

Despite these differences, the domains *are* divided into smaller parts for communication and instructional purposes. From a practical point of view, you should be aware that these areas are discussed at length in the literature, that the category labels can be found in many texts on literacy instruction, and that these smaller **teachable units** are acknowledged and used in many reading systems today. Even for those with a holistic philosophy, the search for answers to why a student experiences a lack of success with literacy tasks must include consideration of these areas so that appropriate instructional opportunities can be developed.

Oral and Written Language Ability. This component of the reading process lies at its core and is of concern when a student performs very poorly on assessment instruments or when a beginning reader has trouble with simple reading tasks. A correlative diagnostic question to be asked when a student performs so poorly is as follows:

- Does the learner demonstrate underdeveloped oral (i.e., speaking and/or listening) and/or written language ability?

Teachers at all levels should ask themselves whether their students have the oral and written language competence needed for a particular reading task, whether students are native speakers of English or nonnative speakers of English reading in their native language or reading English. As the concept of emergent literacy implies, oral and written language competence develops only in a learning environment in which "children have frequent opportunities to use language and to hear or see language being used in meaningful, communicative contexts" (Rhodes & Dudley-Marling, 1988, p. 77). ESL (English as a second language) teachers are especially interested in providing appropriate language environments (see Chapter 3).

Word Recognition. If a student has difficulty with word recognition, more specific information must be sought by asking the following diagnostic questions:

- Does the learner have a word recognition strategy?
- Does the learner have a limited sight vocabulary?
- Does the learner have difficulty in the area of word analysis (decoding)?
- Does the learner have difficulty using context clues?

Answers to these questions tell the teacher where to begin an instructional focus. Chapter 8 details these areas of difficulty in word recognition and provides suggestions for assessment and instruction. The important point to remember here is that any area(s) associated with word recognition can be out of balance for a particular student. Some readers termed *disabled* have difficulties so severe that they are prohibited from reaching the heart of reading—that is, comprehension.

Reading Comprehension and Strategic Reading for Narrative Text. Much has been learned about reading comprehension in recent years and it is clear that comprehension is deeply intertwined with memory, thinking, and language. When a student demonstrates poor comprehension, the following diagnostic questions should be carefully considered:

- Does the learner have a limited meaning vocabulary?
- Does the learner have difficulty with thinking or problem-solving skills associated with comprehension of narrative text, such as identifying story features, predicting events, or evaluating a character's actions?

- Does the learner have difficulty recognizing his or her own inability to understand what was read?

Answers to these questions help the teacher determine a starting point for instruction and choose appropriate instructional strategies.

Some students, especially in the early elementary grades, appear to have trouble with comprehension when the difficulty actually lies in the domain of word recognition. Therefore, when students of any age are experiencing difficulty typically associated with primary-grade students, teachers should ask the following question:

- Does this apparent comprehension problem result from difficulty with word recognition?

Similarly, especially in the upper grades, an apparent comprehension problem may in reality reflect difficulty with strategic reading of expository text and/or study skills. If the student is experiencing difficulty reading content-area material, the following question is suggested:

- Does the learner's apparent comprehension problem result from difficulty in strategic reading for expository text and/or study skills?

This question and the preceding one probably should be considered transitional questions. They demonstrate how reading comprehension affects the other domains discussed. Chapters 9, 10, and 11 provide suggestions for assessment and instruction in the domain of reading comprehension and strategic reading of narrative text.

Strategic Reading for Expository Text and Study Skills. When students have problems in the domain of strategic reading for expository text and study skills, their abilities in this domain warrant deeper analysis. The following questions are suggested:

- Does the learner have difficulty with content-specific vocabulary?
- Does the learner have difficulty with content-specific skills, such as reading visual displays, formulas, or other unique symbols?
- Does the learner have difficulty recognizing whether the text is meaningful to her or him?
- Does the learner have difficulty locating information?
- Does the learner have difficulty organizing information?

The answers to these questions help the teacher decide where instruction should begin, and to choose appropriate instructional strategies. Chapters 10, 12, and 13 provide suggestions for assessment and instruction in the domains of strategic reading for expository text and study skills.

Components Outside the Major Domains: Reading-Related Factors

Almost all physical, psychological, and environmental problems may impede reading progress. For example, an inadequate background of experience, or one divergent from the majority of students in the class, can seriously affect comprehension, attitude toward reading, and perhaps the acquisition of word recognition strategies. Reading-related factors (see Chapter 4) must be considered independent entities that may adversely affect *any* area of the school curriculum, not just reading. These factors warrant considerable study and should be pursued in advanced coursework typically found at the graduate level.

Correlative diagnostic questions associated with reading-related factors include the following:

- Does this learner demonstrate the influence of a factor related to reading?
- Has this learner had opportunities for reading and writing related to her needs and interests? (In other words, is the learner possibly a "victim" of the curriculum or poor instruction?)

Poor attitudes toward and disinterest in reading hinder reading achievement. Teachers must ask questions about their students' attitudes and interests, their own teaching practices, and the curriculum itself, regardless of the domain in which the reading difficulty occurs:

- Does the learner have a negative attitude toward reading?
- Does the learner lack interest in reading?
- If someone asked my students, "What is reading?" what would they say?
- Is my curriculum so skills-oriented that students never have the opportunity to read for their own purposes? (See Appendix F for an instructional environment survey.)
- Have I examined my own beliefs and attitudes about the way this learner might need to learn?
- Have I explored alternative instructional approaches that might benefit this learner?

The answers to the correlative diagnostic questions for these additional components are typically obtained through observation, surveys, interviews, and reflection.

BASIC STEPS IN THE ANALYTIC PROCESS

This section provides information on the basic steps involved in the analytic process. These steps can be used to answer the questions posed for any of the domains, areas, or specific tasks mentioned earlier. The paradigm for the analytic process, mentioned earlier in this chapter, will now be expanded.

Analysis of Reading Behaviors

Step 1: Gathering Information

Many sources of information about students are available to teachers: the learner, cumulative records (containing relevant medical information, test scores, grades), discussion with others who have had opportunities to observe the student inside the classroom (such as a previous teacher) and outside the classroom (such as parents), work samples (daily oral and written work, dated material such as that found in portfolios), and additional assessment measures (results of informal reading inventories, interest and attitude surveys, teacher-made and classroom-based measures). Assembling all available information possible about students in order to better understand their strengths and needs is called *assessment.* This first step involves teacher action; the following steps represent the teacher's thought processes.

Step 2: Evaluating the Information

In Step 2, teachers judge the quality of the information gathered. They try to establish students' instructional reading levels, find a pattern or set of behaviors indicative of students' strengths and needs, and identify possible areas for development or assistance. If only such information as standardized test scores is available, teachers must verify these scores through other means. Most often teachers use classroom-based measures. Chapters 5 and 6 discuss specific assessment measures, and later chapters provide additional suggestions for classroom-based assessment of particular areas.

Steps 1 and 2 together are roughly equivalent to **diagnosis,** or identification of reading difficulties from behaviors. The outcome can range from a global diagnosis, as determined by the first and second levels of analysis, to identification of specific areas of difficulty represented by the third level. The specific areas identified must then be translated into teaching objectives.

Generation of Possible Teaching Hypotheses

Step 1: Determining Alternatives

Once teachers have identified students needing assistance, they need to consider how best to provide that assistance. Numerous instructional procedures are available, and many of these will be detailed in the following chapters. For now, simply consider a **teaching hypothesis** to be a tentative instructional plan based on a student's identified educational need.

Step 2: Selecting a Tentative Hypothesis

The teacher then evaluates the alternatives generated in Step 1 and decides which instructional plan seems best for the particular student. This decision may be influenced by information regarding the student's interests, learning style, self-concept, or other strong intelligence(s). Once an instructional plan is selected, the teacher develops learning activities and the teaching phase begins. These plans are usually most effective when teacher and student(s) develop them together.

Teaching

Although corrective instruction may be designed for an individual's needs, it is often carried out in a group. By providing group instruction to students with similar needs, classroom teachers are implementing effective classroom management. Additionally, there are many alternative models of teaching, all with specific purposes and the power to help students learn (Joyce, Weil, & Calhoun, 2000). Different purposes require different teaching models, so it is important for teachers to develop and use a large repertoire of teaching models. "When teachers are able to use different pedagogical approaches, they can reach more students in more effective ways" (Gardner, 1999, p. 168). Two quite different models are presented here—the nondirective teaching model and the direct instruction model. These examples represent ends of a continuum from student-centered (nondirective) to teacher-centered (direct). At times, teachers need to use both of these models as well as others in between in order to reach all learners.

Nondirective Teaching

When the instructional purpose is to help students set personal educational goals, the **nondirective teaching** model is an ideal choice. "The nondirective teaching model focuses on *facilitating* learning. . . . [Nondirective teaching occurs when] the environment is organized to help students attain greater personal integration, effectiveness, and realistic self-appraisal . . . the teacher's goal is to help them understand their own needs and values so that they can effectively direct their own educational decisions" (Joyce, Weil, & Calhoun, 2000, p. 288). This is accomplished primarily through a nondirective interview, basically a conversation in which the teacher mirrors students' thoughts and feelings. By using reflective comments, the teacher raises the students' consciousness of their own perceptions and feelings, thus helping them clarify their ideas. The sequence of the nondirective interview is as follows.

Phase 1: Defining the Helping Situation. In this phase, the teacher encourages free expression of feelings. Students who have not been successful in literacy learning are likely to have some feelings about their struggles. For example, a student who is having difficulty with writing will likely feel tense or defensive when asked to write. The teacher's first step is to help the learner release those feelings so that other, more positive aspects of his or her writing can be explored. For example, the teacher might say, "When I'm asked to write a report for the school principal I have a hard time getting started—that makes me feel nervous and panicky. How do you feel when I ask you to write?"

Phase 2: Exploring the Problem. In this phase, students are encouraged to define the problem while the teacher accepts and clarifies feelings. Once the problem area has been defined (e.g., writing), the teacher encourages the student to express both positive and negative feelings and to explore the problem. Some teacher questions or responses might include the following:

- "You say you hate writing because it's too hard. Can you say more about that?"
- "Kind of like it doesn't matter what you do, it always turns out the same."
- "I see."
- "Perhaps you feel you won't succeed."
- "You are saying to me that the problem is . . ."

Phase 3: Insight. In this phase, students discuss problems and the teacher supports the student. As students discuss their problems and become aware of the reason(s) for their feelings or behaviors, they can begin to more clearly see possible solutions. These new insights help the students set goals. Questions that might be asked at this step include the following:

- What is difficult for you as a writer (reader)?
- What is easy for you as a writer (reader)?
- What do good writers (readers) do?
- What are your goals as a writer (reader)?

Phase 4: Planning and Decision Making. In this phase, students plan initial decisions and the teacher helps to clarify possible decisions. This is a difficult step for most teachers, who can readily provide suggestions. It is more important for the student to initiate a plan. Helpful comments might include the following:

- "You would do this because . . ."
- "It sounds like your reasons for that are . . ."

- "What do you think of that?"
- "How might that idea help?"

Phase 5: Integration. In this final phase, students begin to take positive actions. These actions initially may be intermittent and/or unfocused but eventually begin to focus on a single area, giving students the direction they need. Thus, students gain further insight and develop more positive actions. The teacher is supportive and can provide approval statements if genuine progress has been made. Approval statements should be used sparingly, though, to avoid a return to an expectation that it is really the teacher who knows best and makes the decisions. Some helpful comments are as follows:

- "That's a very interesting comment and may be worth considering again."
- "I think we are really making progress together."

Because the nondirective teaching model is student-centered, it is less activity-oriented and more a set of principles for interacting with students in response to a situation. Teacher questions and responses are aimed at initiating and maintaining conversation to help students clarify their own thinking. Some additional examples are as follows:

- "How do you feel when that happens?"
- "Maybe you feel you will be wrong."
- "It sounds to me like your reasons for your actions today are (restate student's reasons)."
- "The last idea you had was really strong. Could you explain it some more to me?"

One possible outcome of nondirective teaching is that students will begin to feel more in control of their own learning.

Direct Instruction

Direct instruction refers to a model of teaching that is highly structured and teacher initiated. This model can be particularly effective in helping readers who have difficulty understanding how to read more strategically; the teacher begins the lesson by providing "mental modeling" to share the reasoning processes involved in expert reading (Herrmann, 1988). Direct instruction, also referred to as "strategy lessons" (Slaughter, 1988), is necessary in any reading program. Such lessons are not always completed in one session. More often, strategies will be learned and practiced over a series of sessions. Thus, a lesson may span several days.

Step 1: Orientation or Overview. Students are informed of the purpose of the lesson and teacher expectations. The learning task is clarified and student accountability established.

Step 2: Direct Instruction/Modeling. The direct instruction model requires that the teacher be *actively* involved in the lesson by first explaining and then modeling or demonstrating the new concept or strategy. Thus, once the particular strategy to be modeled has been identified, the teacher must plan how to introduce the lesson, what to say while modeling, and how to best show the reasoning process. Usually, a *thinking out loud* technique is used to reveal the actual reasoning process followed by the teacher while reading. For example, if the strategy to be modeled is prediction making, the teacher may decide to read a story to the class. After reading the title, the teacher stops, thinks out loud what the story might be about, *and states why*. The teacher proceeds with reading the story, stopping and thinking out loud at points that provide information confirming or rejecting earlier predictions, and always stating why the prediction was confirmed or not and how the text is helping to change the teacher's predictions. Usually the teacher will check for understanding (CFU) at this point to be sure the students understand what they will be expected to do before they apply this new information during practice opportunities.

Step 3: Structured Practice. Once the teacher has modeled a strategy, the students must be given the opportunity for **structured practice**—that is, to practice what has been demonstrated with the teacher still directly involved. In this way the teacher begins to determine the accuracy of the teaching hypothesis as well as the effectiveness of the lesson. The teacher is checking to see how accurately students have interpreted the modeling, another instance of checking for understanding. Depending on students' responses, additional modeling may need to occur. Very often an overhead projector is used during structured practice so students can see the applications while having access to the teacher's explanations. This step is also referred to by Routman (2000) as *shared demonstration*. The teacher works interactively with the students to ensure that the task is understood.

Step 4: Guided Practice. Guided practice allows students to apply the new information on their own while the teacher is still available. In this phase the teacher is essentially monitoring students and providing corrective feedback when necessary.

Step 5: Independent Practice. Independent practice provides an opportunity for students to apply what they have learned, without the teacher's help. This kind of practice is often done as homework, and gives further information on the accuracy of hypotheses and effectiveness of the lesson. If students seem unable or unwilling to participate in independent practice, there are several possible reasons: the hypothesis may be inaccurate, the lesson may need to be revised, or students may not have developed the ability to work independently. In any case, providing independent practice gives the teacher additional information.

Step 6: Evaluation Activity. The **evaluation activity** is a way of directly judging the effectiveness of the lesson(s) and the accuracy of the hypothesis. These activities are usually teacher-made and relate directly to the kinds of tasks demonstrated in the modeling and practice. If the hypothesis was appropriate and learning occurred, opportunities for further practice should be provided; if the hypothesis was not appropriate, alternative hypotheses should be considered.

Reexamination of Reading Behaviors

Step 1: Gathering Information

This second examination of reading behaviors differs in several ways from the first. The first time the teacher gathers information about a student, it is essentially new information. This second examination of behaviors, however, follows an instructional sequence of events, making the analysis much more dependent on the teacher's insights and observations. This analysis overlaps considerably with the preceding teaching stage: as the teacher teaches, information is gathered. The teaching is also the assessment.

Step 2: Evaluating the Information

Evaluation is based on feedback provided by the instructional sequence. The teacher must decide whether the lesson was effective and whether the teaching hypothesis was appropriate.

Step 3: Generating Possible Teaching Hypotheses

New hypotheses are needed if the lesson is effective and the desired behaviors are learned. New hypotheses are also needed if the original one was inappropriate, because the teacher will proceed to a new lesson. In both instances, this step depends on the teacher's perceptions of the lesson and the results of the evaluation activity.

Step 4: Selecting a Teaching Hypothesis

Based on *all* the available information, a new hypothesis is selected and a lesson planned. This takes the teacher back into the teaching phase and the whole cycle begins again (refer to Figure 2.2).

FROM TEACHING HYPOTHESES TO LESSON PLANS

Once a teaching hypothesis has been selected, the teacher designs a corresponding lesson plan or set of lesson plans. The lesson plan(s) depicts the manner in which the desired reading behavior is to be achieved. Good lesson plans for corrective reading contain three important elements: (1) specific learner objectives, (2) procedures and materials designed to help the learners achieve the objectives, and (3) activities designed to evaluate whether the pupils have achieved these objectives.

Objectives

When a teacher works with corrective readers, objectives and teaching procedures emerge from his or her knowledge of each student. The typical steps of a directed reading lesson—such as motivation, introduction of new vocabulary, guided silent reading, oral rereading, and skill development—may or may not be used for students receiving corrective instruction. More often, a corrective reading lesson deals with a specific reading strategy. For example, a "lesson" in using context clues may require several weeks or months. It becomes a major teaching strand with long-term goals (for more than one lesson) and specific lesson plan objectives, such as learning to identify certain words in a sentence as clues to what the unknown word might be.

If more than one reading domain is involved, as is likely, each should receive attention through instruction that integrates them as much as possible. Similarly, if several sessions on one area of concern are required, a variety of materials and procedures focusing on that area is needed. Teachers should try to provide diversity in learning activities to achieve the lesson objectives, and to address a variety of intelligences. For example, many instructional formats are available for teaching initial consonant blends: through the use of children's literature (linguistic intelligence), through puzzles and other visual presentations (spatial), through oral problem-solving riddles (logical-mathematical), through manipulatives or sandpaper tracings (bodily-kinesthetic), through songs that teach (musical), and through learning games (interpersonal). The effective teacher takes advantage of several of these techniques, using different materials and procedures until the learner experiences several successful sessions.

Success experiences should always be interspersed within corrective instruction. *Every* lesson should provide opportunities for students to do things they are able to perform well, even though the time spent this way may be minimal. This procedure helps counteract negative feelings the learner may have about the more challenging aspects of the lesson. Thus, each lesson includes learning activities that focus on areas of strength to enhance self-concept and the underdeveloped linguistic intelligence.

Teacher Objectives and Correlated Student Learning Objectives

Teachers, especially beginning teachers, are often understandably confused about objectives because they tend to think about objectives from the teacher's point of view rather than from the student learning point of view. To avoid this confusion, teachers can state objectives from both perspectives. When writing teaching objectives you can begin with the words "To teach . . ." and specify the content you want to teach or the student wants to learn. The correlated student learning objective, which helps the teacher and student focus on student behavior, should be stated in terms of student performance because such objectives lend themselves to evaluation of the lesson's effectiveness. To use the earlier example of a lesson in context clues, the teacher's objective might be:

> To teach use of context clues to aid in figuring out words unknown in print.

The correlated student learning objective might be:

> At the end of this lesson, the student will be given a portion of a language experience story having five sentences, each containing a blank followed by three word choices. The student will be able to underline words in the sentence that help in choosing the one word that correctly completes the sentence. The student should be able to complete 80 percent, or four of the five sentences, accurately.

Writing Student Learning Objectives

Student learning objectives should include three components: (1) the condition, (2) the observable behavior, and (3) the criterion. The *condition* refers to the setting or context in which the behavior will occur. Following are examples:

> Using a 250-word section from a social studies text . . .
>
> Given a 10-item worksheet on sequence of events . . .
>
> Given a 100-word paragraph . . .
>
> Using a list of the 12 vocabulary words . . .
>
> During a silent reading of Taro Yashima's book *Umbrella* . . .

The *observable behavior* refers to that which the teacher expects the student to *demonstrate*. For best results, verbs that express observable behaviors should be used. While several types of observable, or overt, behaviors can be prescribed, they fall into two general categories, motoric and verbal. Verbs that require unobservable, or covert, mental activity should be avoided because the activity cannot be verified easily. Examples of motoric, verbal, and covert verbs are as follows:

> *Motoric:*   point, circle, mark, write, underline
> *Verbal:*   say, read orally, tell, retell, paraphrase
> *Covert:*   know, learn, remember, decide, participate, listen

The primary strength of overt verbal behaviors is their ready accessibility to the teacher in a discussion-recitation setting. Answering the teacher's questions and reading orally are common verbal reading behaviors. Probably the greatest weakness of overt verbal behaviors is that they do not lend themselves to easy record keeping, particularly in a group or informal setting. Recording overt oral behaviors accurately requires that the teacher work with students individually. This may mean working directly with the student or listening to a taped reading by the student.

Motoric behaviors, especially marking or writing by students, have the advantage of being relatively permanent and readily scored. Motoric behaviors also can be recorded for more than one student at a time. Record keeping can be less time-consuming than recording and scoring oral reading behaviors for each student, although interpreting students' written products does require time and thought.

For learners who have not had many opportunities to write, writing words and sentences may be a difficult task. Those who experience reading difficulties often write and spell at a lower developmental level than that of their reading. This is all the more reason for these learners to be given opportunities to write, although the quantity of writing and spelling required to complete an activity might be limited initially until confidence increases. Multiple-choice questions that require marking and questions requiring short written answers are suggested, particularly if a written model is available for copying. If a daily writing journal is employed for instructional practice, students' writing abilities will likely improve more rapidly. (More information about the reading/writing connection can be found in Chapter 7.)

The *criterion* element of a student learning objective serves as the basis for deciding whether the lesson helped the learner reach a higher performance level than earlier behaviors indicated. The criterion itself is a matter of subjective judgment, and the teacher needs to take into account the fact that certain strategies are learned over a period of time. Early in a corrective program the criterion level may be low, but as the student learns, this level is raised. For instance, the teacher and Bill agree that he needs to self-correct his miscues more often. If currently he *never* self-corrects, the initial criterion may call for Bill to self-correct "at least once." Later, after becoming aware of the nature of his miscues (see Retrospective Miscue Analysis discussions in Chapters 6 and 8), this criterion may be raised to "most miscues will be self-corrected." Examples of criteria are as follows:

with 7 out of 10 correct

with 85 percent accuracy

at least 5 times

Following are two complete examples of student learning objectives:

Condition: Following the shared reading of *Bringing the Rain to Kapiti Plain,* and a mini-lesson on *long a* spelling patterns,

Behavior: each student will locate and make a list of words from the story that have a *long a* sound

Criterion: with both of the two *long a* patterns in the story represented *(ai, aCE).*

Condition: Given a 200-word paragraph from his language experience story,

Behavior: Hue will read out loud and show evidence of self-monitoring by verbally correcting

Criterion: at least half his miscues.

The value of student learning objectives is not in their precise writing. These objectives cannot be written at all unless the teacher has thought about the student's needs and how to go about helping the student. These objectives provide direction for the teacher as well as documentation for later reflection. Following a lesson, the teacher should review the student learning objective and ask questions such as, "Was this goal achieved? Why/why not? Is it still an important goal? Did I learn anything new about the student from this lesson? Should the goal be changed?"

Procedures

The heart of every lesson resides in the teaching procedures. Teachers' roles change rather dramatically from analyzing reading behaviors and forming teaching hypotheses to instructing. Teachers also use assessment procedures during their lessons. Wise teachers are constantly evaluating whether students are grasping the various points of the lesson. Teachers who "reflect-in-action" can modify lessons while they are ongoing (Schön, 1987).

When planning the procedures for a lesson, teachers should focus on two considerations: the steps in the lesson and the questions involved.

Planning the Steps

Procedural Steps. Many steps, such as changing learning activities, reviewing the lesson, and preparing for independent practice activities, are procedural in nature. These steps are necessary but only peripheral to the teaching function, which is the focus here.

Teaching Steps. The steps planned for teaching a student something new need to be considered quite carefully. Teachers have options, or alternative techniques, for presenting new concepts. For contrast, two are mentioned here: didactic (deductive) and discovery (inductive) teaching techniques. In **didactic teaching,** also called **deductive teaching,** new information is given to the pupil in a direct fashion. An example is "giving" the student a new word and telling him to learn it.

> *Teacher:* Jimmy, the word is *tray, tray.* Now you say it.

The lesson may continue with the presentation of more new words and appropriate practice activities. This technique is direct and efficient and often works well for specific purposes. It is limited, however, in that it provides little opportunity for students to be actively involved or to learn to generalize the specific word recognition process to other unknown words **(transfer of training).** To be sure, some learners can make their own generalizations and transfer these learnings to other tasks. Typically, however, students having difficulty with reading also have trouble transferring what they have learned from one task to another. The discovery approach to teaching may better help these students learn the process (e.g., analyzing the word) as well as the product (the word itself, in this case).

In **discovery teaching,** also called **inductive teaching,** learners are encouraged to seek generalizations for themselves. The teacher's function is to observe how students carry out this process and to provide reinforcement and additional clues to aid learning as needed. Providing clues helps prevent undue frustration if pupils have trouble making the "discovery." The teacher also helps students learn how to discover knowledge, that is, the transfer process itself. The word *tray* can again be used as an example.

> *Teacher:* Jimmy, you have told me this word in your story is a new word (teacher points to the word *tray* in the sentence, *The cookie tray fell down*). How can you figure it out?
> *Jimmy:* (No response)
> *Teacher:* Look at the rest of the words in the sentence. Do they help you?
> *Jimmy:* (No response)
> *Teacher:* Do you see anything or any part of this word you might already know?
> *Jimmy:* It starts the same as *train.*
> *Teacher:* Good! Anything else?
> *Jimmy:* No.
> *Teacher:* How about the ending?
> *Jimmy:* Well, it ends like *say* and *may.*

Teacher: Yes, go on.

Jimmy: Tr-tr-tr-ay-tray. I think it's *tray.*

Teacher: Very good, Jimmy. Now let's check it out in the sentence to see if it makes sense.

Jimmy: The cookie *tray* fell down. Yes, that makes sense. The new word is *tray.*

Teacher: That's great, Jimmy. You are becoming a good word detective. Let's make a card for your word bank . . . great! Now, on the back of the card I want you to write a new sentence using the word *tray* (or the teacher can write a dictated sentence). Then you can practice this word later so you can read it quickly. If you have trouble remembering this word, turn your card over and read your sentence for help. You might also want to add this word to your personal dictionary with a picture and your new sentence.

Notice how much more teacher time and effort are involved when the discovery approach is used. But notice also that the teacher is getting the pupil actively involved in developing a strategy for analyzing unknown words. The minimal clues given to the learner and the use of ample praise for risk taking help reduce negative feelings of failure and frustration.

Planning the Questions

The second important consideration when planning a lesson is anticipating questions that may help the students during the lesson. The teacher cannot always plan the exact questions but should be prepared to use certain types of questions during the lesson. Two types are discussed in this section, and the use of teachers' questions is addressed frequently throughout the remainder of this text.

Problem-Solving Questions. The use of **problem-solving questions** moves a student from thinking, "I don't know the answer," to a more dynamic frame of mind equivalent to, "How can I try to solve this problem?" An example of this type of question taken from the previous dialogue is as follows:

"How can you figure out the word, Jimmy?"

Often a question of this type signals subtly to the pupil that the teacher is accepting of lack of knowledge—that it is okay if a person does not know the word or answer. The student can then focus on the problem without feeling a sense of embarrassment or failure if a guess is wrong. The teacher thereby increases the probability that active student participation will occur without the learner feeling threatened.

Facilitating Questions. Pupils frequently are not able to solve a problem on their own. A second type of question, called a **facilitating question,** encourages continued thinking. The purpose of facilitating questions is to make discovery easier for the learner. Examples are paraphrased from the previous dialogue:

"Do the rest of the words in the sentence help you?"
"Do you see any part of this word you might know?"

Some facilitating questions encourage pupils to *focus* on a point they may have overlooked:

"How about the ending of the word?"

Other facilitating questions present clues in the form of questions:

"Do you think the new word ends like these that you already know?" (The teacher writes or says appropriate examples.)

Facilitating questions demonstrate the teacher's efforts to guide students to discovery through active participation. In the example, the teacher wants Jimmy to learn the word *tray,* but all that effort to teach one word is hardly justifiable. The underlying purpose of this activity is to help students learn part of the process involved in figuring out new words. The teacher and students focus on the process of analyzing a particular word so that the steps in the thought processes can be learned and so that the general thinking strategy practiced here by Jimmy with the aid of his teacher will eventually transfer to other unknown words that he encounters when the teacher is not present.

One purpose of problem-solving and facilitating questions is to help the pupil actively seek answers to the immediate question. Far more important, however, is their role in helping students develop independent-thinking strategies that can be applied to many other situations.

Assessment and Evaluation during the Lesson

This section has briefly illustrated the teaching task and discussed significant parts of lesson planning. One important issue remains. During the lesson, while the teacher is teaching, the opportunity for direct assessment of student learning is always present. The most expeditious way to assess directly is to ask questions during the course of the lesson that elicit oral responses. The teacher asks a question or a set of questions about each point being taught. Asking for examples or illustrations also provides assessment information. If the teacher is reviewing content recently taught, the lesson should be opened with general questions that start with "Who remembers . . ." or "Can someone tell us . . ." If the students are having trouble, the teacher can give clues or hints, which often can be stated as facilitating or focusing questions.

One good teaching procedure is to provide a brief, structured practice session on the topic, but with new examples for students to solve. Corrective readers often learn content more quickly if they can practice with the teacher and classmates. Misperceptions and incorrect learnings can be corrected immediately. A written worksheet or chalkboard or transparency practice on the topic provides a common focus for the group and helps prepare them for any evaluation activity that may follow.

Once teachers become familiar with their students, they can use practice sessions as a guide to the students' readiness to take a quiz or to participate in some other evaluation activity. If the students do poorly during practice, the evaluation activity should be deferred and further instruction or a second practice period given.

A COMPLETE LESSON

The following outline, representing the basic steps in the analytic process, should serve as a general guide to and summary of this process. It is generally applicable to all components of literacy development.

1. Analyze reading behaviors
   a. Gather information
   b. Evaluate information
2. Generate possible teaching hypotheses
   a. Identify several alternatives
   b. Select a tentative hypothesis
3. Teach (decide upon appropriate teaching model)
   a. Use nondirective teaching

(1) Encourage student catharsis and problem definition
(2) Facilitate student insight
(3) Encourage planning and integration of thought and action
(4) Reflect on interaction with student
  b. Use direct instruction
(1) Deliver orientation
(2) Provide modeling
(3) Allow structured practice with teacher
(4) Provide guided practice
(5) Give independent practice
(6) Provide evaluation activity; reflect on lesson
4. Reexamine reading behaviors
  a. Gather information
  b. Evaluate information
  c. Generate teaching hypotheses
  d. Select a teaching hypothesis

It is important to recognize the link between 3a(4) and 3b(6), the evaluation/ reflection at the end of the lesson, and 4a, 4b, and 4c, the gathering and evaluating of information and generating of new teaching hypotheses. Teaching and assessment often occur simultaneously. Without evaluation or reflection on the lesson, the analytic process is incomplete. Furthermore, if a teacher never examines student artifacts and chooses to use only observational evaluation procedures, judgment of student learning has not been adequately verified. Thus, the teacher *assumes* the lesson was learned, and that assumption is subject to the pitfalls of assumptive teaching. While a written evaluation activity is not needed for every student for every lesson, the risk of falsely assuming that learning has taken place is much higher for students having reading difficulties.

Figure 2.4 presents an example of a plan for one session in a series of sessions in which the K–W–L strategy (see Chapter 12) is being learned. Following a direct instruction model, the teacher has previously modeled the strategy and has provided structured and guided practice with the new strategy. This session represents a review of the student's ability to independently complete a K–W–L strategy sheet. The teacher has also planned an evaluation activity so she can determine how effective the K–W–L strategy was for her student. (Note that the material in brackets in Figure 2.4 is explanatory material for you, the reader, and not part of the lesson plan.)

Figure 2.4   Sample Lesson Plan*

Teacher's Name	Session #14
Date:	Child's Name:
School:	Age: 10, Grade: 5

Intention: *[This is the purpose and rationale for the lesson from the teacher's perspective.]*
   I intend to use this session to complete the K–W–L strategy lesson on Harriet Tubman that we began last week for the purpose of enhancing J.'s comprehension, particularly with informational text. This lesson continues to address Standards 1 and 3. [See NCTE/IRA Standards in Appendix C.] I assume that J. has taken some time over the weekend to review the passage that she read silently at our last meeting (see session #13 for reference), and has continued to record informa-

continued

Figure 2.4 *continued*

tion on the K–W–L strategy sheet. I will also give J. the opportunity to expand her knowledge in particular categories, which she suggested, dealing with the subject.

Procedures: *[How will you go about achieving your goal?]*
1. J. will display the work done on her own at home and we will discuss the items she listed under the heading "What We Learned." (A copy of her chart is available.) We will go on to discuss information about Harriet Tubman that J. would like to investigate further.
2. We will take turns reading particular (i.e., favorite) sections from the Harriet Tubman book aloud. I will choose sections that deal with the topics J. chose as wanting to learn more about.
3. J. will then record suggestions of subtopics for further research in other materials (e.g., encyclopedia, social studies text).
4. I will give J. the opportunity to read, or have read to her, the book *Harriet and the Promised Land,* by Jacob Lawrence.

Evaluation: *[How will you know what the student has achieved? What will the student be able to do to convince you that your lesson was effective; in other words, what is the student learning objective?]*
Given a brief, teacher-made cloze passage, J. will be able to identify and write in the blanks at least five pieces of information on the subject of Harriet Tubman. (Completed passage is available.)

Reflection: *[Reflections provide an analysis of the lesson, not a blow-by-blow description of the lesson's procedures. It is important to discuss the outcome of any evaluation activity, and what those results indicate for the next lesson. It is also important to evaluate your own teaching effectiveness as well as the effectiveness of the procedures you used. Try to summarize from this specific experience to teaching in general—what did you learn that will help you in your professional growth? In addition, discuss any surprises, glitches, and/or adjustments you experienced during the lesson.]*
The K–W–L strategy employed in this lesson to help J. recognize and identify significant information within informational text was apparently quite successful. J. completed the entire cloze passage with 100% accuracy! She was so proud! In addition, I added something to the lesson plan procedures during the lesson: J. was able to compose a list of four facts that she already knew about the subject, Harriet Tubman, and give suggestions about information that might be acquired from an encyclopedia passage (we were able to begin this research project). As J. began to read the encyclopedia passage, she became very excited every time information she was to look for was "right there." Therefore, I believe the "What We Want to Find out" portion of the K–W–L strategy was most beneficial to J. She was able to see that information that she herself suggested had substantial value, and also that this step of the strategy is an important one. The bits of information and the questions that J. posed were able to be answered immediately in the reading. Great instant feedback! From the text *Harriet and the Promised Land,* J. chose to add three new words to her vocabulary file box: *fowl, chariot,* and *disguise.*

I felt so good about this sequence of lessons using the K–W–L strategy. It works great for informational text, especially since this type of text is often difficult and seemingly boring to students. It really provides the student with direction and a purpose for reading. I think I could use this strategy too with my college texts! J. promises she will use her K–W–L charts again—I hope she will. I think the K–W–L lessons went well because I took it slow. I modeled the use of the chart first with a short passage; then we worked together on the Harriet Tubman book. It is also an easy strategy to catch on to. Even though it took three sessions to complete, it was worth it. J. really understands the benefits of using the strategy. That's why I think she just might continue to use it.

I learned how important it is to model new strategies, or really anything you want students to do, so students are clear about what to do. It is also important that they be able to experience some success with the new strategy so they can appreciate its value. Since J. is still interested in this topic, we will continue to search for answers to her questions.

*Special thanks to Stacy Scarpero, a university student, for agreeing to share this lesson plan.

SUMMARY

In this chapter, the analytic process and analytic teaching are defined and explained. The analytic process is contrasted with assumptive teaching and a justification for the process is presented.

A large portion of this chapter discusses the components of the reading process. Three levels of analysis are described and correlative diagnostic questions are provided for the major domains of oral and written language ability, word recognition, comprehension and strategic reading for narrative text, strategic reading for expository text and study skills, and additional components such as linguistic diversity and reading-related factors. Analysis ultimately leads to instruction—for example, learning to use word-order clues within the area of context clues.

Another major section of this chapter deals with moving from the formation of teaching hypotheses to the preparation of lessons. Examples of teacher and student learning objectives are provided. Two teaching models, nondirective and direct instruction, are explained. Procedures for lessons include determining the steps for deductive and inductive teaching. Problem-solving and facilitating questions, designed to promote active learner involvement and transfer of thought processes, are discussed. Finally, a complete lesson plan is presented.

Suggested Readings

Gambrell, L., Morrow, L., Neuman, S., & Pressley, M. (Eds.). (1999). *Best practices in literacy instruction*. New York: Guilford Press.

This scholarly work brings together recent insights from the research on literacy development that have direct implications for classroom practice. Guiding principles and practical classroom-based strategies and techniques are provided.

Herrmann, B. A. (1988). Two approaches for helping poor readers become more strategic. *The Reading Teacher, 42,* 24–28.

This article provides explicit examples of teaching procedures helpful for working with students having reading difficulty. The examples include the actual dialogue between the teacher and student.

Spiegel, D. L. (1992). Blending whole language and systematic direct instruction. *The Reading Teacher, 46,* 38–44.

This commentary discusses the value of systematic direct instruction and attempts to point out that such instruction is not incongruent with the whole language philosophy.

Tancock, S. M. (1994). A literacy lesson framework for children with reading problems. *The Reading Teacher, 48* (2), 130–140.

This article presents an alternative framework for combining instructional components with the flexibility required for addressing individual learners' interests and needs.

White, C. (1990). *Jevon doesn't sit at the back anymore.* New York: Scholastic.

This short monograph is the story of one teacher's efforts to observe and record what happened in her own classroom. She learned that a strong community of learners can be forged when teachers take the time to learn the strengths and differences of individual students.

3 Language Diversity Foundations for Literacy Instruction

John G. Barnitz
University of New Orleans

Objectives

After you have read this chapter, you should be able to:

1. explain the relationship between communicative competence and reading development;
2. describe some of the basic characteristics of linguistic competence and sociolinguistic competence;
3. describe how language characteristics vary across cultural groups;
4. list some specific characteristics of African American English or other language varieties more prevalent in your area;
5. explain implications of linguistic diversity for assessing students' language and literacy abilities;
6. explain basic principles for facilitating children's acquisition of standard English;
7. appreciate and respect the language and culture of all learners.

Key Concepts and Terms

African American Vernacular English (AAVE)
communicative competence
dialects
dialogue journals
discourse
experience-text-relationship method

language experience approach
lexicon
linguistic competence
morphemes
narrative ability
oral interaction
orthographies

phonemes
regional dialects
social dialects
sociolinguistic competence
standard dialects
style shifting
vernacular dialects

Study Outline

> . . . Give me your tired, your poor,
> Your huddled masses yearning to breathe free,
> The wretched refuse of your teeming shore.
> Send these, the homeless, tempest-tost to me.
> I lift my lamp beside the golden door.

Many of us recognize these words from the sonnet "The New Colossus," by Emma Lazarus (1883; reprinted 1993), written in honor of the Statue of Liberty and later put to music by Irving Berlin (1949) in *Miss Liberty* (Sherwood & Berlin, 1949). These words symbolize our nation's welcome and commitment to people from various lands. By extension, these words can symbolize our commitment as teachers to learners of various cultural and linguistic backgrounds, whether indigenous to America, or immigrants. But to what extent do we lift our lamps beside the golden doors of our classrooms? To what extent do we consider and value our students' rich diversity of cultures, languages, and dialects in our literacy instruction?

As teachers in the twenty-first century we are ever mindful of the need to acquire as much professional knowledge as possible about diverse languages, dialects, and cultures if we are going to facilitate literacy acquisition in our increasingly multicultural classrooms. Too often teachers discover that many students struggling in reading are learners whose native tongues are either vernacular dialects of English or another language altogether. This chapter serves as a brief introduction to some foundational concepts of linguistic diversity that will help in our efforts to become successful teachers in diverse instructional settings.

Before proceeding, explore your own personal awareness of linguistic diversity. Activate your own schemata about the many people from various cultures and languages in your life from childhood to the present. My own many experiences in urban, suburban, and rural contexts have shaped my respect for diversity, such as experiences with extended family, schooling and teaching, folk dancing, and riding city buses, to name a few (Barnitz, 1997). Just over the past year I recall hearing diverse languages and dialects in the following contexts:

- reading directions written in several languages on a film cartridge for my camera and for installing a kitchen faucet
- reading menus in restaurants written in various languages with food items from various cultures
- shopping in a Polish delicatessen or bakery and hearing Polish accents

- attending church services that involved at least three languages
- watching a few baseball games and basketball games on television and sitting in the bleachers of neighborhood playgrounds around the metropolitan area and listening to the spectators and players
- watching and listening to the Summer Olympics televised from Australia
- talking with neighbors and friends of various ages who have their own unique features of speech
- watching movies about teachers in urban and rural schools

Standing in line at gas stations, banks, and grocery stores is no longer boring when my ears are tuned in to the diverse pronunciations, sentence structures, and vocabulary of others in line. So take a few moments now to reflect on your exposure to linguistic differences. I am sure you will agree that linguistic diversity is all around us and certainly in our schools.

This chapter provides foundational information in three major areas. First, we will explore the nature of communicative competence, about knowing and using language that is so foundational to reading and writing; next we will explore some ways that particular languages and vernacular differ from standard English; finally, we will outline some general principles and specific strategies for literacy assessment and instruction with linguistic diversity awareness in mind.

COMMUNICATIVE COMPETENCE

Communicative competence is the knowledge and use of language for oral and written interaction—the internalized knowledge of the structures of language and the ability to use language in various social situations. Regardless of dialect or language backgrounds, learners first develop their abilities in speaking and listening and extend that ability to writing and reading. In addition, learners develop communicative competence through the arts—that is, through viewing and visually representing. All the communicative/ language arts involve psycholinguistic processing, or composing and comprehending meaning of oral and written language by using the various thinking processes (memory, knowledge, language, perception, etc.). Communicative competence also refers to the ability to express or compose meaning through talking, writing, and visually representing, and comprehend meaning by listening, reading, and viewing—all for functional purposes.

Communicative abilities involve not only the linguistic knowledge of language structures, but also the strategic and pragmatic use of language. Shuy (1981a) distinguished between linguistic competence and sociolinguistic competence. **Linguistic competence** generally refers to the mastery of the formal system of language (i.e., sounds, sentences, vocabulary), while **sociolinguistic competence** is the use of language "to get things done," which includes language functions and the social strategic use of language to accomplish communicative goals (i.e., pragmatic use). Functional use of language is basic to language production and comprehension and usually precedes the perfection of formal structures. Functional use of language is also crucial to school success (Piper, 1998; Shafer, Staab, & Smith, 1983). Social use of language (active speaking, listening, writing, reading, visually representing, and viewing,) is critical for language and literacy acquisition. Social interaction is especially critical for diverse learners (Au, 1993a; Bloome, 1991; Cary, 2000; Enright & McCloskey, 1988; Freeman & Freeman, 1992; Hiebert, 1991; Rigg & Allen, 1989; Tharp & Gallimore, 1988). Thus reading involves a complex interaction of social, cognitive, and linguistic processes (Bernhardt, 1991; Carrell, Devine, & Eskey, 1988; Ferdman,

Weber, & Ramirez, 1994; Kamil, Mosenthal, Pearson, & Barr, 2000). For a review of re-search on second-language reading, see Bernhardt (2000) and Garcia (2000).

Sociolinguistic competence includes, among other processes, social interaction abilities, language functions, narrative abilities, and style shifting (Shuy, 1981a). **Oral interaction** is a basic social skill that includes conversational abilities, switching topics, taking turns, and strategies for politeness and tact, as well as basic pragmatic abilities such as knowing what and what not to say (or write). Such skills may transfer to reading because literacy is also a social process (Au, 1993a; Bloome, 1991; Cook-Gumperz, 1986; Vygotsky, 1978). Such skills also help us infer, for example, the social motives of an author and better comprehend the oral interactions of characters in a story.

Language functions are crucial to the effective use of language. Language exists because it is useful, and children learn language as they perceive the need. Children from various linguistic backgrounds use a variety of functions. For instance, sixth-grade students can demonstrate a wide range of language functions in their **dialogue journals** (written conversations between child and teacher); reporting opinions and personal and general facts, responding to questions, predicting future events, complaining, giving directives, apologizing, thanking, evaluating, offering, promising, and asking various kinds of questions (Shuy, 1988; Staton, Shuy, Peyton & Reed, 1988). Second-language learners also use language functionally; for example, Zulu speakers (ages 12–16) learning English also used the language functions of teaching, inquiring, joking, informing, scolding, offering, seeking clarification, apologizing, explaining, expressing opinions, conversing, thanking, comforting, and reflecting in their dialogue journals (Lindfors, 1989). Functional language development is essential to literacy development in that the writer must use language to facilitate a certain response in the reader. Conversely, an effective reader is aware of what the author is trying to do with language. Therefore, language ability is central to reading and writing.

Narrative ability includes the functional use of language in fluently expressing and sequencing ideas. Many ethnically diverse learners demonstrate strength in composing oral stories, telling lengthy jokes, and describing events such as traffic accidents. Variations in narrative **discourse** (any oral or written communication longer than a single sentence) have been documented by research. If students have an intuitive awareness of how narrative discourse is ordered in text, they can make meaningful predictions in the reading comprehension process. Students may demonstrate strong narrative abilities (an aspect of linguistic intelligence) regardless of the language or dialect spoken.

Style shifting is another important language skill that refers to the ability of speakers and writers to adapt their language styles to various social contexts (depending on the different settings, participants, and topics). As such, style shifting is certainly a core operation of linguistic intelligence, and can also be considered a facet of interpersonal intelligence. Just as we vary our dress depending on the social situation (i.e., formal, semiformal, casual), so do we shift our language styles. Language variety is a necessary part of language competence. The more variety in our language "wardrobe," the better we can interact in diverse social contexts. We need to express ourselves formally in formal situations (e.g., job interviews, professional presentations) and also informally in casual situations (e.g., visiting with a friend in a coffee shop or sitting on the bleachers of a basketball game).

Communicative abilities in oral and written language are central to any language arts program for both native and nonnative English speakers. In addition, Cummins (1994) argued that second-language learners need to acquire not only conversational abilities in the target language, but also academic language competencies in both oral and written language. Programs for second-language learners especially need to facilitate the acquisition of reading and writing academic discourse. To reach grade-level norms, the acquisition of many competencies in a second language often requires a minimum of two years for conversational English abilities and five to seven years for academic language proficiency (Collier, 1987, 1989; Cummins, 1994). To learn a first and second language requires facilitation of functional social interaction. Within a social context, linguistic competence can be acquired, and second-language acquisition is a natural outcome (Krashen, 1987).

Sociolinguistic competence is the foundation for the development of linguistic competence, which includes the structural components of language. These structural components are the *phonological system,* which includes the sounds **(phonemes)** and sound processes of a language; the morphological system, which includes the meaningful word structures **(morphemes);** the *syntactic system,* which consists of the structures and processes of sentence formation; and the **lexicon,** the systematic set of vocabulary and word meanings. Both linguistic competence and sociolinguistic competence are necessary components of any language and literacy development instructional program. Thus, instruction cannot be isolated from the development of learners' communicative competence, regardless of the variety of languages students bring to school.

Learners of any language and dialect develop a certain degree of communicative competence in their native language or dialect; much of language development and ability is universal or common across all languages. Yet differences do exist and need to be considered by teachers in the development of literacy. These differences can exist between the learner's language and the text, between the learner's language and that of the teacher, between the text and the teacher, and between the learner and other learners in a multicultural classroom community. The challenge is to minimize the impact of the differences in guiding learners in their development of literacy.

SOME LINGUISTIC VARIATIONS

Linguistic variations are generally of two kinds: variations within a language and variations across languages. Variations within a language are called **dialects,** which are value-neutral variations of a language found among speakers of particular regions, social classes, or cultural groups. Variations identifiable to speakers in a particular geographical area are called **regional dialects;** variations identifiable to particular speakers in particular social classes or cultural groups are called **social dialects.**

Dialects usually vary in terms of phonological, grammatical, lexical, and functional dimensions. Phonologically, you can easily identify the many variations in pronunciations of words; for example, how do you, your classmates, or family and friends say, "How now brown cow"? "Boil the oysters in oil"? "Park the car by the river"? "Will merry Mary find someone to marry"? "Give them these, not those"? Many pronunciations exist within a language, and learners bring these various pronunciations to both their reading and spelling of words. Grammatically, can you identify people with variations in sentence structures? For example, have you heard someone say, "Did you bring the camera with"? "Did daddy go a-huntin'"? "My mama, she be tall"? Likewise, do you know people from various regions, cultures, social classes, or age groups whose vocabulary varies? Do you or they say *soft drink, cold drink, soda,* or *pop? Bag* or *sack? Neutral ground* or *median strip? Hoagie, submarine,* or *po'boy? Bad, good,* or *cool?* And what about situational, functional differences in conversations, such as getting straight to the point or talking around a point? Discuss among your classmates or colleagues how dialects and discourse customs differ within your communities. (For more information on dialects, see Wolfram, Adger, & Christian, 1999; and the video *American Tongues,* Alvarez & Kolker, 1987.)

Variations often mark us, sometimes unjustly, as formal or informal; educated or less educated; or prestigious or of less status, depending on the social values and norms about language in a community. The language varieties spoken and preferred by the dominant members of a society for conducting formal affairs are called **standard dialects** (Wolfram, 1991), while the varieties more likely used in informal settings and also pervasive among groups of lower social status are called **vernacular dialects.** It is important to note that vernacular dialects and the many variations among social situations are systematic, rule-governed, sophisticated sociolinguistic systems (Labov, 1975; Wolfram, Adger, & Christian, 1999). Many of these features are also found in other vernacular dialects.

EXAMPLES OF LANGUAGE VARIATIONS

African American Vernacular English

African American Vernacular English (AAVE) is a variety of English spoken in African American communities. AAVE consists of a range of speech from standard English to the vernacular speech found within the community and in informal settings. As in any ethnic variety of English, AAVE is rule-governed, containing a systematic set of phonological and syntactic features, some of which are seen in Table 3.1 (Baugh, 1983; Burling, 1973; Labov, 1975; Sleeter, 1991; Smitherman, 1985; Wolfram, Adger, & Christian, 1999).

In addition, the rich lexical and discourse styles found in the African American community make AAVE a fully developed communicative system that is beneficial to literacy development in standard English. The "ebonics" controversy of the 1990s and the Ann Arbor court decision of the late 1970s have led to our understanding of the advantages of acquiring standard English, but with respect for the legitimacy of native vernacular varieties, which function like any language or dialect. African American varieties of English (like other ethnic varieties) are considered fully developed linguistic systems capable of supporting the development of literacy. (For more information, consult the Web site of the Center for Applied Linguistics at http://www.cal.org/ for additional discussions of dialects and ebonics related to education, as well as Adger, Christian, & Taylor, 1999.)

Table 3.1   Selected Phonological and Syntactic Features of AAVE

Phonological Patterns of AAVE	Examples
Consonant cluster simplification	des (desk)
Deletion of /l/	hep (help)
voiced *th*	den (then)
voiceless *th*	tin (thin)
vowel neutralization before nasal consonants	pin (pen)

Morphological and Syntactic Patterns of AAVE	Examples
Deletion of plural	ten cent (cents)
Deletion of third-person singular	The girl walk fast. (walks)
Deletion of past tense	The man call yesterday. (called)
Existential *it (there)*	It was two cars in the garage. (There were)
Invariant *be*	He be hollin' at us. (He hollers)
Deletion of *be*	My momma name Annie. (name is)

Additional Language Varieties

Nonnative varieties of English are found throughout the United States and the world, and learners of English as a second language (ESL) will likely need some additional assistance from their teachers in learning to read. Many English language learners (ELL) will already have some literacy abilities in their first language and in English. Their native linguistic abilities transfer to English, although the extent of transfer may depend on the specific languages and writing systems involved (Cowan & Sarmad, 1976).

Learners often use the rules from their native language schema in reading English as a second language. Many so-called errors are the result of the influence of the native language rather than linguistic or cognitive deficits (Flores, 1984). Therefore, it is important for teachers to learn about similarities and contrasts between languages. Although languages are too complex to be thoroughly discussed here, some phonological, syntactic, and lexical differences between English and Spanish and between English and Vietnamese are now presented in some detail.

Phonological Variations

Phonological contrasts should be considered when teaching phoneme-grapheme correspondences for learning to read and spell words. Not all languages have the same set of phonemes, and their relationship with the writing system can also vary. Because the phoneme systems vary, certain pairs of English words that normally are pronounced differently are pronounced or heard as homonyms by the native speaker. Geissal and Knafle (1977) explained that linguistically diverse learners use their native phonological systems when processing English and may not hear some of the English sounds or contrasts. This could result in what would seem to be a mispronunciation error by someone not knowledgeable about the particular language diversity. These pronunciations are certainly not the result of a language disorder.

The following consonant contrasts are often *not* made by native Spanish speakers learning English because these contrasts are not made in Spanish (Troike, 1972, p. 312):

Sound	*Examples*
ch/sh	chair/share, watch/wash
s/z	sip/zip, racer/razor
n/ng	sin/sing
b/v	bat/vat, rabble/ravel
t/th	tin/thin
s/th	sin/thin
d/th	den/then, ladder/lather

Spanish, unlike English, has only five vowel phonemes. Thus Spanish speakers do not hear or pronounce contrasts such as the following:

bait/bet/bat

cut/cot

cheap/chip

pool/pull

coat/caught

Here are some more examples, this time from Vietnamese (Grognet et al., 1976). Vietnamese speakers learning English do not contrast such pairs of English words as the following:

Sound	Examples
z/s	flees/fleece, dyes/dice
ch/sh	much/mush
f/p	laugh/lap
p/b	pin/bin
k/g	back/bag
th/t	ether/eater
th/d	weather/wetter/wedder
i/e	pit/Pete
e/a	bct/bat

Nonnative speakers of English (and dialect speakers) do not initially hear or pronounce contrasts not made in the native language. Vietnamese phonology does not allow certain consonant clusters at the ends of words; therefore, in pronouncing English words they may split consonant blends with vowels (e.g., stop becomes suhtop) or delete consonants at the ends of words (e.g., cold becomes col'; called becomes call). Thus, their auditory discrimination and oral reading may be influenced by the phonological organization of the native language. However, this is natural and not a sign of linguistic deficiency or disability (Flores, 1984; Goodman & Buck, 1973/1997). In teaching the reading and writing of words, these pairs of words can be treated like any other set of homonyms; that is, teach them in meaningful contexts first. More contextual support reduces potential linguistic interference from phonological diversity. Therefore, meaning-based, holistic techniques are especially important to successful reading instruction of linguistically diverse learners (see Barnitz, 1985; Carrell, Devine & Eskey, 1988; Enright & McCloskey, 1988; Freeman & Freeman, 1992; Opitz, 1998; Peregoy and Boyle, 1997; Rigg & Allen, 1989; Spangenberg-Urbschat & Pritchard, 1994).

For problem English contrasts for speakers of other languages, see Kress (1993, p. 132); for the Russian language specifically, see http://www.geocities.com/Colosseum/Track/7635/alphabet.html.

Syntactic Variations

Just as phonological systems of native languages influence performance in English, so do the syntactic systems. Davis (1972, pp. 131–132) presented, among other syntactic features, the following sentence structures likely produced by Spanish speakers learning English (also included in a teachers' guide by the New York City Board of Education, *Teaching English to Puerto Rican Pupils in Grades 1 and 2* [1956, 1963] cited by Davis, 1972.).

Sentence Structure	Examples
Deletion of subject pronouns and articles	Is green. Is my sister.
Negative morpheme before verb	Jose not (no) is here.
Adjectives after nouns	The dress green. The dresses greens.
Deletion of /s/ inflections	He go to church. The pencil are here.
Present instead of progressive	He clean now.
Preposition contrasts	In the counter. In First St.
Have for *be*	She have nine years.

Teachers of Vietnamese learners need to be aware of syntactic differences (Grognet et al., 1976). The Vietnamese language does not use suffixes to convey meaning. Meaning is conveyed in other ways, as seen in sentences that translate into English as follows:

I need book.

I need one piece book.

I need three piece book.

I need few piece book.

Plurality is marked by separate words rather than suffixes. Likewise, tense is marked by separate words that are equivalent to the underlined words in the following sentences:

I often drink tea.

I intend to drink tea.

I past tense drink tea.

I about to drink tea.

Because Vietnamese does not use suffixes, its native speakers often omit or ignore them in their speaking, writing, and reading of English. Greene (1981) referred to this as the "morpheme conceptualization barrier," but found that Vietnamese speakers who also were competent in French, a language with suffixes, tended to recognize and produce English suffixes in their writing and reading. Strategies such as sentence expansion, choral reading, the language experience approach, creative writing, and particularly using children's literature can help students become sensitive to new syntactic structures being learned in English (these instructional strategies are discussed in more detail in later chapters).

Lexical Variations

Teachers should also know that vocabulary varies across languages. For example, the Spanish *penitencia, realizar, libreria,* and *chanza* are not equivalent to the English *penitentiary, realize, library,* and *chance,* but rather *penance, accomplish an ambition, bookstore* and *joke* (Thonis, 1976). French speakers learning English need to learn the meaningful contrasts between the English words *cut* and *carve,* for example, because French has only one word for both concepts, *couper.* For teaching vocabulary to all learners, strategies such as semantic mapping and semantic feature analysis are recommended (see Chapter 10). Likewise, idioms and various other figures of speech are also potentially problematic for learners not familiar with the metaphorical use of phrases such as *kick the bucket, factor into the equation,* and *the bottom line.* Because vocabulary and metaphorical language are closely related to meaning, there is a potential for interference with reading comprehension, unless they understand how to use context and/or acquire the nonliteral meanings.

For brief descriptions of various languages of the world, see Comrie (1990), Hallcom (1995), and McWhorter (2000).

Other Variations

Other ways that languages vary include orthographic diversity and discourse diversity.

orthographies   **Orthographies** are writing systems for languages and fall into various categories. Some writing systems have symbols that represent whole word meanings, like Chinese. Most writing systems have symbols that represent levels of the stream of speech; for example, *syllabaries* have symbols representing syllables as in Japanese and Cherokee. The most common writing systems have symbols representing phonemes—for example, various alphabets. These alphabetic writing systems operate based on the spelling system that conveys the particular grapheme-phoneme representations in the language. Most languages of the world have alphabets of various kinds (e.g., Greek, Arabic, Russian), but most alphabetic languages use the Roman alphabet, based on Latin, which spread through imperial conquests and missionary evangelization across many languages of the world. English, a Germanic language, has acquired the Roman writing system, which does not appear on the surface as "regular" as would be found in the Romance languages. Likewise, the directionality of print varies across languages; for example, Arabic, Farsi, and Hebrew speakers read from right to left. Nonnative speakers of English have to grapple with the unique alphabet connections to English. While first- and second-language learners can readily acquire phonemic awareness, the connections to the writing system are more difficult and performance can vary. See Venezky (1999) and Wilde (1997) for discussions of the writing system of English. See Coulmas (1989) for discussions of writing system characteristics of languages around the world.

Oral and written discourse diversity also can influence learners acquiring literacy (See review by Barnitz 1986, 1994, 1998). Research by Au (1993a) has documented the role of culturally unique discourse strategies of co-narration of responses to texts in reading lessons for Hawaiian minority children. Heath (1983) documented the unique "ways with words" of three communities in the Piedmont Carolinas impacting children's literacy if teachers are aware or unaware of the diversity. Discourse variations can be allowed in classrooms that involve children in talking naturally as a strategy for developing authentic literacy (Au, 1993a). Likewise, culture-specific variations in textual organization (Kaplan, 1966; Connor, 1996) can influence the comprehension and composing of texts by learners from various cultures (see Barnitz, 1986).

Taken as a whole, language in any of its variations forms a rich foundation for literacy development. Successful teachers with linguistic knowledge know how to minimize any negative effects of differences on the reading performance of their students. Some guiding principles for literacy development with language diverse learners follow.

INSTRUCTIONAL PRINCIPLES

Respect differences in languages and dialects as natural. Learners have communicative competence in their native dialects and languages upon which to build English literacy. This implies that children can develop literacy if allowed to use their native dialect or language in transition to learning to read and write standard English. Respecting linguistic diversity allows for children to take risks to communicate in the various language arts modes. In our profession, we have come to appreciate linguistic diversity as difference rather than as deficit, for negative attitudes toward language and cultural differences interfere with the success of learners acquiring literacy of standard English and their native language or dialect (Goodman & Buck, 1973/1997). We can minimize any potential negative effects of differences if we have the appropriate theoretical and practical professional knowledge, and attitudes. It is important for teachers to understand and appreciate linguistic diversity as one of the professional knowledge bases for teaching culturally diverse learners. Visit http://www.nabe.org/, the Web site for the National Association for Bilingual Education, and http://www.tesol.org/assoc/k12standards/it/01.html to view the ESL Standards for Pre–K–12 Students.

Use methods that bridge cultural background knowledge and whatever texts are being read. Such techniques allow learners to use the total language system, while it is still developing, in the literacy process. Holistic strategies such as the language experience approach (LEA) (see Chapter 7) and the experience-text-relationship method (ETR) (see Chapter 11) allow learners to make connections between their language and culture and that of the texts they are reading and writing. The **language experience approach** allows developing readers and writers to connect their oral language with the written language. The texts produced in language experience lessons become good "drafts" for further development of linguistic skills and processes (see Rigg, 1989). The **experience-text-relationship method** and related reading process approaches allow learners to use their authentic discourse and cultural background knowledge in constructing meanings for the texts they are reading (Au, 1993a). English language learners have better opportunities to acquire competence in oral and written English when "comprehensible input" (Krashen, 1987) is provided for students in natural language lessons. Teachers can make input comprehensible if they base lessons on students' prior knowledge and use language that is predictable. See http://www.cal.org/ to learn more about the issues related to improving communication through better understanding of language and culture.

Contextualize instruction on language structures and skills within the composing and comprehending process. While process strategies are critical for successful development of language and literacy, second-language learners will also need direct instruction on specific aspects of the language system such as grammar structures, spelling patterns, meaning vocabulary, and discourse patterns. Teachers may choose to use semantic maps or clusters to teach the relevant cultural background knowledge and vocabulary related to a story being read (see Chapter 10), or they may choose to use various graphic organizers or text pattern diagrams to represent the organizational pattern of a text, especially for learners who organize textual meaning differently (see Chapter 11). Teachers may choose to use a variety of authentic approaches to teaching grammar structures (see Chapter 7), especially if the learners come from language backgrounds where the grammar structures are ordered differently (see Weaver, 1998; Barnitz, 1998). Or, through systematic phonics instruction in balanced reading programs, teachers will need to provide direct instruction on the orthographic patterns, especially if the reader comes from a language that does not use an alphabetic writing system, or uses an alphabetic system different from English (see Chapters 7 and 8). Many strategies that are successful with native speakers can also be adapted to nonnative speakers of English when combined with holistic strategies (Barnitz, 1985).

Use authentic materials from the learner's community. Literacy materials are all around us and readily available. Such materials include restaurant menus from ethnic restaurants, church bulletins printed in more than one language, directions for assembling a toy or installing camera batteries or film, and brochures from community businesses written in several languages. Meaningful materials from the community that are used in the classroom support literacy development. These authentic materials can be connected with role-playing strategies for developing communicative competence related to direct use in the community (e.g., learning to order from a menu; also see Chapters 12 and 13). Moreover, authentic materials representing various cultural groups can be used for developing cross-cultural awareness in order to build classroom community and help develop respect among students for each other's languages and cultures.

Design literature-based instruction for developing language competence. Using literature as well as musical lyrics can provide needed variety of language structures and functions that support English language acquisition. Exposure and interaction with literature and lyrics facilitates the acquisition of the various systems of language, multicultural understanding, and various cognitive and social processes. Literature in its various genres as well as literature with artistic illustrations and audio-recorded counterparts provides necessary "scaffolding" for children acquiring the language. Teachers can also have learners read familiar stories (e.g., "Cinderella") that may be represented in different ways and in various languages and cultures (see Chapter 11 for examples of ways to compare and contrast versions of familiar stories). For a review of the many benefits of literature-based instruction, see Barnitz, Gipe, and Richards (1999) and Morrow and Gambrell (2000). Refer also to Appendix D for an extensive list of quality multiethnic children's literature.

Use technological and other communicative arts to facilitate oral and written language acquisition. Speaker and Barnitz (1999) present a vision for a hypothetical culturally diverse classroom in the twenty-first century. Technology provides the multimediated support for language and literacy to be acquired if embedded within a classroom community that is communicatively interactive. Technological processes associated with various mediated language experiences are universal across languages. Native and nonnative speakers of English can view and visually represent ideas in various electronic and linguistic forms in order to communicate. The more learners use whatever communicative systems are available to them, the better the chance that their general communicative abilities will develop. By incorporating the arts into language/literacy instruction, we especially help nonnative speakers of English acquire abilities of constructing meaning. Photography, dance, music, painting, and drama can allow for communicative expressions to occur, which in turn are foundationally related to oral and written language development. Wholesome musical lyrics from audio recordings can also support literacy, especially for learners whose learning styles are attuned to musical ways of representing meaning. Likewise, professionally published or teacher-made audio recordings of literature and content material can also support comprehension and language skills acquisition. Many of the visual and musical arts provide contextual support for oral and written language to occur and develop, in addition to providing an avenue for students whose strong intelligences are bodily-kinesthetic, spatial, or musical in particular (see Chapter 14). The arts, both the performing and technological, are invaluable avenues to facilitating language and literacy abilities of culturally diverse learners. Therefore, teachers need to be advocates for supporting technology and the arts.

Facilitate authentic, functional communication. In classroom communities, functional discourse is encouraged. Using language for various purposes or functions is what drives the language acquisition process (Halliday, 1978). Thus, writing and reading texts related to real purposes, for real audiences, provides natural motivation for literacy. Dialogue journals, mentioned earlier, are one means of incorporating language functions. Whether in print or electronic formats (e.g., e-journals; e-mails), dialogue journals can encourage the development of functional discourse in which the English-speaking adult serves as a model for using the structures and functions of English in the natural writing/reading process. It is through natural, functional discourse that learners of any language or dialect acquire literacy.

Base literacy assessment on authentic language and literacy tasks and events. Through authentic tasks, students use the entire language system to express themselves in real literacy events (Garcia & Pearson, 1991). Potentially negative influences of dialect or language diversity are diminished when there is rich situational and textual context. Whatever a student's dialect, functional language use in narrating or retelling a story can be demonstrated. The following is a retelling by a sixth-grade African American female student of the story *Jumanji* (Van Allsburg, 1981). (Some of the dialect is represented by the spelling, but the focus here should be on the fluent cohesiveness of the narrative summary.)

> This story is about Judy an(d) Peter. Dey (their) mother an(d) father went to a reception; dey left the(m) home by theyself (theirselves). Judy an(d) Peter say it got a little boring; so, so, dey went outside across the street an(d) dey foun(d) a game. Judys, Judy say, "No, let's wait, let's rea(d) de instruction(s)." Judy read the instructions. Den they start(ed) playin the game. Lots of thangs (things) happen(ed) to a game. Den, Peter roll(ed) de dice; den he stopped on a lion; his siste(r) said, "Peter, look behind you!" On top of the piano, they had a big lion lickin his lips. Den it was Judy turn. Den somethin' happen(ed) to her. An den other thangs . . . Judy and dem, um, when Judy and dem finish(ed) the game, they brought it back across the street. Dey (their) fathe(r) and mothe(r) came home; dey were (a)sleep. Judy shoved at Peter to wake him up an den, his mo(ther), they started to finish the puzzles. Then this lady came an say, "My two son(s) don't, dey don't read the instructions," and den the, um the two boys went outside; dey went across the street an dey found a puzzle an brought it back.

At first glance, a teacher might misjudge this student's language abilities by focusing only on the surface dialect features. This short retelling illustrates the student's ability to compose a narrative with an overall gist of the story. (See Irwin and Mitchell, 1983, and Morrow, 1988, for ways of assessing retellings; also refer to Figure 6.1 and Figure 11.1 in this text.) Multiple ways of authentic assessment are needed to understand the full linguistic abilities of children.

In interpreting assessment data, be sensitive to cultural and linguistic variation. [Hall and Freedle (1975) review research demonstrating that students' performance on tests is better if the vocabulary matches their cultural backgrounds.] In Louisiana for example, the word *parish* is equivalent in meaning to *county* used in other parts of the country; the words *carnival, throw,* and *krewe* have particular meanings associated with Mardi Gras; and children play *cabbage ball* instead of 16-inch *softball*. If these items appeared on a standardized vocabulary test, non-Louisianians would probably be at a cultural disadvantage.

In a similar way, various cultural experiences affect the comprehension of prose. In a study by Reynolds, Taylor, Steffensen, Shirey, and Anderson (1981), urban African American students comprehended a passage describing an event in a school cafeteria (involving the discourse style of playing the dozens) differently than agrarian European American students. Andersson and Gipe (1983) found that the creative process required for inferential comprehension by New Orleans–area Catholic school children and New York Greek Orthodox children was influenced by the cultural schemata the children possessed. Put simply, cultural background knowledge influences the comprehension and recall of information in text (see Au, 1993a; Barnitz, 1986; Steffensen, 1987).

Another example of language and cultural influences with respect to assessment can be found in auditory discrimination tests (Geissal & Knafle, 1977). Linguistically diverse students may not hear contrasts between word pairs such as *thin/tin, sherry/cherry, cot/caught, oil/Earl,* and *Mary/merry/marry* because the linguistic rules and patterns of their dialects or native languages do not permit such contrasts. Teachers must know about features of linguistic diversity in order to attribute an "error" to the appropriate cause, that is, an auditory problem versus a dialect variation. In fluent reading, these dialect homonym pairs can be interpreted by context just like other homonym pairs, such as *knight/night*. Dialect differences are not a liability in literacy performance (Goodman & Buck, 1973/1997).

SUMMARY

This chapter provided a brief overview for the linguistically based professional knowledge that teachers use in teaching diverse language learners to read and write standard English, also called the language of wider communication. To facilitate the necessary acquisition of standard English literacy, respecting the native languages and dialects of our students is a necessary first step. Likewise, incorporating literacy strategies that allow diverse learners to connect to the full range of the communicative arts is especially critical to supporting their development of communicative competencies, ever so critical to learning to read and write. Teachers need a solid understanding of the communicative nature of language and the arts, a continually growing understanding of the languages and dialects found among the children they teach; and implementation of principles and strategies that consider the unique cultures and languages students possess. All of this knowledge contributes to classroom decisions that benefit all children in developing language, literacy, life, and liberty. We certainly can lift our linguistic lamps beside the golden doors of our schools and communities.

Suggested Readings

Au, K. H. (1993). *Literacy instruction in multicultural settings.* Fort Worth, TX: Harcourt Brace Jovanovich.

> *The author provides teachers with an understanding of cultural and linguistic considerations for teaching reading and writing. Taking a constructivist approach to literacy instruction, the author also emphasizes the roles of cultural discourse interaction and multicultural literature for teaching writing and reading.*

Brisk, M. E., & Harrington, M. M. (2000). *Literacy and bilingualism: A handbook for all teachers.* Mahwah, NJ: Erlbaum.

> *The authors provide current perspectives on bilingualism and biliteracy at the elementary and secondary school levels. Readers of this book will acquire an understanding of both theory and practice for development of language and literacy in bilingual education.*

Cary, S. (2000). *Working with second language learners: Answers to teachers' top ten questions.* Portsmouth, NH: Heinemann.

> *The author provides reader-friendly chapters to answer the most frequently asked questions by teachers charged with educating linguistically diverse learners. Topics include assessment; making teacher-talk more understandable; motivating reluctant learners to speak English, making difficult texts more comprehensible; helping learners write English better; teaching grade-level content areas; building students' learning strategies; supporting learners' native languages when teachers do not speak those languages; and minimizing cultural communication conflicts in classroom settings.*

Faltis, C. J., & Hudelson, S. J. (1998). *Bilingual education in elementary and secondary school communities: Toward understanding and caring.* Boston: Allyn & Bacon.

> *The authors provide an overview of the advantages of bilingual education in today's schools. Included also are chapters on the nature of bilingual education programs, why it is a schoolwide concern, theoretical frameworks from a second-language acquisition perspective, and implementation in elementary and secondary schools.*

Freeman, D. E., & Freeman, Y. S. (2001). *Between worlds: Access to second language acquisition,* 2nd ed. Portsmouth, NH: Heinemann.

> *This book provides readers with a practical understanding of second-language acquisition inside and outside the classroom worlds of nonnative speakers of English. The authors provide theoretical and practical discussions of language, literacy, and content instruction for linguistically diverse learners.*

McWhorter, J. (2000). *Spreading the word: Language and dialect in America.* Portsmouth, NH: Heinemann.

> *This text is a concise introduction to linguistic diversity found among school populations. The author includes many examples to illustrate linguistic topics teachers need to know about their students' abilities.*

Opitz, M. F. (Ed.). (1998). *Literacy instruction for culturally and linguistically diverse students: A collection of articles and commentaries.* Newark, DE: International Reading Association.

The editor provides a collection of previously published articles from International Reading Association journals, which are grouped into five major thematic categories: awareness and attitudes toward literacy, principles of instruction, enhancing reading comprehension, using writing to develop reading, and selecting and using multicultural literature. Included are invited general commentaries on these themes and articles. An annotated bibliography of multicultural children's literature is also provided.

Peregoy, S. F., & Boyle, O. F. (1997). *Reading, writing, and learning in ESL: A resource book for K–12 teachers.* New York: Longman.

The authors provide a practical guide for elementary school teachers for developing English as another language for their linguistically diverse learners. Particular emphasis is on developing writing and reading through interrelating the language arts across the curriculum.

Spangenberg-Urbschat, K., & Pritchard, R. (Eds.). (1994). *Kids come in all languages: Reading instruction for ESL students.* Newark, DE: International Reading Association.

This edited book provides teachers with an introductory survey of trends in teaching children from diverse language backgrounds. The collection of readings is divided into three sections: issues on linguistic and cultural diversity, organizing for instruction, and instructional practices.

Wolfram, W., Adger, C., & Christian, D. (1999). *Dialects in schools and communities.* Mahwah, NJ: Erlbaum.

The authors provide an invaluable resource on current trends and issues on sociolinguistic variation found in school and community settings. Included are such topics as language variation, dialect variation, and communicative interaction across cultural groups; perceptions and attitudes about dialects and learners who speak them; the impact of variation on oral (speaking, listening) and written (writing, reading) communication performance; and fostering dialect awareness in classrooms.

Recommended Web Sites for Related Professional Organizations

American Association for Applied Linguistics
   http://www.aaal.org/
American Dialect Society
   http://www.americandialect.org/
Center for Applied Linguistics
   http://www.cal.org/
International Reading Association
   http://www.reading.org/
Lindy Boggs National Center for Community Literacy
   http://www.loyno.edu/boggs.literacy.center/

Linguistic Society of America
   http://www.lsadc.org/
National Association for Bilingual Education
   http://www.nabe.org/
National Council of Teachers of English
   http://www.ncte.org/
Teachers of English to Speakers of Other Languages
   http://www.tesol.org/

4 Reading-Related Factors

After you have read this chapter, you should be able to:
1. identify three basic categories of reading-related factors associated with reading difficulties;
2. explain the teacher's role with regard to each of the basic categories of reading-related factors;
3. recognize symptoms of poor general health or possible visual, auditory, or neurological problems;
4. prepare objective anecdotal records;
5. suggest ways to establish a classroom environment that might help students who have difficulties with learning or who have been "labeled," to revalue themselves as learners.

Key Concepts and Terms

ADD/ADHD	auditory perception	physical neglect
affect	bibliotherapy	reading-related factors
anecdotal records	brain-based learning	resiliency
at risk	cognition	sexual abuse
attributional retraining	dyslexia	stuttering
auditory acuity	emotional maltreatment	variables
auditory blending	learning disability	visual acuity
auditory discrimination	nonreading factors	visual perception
auditory memory	physical abuse	visually impaired

HISTORICAL BACKGROUND

For many years educators and others have been concerned because too many students fail to learn to read, or read so ineffectively that eventually the struggle leads to avoidance of reading altogether. All teachers will find such students in their classrooms and should be prepared to help them as much as they can. The list of potential causes for reading failure is long and includes such factors as lack of nurturing experiences, emotional blocking, lack of motivation, poor health, hunger, inability to perceive objects and sounds, dysfunction of the central nervous system, processing problems, low mental activity, and inappropriate teaching. Only one factor in this list, inappropriate teaching, can be directly controlled and substantially changed by educators. The remaining factors (plus many others) are not directly related to teaching reading, but are important to all learning; thus they are referred to as **reading-related factors,** or **nonreading factors.**

The interest in factors associated with reading failure originated to a great extent with clinicians from other disciplines. They observed that many of their clients and patients also had reading problems. These observations suggested further study to determine whether the concomitant factors were causing reading difficulties. Many studies conducted early in the twentieth century compared good and poor readers to determine the incidence of specific factors. In general, these early studies, referred to as "head count" studies, revealed that students labeled "reading disabled" exhibited concomitant nonreading factors more frequently than good readers did. This finding held for several different types of reading-related factors.

More recent correlational studies tend to verify the findings of the earlier "head count" studies. These studies yield relatively high correlations between two factors, or **variables**—the factor of reading development and whatever nonreading factor is being investigated. Unfortunately, many people have misinterpreted the results of these correlational studies. The proper interpretation of high correlation coefficients is that the *relationship* between reading achievement and the other factor is high. The conclusion that the nonreading factor caused the reading difficulty (or vice versa) *cannot* be drawn from a correlational study, because an unknown factor may be influencing both the nonreading factor and level of reading achievement.

Another research approach identifies a large group of people exhibiting a particular nonreading factor and assesses their performance in reading. Such studies often reveal a wide range of reading achievement scores, indicating that some people with the factor read satisfactorily and some do not. Those who read well somehow compensate for the nonreading factor. Therefore, it is extremely important for teachers and others to know that the presence of a particular nonreading factor is no guarantee that the student will not learn to read. It *is* reasonable to conclude, however, that the presence of the nonreading factor may impede reading progress. Furthermore, when a student manifests the presence of two or more nonreading factors, the chances for success in reading are lessened and the student is considered **at risk.** The multiple causation hypothesis (Monroe, 1932; Robinson, 1946) must be considered seriously, but in no way as an excuse for not providing the best instruction for the student.

THREE BASIC CATEGORIES

Factors associated with reading difficulties can be placed in one of three basic categories: physical (including neurophysical or neurological), psychological, and environmental, which includes instructional factors. Teachers, by the very nature of their role and their training, should be held responsible for instructional factors associated with poor reading achievement. Thus, this text focuses on helping teachers identify students making poor progress in reading and provide appropriate instruction for these students. The improvement of reading instruction through better informed teachers is a major goal of this text.

Physical Factors

General Health

Learning to read is a demanding task for many students. A student must be alert, attentive, and capable of working for a sustained period of time. Any physical condition that lowers stamina or impairs vitality can have a deleterious effect on learning. Serious illnesses and prolonged absences from school obviously may result in learning gaps. Many conscientious parents and teachers work hard to alleviate such problems; home instruction is also provided by many school systems for students who are bedridden or otherwise incapacitated for extended periods of time. Today's technology can also be of great assistance in such situations.

More subtle forms of illness and physical problems sometimes elude parents and teachers. Chronic low-grade infections, glandular disturbances, allergies, and persistent minor illnesses such as mild respiratory problems can induce a general malaise and lower the vitality level. Insufficient sleep may inhibit learning, and malnutrition may lower ability to attend and learn.

Teachers, of course, are not physicians and cannot appropriately assume medical responsibilities. Yet they do function as substitute parents while school is in session and must be sensitive to the general well-being of each student in their class. When teachers are concerned about possible health problems, they should seek help from the school nurse and principal. Communication with the parents should be initiated according to local school policies.

Occasionally teachers encounter parents who resist counseling efforts regarding their child's health. Little can be done to help the student directly when this happens. If the problem is serious enough, however, legal procedures can be instigated. Usually other community agencies, such as the child welfare department, become involved in these cases.

When students are not in good health, teachers must try to accommodate their problems as much as possible. Let these students rest, put their heads on their desks, go to the nurse's office, or whatever seems reasonable for the particular problem involved.

Visual Acuity

Visual acuity is keenness of vision. Acuity problems are usually physiologically based and can be corrected by ophthalmologists or optometrists. The role of the classroom teacher is to identify students with visual acuity problems that may have gone unnoticed by parents or other teachers.

While some students learn to read in spite of visual problems, the emphasis here is not so much on the relationship to reading difficulty as it is on comfort and efficiency. When students can deal comfortably with print at normal distance (about 14 to 18 inches), the chances are good that they will be able to attend to a task as long as is necessary. Discomforts such as headaches or burning or watery eyes diminish their chances considerably. Learners who see relatively clearly work more efficiently for longer periods of time without having to direct undue energy to accommodate visual deficiencies.

Assessment Techniques. Some school systems hire reading (or other) specialists who are trained to help identify students with vision problems. Even with special training, however, these people are not vision specialists, and their work should be considered as screening only. Instruments typically used for screening purposes are the *Keystone School Vision Screening Test* (Keystone View) and the *Master Ortho-Rater Visual Efficiency Test* (Bausch and Lomb). Other devices often used for the screening of vision are the *Rader Visual Acuity Screening Chart* (Modern Education Corporation), the *Snellen Chart,* and the *Spache Binocular Reading Test* (Keystone View).

Probably the most important assessment function for classroom teachers is to observe the behavior of their students. The Optometric Extension Program Foundation has compiled an excellent checklist to help teachers make reliable observations of visual behavior that could interfere with academic progress (Figure 4.1). If several of these behaviors are observed, especially within a single category, the teacher should refer the student to an appropriate vision specialist, whether inside or outside the school setting.

Figure 4.1   Educator's Checklist: Observable Clues to Classroom Vision Problems

Student's name _____ Age _____ Date _____

1. Appearance of eyes:
One eye turns in or out at any time _____
Reddened eyes or lids _____
Eyes tear excessively _____
Encrusted eyelids _____
Frequent styes on eyelids _____

2. Complaints when using eyes at desk:
Headaches in forehead or temples _____
Burning or itching after reading or
   desk work _____
Nausea or dizziness _____
Print blurs after reading a short time _____

3. Behavioral signs of visual problems:
A. *Eye movement abilities (ocular motility)*
   Head turns as reads across page _____
   Loses place often during reading _____
   Needs finger or marker to keep place _____
   Displays short attention span in reading
      or copying _____
   Too frequently omits words _____
   Repeatedly omits "small" words _____
   Writes up- or downhill on paper _____
   Rereads or skips lines unknowingly _____
   Orients drawings poorly on page _____
B. *Eye teaming abilities (binocularity)*
   Complains of seeing double (diplopia) _____
   Repeats letters within words _____
   Omits letters, numbers, or phrases _____
   Misaligns digits in number columns _____
   Squints, closes, or covers one eye _____
   Tilts head extremely while working
      at desk _____
   Consistently shows gross postural
      deviations at all desk activities _____
C. *Eye-hand coordination abilities*
   Must feel things to assist in any
      interpretation required _____
   Eyes not used to "steer" hand movements
      (extreme lack of orientation, placement
      of words or drawings on page) _____
   Writes crookedly, poorly spaced, cannot
      stay on ruled lines _____
   Misaligns both horizontal and vertical
      series of numbers _____
   Uses hand or fingers to keep place on
      the page _____

Uses other hand as "spacer" to control
   spacing and alignment on page _____
Repeatedly confuses left-right directions _____
D. *Visual form perception (visual comparison,
   visual imagery, visualization)*
   Mistakes words with same or similar
      beginnings _____
   Fails to recognize same word in next
      sentence _____
   Reverses letters and/or words in writing
      and copying _____
   Confuses likenesses and minor
      differences _____
   Confuses same word in same sentence _____
   Repeatedly confuses similar beginnings
      and endings of words _____
   Fails to visualize what is read either
      silently or orally _____
   Whispers to self for reinforcement while
      reading silently _____
   Returns to "drawing with fingers" to
      decide likes and differences _____
E. *Refractive status (nearsightedness,
   farsightedness, focus problems, etc.)*
   Comprehension reduces as reading
      continues; loses interest too quickly _____
   Mispronounces similar words as
      continues reading _____
   Blinks excessively at desk tasks and/or
      reading; not elsewhere _____
   Holds book too closely; face too close
      to desk surface _____
   Avoids all possible near-centered tasks _____
   Complains of discomfort in tasks that
      demand visual interpretation _____
   Closes or covers one eye when reading
      or doing desk work _____
   Makes errors in copying from
      chalkboard to paper on desk _____
   Makes errors in copying from reference
      book to notebook _____
   Squints to see chalkboard, or requests
      to move nearer _____
   Rubs eyes during or after short periods
      of visual activity _____
   Fatigues easily; blinks to make
      chalkboard clear up after desk task _____

Teachers' Responsibilities. The classroom teacher does not initiate correction of visual acuity problems. These problems are often resolved through proper prescription of glasses. If the vision specialist believes a problem can be corrected through visual therapy, such activities typically are conducted by the parents under a doctor's supervision or by special teachers working with the student on a one-to-one basis outside the regular classroom.

Classroom teachers should ensure the best possible conditions to accommodate the needs of students with mild vision problems. Nearsighted students (i.e., those with *myopia*) should be able to see the chalkboard better when their desks are closer to it. Prescription lenses will reduce this problem, as well as farsightedness (i.e., *hyperopia*) and astigmatism. Ample light is necessary, and students should be reminded occasionally to rest their eyes after lengthy reading assignments. Ease of reading rather than speed should be emphasized.

For students who have been classified as **visually impaired,** sight-saving books printed in large type (12 to 24 point) can be requested for use in regular classrooms (see the "Suggested Readings" at the end of this chapter for sources of large-print materials). Visually impaired students function quite well in a regular classroom. In addition to large-print materials, methods using tactile discrimination and word tracing are useful.

Visual Perception

Visual perception skills include visual discrimination of form, visual closure, constancy, and visual memory. A student may have normal visual acuity skills but underdeveloped visual perception skills.

Visual discrimination of form, commonly called simply *visual discrimination,* requires recognizing similarities and differences between letters and words in reading. For example, the student must be able to distinguish between *H* and *K* or *c, e,* and *o.*

Visual closure is the ability to identify or complete, from an incomplete presentation, an object, picture, letter, or word. The student must identify the whole even though the whole is not provided. For example, the student must be able to recognize that

 needs another feature, or that has teeth missing, or that f_ _tb_ll

represents the word *football.*

Constancy is a factor when a figure, letter, or word remains the same regardless of a change in shape, orientation, size, or color. This concept is critical for reading because many types of print fonts are used and students must not be confused by slight changes— for example, *a* and a. Also, many letters that are the same in shape are different letters because of their orientation, or placement—for example, *b* and *d, p* and *q,* or *n, u,* and *c.* In the world of objects, orientation has never made a difference—a chair is a chair no matter which way you turn it. However, when dealing with letters and words, orientation can make a difference.

Visual memory is the ability to remember the sequence of letters in words. This ability is most obviously reflected in spelling; however, it is also important in reading when words are encountered having the same or many similar letters but a different sequence. For example, a student lacking in visual memory may have difficulty distinguishing between *ate, eat,* and *tea.* Many mature readers have to tax their visual memory skills upon encountering *through, though,* and *thorough.*

Assessment Techniques. Several standardized instruments assess visual discrimination, visual closure, constancy, and visual memory skills. The following are examples:

- *Gates-MacGinitie Reading Tests-Level Pre-Reading (PR),* Riverside
- *Metropolitan Readiness Tests,* Harcourt Brace Educational Measurement
- *Murphy-Durrell Reading Readiness Analysis,* Harcourt Brace Educational Measurement

If teachers know the characteristics of the various visual perception skills, they can develop classroom activities to assess these visual abilities. Worksheets can be easily prepared that request students to identify the "same letter or word" (e.g., o | c o c e; cake | coke cake coke) or the "letter or word that is different" (e.g., b b o b; bed bad bed bed).

Visual closure tasks at an early stage usually involve picture or shape completion tasks. In one example, the student is asked to complete the second drawing so it looks like the first.

Constancy is often assessed as a specially designed visual discrimination task. Again, finding what is "alike" or "different" is the direction—for example, d | b b b d or p | p q p.

Visual memory is more difficult to assess. Initially, the teacher may use a modification of the party game in which several objects are presented on a tray for viewing, then covered, and participants are asked to write down as many as they can remember. For classroom use, three or four objects may be shown. The teacher then covers them, removes one, shows the remaining objects, and asks the student what was removed. Letters and words can be assessed in a similar fashion. A word or letter is shown for about two seconds. The student is then asked to locate the word or letter from a list of words or letters. Consistently poor performance on spelling tests or in written work beyond third or fourth grade may also indicate a need for visual memory practice.

Teachers' Responsibilities. Many practice activities are readily available to teachers in developmental reading texts and activity books for helping students develop visual perception skills. Some of the more representative exercises are provided here.

1. Have the student mark the letter that is like the one at the beginning of the row:
   B | E   B   D

2. Direct the student to identify "what's missing?" in a picture.

3. Direct the student to mark the letter or letter group that looks like the first item in each row:

   ap | pa   la   ap

   bl | lb   bl   bi

4. Show the student a series of letters, remove the series, and have the student write from memory what was seen. Reshow the series if necessary until the student succeeds.

Auditory Acuity

Auditory acuity is keenness of hearing. Students obviously need to hear adequately in school. Students with high-tone hearing deficits have more difficulties learning to read than those with low-tone deficits. The consonants that give distinction and meaning to speech in our language are relatively high-pitched (especially *s*, *l*, and *t*), whereas vowel sounds are lower in pitch. Most teachers of young children are female, and their voices are higher than those of males. Thus, it is understandable why high-tone deficits might be more critical than low-tone deficits when teaching young children to read. Much early reading work involves oral-aural participation. Successful performance with phonics activities also requires good auditory acuity.

Hearing loss is a medical matter best handled by a hearing specialist or otologist. The teacher can be of considerable help, however, by identifying students suspected of having hearing deficits.

Assessment Techniques. Screening for auditory acuity with an audiometer is a reliable procedure. However, teachers must be specially trained in the use of this sensitive instrument, and even then, results should be considered tentative. Students who do not pass the audiometric screening should be referred to a hearing specialist in the school or to other proper personnel for professional diagnosis.

Classroom teachers must be sensitive to and observant of behaviors or physical symptoms that suggest hearing loss. The list of common symptoms in Figure 4.2 will help the teacher identify students who should be seen by the school nurse, speech and hearing specialist, or reading specialist. A decision can then be made whether to suggest medical assistance.

Fortunately, many school systems have speech and hearing specialists. Young children entering school are usually screened by the specialist, and many potential problems are identified early. Teachers find these services helpful, and the speech teacher is usually eager to consult with and assist the faculty with students experiencing hearing loss.

Sometimes teachers can jump to the conclusion that there is a hearing deficit when a student shows particular physical symptoms. Some symptoms may be only temporary because of congestion from colds or an ear infection. The wise teacher observes behavior over a period of time, perhaps three to four weeks, to see whether the behaviors or symptoms persist. If they do, referral should be considered.

Figure 4.2   Checklist of Symptoms of Hearing Difficulties

	Yes	No
Inclines one ear toward speaker when listening		
Holds mouth open while listening		
Holds head at angle when taking part in discussion		
Reads in unnatural tone of voice		
Uses faulty pronunciation on common words		
Has indistinct enunciation		
Often asks to have instructions and directions repeated		
Breathes through mouth		
Has discharge from ears		
Frequently complains of earache or sinusitis		
Has frequent head colds		
Complains of buzzing noise in ears		
Seems to be inattentive or indifferent		
Does poorly in games with oral directions		
Has trouble following trend of thought during oral discussions		

Reproduced by permission of the publisher, F. E. Peacock Publishers, Inc., Itasca, Ill., from Eddie C. Kennedy, *Classroom Approaches to Remedial Reading,* 1977, p. 391.

Teachers can structure activities to help determine hearing loss. Some examples follow.

- *Simon Says.* The teacher plays Simon Says with small groups. The students are told to face away and follow the directions. If a student consistently has trouble keeping up with classmates, the teacher may suspect a hearing deficit.

- *Low voice or whisper test.* The teacher stands about 20 feet away from the student (first on one side, then the other). The student is then asked to repeat the words the teacher says in a normal, clear voice. A student who cannot do this task at 15 or fewer feet may have a hearing deficit. A variation of this procedure is to talk softly (or whisper) while standing just behind a student. If the student does not respond to the same volumes as other students, a hearing deficit may exist.

- *Watch tick test.* The teacher holds a stopwatch or loudly ticking wristwatch about 12 inches from the student's ear, gradually extending the distance to about 48 inches. Students with normal hearing should hear the ticks 40 to 48 inches from the ear (Kennedy, 1977). If the distance is less than 40 inches, a deficit may exist, and the teacher should consider referral.

Results of these assessment procedures vary depending on factors such as noise level of the environment, differences in teachers' voices, and loudness of watches. A good way to judge the adequacy of these procedures is to test several students, and notice those who differ significantly from the overall group. If a student's responses consistently deviate from the peer group, more reliable and sophisticated assessment procedures performed by the appropriate specialist are probably in order.

Teachers' Responsibilities. Corrective work for students with auditory acuity impairments, particularly those who are deaf or hard of hearing, is an intricate task that requires specially prepared teachers. Facilities for these learners are usually provided in special schools or special education classes. However, most students with mild hearing impairments or with deficits corrected by prosthetic devices (e.g., hearing aids) function quite well within the regular classroom. Special provisions need to be considered, such as seating the student close to where the teacher and others are talking. It is also helpful for the speaker to face these students directly so they will have the advantage of watching lips closely if needed. Clear enunciation is essential.

Students who have hearing impairments may have difficulty when oral discussion and recitation are in progress. Listening to others read may be difficult, too. Teachers should stress silent reading and a visual approach to word analysis for these students. Phonics may be difficult or, for some, impossible to learn. Emphasis during instruction in word recognition (see Chapter 8) should be placed on the uses of visual and structural analysis techniques and context clues.

Auditory Perception

As with visual perception, a number of skills are included in the area of **auditory perception,** defined as the ability to discriminate, remember, and blend sounds. **Auditory discrimination** is the ability to distinguish sounds, **auditory memory** is the ability to remember a sequence of sounds, and **auditory blending** refers to the blending of phonemes to form a word.

Assessment Techniques. When their auditory discrimination skills are being assessed, students should face away from the teacher to eliminate the possibility of lip reading. Some common procedures follow.

1. Pronounce word pairs (e.g., *big/pig, pat/pot, some/come, rug/run*). Direct the student to answer "same" if the two words sound the same, or "not the same" or "different" if the two words sound different in any way. Several examples should be given for practice, and enough word pairs to assess all positions reliably (beginning, middle, end); probably about ten pairs are adequate for each position.

2. The same concept can be modified for use with a group of students by providing each student a sheet of paper listing the item number followed by the words *same* and *not the same,* or *yes* and *no* (Figure 4.3). Again, word pairs are pronounced by the teacher (standing behind the group) and students are to circle "yes" or "same" if the two words sound the same and "no" or "not the same" or "different" if they sound different.

The assessment of auditory memory evaluates a student's ability to follow oral directions and remember information presented orally in class. Generally, assessment requires students to recall and reproduce a series of unrelated words. For example, the teacher may say, "Listen to these words and be ready to repeat them in the same order: cow . . . tie . . . bed. Now you say them." With young children, several practice items are needed. The number of words can also be increased if three appear to be too easy.

Assessment of auditory blending requires that the learner articulate the sounds of a word together in order, as in spoken language. Blending is a relatively difficult skill and should not be expected in children prior to age 4. It is also more difficult to blend with noncontinuant-stop phonemes (e.g., *p, b, t*) than it is with continuant phonemes (e.g., *m, s, sh*). Initial consonant sounds are easier to blend than are final consonants. Auditory blending assessments should consist of about 30 words: the first 10 should require the learner to blend two phonemes to pronounce a word (e.g., /i/-/n/ = *in*; /i/-/s/=*is*; /u/-/p/ = *up*); the next 10 should require that three or four phonemes segmented into two parts be blended to pronounce a word (e.g., /m/-/an/ = *man*; /n/-/et/ = *net*; /st/-/ep/ = *step*); the last 10 should require that three or four phonemes segmented into three of four parts be blended to pronounce a word (e.g., /m/-/a/-/p/ = *map*; /th/-/a/-/t/ = *that*; /c/-/l/-/o/-/ck/ = *clock*; /s/-/t/-/ar/ = *star*; /b/-/oo/-/k/ = *book*). This task takes 5 to 10 minutes to administer, and kindergarten children typically achieve an average score of 20 out of 30 correct.

Teachers' Responsibilities. To develop auditory discrimination skill, the teacher should begin with practice in listening for known sounds within known words. This provides not only success for the student but also a better idea of the nature of the task.

Figure 4.3 Sample Items for Protocol Sheet Used in Assessing Auditory Discrimination

1. yes	no
2. yes	no
or	
3. same	not the same
3. same	different
and so on	

The teacher must understand that "poor auditory discrimination is often accompanied by inaccurate or indistinct speech. The child who pronounces *with* as *wiv* is not likely to notice any difference between final *v* and *th* in words. It is hard for many children to discriminate among short vowel sounds because those sounds do not differ greatly" (Harris & Sipay, 1990, pp. 456–457). Therefore, in such cases the teacher must decide whether instruction in auditory discrimination would be time well spent, or whether visual learning should be emphasized until articulation has improved.

Useful activities for auditory discrimination development follow. The first three activities are particularly representative of those currently found in use in classroom settings in which phonics instruction is emphasized.

1. Students are asked to locate or mark pictures that begin or end with a particular sound.
2. Students are asked to listen to pairs of words and determine whether they begin or end with the same sound.
3. Pictures are provided, with a choice of two letters for each picture. Students are to choose the letter that represents the beginning or ending sound of the picture.
4. Using a familiar story or nursery rhyme, the teacher selects words to be changed to new words by altering one or two sounds. The teacher then reads the story slowly while the students listen for words that sound wrong. Students must identify the incorrect word and state what the word should sound like. The teacher then continues reading. Brown (1982) calls this activity "fractured fables" and provides an example:

Little Bo *Beep* has lost her *shape*
And doesn't know where to find them.
Leaf them alone, and they'll come home
Wagging their *tells* behind them. (p. 248)

Auditory memory exercises are designed to develop the ability to attend to, recognize, and recall sequences of numbers, letters, and words. The following are representative activities.

1. Give students a series of numbers to dial on a telephone or type on a typewriter or computer.
2. Require students to repeat clapping patterns (e.g., clap/clap-clap/clap).
3. Require students to decide whether two sound patterns are alike. Claps, taps, or toy flutes can be used (e.g., -/-/-; -/-/—).
4. Pronounce two words for the students, then repeat one of them. Students are required to note whether the repeated word was the first or second word of the pair.
5. Have students repeat a series of three to seven unrelated words in sequence, from memory.

A few auditory blending activities are presented here for explanatory purposes. Auditory blending is also discussed in Chapter 8.

1. Have students join beginning consonant sounds to ending phonograms (e.g., /b/ -ake, /k/ -ake, /f/ -ake, /l/ -ake, /m/ -ake).
2. Combine visuals with the preceding auditory task. While pronouncing /k/ -ake, show the word card for *cake* and continue by covering the initial consonant with the various other consonants, for example, *make*.

3. Provide riddles, such as, "I'm thinking of a word that starts like *man,* /m/, and ends like *lake,* -ake. What is the word?"

Neurological Factors

Neurological, or neurophysical, factors refer to conditions that result in learning problems due to differences in the structure and functioning of the brain. Neurological factors affect approximately 15 percent of the U.S. population, resulting in 2.4 million school children having a learning disability. Of these, 80 to 85 percent experience difficulty in language and reading (International Dyslexia Association, 2000).

Considerable confusion exists concerning students who have learning problems due to neurological involvement. There are a host of terms used to refer to these children: "learning disabled," "dyslexic," exhibiting "undifferentiated attention deficit disorder, or ADD," and "attention deficit hyperactivity disorder, or ADHD." Until recently, distinctions between these labels were not readily made. But these are very distinct conditions, each with its own set of characteristics. If descriptive criteria are unknown, labels of this nature can be counterproductive to helping teachers help students because they focus on deficits to the exclusion of competencies. Teachers must be able to recognize the symptoms of those relatively few instances of dyslexia, the neurological deficit associated with reading difficulty, as distinct from symptoms of attention deficit disorders and other learning disabilities. But teachers also must recognize the specific talents of these children, and they are substantial. MI theory provides a framework for viewing learning disabilities as just one part of a student's intelligences profile.

The Internet is a great source of information about each of these conditions. Visit the International Dyslexia Association (formerly the Orton Dyslexia Society) at http://www.interdys.org/. For ADD information, visit http://www.add.org/ or http://www.chadd.org/. Visit the Learning Disabilities Association of America at http://www.ldanatl.org/.

The International Dyslexia Association defines **dyslexia** as "a neurologically based, often familial disorder which interferes with the acquisition and processing of language. Varying in degrees of severity, it is manifested by difficulties in receptive and expressive language—including phonological processing—in reading, writing, spelling, handwriting, and sometimes in arithmetic. Dyslexia is not a result of lack of motivation, sensory impairment, inadequate instructional or environmental opportunities, or other limiting conditions, but may occur together with these conditions. Although dyslexia is lifelong, individuals with dyslexia frequently respond successfully to timely and appropriate intervention" (in Stowe, 2000, pp. 1–2).

People with dyslexia often excel in areas that require visual, spatial, and motor integration. Thus, they are likely to reveal well-developed spatial, bodily-kinesthetic, and/or musical intelligences (Gardner, 1999).

Dyslexia is essentially a language processing disability. But not all people with dyslexia demonstrate the same symptoms. Some have great difficulty using word-attack skills to read words not already committed to memory. They have trouble breaking spoken words into their component parts to assist their spelling, and have particular difficulty with consonant clusters. Others read more slowly, as they have difficulty blending component parts into words while reading. In oral reading, they often pronounce letter sounds in the wrong order and produce the wrong sound for given letters. For most there will likely be a discrepancy between listening comprehension and reading comprehension. Individuals with dyslexia, being bright, have learned to use their language strengths (e.g., vocabulary, general knowledge, interpretive ability) to compensate for other weaknesses.

There are many signs that indicate dyslexia, but few dyslexics show all of these signs. The more common signs are:

- Lack of awareness of sounds in words, sound order, rhymes, or sequence of syllables
- Difficulty decoding words—single-word identification
- Difficulty encoding words—spelling
- Poor sequencing of numbers or of letters in words, when read or written, e.g.: *b–d; sing–sign; left–felt; soiled–solid;* 12–21
- Problems with reading comprehension
- Difficulty expressing thought in written form
- Delayed spoken language
- Imprecise or incomplete interpretation of language that is heard
- Difficulty in expressing thoughts orally
- Confusion about directions in space or time (right and left, up and down, early and late, yesterday and tomorrow, months and days)
- Confusion about right or left handedness
- Similar problems among relatives
- Difficulty with handwriting
- Difficulty in mathematics, often related to sequencing of steps or directionality or the language of mathematics (*Source:* International Dyslexia Association, 2001, available online at http://www.interdys.org/about_dy.htm)

ADD/ADHD, on the other hand, involves an overall inability to attend during complex tasks that require a high degree of self-monitoring. The characteristics of ADD are as follows: can persist when task is interesting, chronic inattention when task is uninteresting, class clown, impulsive or erratic behavior, failure to start work, sloppy work, ignores rules, seeks attention, noisy and disruptive. ADHD has the added characteristic of hyperactivity.

In general, a student with a **learning disability** demonstrates a severe discrepancy between achievement and intellectual ability in one or more academic areas (e.g., oral expression, written expression, listening comprehension, basic reading skill, reading comprehension, mathematics computation, mathematics reasoning). However, this discrepancy is not the result of visual, hearing, or motor handicaps; mental retardation; emotional disturbance; or environmental, cultural, or economic disadvantage (Mercer, 1997).

It is appropriate to include some mention of children who stutter[1] in this section on neurological factors. While **stuttering** itself is termed a speech disorder, research shows that neurological components are probably involved. Also, stuttering has recently been recognized as a learning disability (National Stuttering Association, 2000). Stuttering affects about 1 percent of adults and 4 percent of children, generally starts between ages 2 and 5, and is five times more likely to affect boys than girls. The degree of stuttering can vary widely, and its cause is unknown. It is also unexplained why people who stutter often do not stutter when they sing, whisper, or speak in chorus, or when they do not hear their own voice. It is important for teachers to have knowledge of stuttering especially with classroom expectations of oral presentations such as reports or other

---

[1]The author wishes to thank Mark Eidem for suggesting that this topic be included.

types of oral classroom participation (e.g. oral reading). While stuttering does *not* reflect any diminished mental capability, it can limit a student's ability to participate in "speaking" assignments (e.g., Readers' Theater) or oral reading situations. These expectations would be very intimidating for students who stutter and could indirectly affect their reading development by associating oral reading activities with negative feelings (e.g., feelings of anxiety, frustration, teasing by classmates). Teachers' responsibilities are to maintain a relaxed pace and moderate rate of speech and expect all classmates to do the same, model good listening behaviors, and provide opportunities for choral reading or singing with others. (For more information on stuttering, visit http://www.nsastutter.org/ or http://www.stuttersfa.org/.)

Personal issues can accompany any of these learning disabilities and the teacher should be aware of these as well. Understandably, students with a learning disability might exhibit a poor self-image. They sometimes have difficulty picking up on social signals from other children. They fear failure and new situations. Their feelings about themselves swing back and forth between positive and negative. They sometimes have trouble finding the right words and remembering sequences of events. Feelings of frustration and anger are common. A caring teacher will watch for these signs and provide the necessary support.

Assessment Techniques. Accurately assessing neurological involvement is difficult even for medical and psychological specialists. Therefore, teachers must be extremely cautious and conservative regarding assessment. A teacher's best assessment technique is observation with the use of anecdotal records (see the next section and also Chapter 6). When neurological involvement is suspected, a teacher who can provide documentation in the form of dated records will greatly assist those specially trained to evaluate the presence of these conditions.

Teachers' Responsibilities. When neurological impairment is suspected, teachers should follow established channels provided by the school system. The school principal will be able to advise the teacher on how to proceed. In addition to documenting the possible symptoms of dyslexia, ADD, and other learning disabilities, teachers might also consider those students who demonstrate such behavioral symptoms as poor balance or awkwardness, delayed speech, extreme distractibility, wide mood swings, and disorganization in time and space (Harris & Sipay, 1990) for referral to the school's reading specialist or school psychologist and the school principal. Together these professionals decide whether to recommend to parents that their child see a family physician or a pediatric neurologist for further evaluation.

Meanwhile, a teacher can help students use their strengths and pursue alternate routes to achieve academic success. As Armstrong (2000) states, "By constructing a perspective of special-needs students as whole individuals, MI theory provides a context for envisioning positive channels through which students can learn to deal with their disabilities. . . . It's interesting to note that braille, for example, has been used successfully with students identified as severe dyslexics who possessed special strengths in tactile sensitivity" (p. 105). Similarly, Schirduan and Case (2000) report on an elementary school curriculum that uses strategies consistent with MI theory as improving the self-concept of students with ADHD.

Relatively new findings from the area of brain research are also having an impact on teaching students with a variety of disabilities. Jensen (1998) has attempted to relate the results of this research to teaching and learning. However, many well-intentioned educators have gone beyond the research in their use of aromatherapy (for calming) and peppermint candy (for invigorating), for example. This emerging theory—referred to as

brain-based learning, or creating instructional environments intended to make the brain more receptive to learning—is an area in need of more research. Applications of brain-based learning need to be tested, much as educators have been testing MI theory (see *http://pzweb.harvard.edu/sumit/*). For up-to-date information on brain research, visit *http://www.sfn.org/briefings/*.

Psychological Factors

Psychological factors refer to processes of the mind or psyche. Two psychological areas of concern to teachers are **cognition,** roughly the equivalent of thinking; and **affect,** which refers to feelings and attitudes. What people think and what they feel often are not the same, although the two processes are frequently so interrelated that it is difficult to separate them. Teachers of reading are primarily concerned with students' thinking, but to be truly effective they also need to be concerned with feelings. These two important psychological factors are considered further in the following sections.

Cognition
Cognition can be broadly conceptualized as reflecting a person's general ability to think, to act purposefully, and to solve problems. Reading is a cognitive process, and the specific aspects of conceptual development, schema theory, and comprehension are discussed fully in Chapters 9–13.

Affect
How people perceive themselves and the world around them is a gauge of their emotional and social adjustment. People who do not feel good about themselves often have problems resolving inner conflicts and relating effectively with others in their environment. This generalization holds true for students who have trouble reading.

Studies of the incidence of emotional maladjustment among effective and ineffective readers in general show no clear differences, although they suggest that serious reading problems are likely to be accompanied by adjustment problems. It would be very dangerous to conclude, however, that emotional instability causes reading problems. A more appropriate conclusion is that adjustment problems are likely to contribute to reading problems. Behavior problems probably interact with other causes of reading failure to make learning to read even more difficult for ineffective readers.

Another issue to consider is the degree of maladjustment. Severe emotional dysfunction hinders progress in learning more than do moderate problems. Deep-seated problems are more difficult to remedy and tend to interfere longer than milder, more transitory problems.

Whether psychological adjustment problems are a cause or a result of reading difficulties is not clear, but the presence of these factors can be safely assumed to inhibit reading progress. Quite often, students who improve in reading also improve in terms of self-concept. Thus, the classroom teacher should make every effort to help students feel good about themselves, to feel successful, *especially* if they have difficulty with academic subjects such as reading.

Teachers' Responsibilities
Responsible classroom teachers are concerned with the well-being of their students, including their social and emotional well-being. Occasionally teachers observe students who seem to exhibit unusually severe maladjustment in these areas. Teachers may have an advantage over parents in identifying contributing social and emotional factors because they are not as close emotionally to the students and also because they can

Figure 4.4   Checklist of Symptoms Associated with Emotional Maladjustment

	Yes	No
General Traits or Behavior		
1. Displays signs of excessive shyness	_____	_____
2. Displays signs of introversion	_____	_____
3. Displays signs of lack of confidence	_____	_____
4. Gives up easily on school tasks	_____	_____
5. Plays alone	_____	_____
6. Daydreams	_____	_____
7. Displays signs of overdependence	_____	_____
8. Seeks approval excessively	_____	_____
9. Has numerous unexplained absences	_____	_____
10. Displays signs of nervousness	_____	_____
11. Does not work cooperatively with classmates	_____	_____
12. Argues and fights with classmates	_____	_____
13. Constantly disrupts class	_____	_____
Reading-Related Traits or Behavior		
14. Shows fear of the reading task	_____	_____
15. Refuses to read orally	_____	_____
16. Displays antagonism toward reading	_____	_____
17. Does not get along with others in reading group	_____	_____
18. Does not attend during reading lesson	_____	_____
19. Does not complete reading assignments	_____	_____
20. Displays fear or nervousness during recitation	_____	_____

compare one student's behavior with that of many others. After teachers have taught for a few years, they have a fairly good idea of what constitutes bizarre or aberrant behavior. While teachers should not dabble in amateur psychology, they should note unusual behaviors in students, particularly when those behaviors are frequent and persistent.

When teachers become aware of possible maladjustment, they should reflect on precisely what the student is doing to cause concern. Figure 4.4 provides a checklist of some of the symptoms associated with psychosocial problems.

Many other behaviors are also possible symptoms. A checklist helps teachers organize their thoughts and prepare a case for referral to the school psychologist, guidance counselor, or school social worker. In many school systems these specialists have a heavy workload and the waiting period after referral can be many months. A well-prepared and documented referral by a thoughtful teacher may expedite response.

Carefully prepared **anecdotal records,** brief written notes that are highly objective in nature (see also Chapter 6), are a teacher's best tool in presenting a case for referral. Behaviors should be described objectively rather than presented as tentative conclusions. Valuable information is lost when conclusions are the only thing noted. The objective details will be helpful in revealing patterns of behavior when anecdotal records are reviewed over time. Consider the following examples:

Date	*Conclusions*	*vs.*	*Objective Description*
11/18	Jennifer had a temper tantrum.		Today, when Jennifer discovered she did not have her paper posted on the "my best effort" bulletin board, she ran up to the board, ripped off several papers belonging to classmates, then began to cry.

| 11/20 | Jennifer fought with Susan in the cafeteria line. | Susan accidentally pushed Jennifer while they were in the cafeteria line. Jennifer then began to hit and kick Susan. Her facial expression frightened both Susan and me. |
| 12/5 | Jennifer refused to participate in the reading group and at other times today. | Jennifer was unusually quiet today. When I asked her comprehension questions, she dropped her head and eyes. I let someone else answer. Later when I tried to re-engage her in the group activity, she still would not respond. I tried several other times to communicate with her today and had no luck. She did not talk with me all day. |

The incomplete-sentence technique is often used to gain insights into the student's feelings about reading and self in general. Typically, a student will be asked to complete twenty to fifty sentence starters either orally or in writing. Some examples follow:

My reading group _____ .

The teacher thinks I _____ .

My books _____ .

Information from such an instrument should be considered tentative and must be verified because students often respond as they think the teacher wants them to. This is a limitation of any self-reporting technique. A frequently used incomplete sentence test was developed by Boning and Boning (1957) and can be found in Appendix H.

Most school systems today have special classes for students displaying social or emotional maladjustment. Some students with relatively mild adjustment problems function quite well within the regular classroom. But sometimes these students do *not* learn well, and their response to failure and frustration from not learning academic subjects interacts negatively with their already negative self-concept, leading to further maladjustment. This can create a negative spiral that worsens with time.

Failure can also have a devastating effect on well-adjusted people. Johnston and Winograd (1985) believe that many of the problems exhibited by readers in difficulty are related to their passive involvement in reading. This indicates that the teacher can make a positive impact by providing a program that ensures active participation, strategy instruction, and **attributional retraining** (teaching pupils to accept responsibility for their successes and failures and that effort and persistence may help to overcome failure) (Borkowski, Wehing, & Turner, 1986). Following are suggestions for helping students displaying evidence of lowered self-esteem, whether from lack of accomplishment in reading or from other sources. They can also be appropriately used with most students.

1. *Create a facilitative learning environment.* The teacher must make special efforts to establish a warm, trusting working relationship with readers in difficulty. Teachers should listen carefully. Often students feel the need to discuss what is bothering them with a trusted adult, but teachers may be so preoccupied that they fail to hear the clues given. Dialogue journals can provide students and teachers a vehicle for "talking" to each other (Staton, 1988). Teachers also must be careful not to use their own values to judge nonreading behaviors, lest they contribute negatively to any maladjustments. On the other hand, learners often need reassurance and specific suggestions, particularly regarding their troubles, whether they are academic or of a different nature. The teacher must

establish a free and open atmosphere but at the same time set certain limits. The teacher should maintain those limits, being pleasant but firm when necessary. The purpose of establishing rapport is to create an environment in which a learner's self-confidence and self-esteem are nurtured.

2. *Create opportunities for success.* The axiom "Nothing succeeds like success" is particularly appropriate for students having trouble reading. Teachers help structure success experiences by ensuring that students work at a difficulty level that is easy enough for them. Find something they can read easily, even if it is their own name. Increasing the difficulty level if it is too easy is healthier than decreasing it after failure.

More difficult tasks can be spaced among easier ones. Students often can work with new and difficult tasks for only a few minutes before becoming too frustrated to continue. Interspersing success experiences among such tasks often relieves undue pressure.

Older students often respond negatively to "baby stuff." This problem can be avoided if teachers use materials that appear more mature than they really are. High interest–low vocabulary books and stories without pictures of younger children are recommended. Some excellent picture books are available that lend themselves to sophisticated uses that will appeal to older students' sensibilities (see Benedict & Carlisle, 1992; Cassady, 1998; Danielson, 1992; Hadaway & Mundy, 1999; Miller, 1998; Neal & Moore, 1991/1992; Polette, 1989; Tiedt, 2000). Cross-age tutoring programs can also be effective ways to help older students gain much needed practice with easier materials (Juel, 1991; Labbo & Teale, 1990; Morrice & Simmons, 1991).

A process called **bibliotherapy** can provide opportunities for troubled students to identify with a character or situation in a book and experience a catharsis or perhaps gain insight into their own problems (Dreyer, 1987). Bibliotherapy, then, can help a student come to grips with personal problems and realize that reading can be a useful activity for personal growth (D'Alessandro, 1990). For example, *Golden Daffodils* (Gould, 1982) is a book about Janis, a fifth-grade student who has cerebral palsy, being mainstreamed into a regular classroom. Students with and without physical handicaps can better understand themselves and others when reading about the obstacles Janis must overcome. Other examples include *My Name is Brain/Brian* (Betancourt, 1993), a story about a sixth-grade boy diagnosed with dyslexia, and *Adam Zigzag* (Barrie, 1994), a novel about a teenage boy with dyslexia.

3. *Provide ample reward and reinforcement.* Because many ineffective readers have less than adequate confidence in their ability to learn to read, they often need more encouragement than other students. Praise students when they succeed or when they attempt a task that is difficult and threatening. Social reinforcement can be given verbally ("very good," "nice try") or nonverbally (a reassuring smile, a pat on the back).

A more structured approach, using behavior modification techniques adapted to individual needs, often helps students having more serious problems. Extrinsic reinforcers applied by the teacher should in time be integrated into the learner's own personality structure. When this occurs, and the student personally feels the reward of accomplishment, the reinforcement becomes the intrinsic satisfaction gained from doing the activity. One consideration often overlooked by teachers is that some students need considerable practice before they can attain a sense of satisfaction. Sometimes teachers try to push too fast for growth, changing learning tasks before the learner reaches the satisfaction of mastery.

4. *Encourage student participation.* Generally speaking, students who are involved in analyzing, planning, and evaluating their own reading are those who profit most from corrective instruction. Teachers should support students in understanding what they need to learn to improve their reading. With teacher help, many students can verify, even if intuitively, the reality of their identified learning gaps. They can also demonstrate to the

teacher their ability to be successful at certain tasks that an original analysis may have suggested were too difficult. Timely, meaningful interaction between pupil and teacher leads to efficient and enjoyable learning.

When students recognize their need and realize their desire to know a variety of reading strategies, their goals become much clearer and attainment of those goals is consequently facilitated. Students like to keep track of their progress in attaining goals, and teachers should encourage them to make progress charts or otherwise keep their own record of their growth. These charts and graphs become concrete evidence of success that helps the learner maintain goal-directed behaviors. They also become an important evaluation tool for both student and teacher. Maintaining a portfolio is a natural way for students to keep track of their own progress and development over time (Clemmons, Laase, Cooper, Areglado, & Dill, 1993; DeFina, 1992; Glazer & Brown, 1993; Johnson & Rose, 1997; Sunstein & Lovell, 2000; Tierney, Carter, & Desai, 1991). For best results, at least four one-to-one teacher-student conferences are required each semester, with student self-analysis occurring more frequently (Farr, 1992).

Environmental Factors

Much of what occurs in the environment, or surrounding world, directly and indirectly influences the people who live in that environment. Environmental factors that have a strong negative influence on school achievement and reading progress include debilitating poverty, unfortunate conditions within the home, schools that are physically inadequate for or unresponsive to students' instructional needs, and societal ills. These environmental factors put students at risk and make them academically vulnerable.

Poverty

In recent years considerable evidence has demonstrated that economic differences have a strong relationship with school achievement. Low income and poverty have a positive correlation with low achievement (Dyer, 1968; Puma et al., 1997). Schools in economically distressed areas, such as ghettos, barrios, urban housing developments, and certain rural areas, generally do not offer the same benefits to students as the more affluent systems characteristic of suburban school districts. Poor students from minority groups, in particular, have been denied the benefits of a good education (Kozol, 1991), which has led to a "pedagogy of poverty" (Haberman, 1991) rather than a humanizing pedagogy with a commitment to social justice.

Students from impoverished circumstances, some perhaps homeless, come to school with experiences and backgrounds that vary considerably from their upper- and middle-class peers. Thus, the content of the school's reading program may be inappropriate for these students. While academically vulnerable due to their economic circumstances, these students are capable learners. They need enhanced and enriching conceptual, experiential, and language opportunities in school to ensure their literacy development. These students must also be made to see themselves as competent readers and writers, and they will do so as teachers help them master literacy tasks. But first, they need teachers who believe in them. Educators need to acknowledge that their own particular values, beliefs, or attitudes undergird the pedagogy and curriculum provided their students. Teachers who seek to implement a framework of education for social justice will not approach children of poverty with preconceived notions about their needs. Nieto (1999) says it well:

> Many students are subjected to stale teaching and irrelevant curricula, but it is especially children of color, [and] those who live in poverty, speak a native language

other than English, or attend poorly financed schools who are affected dispropor-
tionately and negatively by pedagogy and curriculum. This is true for several reasons. First, frequently these students are tracked into low-level ability groups . . .
and very often they are thought by their teacher to need "basic skills" before moving on to more interesting knowledge and creative tasks. Second, teachers in poorly
funded schools tend to be the least experienced and therefore they usually have
scant knowledge of alternative pedagogical strategies or current curriculum thinking . . . Finally, in the case of students with limited English proficiency, the singu-
lar focus on their learning English results in overshadowing all other considerations
of curriculum and pedagogy. (p. 78)

Negative Home Environment

Unfortunate home environments are found in every social, cultural, and economic group.
When a home is unstable and the family setting does not nurture feelings of security,
learning problems may arise. Factors frequently mentioned are broken homes; family
conflicts; sibling rivalry; and quarreling, overprotective, dominating, neglecting, or abusive parents. No one can deny that these factors have negative effects on a child. However, many children exposed to these conditions successfully learn to read. Hence the
response to problems at home is a highly individual, idiosyncratic matter. The more resilient the child, the more likely the child will succeed. **Resiliency** is defined as the
"capacity to spring back, rebound, successfully adapt in the face of adversity, and develop social competence despite exposure to severe stress" (Bowman, R. personal communication, January 23, 1999). (For more information, see the section on resiliency later
in this chapter.)

Negative School Environment

Schools and instructional programs must also share the blame for reading failures. Too
often the common response to reading failures is to increase the amount of testing,
demand national standards, or mandate a particular curriculum (Alexander, 1993; Farr,
1992; Frazee, 1993; Newmann & Wehlage, 1993). Such responses have led to mixed results, sometimes benefiting and sometimes hindering student learning.

Poor teaching is frequently cited as a reason for students not learning to read well
(Shannon, 1989). Among the many complaints, the more common are using unsuitable
teaching methods; using overly difficult reading materials; using dull or otherwise inappropriate reading methods and materials; overemphasizing skills in isolation, especially
phonics; giving too much or too little emphasis to reading skills; and teaching reading
without integrating it into other curricular areas (see Shannon, 1990, for a historical treatment of the philosophies and practices of alternative literacy programs).The sooner educators and other school personnel recognize that there is no one way, no best method, no
"magic bullet," and no "quick fix" for teaching reading, and that teaching approaches
should accommodate students' different ways of knowing, the sooner all learners will
make progress in literacy development (Allington & Walmsley, 1995; Nieto, 1999). Each
learner is unique; even learners within the same cultural group are unique. Every learner
comes to us knowing something, and it is the responsibility of educators to find out what
each learner knows and build upon that knowledge.

Improved instruction can best be facilitated by administrators and teachers working
collaboratively. Administrators can work to alleviate certain rigid school policies that lead
to imbalanced curricula and other inappropriate outcomes. Examples of such policies are
(1) requiring teachers to emphasize reading subskills to the detriment of reading as a
transactive process, (2) overemphasis on the affective domain to the detriment of cogni-

tive learnings, (3) requiring teachers to instruct students in a specific sequence at a specific time, to the detriment of students needing supplementary or corrective instruction, and (4) requiring students to attain a specified level of achievement before they are promoted, to the detriment of students who are doing their best and achieving, but below some arbitrary level. Teachers become frustrated and their efforts are hindered by such unfortunate administrative policies. On the other hand, teachers must work to remain as informed as possible about their students' needs and current pedagogical knowledge. They must also be willing to learn *with* their students to impress upon students that teaching is more about learning than it is about "knowing everything." And finally, teachers must have the courage to be advocates for their students, which will sometimes mean "teaching against the grain" (Cochran-Smith, 1991).

Societal Ills

It is a major challenge of schools today to educate students who are at risk for their personal safety and survival. Teachers must be alert to all aspects of child maltreatment. Areas of child abuse and neglect include **sexual abuse** (sexual exploitation, molestation, child prostitution), **physical abuse** (nonaccidental injury to a child resulting in bruises, burns, broken bones, and/or internal injuries), **emotional maltreatment** (constant belittling, verbal abuse, inappropriate parenting, and neglect), and **physical neglect** (abandonment or inadequate provision of food, clothing, shelter, medical care, and supervision) (Bear, Schenk, & Buckner, 1992/1993).

The National Clearinghouse on Child Abuse and Neglect Information (800-394-3366 or http://www.calib.com/nccanch/) reports that in 1998 approximately 903,000 children were determined to be victims of child abuse and neglect in the United States. Of these victims, 53.5 percent suffered neglect, 22.7 percent physical abuse, 11.5 percent sexual abuse, 6 percent emotional abuse, 2.4 percent medical neglect, and 25.3 percent additional types or other forms of maltreatment (e.g., congenital drug addiction). (The percentages total more than 100 percent because children may have been victims of more than one type of maltreatment.) Many abuse victims are young children; in 1998, 14.8 out of every 1,000 victims of child maltreatment were three years old or younger. Rates also vary by race/ethnic group, with 3.8 out of every 1,000 victims of the same race for Asian/Pacific, 8.5 per 1,000 for White, 10.6 per 1,000 for Hispanic, 19.8 per 1,000 for American Indian/Alaska Native, and 20.7 per 1,000 for African American (U.S. Department of Health and Human Services, 2000, pp. 4-2–4-4).

Child abuse is far too common for teachers not to be knowledgeable about its physical and behavioral indicators (see Table 4.1). Teachers have the best opportunity to identify these students and, having done so, are required by law to report such cases. But a teacher's help doesn't stop there. All the suggestions made earlier with regard to emotional and social adjustment apply here as well (see Bear, Schenk, & Buckner, 1992/1993).

Crack and cocaine have also had a serious impact on today's classrooms, but not in the way one might expect. Waller (1992/1993) and DeSylvia and Klug (1992) estimate that between 400,000 to 700,000 children are born annually to mothers in all socioeconomic and cultural groups who used crack or cocaine during pregnancy. While it is true that these children are at risk for physical, cognitive, and emotional difficulties, rigorous research efforts indicate the infants' ability to compensate. Chasnoff (1991) found that some children prenatally exposed to crack or cocaine exhibit no overt effects, while others exhibit severe effects such as low birth weight, congenital malformations, tremors, excessive crying, or smaller head circumference. But Chasnoff (1992) goes on to state that these children are "more like drug-free children than they are different" (p. 2). Barone's

Table 4.1   Indicators of Child Abuse

	Physical Indicators	Behavioral Indicators	
Physical Abuse	• unexplained bruises (in various stages of healing), welts, human bite marks, bald spots • unexplained burns, especially cigarette burns or immersion burns (glovelike) • unexplained fractures, lacerations, or abrasions	• self-destructive • withdrawn and aggressive—behavioral extremes • uncomfortable with physical contact • arrives at school early or stays late as if afraid	• chronic runaway (adolescents) • complains of soreness or moves uncomfortably • wears clothing inappropriate to weather, possibly to cover body
Physical Neglect	• abandonment • unattended medical needs • consistent lack of supervision • consistent hunger, inappropriate dress, poor hygiene • lice, distended stomach, emaciated	• regularly displays fatigue or listlessness, falls asleep in class • steals food, begs from classmates • reports that no caretaker is at home	• frequently absent or tardy • self-destructive • school dropout (adolescents)
Sexual Abuse	• torn, stained, or bloodied underclothing • pain or itching in genital area • difficulty walking or sitting • bruises or bleeding in external genitalia • venereal disease • frequent urinary or yeast infections	• withdrawn, chronic depression • excessive seductiveness • role reversal, overly concerned for siblings • poor self-esteem, self-devaluation, lack of confidence • peer problems, lack of involvement • massive weight change	• suicide attempts (especially adolescents) • hysteria, lack of emotional control • sudden school difficulties • inappropriate sex play or premature understanding of sex • threatened by physical contact, closeness • promiscuity
Emotional Maltreatment	• speech disorders • delayed physical development • substance abuse • ulcers, asthma, severe allergies	• habit disorders (sucking, rocking) • antisocial, destructive • neurotic traits (sleep disorders, inhibition of play)	• passive and aggressive—behavioral extremes • delinquent behavior (especially adolescents) • developmentally delayed

(1995, 1996) work also offers a more positive prognosis. She challenges us to reexamine our assumptions about children who were prenatally exposed to crack or cocaine as difficult to teach, hyperactive, late developers of language, and even violent. She has found that these children, like other children, respond to a supportive environment. Barone (1995) states that the only instructional recommendation that can be made for teachers is to provide these children the best instruction recommended for all children. Classrooms like those seen in Project Daisy that support holistic, active learning, process-oriented, literature-based reading and writing, students' decision making, and higher level thinking document the success of these approaches with all children including those who have been prenatally exposed to crack/cocaine. (pp. 52–53)

Resiliency

In spite of all the challenges that negative environmental factors present, the resilient child manages to survive and do well. The resilient child has the ability to bounce back. The resilient child is goal-oriented and believes that his or her efforts will lead to positive results. The resilient child can think critically and consider alternative solutions to both cognitive and social dilemmas. The resilient child reflects on and learns from experiences, and is motivated to achieve. It is easy to see that resiliency has a direct relationship to student learning.

But resiliency is a capacity that is learned. Four key systems in a child's environment can either present risk factors or protective factors in the development of resiliency: family, peers, school, and community. The more risk factors present in these four key systems, the greater chance the child will engage in risky behaviors; whereas the more protective factors present in these four key systems, the greater chance the child will develop resiliency. Examples of risk factors grouped according to the four key systems are (1) unclear expectations for behavior; lack of monitoring; tobacco, drug, and alcohol abuse; low expectations for children's success (family); (2) antisocial behavior; rebelliousness; use of tobacco, alcohol, and other drugs (peers); (3) ill-defined or unenforced school policies, lack of student involvement, academic failure, identifying students as "high risk" (school); and (4) economic deprivation, community disorganization, lack of employment opportunities, tobacco and drugs readily available and norms favorable to abuse (community). Examples of protective factors are (1) close bonding with the child, values and encourages education, clear expectations, nurturing and protective, shares family responsibilities (family); (2) respects authority, involved in drug-free activities (peers); (3) nurturing caretakers, encourage goal setting, high expectations, active student involvement, involves parents, fosters cooperative learning (school); and, (4) access to resources such as child care and job training, supportive networks, opportunities for youth in community service (community). Research by the Search Institute (1997) found that having at least one caring adult in a young person's life led to resiliency. They identified 40 assets, or protective factors, that lead to resiliency. The more protective factors possessed, the greater the chance for healthy, caring, responsible, resilient youth. It was also found that even if a child only possessed just over half (or 21) of the 40 assets, he or she would be likely to succeed in school. Likewise, those with very few assets (0–10) had below a C average.

Teachers' Responsibilities

It is very difficult to designate a specific environmental factor as the *cause* of a student's reading difficulties. Rather, this factor should be considered as a possible contributor to reading difficulties. Teachers are not sociologists or social workers, and few have been trained in techniques that pinpoint contributing factors. The role of the teacher is one of identifying *possible* contributing factors and referring the student to appropriate specialists or agencies according to school policies. School districts often have social workers, counselors, and nurses to help teachers in the decision-making process.

Many schools have special programs for students who live in poverty, such as government-subsidized breakfast and lunch programs. Many communities today have mental health clinics that deal with family adjustment problems on a sliding fee basis. Community welfare agencies often have child welfare departments concerned with children caught in untenable living conditions, including homeless or abusive situations. Thus, a major responsibility of teachers is to be knowledgeable regarding community services available to the students they teach and to their families.

To assist any possible future referral, anecdotal records should be used to document teacher observations with a high level of objectivity. This means the teacher must be careful to describe behaviors rather than simply assign labels, such as "This child's father is abusive." Teachers must remember not to overlook the privacy rights of students and their families. *Anecdotal records must never read like gossip.*

Teachers also must examine their own attitudes and beliefs about the students they teach. I agree with Sonia Nieto (1999) when she says, "Teaching and learning are primarily about relationships. . . . Consequently, teachers' beliefs and values, how these are communicated to students through teaching practices and behaviors, and their impact on the lives of students—these are the factors that make teaching so consequential in the lives of many people. . . . If we understand teaching as consisting primarily of social relationships and as a political commitment rather than a technical activity, then it is unquestionable that what educators need to pay most attention to are their own growth and transformation and the lives, realities, and dreams of their students" (pp. 130–131).

In addition, it is the responsibility of teachers to make every effort to involve each student's parents in their child's literacy development. The very best advice to give parents is to read aloud with their child and to talk about the books their child is reading. Parental involvement is critical to student achievement. Parents and teachers who work together can make an outstanding positive contribution to a student's educational experiences. But sometimes parents need guidance and support to become effectively involved in their child's literacy development. Progress reports (see Appendix A) are one way to inform parents of what their child is experiencing in the classroom. Morningstar (1999) suggests the use of home response journals as a way for parents and teachers to communicate about a child's home and school language/literacy experiences. Other ways to keep parents informed include personal letters, especially positive notes about their child; classroom newspapers or newsletters; and invitations to visit the classroom at their convenience (Thomas, Fazio, & Stiefelmeyer, 1999a, 1999b). It is important to be prepared for parents' questions (see Figure 4.5). Also, when meeting with parents for a conference, teachers should:

1. Talk specifically about their child and use specific examples. Especially mention their child's strengths.
2. Mention things that their child is enthusiastic about.
3. Ask parents for information about their child's interests and achievements at home.
4. Offer possible solutions to any problems. Engage their cooperation in joint efforts to help the child.
5. Discuss your criteria for grades (e.g., what does "B" mean in your class), and state what you think is important about the report card or the student's progress report. The most important thing is to keep the lines of communication open. Positive communication encourages further involvement between teacher and parents, removes barriers, and provides the school with greater parental support (Batey, 1996; Rasinski, 1995).

The following list shows U.S. publishers of large-print editions of adult general interest or young adult books:

The American Printing House for the
    Blind, Inc.
1839 Frankfort Avenue
P.O. Box 6085
Louisville, KY 40206-0085
E-mail: info@aph.org
Internet: http://www.aph.org/
Phone: 502-895-2405
Fax: 502-899-2274
Customer Service: 800-223-1839 (U.S. and
    Canada)
Marketing/Sales: 800-572-0844 (U.S. and
    Canada)

Baker Book House
P.O. Box 6287
Grand Rapids, MI 49516-6287
Phone: 616-676-9185
Fax: 616-676-9573
800-877-2665
Orders Only: 800-398-3110 Fax

Bethany House Publishers
11400 Hampshire Ave. South
Minneapolis, MN 55438
E-mail: info@bethanyhouse.com
Internet: http://www.bethanyhouse.com/
Phone: 612-829-2500; 800-328-6109
Fax: 612-829-2768

Kregel Publications
P.O. Box 2607
Grand Rapids, MI 49501-2607
E-mail: kregelbooks@kregel.com
Internet: http://www.kregel.com/
Phone: 616-451-4775; 800-733-2607
Fax: 616-451-9330

Lutheran Braille Workers
Large Print Division
P.O. Box 5000
Yucaipa, CA 92399
Phone: 909-795-8977
Fax: 909-795-8970

Rainbow Books, Inc.
P.O. Box 430
Highland City, FL 33846-0430
E-mail: rbibooks@aol.com
Phone: 941-648-4420; 800-356-9315 or
    888-613-BOOK
Fax: 941-647-5951

Random House Large Print
1540 Broadway
New York, NY 10036
E-mail: jfrost@randomhouse.com
Internet:: http://www.randomhouse.com/
    features/ largeprint/
Phone: 212-782-9489
Fax: 212-782-9600

Walker & Co.
435 Hudson St.
New York, NY 10014
E-mail: georgegibson@walkerbooks.com
Phone: 212-727-8300; 800-AT-WALKER
Fax: 212-727-0984

5 Reading Assessment
Indirect Measures

Objectives
Objectives

After you have read this chapter, you should be able to:
1. define and describe briefly the following measurement terms: *validity, reliability,* and *standard error of measurement;*
2. interpret these scores: grade equivalent, percentile, NCE, and stanine;
3. describe the differences between norm-referenced and criterion-referenced tests.

Key Concepts and Terms

assessment	high-stakes testing	reliability
at-level testing	indirect assessment	standard deviation
construct validity	mastery tests	standard error of
content validity	norm-referenced tests	measurement
correlation coefficients	normal curve equivalent	standard scores
criterion-referenced tests	(NCE) scores	standardized tests
direct assessment	norms	stanine scores
evaluation	out-of-level testing	validity
formal tests	percentile scores	
grade-equivalent scores	performance assessments	

Educational assessment, in its current stage of development, is generally of two types: large-scale achievement testing and performance assessment. Large-scale testing remains in the forefront due in large part to the backlash against constructive, integrated, and holistic approaches, and now the mandates of specific methods for instruction by state legislatures.

On the other hand, many school districts and schools would support moving away from assessing the kinds of isolated pieces of knowledge evaluated in standardized tests and toward **performance assessments** in which students read, write, and solve problems in genuine ways such as taking and supporting a point of view on a specific issue. In particular, Arizona, Colorado, Connecticut, Kentucky, Maryland, Michigan, New York, and Oregon have worked toward making large-scale performance assessments more authentic regarding the texts, tasks, and contexts of reading (Hymes, 1991; Valencia, Hiebert, & Afflerbach, 1994).

This is not an easy period for administrators, teachers, and all those struggling to create new forms of assessment that reflect emerging curricula and standards. For example, we teachers even need to reexamine the language we use when we talk about assessment. As Peter Johnston (1992) points out,

> we refer to our own observations as "subjective," "informal," and "anecdotal," whereas we refer to tests as "objective" and "formal." Our own language devalues the close knowledge we have and values distance. It would be more helpful if we referred to our own assessments as "direct documentation" and test-based assessments as "indirect" and "invasive." These uses of language are far from trivial. They show that we do not value our own assessment knowledge. Our unfortunate cultural concern for control, distance, objectification, and quantification . . . does not favor teachers, whose knowledge is often intuitive, usually nonnumerical, more inclined to the narrative, and gained through personal involvement. . . . Detailed knowledge comes from proximity and involvement, not distance. (p. 61)

As I reflect upon Johnston's words and the work of others (Wolf, 1993), I, too, find it more accurate to use the term **indirect assessment** to refer to the standardized, norm-referenced types of tests discussed in this chapter, and the term **direct assessment** to refer to the classroom-based, or teacher-based, assessment techniques discussed in Chapter 6.

Currently, the indirect measures, while less meaningful to the teacher in terms of instructional planning because of their distance from what happens in the classroom, *are* administered in schools and *are* likely to be around for some time to come, as there continues to be a need for large-scale testing within school districts. For example, large-scale testing results remind us that there is an achievement gap for poor and minority children (Raines, 2000). While large-scale testing can provide information about achievement that we need to be aware of, the increasing reliance on a single test score to make important and substantial educational decisions (i.e., **high-stakes testing**) is a disturbing trend. (For more information and the International Reading Association's position on high stakes testing, see http://www.reading.org/advocacy/policies/high_stakes.html).

This chapter is informative of the basic concepts related to indirect measures, enabling teachers to better decide for themselves how valuable a particular test score may or may not be. Also, the information found here should help teachers better discuss standardized test results with parents.

A review of the basic concepts of assessment and evaluation includes definitions, measurement concepts, a brief discussion of different kinds of scores, and, more specific to the goal of this text, purposes of testing in reading. After this review, the chapter proceeds with a discussion of particular published reading tests.

ASSESSMENT AND EVALUATION: BASIC CONCEPTS

Definitions

Both assessment and evaluation are critical to the analytic process. Many educators use the terms interchangeably; however, **assessment** usually refers to the process of gathering data about a learner's strengths and difficulties, while **evaluation** refers to the process of judging achievement or growth, or of decision making. Thus, evaluation implies the need to use assessment techniques to obtain information for making judgments or decisions.

In schools, reading achievement is frequently evaluated through the use of standardized achievement tests. **Standardized tests** are so called because they have been administered in the same way to a large group of students (who represent students for whom the test was designed) in order to establish a reference or norm group. The scores of these students then become the **norms** and can be used for comparison with the scores of other students taking the test. Thus, the term **norm-referenced test** is also used to describe a standardized test. Part of the standardization procedure involves preparing a standard set of directions for administration that includes directions to students and time allotment for completing subtests. This standard set of directions is another reason these tests are called standardized, and because the directions for administration must be strictly adhered to, the tests have also become known as **formal tests.**

Several other terms associated with standardized testing will be used throughout this chapter. Those related to interpreting standardized test scores will be defined here. Other important terms are defined in the next section. Because a standardized test is norm-referenced, norm tables are included in the test manual to tell you how the raw scores are converted into normed scores. These normed scores include percentile scores,

Figure 5.1   The Normal Distribution, Percentiles, and Selected Standard Scores

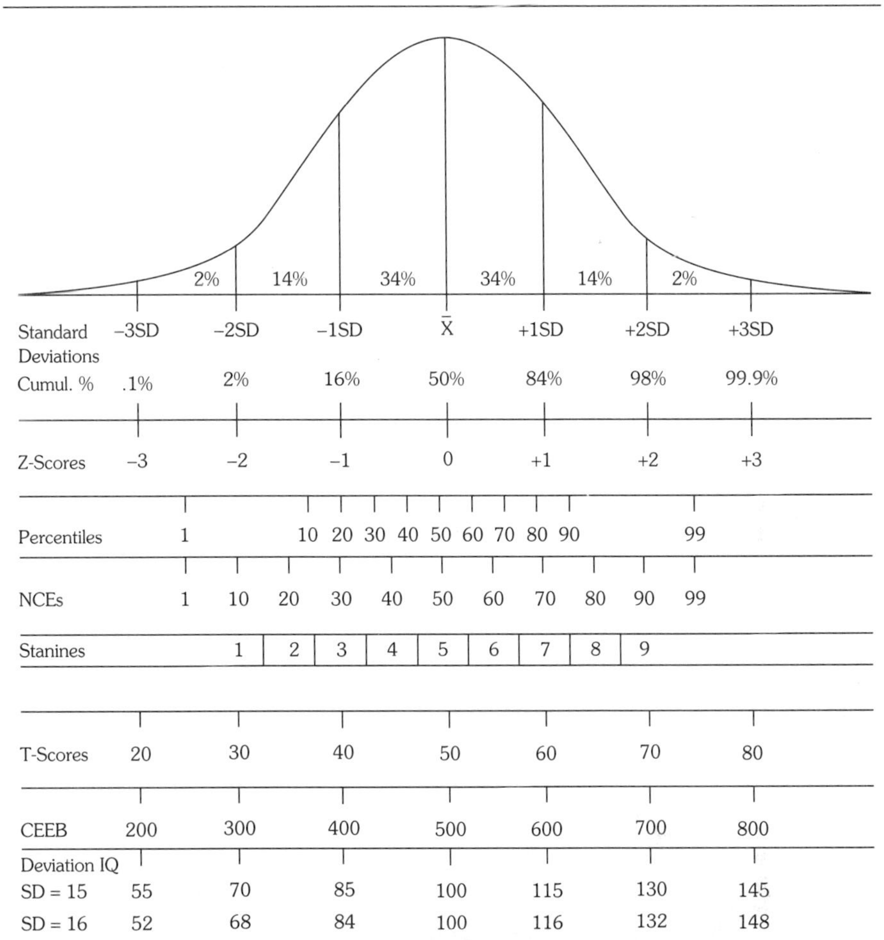

	2%	14%	34%	34%	14%	2%	
Standard Deviations	−3SD	−2SD	−1SD	X̄	+1SD	+2SD	+3SD
Cumul. %	.1% 2%	16%	50%	84%	98%	99.9%	
Z-Scores	−3	−2	−1	0	+1	+2	+3
Percentiles	1	10 20 30 40 50 60 70 80 90				99	
NCEs	1	10 20 30 40 50 60 70 80 90 99					
Stanines		1 2 3 4 5 6 7 8 9					
T-Scores	20	30	40	50	60	70	80
CEEB	200	300	400	500	600	700	800
Deviation IQ SD = 15	55	70	85	100	115	130	145
SD = 16	52	68	84	100	116	132	148

Reproduced by permission from *Test Service Bulletin No. 148,* 1986. The Psychological Corporation, San Antonio, Texas.

standard scores such as stanines and normal curve equivalent scores, and grade equivalent scores. Each will be defined here. For help in seeing how some of these scores and others relate to the normal curve, refer to Figure 5.1.

Percentile Scores

Percentile scores, converted from raw scores, compare students only with others of the same grade or age. Students who receive a percentile score of 63 have done as well as or better than 63 percent of students in the norm group. The percentile scores *do not* represent the percentage of items answered correctly. Percentile scores can range from 1 to 99 (Figure 5.1) and can be compared directly with other subtests or tests taken previously. Interpretation of percentile scores is limited, however, to comparing students with those in the norm groups or those in the same classroom or school. For example, if fourth-grader Georgia's raw score of 17 converts to the 12th percentile on the reading comprehension subtest, the proper interpretation is that Georgia has done as well as or better than 12 percent of a large sample of fourth-grade children who took this test. If her score on the vocabulary subtest converted to the 6th percentile, the teacher can say that Georgia performed slightly better in reading comprehension than in vocabulary. The teacher *cannot,* however, average the two percentiles and say that, overall, Georgia scored at the 9th percentile. That is an inaccurate statement because of the way percentiles bunch up in the middle of a normal distribution; distances between scores are not equal. The teacher may also compare Georgia's score with those of her classmates who took the same test or with her previous scores on this test. That information might help the teacher place Georgia into an initial group for instructional reading purposes, but is not at all helpful for deeper-level analytic purposes. Therefore, the teacher must still rely on other means of assessing reading behaviors to help identify Georgia's specific areas of reading strength and difficulty.

Standard Scores

Standard scores are derived from raw scores in such a way as to obtain uniformly spaced scores. Standard scores indicate an individual score's distance from the average, or mean, score in terms of the variability of the distribution of all scores. Variability is indicated by a number called the **standard deviation.** (The higher the standard deviation, the more variability in the scores.) Standard scores allow comparisons to be made among scores on different tests and subtests. Some standardized achievement tests convert raw scores according to an average standard score of 50 with a standard deviation of 10 (see T-scores, Figure 5.1). For example, if Jerry earned a raw score of 52 on a math test and 42 on a reading test, the scores cannot be directly compared because they do not reflect anything about the total distribution of scores for all the students taking the tests. By converting the raw scores to standard scores, each of Jerry's scores can be considered in relation to an average score of 50 and a standard deviation of 10. Jerry's scores convert to a standard score of 80 on the math test and 48 on the reading test. Jerry therefore did much better on the math test than on the reading test, but the raw scores did not indicate such a large difference. Jerry also scored well above average on the math test. The average is 50; thus 80 is 30 points or 3 (30 divided by 10) standard deviations above the mean. On the other hand, Jerry did just about average on the reading test.

Stanine Scores

Stanine scores are standard scores for which the raw scores have been converted into nine equally spaced parts, with a stanine of 1 being low and 9 being high. A stanine of 5 is considered average, and the standard deviation is approximately 2 (Figure 5.1). Stanine scores are interpreted similarly to percentiles, with the major difference being the number and size of units involved; there are 99 percentile units and only 9 stanines. For interpretation purposes, stanines 1, 2, and 3 reflect poor performance, stanines 4, 5, and 6 reflect average performance, and stanines 7, 8, and 9 reflect good performance on a test.

NCE Scores

Another kind of standard score based on a normal curve, **the normal curve equivalent (NCE) score,** is a norm that has more recently come into use. NCE scores range from 1 to 99 with a mean of 50, and in this way they are similar to percentile scores. The points in between are different from percentiles, however. Percentile scores tend to pile up around the mean and spread further apart upon approaching the extremes; NCE scores are in equal units. Therefore, NCE scores are interpreted just as the T-scores discussed earlier in the example of Jerry.

Other standard scores that are seen in Figure 5.1 are Z-scores, CEEBs, and Deviation IQs. Z-scores simply specify standard deviation units with a mean of 0 and a standard deviation of 1. Thus Z-scores may be positive or negative. CEEBs are college board scores reported for such tests as the Scholastic Assessment Test (SAT) or the Graduate Record Exam (GRE). Their mean is 500 with a standard deviation of 100. The Deviation IQs are intelligence test scores for such tests as the Wechsler or Stanford-Binet intelligence tests. The mean is 100 with a standard deviation of 15 (Wechsler) or 16 (Stanford-Binet).

Grade-Equivalent Scores

Grade-equivalent scores are usually stated in terms of years and tenths of years. For example, if the average raw score of beginning fourth-grade children in the norm group is 33, then 33 is assigned the grade equivalent of 4.1 (fourth grade, first month). Any child who scores 33 raw-score points receives a grade-equivalent score of 4.1.

Grade-equivalent scores *appear* easy for teachers to interpret because the reference point is a grade in school, but interpretation actually has some serious limitations. The further away a pupil's score is from the average, the greater the chances are that the grade equivalent will be misinterpreted. Grade-equivalent scores for average children are probably accurate, but low or high scores are susceptible to error of interpretation. It is particularly important for teachers of students who are reading poorly to remember this. To continue with the example of the fourth-grader, if Georgia scores 17 raw-score points (a fairly low score), which converts to a grade-equivalent score of 2.1 according to the norm table found in the test manual, the teacher should *not* conclude that Georgia is reading in a manner similar to a beginning second-grade child. All that can be said is that Georgia is reading poorly compared to her fourth-grade classmates and that she earned the same raw score as the average of second-graders in the first month of second grade.

Grade-equivalent scores do *not* indicate grade placement for a student. For example, suppose Tommy, a third-grader, takes the test containing second-, third-, and fourth-grade material and receives a grade-equivalent score of 5.3. This does *not* mean that Tommy is able to handle fifth-grade, third-month material because he was never tested on fifth-grade material. It only means that Tommy can perform second-, third-, and fourth-grade tasks in the test as well as average students in the third month of fifth grade can perform these (below-grade-level) tasks.

Grade-equivalent scores have been so seriously misinterpreted that in 1981 the International Reading Association passed a resolution calling upon publishers to eliminate grade equivalents from their tests. Therefore, percentile scores, stanines, or NCEs are recommended for comparing a student's performance to that of the norm group.

Basic Measurement Concepts

Successful assessment and evaluation in reading depend considerably on the tools teachers use. These tools can be called tests in the broadest sense of that term, but tests can range from informal reading inventories, to teacher-made spelling tests, to the highly structured standardized achievement tests. Some concepts are basic to all measurement systems, regardless of how they are constructed or used. Among the more important concepts are validity, reliability, and standard error of measurement.

Validity

The most important of all measurement characteristics is **validity.** A test is valid if *it measures what it claims to measure and does the task for which it is intended.* The critical question for the teacher to ask is: Does this test measure what I have been teaching? Sternberg (1991) reminds us that "we need to be considerably more cautious in our use of test scores and that we need at least to think about creating tests that are more realistic simulations of people's behavior in the kinds of situations in which they use the aptitudes and achievements that we measure. . . . Reading tests [are] considerably less valid as measures of real-world reading behavior than most people have wanted to believe" (p. 540).

Test content that matches a teacher's instructional objectives is said to have **content validity.** If the match is poor, the test is an invalid measure of those particular instructional objectives. For example, a teacher has been concentrating on teaching reading comprehension for the past three months and now wants to test the pupils. A test measuring reading comprehension would be valid; one measuring phonics knowledge would be invalid because the test would not measure what had been taught. The phonics test is not a bad test in and of itself; rather, it is inappropriate for the purpose intended. Kavale (1979) suggests that teachers can best determine content validity by actually taking the test.

Teachers are unlikely to make an error in situations in which the validity issue is so clearly apparent, as in the preceding example, but occasionally the matter is more subtle. Consider, for instance, the use of a test called "Vocabulary Knowledge" when the match between the test and the lessons taught is a matter of approach. If the teacher has used a modified cloze procedure approach, and the test measures vocabulary from a synonym-matching approach, the test would not be highly valid because it does not assess vocabulary as it was taught. Teachers and school administrators must be jointly responsible for choosing appropriate tests.

Another type of validity, **construct validity,** refers to the degree to which a test measures a certain ability or trait. For example, an intelligence test is said to have construct validity to the extent that it actually measures intelligence. Because most traits cannot be measured directly, tests having construct validity measure behaviors believed to reflect the trait. The titles of some tests imply construct validity without providing empirical information in the test manual to support the existence of the validity (Sax, 1980). Such a practice is misleading to teachers and to others who may not be knowledgeable about measurement concepts. A test on reading comprehension, for example, should provide evidence that the test, in fact, measures reading comprehension.

Many tests designed to measure word recognition skills have been questioned on the basis of their construct validity. If a syllabication subtest asks students to identify the number of syllables in various words, and the words are spoken by the examiner, the construct validity of the test can be questioned. In the real reading situation, the students *see* and do not *hear* the words that they must syllabicate. Thus the question is whether the behaviors measured by oral presentation measure the same trait required during the process of silent reading.

Construct validity is typically supported by **correlation coefficients,** which indicate how strongly two variables are related. To be of most value for assessment, the subtests involved must be relatively independent, as reflected by low correlation coefficients ranging from 0.00 to 0.70. A high correlation (0.70 to 1.00) indicates a strong relationship between the subtests; in that case, the subtests are too interrelated to measure the different aptitudes they purport to measure.

Statistical procedures are available to determine test validity, but they are not directly related to the major purposes of this book. They are vital, however, for teachers who are asked to evaluate and select standardized tests for their school or school district. Both George Spache (1976) and Kenneth Kavale (1979) add important issues relevant to selecting standardized tests in reading. These readings are highly recommended for those who select and use such instruments.

Reliability

The consistency or dependability of a test and its measurements denotes its **reliability.** If a teacher were to give the same test to a group of students more than once (test-retest) within a short time frame (so that growth isn't being measured), and the scores on the tests are nearly the same for each student, the test is considered reliable because it yields essentially the same score each time it is given.

Reliability is also expressed through a correlation coefficient. The higher the correlation coefficient, the more dependable the scores obtained from the test. A coefficient of 0.90 or more is considered very reliable; if it is below 0.80, the teacher should be cautious in making decisions about individual students. Reliability can be estimated in a number of statistical ways, and each has a different name. Test manuals indicate the type of reliability by using terms such as *split-half reliability, parallel forms reliability,* and *Kuder-Richardson reliability.* In any case, a high correlation coefficient is desirable.

No reading test is perfectly consistent. Some common conditions affecting reliability are objectivity in scoring, needed variability among scores of students being tested, number of items on the test, difficulty level, and standardization of test administration and interpretation (Sax, 1980).

Objectivity in scoring is critical. If different teachers independently score the same test but arrive at different scores, reliability cannot be very high. Multiple-choice tests are relatively free from problems of this type compared to more subjective measures, such as essay tests.

Reliability also depends on the variability of the students taking the tests. If everyone taking the test functions at the same level and gets the same score, reliability of that test is zero, because student variability is lacking.

The easiest and most efficient way to improve reliability is to increase the number of items on the test, provided that the added items consistently measure what the original items measure. This explains, in part, why some tests are so long. In instances of behavioral observation, the teacher must increase the number of times the student is observed performing a specific task.

Difficulty level also affects reliability. A very easy or very hard test does not measure individual differences because all student responses tend to be the same (Sax, 1980). Clearly such a test cannot be used for analytic purposes.

Standardization of test administration and interpretation, or criteria for scoring and interpreting, provides more reliable information. Tests and assessment measures that lack such clear guidelines result in interpretations that are highly dependent on the person making the assessment.

Standard Error of Measurement

When a score is obtained for a student, the teacher should ask how much confidence can be placed in it as the student's *true* score. Many test manuals describe a statistic known as the **standard error of measurement** (SEmeas or SEM). This statistic indicates the extent to which an individual's score can be expected to vary each time the test is taken. In other words, standardized tests are not precise instruments and there is error associated with any score. The *true* score is the score that would result if the same test were taken many, many times and those scores averaged. Since this isn't possible, the standard error of measurement is reported for the test and it is used to determine a range within which the true score lies. This range is called the *band of probability* or the *confidence interval.* This band identifies the highest and lowest scores that the true score falls between two-thirds of the time. For example, let's say the SEM is 10 standard score points, and in this example the raw score converts to a true T-score between 60 and 80. The SEM of 10 was added and subtracted from the obtained T-score of 70 to achieve the band of probability for the true score. If we then convert these scores to percentiles (refer to Figure 5.1), the interpretation would be that for two out of three testings, the true score would fall between the 82nd and 99th percentiles. In one of three testings, the score could fall below the 82nd (for percentiles the 99th is the highest score) (Fry, 1980).

Since the range or band of probability for a test score can be fairly wide, ideally we would like to use a test with high validity, high reliability, and a small SEM. The concept of the SEM is not restricted to standardized tests, however. Teacher observations, surveys and checklists, informal reading inventories, criterion-referenced tests, and text-related tests, which will be defined a little later, also have a potentially large SEM because they have not been given to large groups of students with the intention of revising to lower the SEM. Thus there is considerable potential for error with direct measures as well as with indirect measures. Before making a decision about a student's ability, the teacher must consider a variety of information (e.g., test score plus informal observation plus work samples). The nature of assessment is multidimensional, much as literacy is a multi-dimensional process.

PURPOSES OF TESTING IN READING

Testing has many different purposes and many tests are available, so care must be taken to choose a test appropriate for a specific purpose. As Kavale (1979) says, "If the uses for the test results are not known in advance, the best test to use is none at all" (p. 9).

Test selection should be based on answers to the questions *what, who, by whom,* and *for what* (Merwin, 1973). Kavale (1979) provides some examples of how these questions might be answered. For instance, a test is needed to:

1. Assess reading achievement *(what)* of [an eighth-grade student] *(who)* by the teacher *(by whom)* to help determine the student's instructional reading level *(for what)*

2. Assess word attack skills *(what)* of a [second-grade child] *(who)* by the teacher *(by whom)* to determine whether particular phonics knowledge is needed *(for what)*

3. Assess gain in reading achievement *(what)* of a group of fourth-grade students *(who)* by a curriculum supervisor *(by whom)* to determine the effectiveness of a new set of instructional materials *(for what)* (p. 10)

Using Merwin's guidelines, the answer to the *for what* question represents the specific purpose for testing, but the other questions are equally important to the selection of a test.

Because of the great number of purposes for testing in reading, all cannot be listed; however, some examples are particularly relevant for classroom teachers:

1. Organizing the class into reading, skill, or interest groups

2. Assessing reading levels of individual students

3. Identifying specific reading difficulties in areas such as word identification, inferential comprehension, or vocabulary development

4. Evaluating individuals or small groups

PUBLISHED READING TESTS

A number of standardized tests are available for use in assessing reading. Along with the tests themselves, publishers provide examiner manuals and several additional aids, such as scoring keys and record sheets. A test's technical manual or examiner manual contains vital information that must be studied before giving the test. A good test manual contains directions for test administration and scoring, and information to aid effective interpretation of the scores. Additional information of a statistical and technical nature, such as validity and reliability coefficients and the SEM, are usually found in the technical manual.

Teachers must carefully follow directions when administering standardized tests. Tests are designed to give every pupil, as nearly as possible, the same chance when taking the test. If teachers do not follow standardized directions, scores cannot be used reliably and validly. Directions should never be rushed or examples omitted. On the other hand, teachers should never give more information to pupils than is specified in the test manual. Deviations from the directions or test time will put the pupils in a context different from the norm group, and norms for the test will not be appropriate. It is imperative, therefore, that teachers follow instructions precisely or note any deviations from the standardized procedures.

The testing environment is an important consideration because classroom conditions affect the reliability of test results. The classroom should be well lighted, ventilated, and free from undue noise or interruptions. A sufficient number of tests, answer sheets, and marking pencils should be readily available. Pupils unaccustomed to taking tests should be briefed beforehand regarding such test-taking behaviors as no talking, no helping, and no drinks of water. In classrooms in which cooperative learning groups and conversation are the norm, these testing requirements can certainly affect results (McAuliffe, 1993). Most students would benefit from a practice session using practice booklets, which are often available with standardized tests. At times teachers have difficulty maintaining the neutral role needed during the testing period, but the temptation to help students must be resisted. The roles of teacher and tester are *not* the same.

Standardized Reading Survey Tests

Standardized tests most widely used in schools today are achievement test batteries such as the *Comprehensive Test of Basic Skills (CTBS), Iowa Tests of Basic Skills (ITBS), Metropolitan Achievement Tests (e.g., Metropolitan 8),* and *Stanford Achievement Tests* (e.g., *Stanford 9*). Designed to sample broad knowledge in a given area, these batteries typically yield two or three reading scores plus scores for other subject areas, such as arithmetic and social studies. Common areas assessed in reading are vocabulary, comprehension, total reading (often a combination of the vocabulary and comprehension scores), and, less frequently, measures of study skills and rate of reading.

Survey reading tests are similar to the reading subtests on achievement test batteries. When general reading is the focus of testing, a survey test saves time and money because other content areas are not included. These tests help in placement and are often used in pre- and post-intervention assessments to determine whether students have benefited from that particular intervention. Two examples of survey reading tests are the *Gates-MacGinitie Reading Tests,* 4th ed. (MacGinitie, MacGinitie, Maria, & Dreyer, 2000), available for K–12 and adult, and the *Nelson-Denny Reading Skills Test* (Brown, Fishco, & Hanna, 1993), for high school, college, and adult, with an electronic version of the survey test made available in 2001. Teachers should be aware, however, that scores from these tests probably reflect either maximum or minimum performance on the part of many students. They usually either try hard to do their best on tests of this type, or give up altogether and answer questions randomly. In either case, their scores tend to reflect a level of concentration and performance not typical in their day-to-day reading activities.

While survey reading tests can help teachers with level 1 analysis, identifying those students who may need assistance in their reading development, and perhaps with level 2 analysis, identifying the major domain in which reading difficulties are occurring, they are not designed to do more than this. Other tests and assessment procedures are more helpful for analyzing reading behaviors at levels 2 and 3 (areas of difficulty), and they can supplement data obtained from survey tests. Also consider that there are students who are effective readers but never do well on standardized tests.

Most survey reading tests are designed to be administered in one of two ways. The first, called **at-level testing,** uses a single level of the test for a specified grade level. For example, level A of the test is to be used for first and second grades, level B for third and fourth grades, and level C for fifth and sixth grades. A third-grade teacher would administer the level B test to all students in the class.

The second option, called **out-of-level testing,** allows the teacher to select the level of the test that best reflects the average achievement of the class. For example, a teacher of students whose average achievement is atypically low or high could select a level better suited to the students, thus increasing reliability. If out-of-level testing is desired, be sure to check the teacher's manual for further information about the test being used.

Standardized Diagnostic Reading Tests

The major purpose of standardized diagnostic reading tests is to measure discrete reading subskills. These tests are sometimes used by teachers to identify students' specific areas of strength and difficulty. A graphic profile is used to compare subtest scores for individuals and to determine level of ability in the reading areas. Because diagnostic assessment is directed at identifying specific strengths and areas of difficulty, the total test score is much less meaningful than the profile because it represents a composite performance. Reviewing the profile for an entire class can aid appropriate grouping for instruction. In the class summary profile for a fourth-grade urban classroom seen in Figure 5.2, the teacher circled stanines that are in the low range (1, 2, and 3). Such a procedure helps a teacher readily identify students who may need assistance in one reading domain (e.g., Marcus T., reading comprehension), or several (e.g., Irwin J., all domains). The teacher can also begin to form tentative hypotheses for instruction and groupings (see comments in Figure 5.2).

The most common diagnostic reading test used by classroom teachers is the *Stanford Diagnostic Reading Test,* 4th ed. (Karlsen & Gardner, 1995), also available in a braille edition. The Stanford (SDRT 4) provides six levels for assessing reading competence, with a single form for the first three levels and two parallel forms for the three upper levels. The six levels are designated by color: (1) red level for grades 1.5–2.5, (2) orange level for grades 2.5–3.5, (3) green level for grades 3.5–4.5, (4) purple level for grades 4.5–6.5, (5) brown level for grades 6.5–8.9, and (6) blue level for grades 9.0–13.0. In addition, SDRT 4 offers teachers three optional assessment tools: (1) Reading Strategies Survey, for determining which reading strategies students understand and use; (2) Reading Questionnaire, for assessing attitudes, interests, and factors affecting comprehension; and (3) Story Retelling, which uses a scoring rubric (see Chapter 6) to assess either an oral or written retelling.

This newest edition of the Stanford Diagnostic Reading Test reflects an effort to respond to current instructional approaches. The SDRT 4 includes new reading selections written by published authors that parallel the type of literature used in classrooms today. There is also a new focus on assessing reading strategies in addition to literal, inferential, and critical comprehension.

Figure 5.2   Graphic Profile for Comparing Subtest Scores

Teacher _____Ms. B._____   Grade _____4_____   Date _____October_____

Pupil's Name	Auditory discrimination	Phonic analysis	Structural analysis	Auditory vocabulary	Literal comprehension	Inferential comprehension	Total comprehension	Comments
Duane B.	(3)	4	5	4	4	4	4	VERIFY AUDITORY DISCRIMINATION
Elizabeth B.	6	4	6	5	5	4	5	COULD PEER TUTOR?
Isaiah D.	5	5	(3)	(3)	4	(3)	(3)	VOCABULARY AND INFERENTIAL COMP.
Rebeka D.	8	6	7	8	7	7	7	COULD PEER TUTOR?
Irwin J.	(1)	(2)	(3)	(3)	(2)	(2)	(2)	COMPREHENSION STRATEGIES 1ST
Austin J.	4	4	4	4	(2)	(1)	(2)	COMP. STRATEGIES- FOCUS INFERENTIAL
Brandon M.	5	5	(2)	(2)	4	4	4	COMBINE VOCAB. AND AFFIXES
Latasha M.	5	5	4	4	(1)	(1)	(1)	COMPREHENSION, DOES LATASHA RELY
Natasha M.	5	(3)	6	5	5	5	5	TOO MUCH ON HER TWIN, NATASHA?
Kalisha M.	(3)	4	6	(3)	(3)	(1)	(2)	FOCUS ON INFERENTIAL COMP.
Paul M.	5	4	5	(3)	(3)	(3)	(3)	SOME COMP. ASSISTANCE
Bichhuy N.	(2)	(2)	4	5	5	5	5	LANGUAGE INTERFERENCE?
Julius P.	7	9	9	9	9	8	8	COULD PEER TUTOR?
David P.	4	(1)	4	(1)	(1)	(1)	(1)	COMP. STRATEGIES LEA? VERIFY STRUCT.
Eric T.	(1)	(2)	5	(2)	(2)	(2)	(2)	COMPREHENSION 1ST/ VERIFY STRUCTURAL
Marcus T.	5	4	4	4	(2)	(2)	(2)	COMPREHENSION STRATEGIES
Brian T.	4	(1)	5	4	(3)	(3)	(3)	VERIFY PHONIC SCORE
								10/17 NEED
								COMPREHENSION ASSISTANCE

The areas included in the SDRT 4 are phonetic analysis, vocabulary, reading comprehension, and scanning for information. More specifically, the red level measures phonetic analysis, auditory vocabulary, word recognition, comprehension of sentences, riddles, cloze paragraphs, and short paragraphs with questions. The orange level measures phonetic analysis, auditory vocabulary, reading vocabulary, comprehension of cloze paragraphs, and paragraphs that represent recreational, informational, and functional types of text. The green level measures phonetic analysis, reading vocabulary, and reading comprehension of paragraphs representing various types of text. The purple, brown, and blue levels measure reading vocabulary, comprehension of various types of text, and scanning to locate information.

While several of the subskills tests are administered over most levels, the specific subskills are measured differently. For example, the phonetic analysis subtest for the red level measures students' abilities to discriminate among consonant sounds represented auditorially by single consonant letters, consonant clusters, and digraphs in the initial and final positions, while the same subtest for the green level measures whether the reader can recognize the same consonant sounds represented by the same spelling or two different spellings (e.g., *f*ace and *r*ain; *f*oam and gra*ph*; *p*ie and rep*ly*; *s*ugar and na*ti*on). The changes in what is measured from level to level are intended to reflect the developmental characteristics of the reading process. Teachers will have to decide whether these subtests provide valid (content validity) assessments for their students.

Criterion-Referenced Tests

A **criterion-referenced test** measures how well an individual performs a specific task following instruction for that specific task. Usually a desired level of performance is specified, thus the term *criterion*. Criterion-referenced tests, or skills management systems, are assessment/instructional materials that focus on reading subskills. They are also referred to as **mastery tests** because students are said to have mastered a subskill when they attain the specified criterion. Teachers have actually been using the concept of a criterion-referenced test for years. Any time they develop a test to measure some specific instructional objective and designate a specific grade as passing, they are using the concept of criterion-referenced testing. For example, the content of a criterion-referenced test may be final consonant sounds. In order to say that Jimmy knows final consonant sounds, he may have to respond correctly to 90 percent or more of the test items. Jimmy's performance is not compared with group performance. Teachers set the criterion level to coincide with their expectations for a particular individual.

The assumption underlying criterion-referenced tests and the manner in which they are constructed is different from norm-referenced tests. Criterion-referenced tests focus on whether a student (or group of students) has learned a particular set of reading subskills. This is different from the norm-referenced test that compares learners with a norm group on general ability in the major reading domains. Table 5.1 compares and contrasts norm-referenced and criterion-referenced tests.

For criterion-referenced or mastery tests, interpretation of the results appears quite simple and straightforward in that 80 percent indicates passing or mastery of a subskill and less than 80 percent indicates failure or nonmastery. The decision-making process is simplified for teachers. Using the score as a basis, they decide whether a student has learned the subskill; if mastery is attained, the next decision is whether to move on to another subskill or to a higher level of difficulty for the subskill under consideration. If the student has not mastered the subskill, the teacher decides either to reteach or to review the particular subskill involved.

Teachers also should be aware that some students learn their reading subskills well but still cannot read adequately, if at all. Likewise, some students read adequately but still fail reading subskills tests (Jackson, 1981; McNeil, 1974). A pure subskills approach to teaching reading can lead to troubled readers just as a no-skills approach can.

Table 5.1   Comparison of Norm- and Criterion-Referenced Tests

Norm-Referenced	Criterion-Referenced
1. Norm-referenced tests assess the student's knowledge about the particular subject or content being tested.	1. Criterion-referenced tests assess the student's ability to perform a specific task.
2. Norm-referenced tests compare a student's performance with that of the norm group. (During the last phase of test construction, a final draft form is given to a large number of students who are representative of the students for whom the test was designed. This is the *norm group*.)	2. Criterion-referenced tests determine whether students possess the skills needed to move to the next level of learning.
3. Norm-referenced tests can be used annually as pretests and post-tests to determine student gain while comparing these gains to those of the norm group.	3. Criterion-referenced tests can be used as pretests and post-tests to determine which skills need to be taught and which skills have been mastered.
4. Norm-referenced tests contain items that are considered to be precise, valid, and reliable in order to discriminate among the weakest and best students.	4. Criterion-referenced tests contain items that determine whether the student is able to use the learned skill in particular situations.
5. Norm-referenced tests have a high degree of validity.	5. Criterion-referenced tests have only content validity; the items assess the ability needed to perform a given behavior.
6. Norm-referenced tests have a high degree of reliability. They consistently measure the same behavior with each administration of the test. This factor is *essential* for norm-referenced tests.	6. Criterion-referenced tests are not concerned with statistical calculations of reliability. If students are retested, they should not make the same score.
7. Interpretation of the student's score on norm-referenced tests depends on the scores obtained by the norm group.	7. Interpretation of the student's score on criterion-referenced tests depends upon whether the student is able to perform a specific task.
8. Norm-referenced test scores yield global measurements of general abilities.	8. Criterion-referenced test scores yield exact measures of ability to achieve specific objectives.
9. Norm-referenced test scores are interpreted in terms of norms that have been statistically listed in the test manual by the author or the publisher.	9. Criterion-referenced test scores are interpreted in terms of a score that is considered acceptable by the teacher, and by examining specific items that were correct or incorrect.
10. Norm-referenced test items are written to create variability among the individual scores in a particular group.	10. Criterion-referenced test items are designed to assess ability to perform a specific task as stated by a behavioral objective.

From Eddie Kennedy, *Classroom Approaches to Remedial Reading,* 1977, pp. 82–83. Adapted by permission of the publisher, F. E. Peacock, Publishers, Inc., Itasca, IL.

SUMMARY

The early part of this chapter reviews the state of fundamental change that assessment is undergoing. New ways of thinking about assessment and evaluation are introduced. Several important measurement concepts, such as content and construct validity, reliability, and standard error of measurement, are discussed.

The second part of the chapter discusses a specific published diagnostic reading test that is easily administered and currently used by classroom teachers. Criterion-referenced tests are also briefly explained and contrasted with norm-referenced tests.

Suggested Readings

Farr, R. (1992). Putting it all together: Solving the reading assessment puzzle. *The Reading Teacher, 46,* 26–37.

Distinguished educator Roger Farr has written extensively on reading assessment. In this article, Dr. Farr discusses conflicting views on reading assessment and proposes linkages among various approaches as a solution.

Hymes, D. (with Chafin, A., and Gonder, P.). (1991). *The changing face of testing and assessment: Problems and solutions.* Arlington, VA: American Association of School Administrators.

This report deals with issues related to recent reform efforts in assessment, and specifically explores the value of both standardized tests and performance-based assessments.

Johnston, P. (1992). Nontechnical assessment. *The Reading Teacher, 46,* 60–62.

An informative summary of assessment issues and content of Johnston's larger work, Constructive Evaluation of Literate Activity *(1992, Longman). He stresses the need to know reading and writing better, to know our students better, and to become more reflective.*

6 Reading Assessment
Direct Measures

Objectives

After you have read this chapter, you should be able to:

1. compare and contrast the following direct measures: informal reading inventories, running records, cloze procedure, checklists, observations, conferences, and performance samples;
2. administer and interpret an informal reading inventory, cloze passages, story retellings, and interest and attitude surveys;
3. discuss the value of the information obtained through direct measures for use at analytical level 3.

Key Concepts and Terms

basic story features	instructional reading level	passage dependent
cloze procedure	interactive assessment	protocol
end-of-unit tests	kidwatching	qualitative analysis
frustration reading level	learning centers	quantitative analysis
independent reading level	listening capacity	running records
informal reading inventory (IRI)	maze technique	scoring rubric
	miscue	story retelling
	miscue analysis	text-related tests

For many years teachers have felt that standardized measures in reading do not give sufficient information for instructional decision making. The main justification for using classroom-based tests and measures is that they supply useful information for direct teaching applications. Because these measures often involve the actual materials and tasks used in the classroom, the teacher obtains a more realistic view of how the reader functions within the instructional setting.

Direct assessments occur frequently; thus the reliability of such assessments is increased. If standardized reading tests were given as often, the process would be extremely time-consuming, subtracting substantially from available teaching time, already at a premium in the classroom. Furthermore, the cost would be prohibitive. Also, the information yielded by many standardized tests is not the type that teachers want most; that is, information that tells whether specific strategies have been learned or the particular strengths of an individual student relative to his or her curriculum and instructional program.

A number of direct measures that help teachers assess and evaluate students' reading behaviors will be explained in this chapter. No one technique is sufficient, nor should the results of standardized, or criterion-referenced tests be ignored. In the words of Emily Grady (1992), "education needs accountability, but accountability must contribute to the growth of students. . . . Teachers must be central to the assessment process; they must be the documenters and reviewers of their students' learning. Students [also] must enter into the assessment process in order to gain insight and confidence in controlling their own learning" (p. 29).

Additionally, assessments "should accommodate the full spectrum of the intelligences, allowing students choices based on how they feel they can demonstrate that they have mastered the required material" (Lazear, 1994, p. 94). Figure 6.1 provides a variety of suggestions to assist teachers in designing opportunities for all students to demonstrate what they know and what they can do.

COMMONLY USED DIRECT MEASURES

Text-Related Tests

In addition to core materials found in many classrooms (e.g., basal readers, workbooks, and teacher's manuals), most publishers provide ancillary materials, including tests, to help assess student learning. These **text-related tests** measure acquisition of strategies and subskills emphasized in a reader or text at a particular level. Such tests have the advantage of content validity, because they are intended to measure the content learned from the reading materials just completed. While carefully constructed, they usually have not been normed, like previously discussed standardized tests. They also measure a smaller number of subskills and objectives. Good students may not have a chance to show what they can do; they often *top the test* (i.e., obtain very high scores). The tests can, however, indicate students who need assistance. Thus they can have considerable analytic value for the classroom teacher.

Many basal systems contain **end-of-unit tests** in the teacher's manual or in the student workbooks. These tests should not be overlooked by teachers; they provide useful information regarding student accomplishment of relatively small learning segments. Extension procedures are often recommended for students who do not perform well on these tests.

Informal Reading Inventories

The **informal reading inventory (IRI)** is probably the most widely known nonstandardized, direct measure. Major purposes for using this measure include (1) to help the teacher observe a student's strategic reading behaviors with material of various grade levels, (2) to aid the teacher in choosing appropriate texts, readers, or other reading materials for each student in the class, (3) to aid the teacher in identifying three different reading levels—the independent reading level, the instructional reading level, and the frustration reading level, and (4) to aid the teacher in learning more about each pupil's reading strengths and needs. An individually administered, nonstandardized instrument enables the teacher to assess reading strategies that can be assessed only through direct observation, such as the ability to monitor and self-correct oral reading miscues. Other advantages include the flexibility to modify or clarify directions for some students and the opportunity to observe other behaviors, in addition to reading, in the context of assessment.

The traditional IRI consists of a series of graded passages that students read and answer questions about. Inventories can be (1) published instruments, in which passages and questions are carefully constructed to reflect reading grade levels accurately, (2) teacher-made, with passages selected from the reading materials used in the school, or (3) constructed by a publisher to accompany a particular basal reader series. Lists of words graded by difficulty are often used as quick screening devices to determine a starting point for reading passages. Passages are then read orally, silently, or both, depending on the teacher's purpose. Word recognition errors are recorded for the oral selections, while comprehension is checked for passages read orally or silently. Rate of reading can also be obtained by recording the time spent reading the passages.

Figure 6.1 Multiple Intelligences Assessment Menu

Verbal-Linguistic Intelligence
(Language Arts–Based Assessment Instruments)

- written essays
- vocabulary quizzes
- recall of verbal information
- audiocassette recordings
- poetry writing
- linguistic humor
- formal speech
- cognitive debates
- listening and reporting
- learning logs and journals

Logical-Mathematical Intelligence
(Cognitive Patterns–Based Assessment Instruments)

- cognitive organizers
- higher-order reasoning
- pattern games
- outlining
- logic and rationality exercises
- mental menus and formulas
- deductive reasoning
- inductive reasoning
- calculation processes
- logical analysis and critique

Visual-Spatial Intelligence
(Imaginal–Based Assessment Instruments)

- murals and montages
- graphic representation and visual illustrating
- visualization and imagination
- reading, understanding, and creating maps
- flowcharts and graphs
- sculpting and building
- imaginary conversations
- mind mapping
- video recording and photography
- manipulative demonstrations

Bodily-Kinesthetic Intelligence
(Performance–Based Assessment Instruments)

- lab experiments
- dramatization
- original and classical dance
- charades and mimes
- impersonations
- human tableaux
- invention projects
- physical exercise routines and games
- skill demonstrations
- illustrations using body language and gestures

Musical-Rhythmic Intelligence
(Auditory–Based Assessment Instruments)

- creating concept songs and raps
- illustrating with sound
- discerning rhythmic patterns
- composing music
- linking music and rhythm with concepts
- orchestrating music
- creating percussion patterns
- recognizing tonal patterns and quality
- analyzing musical structure
- reproducing musical and rhythmic patterns

Interpersonal Intelligence
(Relational–Based Assessment Instruments)

- group "jigsaws"
- explaining to or teaching another
- "think-pair-share"
- "round robin"
- giving and receiving feedback
- interviews, question-naires, and people searches
- empathic processing
- random group quizzes
- assess your teammates
- test, coach, and retest

Intrapersonal Intelligence
(Psychological–Based Assessment Instruments)

- autobiographical reporting
- personal application scenarios
- metacognitive surveys and questionnaires
- higher-order questions and answers
- concentration tests
- feelings diaries and logs
- personal projection
- self-identification reporting
- personal history correlation
- personal priorities and goals

Naturalist Intelligence
(Natural World–Based Assessment Instruments)

- classifying leaves
- sorting animal pictures
- planting seeds
- caring for a classroom pet
- developing an ecology project
- matching animal characteristics to human traits
- maintaining a garden or terrarium
- correlating animal sounds to human emotions
- tracking star locations and constellations
- reporting on biological inventions such as cloning or genetically-altered foods

Adapted from Multiple Intelligence Approaches to Assessment, © 1994 Zephyr Press, Tucson, Arizona. Reprinted with permission.

Probably the greatest disadvantage of many published IRIs is that they assess reading comprehension—the heart of reading—using as few as five test items per level. The reliability of test results can be seriously questioned when so few items are used. The questions are not always well written, nor do they necessarily discriminate between good and poor readers (Davis, 1978). Some inventories also claim to provide information on comprehension subskills (e.g., determining main ideas, recalling details, identifying cause and effect, inferring word meanings from context); however, research shows they do not, so IRIs should not be used for this purpose (Duffelmeyer & Duffelmeyer, 1989; Duffelmeyer, Robinson, & Squier, 1989; Schell & Hanna, 1981). Furthermore, comprehension is frequently assessed on *oral* reading of the passages. This is of particular concern with ineffective readers and readers in the early elementary grades, who may expend their cognitive abilities trying to do well reading aloud, thereby diverting attention from constructing meaning.

IRIs can be time-consuming to administer and interpret, especially if administered to an individual to record oral reading behaviors. Average administration time per student is 30 minutes. Interpretation time can be at least as much and probably more. However, not every student needs to be assessed with an IRI.

Many teachers are choosing to use published IRIs because of the time required to construct an IRI. Examples of some published inventories are the *Analytical Reading Inventory* (Woods & Moe, 1999), the *Basic Reading Inventory, Preprimer–12* (Johns, 1997), the *Classroom Assessment of Reading Processes* (Swearingen & Allen, 1997), the *Ekwall/Shanker Reading Inventory* (Ekwall & Shanker, 1999), the *Flynt-Cooter Reading Inventory for the Classroom* (Flynt & Cooter, 1998), the *Informal Reading Inventory: Preprimer to Twelfth Grade* (Burns, 1998), the *Qualitative Reading Inventory* (Leslie & Caldwell, 2000), and the *Stieglitz Informal Reading Inventory* (Stieglitz, 1997). As with standardized tests, reliability and validity must be considered. For individual assessment purposes a desirable reliability coefficient is 0.90. Authors of published IRIs should provide this information in their administration manuals.

The question of validity is most critical. Does the IRI measure what it is intended to measure? To answer this question, you must recall the four major purposes for administering an IRI and remember that the issue of validity differs somewhat for each one. For example, if the purpose is to aid the teacher in placing a pupil in an appropriate reader, then a publisher-constructed or teacher-made IRI based on the reading series being used may be more valid.

Another validity issue is related to the purpose of identifying the three reading levels that IRIs purport to establish. For some time, writers and users of informal reading inventories have chosen to use the arbitrary criteria set up by Betts (1946) to distinguish the independent (99 percent word recognition, 90 percent comprehension), instructional (95 percent word recognition, 75 percent comprehension), and frustration (90 percent or less word recognition, 50 percent or less comprehension) reading levels discussed in the next section. These criteria were based on data obtained from 41 fourth-grade students who read the passages silently before reading them aloud. Not until 1970, when William Powell adjusted these criteria to be dependent on the grade level of the child being tested, were the Betts criteria challenged. Powell (1970) found that children who could comprehend material reasonably well (70 to 75 percent comprehension) achieved average word recognition scores ranging from 83 to 94 percent across grades 1 through 6. Older readers were even more accurate in word recognition. Unfortunately, too little research evidence is available either to support the Betts criteria (Roberts, 1976) or to define appropriate criteria for establishing the three reading levels. (See also the "Interpreting IRIs" section later in this chapter, specifically Figure 6.5 and Table 6.1.) Published IRIs are generally consistent in using the Betts criteria, with only a few exceptions. Regardless, the scoring criteria are clearly noted in each inventory's administration section.

It is important to remember that IRIs are nonstandardized measures and thus can be used flexibly. Published IRIs provide what sound like rigid procedures for administration; however, teachers using published IRIs understand their own purpose(s) for using the IRI, employ good judgment, and rely on their knowledge of the reading process. For example, a study by Cardarelli (1988) points out that by allowing students to look back at a passage to answer the comprehension questions, more than half of these students increased their scores sufficiently to change frustration reading levels to instructional reading levels. This procedure makes good sense if a teacher normally allows students to look back in their textbooks for answers to questions rather than insisting that the students answer the questions from memory as directed in most IRI manuals.

In any event, teachers must use other direct assessment procedures to supplement results of IRIs on comprehension. For instance, the student being assessed should be encouraged to recall as much about the passage or story as possible *before* questions are asked. This procedure is called **story retelling.** General comprehension questions can be asked if the student does not respond freely. For example:

Tell me about . . .

Who was in the story?

What happened?

Where did this happen?

How did it happen?

Why do you think the story was written?

Teachers may choose to record a student's story retelling by making check marks on a previously prepared outline of the story that identifies major points from the passage related to characters, events, plot, and theme (Figure 6.2; see also Figure 10.1). This outline, record sheet, or **protocol,** is also called a *scoring rubric.* Scoring rubrics are discussed later in this chapter. If the items listed are not mentioned by the student, the teacher asks questions, also prepared in advance, to help elicit desired information. This is called *prompting.* Questions about retellings should not supply information or insights the reader did not provide in the retelling. Most questions should be of the *Wh–* variety and refer to information already given by the reader. These questions, when asked following a story, should be keyed toward the elements of a story. For example, as modified from Weaver (1994, pp. 247–249):

Characters:

What else can you tell me about (name of character(s) provided in the retelling)?

Who else was in the story besides (the characters mentioned)?

Events:

What else happened?

What happened after (event provided in the retelling)?

Where (or when) did (event mentioned in the retelling) happen?

How did (event mentioned in the retelling) happen?

Figure 6.2   General Scoring Rubric for Story Retelling

Name: _____   Grade: _____   Date: _____
Story Title (and Author): _____
Context: Story Read by Child _____   Story Read to Child _____

Main Points for Retelling	Unprompted	Prompted
CHARACTERS (_____ points each)		
1. _____	_____	_____
2. _____	_____	_____
3. _____	_____	_____
4. _____	_____	_____
5. _____	_____	_____
SETTING (_____ points each)		
1. _____	_____	_____
2. _____	_____	_____
3. _____	_____	_____
4. _____	_____	_____
EVENTS/PLOT (_____ points each)		
1. _____	_____	_____
2. _____	_____	_____
3. _____	_____	_____
4. _____	_____	_____
5. _____	_____	_____
6. _____	_____	_____
7. _____	_____	_____
8. _____	_____	_____
9. _____	_____	_____
10. _____	_____	_____
RESOLUTION/THEME (_____ points each)		
1. _____	_____	_____
2. _____	_____	_____
3. _____	_____	_____

TOTAL POINTS: _____ /100 = _____ %   _____/100   +   _____/100
Evaluative Comments: (e.g., awareness of story features; story structure; understands story theme(s), etc.)

Plot:

Why do you think (action(s) mentioned in the retelling) happened?

What was the main problem for (character mentioned in retelling)?

Theme:

How did you feel when (event mentioned in the retelling) happened?

What do you think the author might have been trying to tell us in the story?

Setting:

Where/when did the story take place?

How was (character or event mentioned in the retelling) important to the story?

These questions can easily be modified for retellings of expository material. For example:

- What else can you tell me about (topic of passage mentioned in retelling)?
- What else was this passage/section about besides (the topic mentioned)?
- What other information did the author provide about (topic or important concept briefly mentioned in the retelling)?
- What happened after (event mentioned in retelling)?
- What do you think the authors are trying to tell us in this section?
- How was (event or fact mentioned in the retelling) important to this passage?
- How do you think you might use this information?
- How is this information like anything you have read about before?

For both narrative and expository passages, teachers also should ask questions related to the reading event. As found in Weaver (1994, pp. 248–249), these questions are modified from the *Reading Miscue Inventory: Alternative Procedures* (Goodman, Watson, & Burke, 1987):

Is there anything you'd like to ask me about this (story, passage)?

Were there any (concepts, ideas, sentences, words) that gave you trouble? What were they?

Why did you leave this word out?

Do you know what this word means, now?

Were there times when you weren't understanding the story? Show me where.

Tell me about those times.

Remember when you said the kid was a "typeical baby"? What is a "typeical baby"? (Ask about key words that were mispronounced or otherwise miscued, to see if the reader got the concept despite the miscue.)

In addition to demonstrating an understanding of story structure, story retellings reveal the reader's ability to remember facts, make inferences, and recall sequence (Morrow, 1985a, 1985b). To evaluate retellings, a scoring rubric is recommended (refer to Figure 6.2 and Figure 10.1). Many IRIs include story retellings in their procedures and provide scoring rubrics. To assess silent reading for groups or for students in the upper grades, a written retelling is possible (Smith & Jackson, 1985). The use of a story frame or a paragraph frame (see Chapter 10) also lends itself well to this purpose.

The "think-aloud" procedure (Brown, 1985; Kavale & Schreiner, 1979; Olshavsky, 1976/1977) addresses the criticism that comprehension questions do not assess the process of comprehension. This procedure requires readers to verbalize their thoughts while reading. These verbalizations provide insights into the ways individual readers derive meaning from text.

Three Reading Levels

Three reading levels relevant to classroom teaching can be estimated from administering and interpreting IRIs. The first level, the **independent reading level,** refers to the difficulty level at which a learner reads comfortably without teacher help. Students should be reading library books and other materials for pleasure at this level, with little or no diffi-culty recognizing words or comprehending. School reading to be done at home should be at students' independent reading levels. Students learn to read for fun and enjoyment when they read easy materials. At this level they develop favorable attitudes toward and positive interests in reading.

At the **instructional reading level,** students read with some direction and super-vision. Students are usually placed in basal readers written at their instructional reading levels, but most other materials pupils read *should not* be this difficult unless a teacher or someone else is available to help them. Without help, tension and other unfortunate out-comes may result (Arnold & Sherry, 1975). Too often, a single content-area textbook is used for instructional purposes. This practice assumes that all students in a class have the same instructional reading level.

The **frustration reading level** is one at which reading deteriorates and students cannot continue reading because the material is too hard even with instruction and guid-ance. Physical behaviors frequently associated with frustration include frowning, crying, squirming, whispering, or rebelliousness. Teachers should guide students away from this level of reading material.

Constructing and Administering IRIs

The informal reading inventory is constructed using materials typically read in the school, including content-area textbooks. The selections, chosen from the variety of material read, might range from 50 words at the primer level to 100–150 words in grades 1 through 3, to 200–250 words or so beyond grade 3. Stories should be well formed and co-hesive enough to allow development of comprehension questions. These questions should be **passage dependent,** that is, answerable upon reading the passage, and balanced between literal and inferential comprehension. For help in writing questions, Dantonio (1990), Pearson and Johnson (1978), and Valmont (1972) are recommended readings. Also, longer selections and more comprehension questions increase the relia-bility of the results.

In order to assess retellings, a list of the main points of each selection will need to be prepared (refer to Figure 6.2). The selections, list of main points, and questions are typed on separate sheets of paper and duplicated. These pages become the protocol, record sheet, or rubric, that the teacher uses for assessment purposes. The teacher may, with permission from publishers, reproduce the pages from the texts and bind them to-gether in a notebook. A sample of about twenty words introduced in each text can be placed in list format to be used for "quick" screening purposes. These procedures are time-consuming and explain why many teachers prefer published IRIs.

Once the protocols and the student's notebook are assembled, the IRI is given. With a published inventory, begin by asking the learner to read the word lists or sentences, as in the Flynt-Cooter (1998), starting with the lowest-level list available. If the first list is read with at least 80 percent accuracy, the next level can be tried. The student continues to read the word lists until the 80 percent criterion is *not* met. At this point the student is asked to read the selection corresponding to the highest-level word list on which he or she scored 100 percent. Beginning at an easier level helps to ensure that the first selection will be read successfully. When using a published inventory, the criteria for determining starting points may vary. You should carefully read the directions for administration found at the beginning of the inventory being used.

The student reads selections of increasing difficulty while the teacher codes behav-iors in oral reading and comprehension. There are two popular ways to code passages read orally: by using traditional miscue codes, which are similar to an editor's proofreading symbols, or by using **running records,** a combination of proofreading symbols and check marks (Clay, 2000). Figure 6.3 provides an example of a coded IRI passage using traditional miscue codes. Figure 6.4 shows the same passage recorded, scored, and analyzed as a running record. It should be noted that the use of running records does *not* require a protocol. Thus, running records can be used with any material a student is reading, making it a most adaptable method for assessing oral reading behaviors. As long as the teacher has paper

Figure 6.3   Example of a Traditionally Coded IRI Passage

FORM A: LEVEL 1 ASSESSMENT PROTOCOLS

You Cannot Fly! (96 words)

PART I: SILENT READING COMPREHENSION

Background Statement: "Have you ever wished you could fly? A boy named Sam in this story wants to fly. Read this story to find out if Sam gets to fly. Read it carefully because when you're through I'm going to ask you to tell me about the story."

Teacher Directions: Once the student completes the silent reading, say, "Tell me about the story you just read." Check off any answers to the questions below that the student provides during the retelling. Ask all remaining questions not addressed during the retelling.

Questions/Answers	*Story Grammar Element/ Level of Comprehension*
✓ 1. Who was the story mainly about? *Sam* *(Sam)*	character–characterization/ literal
— 2. What was Sam's problem? *he kept falling off his bed* *(Sam wanted to fly, but couldn't)*	story problem(s)/literal
— 3. What were two ways Sam tried to solve his problem? *he tried to fly and he got a letter* *(jumping off his bed and a box)*	problem resolution attempts/literal
— 4. How was Sam's problem finally solved? *everybody laughed* *(Sam got to ride on an airplane)*	problem resolution/inferential
✓ 5. What did the family and Sam do after reading the letter? *they laughed* *(laughed)*	problem resolution attempts/literal
— 6. Where did the story take place? *DK* *(Sam's house)*	setting/inferential
— 7. What lesson did Sam learn? *letters make you laugh* *(responses will vary, accept plausible ones)*	theme/evaluative
✓ 8. What words would you use to tell someone what kind of boy Sam was? *nice, happy* *(responses will vary, accept plausible ones)*	character–characterization/ evaluative

PART II: ORAL READING AND ANALYSIS OF MISCUES

Directions: Say, "Now I would like to hear you read this story out loud. Please start at the beginning and keep reading until I tell you to stop." Have the student read orally until he/she reaches the oral reading stop-marker (//). Follow along on the Miscue Grid marking any oral reading errors as appropriate. Then complete the Developmental/Performance Summary to determine whether to continue the assessment. (*Note:* The Miscue Grid should be completed *after* the assessment session has been concluded in order to minimize stress for the student.)

Adapted with permission from Flynt/Cooter, *Reading Inventory for the Classroom.*

Figure 6.3   *continued*

	MIS-PRONUN	SUB-STITUTION	SELF-CORRECT	INSERTION	TCHR ASSIST	OMISSION	MEANING DISRUPTION
You Cannot Fly!							
Once a boy named Sam wanted to *want*	1						
fly. His mother and father said,							
"You cannot fly." His sister said,						1	1
"You cannot fly." Sam tried jumping *to jump*	1			1		1	1
off a box. He tried jumping off *to jump*	1			1			
his bed. He fell down each time. *eight times*	1	1					
Sam still tried hard but he still *heard*		1				1	1
could not fly. Then one day *The (SC)*	1		1				
a letter came for Sam. The letter							
said, "Come and see me, Sam, on						1	1
the next airplane." It was from							
his grandfather. Sam went to his							
family and read the letter. Sam *father*		1					1
said, "Now I can fly." Sam and his							
family all laughed together. // *TA*					1		
TOTALS	5	3	1	2	1	4	5

Notes:

Student's miscues for the most part aren't serious, but a few were crucial to a lack of understanding this passage. Confidence level was high, but student never made the connection that his grandfather lived somewhere far enough to fly to.

Figure 6.3   *continued*

Examiner's Summary of Miscue Patterns:

PART III: DEVELOPMENTAL/PERFORMANCE SUMMARY

Silent Reading Comprehension   *Oral Reading Accuracy*

_____   0–1   questions missed = Easy   _____   0–1   oral errors = Easy

_____   2   questions missed = Adequate   _____   2–5   oral errors = Adequate

_5_   3+   questions missed = Too hard   ✓   6+   oral errors = Too hard

Continue to next assessment level passage?   _____ Yes   ✓ No

Examiner's Notes: I would like to try RMA
procedures with this passage,
focusing on the miscue of <u>can</u>
for <u>cannot</u>.

FORM A   LEVEL 1 ASSESSMENT PROTOCOLS

Figure 6.4 Level 1 Passage Scored and Analyzed as a Running Record

Errors*		MIS-PRONUN	SUB-STITUTION	SELF-CORRECT	INSERTION	TCHR. ASSIST.	OMISSION	MEANING DISRUPTION
	You Cannot Fly!							
1	✓✓✓ ✓ ✓ wan ✓ Once a boy named Sam wanted to							
0	✓ ✓ ✓ ✓ ✓ fly. His mother and father said,							
1	✓ can ✓ ✓ ✓ ✓ "You cannot fly." His sister said,							
3	✓ can ✓ ✓ ✓ to jump "You cannot fly." Sam tried jumping							
2	✓✓✓ ✓ ✓ to jump ✓ off a box. He tried jumping off							
2	✓ ✓ ✓ ✓ eight times his bed. He fell down each time.							
2	✓ ✓ ✓ heard ✓ ✓ — Sam still tried hard but he still							
1	✓✓✓ the ✓ ✓ could not fly. Then one day							
0	✓ — R ✓ ✓ ✓ a letter came for Sam. The letter							
1	✓ ✓ ✓✓ — ✓ ✓ said, "Come and see me, Sam, on							
0	✓ ✓ ✓ ✓✓ ✓ the next airplane." It was from							
0	✓ ✓ ✓✓✓✓ his grandfather. Sam went to his							
1	father ✓ ✓ ✓ ✓ ✓ family and read the letter. Sam							
2	✓ — ✓✓ ✓ now ✓✓✓ said, "Now I can fly." Sam and his							
1	T ✓ ✓ ✓ family all laughed together. //							
17	**TOTALS**							

Notes:

* Based on criteria and directions for scoring as outlined in Clay (1985, pp. 19-21, 115)

$$\frac{\text{Running Words}}{\text{Errors}} = \frac{96}{17}$$

$$\text{Accuracy} = 100 - \frac{17}{96} \times \frac{100}{1} \%$$
$$= 82\%$$
$$= \text{Hard Text}$$
$$(< 90\% = \text{too difficult})$$

$$\text{Error Rate} = 1 : 5.65$$

Adapted from Flynt/Cooter, *Reading Inventory for the Classroom.*

and pencil handy while observing the student reading, a running record of that reading can be made and later scored and analyzed. A tape recording allows the performance to be reviewed to verify the codings and scoring estimated during the administration. Reading continues until the student reaches the criteria associated with the frustration level. At this point, in addition to *not* achieving a minimum level of word recognition and comprehension, the student usually exhibits other symptoms, such as squirming in the chair or facial contortions.

For novice users of informal reading inventories, all these directions for administration may seem quite formal and intimidating. Keep in mind, however, that the essential point in all assessment is to learn more about the student as a reader—not merely to identify reading levels. Brozo (1990) makes a case for **interactive assessment,** in which the teacher tries "to discover the conditions under which a student will succeed in reading" (p. 523). Using an informal reading inventory as an example, Brozo illuminates the much less testlike procedures of interactive assessment, which, briefly, include beginning with a diagnostic interview to learn about interests, attitudes, and students' goals and perceptions about reading, and moving through the steps of IRI administration in an instructional manner rather than a test-taking manner. Kletzien and Bednar (1990) support this approach to assessment when they describe the value of what they term *dynamic assessment:*

> When the at-risk reader is made an active participant in the assessment, the reader gains greater confidence and a sense of control over reading strategies. The social interaction between the examiner and the reader is particularly important for these learners. Too often, they simply give up on a standardized test and receive a very low score, further depressing an already low self-concept. [Dynamic assessment/ interactive assessment] acknowledges what the reader actually can do, and thus provides a positive experience. (p. 532)

Such views of assessment have led to instructional procedures teachers can use to provide students with feedback about their miscues. One of these procedures is called *Retrospective Miscue Analysis* (Y. M. Goodman, 1996; Goodman & Marek, 1996), and users of this text are urged to examine the source provided in the list of recommended readings at the end of this chapter.

As teachers gain experience in IRI administration and begin to appreciate the flexible uses of IRIs and other assessment tools, interactive assessment procedures may have more appeal. Remember the important goals of assessment, to learn students' capabilities and to guide instructional planning, as you proceed through the rest of this chapter.

Scoring IRIs

IRIs are rather easy to score for placement purposes. One scoring system for oral reading accuracy is suggested by Harris and Sipay (1990, pp. 227–228).[1]

The following should be counted as one error each:

1. Any word used that deviates from the text and disrupts the meaning

2. Any word pronounced by the teacher after the child has hesitated about five seconds

The following should be counted as only one error, regardless of the number of times the error is made:

1. Repeated substitutions (one word substituted for another, such as *when* for *then*). Flynt and Cooter (1998) follow Clay's (2000) guidelines, which are to count this substitution as an error each time it is made. Repeated substitution errors of proper names are counted only once (e.g., *Bobby* for *Billy*).

---

[1]Adapted from *How to Increase Reading Ability* by Albert J. Harris and Edward R. Sipay. 9th ed. Copyright 1940, 1949, 1956, 1961, 1968, 1970, 1975, 1980, and 1990 by Longman, Inc. Reprinted by permission of Longman, Inc., New York.

2. Repetitions (individual words or groups of words that are said more than once). There is disagreement on counting repetitions as errors. For example, Spache (1976) counts two or more words repeated as a repetition error; Ekwall and Shanker (1996) think *all* repetitions should be counted as errors; Clay (2000) and Taylor, Harris, and Pearson (1988) do *not* count repetitions as errors at all; Flynt and Cooter (1998) do not even record repetitions. Generally I favor noting repetitions but *not* counting them as errors. Repetitions usually occur for a reason and demonstrate that the reader is concerned with maintaining understanding of material read. However, if there are a great number of repetitions this may indicate the material is too difficult.

3. Repeated errors on the same word, even though the errors themselves may be different. Again, variation among authors of published inventories exists. For example, Leslie and Caldwell (1995) count once as an error a repeated miscue that maintains meaning (e.g., *phone* for *telephone*), but count as errors each miscue on the same word when the pronunciation changes the meaning (e.g., *expect* and *export* for *expert* would count as two errors).

The following should *not* be counted as errors:

1. Pronunciations or miscues that reflect cultural or regional dialects
2. Spontaneous self-corrections
3. Hesitations
4. Ignoring or misinterpreting punctuation marks

The total errors are counted and converted to a percentage score based on the number of words pronounced correctly and the total number of words in the selection.

In addition to recording oral reading behaviors, retellings and responses to comprehension questions asked after each selection are also recorded. Sometimes these responses can be scored as the student answers the questions. More often, however, judgment about performance can only be made in relation to what the student read and how the student has responded. Therefore, it is best to analyze these responses carefully at a later time.

Interpreting IRIs

Establishing Reading Levels. Once the teacher has obtained scores on (1) oral reading behaviors and (2) comprehension of silent or oral reading or both for the selections read, the scores are assembled in a table such as that in Figure 6.5 to aid interpretation of results. All published inventories provide a similar table, usually called a *summary sheet*. When interpreting results of an IRI, remember that these inventories are subject to error of measurement. Thus, the criteria for establishing the independent, instructional, and frustration reading levels must be interpreted judiciously. The teacher surveys the assembled scores and makes judgments about the estimated reading levels based on the progression of scores as well as the scores themselves. Results of research by Powell and Dunkeld (1971) and Cooper (1952) would indicate that the student's grade level should also be a consideration (see Table 6.1). As indicated earlier, there is not absolute agreement on the criteria to be used to determine reading levels.

Almost always, interpretation requires some estimating and interpolating. In interpreting Sandra's scores (Figure 6.5), chances are good that Sandra's independent reading level is third grade and that the 80 percent comprehension score obtained at the 2^2 reader level for oral reading reflects error of measurement. The instructional reading level is

Figure 6.5 Sample Table to Aid Interpretation of Scores for Reading Accuracy and Comprehension

Summary of Results of Informal Reading Inventory

Name: _____ Sandra _____   Grade: _____ Beginning 4th _____

Level of Text	Oral Reading		Silent Reading	Reading Level
	Percent Accuracy	Percent Comprehension	Percent Comprehension	
2^1	99	100	100	Independent
2^2	97	80	90	Instructional
3^1	98	100	100	Independent
3^2	94	80	100	Instructional
4	93	80	90	Instructional
5	88	50	70	Frustration

Estimated independent reading level: 3^1
Estimated instructional reading level: 4*
Estimated frustration reading level: 5

*or 3^2–4, if a range is desired.

probably fourth grade, the higher of the two sets of scores yielding that outcome, especially in light of the silent reading comprehension score. Notice also that the 94 and 93 percent accuracy scores are slightly below the Betts criterion of 95 percent, but are acceptable for the instructional level according to both the Powell and Dunkeld and the Cooper criteria.

Once reading levels have been estimated, the teacher verifies these tentative working hypotheses (i.e., independent reading level equals beginning third grade; instructional reading level, fourth grade; frustration reading level, fifth grade). This is accomplished by placing Sandra in fourth-grade-level materials to see if she can deal effectively

Table 6.1 Powell/Dunkeld and Cooper Criteria for Determining Informal Reading Inventory Instructional Reading Levels

Powell and Dunkeld Criteria for Instructional Level

Grades 1–2   88–97.9% word recognition
                    70–89% comprehension
Grades 3–5   92–97.9% word recognition
                    70–89% comprehension
Grades 6+   94.4–97.9% word recognition
                    70–89% comprehension

Cooper Criteria for Instructional Level

Grades 2–3   95–98% word recognition
                    70% minimum comprehension
Intermediate   91–96% word recognition
  grades   60% minimum comprehension

with the texts and accompanying lessons. Verification of placement in materials is critical to effective analysis and instructional planning. Without verification, all the analytic effort may be for naught.

Work by Beck (1981), Berliner (1981), Gambrell, Wilson, and Gantt (1981), and Jorgenson (1977) suggests that student achievement in reading, especially for developing readers, is positively affected if a large portion of instructional time is spent with relatively easy material (error rates of 2 to 5 percent), with regular exposure to more difficult material. Beck (1981) explains that in this way the reader is allowed "to develop fluent and automatic responses in less difficult text while encountering a challenge to develop new knowledge and strategies in more difficult text" (p. 89).

The best advice might be to be conservative. If reading levels are unclear or other characteristics about a student deserve consideration (e.g., immature personality, general academic difficulty, poor work habits, or disruptive home background), the student should be placed in the easier material under consideration (Haller & Waterman, 1985).

Analyzing Results of the IRI. Analysis of IRI results beyond establishing the three reading levels provides a wealth of information. Oral reading behaviors and comprehension performance can be examined further to find patterns in a student's reading behaviors and shed light on that student's reading strategies. Borrowing heavily from the *Reading Miscue Inventory* developed by Goodman and Burke (1972), coded oral reading behaviors can be thought of as miscues. A **miscue** is defined as an observed response that differs from the expected response—that is, the reader does not say exactly what is written. With this inventory, Goodman and Burke introduced the notion of **qualitative analysis;** rather than simply count errors **(quantitative analysis),** the examiner attempts to analyze the reader's strategies.

The rationale for analyzing miscues is that not all unexpected responses are equally serious. For example, if the reader inserts *very* before the word *happy* in the sentence *Tom was not happy,* the meaning of the sentence has not been seriously altered. The teacher may overlook miscues if meaning is not changed. This kind of qualitative analysis often reveals that students are extracting meaning from what they read despite apparent word recognition errors. This is especially relevant for linguistically diverse learners. If nothing else, the qualitative analysis makes the teacher aware of the language functioning of the student who speaks a dialect variation (see Chapter 3). At its best, the qualitative analysis makes the teacher aware of the student's reading strategies.

A detailed **miscue analysis** is not necessary for every reader, not even for every reader experiencing difficulty. A thorough miscue analysis might be done only for readers who demonstrate especially perplexing reading miscues. For such cases the teacher is referred to Goodman and Burke's *Reading Miscue Inventory Manual* (1972).

To determine the instructional needs of most students, a simple form of miscue analysis is extremely useful. A partial analysis that looks at the use of graphophonic, syntactic, and semantic cues and asks whether the reader views reading as a meaning-making process provides valuable information about areas of strength and need. This underlying philosophy of determining whether the reader is reading for meaning and what strategies the reader is using is essential in miscue analysis.

A brief set of questions can be asked about miscues to provide insight into the reader's use of language cues and reading strategies. These questions should (1) emphasize that reading for meaning is more important than exact reproduction of the surface structure, (2) aid the teacher in identifying both a reader's strengths and needs, and (3) acknowledge the importance of self-corrections of miscues that do not fit the context. Figure 6.6 shows the results of such an analysis.

Figure 6.6   Example of Miscue and Comprehension Qualitative Analyses Based on a Fifth Grader's Oral Reading of Passages from the Woods and Moe *Analytical Reading Inventory*

Student: Jason   **Miscue Analysis Chart**

Level of Passage	Miscue in Context	Acceptable		Unacceptable	Self-Correction of Unacceptable Miscues	Graphic Similarity			Unknown Words
		Syntax	Semantics			Initial	Medial	Final	
3	Suddenly he dashed home and soon returned with a bucket of yellow (paint) one of black, and several brushes.			✓					
3	I thought you might want to paint your *and* (so) clubhouse yellow with black stripes.			✓	✓				
4	Con-di-tion The pony's condition was growing worse as his breathing grew louder and harder.	✓	✓			✓	✓	✓	
4	bucket At nightfall Jody brought a blanket from the house so he could sleep near Gabilan	✓		✓		✓		✓	
4	blizzards Looking up he saw buzzards, the birds of death, flying overhead.	✓		✓		✓		✓	
4	blizzard perching A buzzard was perched on his dying pony's head.	✓		✓		✓		✓	
		✓	✓			✓	✓		
	Column Total	5	2	5	1/5	5	2	4	0
	Total No. of Miscues Analyzed	7	7	7		7	7	7	7
	Percentage	71%	29%	71%	20%	71%	29%	57%	0%

In a much abbreviated version of miscue analysis, a teacher might simply ask whether the miscue changed meaning (unacceptable), whether it was acceptable in context, or whether it was corrected. A simple form also might be used for periodic assessments of oral reading behaviors (Figure 6.7). With this form, the teacher can compare the responses to these questions. If "Yes" is checked for question 3 and "No" or "Sometimes" for question 1, the student may be relying too heavily on graphophonic cues. Instruction in the use of syntactic and semantic context clues would be in order. On the other hand, if "Yes" is checked for question 1 and "No" or "Sometimes" is checked for question 3, the student may be relying too heavily on context clues. Instruction in phonics or structural analysis would be advisable. This instruction might include such facilitating questions as "Do you see any part of the word that you know?" (e.g., *run* in *running*), or "What word do you know that starts with_____, and would make sense?"

As the miscue analysis and evaluation of comprehension performance are being conducted, factual summary statements for observed reading behaviors and strategies can be made. Instructional goals will become more evident from examination of these summary statements. Examples of summary statements can be found in Figure 6.8.

Figure 6.6   *continued*

Comprehension Analysis Chart

Lower Level				Higher Level			
Level of Passage		Oral	Silent	Level of Passage		Oral	Silent
2	No. Correct	3		2	No. Correct	3	
	Total Possible	3			Total Possible	3	
	Percentage	100%			Percentage	100%	
3	No. Correct	4		3	No. Correct	3	
	Total Possible	4			Total Possible	4	
	Percentage	100%			Percentage	75%	
4	No. Correct	3		4	No. Correct	3	
	Total Possible	4			Total Possible	4	
	Percentage	75%			Percentage	75%	
5	No. Correct	2		5	No. Correct	2	
	Total Possible	4			Total Possible	4	
	Percentage	50%			Percentage	50%	
	No. Correct				No. Correct		
	Total Possible				Total Possible		
	Percentage	LISTENING			Percentage	LISTENING	
6	No. Correct		1	6	No. Correct		2
	Total Possible		4		Total Possible		4
	Percentage		25%		Percentage		50%
5	No. Correct		4	5	No. Correct		3
	Total Possible		4		Total Possible		4
	Percentage		100%		Percentage		75%
	No. Correct				No. Correct		
	Total Possible				Total Possible		
	Percentage				Percentage		
Total No. Correct		12		Total No. Correct		11	
Total No. Questions		15		Total No. Questions		15	
Total Percentage		80%		Total Percentage		73%	

Summary statements can be written for each level of material, the type of material (i.e., narrative or expository), listening comprehension, and any other relevant observations such as written language samples and oral language samples (discussed later in this chapter).

Listening Capacity

Another piece of information that can sometimes be estimated by an IRI is **listening capacity,** also called the listening comprehension level. This is the highest level at which

Figure 6.7   Form for Assessing Oral Reading Behavior

	Yes	No	Sometimes
1. Do the reader's miscues make sense in context?			
2. Does the reader correct unacceptable miscues?			
3. Does the reader pay too much attention to graphophonic cues and not enough to syntactic or semantic cues?*			

*A miscue may be graphically similar in the initial, medial, or final position (or some combination) and be unacceptable in terms of meaning. For example, a reader paying more attention to graphophonic cues than semantic or syntactic cues might substitute *his* for *this* in the sentence *This time it was ready.*

the student can understand 75 percent of the material read aloud by the teacher. The teacher reads and asks questions about a selection beginning at the next level above the frustration reading level. This score is sometimes used as an indication of a learner's ability to understand oral language.

Listening comprehension is sometimes considered an estimate of reading expectancy; that is, if the student were able to read the material, the listening comprehension level, or listening capacity, represents the level at which it could be understood. However, listening comprehension is probably not a valid indicator of reading potential for primary-grade children. For other learners, if the listening comprehension level is higher than the instructional reading level, the student may be reading below what can be expected, or the student may need to develop reading comprehension skills.

Similar results were found in research by Sticht and Beck (1976); that is, listening comprehension surpasses reading comprehension until about grade 7. First-graders are struggling with word recognition. Likewise, second- and third-graders may sometimes be unfairly labeled as underachievers if listening comprehension is found to be higher

Figure 6.8   Summary Statements Based on the Miscue and Comprehension Analysis Charts for Jason

SUMMARY STATEMENTS

Name:	Jason	**Date:**	December
Age:	10	**Level of Material:**	3–6
Grade:	5	**Type of Material:**	Narrative

1. The majority of Jason's miscues (71%) are unacceptable; that is, they change meaning.
2. Jason self-corrected only 20% (1 out of 5) of his miscues.
3. The majority of Jason's miscues (71%) are acceptable syntactically; that is, they maintain the same part of speech as the original text.
4. Jason is aware of context clues, but does not use these clues consistently.
5. Jason's substitutions are usually graphophonically similar to the initial and final position of the word in text.
6. Jason's substitutions involve words of more than one syllable (4 out of 5).
7. Jason's substitutions involve words that may not be in his meaning vocabulary.
8. Jason's oral reading comprehension is consistent for both lower and higher levels of questions.
9. Jason's oral reading comprehension level is consistent with his word recognition abilities.
10. Jason's listening comprehension is approximately one year higher that his oral reading comprehension.

than reading comprehension. As students learn to read, which appears to take longer (grades 6–8) than the traditionally designated primary grades (1–3), their reading comprehension skills overtake their listening comprehension skills. As stated by Sticht and James (1984), "precisely what is happening that makes this additional time necessary is not certain, though it may be that in the first three or four years of school, children learn the rudiments of reading-decoding . . . while an additional two to three years of practice is required for the automaticity of reading to equal that of auding [listening comprehension]" (p. 307).

Cloze Procedure

Another measure that is used for initially determining or verifying the instructional reading level is the **cloze procedure.** This requires a reader to fill in blanks for words that have been systematically deleted from the written selection. In the most common form of cloze test, every fifth word is deleted. These tests are more typically administered to groups of students in the upper elementary and secondary levels to assess suitability of textbook material (see Appendix E).

Cloze tests are relatively easy and inexpensive to construct, administer, and interpret. The following steps are suggested in preparing a cloze test passage.

1. Select a passage containing 250 to 300 words (Bormuth, 1975). Be sure the passage does not depend on information presented earlier in the text (i.e., a passage with many pronouns). The passage should be representative of the content of the book.

2. Keep the first sentence intact.

3. Beginning with the second sentence, delete words at a consistent interval (e.g., every fifth, seventh, or tenth word) for a total of fifty deletions (Bormuth, 1975). Replace the deleted words with blanks of equal length. Duplicate the desired number of copies.

4. If the blanks are numbered, prepare an answer sheet with corresponding numbers for students to use in recording their responses.

5. If desired, students can write their responses directly on the blanks.

Administration of the cloze test is fairly straightforward. Students who have never experienced a cloze test should be given some practice with the procedure first. This practice test should use material easy for the students to read and should contain at least ten deletions (Pikulski & Tobin, 1982).

Instructions for the cloze test *must* direct the students to read through the entire passage before trying to fill in the blanks. Students should also be told that only one word goes in each blank and that misspellings are not counted as errors. Although the test is untimed, the teacher may want to set a reasonable time limit.

Scoring a cloze test is an often misunderstood procedure. Only exact words should be considered acceptable as correct responses. This decision is not arbitrary; it is based on considerable research (Gallant, 1964; Henk & Selders, 1984; McKenna, 1976; Miller & Coleman, 1967; Ruddell, 1964; Taylor, 1953) in which exact-word replacement scores were compared to synonym replacement scores. The synonym scores were higher than the exact-word scores, but the two scores were highly correlated (.95 and above). Because students essentially ranked the same using either technique, giving credit for synonyms has no advantage when the purpose of the test is to estimate students' instructional levels. Preparing a list of acceptable synonyms as part of cloze test preparation would simply not be worth the time or effort (Pikulski & Tobin, 1982).

In addition to yielding slightly higher scores, synonym replacements would invalidate the scoring guidelines. Criterion scores have been established for determining independent, instructional, and frustration reading levels using exact word replacement scores. Thus, to allow synonyms would yield an inflated score and the available criteria could not be used appropriately. Pikulski and Tobin (1982) have synthesized the research on criterion scores and suggest the following guidelines:

Independent level: Students who obtain cloze scores of at least 50 percent should be able to read the material with relative ease. No teacher guidance should be necessary. Consequently, this material should be appropriate for homework assignments and other types of independent projects.

Instructional level: Students scoring between 30 and 50 percent should be able to use the material for instructional purposes. However, some guidance will be necessary to help them master the demands of the material.

Frustration level: Students scoring lower than 30 percent will usually find the material much too challenging. Since there is almost no potential for success, the material should be definitely avoided. (pp. 53, 54)

The disadvantage of the cloze procedure is that its effectiveness as an assessment tool is not clearly established. Carefully constructed cloze tests could potentially provide helpful information regarding a reader's use of syntactic and semantic cues during silent reading. But teachers still need to observe other dimensions of the reading process. In addition to textbook selections, cloze passages can also be constructed from students' own written stories or other familiar materials and used instructionally to show readers how to use the syntactic, semantic, and graphophonic cue systems. When used for instructional purposes, cloze passage construction can be modified in many ways to suit specific purposes. Cloze as an instructional tool is discussed in more detail in Chapter 8.

A popular variation of the cloze procedure is the **maze technique.** Instead of deleting words from a passage, the maze procedure gives the reader a number of words from which to choose. While this format may have more appeal for the test taker, construction of the test is more time-consuming and more prone to error than the cloze procedure. Guthrie, Siefert, Burnham, and Caplan (1974) suggest the following guidelines for constructing a maze test.

1. Select a representative passage of about 120 words.
2. Beginning with the second sentence, replace words at constant intervals (e.g., every fifth or tenth word) with three word choices. These should include the correct word itself, a word that is the same part of speech as the correct word, and a word that is a different part of speech.
3. Vary the position of the correct word.
4. Duplicate copies.

As of yet, little research has been done on the maze technique, and criterion scores should be considered tentative. Guthrie et al. (1974) suggest that 85 percent or higher accuracy reflects an independent level; 60 to 75 percent, an instructional level; and below 50 percent, the frustration level. More research is needed on the maze technique before its use as a placement tool is recommended. As with the cloze procedure, the maze technique can be a most effective tool for improving word recognition (see Chapter 8).

Assessment by Observation, Conferences and Interviews, and Performance Samples

Observation

During the first week of school, analytic teachers observe their students and document through anecdotal notes or checklists what they discover about their students' unique talents and intelligences, preferred ways of learning, strengths, and instructional needs. At the same time, analytic teachers notice peer interactions and relationships, students' interests, thinking abilities, and oral language patterns, as well as each student's level of self-esteem and ability to complete assignments. Suggestions for a week of student observation include the following:

1. *Free time.* Who interacts with whom? Who reads and writes independently? Who needs structure or freedom? Who prefers to interact with group members? Who enjoys some time alone? Who enjoys working with computers? Who is sensitive to the moods and feelings of others?

2. *Reading groups (randomly assigned).* Who can identify ideas or words they don't understand? Who uses background knowledge and context to determine unknown words? Who monitors his reading comprehension? Who understands that the main goal of reading is comprehension? Who identifies with story characters? Who asks questions?

3. *Playground.* Who displays leadership abilities? Who appears to be a follower? Who needs to learn to take turns? Who is able to empathize and get along well with others? Who likes to show others how to do something? Who is particularly well-coordinated physically?

4. *Lunchroom.* Who appears overly hungry? Who needs to learn table manners? Who appears lethargic or tired? Who has difficulty staying still in her seat?

5. *Class meetings.* Who speaks in complete sentences? Who has a sense of humor? Who listens carefully? Who understands and participates in problem solving or brainstorming activities? Who has difficulty hearing? Who is shy? Who offers helpful suggestions? (See Glasser, 1969, for a thorough discussion of class meetings.)

6. *Sustained silent reading (SSR) or DEAR (Drop Everything and Read).* Who can choose books on his independent reading level? Who "mouths" words when reading silently? Who becomes easily distracted? Who points to words and sentences and might find a sentence marker useful? Who chooses books that complement her personal interests?

7. *Small groups.* Who completes learning tasks? Who cooperates? Who works to his best abilities? Who assists "others in using a skill after mastering it themselves" (Biemiller, 1993, p. 14)? Who appears to be an auditory, visual, or kinesthetic learner? Who communicates ideas that especially contribute to the group's understanding of difficult concepts? Who is quick at solving a variety of problems?

8. *Visual and performing arts activities.* Who displays exceptional artistic, imaginative, or creative abilities? Who needs to learn how to use visual-art media (e.g., tempera paints, watercolors, fine and broad markers, crayons, colored pencils, glue, scissors, chalk)? Whose artistic accomplishments are not commensurate with age or grade level? (See Lowenfeld, 1970, for a discussion of the stages of children's art.) Who is interested in performing plays and puppet productions?

9. *Teacher reading aloud.* Who listens and remembers? Who needs opportunities to develop appropriate background knowledge in order to comprehend and appreciate

stories? Who understands the relationships among **basic story features** (characters, setting, problems, and solutions) and their connections? Who identifies with story characters? Who recognizes how authors portray story characters (Richards & Gipe, 1993; Richards, Gipe & Necaise, 1993)? Who recognizes and understands inferential language (e.g., metaphors, similes, and idioms)? Who doodles during this and similar class activities?

10. *Creative writing.* Who is willing to use developmentally appropriate invented, or constructed, spelling? Who is interested in unusual words? Who uses written language in particularly appealing ways? Who uses drawings, "speed writing," semantic maps, outlines, or conversations with peers to help plan her compositions? Who proofreads? Who is ready to learn about punctuation or paragraphing? (Please refer to Chapter 7 for a detailed discussion of student writing, activities, and lessons.)

11. *Independent literacy activities.* Who likes to read stories that are accompanied by recorded book tapes? Who demonstrates impulsivity or reflective tendencies? Who likes to work with multisensory materials such as flannel boards and story character cutouts, filmstrips, tape recorders, hand puppets, art supplies, or literacy games? Who enjoys creative bookmaking? Who can remember songs or rhymes easily?

As you can see, a large amount of information about students can be obtained through observation. Instructional decisions should never be made on the basis of one observation, however. Teachers who try to organize the instructional setting specifically to improve and enhance behavioral observation increase the reliability of those observations. For example, the more opportunities students have to show the teacher that they know the initial consonant blend *st* or that they can use word order clues to predict the next word in a sentence, the more reliable the information. *More opportunities* is analogous to *more items* on a test, an important way to achieve reliability.

Observing students, or kidwatching, is a skill that teachers develop over time through practice. According to Yetta Goodman (1996), who popularized the term in the late 1970s, **kidwatching** is "careful and knowledgeable observation of students as they are immersed in their own learning and language use" and "is a conscious process on the part of teachers as they take field notes" (p. 209) or mark miscues. Also, through observation and the use of anecdotal records, teachers can record "learning in action" (Drummond, 1994, p. 89). These records can then be used to (1) identify and understand each student's modes of learning or intelligences, (2) form general ideas or hypotheses about students, (3) plan instruction that meets students' needs and uses their individual strengths, and (4) communicate more effectively with parents about a student's learning. Considering the busy nature of classrooms, the key to successful kidwatching is developing a system for maintaining written records of observations.

Checklists. Many teachers use *anecdotal records* (informal notes to aid recall of observed behaviors; see also Chapter 4) that they later compile for assessment and evaluation purposes (see Figure 6.9). Other teachers prefer to use checklists that they have developed or have found in various professional resources (see Figure 6.10 for an example). Checklists are especially helpful for novice teachers who are still developing a strong knowledge base about literacy development. The checklist can provide guidance for what to observe. It is important that checklist usage allow for multiple observations over time and in a variety of contexts. There should be a place for the teacher to note not only the date of the observation, but the context of the observation—such as the type of material read, the purpose for reading, and whether it was student- or teacher-initiated reading—as well as the instructional conditions (e.g., the teacher's instructions or type of program). Figure 6.11 represents one attempt to guide observation of early reading development.

Figure 6.9   Example of an Anecdotal Record

Name: *Keyotta*

12/3/01	Is learning to use her background knowledge and the context of a passage to determine unknown words in text.
1/4/02	Is becoming a motivated, wide reader. She has read three books this week—topics: outer space, baby animals, African Americans of achievement.
1/14/02	Still needs to develop confidence in her abilities to use her background knowledge and the context of a passage to determine unknown words. Appears to use both auditory and visual modalities to process new information.
1/29/02	Has become interested in wild animals and their habitats (assemble literature on this topic). Is especially competent working with musical and spatial (e.g., puzzles) activities.
2/14/02	Created and presented a play to the kindergarten—topic: animals and Africa.

A checklist can also be used to summarize the performance of several students at once. This procedure is useful because teachers are usually working with groups of students functioning at different levels. The checklist in Figure 6.12 can be used to record the progress of a group of students using a particular set of reading materials or receiving instruction at a level different from other classmates. Students can also use checklists for self-evaluation purposes (see Figure 6.13).

While observation, anecdotal records, and checklists provide much information about literate behavior, a system must be organized to aid interpretation of what has been observed. Such systems are referred to as rating scales and scoring rubrics.

Rating Scales. While checklists ask teachers to note the presence of a particular behavior on a particular date, rating scales assist in summarizing such data. A rating scale asks

Figure 6.10   Example of a Teacher-Developed Checklist

Name: _____*Scotty*_____   Date: _____*October 10*_____

	Yes	No	Comments
Enjoys listening to literature selections	✓		*always listens closely and gives opinions on story content*
Responds enthusiastically to literature heard or read by creating art projects, writing in literature response journals, creating stories, books, and drama activities	✓		• *Created a dinosaur diorama* • *Writes daily in his literature response journal* • *Actively participates in our playwriting interest group*
Is developing reading independence			
Is learning to use reading comprehension strategies according to need (e.g., word identification, K–W–L, It reminds me of)		✓	*still over-reliant on graphophonic cues to determine unknown words (review three-step word identification plan)*

Figure 6.11 Checklist for Appraising Early Reading Development

Student _____ Age _____ Grade _____

CHARACTERISTICS	Date Observed	Context	Date Observed	Context
Cognition				
1. Understands grade-level material read aloud	_____	_____	_____	_____
2. Remembers new words used in class	_____	_____	_____	_____
3. Remembers content of stories discussed in class	_____	_____	_____	_____
Language				
1. Speaks in complete sentences	_____	_____	_____	_____
2. Speaking vocabulary is adequate	_____	_____	_____	_____
3. Speaking vocabulary is advanced	_____	_____	_____	_____
4. Speech is normal	_____	_____	_____	_____
5. Hearing is normal	_____	_____	_____	_____
General Reading				
1. When being read to, the child:				
a. sometimes finishes the sentence (anticipates what is next)	_____	_____	_____	_____
b. sometimes follows along with finger	_____	_____	_____	_____
c. pays attention	_____	_____	_____	_____
2. Recognizes signs (e.g., stop signs), labels (e.g., "Wheaties"), or logos (e.g., "McDonald's")	_____	_____	_____	_____
3. Recognizes his/her name	_____	_____	_____	_____
4. Recognizes letters in *(state what context)*	_____	_____	_____	_____
5. Recognizes words in *(state what context)*	_____	_____	_____	_____
6. Remembers words taught as whole words	_____	_____	_____	_____
7. Attempts to blend sound units	_____	_____	_____	_____
8. Can guess new words from context	_____	_____	_____	_____
9. Skips words when reading in order to use context	_____	_____	_____	_____
10. Skips unknown words totally in order to maintain comprehension	_____	_____	_____	_____
11. Reads fluently	_____	_____	_____	_____
12. Reads with little or no transposing of letters/words	_____	_____	_____	_____
13. Observes punctuation in oral reading	_____	_____	_____	_____
14. Reads silently with little or no finger pointing to text	_____	_____	_____	_____
15. Reads silently with little or no subvocalizing	_____	_____	_____	_____
16. Recalls facts of material read	_____	_____	_____	_____
17. Can summarize main points of material read	_____	_____	_____	_____
18. Can locate answers to questions	_____	_____	_____	_____
19. Comprehends narrative material	_____	_____	_____	_____
20. Comprehends expository material	_____	_____	_____	_____
21. Adjusts reading speed according to reading purpose or difficulty of material	_____	_____	_____	_____
Motivation				
1. Enjoys being read to	_____	_____	_____	_____
2. Knows that books have a top and bottom, and turns pages front to back	_____	_____	_____	_____
3. Talks about books he/she listened to or read	_____	_____	_____	_____
4. Looks at books on his/her own	_____	_____	_____	_____
5. Has favorite book(s)	_____	_____	_____	_____

Additional Comments and Observations:

Figure 6.12   Checklist of Oral Reading Characteristics for a Group of Students

Date: Names:	Harry	Susie	Leroy	Mark	Daisy	Kenya
Comprehension						
Recalls facts						
Makes inferences						
Word Recognition/Decoding						
Has adequate sight vocabulary						
Needs few or no words pronounced						
Mispronounces few words						
Omits few or no words						
Inserts few or no words						
Uses context adequately						
Uses strategies in addition to context						
Knows high-utility words						
Analyzes word visually						
Knows symbol-sound associations						
Can blend sounds						
Fluency						
Has few or no hesitations						
Has few or no repetitions						
Phrases appropriately						
Reads phrases or groups of words						
Pays attention to punctuation						
Reads at an appropriate rate						
Usually or always keeps place						
Demonstrates proper use of voice						
Demonstrates proper enunciation						
Demonstrates proper expression						
Uses proper volume						
Observations						
Seldom shows signs of tension						
Reads with little or no finger pointing						
Holds book at appropriate distance						
Concentrates on task at hand						

Comments:

Figure 6.13 Example of a Student Self-Evaluation Checklist

Name: _Mary Alice_   Date: _May 4_

	Yes	No	My Explanation
I completed my reading goals for this week	✓		I finished the first chapter of _Sarah, Plain and Tall_
I monitored my reading comprehension		✓	I forgot to write down what I didn't understand
I learned something new as I read	✓		Sarah was a mail-order bride. Long ago, people lived very far away from each other, so they didn't get to meet each other. When they wanted to get married, men would sometimes advertise for a bride.
I helped someone with his or her reading	✓		I gave Angela a suggestion for her creative dinosaur book
I connected reading with other learning activities	✓		I created a mural showing Sarah as a mail-order bride. I also used the Internet to find some facts about how farm people lived long ago.

MacLachlan, P. (1985). _Sarah, Plain and Tall_. New York: Harper and Row.

the teacher to judge the degree to which or frequency with which a behavior is exhibited. A five-point scale is common, with ratings similar to the following:

1 = not exhibited

2 = rarely exhibited

3 = sometimes exhibited

4 = often exhibited

5 = always exhibited

The rating scale in Figure 6.14 can be used to summarize the observations associated with the eight multiple intelligences (Lazear, 1994).

Scoring Rubrics. A **scoring rubric** is a record sheet that indicates a set of criteria used for rating students' performance samples, portfolios, or tests. Scoring rubrics communicate the standards used in evaluating students' works to the students themselves, other teachers, parents, administrators, and/or other interested parties. According to Hart, "a scoring rubric describes the levels of performance students might be expected to attain relative to a desired standard of achievement. These descriptors, or performance descriptions, tell the evaluator what characteristics or signs to look for in a student's work and then how to place that work on a predetermined scale" (1994, p. 70).

Figure 6.14 Student Behavior Log

Student Name: _____

Age: _____ **Date of Observation:** _____

Indicate the degree to which you observe the stated behavior or characteristic in each student, using the following scale: 0 = uncertain; 1 = does not fit at all; 2 = fits slightly; 3 = fits moderately; 4 = fits strongly

Verbal-Linguistic Behaviors

Loves talking, writing, and reading almost anything	0	1	2	3	4
Precisely expresses self both in writing and talking	0	1	2	3	4
Enjoys public speaking	0	1	2	3	4
Is sensitive to impact of words and language on others	0	1	2	3	4
Understands and enjoys plays on words and word games	0	1	2	3	4

Logical-Mathematical Behaviors

Is good at finding and understanding patterns	0	1	2	3	4
Is quick at solving a variety of problems	0	1	2	3	4
Can remember thinking formulas and strategies	0	1	2	3	4
Likes to identify, create, and sort things into categories	0	1	2	3	4
Is able to follow complex lines of reasoning and thought processes	0	1	2	3	4

Visual-Spatial Behaviors

Frequently doodles during class activities	0	1	2	3	4
Is helped by visuals and manipulatives	0	1	2	3	4
Likes painting, drawing, and working with clay	0	1	2	3	4
Has a good sense of direction and understanding of maps	0	1	2	3	4
Creates mental images easily; likes pretending	0	1	2	3	4

Bodily-Kinesthetic Behaviors

Has difficulty sitting still or staying in seat	0	1	2	3	4
Uses body gestures and physical movement to express self	0	1	2	3	4
Is good in sports; is well-coordinated physically	0	1	2	3	4
Likes to invent things, put things together and take them apart	0	1	2	3	4
Likes to demonstrate to others how to do something	0	1	2	3	4

Musical-Rhythmic Behaviors

Hums quietly to self while working or walking	0	1	2	3	4
Taps pencil, foot, or fingers while working	0	1	2	3	4
Can remember songs and rhymes easily	0	1	2	3	4
Likes to make up tunes and melodies	0	1	2	3	4
Senses musical elements in unusual or nonmusical situations	0	1	2	3	4

Interpersonal Behaviors

Has an irresistible urge to discuss almost everything with others	0	1	2	3	4
Is good at listening and communicating	0	1	2	3	4
Sensitive to the moods and feelings of others	0	1	2	3	4
Is a good, effective team player	0	1	2	3	4
Is able to figure out the motives and intentions of others	0	1	2	3	4

Intrapersonal Behaviors

Is highly intuitive and/or "flies by the seat of pants"	0	1	2	3	4
Is quiet, very self-reflective and aware	0	1	2	3	4
Asks questions relentlessly; has avid curiosity	0	1	2	3	4
Is able to express inner feelings in a variety of ways	0	1	2	3	4
Is individualistic and independent; is not concerned about others' opinions	0	1	2	3	4

Naturalist Behaviors

Is sensitive to things in nature	0	1	2	3	4
Enjoys caring for classroom pets or plants	0	1	2	3	4
Likes animals and talks about own pets	0	1	2	3	4
Knows about plants, animals, and living things	0	1	2	3	4
Is concerned with the environment; is ecologically aware	0	1	2	3	4

Multiple Intelligence Approaches to Assessment, © 1994 Zephyr Press, Tucson, Arizona.

The following example of a scoring rubric provides for consistency in evaluating students' written responses to a particular question by establishing five levels for scoring, each defined by a set of characteristic behaviors, or criteria. Scores of 4 and 2 were given for responses that fell somewhere in between 5 and 3 or 3 and 1, respectively.

5   Focus of response is clear; ideas flow smoothly; supporting details are evident and relevant; references are appropriate and adequate

3   Response lacks focus but remains on topic; reader can follow flow of thought somewhat; supporting details are not relevant; references are insufficient

1   Response has no focus and is off topic; little or no flow among ideas; supporting details are not provided; no references provided

(See also Figure 10.1 for a completed story-retelling scoring rubric.) Checklists, rating scales, and scoring rubrics are good sources of information for planning instruction as well as evaluation.

Conferences, Interviews, and Interest and Attitude Surveys

Even teachers who carefully plan opportunities for observation will have unanswered questions about the progress of some students. Thus the teacher must structure short periods of time to focus more directly on behavioral responses of individual students. These periods are usually called teacher-student conferences, or interviews.

The teacher arranges a conference any time during the day when five to twenty minutes can be spared for an individual student. A variety of assessment procedures (IRIs, a written lesson, teacher-made exercises) can be used to gather information, but usually the teacher is interested in finding answers to the specific questions that motivated the conference. For instance, if the student has made inconsistent responses (e.g., sometimes observing punctuation and sometimes not) during the instructional period or on written work, the teacher will want to know whether meaning is being affected for the student.

Conferences and *interviews* between the student and the teacher may reveal potential areas of instructional need. If these are identified early, the effectiveness of a corrective reading program will be enhanced. Most learners, including high achievers, falter from time to time in their learning. Brief, timely conferences pay great dividends because they identify areas of difficulty before they become serious reading problems.

Interests and attitudes are also important student characteristics that are neither easily nor quickly determined by observation. Asking requires the least time and effort. Teachers can gather the information in casual conversations with students or, more efficiently, during an interview through the use of interest and attitude surveys. These surveys can be conducted as oral interviews, in written format, or some combination of each.

Interest and attitude surveys suggest instructional techniques that may be useful in working with the student. If interests are known, the teacher uses materials that deal with those interests. If the student has a negative attitude, expected in students having serious reading difficulties, the teacher makes special efforts to motivate the learner and improve attitudes toward reading.

Obtaining information on interests consists of asking a series of questions regarding students' favorite activities, whether they have pets or hobbies, what television programs they watch, and so forth. An example of an interest inventory is presented in Figure 6.15.

Attitude surveys also ask questions, but of a different nature. Usually students respond yes or no, or indicate some degree of feeling (e.g., strongly agree, agree, don't know, disagree, strongly disagree). Figure 6.16 contains representative items from an attitude survey appropriate for primary grades.

Figure 6.15 Sample Interest Inventory

Inventory of Pupil Interests and Activities

Name _____ Age _____ Grade _____

School _____ Date _____ Interviewer _____

1. What is your favorite TV show?
2. Who is your favorite TV character?
3. If you could make up a TV show, what would it be about?
4. Do you have a favorite movie?
5. Do you have any pets?
6. What is your favorite animal?
7. If you could be any living thing, what would you be?
8. Where have you traveled? Name three places.
9. Name all the different types of transportation you have experienced (train, bus, auto, boat, wagon, airplane, jet, truck, buggy, subway, bicycle, ship).
10. If you received two airplane tickets for anywhere in the world, where would you go?
11. If you had a time machine for any time and place in the past or future, where would you go and when?
12. What is your favorite subject?
13. What is the latest book you've read? Did you enjoy it? Why or why not?
14. What kind of books do you read at home?
15. If it were a rainy day at home, what would you do?
    If it were a sunny day at home, what would you do?
16. What is your favorite sport?
17. What is your favorite hobby?
18. If I gave you $100 to buy whatever you wanted, what would you do with the money?

Attitude surveys should also address students' perceptions of reading as a process and perceptions of themselves as readers. For example, an interview format can be used to provide teachers relevant information about students' perceptions of themselves as readers and writers. The interview might include some of the following key questions:

- Do you like to read (write)?
- What is your favorite book (or who is your favorite author)?
- When do you read (write)?
- Do you think you are a good reader (writer)? Why or why not?
- Who is the best reader (writer) you know? Why?
- When you get to a word you do not know, what do you do?
- If someone asked you for help figuring out a word, how would you help?
- When you do not understand what you read, what do you do?
- Would you rather read a story or write a story?
- Would you rather read (write) or ride a bike?
- Would you rather read (write) or watch TV?
- Would you rather read (write) or sleep?
- Would you rather read (write) or draw?
- Would you rather read (write) or do arithmetic homework?

Figure 6.16   Primary Grades Attitude Survey

(Teacher: Before administering this survey, be sure children can distinguish the three faces as feeling happy, don't care, and feeling sad, respectively. You might want to ask a few practice questions, such as "How do you feel about Christmas?" or "How do you feel about going to bed early?" Feel free to add items to the survey. For group administration, students can either color in or mark the face that represents the way they feel about each question. Individuals can either point to or hold up individual face cards to indicate their feelings.)

1. How do you feel when your teacher reads a story to you?

2. How do you feel about reading out loud in class?

3. How do you feel about going to the library?

4. How do you feel when you come to a new word in your book?

5. How do you feel about your reading group?

6. How do you feel about getting a book for a present?

7. How do you feel when you read at home?

8. How do you feel when you read to your mom, dad, or a friend?

9. How do you feel about reading a story before bedtime?

10. How do you feel when you don't understand what you read?

- Would you rather read (write) or help do the dishes?
- When you write, what kinds of problems do you have? What do you do about them?
- Do you ever make changes in what you write? What kind of changes?

Open-ended statements are also used to assess attitudes. For example, the student might be asked to complete the following sentences:

Reading is . . .

I think reading . . .

Most books . . .

My parents . . .

Teachers . . .

The entire *Incomplete Sentence Projective Test* (Boning & Boning, 1957) can be found in Appendix H.

Valid and reliable interest and attitude surveys for reading and writing are available for use or modification by teachers. Some of these are listed at the end of the chapter. In addition, a standardized instrument, the *Estes Attitude Scales* (Estes, Estes, Richards & Roettger, 1981) is available in both elementary and secondary forms. As reviewed in the *Ninth Mental Measurements Yearbook* (Mitchell, 1985), the Estes Attitude Scales measure attitudes toward school subjects. The elementary form for grades 2–6 includes items for math, reading, and science; the secondary form for grades 6–12 includes items for English, math, reading, science, and social studies. The scales take twenty to thirty minutes to administer. Reliability is reported as .76–.88 for the elementary scale and .76–.93 for the secondary scale, which is quite respectable for measures of this sort. The *Estes Attitude Scales* would be useful for obtaining affective data for comparisons at local levels.

This instrument is especially valuable in light of the research that shows the importance of considering attitudes toward content areas at the middle and secondary levels (Alexander & Cobb, 1992). A positive attitude toward reading in a content area undeniably has an impact on achievement in that subject.

Performance Samples

Teachers have many options for regularly assessing literacy development as students complete a variety of school assignments. Any tangible products such as journals, videotapes, audiotapes, art, drama productions, songs, and graphic organizers can be analyzed for oral and written language development. In this way the teacher has the means to assess students' needs on a continuing basis. Additionally, students have the opportunity to see their own development if they are keeping portfolios (refer to the "Suggested Readings" at the end of this chapter, also see Chapter 7 for types of portfolios). Because instruction and assessment overlap to a great extent, the instructional suggestions presented in the following chapters can also serve as assessment measures.

One good way to sample students' oral and written language is to ask them to draw, talk, and then write about what they have produced. After the drawing and writing are complete, ask the student to read what was written. If a student seems reluctant, the teacher might invite the student to draw a picture of her family and write something about each member.

Wordless picture books are a good source of oral language samples as well as written samples for any age student, including older and adult students (for suggested titles, see Bloem & Padak, 1996; Danielson, 1992; Johnson-Weber, 1989; Neal & Moore, 1991/1992; Polette, 1989; Rutland, 1987; Tiedt, 2000). Oral language samples can be tape-recorded for later transcription, and written samples, with teacher notations, collected and dated to document growth.

Sulzby (1985) has developed a seven-point scoring rubric for assessing various levels of sophistication in students' attempts at rereading their own written language. For example, a score of 2 is given to the behavior of the learner producing random marks on paper but refusing to reread them; a score of 4 is given for a learner attempting to reread what was written, but not keeping eyes on the print; and a score of 7 is given when the learner's eyes are following the print and there is a match between voice and print. This type of assessment not only can inform the teacher about a student's understanding of literacy concepts, but can also promote students' literacy development by drawing their attention to the distinctions between oral and written language.

Writing also plays an important role in learning our alphabetic system—that is, graphic symbols representing oral language. Writing forces learners to attend to the visual features of print, which in turn helps them become aware of letter-sound patterns and their relationship to words. As young children hear and see stories read over and over, learn letter names, print or spell words, and try to read and write new words, they will learn, naturally, the written English alphabetic system. Of course, progress can be enhanced with encouragement, modeling, and instruction geared toward the student's current level of understanding about print. An analysis of students' invented spellings reveals development of such phonic skills as segmentation (breaking words into parts), blending (putting sounds together to form words), and letter-sound correspondences. (See Appendix I for stages of spelling development and a spelling test that can be used to sample students' spelling.)

In addition to analyzing spelling, a more focused analysis of written language samples can reveal students' knowledge of writing. Examination of writing samples should be made with the intention of providing feedback to students that will help them become more skillful writers. A system that looks at the qualities of good writing as well as the process of writing might serve a teacher's needs best. Appendix J provides guidelines for evaluating and scoring writing and an example for two different approaches to analyzing a writing sample. Chapter 7 also provides suggestions for instructional/assessment practices that support a reading-writing connection.

Students build their own rules for oral grammar and written language based on their observations and explorations with print (Noyce & Christie, 1989). By listening to students speak and by examining their writing samples, we gain insight into what they have already learned about oral and written language.

DOCUMENTATION AND RECORD KEEPING

It is important for teachers to keep records in order to monitor students' literacy progress and their changing interests. As seen throughout this chapter, documentation includes the nature and content of student-teacher conferences (Figure 6.17), records of teacher observations, examples of students' work, comments and suggestions, and notes on specific reading comprehension and writing strategies employed by students. Documentation can be accomplished through checklists, anecdotal records, student self-evaluation, examples of students' work gathered in *working* and *showcase portfolios* (see Chapter 7), tape recordings, videos, photographs, and students' comments about their achievements and instructional needs.

Figure 6.17   Example of Student-Teacher Conference Documentation

Name: _Jo Ellen_   Date: _March 12_

Topics of Discussion:	Teacher's comments;
Literature read or heard	Is reading *Cousins* by Virginia Hamilton
Reading comprehension strategies	Explained that she uses prediction strategies often
Achievements	
Problems	
Behavior	
Weekly goals	1. Complete *Cousins* 2. Begin writing a play based on the main characters in *Cousins*
Long-term goals	1. Write and direct a three-act play

Hamilton, V. (1990). *Cousins.* New York: Putnam and Grosset.

Documentation and record keeping also provide the information a teacher needs for evaluating a student's progress. While teachers know that continual assessment of each student's literacy progress is essential in determining future instruction, teachers are also expected to evaluate students' efforts and assign grades. Student evaluation should be based on the following:

1. Motivation for reading and writing
2. Growth in ability to read for comprehension and write for authentic purposes
3. Growth in ability to employ word identification strategies
4. Growth in ability to recognize and understand basic story features and their connections
5. Growth in ability to appreciate and judge the quality of literature read or heard
6. Growth in ability to compare and contrast the structure of poetic and expository text
7. Growth in ability to use reading comprehension and writing strategies based upon need
8. Growth in ability to monitor reading comprehension
9. Development of wide reading interests
10. Growth in ability to write on a wide range of topics using different *voices of composition* (see Chapter 7)
11. Growth in ability to evaluate the quality of personal literacy efforts

Teachers recognize that it is especially important for students to learn how to evaluate their own literacy achievements and progress. Students who can evaluate their own work in terms of strengths and needs develop responsibility for their own learning (Tierney, Carter, & Desai, 1991). Teachers must work to provide the "risk-free environments necessary in order for this to happen" (Glazer, 1993, p. 108).

Putting It All Together

The vignette that follows will demonstrate the analytic process as it was implemented by one classroom teacher at the beginning of a school year.

The School Context

An urban, public elementary school with a diverse, at-risk, lower socioeconomic student population has 32 students in the third grade.

The Teacher

Ms. Johnson, a dedicated teacher who has helped make the classroom an inviting, exciting place, has been teaching for four years.

Ms. Johnson has collected a wide variety of literature at different grade levels and has created an attractive area for individual silent reading. She displays students' work, including art projects, language experience stories, and students' creative books. Learning centers are interesting, appealing, and orderly. Ms. Johnson believes that reading quality fiction and nonfiction to her students enhances their love of reading, reading comprehension, oral language, and writing abilities. She also supplies multiple copies of literature selections for her students so that she can teach reading using quality fiction and nonfiction. Occasionally she uses basal text stories with her reading group if they are pertinent to a thematic unit being studied.

Ms. Johnson also observes her students carefully and notes their particular talents and literacy instructional needs. She then forms temporary groups according to student needs (e.g., helping students understand paragraphing or learn the importance of predicting and hypothesizing about text ideas and events). Ms. Johnson sincerely likes her students and her job. She is energetic, empathic, open to new ideas, and is confident in her abilities to influence her students in positive ways and in her abilities to make sound educational decisions.

Ms. Johnson conducts daily whole class meetings and encourages her students to discuss problems, pleasures, and reading goals.

During the first week of school, Ms. Johnson carefully observed each of the students in her classroom during free time, reading groups, lunch, whole group instruction, art, music, independent reading, and morning class meetings. She placed each student's name on an individual page of a large notebook. She noted peer interactions, language ability, ability to complete assignments, and apparent feelings of self-esteem for each student. She also made tentative notes concerning each student's apparent listening abilities and reading and writing strengths, and began to classify observations on the Student Behavior Log (see Figure 6.14).

Also during the first week of school, Ms. Johnson asked for her students' help. She explained that she would meet individually with each student to discuss personal reading goals and interests. She also told her students that she wanted them to experience as much success as possible. Ms. Johnson discussed the reasons for flexible reading groups and student conferences as well.

Jamika

One of Ms. Johnson's students was Jamika. During the first week of school, when Ms. Johnson wrote her initial ideas about students in her notebook, she made the following notes on Jamika.

Jamika (Birthdate: 3/13/93)

1. Quiet
2. Cooperative

3. Polite

4. Appears to have adequate oral language abilities

5. Appears interested in class activities

6. Appears healthy

Ms. Johnson observed Jamika further and added notebook comments.

7. Does not volunteer to share ideas and opinions about literature heard or read

8. Follows along carefully as teacher reads

9. Understands basic story features and their connections (see Chapter 7)

10. Often doodles and enjoys drawing

Ms. Johnson began to formulate some questions about Jamika. She asked:

- Why does Jamika exhibit apparent passive behavior?
- Does Jamika lack self-confidence and self-esteem?
- Is the reading material too difficult for Jamika?
- What reading comprehension strategies might help Jamika?

Ms. Johnson decided to look at Jamika's cumulative folder and then make additional notebook comments.

11. Youngest of three siblings

12. Above average grades in first and second grades

13. Average and slightly below average standardized test scores

14. Many absences in first and second grade because of illness

Ms. Johnson decided to have a conference with Jamika. Because the teacher was an active, empathic listener and communicated with Jamika in a nonjudgmental manner, Jamika felt comfortable in sharing her thoughts. After the conference Ms. Johnson wrote:

15. Brother and sister both high achievers

16. Believes that she is not as "smart" as her siblings

Ms. Johnson decided to gather some definite information about Jamika's literacy abilities. She wanted some answers to these questions:

- Is Jamika reading to her fullest potential?
- What is Jamika's instructional reading level? Independent reading level? Listening comprehension level?
- Is Jamika a corrective reader, possibly because of missing reading instruction due to illness?
- What are Jamika's general writing abilities?
- What writing behaviors does Jamika exhibit? (see Chapter 7)
- What perceptions does Jamika have about reading and writing?
- What perceptions does Jamika have about herself as a reader and writer?
- What are Jamika's interests?

Ms. Johnson decided to get some ideas about Jamika's interests and reading ability using an interest inventory and an informal reading inventory. She worked with Jamika while the class was actively involved in learning center activities. Afterwards she recorded the results in her notebook.

17. Interested in dinosaurs and baby animals
18. Adequate sight vocabulary commensurate with third grade
19. Reading independently at second grade
20. Reading instructionally at third grade
21. Listening comprehension level is fifth grade

Ms. Johnson then invited Jamika to write an informal letter or story of her choice, which she could then illustrate. As Jamika wrote, Ms. Johnson observed her and made notes about her writing behaviors.

22. Jamika wrote in the expressive voice (see Chapter 7). She wrote about a trip to Disneyworld.
23. Jamika used standard and transitional spelling commensurate with her age and grade (e.g., "Dizneewrld").
24. Jamika wrote legibly and was overly concerned with forming letters correctly.
25. Jamika used appropriate capitalization and punctuation at the end of sentences.
26. Jamika did not use a plan for writing nor did she reread her work or revise.
27. Jamika appeared to be very anxious as she wrote, but was eager to illustrate her story.

Next, Ms. Johnson interviewed Jamika to determine her perceptions about reading and writing. She asked Jamika questions such as: Do you like to read? Why or why not? What do you do when you come to a word that you don't know? How do you figure it out? Do you think that you are a good reader? Why or why not? Why do people write? How do you decide what to write? What part of writing do you like the most? The least? Why? Are you a good writer? Why? Why not? (See earlier section in this chapter for additional questions.)

After examining Jamika's responses to these questions, Ms. Johnson wrote the following tentative hypotheses in her notebook:

- Needs to develop motivation to read
- Needs to develop confidence in herself as a reader and writer
- Needs to learn word identification plans (see Chapter 8)
- Needs to learn to read for comprehension and actively seek meaning (see Chapter 10)
- Needs to learn some prewriting strategies (see Chapter 7)
- Needs to learn editing techniques

After analyzing and reflecting upon Jamika's IRI results, the Student Behavior Log, writing behaviors, perceptions about writing, oral language abilities, and affective dimension behaviors, Ms. Johnson decided that Jamika probably had far greater reading and writing potential than she demonstrated. Ms. Johnson added the following to her tentative hypotheses:

- Lack of motivation, possibly due to poor self-esteem; lack of confidence; lack of reading and writing success in first and second grades.

- Possible feelings of inadequacy because of high-achieving older siblings
- Insufficient knowledge about the processes of reading and writing
- Focus on talent in visual/spatial intelligence

Ms. Johnson decided to plan a program of reading/writing instruction together with Jamika. After the planning conference, she wrote the following instructional alternatives for Jamika.

Literacy Instructional Plan

1. Place in temporary groups focusing on word-identification plans and reading comprehension techniques
2. Assign creative bookmaking
3. Assemble literature that meets Jamika's interests (i.e., dinosaurs and baby animals)
4. Teach reading comprehension techniques that help Jamika learn to read for meaning
5. Provide opportunities for Jamika to engage in collaborative writing and bookmaking activities
6. Help Jamika engage in numerous nonstructured writing activities
7. Establish dialogue journal with Jamika to foster a reading/writing connection and provide a risk-free opportunity for Jamika to write
8. Provide teacher-guided writing lessons such as "Writing Cohesive Paragraphs" (see Chapter 7)
9. Arrange physical examination, including visual and auditory acuity
10. Schedule student-parent-teacher conference

Ms. Johnson will continue to observe Jamika's literacy progress throughout the school year. She plans to continue student-teacher conferences and informal communication, teacher support, and providing for Jamika's success as a reader and writer.

SUMMARY

A variety of direct measures have been presented. These classroom-based assessment procedures are valuable to the teacher for gathering information and verifying tentative teaching hypotheses in the analytic process. Appropriate use of both classroom-based and standardized measures is most effective in learning students' reading needs. The chapter ends with an example of one teacher's implementation of the analytic process.

Suggested Readings

Afflerbach, P. (1993). Report cards and reading. *The Reading Teacher, 46,* 458–465.

It is one thing to gather information through direct assessments and another to report the results of such information to parents. This article discusses key issues in developing report cards that are more consistent with use of direct assessments.

Bridges, L. (1995). *Assessment: Continuous learning.* York, ME: Stenhouse.

This resource provides a wealth of information about authentic assessment and kidwatching, as well as practical suggestions for assessment tools and portfolios.

DeFina, A. A. (1992). *Portfolio assessment: Getting started.* New York: Scholastic.

This most readable book, written by a classroom teacher/teacher educator, provides detailed information about portfolios for beginners or those wishing to refine or expand their use of portfolios. Numerous charts and examples give the specifics needed for assessing reading and writing abilities.

Goodman, Y. M. (1996). Revaluing readers while readers revalue themselves: Retrospective miscue analysis. *The Reading Teacher, 49,* 600–609.

Yetta Goodman further explains Retrospective Miscue Analysis (RMA), introduced in 1989, and several variations in this article. RMA also serves a self-assessment function in that it invites readers to reflect on their own reading process.

Nolan, E. A., and Berry, M. (1993). Learning to listen. *The Reading Teacher, 46,* 606–608.

This brief article shares the very real concerns associated with one teacher's movement to reliance on more direct measures of assessment. The importance of communicating with parents is made clear.

Rhodes, L. K., and Nathenson-Mejia, S. (1992). Anecdotal records: A powerful tool for ongoing literacy assessment. *The Reading Teacher, 45,* 502–509.

This article provides detailed discussion of anecdotal records for process assessment. Samples with corresponding analyses show how anecdotal records support the analytic process of gathering information to advise instructional planning and in turn generate new teaching hypotheses.

The following sources provide some valid and reliable interest and attitude surveys for reading and writing available for use or modification by teachers.

Bottomley, D., Henk, W., & Melnick, S. (1997/1998). Assessing children's views about themselves as writers using the Writer Self-Perception Scale. *The Reading Teacher, 51,* 286–296.

Gambrell, L. B., Palmer, B. M., Codling, R. M., & Mazzoni, S. A. (1996). Assessing motivation to read. *The Reading Teacher, 49,* 518–533.

Henk, W. A., & Melnick, S. A. (1995). The Reader Self-Perception Scale (RSPS): A new tool for measuring how children feel about themselves as readers. *The Reading Teacher, 48,* 470–482.

Kear, D. J., Coffman, G. A., McKenna, M. C., & Ambrosio, A. L. (2000). Measuring attitude toward writing: A new tool for teachers. *The Reading Teacher, 54,* 10–23.

McKenna, M. C., & Kear, D. J. (1990). Measuring attitude toward reading: A new tool for teachers. *The Reading Teacher, 43,* 626–639.

Tullock-Rhody, R., & Alexander, J. E. (1980). A scale for assessing attitudes toward reading in secondary schools. *Journal of Reading, 23,* 609–614.

PART II

The Major Domains

CHAPTER

7 The Reading/Writing Connection

Janet C. Richards
University of Southern Mississippi–Gulf Park

Objectives

After you have read this chapter, you should be able to:

1. explain how reading and writing are mutually supportive processes;
2. discuss how writers gain valuable knowledge about reading;
3. discuss the importance of a writing program for struggling readers;
4. define the role of an effective writing teacher;
5. explain how to implement writing lessons and activities in a corrective reading program;
6. define and explain the differences and benefits of nonstructured, collaborative, teacher-guided, and creative writing;
7. explain the relationship between writing instruction and writing assessment;
8. discuss the value of helping students learn to assess their own writing.

Key Concepts and Terms

artifacts	genre	quickwrites
author's chair	invented spelling	recursive nature of writing
collaborative writing	language conventions	showcase portfolio
conventional spelling	language functions	teacher-guided writing
creative writing	nonstructured writing	lessons
emergent writers	personal dictionary	working portfolio

S tudents in our after-school corrective reading program write as much as they read. Connecting the literacy learning modalities of reading and writing makes sense. Both are thinking, meaning-making processes. Each supports, complements, and contributes to the other's development (Ross & Roe, 1990).

Children's awareness and understanding of reading and writing develop concurrently. Experts in children's emergent (i.e., early) literacy behaviors note that young

---

Author's Note: This invited chapter by Dr. Richards presents the concepts and practices of the reading/ writing connection by sharing the workings of an actual program in progress. Those readers who are also currently working with students may therefore find this chapter especially helpful for getting started. In the learning context described in this chapter, elementary education majors enrolled in a corrective reading methods course each work with a group of three to five students for one hour twice weekly throughout a semester. As teacher educators, we are firmly committed to the idea that all students learn best when they have opportunities to read, write, and share ideas as part of a supportive community of language learners and users. "Learning is a social process that is made more powerful when learners are encouraged to interact and think with others" (Short, 1993, p. 156).

children spontaneously engage in pretend reading and writing in their individual and group play. For example, when my granddaughter, Elizabeth, was 3 years old, she enjoyed role-playing the part of a McDonald's waitress. She "wrote" her family's orders for Big Macs and Happy Meals, "read" the orders, and "served" the food.

Knowledge of reading does not precede knowledge of writing (Bromley, 1989). It is interesting to note that at age 11, Elizabeth's preferred learning style is still through writing. Writing promotes reading. Writers read extensively to gain information about writing topics and to revise their writing. They also read when they write collaboratively with a partner and when they share their work with others (Atwell, 1987).

Writers become familiar with different **language functions** (i.e., purposes) and **genre** (i.e., styles) or **symbol systems** (i.e., any form of writing that offers meaning) such as poetry, grocery lists, news articles, personal diaries, letters of invitation, stories, reports, and Web pages. Further, as they write, observe others write, and read, they construct knowledge about **language conventions** such as spelling, punctuation, capitalization, and paragraphing. For example, as one 6-year-old in our program journaled with her university tutor, she commented, "I'm making dots at the end of sentences just like you do." Another student in second grade recently became aware of quotation marks. "I know you don't put these marks around every word," he told his university tutor. "I think you only do that when people say something."

Writers are "less likely to be intimidated by written language" (Newkirk, 1982, p. 457). By becoming authors themselves, young students learn that written language can be changed, deleted, or expanded. It is not something that is rigid and beyond criticism. Studies show that in classrooms where students write extensively, reading scores go up (Graves & Murray, 1980). "Daily writing promotes and enhances reading" (Dionisio, 1989, p. 747).

It is especially important to connect reading and writing instruction for struggling readers. Many of these learners have had few positive writing experiences. Therefore, they write as little as possible. Since reading and writing develop simultaneously, and strengthen and build upon each other, it is imperative that students with reading difficulties have opportunities to write and observe others as they write (Wiseman, 1992). For these (and all) learners, "reading and writing instruction shouldn't be separated, nor should writing instruction be postponed until students are able readers" (Rhodes & Dudley-Marling, 1988, p. 14).

THE ROLE OF THE TEACHER IN A WRITING PROGRAM FOR STRUGGLING READERS

The role of the teacher in a writing program for struggling readers is no different from the role of good writing teachers in any program. Good writing teachers are writers themselves (Graves, 1988; Solley, 2000). They are enthusiastic about writing and wholeheartedly

---

Also, we have found that with some slight modifications, the techniques described in this chapter are as applicable to secondary students as they are to elementary and middle school students. Secondary teachers can easily adapt the ideas discussed to suit their students' literacy instructional needs and interests.

We sincerely thank the students whose writing samples you will see throughout this chapter. Also, the brief explanations of "Add a Paragraph/Write a Book" and "Writing Cohesive Paragraphs" were previously discussed in *READ: Exploration and Discovery,* a journal of the Louisiana Reading Association. The editors of *READ* have graciously given their permission to include these lessons in this chapter. We also wish to thank all of the wonderful university students whose professional development is displayed in this chapter.

"believe that their children can write" (Daniels, 1991, p. 169). They know it takes time to move through the writing process to include prewriting, drafting revising, and editing, so they give their students the time they need to write. These teachers know that writing creatively is a complex, problem-solving process in which writers move back and forth between planning, composing, and revising their work. They recognize and support the developmental nature of children's spelling (please refer to Appendix I), and know where their "students fall along the [spelling] developmental continuum" (O'Flahavan & Blassberg, 1992, p. 409). Good writing teachers understand that students learn how to spell in conventional ways by engaging in meaningful reading and writing activities (Bartch, 1992; Pappas, Kiefer, & Levstik, 1999). They understand that the "stage of writing is set by what the teacher does, not by what the teacher says" (Graves, 1988, p. 12). Therefore, teachers are learners about writing along with their students. They demonstrate and model the various functions of writing and freely share their writing experiences (Juliebö & Edwards, 1989).

Good writing teachers also understand that students learn about writing by writing for their own purposes and audiences as part of a larger community of language users. Consequently, they never require their students to complete meaningless, isolated writing tasks, such as copying sentences from the board or writing weekly spelling words five times each. Instead, they create a learning context in which students feel free to take risks, experiment with writing, and use writing to communicate meaning (Anderson, Raphael, Englert, & Stevens, 1992). Most important, good writing teachers know that "the key to helping readers [and writers] in trouble is to help them revalue themselves as language learners and users" (Goodman, 1982, p. 88).

IMPLEMENTING THE WRITING PROGRAM

Students in our after-school reading program begin writing, and thinking and talking about writing, at their first tutoring session. In order to get an idea about the general writing abilities of each new group of students, their university tutors invite them to write an informal letter or story on a subject of their choice (Figure 7.1). We never tell students what to write, but encourage them to self-select their writing topics, using their own ideas to write about what is important to them. The tutors encourage **emergent writers** (i.e., beginning writers) to write any words, alphabet letters, numbers, or symbols they know, or to convey a message by scribbling or drawing a picture (Figure 7.2). As the students write, their tutors continually reassure them that their writing samples will not be graded but will be used to help plan future writing lessons and activities. If students request help in spelling, their tutors encourage them to use invented spelling, or constructed spelling, by saying, "It's okay to spell words your own way. When you are finished writing we can read your story together." As discussed later in this chapter, spelling is important, but should not be a concern until students are working on final drafts of their writing.

Observations, Initial Assessments, and Instructional Decisions

As the students write, their university tutors carefully observe and make notes about each student's writing behaviors (e.g., "John re-read and revised his story"; "Melissa spoke aloud to herself as she wrote"; "Matt erased extensively and used body language indicating that he was anxious and frustrated about writing"; "Andy planned his composition

Figure 7.1   Antonia's Story for Assessing General Writing Abilities

If a dinosaur came to lunch
I would screm. I would feed
hem frinck fisee and I would
feed him auntil he snuwsd
and I would snike out and
win he wack up he would
eat and eat he would
eat donunuts a cake and
Milk and cuokise and popsikls
and pop tort and it would
eat eveyting in the word
he defuntle eat he.

using his artistic abilities. He drew pictures"). Later, the tutors analyze the writing samples (Figure 7.3), guided by a developmental writing checklist (Figure 7.4).

At this first session, the university tutors also attempt to determine their students' perceptions about writing by recording students' responses to questions on a writing perception survey (Figure 7.5). The tutors then carefully reflect upon these three sources of information (observation notes, writing sample analysis, and student's responses to

Figure 7.2   Emergent Writer's Initial Writing Sample

Theis dig da y My name
1234561 89 10 1112 13 145161189
20Cat.dogg igsup.
The

Figure 7.3   Tutor's Analysis of Antonia's First Writing Sample

ANTONIA

Antonia is eight years old. Her completed composition follows a logical progression and is interesting/enjoyable for the reader. Antonia wrote in both the expressive and imaginative voices. She wrote about herself (i.e., "I"), and created an imaginary story about a dinosaur. Antonia used standard and transitional spelling (e.g., "screm" (scream), "hem" (him), "frinck fisee" (french fries), "auntil" (until), "snuwsd" (snoozed), "snike" (sneak), "wock" (woke), "donunuts" (doughnuts), "cuokise" (cookies), "pop tort" (Pop Tarts), "eveyting" (everything), "word" (world), "defuntle" (definitely). Antonia wrote legibly and formed graphemes correctly. She capitalized the first word of the composition and *I* appropriately.

Antonia did not use a plan for writing. She completed her first draft and did not reread or revise. Antonia did not write for a specific audience. She did not title her composition nor include any punctuation until the end of the composition. The entire piece consists of one long sentence with "and" used as a connector throughout.

INITIAL INSTRUCTIONAL DECISIONS

1. Encourage Antonia to participate in many nonstructured writing activities. She expresses herself well and combines *voices* effectively. We need to encourage her creativity and help her write for her own purposes and for her own audiences.
2. Develop Antonia's awareness of *audience* (i.e., to whom is she writing?).
3. One of Antonia's immediate writing needs is using appropriate punctuation. In structured writing activities, point out the use of punctuation. Explain to Antonia how punctuation helps readers understand an author's writing.
4. Consider initiating a small unit on dinosaurs. Antonia is very interested in this topic.
5. Antonia is a good storyteller. She would probably enjoy participating in *Add a Paragraph/Write a Book.*
6. Model use of punctuation in dialogue journal activities.
7. Use teacher dictation to help draw Antonia's attention to punctuation.
8. Antonia would probably enjoy reading about dinosaurs. Assemble a literature collection composed of dinosaur books (fiction, nonfiction, poetry, jokes).
9. Antonia's story could contain two paragraphs (e.g., first paragraph: "If a dinosaur came to lunch I would scream. I would feed him french fries and I would feed him until he snoozed"). Use teacher-guided activities, and introduce *cohesive paragraphs* to demonstrate the concept of paragraphing.
10. Antonia uses interesting, descriptive vocabulary (e.g., snoozed; definitely). Compliment Antonia on use of interesting words. Consider *rephrasing* activities.
11. When reading, draw Antonia's attention to titles of stories and books. Discuss how authors choose titles for their work. Discuss why authors title their compositions, stories, and books.
12. Perhaps Antonia would like to learn the standard spelling of some of the descriptive words she used in her composition.
13. Continue to observe Antonia daily in order to revise/extend instructional decisions.

questions on the writing perception survey) to get a sense of what each student knows and thinks about written language. This information, coupled with data gathered from an informal reading inventory and an interest survey (refer to Chapter 6), gives us insight into each student's literacy development, interests, and experiences.

At the same time, however, we recognize that students' writing abilities and understanding about writing grow daily. Therefore, ongoing observation is a necessity. In order to ascertain each student's ever-changing writing (and reading) instructional needs, a rich source of information is close attention to students as they respond to instruction (Rhodes & Dudley-Marling, 1996).

Figure 7.4   Developmental Writing Checklist

Name: _____   Date: _____

UNDERSTANDS THE WRITING PROCESS		DEVELOPMENTAL STAGE OF SPELLING
1. Developed and used a plan for writing (e.g., semantic map, lists, outline, drawings, notes) (Circle which apply.)	YES NO	(Circle which stage most applies and give examples.)
2. Referred to a plan when writing	YES NO	1. prephonemic 2. early phonemic 3. letter name 4. transitional 5. standard
3. Re-read first draft and revised writing	YES NO	KNOWLEDGE OF MECHANICS
4. Rearranged words, sentences, and paragraphs	YES NO	1. Titled the composition — YES NO
		2. Used periods appropriately — YES NO
5. Revised vocabulary to include descriptive words and a variety of verbs	YES NO	3. Used question marks appropriately — YES NO
		4. Used commas appropriately — YES NO
6. Wrote for a specific audience (e.g., teacher, family, friend)	YES NO	5. Used exclamation marks appropriately — YES NO
7. Completed composition follows a logical progression	YES NO	6. Used quotation marks appropriately — YES NO
		7. Used appropriate capitalization — YES NO
8. Completed composition is interesting/enjoyable for the reader	YES NO	8. Indented paragraphs — YES NO
		9. Wrote in complete sentences — YES NO
9. Used expressive *voice;* imaginative *voice;* expository *voice* (Give examples.) (Circle which *voices* apply.)	YES NO	10. Wrote legibly — YES NO
		11. Formed graphemes correctly — YES NO
10. Combined *voices* appropriately (Give examples.)	YES NO	(Items suggested by Tompkins & Hoskisson 1991; Rhodes & Dudley-Marling, 1988)

Figure 7.5   Writing Perception Survey

Name: _____   Date: _____

1. Why do people write?
2. How can you learn to write stories?
3. What stories would you like to write? Why?
4. What is the difference between writing a story and writing a composition that explains or describes or tells somebody how to do something?
5. If you were teaching someone to write well, what would you tell them to do?
6. When you write, what do you do first?
7. How do you decide what to write?
8. What part of writing do you like the most? Why?
9. What part of writing do you like the least? Why?
10. When you are writing and get stuck, what do you do?
11. How do you know if your writing is any good?
12. If you were writing your own books, what would you write about?
13. Do you think you are a good writer? Why? Why not? (Rhodes & Dudley-Marling, 1988, p. 62)

See also Hansen, 1987; Tompkins & Hoskisson, 1991.

Nonstructured Writing Activities

There are always personally important reasons to write during our tutoring sessions. When writing is a natural and purposeful activity, everyone wants to write. For instance, a student may decide to take stock of all the books he has written (Figure 7.6); a group may create a mural illustrating and telling a favorite story; two friends may spontaneously exchange informal notes concerning their feelings (Figure 7.7); or a student may write a list of rules for her friends to follow when they come to her house to play (Figure 7.8). These types of **nonstructured writing** activities are "primarily student-centered with pupils writing about what is of most interest and concern to them" (Templeton, 1991, p. 218). By participating in nonstructured writing activities, students gain knowledge about written language without direct instruction. Nonstructured writing activities also help foster a supportive, risk-free environment that in turn encourages students to write.

Structured Writing Lessons and Activities

Throughout the semester our students also engage in more structured writing lessons and activities that we categorize as (1) collaborative writing, (2) teacher-guided writing, and (3) creative writing. In these more focused writing endeavors, "the [student's] purposes come first but the teacher deliberately creates a setting in which writing in different forms can be perceived as useful" (Nathan, Temple, Juntunen, & Temple, 1989, p. 93).

Figure 7.6   Student's Writing Record

Here is all my books I wrotin.

Beauty and the Beast.
The Lizrd.
Michelle and the Casle.
The rabbit who had no friends.
The cat who ate all the fish.
Once I was taking a nap.
My bedroom and bed.

All my dogs.

Figure 7.7 Informal Notes Between Two Students

~~Aptie~~ 7, 1993

Dear Ria,

I was going to let you have my egg But you can Just Say I am fired.

no you are not. I'am You'r friend Be mine too O.K. I like you now. You are my two Best friend!

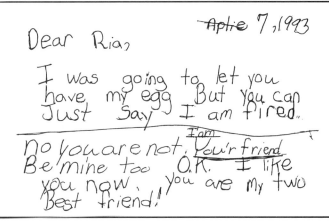

Collaborative Writing Activities

Language is facilitated in social situations that include genuine conversations (Bloome & Egan-Robertson, 1993; Pappas, Kiefer, & Levstik, 1999). **Collaborative writing** activities give our students opportunities to enjoy writing with a partner, or a group of friends, and a university tutor who serves as a role model. When writers plan, discuss, respond to one another, and write together, they spark one another's creativity and become less anxious

Figure 7.8 Betsy's List of Rules for Her Room

Rules of the room
do What the rules say
be good
do not be bad
do not hrut little kids
do not be mean to bothers and siters
clen up after your slef
be nice
take one toy out
do not tak a nour toy oet till you put the ather toy a way.
do What I say
if you do not go home.

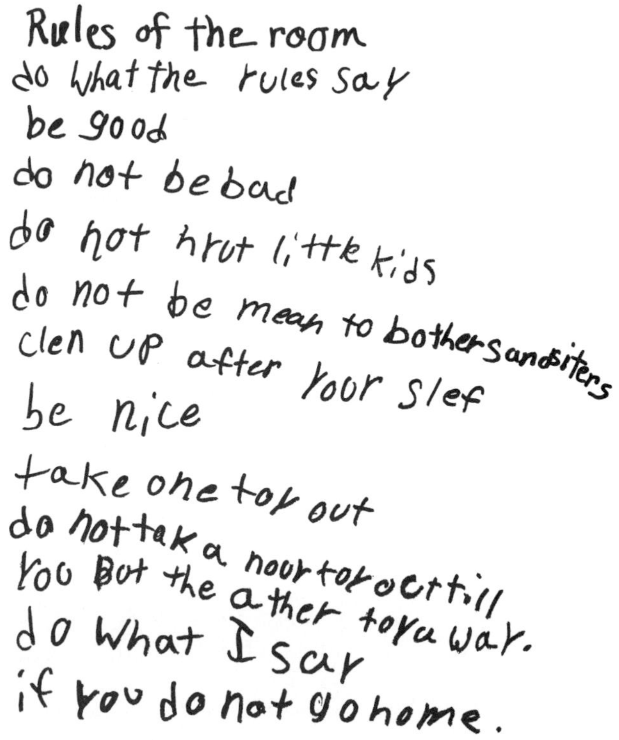

about individual performance (Newman, 1985). Four collaborative writing activities our students particularly enjoy are (1) Write a Sentence/Make a Story, (2) Add a Word/Stretch the Sentence, (3) Add a Paragraph/Write a Book, and (4) dialogue journaling. The tutors model each of these activities for their students before having their students participate.

Write a Sentence/Make a Story. This activity links reading and writing and helps develop students' understanding of basic story features and their connections (i.e., characters, setting, problems, and solutions). To begin this activity, three to five students and their university tutor sit in a circle around a table. On a large sheet of paper each participant writes his or her idea for the first sentence of an imaginative story. If there are six participants, there are six different sentences (e.g., "Joanne got a rabbit for her birthday" or "Shane loved to play baseball"). Participants then pass their papers to the person on their right, who reads the sentence and adds a second sentence to the story (e.g., "One day Joanne took her rabbit to the playground" or "Shane played baseball every day with his friends").

interpersonal

Participants continue passing their papers, adding one additional sentence to each of the stories until they receive their original papers. Group members may pass their papers around the circle a second or third time if they decide that their stories need further development. Emergent writers, those just beginning their writing development regardless of age, participate in Write a Sentence/Make a Story by drawing sentence pictures or dictating their sentence ideas to their tutors.

spatial

At the end of the activity, participants read their collaboratively created stories aloud for everyone's enjoyment. Tutors also lead a discussion about the characters, setting, problems, and solutions in each story, and how these basic story elements connect to one another. Figure 7.9 shows an example of a collaborative story for a tutor and two students.

Add a Word/Stretch the Sentence. This activity promotes a reading/writing connection, helps students construct knowledge about the subtle interplay and interconnectedness of *syntax* and *semantics* (i.e., word order in sentences and meaning, respectively), improves students' control of written syntax, and helps students construct more elaborate written sentences.

Figure 7.9 Example of a Collaborative Story

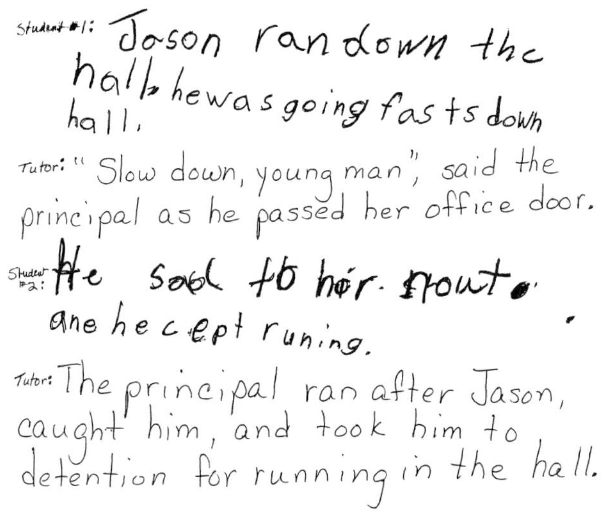
Student #1: Jason ran down the hall, he was going fasts down hall.
Tutor: "Slow down, young man", said the principal as he passed her office door.
Student #2: He sad to hor. flout. ane he cept runing.
Tutor: The principal ran after Jason, caught him, and took him to detention for running in the hall.

To start the activity, students and their tutor sit in a circle around a table. On a large sheet of paper each participant creates a beginning sentence of a written discourse in any *composing voice.* For example, "I love tutoring class" is written in the *expressive voice;* "The zoo has a dinosaur exhibit" is written in the *expository voice;* "Once there lived three little puppies" is written in the *imaginative* or *poetic voice* (see Britton, Burgess, Martin, McLeod & Rosen, 1975, for a thorough discussion of voices of composition). Next, participants pass their papers to the person on their right, who reads the last sentence and rewrites it, adding one additional word in any appropriate place in the sentence (e.g., "I really love tutoring class" or "The zoo has opened a dinosaur exhibit"). Emergent writers participate in this activity by dictating their original sentence and each of their "stretched" sentence ideas to their university tutors.

At the end of the activity, students and tutors take turns reading aloud their original sentence and each of the "stretched" sentences for the group's enjoyment. They also discuss how the meaning of each original sentence was expanded or changed (Figure 7.10). Tutors also look for opportunities to teach other skills (e.g., everyday vs. every day).

Add a Paragraph/Write a Book. This activity promotes a reading/writing connection, alleviates writers' anxieties, and helps students construct knowledge about basic story features and their relationships. To initiate this activity, tutors place the first paragraph of an imaginative story at the beginning of a book made from blank pages stapled together. When time permits, individual students and their tutors add either an anonymous or an author-signed paragraph to the story. As the story progresses, students and tutors take turns reading the partially completed story aloud for the group's enjoyment. They also discuss their ideas for further story development. Once the book is completed, participants add visual art to clarify and highlight the story's ideas and stimulate readers' imaginations. We also provide additional opportunities for students to exploit their special intelligences by encouraging them to create dances, songs, or drama productions that accompany and offer new insights about their stories (Armstrong, 2000; Gardner, 1995, 1999). Then they share their collaborative authorship efforts with peers in the tutoring program and in their regular classrooms. (See Appendix K for an example of a completed book.)

spatial

bodily-kinesthetic
musical

Dialogue Journals. Tutors in our program journal with each of their students at every tutoring session, or we arrange for an e-mail pen pal so students can journal with another student in another location. The journal entries are private and are read only by the two journal partners. Dialogue journaling provides a way for tutors and individual students to

interpersonal

Figure 7.10   Example of "Stretched" Sentence

Nan can read.
Nan can read Books
Nan can read many books
Everyday Nan can read many books.

"carry on a conversation over time, sharing ideas, feelings and concerns in writing" (Staton, 1987, p. 47). (Dialogue journals also provide an excellent vehicle for risk-free writing. These journals are *never* graded, and since the teacher responds in writing, a model for spelling and handwriting, as well as grammar and sentence structure, is always available to the student.) Students write in a bound notebook to their teacher about anything they want (early or emergent writers may draw pictures to get across a message). The teacher writes back in the same notebook, responding naturally, as in conversation. E-mail journals can be used for the same purpose as dialogue journals, and may provide a more motivating venue for upper elementary and older students especially (Seaborg & Sturtevant, 1996).

Journaling also fosters a reading/writing connection and motivates students to write. Writing collaboratively with an equal partner enhances students' informal writing abilities and writing confidence as well. For instance, because of insecurity or lack of writing experience, some of our students initially choose to convey a journal message by drawing a picture or dictating a message. However, as the semester progresses, these students begin to feel more comfortable about writing and have learned a great deal about written language. Many of our students model and imitate the language functions (e.g., reporting facts or opinions, asking questions) and language conventions (e.g., using exclamation marks or closing entries by writing "love") their tutors use in their own journal entries.

As shown in the series of three nonconsecutive days of journaling seen in Figure 7.11, when Tonya entered our program she wrote just a few words and drew hearts to show her feelings. Two weeks later she answered her tutor's question, attempted to write complete sentences, and modeled her tutor's use of question marks. Six days later Tonya wrote a long journal entry in which she shared a considerable amount of information and feelings.

Journal writing is never considered a writing assignment. Therefore, the university tutors never correct their students' spelling, punctuation, or capitalization. Instead they try to be particularly responsive to what their students write. They never ask their students too many questions or write only about their own interests and concerns. Rather, they compliment their students' work (e.g., "I liked your story about wolves"), support and affirm their students' efforts (e.g., "You really are trying hard and it shows!"), and write honest, interesting, personal messages that encourage and entice their students to respond (Young & Crow, 1992).

Teacher-Guided Writing Lessons

Many teachers recognize that, in order to become proficient writers, students experiencing serious difficulty usually need to engage in activities that draw their attention to certain aspects of language they may otherwise disregard or overlook. Short, **teacher-guided writing lessons** provide a way to help students focus upon and practice "new writing skills without being overwhelmed" (Bryson & Scardamalia, 1991, p. 164). These types of lessons concentrate on discrete aspects of written language such as spelling, punctuation, and capitalization, and also include more global aspects of composing such as prewriting strategies, paragraphing, and editing.

The university tutors design teacher-guided writing lessons based upon their students' immediate writing needs. Therefore, the students view these types of mini-lessons as personally useful and meaningful because they immediately are able to apply the concepts they learn in their own independent writing and revision efforts. Three teacher-guided writing lessons particularly effective for our students are Teacher Dictation, Rephrasing, and Writing Cohesive Paragraphs. Features of these three lessons can easily be modified or adapted to suit the writing needs of diverse groups of learners in any educational setting.

Figure 7.11   Dialogue Journal Entries

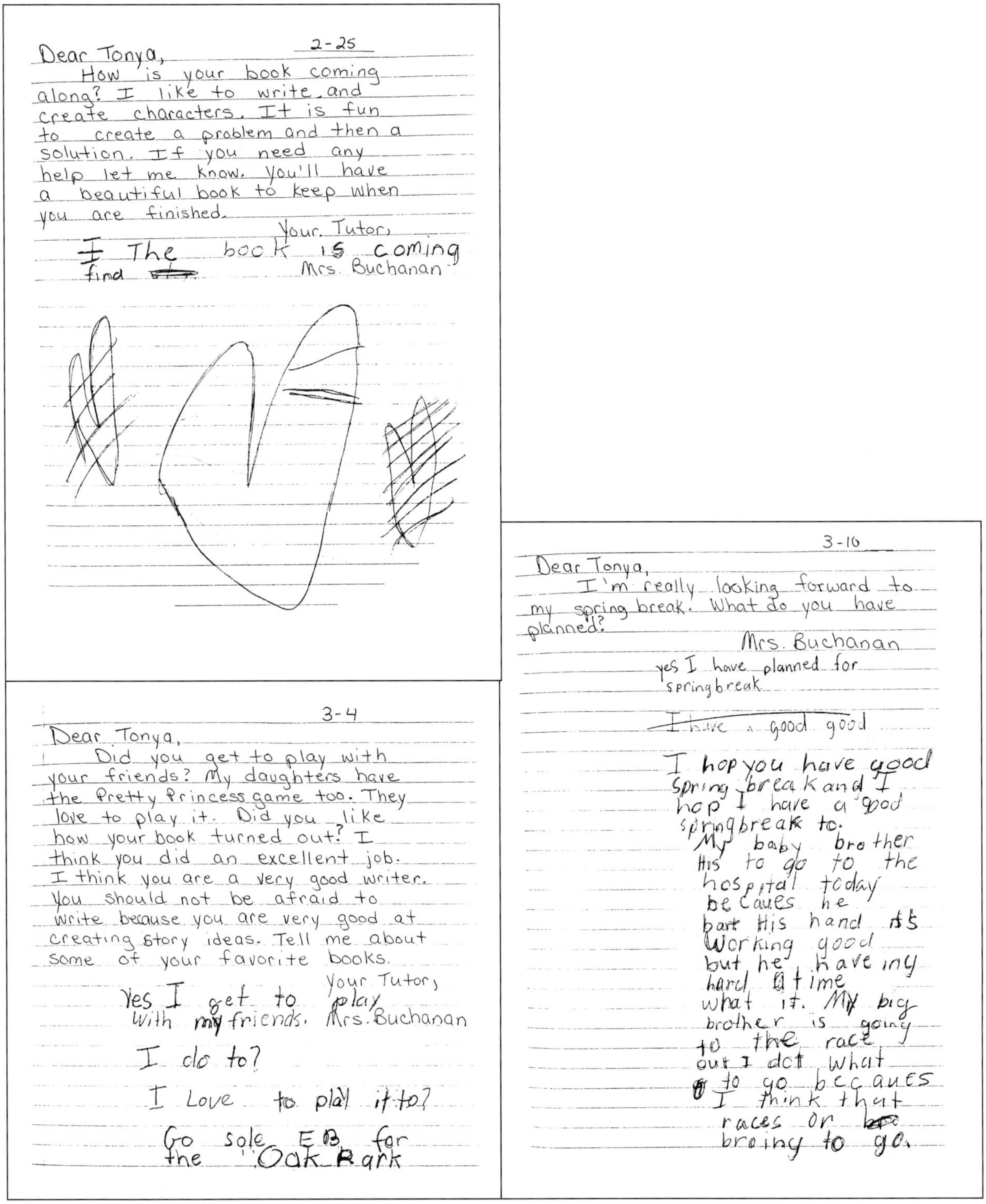

Dear Tonya,   2-25
    How is your book coming
along? I like to write and
create characters. It is fun
to create a problem and then a
solution. If you need any
help let me know. You'll have
a beautiful book to keep when
you are finished.
                          Your Tutor,
    ⫢ The book is coming
    find ⫢   Mrs. Buchanan

Dear Tonya,   3-4
    Did you get to play with
your friends? My daughters have
the Pretty Princess game too. They
love to play it. Did you like
how your book turned out? I
think you did an excellent job.
I think you are a very good writer.
You should not be afraid to
write because you are very good at
creating story ideas. Tell me about
some of your favorite books.
                          Your Tutor,
    Yes I get to play
    with my friends. Mrs. Buchanan

    I do to?

    I Love to play it to?

    Go sole EB for
    the 'Oak Bark

Dear Tonya,   3-16
    I'm really looking forward to
my spring break. What do you have
planned?
                    Mrs. Buchanan
yes I have planned for
spring break

    I have a good good

    I hop you have good
    spring break and I
    hop I have a good
    springbreak to.
    My baby brother
    His to go to the
    hospital today
    be caues he
    bark His hand As
    Working good
    but he have iny
    hard a time
    what it. My big
    brother is going
    to the race
    out I dot what
    to go becaues
    I think that
    races or
    broing to go.

Figure 7.12   Example of Oral Rephrasing

Tutor: The boys and girls cooked a meal.
Barbie: The children fixed cocoa.
Tonya: The kids made a cake.
Brad: The children made a pie.
Chris: The kids made sweet potatoes for dinner.
Jessica: The friends made dinner.
Marian: The kids made biscuits.

Teacher Dictation. This teacher-guided lesson connects the processes of listening, writing, and reading, and enhances students' understanding of language conventions at the sentence level (i.e., spelling, punctuation, and capitalization). Studies show that language conventions such as punctuation are a particular problem for students having serious difficulty (Norton, 1993). To begin this teacher-guided lesson, students listen carefully as their tutor dictates a sentence that contains particular aspects of language that students are ready to address in their independent writing. For example, if some students are ready to learn about capitalizing the first word of a sentence, a tutor might dictate the sentence "Wild animals live in the zoo." Students then write the dictated sentence. Their tutors also write the sentences on a large chart or chalkboard while modeling their thinking aloud (e.g., "I need to begin a sentence with a capital letter"). Tutors then read aloud the dictated sentence as students follow along.

The next step is a discussion of the particular language conventions pertinent to the sentence (e.g., "The word *Wild* begins with a capital letter because it is the first word of the sentence"). To complete the lesson, tutors help their students edit or "fix" any problems in their sentences such as adding a period or editing spelling. As the semester progresses students take over the tutor's role and dictate sentences to the group. As extensions to this activity, tutors help students focus on the particular patterns, structures, and spelling features of any spelling words they have missed. Students also enter their "missed" words in their personal dictionaries (see the section on spelling in this chapter).

Rephrasing. This teacher-guided writing lesson connects listening, writing, and reading; enhances and expands students' vocabularies; and helps students generate language and construct knowledge about how language works. The procedure for this lesson begins with the Teacher Dictation activity described in the previous section: (1) teacher dictates a sentence, (2) students and teacher write the sentence, (3) teacher reads the dictated sentence aloud as students follow along, and (4) if necessary, students edit their writing with their teacher's help.

Following the editing of the sentence, students take turns orally rephrasing the sentence by creating variations in vocabulary and attempting to keep the original meaning of the sentence intact. For example, participants might rephrase the sentence, "Today is Tuesday" as "This is the third day of the week"; "This is the day before Wednesday"; "This is the day after Monday"; or "This is the day before the fourth day of the week." Rephrasings can also be done in writing instead of orally. Participants then share all their rephrased sentence ideas and discuss any possible meaning changes that may have occurred. Groups often write and display all their sentence variations on sentence strips or charts in order to share their work with others (Figure 7.12).

spatial

Writing Cohesive Paragraphs. This lesson provides a strategic plan students can follow independently to improve their abilities to write paragraphs that focus on a central theme. To begin the lesson, tutors help their students develop a prewriting semantic map

Figure 7.13   A Prewriting Semantic Map Created with *Inspiration*

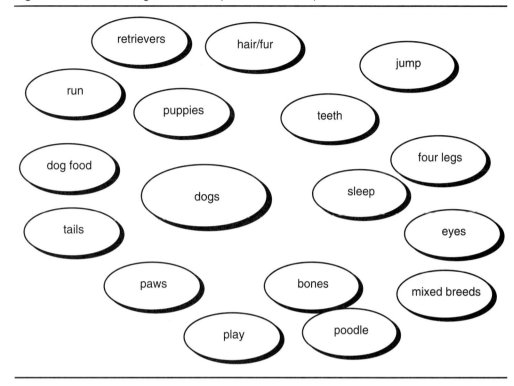

logical-
mathematical

spatial

logical-
mathematical

on a topic of the student's choice, such as the map about dogs that was prepared using Inspiration[1] software (Figure 7.13).

Next, tutors help their students categorize and link the concepts in the map. Most students usually require considerable help in this step, but the Inspiration software makes it easy to change categories and experiment with the arrangement of categories for writing purposes. Students then rank the categories according to the order in which they might place the information in a composition (Figure 7.14). (See also the section on K–W–L Plus in Chapter 12.)

Tutors then help their students think about how to organize the composition into an opening paragraph, subsequent paragraphs, and a closing paragraph. For example, in an expository voice composition about dogs, the student may decide that the opening paragraph might present a short history of dogs. Subsequent paragraphs may equal the number of categories included in the conceptual map (e.g., a paragraph about the breeds of dogs, dogs' physical attributes, dogs' activities, and preferred foods of dogs). A closing paragraph might present a summary of ideas in the composition.

Since writers usually discover new or "just thought of" ideas as they write, the university tutors encourage their students to incorporate these new ideas into the appropriate categories of their semantic maps. If necessary, students may decide to create an

---

[1]Inspiration is a software prewriting tool used for developing ideas and organizing thinking. Users can easily brainstorm and create maps, diagrams, and webs that may be converted to conventional outlines with just the click of a mouse. Inspiration is available from Inspiration Software, Inc., 7412 SW Beaverton, Hillsdale Hwy., Suite 102, Portland, OR 97225-2167. 1-800-877-4292 or http://www.inspiration.com.

Figure 7.14   Categorizing and Outlining from Semantic Map on Dogs using *Inspiration*

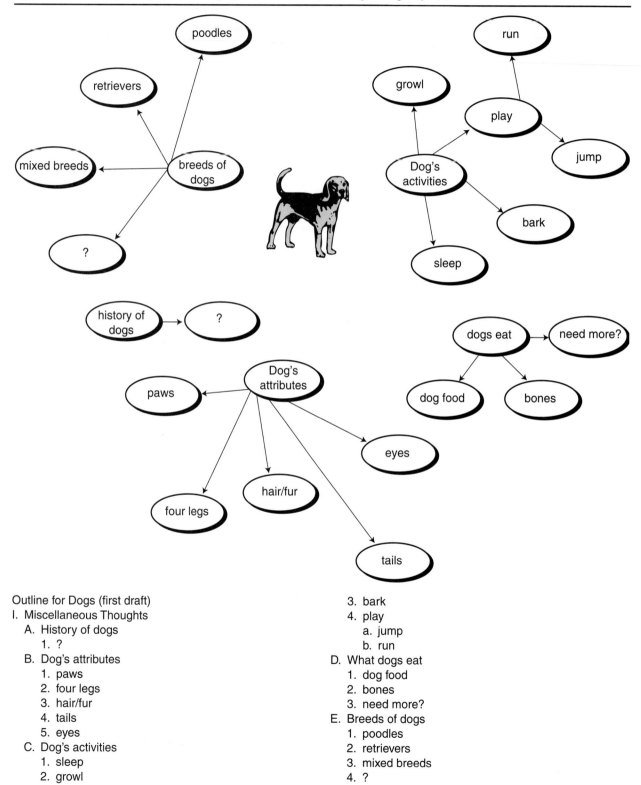

Outline for Dogs (first draft)
I. Miscellaneous Thoughts
   A. History of dogs
      1. ?
   B. Dog's attributes
      1. paws
      2. four legs
      3. hair/fur
      4. tails
      5. eyes
   C. Dog's activities
      1. sleep
      2. growl

      3. bark
      4. play
         a. jump
         b. run
   D. What dogs eat
      1. dog food
      2. bones
      3. need more?
   E. Breeds of dogs
      1. poodles
      2. retrievers
      3. mixed breeds
      4. ?

additional category for a new idea. In this way, they consciously choose to use the new information by inserting these ideas into the appropriate paragraphs in the composition.

The Creative Writing Process

Recognition of writing as a process began in the early 1970s. Researchers became less concerned with students' final writing products and more aware of the thinking processes students employ as they write (Solley, 2000). Through observations of pre-kindergarten–twelfth-graders, it was learned that writers ask themselves questions, determine what specific word and sentence structure choices to use in their compositions, and deliberately change the order of words, sentences, and paragraphs (Elbow, 1973; Emig, 1971). In the early 1980s, models of the writing process were developed that included planning, writing first drafts, and reviewing the developed composition (Harste, Woodward, & Burke, 1984). A second, more detailed model of the writing process evolved in the late 1980s that has great implications for classroom teachers. Termed *social constructivism* (Rhodes & Shanklin, 1993), this model focuses on the **recursive nature of writing** (i.e., writers discover "new" or just-thought-of ideas as they write and must go back and work those ideas into previously written material, as mentioned previously). The model also notes that good writing evolves from authentic experiences within a social community of learners where freedom of expression is encouraged (Calkins, 1983; Graves, 1983). From this social *contextualist* perspective, the writing process model was extended to include rehearsal (i.e., trying out ideas for writing), drafting, revising, and editing (Solley, 2000).

constructivist

Following social constructivism tenets, we believe that all good writing (i.e., authentic, honest, meaning-oriented) starts with experiences. Therefore, the starting point in our **creative writing** program is to provide diverse experiences for our students that give them a "natural thing to write about next" (Allen, Brown, & Yatvin, 1986, p. 463). The experiences we provide for our students complement their individual strengths and help develop their linguistic intelligence (Gardner, 1983, 1995, 1999). Some of the experiences we provide for our students include (1) reading, listening to, and discussing quality fiction and nonfiction; (2) inviting guest speakers to talk on wide-ranging topics such as dinosaurs, Great Britain, and rabbits; (3) designing, creating, and flying kites; (4) making and eating cakes and banana splits; (5) preparing a tea party for others; (6) presenting plays and Readers' Theatre productions for others to enjoy; (7) making a substance similar to Play-Doh to use as sculpture material; (8) creating and playing literacy board games; (9) walking outside to view clouds, toads, flowers, rain, or shadows; and (10) planning and participating in a Literacy Celebration Day at which food is served, students' work is displayed, and students, tutors, parents, grandparents, and classroom teachers have an opportunity to celebrate our students' literacy successes.

**logical-
mathematical
bodily-kinesthetic**

**spatial
naturalist**

interpersonal

Prewriting. Prewriting strategies help students generate ideas for writing and determine what they know or need to know about a creative writing topic. Several prewriting strategies our students especially enjoy are presented here.

1. *Drawing.* Often, our students explore ideas for writing and begin the writing process by representing their ideas through drawing. Drawing is a natural, visual prewriting strategy that all students find beneficial. More important, drawing is "especially motivational for youngsters who otherwise might be unreachable" (Sautter, 1994, in Sidelnick & Svoboda, 2000, p. 176) (also see Chapter 14). As Blecher and Jaffee (1998) note, drawing helps support "those students who are still in the margins" (p. 95). Drawing provides opportunities for students with special writing needs to represent what they want to write through another modality or symbol system other than print (Richards, Goldberg, & McKenna, accepted for publication). Drawing also allows students to sequence story events and keep track of details.

spatial

A Focus on SLL: The Language Experience Approach

With the language experience approach, the teacher takes advantage of students' experiences to motivate oral expression and develop reading skill. Students, either individually or in small groups, are led to dictate a story about a common experience to a teacher who functions as a scribe, editor, and language expander. The teacher interacts with the students to elicit elaborations when appropriate. Once the story is written down, the teacher and students analyze it for specific functions and structures. The first draft becomes an invaluable first step in language expansion.

For example, they can expand the syntax of the first draft. Starting with a sentence such as *The boy ran,* students can be led to add words for various slots and yield a sentence such as *The happy boy ran slowly through the yard.* Students can also expand their sentences by adding other clauses, or by applying sentence-combining activities.

Teachers also ask questions with the language experience approach that elicit more descriptive words or phrases or alternative ways of expressing thoughts, including standard English equivalents to vernacular dialects. Teachers can also teach vocabulary and comprehension through the use of semantic maps. In this way, the language experience approach is invaluable in teaching reading to linguistically diverse students. After discussion of an experience, these students can dictate a story in their vernacular that is written down in the native dialect with standard spellings. For example, notice the following hypothetical sample developed through students' experiences with an event, in this case a parade.

> My friend, he went to the parade. He don't like the crowd. He climb a tree and he saw the band. And he saw the float.

In order to elicit a first draft, the teacher asks facilitating questions to lead students to generate thinking and use language in social settings. The teacher could ask questions such as "Who went to the parade?" "What did he see or hear?" Students should be encouraged to express themselves in their natural language or dialect to generate language for a first draft of an experience story. Then, the teacher and students *together* revise the language by rephrasing or expanding on it. This leads the students to learn editing skills as well as develop an awareness for edited standard English. The teacher leads the students to produce a revised draft of their emerging text through discussion and questioning. For example, "Does this sound like 'school' language?" "Could we add new sentences or new information?" "Could we add some words, or take some out?"

> My friend went to the parade. He doesn't like crowds. He climbed a tree. He saw the bands. He saw the floats.

The teacher continues to ask questions to elicit responses for further revision and elaboration. For example, "Who is your friend?" *(Nathan)* "What kind of parade?" *(Mardi Gras parade)* "What kinds of bands and floats?" "Can we say/write some of these ideas in one combined sentence?" This will yield an elaborated text with more description and connective words:

> My friend Nathan went to the Mardi Gras parade. Since he doesn't like large crowds, he climbed an oak tree on the street corner. Then he saw the marching bands and the decorated floats.

The language experience approach uses the following five steps: discussing an experience, dictating, accepting without correcting, revising, and follow-up. Within each of these steps, the teacher engages the students through questioning and dialogue. The teacher may also use various adjunct aids, such as webs and maps for helping students organize their thoughts. Students learn their language skills through the writing-reading process in the social context of a classroom community.

2. *Drama enactments.* Drama is another way of preplanning and representing writing ideas that our students find helpful (see Chapter 14). In our program, individual students may perform or tell stories they want to write. In addition, small groups of students may collaborate and present a drama enactment that offers multiple perspectives about a single topic. For example, four sixth-graders recently worked together to plan their expository compositions about the November 2000 U.S. presidential debates and national election. Prior to writing, each student took a different perspective and played the part of one of the candidates.

interpersonal

3. *Speed writing. Speed writing,* also known as *free writing* or **quickwrites,** alleviates writers' anxieties about composing, helps writers generate ideas for writing, and frees writers from worrying about language conventions (Norton, 1993).

Figure 7.15   Story Features Map

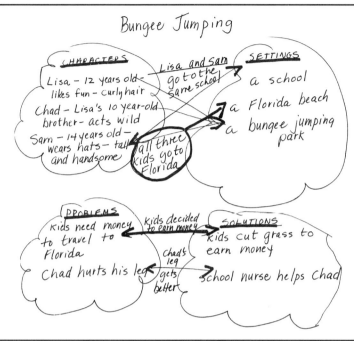

Participants in *speed writing* write nonstop for a certain amount of time (e.g., two to five minutes) without erasing, crossing out, or requesting help with spelling. The idea is to relax and let ideas emerge.

At the end of the designated writing time, authors share their efforts with the group. Listeners ask questions and offer comments and suggestions that may help authors clarify or further develop their work. As an extension to speed writing, we often write individual notes to students or tutors who have shared their speed writing to tell about sad, confusing, or worrisome times in their lives. For example, a student recently wrote about the death of her pet. When she finished reading her writing to our group we immediately created sympathy cards to offer her our support and express our concern.

interpersonal

4. *"Story features and their connections."* "Story Features and Their Connections" is a prewriting strategy that helps writers plan their imaginative stories in a thoughtful, organized, and interesting way by considering the four basic story features of characters, settings, problems, and solutions. To implement this strategy, tutors help their students fill in semantic maps based on their ideas about the specific feature they might include in a story. The story features map pictured in Figure 7.15 was created by a group of sixth-graders. The group decided to portray three characters named Lisa, Chad, and Sam; include three settings (i.e., a school, a Florida beach, and a bungee-jumping park); create two problems (i.e., a group of students needs money for a trip and Chad hurts his leg); and offer a solution for each problem.

spatial

When the story features map was filled in, the sixth-graders brainstormed how their story features might connect to one another. The map shows that the three characters connect to the Florida beach (i.e., a setting) because the characters travel to Florida. The map also illustrates how the problem of "needing money" is solved when the three characters earn money by cutting grass.

**logical-
mathematical**

After completing the map and determining the connections among the story features, the sixth-graders wrote a first draft of their story and titled it "Bungee Jumping." Once our students have a sound understanding of the four basic story features and their interconnections, their university tutors help them focus on other important parts and connections of well-formed stories such as episodes (i.e., a series of actions and happenings), and a resolution (i.e., the final outcome of a story). Tutors also assist their students in constructing the implied story themes pertinent to their story (i.e., the underlying ideas that tie the characters, goals, setting, and episodes together). For example, the students who composed the story "Bungee Jumping" decided that the themes of their story were, "Friends are important," "Friends help one another," "Never give up," and "Be a problem solver."

Drafting/Composing and Sharing for Feedback. As our students write first drafts of their imaginative stories, books, plays, and poems; write letters to favorite authors; and create recipes (Figure 7.16), we encourage them to concentrate first on their messages and to "spell and punctuate as they think best" (Allen, Brown, & Yatvin, 1986, p. 463). Good writers seldom worry about correct language conventions (i.e., spelling, punctuation, capitalization, and paragraphing) until they are ready to edit their work. During these composing sessions the university tutors circulate and interact among their students, offering encouragement and providing guidance if asked. The tutors also ask their students questions designed to encourage them to experiment with writing and further develop their work (e.g., "Tell me more about this new character in your story. I want to know what he looks like so that I'll recognize him if I meet him") (Graves, 1983). Additionally, we model with our own students how to use such reviewer forms as PQP **interpersonal** (Figure 7.17) so that writers can get necessary feedback for revision.

Revising and Editing. Revision is concerned with content; editing is concerned with mechanics. "Overemphasis on the mechanics of writing and neatness in the early stages of writing development often overshadows the ideas students are trying to express" (Searfoss, 1993, p. 12). Therefore, when our students' first drafts are completed, editing decisions are guided by each student's evolving literacy development and corresponding ability to complete revision tasks. It makes no sense to require a student to conduct extensive, personally meaningless revisions if she (1) is anxious and hesitant about writing, (2) has just begun to commit personal thoughts to paper, (3) is developmentally not ready to use conventional spelling or punctuation, or (4) has just begun to believe in herself as a writer.

Spelling problems especially "tend to inhibit many students who would otherwise be imaginative, intelligent writers" (Silva & Yarborough, 1990, p. 48). Therefore, we provide private spelling guidance for our students during editing conferences (see the section on spelling later in this chapter).

Publishing/Sharing. After our students complete any developmentally appropriate revision tasks and are satisfied with their work, the university tutors invite them to share their writing efforts with peers. In these sharing sessions, often using the format of the **author's chair,** students and tutors offer positive feedback to each writer (e.g., "I really liked the part in your story where the giant meets the wicked prince"), and each writer's efforts are applauded and celebrated as a literacy accomplishment. Following sharing, final revisions are made and final products published and are made available for others to enjoy (see James's book in Appendix K).

Implementing a Spelling Program

In developing students' competencies "spelling, although a small piece of the writing process, is of great concern [and presents some confusions] to teachers, parents, and the

Figure 7.16   Student Letter to a Favorite Author and Student Recipe for Cooking Turkey

thurs- 1-28-93
dear tomie depapla i hope you write
more stre ga nona Books. I like fin' mcod
and wath out for the chicken feet in
your soup. love sam yeur in tresdid reader

important sam's resahpeay
to coek a turkey you need a turkey

step 1. freze it!
step 2. thale it!
step 3. put sauce on it!
step 4. put it in the oven!
step 5. cook it for a Hour!
step 6. eat it!

Figure 7.17   Using Praise, Question, and Polish in the Revising/Editing Stage of the Writing Process

---

PQP Form for Peer Feedback

Writer/Author _____

Person Reviewing _____

Title of Writing _____

PQP = Praise, Question, Polish

1. PRAISE
    These are the things I particularly like about what you wrote:

2. QUESTION
    These are the questions I have about what you wrote:

3. POLISH
    I have these suggestions for making what you wrote even better.

general public" (Wilde, 1996, p. x; also see Solley, 2000). We believe that children's spelling is an extension of their overall language development and follows a natural progression from nonstandard to **conventional** (or "correct") **spelling** (Pappas, Kiefer, & Levstik, 1999). Students progress at their own pace. Therefore, we view our students' developmentally appropriate **invented spelling** (i.e., constructed by listening to the sounds heard in a word, and temporary until the conventional spelling becomes known) as an important part of their written language growth. Gentry (2000) states, "Like miscues in reading, invented spelling may be "windows into the mind" (Goodman, 1979, p. 3) that allow the observer to assess and teach not only spelling, but also important aspects of phonemic awareness, phonics [see Chapter 8], writing, and other essential elements of literacy" (p. 318).

We encourage our students to view themselves as writers who are capable of using interesting and dynamic words rather than confining themselves to just the spelling words that they have memorized. Consequently, we support students' use of individually constructed spellings in their dialogue journals, in their literature and prediction logs, and in initial drafts of their compositions. At the same time, we believe that our students need to develop an interest in spelling and that they should learn to value using conventional spelling in their "public" work so that others can read their writing. Thus, we also provide both nonstructured and structured spelling activities and lessons, and offer different strategies for students who have difficulty acquiring spelling naturally and effortlessly.

Nonstructured Spelling Activities. Since "writing provides the purpose for learning how to spell" (Bolton & Snowball, 1996, p. 1), many of our spelling lessons are placed within the context of each student's developmentally appropriate spelling needs during individual writing conferences. We also promote informal discussions about particular spellings of unusual words and talk about words that do not follow a particular spelling pattern when these words occur during instruction. Thinking and talking about spelling and focusing attention on words help our students become more proficient spellers and enhance their oral language and vocabulary as well.

Students also find it useful to record interesting words, words that do not follow a typical spelling pattern, past tense words, and words and their synonyms and antonyms in a word study notebook or personal dictionary (see the following section). Additionally, we serve as role models, demonstrating to our students how we value conventional spelling by proofreading and self-correcting our own spelling, using such resources as a dictionary, a thesaurus, and a computer spell-check system.

Structured Spelling Activities. Some structured spelling activities that our students find particularly helpful are *personal dictionaries, word categories* (also called *word sorting*), weekly *spelling meetings,* word games (e.g., "Begins With. . ."), and *cheerleader spelling.* These activities can easily be altered to suit the spelling needs of different age groups, SLL students, or students with special learning needs.

1. *Personal dictionaries.* **Personal dictionaries** provide a place where students can record new and unusual words they have discovered during tutoring sessions (e.g., reading or listening to quality children's literature and interacting with peers, tutors, and guest speakers), or words that they "absolutely" must have when they are composing. Personal dictionaries also facilitate students' gradual transitions from invented spelling to standard spelling by developing their awareness of spelling conventions and focusing their attention on the specific features of words such as number of syllables, affixes, medial vowels, and patterns.

intrapersonal   We make personal dictionaries for our younger students by stapling twenty six blank sheets of paper together and placing one alphabet letter (A to Z) on each blank

Figure 7.18   Example of a Personal Dictionary Page

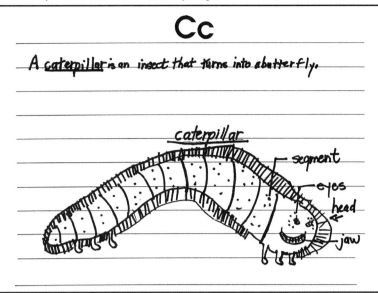

page. We cover the dictionaries with sturdy paper and print our students' names on the front (e.g., "Suzie's Dictionary"). Our older students prefer to use hardcover notebooks or binders with looseleaf paper to record their spelling words and organize them alphabetically. If necessary, we help students turn to the appropriate page to enter their new words in meaningful sentences in their dictionaries. Each new word is highlighted or underlined. For example, during a unit on marsupial animals, some of our students entered the word *marsupials* in their dictionaries on the M page by writing sentences such as *Marsupials are pouched animals* or *Pandas are marsupials.* In order to encourage students' explorations of multiple learning modalities (Bridges, 1995), we help our emergent writers draw illustrations next to each word to serve as a memory aid (see Figure 7.18). We provide time each week when students can share the words they have entered into their personal dictionaries. Students also discuss the meanings of their newly entered words and the various ways these words can be used in different contexts. Tutors use many of the words in students' personal dictionaries in the "Teacher Dictation" lessons described previously.

spatial

2. *Word categories.* "Word Categories" is a word sorting activity in which students develop a list of weekly spelling words relating to literature or to a thematic unit. Students then analyze and categorize the words in terms of their similarities, differences, and discrete or unusual aspects. For a list of fifteen to twenty words it may be possible to devise twenty to thirty categories. For example, after reading and discussing the story *Too Many Tamales* (Soto, 1993), a story about a Hispanic girl named Maria who takes her mother's diamond ring to "wear just for a minute," a group of third-graders developed the following list of spelling words: *desperate, tamales, diamond, Christmas, cousins, necklace, Hispanic, confess, stomach ache, bossy, scared, worried, demanding, celebration,* and *multicultural.* With their tutor's help, the students sorted the words into twenty categories: one-, two-, three-, four-, and five-syllable words; words that describe feelings; words that describe people; nouns; adjectives; words for holidays; words for jewelry; synonyms; words containing "silent" alphabet letters; words ending in *-ed;* words ending in *-ing;* compound words; words that begin with a consonant blend; more than one word;

**logical-
mathematical**

Figure 7.19   Cheerleader Spelling for the Word *They*

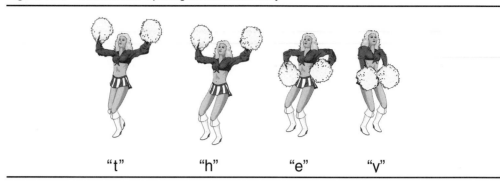

"t"   "h"   "e"   "y"

words with double consonants; and words for food. Students chose five of these words to enter into their personal dictionaries.

3. *Spelling meetings.* Scheduled weekly spelling meetings promote a spirit of genuine inquiry about spelling, encourage students "to be curious about words and to have a respect for the language they will use . . . [in their writing]" (Laminack & Wood, 1996, p. 81), and provide opportunities for students to explore the conventional spellings, letter-sound relationships and patterns, and unusual spelling attributes of interesting words they have discovered during the week as they read, write, and interact with peers, tutors, and visitors. In a typical fifteen-minute weekly spelling meeting, the focus is not on students' spelling errors (Bolton & Snowball, 1996). Rather, students and tutors explore useful strategies for figuring out how to spell difficult words (e.g., see Topping's [1995] cued spelling and Zutell's [1996] Directed Spelling Thinking Activity), and talk about words that are spelled in unexpected ways (e.g., *elephant, broccoli,* and *lettuce*). Students choose five of these words to enter into their personal dictionaries.

4. *"Begins with."* This game focuses students' attention on beginning components or sounds and spellings of words and expands students' vocabulary. To initiate the game, university tutors and their students sit in a circle. Then, a tutor or a student volunteer says, "Tell me all the words you can think of that begin with *c-a-n*" (or *p-e-n, p-r-e, a-c-t, b-e,* and so forth). Students take turns giving all of their ideas. For example, fifth-graders responded to words beginning with *c-a-n* with the following single-syllable and multisyllabic words: *can, candle, cannot, canoe, canvas, canopy, cantaloupe, canteen, canary, cancel,* and *Canada.*

5. *Cheerleader spelling.* Especially helpful for the bodily-kinesthetic learner, cheerleader spelling involves the entire body toward the goal of learning to spell conventionally. In cheerleader spelling (Rogers, 1999), students position their hands and arms either above their heads, at their waist, or to the floor to correspond to each letter in the word according to whether, when written on lined paper in lower case form, it is an ascender (i.e., *b, d, f, h, k, l, t*), between lines (i.e., *a, c, e, i, m, n, o, r, s, u, v, w, x, z*) or a descender (i.e., *g, j, p, q, y*). (See Figure 7.19 for the cheerleader spelling of the word *they.*) This activity requires that the student look carefully at the word, think about the letters and how they are written, and to engage in the physical movements that match each letter formation. Through cheerleader spelling, the form of the word can literally be felt, and the visual patterns of the words spelled in this way more readily recalled.

WRITING INSTRUCTION AND AUTHENTIC ASSESSMENT: A CONTINUOUS PROCESS

We agree with literacy experts who state that "writing is a developmental process that evolves much like oral language" (Glazer & Brown, 1993, p. 47; Pappas, Kiefer, & Levstik, 1999). Daily, systematic authentic assessment, conducted as our students write and respond to literacy lessons and activities, allows us to observe and understand the writing behaviors and processes our students employ. This ongoing approach to assessment also helps us concentrate on an individual student's progress over time rather than measure one student against another at one point in time.

Authentic assessment that takes place within the context of teaching and learning requires university tutors to (1) observe their students carefully as they write and interact with one another, (2) celebrate their students' writing strengths rather than concentrate on deficiencies, (3) "note what a student is developmentally ready to learn" (Glazer & Brown, 1993, p. 52), (4) document students' writing progress and the writing processes they employ guided by observation notes and writing checklists (such as the developmental writing checklist in Figure 7.4), and (5) reflect upon and consider what each student knows about written language. Studying this information provides university tutors with directions for future writing lessons. Thus, writing instruction and assessment merge and become a mutually supportive, continuous process (Glazer & Brown, 1993; Snider, Lima, & DeVito, 1994).

We have found that weekly spelling tests do not provide an accurate picture of what our students know about spelling. Therefore, we use other data to help us determine our students' ongoing spelling competencies. We particularly learn about our students' spelling growth by observing and recording information as our students write. Through careful observation we learn (1) whether our students attempt to spell unknown words, (2) whether our students use their personal dictionaries as spelling resources, (3) what strategies our students use when they attempt to spell unknown words, (4) whether our students proofread their work for spelling errors, and (5) students' developmental spelling stages. This type of authentic assessment focuses on students' spelling proficiencies and considers what students are ready to learn next about spelling. If a standard for reporting spelling progress is needed, the spelling tests provided in Appendix H can be used.

We also agree on the importance of helping students learn how to assess their own writing progress. "By engaging students in self-assessments students learn they are ultimately responsible for their own learning" (Tierney, Carter, & Desai, 1991, p. 59). We use four different formats to increase our students' involvement in self-assessing their writing: (1) shared observations, (2) postwriting questionnaires, (3) spelling questionnaires, and (4) portfolios.

Shared Observations

Students cannot begin to monitor or assess their own writing behaviors and progress until they know something about the processes good writers use, recognize their own composing behaviors, and "have some sense of their own [writing] success and growth" (Bridges, 1995, p. 8). Therefore, university tutors share their observation notes with each of their students in short, informal conferences (e.g., "Today I noticed that you re-read your story and edited your punctuation and spelling. All good writers edit punctuation and spelling when they are satisfied with the message they have written. Good for you").

Figure 7.20   A Self-Assessment Postwriting Questionnaire

Name: _____   Date: _____

This Piece of Writing
1. What part of the writing process was most successful for you (e.g., brainstorming ideas, composing, editing)?
2. What writing strategies did you use (e.g., "Story Features and Their Connections," semantic mapping, speed writing)?
3. What part of the writing process was least successful for you (e.g., brainstorming ideas, first draft, editing)?
4. What pleases you most about this piece of writing?
5. In which *voice* did you write?
6. Are you comfortable with this *voice* of composing? Did you choose to write in this *voice?*
7. What is the topic of this piece? Have you written before on this topic? Why did you choose to write on this topic?
8. How did you organize your writing?
9. What type of mechanical errors caused you the most trouble in this piece (e.g., capitalization, paragraphing, punctuation, spelling)?

Your Next Piece of Writing*
1. What topic interests you for your next piece of writing? Why?
2. For which audience will you write this next piece? Why?
3. How do you plan on gathering information for this topic?
4. How do you plan on organizing this piece of writing?

Or consider the following set of questions for younger writers.**
1. What's good about this writing?
2. What problems did you have as you wrote?
3. What prewriting strategies did you use?
4. What postwriting strategies did you use?
5. What would you like to try in your next piece of writing?

---

*See Norton, 1992.
**See Graves, 1992.

Postwriting Questionnaires

While not expected for every piece of writing, our students find it helpful to occasionally respond to a postwriting questionnaire when they have completed a piece of writing. Postwriting checklists (see also Glazer & Brown, 1993) and questionnaires serve as self-monitoring tools that help emerging writers of any age develop an awareness about their **intrapersonal**   writing behaviors (Figure 7.20). Such self-assessments can also be useful for portfolio assessments if completed at regular intervals (e.g., beginning, middle, end of a school year).

Spelling Questionnaires

Questionnaires designed to help students assess their spelling achievements and goals vary according to students' ages, the developmental stages of students' writing, and what teachers consider important about students' spelling. With their tutors' help, our students fill in the questionnaire shown in Figure 7.21 at least three times throughout the semester.

Figure 7.21 Spelling Questionnaire

Name: _____ Date: _____
Teacher: _____

_____ I am willing to attempt unknown words. (Bolton & Snowball, 1996, p. 36)
_____ I use invented spelling in first drafts of compositions.
_____ I know how to spell (easy) (some) (many) (difficult) words.
_____ I record interesting and unusual words in my personal dictionary.
_____ I am interested in learning how to spell words.
_____ I participate in our weekly spelling meetings.
_____ I try to edit my writing so that others can read my work.
_____ I try to notice how unusual words are spelled.
_____ I care about being a good speller.

Comments:

Portfolios

Our students keep all of the writing they accomplish throughout the semester in two different folders labeled "working portfolio" and "showcase portfolio" (Tierney, Carter, & Desai, 1991). **Working portfolios** house (1) the student's writing in progress, (2) work that may never be completed, (3) first drafts, (4) revision pages, (5) work generated during writing lessons and activities (e.g., speed writing efforts), (6) ideas for possible future writing (e.g., drawings, notes, concept maps, and pictures), and (7) copies of completed postwriting questionnaires. The working portfolio documents all of the student's writing during nonstructured, collaborative, teacher-guided, and creative writing activities.

Showcase portfolios contain examples of writing chosen by students because the work is special to them in some way. For example, each writing sample included in the showcase portfolio is accompanied by a short statement or caption that explains why the writer chose that particular piece for inclusion (e.g., "This is the first story I ever wrote"; "I worked very hard on the ending of this story"; "I want to be a ballerina when I grow up so I wrote a story about a dancer," or "This story is very special. I included an audio tape of two songs I created about the characters in my story.") We also encourage our students to include pieces in their showcase portfolios that represent their abilities to explore, use, and combine intelligences (Bridges, 1995; Collinson, 1995). For example, students may include samples of their drawings and paintings or photographs of their sculptures, murals, and dioramas that complement their creative writing efforts and combine verbal/linguistic and visual/spatial intelligences (Gardner, 1995, 1999). To further personalize their work, our students decorate the front covers of their showcase portfolios and include a reflective introduction to their portfolio (see Figure 7.22), a table of contents, photographs of themselves, and an autobiography (Collinson, 1995).

With our students' permission, both types of portfolios, working and showcase, are displayed during Literacy Celebration Day. Students' writing accompanied by **artifacts**

intrapersonal

spatial

Figure 7.22   Child's Reflective Introduction for a Showcase Portfolio

Introduction*

My name is Arthur. I will be entering the fifth grade at XX School. I created this portfolio during my summer tutoring session at the University of New Orleans. My tutor's name is Marcia L. I began making things for my portfolio on June 21 and completed it on July 20. I began deciding what to include in my portfolio on July 16.

I picked items that were important to me to include in this portfolio. I wanted to show what I had learned and I put all of my favorite projects in the portfolio. I also wanted to show that I am a hard worker.

The way I decided which things would go first in my portfolio was easy, I picked my favorite thing first. I had a list of everything I wanted in my portfolio and I just put it in order starting with my favorite item.

This portfolio shows that I kept a book list for my readings. It also shows that I have a prediction log that I use when I am reading stories. My portfolio shows what I learned through reading. I learned about hurricanes and sand dollars. It also shows that there are some things about my reading that I have to work on still.

My portfolio also shows the different types of writing I can do. I included a book that I wrote and illustrated. I also included some comic strips that I wrote the story for as well as a story that uses new vocabulary.

I think that my best items are the comic strips, my hurricane report, and my movie review. These activities were all fun and I learned a lot from completing each of these.

My portfolio shows the improvements I have made this summer. It shows what I can do. I can write a book if I use my imagination! It shows I can improve with practice and it shows that I am a hard worker.

*All names have been changed for purposes of privacy.

(i.e., products that complement students' writing, such as photographs or tapes of students' visual and performing arts accomplishments), provide our students and us with concrete evidence concerning individual students' improvements, efforts, personal writing interests, and perceptions about themselves as writers. More important, portfolios provide a way for our students to take some responsibility for organizing their work and help them self-evaluate their achievements and writing instructional needs.

SUMMARY

It makes sense to connect reading and writing instruction. Students' paths to literacy learning differ and the literacy learning modalities of reading and writing support and contribute to each other's development. It is especially important to connect reading and writing instruction for struggling readers, regardless of age. Many of these learners write very little because they have had few positive writing experiences. Because reading and writing develop concurrently, strengthening each other, it is crucial that students with reading difficulties have opportunities to write.

The role of the writing teacher in a corrective reading program is no different from that of all good writing teachers. Good writing teachers recognize that writing is a social process. They understand that their students learn about writing by writing for their own purposes and audiences.

Implementing a writing program for struggling readers entails collecting information about each student's knowledge and preconceptions of written language. Ongoing observation is also a necessity in order to assess students' everchanging progress and the processes they employ as they write.

Corrective reading students enjoy participating in nonstructured writing activities that allow them to write about subjects that interest and concern them. They also benefit from more structured writing lessons and activities categorized as collaborative, teacher-guided, and creative.

Portfolios provide a way for students to keep a record of their writing efforts. Artifacts (e.g., visual art, music tapes, or photographs) help complement students' writing and document students' abilities to combine intelligences. Most important, selecting and categorizing work to include in portfolios and making decisions about why the work is important gives students' opportunities to self-assess their writing.

Suggested Readings

Bolton, F., & Snowball, D. (1995). *Teaching spelling: A practical resource.* Portsmouth, NH: Heinemann.

Although writing provides the purpose for learning how to spell, students will not necessarily become competent spellers just by writing frequently. Students need to form hypotheses about how words are spelled, try out their ideas about how to spell words, receive feedback, and refine their hypotheses accordingly.

Bridges, L. (1995). *Assessment: Continuous learning.* York, ME: Stenhouse.

The art of teaching is knowing how to respond effectively at any given moment to students' instructional needs. Authentic assessment informs every aspect of teachers' decisions about student instruction.

Graves, D. (1992). Help students learn to read their portfolios. In D. Graves & B. Sunstein (Eds.), *Portfolio portraits* (pp. 85–95). Portsmouth, NH: Heinemann.

Before students can evaluate their own writing, they need to understand the characteristics of good writing. Graves

offers four approaches designed to help students learn to self-assess their writing.

Laminack, L., & Wood, K. (1996). *Spelling in use: Looking closely at spelling in whole language classrooms.* Urbana, IL: National Council of Teachers of English.

An informed, attentive teacher can create a powerful effective writing curriculum in which spelling grows out of students' own explorations with spelling as they write.

Pappas, C., Kiefer, B., & Levstik, L. (1999). *An integrated language perspective in the elementary school: An action approach* (3rd ed.). New York: Longman.

The authors offer theory, practical strategies, and ideas for thematic units that revolve around an integrated language perspective in elementary education. Readers learn how to foster students' authentic written language and the importance of integrating reading, writing, listening, speaking and thinking.

8 Word Recognition

After you have read this chapter, you should be able to:

1. explain the difference between products of word analysis instruction and the process of word recognition;
2. list the major areas of skill development for word recognition;
3. develop a sequence for instruction of a word unknown in print;
4. choose and develop materials and exercises appropriate for instruction in the process of word recognition;
5. devise an instructional program in word recognition for a student struggling in this area.

alphabetic principle	meaning clues	productive language
analytical vocabulary	meaning vocabulary	psychological set
automaticity	onsets	reading vocabulary
context	outlaw words	rimes
decodable text	perceptual unit	scriptal information
expectancy clues	phonemic awareness	sight vocabulary
fluency	phonics	sight words
grapheme	phonological awareness	structural analysis
key words	picture clues	syndrome
listening vocabulary	predictable text	visual synthesizing

Study Outline

I. Listening vocabulary
   A. Assessment
   B. Instruction
II. Sight vocabulary
   A. Assessment
   B. Instruction
      1. LEA
      2. VAKT
      3. Intensive word practice
III. Fluency
   A. Predictable language method
   B. Neurological impress method (NIM)
   C. Repeated readings
   D. Echo reading
   E. Readers Theater
IV. Word recognition strategies
V. Use of context clues
   A. Expectancy and picture clues
      1. Assessment
      2. Instruction
   B. Meaning clues
      1. Assessment
      2. Instruction
VI. Visual analysis
   A. Monosyllabic words
   B. Polysyllabic words
   C. Assessment
   D. Instruction
VII. Knowledge of word parts
   A. Assessment
   B. Instruction
VIII. Blending and synthesizing
   A. Assessment
   B. Instruction
IX. Summary
X. Suggested readings

Figuring out words unknown in print is only one of many processes used in constructing meaning from print. These processes are dynamic and interactive, changing as a student's knowledge and skills increase. For example, word analysis and word identification influence a reader's ability to understand what is read. What a reader understands in a passage or sentence influences the ability to decode other unknown words. These processes are symbiotic, reciprocal, and interactive. Thus, in this chapter, word recognition is conceptualized as an interaction among the skills learned (the *product* of word analysis instruction) with the way the student analyzes the unknown words (the *process* of word recognition). The more knowledge and skills readers have, the easier and more efficient word recognition will be, and the more fluent their reading will become. Further, the more background and understanding readers bring to the reading passage, the better will be their use of contextual analysis to decode unknown words.

The size of visual stimuli used for analysis is often referred to as the **perceptual unit** or unit of analysis. Reading instruction has a long methodological history, with method being closely related to the unit of analysis. Different methods have emphasized teaching symbol-sound correspondence using letters of the alphabet, syllables, words, sentences, or whole stories. Historically, students have learned to read successfully with each method.

Likewise, some students have trouble learning to read with each method, and different methods tend to yield different types of reading difficulties. You will find exercise examples in this chapter that focus on small units of analysis, such as word parts, but you will also find suggestions for teaching that use larger analytical units typically associated with a holistic or psycholinguistic view of teaching reading. Invariably, the goal of all decoding instruction is to develop independent readers who not only comprehend what they read but who also choose to read. We do not want to make decoding instruction so boring or laborious as to "turn kids off" to reading.

I believe that students with word recognition difficulties profit from learning a variety of analytic units, depending largely on the individual's specific strategy needs. I also believe that many, if not all, beginning readers must learn to analyze words, but that this analysis is only effective when they already know the words' meanings. If the word meaning does not exist in the student's *listening* (or understanding) *vocabulary,* all the effort to analyze the word is wasted because it does not trigger a meaningful response. Unfortunately, beginning readers and many corrective readers do not know whether the word exists in their understanding vocabularies until *after* they have worked to analyze the word. Only when they are sure their efforts have identified the correct word do they feel the possibility of success.

Sadly, these students have no sure way of determining whether they have misanalyzed a word or the word is new to them in terms of meaning. This dilemma facing the young or corrective reader disappears or lessens only with maturity in reading. The best defense against this dilemma is to *develop in the student, from the very beginning, the need to demand meaning from what is read.* If meaning does not result from analytic effort, the student must seek help. Further, students should have a balanced set of word analysis strategies and varied techniques to allow them to approach problem solving of unknown words with flexibility.

Teachers are advised to focus instruction on three long-term goals involving word study: (1) building a listening vocabulary, (2) building a sight vocabulary, and (3) building a balanced set of word recognition strategies. As a prerequisite for building a set of word recognition strategies, teachers need to be sure their students have well-developed phonemic awareness abilities (see the section on inadequate visual analysis later in this chapter).

LISTENING VOCABULARY

All teachers wish to support students in gaining knowledge. Frequently this means teaching new concepts and elaborating on more basic ones. Words reflect these concepts. When students have opportunities to experience new areas of knowledge, they learn new words and their meanings, thereby expanding their **meaning vocabulary.** This is referred to as **listening vocabulary** when the word is heard and understood in speech and as **reading vocabulary** when the word is read and understood in printed form.

Many students come to school with good listening vocabularies; they continue to add to their store of concepts and word meanings as they proceed through the curriculum. Some students, however, have limited knowledge of the world or nontraditional knowledge that is at odds with traditional expectations. World knowledge affects a student's attempts to analyze words unknown in print. No matter how hard students try to analyze a word, and no matter how accurate their analytical skills may be, they cannot trigger a meaningful response if the word is not in their listening vocabulary. To illustrate the point, try to pronounce the following words: *miscreant, putative, egregious*. If you have previously heard these words, chances are good that you will feel secure with their pronunciation. If not, chances are equally good that your pronunciation will be incorrect. Make several guesses (hypotheses) about the pronunciation of the words. For fun, if you don't know the meanings of these words, try to guess the meanings from the words provided.

miscreant	*putative*	*egregious*
mistake	reputed	helpful
hero	punishable	dreadful
degenerate	ugly	powerful
relapse	childlike	tolerable

If you still feel a bit insecure with their meanings, read the following sentences, which may help clarify them.

The *miscreant* defaced Michelangelo's *Pieta*.

Charles's terrier is the *putative* sire of the litter of pups.

Crashing into the train was an *egregious* mistake.

If you knew all the other words in the sentences, you may have used the context to identify the *meaning* of each word and thus you were able to understand the sentence. In all cases, however, the context may not be sufficient. Regardless, you *still* do not know how the word is pronounced because it is not yet in your listening vocabulary. Therefore, it is not in your meaning vocabulary; that is, outside of a textual presentation you are not able to associate a meaning with the word until you hear it used in a context from which you can derive its meaning. In reality, upon encountering such words while reading, mature readers attempt to use context and apply their graphophonic knowledge and do whatever is necessary to maintain the meaning of the passage. Sometimes the word is not important to the overall understanding of the passage and so mature readers skip it. If it turns out the word *is* important, mature readers consult a dictionary or ask someone. This kind of thoughtful behavior, a strategy, is something we need to teach students.

Assessment

Limitations in listening vocabulary are often detectable during oral reading and present a typical **syndrome,** or set of observable behaviors or signs. These readers seem quite successful in analyzing words except for a notable exception. When asked to figure out a word, they demonstrate knowledge of word analysis, blending skills, and use of context clues, coming close to an acceptable pronunciation, but still cannot come up with the word. This suggests that they do not know the meaning of the word being analyzed. Frequent occurrence of this behavior suggests that these students are meeting too many words with meanings they should but do not know.

If using standardized test results, teachers can compare vocabulary subtest scores and subtest scores that assess word recognition skills. When vocabulary knowledge is considerably weaker than other word analysis skills, a limitation has been identified. The *Stanford Diagnostic Reading Tests* (Karlsen & Gardner, 1995) are one of the few group standardized tests available that can be used for this purpose. Finally, another assessment procedure is to ask students directly if they know what a word means.

Instruction

Following are examples of activities recommended to expand listening vocabularies. These activities encompass many areas of the curriculum, so they are appropriate for any age/grade level.

1. Provide many and varied first-hand experiences.
   a. Arrange field trips, preceded and followed by discussions that are deliberately planned to use and review relevant vocabulary. As Durkin (1978) states, "Experience and vocabulary do not grow together automatically. . . . Teachers should have made some decisions beforehand about the concepts and words that ought to come alive as a result of the experience" (p. 380).
   b. Develop interest centers in the classroom, arranged and maintained by both teacher and students, using appropriate charts and labels. Such interest centers also provide discussion topics.
2. Provide vicarious experiences.
   a. Invite speakers to talk about relevant areas of study. Before and after the presentation, initiate discussion and elaborate on important concepts and vocabulary.
   b. Make full use of carefully selected appropriate media—for example, films, filmstrips, transparencies, tapes, models, and computer simulations.

spatial

3. Provide increased opportunities for silent reading of relatively easy materials and for reading aloud to students. Explanations and elaborations by authors frequently add dimensions of meaning. This activity is particularly important for more mature readers who lack experience in a particular area; such an activity could be conceptualized as learning about the world through books. Authors often help by giving context clues that define words or terms and elaborate meanings.
4. Guide the development and use of dictionaries that relate either to a topic of special interest to the student or to a group project or thematic unit.

spatial

   a. Have young children construct personal picture dictionaries.
   b. Have students construct personal spelling dictionaries (see Chapter 7).
   c. Have students construct personal vocabulary notebooks.
   d. Have students prepare alphabet books for a particular topic (e.g., see *Animalia* [Base, 1986], suitable for upper grades, or *The Icky Bug Alphabet Book* [Pallotta, 1986], suitable for younger students. Many alphabet books are available on a wide variety of topics to serve as models.).
5. Guide the direct study of words through such activities as listing synonyms, antonyms, or affixes and searching for word derivations.
6. Read aloud books emphasizing sensory impressions (selected children's literature can provide the stimulus for such exercises, e.g., *Click, Rumble, Roar: Poems about Machines* [Hopkins, 1987] and scores of books about animals).

musical

SIGHT VOCABULARY

Sight vocabulary refers to words in print that are recognized instantly and effortlessly. Mature readers perceive most words they encounter in this fashion. Most children entering school, on the other hand, begin with few or no words that they can read quickly with ease.

Students seem to learn words in three phases. At first encounter they do not recognize the word in print, although it may exist in their listening vocabularies. Then, with repeated exposure, they recognize it partially but still need to analyze its representation in graphic form. (These words make up the **analytical vocabulary;** the student says the word correctly but *not* quickly.) Finally, after several encounters, the word is recognized instantly. Every word that students read should be considered a candidate for their sight vocabularies, with the possible exception of rare, unusual, or foreign words. As a student reads more and more, words accumulate in the student's sight vocabulary and need no further study because they are recognized automatically (LaBerge & Samuels, 1974). The concept of **automaticity** is emphasized at both the word and word-element levels, because the efficient reader must learn these units so thoroughly that little effort is needed to recognize a new word or word part. Of course, automaticity is best achieved by practice in reading whole, meaningful text, not by isolated word drills.

The term *sight vocabulary* should not be confused with that of **sight words.** The latter term refers to a relatively small set of words in our language that do not conform to rules of pronunciation (also known as **outlaw words**), or to analytical techniques learned by children beginning to read, but that need to be made a part of one's sight vocabulary. Examples are *to, of, are, come,* and *you.* Also included are words that appear so frequently that they must be thoroughly learned as soon as possible. The Dolch (1953) list of 220 words and the Moe (1972a, 1972b) list of 210 high-frequency words account for over 50 percent of the words found in reading materials for children (and adults). Other lists of high-frequency words include the *Harris-Jacobson Core Words* (Harris & Jacobson, 1972), the *ESA (Educational Service Associates) Word List* (1977), the *Great Atlantic and Pacific Word List* (1972), and the Fry list of *Instant Words* (Fry, Kress, & Fountoukidis, 1993).

Sight words should be given high priority for every young child's sight vocabulary, but they should not be considered the only words to be learned to the point of instant recognition. Since sight words are usually words whose function is to connect other words, they often have no concrete referent. For this reason, use of phrases rather than isolated words provides a more meaningful presentation (e.g., *be good; here is a(n) . . .; there are . . .*). For a list of phrases based on the Dolch word list, see Rinsky's (1993) *Teaching Word Recognition Skills* (p. 73). Rinsky also makes a point of including words associated with the computer age as an essential part of sight vocabulary. She provides a list of about 130 such words (Rinsky, 1993, p. 75).

Assessment

Students who have not committed words to their sight vocabularies are relatively easy to spot. They do not recognize many words on a page. They frequently are word-by-word readers. When reading orally they analyze nearly every word, sounding out words or word parts with painful slowness. By the time they reach the end of the sentence they often have forgotten much, if not all, of what they read.

A sight vocabulary word can be recognized in about one-half second or less. The classroom teacher can assess this speed in several ways. A good source for words is the glossary found in the student's present texts, one of the high-frequency word lists, or words the student has been working on recently, such as words used in a language experience story or in a new thematic unit.

The following is a good group procedure for screening purposes. Construct a test using words from the texts available for student use, from graded word lists such as the *ESA Word List* (1977) or the *Basic Elementary Reading Vocabularies* (Harris & Jacobson, 1972), or from the word lists from a published informal reading inventory. On each line, type three or four words (depending on the maturity level of the group) of approximately the same difficulty level. Test item difficulty is increased by using words that are visually similar (e.g., *though, through, thought*) and decreased by using visually dissimilar words (e.g., *though, paper, statue*). Make copies for each member of the group and one for yourself to use as a key. A practice test is always a good idea, especially with young children, to help them know what to do when the test is given.

To prepare students for a speed test, the teacher should tell them the following:

1. This is a speed test, and not like real reading when you can look back and forth as much as you want.

2. You will have to hurry your looks (fixations). You may only have time to glance once at each word, then mark the one I say.

3. Some of you may have trouble with this test, but don't worry. If you do, we'll schedule some time to practice these and other words. It's okay if you don't do too well.

4. If you miss a word, be ready to go on to the next line.

In administering the test the teacher says the stimulus word twice, then allows about five seconds for pupils to respond before proceeding to the next item.

Scoring procedures are straightforward, with the number of items correct indicating the performance level. More important for screening purposes, however, is locating the stragglers in the group. Those who have done poorly on the group test should be further observed individually.

To assess individual students, make two typewritten copies of the words in list format (one word per line) and give one copy to the student. Ask the student to read the words to you as quickly as possible, while you check accuracy and rapidity from your copy (this reading might be tape-recorded for later analysis). Remember, accurate but slow is *wrong* for sight vocabulary. Words must be read accurately and quickly. For differentiation, words read correctly but slowly are referred to as being in a student's analytical vocabulary.

A second procedure is to make small typewritten or neatly printed flash cards from the word list and show them for about one-half second, allowing the student a moment to respond. If necessary, record the response on your copy of the word list from which the flash cards were made. These words can be used in sentences on the back of each card to test for recognition in context.

Instruction

Repetition and practice are key concepts for the improvement of sight vocabulary. Many students attain speed and accuracy simply by reading often and meeting the words in their books. Probably the most natural way of meeting common words repeatedly is through extensive recreational reading of relatively easy materials or materials chosen by the students, as in a literature-based program. This type of reading exposes the student to many known words that will assist recognition of those that are unknown. Books with **predictable text** (such as Eric Carle's *The Very Hungry Caterpillar,* 1987, or Bill Martin's *Brown Bear, Brown Bear,* 1982) contain a lot of repetition and provide an excellent source of easy reading, as do language experience stories and CD-ROM story books such as the *Living Books* series by Random House/Broderbund. The value of predictable language to reading fluency is further discussed later in this chapter. Predictable books are more like real language, while books with **decodable text** restrict the language used to words that are easily decoded (i.e., phonetically regular). There are relatively few examples of decodable books that provide meaningful text, which young readers need in order to learn how to use all the language cue systems together. Dr. Seuss books and *Fun with Zip and Zap* (Shefelbine, 1998) are examples of meaningful decodable books. Cunningham (1999) makes the point, "It is very hard to make much meaning if the text you are reading can only contain words you can decode and if you have only learned a few elements . . . 'Dan is in the van. Jan is in the van. The van is tan. Dan ran the van. Jan fans Dan.' Children learned to read this and did apply their decoding, but what did it mean? . . . If a child is just learning to read and the text being read makes no sense but is just there to practice decoding, some children will get in the habit of turning the meaning-making part of their brains off when they read" (p. 71). While there is sometimes a need to use decodable books for supporting a reader struggling with matching visual patterns with sounds, they must be supplemented frequently with real literature so students do not lose sight of the purpose for reading.

A more direct approach may be needed for students with more serious sight vocabulary deficiencies. These students often have had an unfortunate experience with a reading program or teacher overemphasizing analytical techniques or synthetic phonics. These students acquire the bad habit of looking for parts in all words rather than just unknown words. They try to sound out everything. Exercises that ask them to analyze words into smaller units *should be avoided*. Techniques that promote fluent reading, such as neurological impress, echo reading, repeated readings, and Readers Theatre (see the "Fluency" section in this chapter) are recommended.

Direct teaching of sight vocabulary words might proceed as follows (McNinch, 1981). The teacher recites a sentence containing the word to be learned and then writes the word, followed by several more sentences using the word, on the chalkboard, overhead transparency, or on sentence strips.

Teacher: "I *heard* you were sick."

(teacher writes)

heard

Mary *heard* a new joke.

Have you *heard* anything else?

John said he *heard* what you said.

Next, the teacher draws attention to the word in isolation by asking questions about it and providing practice in writing it, such as:

What letter does the word begin with?

What's the last letter in the word?

How many letters are in this word?

Spell the word.

Trace the word in the air.

Spell, say, spell, write the word.

Following this focus on the word's graphic form, students must read the word in a phrase or sentence or use it in a phrase or sentence created by the student. Students should also practice reading the word in whole text. The text might be one developed by the teacher or a book, poem, or language experience story.

Finally, independent practice must be provided. The word might become part of a game or the student could be asked to find the word used in other printed material such as books, magazines, or newspapers.

Three effective programs for increasing sight vocabulary are the language experience approach (LEA), Fernald's (1943) VAKT (visual, auditory, kinesthetic, tactile) approach, and intensive word practice (Moe & Manning, 1984). While the LEA can also be used to teach a word recognition strategy, the VAKT approach and intensive word practice are used specifically to help students learn *troublesome* sight words.

LEA. Many ineffective readers are motivated to increase their knowledge of the word recognition process when material that they have dictated is written down or typed for them. With the LEA, the teacher is also assured that the words used in follow-up activities are part of the student's listening vocabulary.

Any language experience material should be the result of a direct experience of the learner (or learners, in the case of a group production; see also the "Focus on SLL" box in Chapter 7). In addition to developing stories and accounts about field trips, an unusual classroom event, or the actions of a classroom pet, teachers plan many interesting *experiences* for students to write about. Some examples might include reading an exciting book to the students, working with clay or Play-Doh, making no-bake cookies, painting pumpkins for Halloween, performing a science experiment, or sharing family pictures. In the example that follows, the teacher gave each student a marshmallow and directed them to think about how it looks, feels, smells, and tastes. Then a group account was dictated.

The Marshmallow

A marshmallow is soft, white, and fluffy. It is shaped like a drum. It looks like a pillow. It's too small for a pillow. It can roll. The marshmallow smells sweet, airy, and delicious. It's squeezable. It's sticky. There is powder on the outside of it. It tastes like a sponge. It makes you want another one.

Following dictation, the teacher reads the entire account back to the students as they follow along. Any changes students wish to make to the account should be made at this time. (Note that this step also provides the teacher many teaching opportunities. For example, students may notice many uses of *it* and *it's*. If not, the teacher should point them out. The teacher can then ask about the referent for *it* and discuss the nature of pronouns in a real and meaningful context, since the students themselves created the account. In this particular example, a discussion of adjectives would also be appropriate. Additionally, features of words might be important to point out. In this example, features such as compound words, syllabication between two consonants, the vowel–consonant–silent *e* pattern, and the vowel-consonant pattern are among the possibilities. The teacher can also take this opportunity to expand conceptual knowledge by introducing material that discusses the marshmallow plant (see "Marshmallow" in *Childcraft: The How and Why Library*, 1971, p. 177).

Once material has been dictated and read by the teacher, the student reads it. Even if the material is just a caption for a picture drawn by the student, the words from the material are used in many ways to ensure repeated exposures. First, the student should write each word in a personal dictionary with a self-generated sentence or picture or both. In this way, if the student comes across one of the words again and cannot remember it, the teacher can direct the student to his personal dictionary to find the word. The sentence and/or picture will provide the needed help. Not only are new words learned through this approach, but alphabet knowledge and dictionary skills begin to develop, as does a strategy for becoming an independent reader.

Additional activities, such as matching words from students' stories put on cards to words found in other printed material (e.g., basal readers, story books) and playing sight vocabulary games such as a vocabulary version of bingo, are appropriate. The teacher should insist that the word be pronounced each time it is matched, or encountered in the game. Arranging word cards to form sentences also reinforces recognition of the words in other contexts. Any teacher concerned that the words students use in their language experience stories will not help them in other reading tasks need only compare those words to a word list such as Fry's.

As soon as possible, students should do their own writing of stories. Students' efforts at writing will not only help them learn the nature of written language, but writing also focuses [students'] attention on the visual features of print, aiding letter and word recognition" (Noyce & Christie, 1989).

Students with very limited sight vocabularies can be provided sentence starters to get them going. Initially, high-frequency words can be used to create *pattern books*. These are merely sheets of paper stapled together. For instance, the teacher might provide several sheets of paper with *I like to eat* _____. written on each. The student then draws a picture of the food and the teacher writes the word for the food item on the blank line. This is done for each page. When completed, a cover with a title such as *"Things I Like to Eat* by Kalisha" can be created and attached to the stapled sheets. Of course, Kalisha then reads the book. Many words can be taught this way. Other examples of sentence starters are:

I like to play _____.

I like to go _____.

_____ are big.

_____ are little.

My favorite _____ is _____.

bodily-kinesthetic   **VAKT.** The VAKT approach begins with the teacher eliciting a word from the student that the student wants to learn. This word is written or printed in crayon on a strip of paper, in letters large enough for the learner to trace by direct finger contact. The student is then shown how to trace the word and told how to pronounce it at the same time. Following the teacher's example, the student traces and pronounces the word. This continues until the student feels ready to write the word from memory. If the student is successful, the session is terminated. If not, tracing continues. Words successfully written from memory should be checked for recognition later in the day or the next day.

After a period of time that varies from learner to learner, the student reaches a point at which tracing can be eliminated. Instead, someone pronounces the word and the student looks at it and repeats it as often as necessary, until she can write it from memory. If the written word is incorrect, the student looks at the word more carefully while pronouncing it and tries once more to write it from memory. Strict use of the VAKT approach, which includes charting the number of times a word needs to be traced before it is learned, is probably not necessary for most students. Usually the tracing technique itself is sufficient.

Intensive Word Practice. Intensive word practice (Moe & Manning, 1984) also uses a multisensory approach. Usually, three to six new or troublesome words are randomly placed among other words in each of four sections on a word practice sheet (Figure 8.1). Sentences using the new words in a meaningful context are placed beneath the four sections. The procedure emphasizes listening skills and following directions as well as practicing troublesome words, and can be used with a group.

First, the students are directed to fold the paper on the bottom line to separate the sentences from the word boxes. They should see only the numbered boxes. Next, the students are instructed to fold the paper again on the line that separates boxes 1 and 2 from boxes 3 and 4. Finally, the students are directed to fold the paper on the vertical line so they can only see box 1.

The teacher has previously prepared large word cards, each containing one of the new words to be learned; for this example, cards are needed for *this, was,* and *in*. The teacher gives the directions for box 1, instructing the students to mark in some way each of the new words while the teacher pronounces the word and shows the word card. Two repetitions of the word should be sufficient. For example, while showing the word card for *this,* the teacher might say, "I want you to draw a circle around *this.* Draw a circle around *this.*" While showing the word card for *was,* the teacher might say, "Put a line under *was.* Put a line under *was.*" Likewise, for the word card *in,* the teacher might say, "Draw a box around *in.* Draw a box around *in.* Now turn your paper over so you just see box 2."

The directions for box 2 also instruct the students to mark the new words. This time, however, the teacher shows but does not pronounce the word. It is hoped that the

Figure 8.1   Example of an Intensive Word Practice Sheet for Three New Sight Words: *this, was, in.*

1			2		
	boy	was		this	on
	on	in		was	the
	the	this		in	boy
3			4		
	on	in		boy	on
	the	was		in	was
	this	boy		the	this

1. My milk is in this cup.
2. Mother was in the house.
3. This is the dog I like.

students are mentally pronouncing the words as they look back and forth from word card to paper. The directions proceed as follows: "Put a line under _____" (while showing *was*). "Draw a box around _____" (while showing *this*). "Draw two lines under _____" (while showing *in*). Students are then directed to refold their papers so only boxes 3 and 4 can be seen.

For box 3 the teacher pronounces the word but does not show it. All directions are oral. "Put a line under *this*." "Draw a circle around *in*." "Draw a box around *was*."

For box 4 the students are simply told to circle the three words practiced in the lesson. Success with box 4 indicates that the student has at least visual memory for the words taught. Not until the sentences are read at the bottom of the page can the teacher judge whether the students have learned to pronounce the words as well. Students are asked to underline the new words in the sentences and to read the sentences.

The following exercises, and many like them found in developmental texts, activity books, and microcomputer software, are used to develop the habit of looking at words rapidly, and can readily be developed into learning game formats.

spatial

1. Read along with interactive CD-ROM stories, or "talking books." Many excellent interactive animated stories are available that highlight the words while they are being read aloud for students to follow. CD-ROM storybook software assists readers in constructing meaning (Glasgow, 1996) and "enhance[s] literacy acquisition, especially for SLL and students experiencing difficulties with the code" (Nikkel, 1996). Labbo (2000) lists twelve things to do with a talking book in a classroom computer center. Recommended publishers are Random House/Broderbund (415-382-7818) and The Learning Company (800-227-5609).

2. Exercises emphasizing expectancy or context clues.
   a. A snowman melts in the _____.
      sun   cold   man
   b. The bird is in the _____.
      boy   tree   table

3. Exercises requiring quick scanning of a group of words.
   a. See how fast you can find the word that does not belong in each list. Put a line through it.

1	*2*	*3*
boy	dog	pie
girl	look	cake
pipe	bird	much

   b. Put an X by the things you can find in the food store.

meat	soup	dogs
house	candy	cans
eggs	truck	milk

4. Activities and games using individual words.
   a. *Fish pond.* Make word cards with a new (or review) vocabulary word on one side and an easy sentence on the other side with the word underlined. Affix a paper clip to each. Attach to multiple varieties of paper fish created by students. Put in fish pond. Attach a small magnet to the end of a fishing pole. If a player fishes out a word and reads it correctly and quickly, 2 points are scored; if the sentence helps the player say the word, 1 point is scored. Any number of students can play.

spatial

b. *Star Trek.* Invite students to create a large poster board with slots to hold cards placed at appropriate intervals representing the route of a space trip to a worm hole (or wherever). Make a stack of cards, writing a sentence on each one containing the word being practiced. The word should be underlined and in isolation above the sentence. Students take turns drawing from the stack of cards. If they read the word correctly, they put the card in the appropriate slot marking the next step in a trip through the galaxy. This game is best played with two to five students, depending on the number of slots; if more than one poster is created, teams could compete.

c. *Bang.* Make a "bang" card for every five word cards. The word cards have the word of interest on one side and a sentence using the word on the other. (This 5-to-1 ratio can be changed depending on how long you want the game to last: the more "bang" cards, the longer the game will last.) Cards are placed in a bag or box and students take turns drawing them out one at a time. If a word card is drawn and the word pronounced correctly within two seconds (one student acts as a timekeeper in charge of the stopwatch), the card is kept. If the sentence needs to be read to pronounce the word, that one card is returned to the bag. If a "bang" card is drawn, *all* word cards collected up to that point are placed back in the bag. This element of chance enables learners of different abilities to play together and also provides the necessary repetition of new words. The first player to collect five (or three or ten) words is the winner. Several students could play together as teams.

5. *Activities for adolescent readers.* While the Bang game may be suitable for any age, students in upper elementary and middle school generally require more age-appropriate activities for practicing words, even though their abilities may be closer to those of much younger students. Curtis and McCart (1992) present several gamelike activities using words that are more challenging both linguistically and cognitively (e.g., *flammable, combustible, rayon, crayon, mayonnaise*). Their suggestions often have students working in pairs, which further encourages the students to want to work hard. One of their examples is Beat the Clock, a speeded word recognition activity. Student pairs record the time it takes them to read through the words. Timings at the beginning and end of the week give a gauge of progress. Points can be awarded (p. 398).

FLUENCY

Fluency refers to more than just smooth, automatic reading, or to a quick reading rate, it also includes the "ability to read in expressive rhythmic and melodic patterns" (Richards, 2000, p. 535). As such, there are three interactive aspects to fluency: rate or pace, smoothness or automaticity with accuracy, and *prosody,* or reading with expression, natural intonation and appropriate phrasing. One common goal of corrective reading instruction is to develop fluent readers.

The instructional methods provided here are intended to increase reading fluency, which in turn should enable the ineffective decoder of any age or grade level to focus more on meaning than on individual words (Samuels, 1988). The increased amount of practice in reading whole text should also increase the automatic recognition of words.

Predictable Language Method

musical

The predictable language method takes advantage of the rhythmic, repetitive, and redundant language structures in children's storybooks and nursery rhymes (Walker, 2000). It assumes that word identification is facilitated by the predictive nature of the material.

Choose a book that contains a predictable pattern such as Bill Martin's (1970) *The Haunted House* ("One dark and stormy night I came upon a haunted house. I tiptoed into the yard. No one was there. I tiptoed onto the porch. No one was there. . . ."). The material should first be read aloud to the students completely through so they can hear the whole story. During this reading, emphasize the predictable parts using an enthusiastic voice. Now the students are ready for a second reading. During the second reading, ask the students to join in whenever they feel they know what to say. During subsequent readings, an oral cloze procedure can be used to give students practice in predicting upcoming words in text. Finally, students are ready to read the book on their own, using the predictable language pattern and picture clues to aid them. Students can also be asked to write their own story, using the same predictable pattern found in the book but changing the characters and/or setting. For example, the haunted house might become *The Haunted School* with a whole new set of spaces and rooms to tiptoe through.

Neurological Impress Method (NIM)

In the neurological impress method (NIM), the student and teacher read orally in unison (Heckelman, 1969), sitting side by side, with the teacher slightly behind on the right side in order to read into the student's right ear. The teacher's voice will actually be a bit ahead of the student's, especially if the student has a limited sight vocabulary. The teacher thus models fluent and expressive reading and allows the student to experience the way that feels. The teacher does not stop when the student falters. The student is directed to continue to read with the teacher as much as possible. The teacher should move a finger along the line of print being read so the student can follow more easily. This method does take some getting used to; initially using short, rhythmic, and repetitive materials, such as poems or song lyrics, might prove helpful.

Bedsworth (1991) reports impressive gains for middle school students who used NIM only ten minutes each day for nine weeks. All three students made significant gains—3½ years in nine weeks for silent reading. In addition, students' attitudes and perceptions about their reading became more positive. Bedsworth speculates that NIM works because it provides a nonthreatening reading experience; it is a novel approach; the attention of the learner is focused through visual, auditory, and kinesthetic-tactile modalities; and students read in units rather than word by word.

The opportunity for students to read or follow along with an expert reader also exists through the use of audiobooks. In addition to freeing the teacher to work individually with a larger number of students, Baskin and Harris (1995) provide information on many other benefits of using audiobooks, especially in the secondary classroom. Audiobooks will enable older students to experience age-appropriate literature as well as enhance their reading fluency if they attempt to read along with the recording.

Repeated Readings

In repeated readings, a self-selected passage is re-read orally until it is read accurately and fluently (Samuels, 1979/1997). Repeated readings encourage the use of contextual meaning and sentence structure to predict upcoming words and to correct miscues. The student chooses the material to be read. The teacher should make a copy of the passages that will be used for repeated reading so that notations can be made as the student reads. The student reads and the teacher records errors and speed. These numbers are charted on a graph. The student then practices re-reading the material silently. (During this time the teacher can work with another student.) The student then re-reads the passage aloud for the second time while the teacher records errors and speed using a different ink color. Again these numbers are charted and any progress noted. This procedure is followed until a speed of 85 words per minute is achieved. A substantial amount of research shows that the process of repeated readings "helps students remember and understand more, increases their oral reading speed and accuracy, and seems to improve students' oral reading expression" (Dowhower, 1989; National Reading Panel, 2000). Additionally, a modification that supports a cooperative learning approach through the use of partners, called *paired repeated reading* (Koskinen & Blum, 1986), also seems to be effective and easy to manage in regular classrooms.

Echo Reading

Echo reading is similar to both the neurological impress method and the repeated readings procedure in that the student is following a teacher's model and may need to repeat the reading that is being imitated. In echo reading (Walker, 2000), the teacher reads one sentence of text aloud with appropriate intonation and phrasing. The student then tries to imitate this oral reading model. The text reading continues in this fashion until the teacher feels the student can imitate more than one sentence at a time. This technique allows students to read text fluently that they otherwise may not have been able to handle. This technique can also be used in conjunction with repeated readings or the neurological impress method to model particularly troublesome sentences. Echo reading is quite helpful for the student who needs a model of fluent reading—for instance, students who focus too much on the words in a passage rather than the meaning, or those who show no concern for whether their oral reading sounds like fluent language.

Readers Theatre

Readers Theatre provides a realistic opportunity for students to read orally and practice their use of intonation, inflection, and fluency. In Readers Theatre (Sloyer, 1982), students present a dramatic interpretation of a narrative passage through an oral interpretive reading. Character parts are assigned or selected by participating students, and appropriate parts for oral reading are identified and then practiced silently. Following practice, the students read their scripts orally for an audience. (Props and costumes are not necessary.) The mood of the story is conveyed through proper intonation and phrasing. This technique is especially helpful not only for fluency, but also for comprehension. When deciding what should be included in the script, the students must decide what is important in terms of dialogue and narration to the understanding of the story. Once again, the opportunity for repeated readings is present. Research by Martinez, Roser, & Strecker (1998/1999) demonstrates that use of Readers Theatre increases reading rate. For more on Readers Theatre, visit http://www.acs.ucalgary.ca/,dkbrown/readers.html and http://www.aaronshep.com/rt/.

WORD RECOGNITION STRATEGIES

The following word recognition strategies give students the needed flexibility to identify and analyze unknown words. Sometimes students need to use only one of these processes. At other times, two or more are needed and are used either separately or together as parallel processes. The five word recognition processes to be discussed are as follows:

1. Context clues
   a. Expectancy clues
   b. Picture clues
   c. Meaning clues
2. Visual analysis
3. Knowledge of word parts
   a. Structural analysis
   b. Phonic analysis
4. Blending and synthesizing
5. Dictionary skills

Parallels can readily be seen between these word recognition processes and the major skill strands recognized by many reading instructional systems today: namely, sight vocabulary, contextual analysis, phonic analysis, structural analysis, and dictionary skills. The skills are usually sequenced from easy to difficult, according to an author's or a curriculum committee's logic and experience. Thus, skill sequences vary from one school district to another, with differences ranging from slight to considerable. When a student changes from one district to another that is quite different, the teacher must monitor progress carefully to ensure that the student does not experience learning gaps during the transition.

Most reading curriculum guides indicate a scope and sequence of word recognition skills (Figure 8.2). Teachers must know the scope and sequence used in their school, particularly the skills taught in immediately preceding and subsequent years. If a school system does not provide scope and sequence information, teachers must do their own analyses and assume that, in general, the students have received skills instruction randomly or on a basis other than that represented here. In whole-language classrooms, these skills are generally learned when opportunities present themselves, and always in the context of whole text (see Mills, O'Keefe, & Stephens, 1992).

USE OF CONTEXT CLUES

Expectancy and Picture Clues

Two important context clues, **expectancy clues** and **picture clues,** relate directly to understanding what is about to be read. Expectancy clues are related to **psychological set;** that is, when people are introduced to a topic, certain related concepts rise to the thresholds of their minds. These ideas, especially the words associated with them, become more readily available from memory storage. In essence, the nonvisual information, or schemata, that the reader has for a topic is activated. When teachers introduce new material to develop background and experiences, they promote the use of expectancy clues. For example, when students know they will be hearing a selection about how birds build their nests, the words they expect to hear are quite different from those expected in a story about a fire in the basement. Teachers might begin by asking students what they already know about birds building nests, and then writing these ideas down so the students can see the words they have used.

Pictures also function as clues to readers, suggesting certain sets of words that might occur in the story. A picture of two youngsters playing on a raft in a pond elicits many

Figure 8.2   One Curriculum's Scope and Sequence for Word Recognition Behaviors

Emerging Abilities
1. Learning letter names
2. Developing awareness of letter-sound relationships
3. Hearing similarities and differences in beginning and ending phonemes
4. Recognizing rhyming sounds
5. Demonstrating left-to-right orientation
6. Tracing, matching, and copying letters and words
7. Demonstrating awareness of word boundaries in writing
8. Pointing to known words while being read to

First Grade
1. Begin alphabetizing skill (picture dictionary)
2. Begin using initial consonants in a modified cloze (use of context)
3. Begin consonant digraphs with context
4. Begin consonant blends with context
5. Begin short vowels with context
6. Begin spelling patterns
7. Begin final consonants with context
8. Begin initial and final consonant substitution with context
9. Begin common inflectional endings with context
10. Begin long vowels with context
11. Begin common suffixes with context
12. Begin compound words with context

Second Grade
1. Review previous letter-sound correspondences
2. Begin unusual consonants and consonant digraphs (*c, g,* silent *t*) with context
3. Begin unusual vowels *(y)* with context
4. Begin vowel digraphs and diphthongs with context
5. Introduce schwa with context
6. Begin *r*-controlled and *l*-controlled vowels with context
7. Introduce concept of syllabication (# of vowel sounds = # of syllables)
8. Continue compound words
9. Continue suffixes
10. Begin prefixes with context
11. Begin spelling changes involved in suffixes and inflected endings

Third Grade
1. Review previous letter-sound correspondences
2. Begin difficult consonant blends (triple letters)
3. Begin unusual and difficult vowels and vowel clusters
4. Introduce structural analysis (concept of roots and affixes, compounds)
5. Introduce more complex spelling patterns
6. Introduce two- and three-syllable words (syllable patterns)
7. Begin inductive teaching of consistent phonics rules and their application
8. Begin dictionary skills using diacritical markings and pronunciation spellings

words in the mind that are different from a picture of the same children working to build a raft for the pond. Thus, both expectancy and picture clues help the reader anticipate words that might occur in a selection or segment of a story. These concepts are closely related to ideas regarding a reader's ability to organize mentally the material about to be read. Obviously, this ability is also related to background and experience, or **scriptal information** (Pearson & Johnson, 1978), as will be discussed in Chapter 11. Some students who have difficulty using context clues often do not have the conceptual development for dealing with the ideas found in many classroom reading materials. Understanding is thus unlikely, and decoding such content has little value. More familiar material must be used in these cases. Students' own language experience stories are an appropriate beginning.

Assessment

Students will have problems with expectancy and picture clues if they cannot anticipate what may happen (what words may be present) in a story about a given topic, a given set of illustrations, or both. A good way to directly assess a student's ability to use these clues is to ask questions before reading.

> "The selection we are going to read today is about Neil Armstrong, the first man on the moon. What special words do you think we will meet in this selection?"
>
> "This paragraph will tell us how the pioneers kept warm in the winter. Before we read, let's guess how they might have done it."
>
> "You're right, Shayne. This is a picture of the wolf in bed waiting for Little Red Riding Hood. What words do you think we will need to know in this part of the story?"

Notice that these questions are to be answered orally; while the teachers have no objective measures of expectancy, still they can identify those who are having considerable trouble anticipating forthcoming events and the words possibly associated with them. Difficulty may be the result of not being able to use expectancy clues adequately, or inadequate experiential, conceptual, or language background. The best way to differentiate among these is to sample behavior across a wide variety of content.

Instruction

Techniques to improve the use of expectancy clues generally give the stimulus (the subject or topic of concern or a picture portraying it) and call for **productive language** from the student—that is, generating or identifying possible words that may appear. This process differs from reading, which is a receptive language process. The following activities are suggested.

1. Activities to develop use of expectancy clues
   a. Have small groups or individuals prepare to write a story about a given topic of interest. Before students begin writing, the teacher should promote a discussion of words to be used in the story, writing some on the chalkboard as the discussion proceeds.
      (1) For beginning readers, use techniques involved in the LEA, in which the teacher does the writing.

bodily-kinesthetic
      (2) The Fernald (1943) technique or modifications thereof should be used as soon as possible.
   b. Use exercises requiring knowledge of a particular topic.
      These words are about cars, airplanes, or both. Mark the words about cars with a *C;* mark the ones about airplanes with an *A;* and mark those about both with a *B*.

_____ hood	_____ landing	_____ engine
_____ wings	_____ wheels	_____ garage
_____ body	_____ bumper	_____ tail

2. Activities to develop expectancy through use of picture clues

spatial
   a. Display a picture with several different items on it, such as the produce in a market, candies in a store window, or a barnyard scene. Ask the students to name the items;

write them down for further reference. Or use students' own drawings prior to writing about them.

b. Show a set of two to four pictures (comic strips are a good source). Tell the students the pictures can be arranged to tell a story. Ask them to arrange the pictures. They may then choose partners and tell each other (or the teacher) their stories.

c. Call attention to a picture and talk about what may be expected to come next in the story. Verify predictions after the story is read.

Meaning Clues

Meaning clues are more specific to the content being read than expectancy and picture clues. **Context,** as related to meaning clues, is defined as the words surrounding a target word. The target word represents the unknown word to be decoded. Meaning clues often exist within the sentence being read, but they can also exist within phrases or other sentences. Context usually restricts alternative words that fit meaningfully into the slot represented by the target word. Consider the following examples:

As the _____ began to rise into the air, his pole bent.

She put the cake mix in the bowl, then _____ one-half cup of water.

Meaning clues can be used effectively for analyzing unknown words only if the surrounding words are easily read. When the reading matter is too difficult, the reader becomes discouraged and may guess more and demand less meaning from the passage.

Assessment

Students who do not use meaning clues might lack scriptal data or have poorly developed language skills, but more likely they have not been shown how to use such clues. These students can be identified by comparing their analysis of unknown words in isolation to their analysis of unknown words in context. Analysis of a word in context should be easier than analysis of the same word in isolation because language and context limit the word choices that fit meaningfully. If students have learned to *demand meaning* from every sentence they read, they are more likely to be aware of their difficulty and of the unknown word. If not, a major teaching task has been identified (see Chapter 10 for strategies to teach use of context clues to infer word meanings).

Teachers should suspect inadequate use of context when a student makes wild attempts at an unknown word. Wild guessing indicates misuse of context and lack of word analysis skills. Also, many substitutions that graphically resemble the actual word but are semantically incorrect (e.g., *horse* and *house*) and substitutions that are not self-corrected indicate inadequate use of meaning clues.

Teachers can structure a set of tasks to evaluate the student's ability. Select a few words the student does not know, using one of the methods discussed earlier in this chapter. Present the words first in isolation, then in context. If trouble with the words occurs consistently *in both settings,* the student is probably not using context as an aid to word recognition. The following illustrates the two settings, words in isolation and words in context.

Words in Isolation	*Words in Context*
train	We heard the whistle as we walked along the _____ tracks.
night	It was very dark that _____.
stone	Tim felt a sharp _____ under his foot.
wrong	The car was going the _____ way down the one-way street.

Instruction

Techniques for developing the use of meaning clues should be presented in larger discourse units in order to take advantage of all available language clues. It is advisable to begin with easy materials. If the student has to guess too many words, language clues will be obscured. I recommend beginning with a ratio of about one target word for every fifteen to twenty words. Once students understand how the process works and what they are supposed to do, the ratio can be decreased.

The standard deletion ratio of one deletion every fifth word suggested for *assessing comprehension* (Bormuth, 1967, 1968a, 1968b; Rankin & Culhane, 1969) is inappropriate for teaching the use of context clues as an aid for analyzing unknown words because it distracts from the analytical task at hand and asks the student to guess too frequently. The task can be discouraging for readers who are already frustrated with the reading task. Alternatives to reduce this frustration include using a sentence or two with one word deleted, using a multiple-choice format (maze), and adding letters or other word parts to the slot. The following are representative activities.

1. Exercises using thought units of a paragraph
   One day when the lion was looking for food, he walked into a trap. The trap was made of strong _____, and the lion couldn't get out. The lion jumped this way and that way. He tried and tried. All day _____, the lion worked to get out of the trap. But he couldn't get _____.
2. Riddles with meaning clues that give the answer
   It has four legs.
   It has a back.
   You sit on it.
   It is a _____.
   dog   cat   chair
3. Exercises using the meaning of a sentence
   a. He climbed it to paint the ceiling.
      lake   looking   ladder
   b. The car is in the _____.
      house   church   garage
4. Exercises using context and word parts of the target word
   a. The car is in the g_____.
   b. He is cl_____ing the ladder.

For all of these exercises, the most important aspect is incorporation of a teacher-led discussion (Valmont, 1983). This discussion points out the clues that lead to a certain word being suggested. For example, in the riddle exercise, the first two clues (four legs, a back) also describe a dog, cat, or other animal. You must have the third clue (something to sit on) before *dog* and *cat* are eliminated and *chair* becomes the answer. Any unknown word can be approached the same way. The context provides certain clues, and several words are suggested. The teacher is responsible for leading a discussion of what the clues are, why some words fit better than others, and which words are equally acceptable.

Using context and other meaning clues alone is not enough for effective, efficient word recognition, however. Both younger readers and readers having difficulty may rely too heavily on context (Gough, 1984; Nicholson, Lillas, & Rzoska, 1988; Stanovich, 1980; (Yoon) Kim & Goetz, 1994). Overemphasizing these and neglecting other decoding skills can lead to unfortunate learning outcomes. When this happens, students guess too often when they encounter words unknown in print, resulting in a distorted or misunderstood message. This outcome must be addressed immediately; if it is allowed to continue, the student may develop the bad habit of *not* expecting meaning from the passage.

VISUAL ANALYSIS

During the course of reading, students may become aware that they do not know a word after they have looked at it. The symbol (word) has not cued a meaningful response, and the context has not been a sufficient aid; therefore, they must figure out the word some other way. First, they must visually inspect the word and try to recognize smaller parts or spelling patterns that can then be pronounced. Thus, visual analysis precedes phonic or structural analysis, although it is possible that the "smaller parts" might also be structural elements. Phonic exercises that emphasize "sounding it out" as a first step fail to communicate to students that they have to segment visually before they sound.

Visual segmentation of an unknown word embedded in a sentence providing no helpful context clues presents especially difficult analytic problems. Durkin (1978) claims that decoding in such circumstances occurs at the syllable level, where only visual clues can be used. She identifies eight syllabication generalizations that help decode syllables. A problem with this procedure is that the students must memorize and be able to apply all of the rules before precision can be attained—an unrealistic expectation for students already in reading difficulty. The following might be a simpler, although less precise, set of *content rules* to help students begin visual segmentation of words into syllables:

1. Every syllable has one vowel sound.
2. Syllables contain *about* three letters (plus or minus two letters).
3. Syllables are often divided between two consonants *(plan-ter, pic-ture)*.
4. In a syllable with more than one vowel letter, the final *e* or the second vowel is often silent.

These four content rules, plus basic knowledge of letter-sound correspondences, are needed before students can begin to analyze unknown words independently. (For a listing of the more consistent phonic and syllabication content rules, see Appendix L.) Note, however, that these rules are useful in that they capture patterns of spelling. Productive use of these rules lies in relevant experiences, not in rote memorization.

Visual analysis that uses an analogy strategy is also effective. By accessing memory for **key words,** or familiar words containing patterns that resemble the new word, the reader can figure out the word. For example, if the new word is *screen* and the reader already knows, and can access, *green* and *scream,* the new word can be more readily pronounced. Some readers will have difficulty doing this and must be directly shown, while students with a strong naturalist intelligence may notice the patterns very quickly. Work by Ehri (1992); Gaskins, Ehri, Cress, O'Hara, and Donnelly (1996/1997); and Perfetti (1991) stresses the value of fully analyzing "the sounds in the spoken word and [matching] those sounds to the letters in the printed form of words" (Gaskins et al., 1996/1997, p. 315). Strickland (2000) also reminds us that "struggling readers benefit from focused instruction and direct experiences applying the alphabetic code . . . [and that] the examination of textual features and linguistic patterns helps to support [their] reading and spelling" (p. 105).

It must be noted here that use of these visual analysis processes and those that follow assume **phonological awareness,** that is, an awareness of words, that words are made up of parts, or syllables, and of individual sounds, or phonemes. The aspect of phonological awareness that occurs last developmentally, the awareness that words are made up of individual sounds, is called **phonemic awareness** (Opitz, 2000). Griffith and Olson (1992, p. 518) define phonemic awareness as "an understanding of the structure of *spoken* language." This definition implies an ability to manipulate the sounds of language, and it is an essential skill for learning phonics (Cunningham, 1999; National Reading Panel, 2000). "Phonemic awareness is strictly an oral ability and does not involve recognizing or naming letters or knowing which letters make which sounds [i.e., phonics]" (Cunningham, 1999, p. 69). It includes such abilities as orally/aurally recognizing and producing rhyming words, matching sounds, blending and segmenting phonemes, splitting syllables (e.g., *m* + *ake* = *make* and *cow* + *boy* = *cowboy*), and manipulating sounds to create new words (c.g., Change the /*m*/ in make to /*b*/—what is the new word?). It is *not* the same as phonics (learning letter-sound correspondences), but can be considered a prerequisite to success in phonics instruction (Adams, 1990; Juel, 1988; Mercer, 1997).

Activities that foster phonemic awareness include reading aloud books that emphasize rhyme or alliteration, or asking learners to listen for, and clap when they hear, a particular sound during the oral reading. The emphasis is on hearing and reproducing the sounds that they will need to match to printed symbols in order to decode. Once learners understand the concept of *word* (e.g., "I am going to say two words and I want you to tell me which word is longer: *dinosaur* or *dog?*"), recognizing rhymes is the easiest phonemic awareness task, followed by producing rhyming words. Syllable-level tasks are easier than phoneme-level tasks (e.g., "Clap the parts of the word *cowboy*." [/clap/ /clap/ = *cow* + *boy*] versus "How many sounds do you hear in cowboy?" [4 = /k/ + /ow/ + /b/ + /oy/]). Also, blending syllables and beginning sounds (e.g., "Put /st/ and /ick/ together to get the word *stick*") is easier than segmenting sounds as in the previous example. Substituting and manipulating beginning sounds is easier than substituting and manipulating middle and ending phonemes (e.g., *make* to *bake* as in a previous example versus *make* to *Mike* or *make* to *man*).

Use of children's literature assists students in alliteration, rhyming, blending and segmenting, and manipulation of phonemes (see Griffith & Olson, 1992, for further information). Some examples are *Animalia* (Base, 1986), with its "Lazy lions lounging in the local library"; *Sheep on a Ship* (Shaw, 1989), with "It rains and hails and shakes the sails. Sheep wake up and grab the rails"; the *Jamberry* poem (Degen, 1983), containing "Hatberry/ Shoeberry/In my Canoeberry"; and *Don't Forget the Bacon!* (Hutchins, 1976), in which "a cake for tea" becomes "a cape for me" becomes "a rake for leaves."

Monosyllabic Words

Students can be helped to apply at least three basic phonic process rules. The following process rules are adapted from Durkin's (1978) discussion on blending syllables. They are included in this section on visual analysis because they may be of help to students who have unsuccessfully tried to use the *initial consonant plus context clues* strategy and are unaware of how to continue. The next step in an analytical strategy must begin with visual segmentation of unknown words and then proceed to sounding and blending. The basic phonic process rules are as follows:

1. Separate the beginning consonant(s) from the rest of the word.
2. Say the sounds indicated by the spelling pattern, or rime, to include any final consonant(s).
3. Add, and say, the sound for the beginning consonant(s), or onset.

This strategy is illustrated in Figure 8.3 for monosyllabic words, where only the first syllabication content rule is needed.

Figure 8.3   Applying the Process Rules in Analyzing Unknown Words

Step	Analyzing Monosyllabic Words	Example Words				
1.	Separate the beginning consonant(s) from the rest of the word.	l - ed l	fl - ame fl	c - art c	g - o g	w - ait w
2.	Say the sounds indicated by the spelling pattern, or rime, to include any final consonants.	led ↓↓ ĕd ↓	flame ↓↓↓ āme ↓	cart ↓↓ art ↓	go ↓ ō ↓	wait ↓↓ āit ↓
3.	Add and say the beginning consonant(s), or onset.	lĕd	flāme	cart	gō	wāit
4.	Check if the word makes sense in the sentence.	It fits.	It fits.	It fits.	It fits.	It fits.

Step	Analyzing Polysyllabic Words	Example Words			
		vccv penguin ↓ ↓	vcv visit ↓↓	v cvc cvc apartment ↓ ↓ ↓	vcv cc vccv caterpillar ↓ ↓ ↓ ↓
1.	Find the vowels.	e ui	i i	a a e	a e i a
2.	Try to make syllables.	pen - guin	vis - it	a - part - ment	cat - er - pil - lar
3.	Say the trial syllables.	pen - guin	vis - it	a - part - ment	cat - er - pil - lar
4.	Blend the trial syllables.	pen ‿ guin	vis ‿ it	a ‿ part ‿ ment	cat ‿ er ‿ pil ‿ lar
5.	Check if the word makes sense in the sentence.	It fits.	It fits.	It fits.	It fits.

Polysyllabic Words

As students become facile at analyzing unknown monosyllabic words, the focus of the strategy changes to polysyllabic words. The remaining three syllabication rules must then be learned. This process is quite difficult for some students, and they simply give up when asked to analyze polysyllabic words. They must be encouraged to use the following process rules:

1. Find the vowels.
2. Try to make syllables using the consonants before and after the vowels (use process content rules 2 and 3 for monosyllabic words).
3. Say the trial syllables.
4. Blend the trial syllables.
5. Verify with the meaning of the sentence.

This strategy, while helpful, is not precise, and students must be cautioned that if the word they come up with does not fit, they must try to segment the syllables in another way or try different possible vowel sounds. However, after several unsuccessful efforts it is likely the word is not part of the student's listening vocabulary. The word should then be pronounced for the student and recorded for discussion of its meaning following the reading of the text.

Once a student begins using the steps, another word or word part may be recognized, and the steps may be short-circuited somewhat. The identification of vowels and addition of consonants frequently triggers this recognition. For example, a student may easily recognize *ment* in *apartment* once analysis begins. Such short-circuiting should be encouraged. Notice, also, that the division of *apartment* in step 2 is technically incorrect, but the student comes up with the word anyway.

As students develop a word recognition strategy, they are constantly adding to their skills repertoire. Consider the following possible strategies for figuring out a new word as a student adds analytical units (the products of instruction) to the memory store. In the example, replacing an *X* with letters implies that the student can visually identify and say that word part.

Target sentence:

I want something to eat.

When a child can read a few words but does not yet have any word analysis skills:

I want xxxxxxxxxx to eat.

(Child skips word or stops at unknown word.)

Add visual segmentation and ability to sound beginning consonants:

I want sxxxxxxxx to eat. "I want spaghetti to eat."

(Child fails, but the guess is sensible.)

Add knowledge of common word endings:

I want sxxxxxxing to eat. "I want s-s-s-ing to eat."

(Child fails.)

Add knowledge of one common word:

I want somexxing to eat. "I want some-ing—something—to eat."

(Child succeeds by approximation.)

Add knowledge of two common words:

I want something to eat. "I want some-thing to eat."

(Child succeeds.)

Another form instruction might take is for the teacher to demonstrate and model the most appropriate word analysis process to use. For example, the teacher might model for students by beginning with one of the following statements:

1. This word is best decoded by its syllables.
2. This word is best decoded by using phonics.
3. This word is best decoded by looking for a prefix and/or suffix.

For details of this method see Rinsky, 1993, p. 116.

Two important abilities develop when visual analysis skills are learned: discrimination and memory. Visual discrimination training helps the learner see differences between letters, word parts, and words, while memory helps the learner recall these differences quickly without having to resort to a slower, more analytical approach. (For more information on these abilities, see Chapter 4.)

Assessment

Assessment activities for phonemic awareness are essentially the same as instructional activities, but several published assessment tools are available for use with individual students. One that uses colored blocks for showing sequences of sounds in nonsense syllables and is useful for a range from kindergarten to adult is the *Lindamood Auditory Conceptualization Test* (Lindamood & Lindamood, 1979). A norm-referenced test that provides percentile scores for phoneme awareness, blending, memory, and rapid naming is the *Comprehensive Test of Phonological Processes* (Wagner, Torgesen, & Rashotte, 1999). There are two forms of this test—one for ages 5–6 and another for ages 7–18. A valid and reliable measure for the phonemic awareness area of segmenting is the *Yopp-Singer Test of Phoneme Segmentation* (Yopp, 1995), intended to be used with kindergarten and first-grade students. For blending, the *Roswell-Chall Auditory Blending Test* (Roswell & Chall, 1997) is available to assess the blending ability of two and three sounds. Second-language learners should be assessed in their native language. A teacher who is aware of instructional activities for phonemic awareness can easily devise tasks that can serve as assessments.

Students having problems with visual analysis often have been taught letter-sound correspondences but cannot visually identify them when they are embedded in new words or in other materials. Sometimes this is inappropriately considered a lack of ability to apply phonics skills when, in fact, it reflects inability to visually segment word parts. For example, Damien has learned several consonant sounds as well as some words. He has just successfully completed an exercise in consonant substitution with the following phonograms (rimes): *an, et,* and *ill.* His efforts to read orally proceed as follows for the sentence *Will you let Dan go with me?*

Damien: No response. Then, "I don't know the first word."
Teacher: "Think about our lesson this morning."
Damien: No response.
Teacher: "What is the first letter?"
Damien: "W."
Teacher: "Good! Now what does the rest of the word say?"
Damien: "Ill."
Teacher: "What sound does the first letter make?"
Damien: "Wah, as in want."
Teacher: "Now sound them together."
Damien: "Wah-ill—will. Will you . . ." Student does not continue.

Teacher returns to original strategy, noting that Damien had done his earlier lesson satisfactorily, but cannot independently segment the initial consonant or phonogram from the whole word. Practice in this ability is considered advisable as it may represent a lack of phonemic awareness (see earlier discussion).

Another indication of a need for visual analysis practice is continued use of inappropriate word parts even when they do not work. Trying a word element is acceptable, but if it does not work, it should be rejected and another tried. Inflexibility may suggest rigid instructional procedures. The following is an example of flexibility in efforts to analyze a word, trying different word parts.

Target sentence: Yes, you may go with father.
Student's first trial: "Yes, you may go with fat-her." (Student rejects this trial because sentence does not make sense.)
Student's second trial: "Yes, you may go with fa-ther, no, father." (Student accepts this trial because the sentence makes sense.)

(*Note:* This example indicates an opportunity to teach a mini-lesson on consonant digraphs, specifically *th*.)

Instruction

Some useful instructional activities for the areas of phonemic awareness follow. While reading books to or with students, point to each word as it is read. Once a selection has been completed, go back to interesting words and frame them—either by cupping hands around the word or by using pieces of poster board cut to surround the word. Many books of rhyming poetry and stories are written in rhyme (e.g., Dr. Seuss books) that can be read and explored. Pictures can be cut from magazines that show words that rhyme. Thumbs up/thumbs down as an every-pupil response technique can be used with rhyming words. Card games can be created that show pictures of rhyming words, and matches can be sought to form pairs. To emphasize the sounds in words, use a "rubber banding" technique in which the teacher stretches out the sounds within the word while keeping the sounds in the word connected (e.g., "mmmuuuunnnkkkkeeee"). Have the students count the sounds they hear in these rubber-banded words. Again, an every-pupil response technique can be employed for a group of students by providing them with a set of five cards that have the numbers 1, 2, 3, 4, or 5 on them so they can hold up the appropriate card for the number of sounds heard. A variation of counting sounds is the use of Elkonin boxes (named after a Russian researcher) for which the learner places a marker (e.g., a button or a coin) within a box for each sound heard in a word pronounced orally (see Figure 8.4). Words can also be represented by pictures at first, and eventually the word itself can be used to begin a transition to phonics. This will also help the learner realize the **alphabetic principle;** understanding that each speech sound or phoneme has its own distinctive graphic representation, or **grapheme.** In other words, phonemes are represented by graphemes. The results of the Elkonin boxes activity can be expanded to a graphing activity that would appeal to the learner whose strong intelligence is logical-mathematical (see Figure 8.5). An activity for blending sounds that would engage the bodily-kinesthetic learner is called *arm blending* (Fox, 2000). This involves a motion of sweeping one arm down the length of the other as the sounds in a word are being pronounced. The motion parallels what the voice does when blending sounds together. Connecting each sound to a placement on the arm also seems to help the learner remember where the sound occurs in the word for spelling purposes as well. For example, to blend /h/ /o/ /t/, place the hand on the opposite shoulder and say /h/, move the hand down to the elbow and say /o/, and finally down to the wrist to say /t/. These same activities can be made appropriate for older learners by using song lyrics instead of Dr. Seuss books, or age-appropriate magazine or catalog pictures (see Yopp & Yopp,

logical-mathematical

bodily-kinesthetic

Figure 8.4   Using Elkonin Boxes for Phonemic Awareness

The teacher pronounces a word, stretching out the sounds so the student can determine how many sounds are heard in the word. The student then moves a marker into a box for each sound heard, while repeating the word and streching out its sounds. For example:

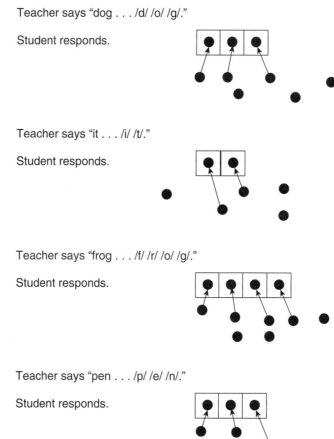

Teacher says "dog . . . /d/ /o/ /g/."

Student responds.

Teacher says "it . . . /i/ /t/."

Student responds.

Teacher says "frog . . . /f/ /r/ /o/ /g/."

Student responds.

Teacher says "pen . . . /p/ /e/ /n/."

Student responds.

musical

1996). In addition, the rhyming game of Hink Pink (similar to the Rhyme Time category on *Jeopardy*) is good not only for phonemic awareness but for vocabulary development as well (e.g., "What is the dance of a hog? A pig jig.") Note that Hink Pinks are two words that rhyme and that both have one syllable. There are also Hinky Pinkys and Hinkity Pinkitys, for two- and three-syllable words respectively. This game would be especially useful for older students still experiencing difficulty with phonemic awareness. Experimenting with the sounds of our language serves to make all students more phonemically aware.

Instruction in visual analysis encourages students to look for known parts embedded in unknown words and then try to segment other *reasonable* word parts—that is, elements that may represent a word part. (Recall the content and process rules described earlier and begin instruction by helping learners discover these rules if needed.)

It should be noted that daily events in most classrooms provide ample opportunity for visual analysis practice within a meaningful context. In Tim O'Keefe's classroom (Mills, O'Keefe, & Stephens, 1992, p. 5), students made the following "discoveries" simply from examining their student attendance sign-in sheets.

Figure 8.5   Graphing Sounds Hear in Twenty Words Following the use of Elkonin Boxes

Following the Elkonin box activity seen in Figure 8.4, students can gain additional practice identify-ing the number of sounds in words by completing a graph. This graphing activity would be espe-cially appealing for the student with a strength in the logical-mathematical intelligence. The twenty words used for the Elkonin box activity were: <u>dog, it, pen, frog, treat, she, lamb, clock. see, cake, pot, Dad, fish, fly, boat, nest, book, brick, lunch, the.</u>

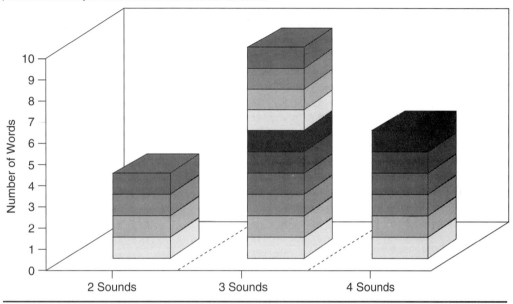

Chiquita and *Charles* both have the letters *ch* at the beginning of their names.

Justin noticed that *O'Keefe* has two *e*'s together, like in Kareem's name. Then he looked around the room and saw the color words collage. He added *green* to his list of words that have two *e*'s together.

Amanda noticed that she, Justin, and Vania all have *r*'s in their last names.

Similarly, the words that students encounter on a daily basis as part of their ongoing reading, writing, and content learning are candidates for "word walls" (Cunningham, 1991, 1999). The word wall developed during the semester described in Chapter 1 con-tained words related to the theme of "At the Beach." The words from this wall can be seen in Figure 8.6. Since students of varying literacy needs in this multi-age setting con-tributed words to the word wall, a wide variety of purposes existed for word study. For example, words beginning with single consonants could be grouped (e.g., *fin, pail, cod, kelp, sand*) as could words beginning with consonant blends (e.g., *blubber, trench, crab*), or consonant digraphs (e.g., *whales, shark*). In addition to many other phonic elements, words could be grouped in various ways related to their meaning (e.g., animals, plants).

The following activities can also aid instruction in visual analysis.

naturalist

1. Give students sets of unknown words that contain word parts they already know.
   a. After a lesson on variants (discussed later), provide exercises such as the following: Draw a circle around the word endings you see. Then use each word to complete the sentences.
      look   looks   looking
      Johnny _____ very tired today.

Figure 8.6   Words from the "At the Beach" Word Wall

cetacean	submarine	sand shark
fin	dolphins	trench
monk shark	conch	oil tankers
pail	sun	beach
moon jellyfish	lifeguard	water
common sand dollar	sand	jelly fish
mackerel	schooners	flying fish
octopus	pontoon bridge	blowfish
medusa	raft	nurse shark
whales	sand crabs	sand dollar
blubber	sea snakes	sea
plankton	surfing	arrowhead sand dollar
starfish	dogfish	sailboats
cod	five-hole sand dollar	dunes
tsunami	sea turtle	yellow sting ray
hotwater vent	crab	beach ball
continental shelf	seaweed	kelp
submersible	continental slope	cowrie
shark	whelk	reef
seagulls	coral	seahorse

"_____ out!" shouted Susan, as the car came speeding toward them.

"What are you _____ for?" asked Mother.

b. After lessons on initial consonant blends, provide exercises such as this: Here are some words. If they start with a consonant, mark a *C* and circle the consonant. If they begin with a consonant blend, mark a *B* and circle the blend.

_____ cat   _____ slip
_____ bring   _____ sing
_____ try   _____ wall

c. After lessons in various structural analysis (also called morphemic analysis) elements, ask students to look for the relevant unit in the unknown words.

(1) Put a line between the two words in each of these compound words.

sweetheart   playground   nighttime

Then write a sentence for each of these compound words in your notebook.

(2) Draw a circle around each affix. Then complete each sentence using the base (or root) word.

rewrite   careful   happiness

The little boy touched his new baby sister with _____.

I will _____ a letter to grandmother.

Dad told me I did a good job and that made me _____.

Students soon learn that if they segment the word in the wrong place, they may not be able to sound the "odd" word parts. They should be encouraged to try again and break the word apart in a different place, always keeping the context in mind.

"Here are some words that have been divided for you. Which one helps you most to sound it out? Put an X on that word."

t/hi/nk   th/in/k   th/ink   Be sure you *think* before you speak.
spr/ing   s/pri/ng   sp/ri/ng   Today is sunny and warm and feels like *spring*.

This exercise has no right or wrong answer, especially if the student arrives at the correct pronunciation. This type of practice is probably best done in an individual setting, where the teacher can encourage the learner to resegment the word if it was inappropriate on the first trial.

A Focus on SLL: Word Configuration Boxes

Similar to the cheerleader spelling idea presented in Chapter 7, word configuration boxes help second-language learners visualize the orthography of the English language.

Not only useful for spelling, but for visual patterns that onsets and rimes provide, word configuration boxes draw attention to these visual elements.

Word Configuration Boxes

Write each word in the correct word box.

1. walk

2. judge

3. fasten

4. could

5. knife

6. write

7. bridge

8. half

9. lodge

10. edge

11. should

12. thumb

13. watch

14. sign

15. wrong

KNOWLEDGE OF WORD PARTS

When students cannot figure out an unknown word from meaning clues alone, they must resort to analysis. Essentially, this means they must look for a word part that they already know. Using the pronounceable word part strategy, students can be asked, "Is there any part of this word that you know?" (Gunning, 1995, p. 488; see also Gunning, 2001, pp. 50–51). Common word parts are presented in Figure 8.7. Two major instructional units concerned with this knowledge are phonics and structural analysis. **Structural analysis** deals with such meaningful word parts as derivatives (affixes), variants (word endings), and compounds. **Phonics,** on the other hand, deals with letter-sound relationships or word parts that do not necessarily have meaning. Examples include consonants, vowels, digraphs, and many syllables. With phonics, students focus on learning what various word parts say, whereas with structural analysis the focus can be twofold: what the word part says and what it means.

The goal of instruction in phonics and structural analysis is for common word parts to become so well known that students can recognize them instantly and automatically (LaBerge & Samuels, 1974). When this level is attained, students do not have to spend an unusually long time analyzing unknown words. With practice, students in primary grades continually add word parts to their *instant recognition* repertoires. Notice the similarity of the concept to that of sight vocabulary, words that have become so familiar they can be recognized instantly and automatically.

Practice is the key to automaticity. Some students quickly attain the level of instant recognition, but others need much practice with written language before these word parts become second nature. Teachers must be diligent in providing ample practice that does not become deadly dull drill. The best solution may be to provide many opportunities to write for authentic purposes (e.g., pen pal letters, journals, lists, and messages; refer to Chapter 7) and to read easy and interesting material.

Assessment

Teachers must answer three questions about students learning word parts:

1. Does the learner know the word part?
2. Can the learner recognize the word part quickly?
3. Can the learner identify the element embedded in an unknown word?

Knowledge of word parts (Figure 8.7) is assessed directly through examination of writing samples, observation of oral reading during conferences, and use of the subtest of the SDRT (Karlsen & Gardner, 1995).

Automaticity requires accuracy as well as alacrity. To assess knowledge of word parts with a group of young students, an exercise similar to the one that follows, which provides three or four word elements per line, is recommended. The teacher gives the stimulus, silently counts to three, and goes on to the next element without giving students time to be analytical.

Teacher says	*Student marks element*		
1. mm—man—mm	h	m	b
2. ing—laughing—ing	ed	s	ing
3. tion—motion—tion	tion	ilk	ton

Figure 8.7 Common Word Elements

1. Consonants
a. *one sound (usually)*
b, d, f, h, j, k, l, m,
n, p, q, r, t, v, y, z
b. *more than one sound*
c: cat, city
g: get, gem
s: sit, his, sure
x: box, exam, xylophone

2. Consonant blends
bl, br
cl, cr
dr, dw
fl, fr
gl, gr
pl, pr
sc, sch, scr, shr, sk,
sm, sn, sp, spl, spr,
st, str, sw
thr, tr, tw

3. Consonant Digraphs
a. *one sound (usually)*
ck, gh, ng, nk, sh
b. *more than one sound*
th: thing, they
wh: when, who
ch: chair, chorus, choir

4. Vowels (long, short, or controlled)
a, e, i, o, u, (y)

5. Vowel clusters
ai: mail, said
ay: say
ea: heat, head
ee: sheep
ei: receive, weigh
ie: believe, tie
ew: few
ey: key, they
oa: road, broad
oe: hoe
oi: boil
ou: though, bough, bought
ow: mow, now
oy: toy
ue: blue

6. Prefixes
ab, ad, ante, anti, auto,
be, bi, com, con, co,
de, dis, en, ex,
in, im, inter, ir,
mis, non, op, out,
per, post, pre, pro,
re, sub, super,
trans, un

7. Suffixes
able, age, al, ance, ate, ble, ence,
er, est, ful, ible, ise, ize, ish,
ist, ite, ity, ly, less,
ment, ness, our, ship, some,
tion, ure, ward

8. Phonograms (Rimes)

a	e	i	o	u
ab	ear	ib	ob	ub
ack*	eat*	ick*	ock*	uck*
		ice*		
		icle		
ad	ed	id	od	ud
		ide*	ode	
		if		
ag	eg	ig	og	ug*
		ight		
ain*				
ake*		ike	oke	
all*	ell*	ill*		
ale*				
am	em	im	om	um
ame*			ome	upm*
an*	en*	in*		un
		ine*		ung
		ing*		
ank*		ink*		unk*
ap*		ip*	op*	up
are		ir*	or*	
			ore*	
ash*	est*	is		us
at*	et	it		ush
ate*				ut
awe				
aw*				
ay*				
	ez	iz	ow	

9. Variants
ed, es, ing, s, 's

*Especially useful phonograms, or rimes

With practice in this type of exercise, students soon learn to work as quickly as they can. Those who have difficulty with this activity should be further observed. The stimulus in this exercise is the sound and not the symbol and, therefore, it is not exactly like real reading. Measurement specialists are critical of assessment techniques of this nature, citing lack of construct validity; however, if the student can match the written version to the oral version, the teacher can be more certain that the student can also produce the oral equivalent for the written word.

The easiest and most accurate way to determine speed is to give the student a list of words containing elements recently explored and ask for the list to be read as quickly as possible. If the elements on the list can be pronounced quickly, one after another (about one-half second per unit of analysis), the student has attained the desired level of instant recognition. Such elements are easy to incorporate into a learning game format.

The teacher must observe a student reading orally to assess the use or application of knowledge of word parts embedded in unknown words. This is best done in situations enabling the teacher to note when a student comes to a word that should be easy to analyze but is not. This may occur during a reading lesson or any other time when oral reading is done. Similar behavior occurs when the student comes to the teacher to ask for a word that is not known but should be. If frequent, this behavior may suggest ineffective knowledge of word parts, inability to use meaning clues, or both.

Tests or subtests assessing knowledge of word parts are available, such as the *Stanford Diagnostic Reading Test* (Karlsen & Gardner, 1995). This test assesses accuracy but not speed. Teachers must use their own judgment regarding this ability, or they can assess this knowledge using the revised version of the *Names Test* (Duffelmeyer, Kruse, Merkley, & Fyfe, 1994; Duffelmeyer & Black, 1996).

Instruction

A natural way to support students in their developing knowledge of the graphophonic system is through the use of children's literature. Trachtenburg (1990) proposes a three-step whole-part-whole strategy in which the first step is the reading of a literature selection that contains many examples of a particular graphophonic element, such as *Bringing the Rain to Kapiti Plain* (Aardema, 1981). In the second step, the teacher draws attention to the particular phonic or structural analysis element for which the selection was chosen. (In *Bringing the Rain to Kapiti Plain* this might be the long sound of *a* as represented by the *ai* and *aCe* spelling patterns.) The third step involves reading another literature selection that contains examples of the element introduced in step two (e.g., *The Lace Snail,* Byars, 1975), so students make the connection that these graphophonic patterns occur throughout all reading material. (See Trachtenburg, 1990, for a list of trade books that repeat long and short vowel sounds.) Similarly, Moustafa & Maldonado-Colon (1999) support starting phonics instruction with a story and the use of familiar language. They remind us that while English can be analyzed into phonemes, onsets and rimes, or syllables, Spanish is not an onset/rime language, with the unit in Spanish being the syllable (e.g., ca + sa = casa). They also support the use of analogies between familiar and unfamiliar words, predictable text, and word walls. Many good follow-up activities are useful in providing practice with word parts.

The instructional examples that follow are organized around the scope and sequence chart in Figure 8.2. Teachers designing lessons for word parts should present them within the context of familiar, meaningful language. Initial instruction in specific phonic or structural analysis elements should follow inductive, or inquiry, procedures (see Chapter 2).

1. Activities to support learning of initial consonants

spatial

   a. *Personal dictionaries.* As young children use and select new or interesting words from their language experience stories or journals, or come across them in reading their storybooks, place these words on alphabetically ordered pages to create a dictionary. A sentence and a picture should accompany each word. Even older students can create personal dictionaries for specialized topics. For example, seventh-graders studying the Middle Ages could create a medieval dictionary based on a literature selection such as *Illuminations* (Hunt, 1989) with words such as *Normans, portcullis, troubadour,* and *zither.*

spatial

   b. *Alphabet books.* Students of all ages can create alphabet books on a particular topic of interest, or as part of a content area unit. For example, one student chose to create an alphabet book on "Life in the Sea" and proceeded to locate a sea creature for

naturalist

   each letter of the alphabet (e.g., a = anemone; b = barnacle; c = clown fish; etc.), illustrated each page, and provided a brief commentary for that creature. These books can become quite involved and sophisticated.

   c. *Choosing the beginning letter.* Instruct students to read the sentence in order to write in the missing letter. The source material has previously been read to the students and they are familiar with it.

   The cow jumped over the _____oon.
   r   n   m

   Humpty Dumpty sat on a _____all.
   w   t   c

   d. *Practice with rimes.* Instruct students to read the sentence in order to write in the missing word. Again, the material is familiar.

   Sam ate the _____.
   ram   ham   slam

   Jack and Jill went up the _____.
   bill   will   hill

2. Activities to support blending of initial consonant clusters

   a. *Use these letters to make a word for each of the sentences.*

   <u>br</u>   <u>sl</u> <u>cl</u>   <u>ch</u>   <u>wh</u>   <u>sh</u>
   The _____ock struck one.   _____icken Little said, "The sky is falling!"
   He _____oke his crown.   Mary's lamb was _____ite as snow.
   Don't _____am the door.   Cinderella lost her _____oe.

interpersonal

   Half the students can receive the initial consonant cluster, while an equal number receive the partial sentence. Students then try to find their "partner," or the person who needs the piece they hold. Once partners have found each other, they work together to act out their sentence for the rest of the class.

   b. *Make a word for the one missing in each sentence that starts like the word that has a line under it.*

   We have a good <u>place</u> to _____.
   Let's <u>try</u> to _____ the squirrel.
   I <u>think</u> he is in _____ grade.
   <u>When</u> did the bicycle _____ break?

   Similar activities can easily be created by students for placement in classroom learning games or for other students.

intrapersonal

   Instruction using Retrospective Miscue Analysis, or RMA (Goodman, 1996) is most helpful for encouraging readers to explore their own reading processes, and to revalue themselves as readers. Teacher and student together examine reading miscues for their quality and patterns that reveal the reader's strategies and knowledge of the language cue systems. Questions like these are common: "Did the miscue make sense?" "Why did you make the miscue?" "Does the miscue look like the word in the text?" "Did the miscue affect your understanding of the text?" "Should it have been corrected?" "Did you correct the miscue?" "How did you figure it out?" "When readers are in environments that encourage risk-taking with teachers who respect them as knowledgeable about their own reading, they begin to depend on themselves as the most important resource to answer their questions as they read" (Goodman & Marek, 1996, p. 205).

BLENDING AND SYNTHESIZING

As students learn to segment words visually and say the word parts, they also learn to reassemble the parts to form a recognizable word. This reassembly process is referred to as blending and synthesizing. *Auditory blending* refers to a sounding process: the student says the word parts and blends them together to cue a meaningful response. This process is generally used by emerging readers when they are first learning to read, and it is a very important skill at that level of learning. **Visual synthesizing** is a more mature process and is used by readers who can analyze words mentally, without having to resort to overt sounding and blending of word parts. For typical learners, a gradual shift from auditory blending to visual synthesizing occurs as the analytical techniques and word parts become automatic. Visual synthesizing is faster than auditory blending and should be the ultimate goal.

Some students have trouble with blending and synthesizing because their reading program has overemphasized learning word parts in isolation; a few students may not be able to blend sounds orally and must learn to rely solely on visual synthesizing.

Assessment

A learner who cannot yet pronounce various word parts or remember a sequence of sounds obviously cannot blend these sounds together. Assuming that the word parts are known, students who are having difficulty with auditory memory or auditory blending can be identified relatively easily. The teacher says the word parts slowly, with a one-second interval between parts, and asks the student to respond by saying the whole word. Following is an example of auditory blending:

Objective	*Teacher*	*Student*
letters	s–a–m	sam
letters and phonogram	s–am	sam
syllables	sam–ple	sample
combination	s–am–pling	sampling

Both the stimulus and response are at the oral level; a student who does this task successfully still may not be able to do it effectively while reading. Therefore, a stimulus must also be provided in printed form, separating the letters or word parts with dashes and spaces. Following is an example of auditory blending when the stimulus is in print:

Student reads and says	*Student says*
tr–ack	track
d–an–cing	dancing

When the student says the parts out loud and blends them together, the process is auditory blending. When the student simply looks at the word parts and rather quickly says the whole word aloud without sounding out the parts, the process is visual synthesizing.

Instruction

Instruction in auditory blending should begin at the level of the syllable (Ericson & Juliebo, 1998). Slow and exaggerated pronunciation of the syllable, or phoneme, is helpful. Practice in segmentation of sounds is also helpful for then combining individual sounds to form words, or auditory blending. Start with compound words like *football* and *raincoat* before blending words of two syllables, like *sister* or *baby*. Move from this syllable level to blending initial consonants with the rest of the syllable in a one-syllable word. For example, "I am going to make some sounds and I want you to tell me what word I am trying to say. Listen. *m-an, m-an.* What word is that?" Continue development by increasing the number of phonemes spoken in isolation (see assessing auditory blending section). This instruction can take the form of a guessing game ("I am thinking of a word that is the color of Cory's pants. It is */b/-/l/-/ack/.*"). Songs can also be adopted as blending activities, such as the song "Bingo."

musical

One of the conclusions in *"Beginning to Read: Thinking and Learning about Print"* (Adams, 1990) states, "because children have special difficulty analyzing the phonemic structure of words, reading programs should include explicit instruction in blending" (p. 126). The use of **onsets** (single consonants, consonant blends, and consonant digraphs occurring at the beginning of words) and **rimes** (the vowels and consonants at the end of a syllable, also called phonograms or word families) may be most helpful in this regard (Goswami & Mead, 1992). The biggest advantage in using rimes lies in the relatively high stability of vowel sounds within most end rimes (i.e., *-ean* as opposed to *bea-*). Rimes are far more generalizable than isolated vowels or even vowel teams. Of 286 phonograms appearing in primary-grade texts, 95 percent were pronounced the same each time they were met (Durrell, 1963). In fact, nearly 500 early elementary words can be derived from the phonograms marked by an asterisk in Figure 8.7 (Fry, Kress & Fountoukidis, 1993; Wylie & Durrell, 1970).

Gunning (1995) describes a word-building strategy for teaching phonic elements within the context of naturally occurring text that relies on adding onsets to rimes. He suggests that students are more likely to recognize pronounceable word parts if phonic elements are taught in natural clusters, such as onsets and rimes.

Use of rimes will mediate the following obstacles to blending:

1. Analyzing rimes into component parts
2. Unawareness that different onsets can be placed before the same rime to make many different words
3. Analyzing complex onsets (e.g., *tw, cl, wh, squ, sch, thr*) into individual phonemes.

With initial instruction, the following procedures are modeled for students. Separated word parts containing rimes are presented to the student to reassemble. Begin with known word parts in known words so that the learner understands the task.

m–eat   meat
sh–ell   shell

If the word parts are pronounced by the teacher and the student responds by saying the whole word, this is auditory blending, with the stimulus and the response both at the oral level.

Perceptual unit	Teacher says	Student says
syllables	bask–et	basket
structural elements	some–thing	something
phonic elements	p–ain–ter	painter

It is best to begin with natural word divisions represented by syllabic utterances as found in rimes and then proceed to more artificial phonic elements. Students need practice with these elements, because they are likely to segment words into elements other than syllables (e.g., mo–ney); therefore, they must be able to blend them to cue an appropriate response.

When the stimulus is changed from word parts spoken by the teacher to written word parts read by the students, the task is considered either auditory blending or visual synthesizing, depending on whether the response is primarily auditory or visual. The following exercises develop both skills.

1. When the words are in isolation:

Print	Student reads
gra vel	gravel
gr avel	gravel
gr av el	gravel

2. When the words are in context:
    a. The men walked toward the <u>gra</u> <u>vel</u> pit.
    b. Add the right word part.
        The men walk _____ toward the gravel pit.
    c. End-of-line segmentation
        The men walked <u>to</u>-
        <u>ward</u> the gravel pit.

Use of children's books, such as the Dr. Seuss series, that contain many examples of phonograms can provide much needed practice with blending in a meaningful context. *Green Eggs and Ham* (Seuss, 1960), available on an interactive CD-ROM (Living Books by the Random House/Broderbund Company, 1996), provides good aural reinforcement of several useful rimes.

SUMMARY

Word recognition is presented as an interaction between the *process* of figuring out words unknown in print and the *products* of instruction, or knowledge of word parts. Several factors influence this interaction. One of the most important is that the word exist in the reader's listening vocabulary. The text also must be sufficiently easy to permit the reader to use context clues. Readers cannot use their understanding of language when material is too difficult, and they are forced to resort to more artificial analytical techniques.

Another factor influencing this interaction is the size of the student's sight vocabulary. As sight vocabulary increases, the number of unrecognized words decreases.

Eventually, the student encounters few unknown words; when they are encountered, they are probably not in the student's meaning vocabulary. Analytical techniques seldom help mature readers who encounter unknown words, because the problem is probably lack of meaning rather than lack of appropriate word recognition facility.

Context clues such as expectancy, or anticipation of words likely to occur in the selection, play an indirect but vital part in the word analysis process. Meaning clues, or knowledge of the language surrounding an unknown word, also contribute immeasurably to an analytical strategy.

For the beginning reader, however, knowledge of word parts is an important way of relating visual symbols to words that are already in the meaning vocabulary. Disregarding context clues for the moment, the process of word recognition probably includes the following steps or stages:

1. The reader knows by looking that the word is not recognized.

2. The word is segmented visually into parts.

3. Some of the parts may be recognized.

4. The reader attempts to analyze the remaining unknown parts. The more techniques the reader has for doing this, the more successful the outcome.

5. The word is reconstructed by auditory or visual means, or both, to approximate the word and cue a meaningful response.

6. The word is confirmed or rejected based on the meaning of the sentence when the word choice is made.

Students *without* reading difficulties probably use bits and pieces of this process intuitively. However, students *with* reading difficulties often need direct instruction to clarify the process at points where their strategy breaks down. The teacher must use the analytic process to help identify areas of strength and need. Ultimately, students assume responsibility for analyzing words independently, always checking for sentence sense and understanding of the passage being read.

Suggested Readings

Allen, L. (1998). An integrated strategies approach: Making word identification instruction work for beginning readers. *The Reading Teacher, 52,* 254–268.

   This article describes, through sample lessons, an instructional framework that focuses on a whole-part-whole approach for word identification development. The integration of skills instruction and children's literature provides a real purpose for learning word identification strategies as well as motivation to read.

Bear, D., & Templeton, S. (1998). Explorations in developmental spelling: Foundations for learning and teaching phonics, spelling, and vocabulary. *The Reading Teacher, 52,* 222–242.

   This article provides a thorough summary of current thinking in the field about how spelling, phonics, and vocabulary are related and how they can best be taught.

   Two main points are addressed: What do we know and what are the instructional implications for word study?

Goodman, Y. (1996). Revaluing readers while readers revalue themselves: Retrospective miscue analysis. *The Reading Teacher, 49,* 600–609.

   Yetta Goodman explains several instructional variations of Retrospective Miscue Analysis in this article. The emphasis is on helping readers realize that they are using strategies that support meaning construction as they read.

Mills, H., O'Keefe, T., & Stephens, D. (1992). *Looking closely: Exploring the role of phonics in one whole language classroom* (Chapter 2). Urbana, IL: National Council of Teachers of English.

   Chapter 2 in this interesting monograph takes the reader through a day in Tim O'Keefe's classroom, highlighting the role of graphophonemics. This monograph is meant to reassure those teachers who think whole-language classrooms ignore phonics instruction by showing how phonics is addressed within the context of authentic reading, writing, and learning experiences.

Routman, R. (1992). Teach skills with a strategy. *Instructor* (May/June), 34–37.

This article focuses on the difference between skills and strategies and presents ideas for teaching phonics strategically. A self-evaluation for teachers is also included to *help those who want to move toward teaching for strategies in reading.*

Trachtenburg, P. (1990). Using children's literature to enhance phonics instruction. *The Reading Teacher, 43,* 648–654.

A most helpful article for teachers who want to include more children's literature in their reading programs but are worried about addressing phonics instruction. The author provides an instructional scenario for doing just this, as well as a list of trade books to support teachers' efforts at linking children's literature and phonics instruction.

9 Reading Comprehension
Foundations

After you have read this chapter, you should be able to:
1. list and describe the major factors affecting the comprehension process;
2. explain the various theories and models of the comprehension process;
3. tell what behaviors a less skilled comprehender is likely to exhibit;
4. describe several general reading comprehension strategies for assessment and instruction.

Key Concepts and Terms

abstract referent	microprocessing	replaced words
attentive listening	phonological system	schema
auditory comprehension	picture walk	scriptally implicit
concrete referent	process of	semantic system
directed reading-thinking	comprehension	semantic webbing
activity (DRTA)	question-answer	structured
integrative processing	relationships (QARs)	comprehension
listening	rauding theory	syntactic system
macroprocessing	reciprocal question-	text organization
mapping	answer relationships	textually explicit
phase-out/phase-in	(ReQARs)	textually implicit
strategy	repeated words	transactional model

BACKGROUND

Concern for understanding reading comprehension is not new, and many attempts have been made to define it. Early scholars such as Edmund Burke Huey (1908/1977) stated that to understand reading would be to understand the most intricate workings of the mind; Thorndike (1917/1971) defined reading as thinking.

Historically, reading experts have tried to explain reading comprehension by identifying what successful comprehenders do. A frequently cited study by Davis (1944) lists nine skills considered basic to successful comprehension:[1]

1. Knowledge of word meanings

2. Ability to select appropriate meaning for a word or phrase in the light of its particular contextual setting

3. Ability to follow the organization of a passage and to identify antecedents and references in it

---

[1]From F. B. Davis, "Fundamental Factors of Comprehension in Reading." *Psychometrika* 9 (1944): 186. Used with permission.

4. Ability to identify the main thought of a passage

5. Ability to answer questions that are specifically answered in a passage

6. Ability to answer questions that are answered in a passage, but not in the words in which the question is asked

7. Ability to draw inferences from a passage about its contents

8. Ability to recognize the literary devices used in a passage and to determine its tone and mood

9. Ability to determine a writer's purpose, intent, and point of view—that is, to draw inferences about a writer (p. 186)

These skills, and similar listings, are considered products of comprehension. Traditional skills-centered approaches to reading comprehension deal predominantly with the products of comprehension. Following is a representative scope and sequence listing for such an approach (Rosenshine, 1980, p. 537).

1. *Literal*—locating details

2. *Simple inferential*—understanding words in context; recognizing the sequence of events; recognizing cause and effect; comparing and contrasting

3. *Complex inferential*—recognizing the main idea, title, topic; drawing conclusions; predicting outcomes

Consider the following example. Through an assessment technique Banetta is found to have difficulty drawing conclusions from a passage, a *product* of comprehension. The usual procedure is to give Banetta additional practice in drawing conclusions. Unfortunately, whether such practice affects the *process* of drawing conclusions is not certain. On the other hand, if the underlying tasks involved in drawing conclusions were known, the procedure would be to determine the stage at which the process broke down and proceed with appropriate instruction from that point. What is really needed, then, is a better understanding of comprehension processes.

FACTORS AFFECTING THE COMPREHENSION PROCESS

Before discussing specific characteristics of the less skilled comprehender, the **process of comprehension** must be examined to learn what strategies are used by the skilled comprehender. In this way, areas of difference between skilled and less skilled comprehenders will be easier to recognize. The ultimate goal is to design appropriate reading comprehension instruction for the less skilled comprehender. Key factors of the comprehension process are best grouped into three categories: (1) factors within the reader, (2) factors within the written message, and (3) factors within the reading environment (Pearson & Johnson, 1978).

Factors within the Reader

Some factors within the reader that affect reading comprehension are linguistic competence, decoding ability, prior knowledge or experience, and interests and attitudes.

Linguistic Competence

Linguistic competence refers to what the reader knows about language. Three systems are involved in learning language: phonological, syntactic, and semantic. The **phonological**

system refers to knowledge of individual sounds in the language, knowledge of how these sounds are blended together to make words, and knowledge of stress, pitch, and juncture. Briefly, stress refers to such differences as:

The DOG broke the cup. (not the cat)

The dog BROKE the cup. (as opposed to just knocking it over)

Pitch refers to intonation differences:

We'll leave in an hour.

We'll leave in an hour!

We'll leave in an hour?

Juncture refers to the differences between *nitrate* and *night rate* or between *icing* and *I sing.*

K. S. Goodman (1996) terms this first important system the graphophonic system and says that it includes the orthographic and phonic systems as well as the phonological. Because the cues in reading are also visual, the reader must have knowledge of the particular orthography of the language being read. In English this is an alphabetic system, as compared to Japanese, for instance, which uses a combination of Chinese characters and syllabic orthography. Additionally, the reader must have knowledge of the relationships between oral and written language using an alphabetic system, better known as phonics.

The **syntactic system** refers to word order in sentences, punctuation, and the use of capital letters. Syntactic knowledge helps the reader determine whether a string of words makes a grammatically acceptable English sentence. For example:

The dog chased the cat.
    or
Chased dog the cat the.

Syntactic knowledge, sometimes called *sentence sense,* also helps the reader know that two different word orders have the same meaning:

The dog chased the cat.
    or
The cat was chased by the dog.

His friend said, "The doctor is ill."
    or
"The doctor," said his friend, "is ill."

Knowledge of syntax even enables the reader to use context clues to read and answer questions on material that has no real meaning:

The ill zoo was a bab. That forn, the sossy ill zoo larped and was mitry.

What was the ill zoo? When did the sossy ill zoo larp? Who was sossy?

In short, syntax is the primary means by which the reader determines relationships between words.

Simply being able to pronounce words and answer certain questions correctly does not ensure that understanding has occurred. Because the sentences about the ill zoo had no real meaning (readers are not able to relate the nonsense words to anything already available in their minds), the importance of the semantic system becomes obvious. The **semantic system** refers to knowledge of word meanings, the underlying concepts of words, and the interrelationships between concepts. Semantic knowledge enables the reader to organize the text into a coherent structure and determine the relative importance of the various concepts found in text (e.g., main ideas versus supporting details).

Pragmatic knowledge is sometimes considered a part of this system along with schematic knowledge. Pragmatic meaning is always partly found in the text and partly found in the context of the literacy event. The reader's schemata must be called upon to achieve pragmatic comprehension (e.g., understanding the humor in a comic strip).

In summary, if the phonological, syntactic, and semantic information provided for the reader on a page of print closely matches the phonological, syntactic, and semantic abilities available in the reader's mind, understanding is likely.

Decoding Ability

When a reader approaches text in order to construct meaning, decoding will occur naturally. However, the construction of meaning will be difficult if the reader cannot readily pronounce many of the words in the passage, or is overly concerned with accurate word pronunciation. The reader who has to devote too much attention to decoding or to correct pronunciation, as in the case of oral, round-robin reading, cannot also attend to processing the meaning of the material (LaBerge & Samuels, 1974; Opitz & Rasinski, 1998; Stanovich, 1980). Readers who identify words quickly and automatically, on the other hand, do not have to focus on decoding and can give their full attention to comprehension, especially when reading silently.

Difficulty with decoding does *not* imply, however, that comprehension cannot occur. In fact, comprehension *must* be the goal for decoding to occur more readily. Consider the following argument presented by Pearson and Johnson (1978).

> Comprehension helps word identification as much as word identification helps comprehension. That is, having understood part of the message helps you to decode another part. In short, context can help to short-circuit the amount of attention you have to pay to print. (p. 15)

Decoding ability has been discussed in detail in Chapter 8, but you may conclude from this brief discussion that decoding is made easier if the reader is reading for meaning. Concern with comprehension instruction is important at every stage of reading development. The reader must *expect* and *demand* that material read *makes sense*.

Prior Knowledge or Experience

What readers bring to the reading task is critical to their understanding of what is read. A reader's background gives personal meaning to the printed page; thus not all readers comprehend material in exactly the same way. For example, if a young reader who has never been out of the city tries to read a book about life on a farm, so many words and events will be unfamiliar that the reading will probably become more of a word-calling situation. Even if this reader uses all of his linguistic competence to make predictions about what will occur in print, words such as *silo, harvester,* and *trough* and events such as birthing a calf or hauling hay will have little or no meaning. Adult readers experience the same frustrations if they try to understand material in an area they are unfamiliar with, such as a physics text, a medical journal, or legal documents. This does not imply that the reader cannot understand material concerning something not experienced, but rather that a reader must have a repertoire of relevant concepts to interpret the printed page. Consider another young reader who has always lived in the Deep South and has never experienced heavy snows. This reader is asked to read a story about a blizzard. Even though the reader has never experienced a blizzard, some relevant concepts available to the reader might be ice, the wind of a hurricane, and the possible tragedy of its aftermath.

In summary, for maximum comprehension to occur, the reader must be able to relate the printed material to personal experiences. Direct, firsthand experiences are usually best. At the very least, vicarious or secondhand experiences, such as listening to stories on a variety of concepts, seeing relevant pictures, and watching films or video clips, must be provided.

Interests and Attitudes

Closely related to prior knowledge and experience are interests and attitudes. Shnayer (1969) reports that interest in a topic enables readers with reading ability from two years below grade level to one year above grade level to read beyond their measured ability. Thus, a reader will better understand a book about explorers if she has an interest in history and the concept of exploration. Readers' attitudes are closely related to their interests. Attitudes are learned and probably reflect previous experiences. A reader with a poor attitude toward reading on any subject has little motivation to pick up a book and read, much less comprehend (Alexander & Cobb, 1992). Because attitude is influenced as much by factors within the reading environment as by factors within the reader, interests and attitudes are addressed further in Chapters 4 and 6.

Factors within the Written Message

As Smith and Johnson (1980, p. 133) state, "Reading comprehension is not entirely dependent on the reader." Elements in the written message must be considered, including the words themselves, sentences, paragraphs, and longer units of discourse, such as stories.

Words

What makes some words easier to learn than others? The most researched characteristics of words are frequency and imagery. Frequency refers to how often a word occurs in the language. Several studies (Ekwall & Shanker, 1988; Jorm, 1977) have demonstrated that passages containing words that occur frequently in the language are more easily comprehended than passages containing words that do not occur frequently.

Imagery refers to how easily a word is visualized. A word with a **concrete referent,** such as *dog,* is probably easier to learn than a word with an **abstract referent,** such as *way.* Passages containing a heavy concentration of words with low imagery (abstract words) will probably be more difficult to understand than passages containing a large number of words with high imagery (Thorndyke, 1977).

The results of a study by Jorm (1977) are particularly relevant. Jorm analyzed the effects of word imagery, length, and frequency on the reading ability of good and poor readers ages 8–11. While word length had little effect on either type of reader, Jorm found that high-frequency words were easier to read for both good and poor readers. He also found that imagery facilitated word recognition only for poor readers. Jorm explains that ineffective readers are more likely than good readers to use a whole-word method for word recognition, and visual imagery is an aid for this type of learning. On the basis of this information, teachers are advised to carefully examine materials to be used with readers having difficulty for the occurrence of high-imagery words.

Teachers working with struggling readers must be concerned with the difficulty of material. The ratio of known words to unknown words is most important. In fact, the ratio of difficult words in a text is the most powerful predictor of text difficulty (Anderson & Freebody, 1981), and a reader's knowledge of key vocabulary predicts comprehension of text better than reading ability or achievement (Johnston, 1984). (See Chapter 10 for a discussion of meaning vocabulary and its relationship to comprehension.) When students are provided material at their instructional reading level, the number of known words approximates 95 out of 100. Students are often taught the *five-finger method* to determine whether a library book is easy enough for them to read. This idea is analogous to the instructional reading level criterion: If the student counts more than five unknown words on a page, the book is probably too difficult. (See Goldilocks Strategy in Chapter 11, and Appendix E for help in determining readability of text material.)

Sentences, Paragraphs, and Longer Units

Comprehension of written material demands much more than understanding each word in the selection. Words must be understood in relation to other words. Likewise, readers seldom read isolated sentences, but they must comprehend relationships within sentences if they are to comprehend a paragraph (called **microprocessing;** see Irwin, 1991, p. 2). Just as sentence comprehension is more than understanding each word, paragraph comprehension (called **integrative processing;** Irwin, 1991, p. 3) is more than understanding individual sentences. Paragraphs are structured to function in longer units of written discourse. To understand a paragraph, the reader must recognize who or what the paragraph is about. The reader must also recognize the relations existing within and between paragraphs, such as cause and effect, question and answer (or problem and solution), sequence, enumeration, description, or comparison and contrast (Meyer, 1984; Sinatra, 1991). Englert and Thomas (1987) report that for instructional purposes, sequence is easiest, followed by, in order of difficulty, enumeration, description, and compare-contrast.

As with sentences, a reader does not often read isolated paragraphs. Paragraphs exist in the context of longer selections. According to Robinson (1983, p. 92), paragraphs serve specific functions: introductory, expository, narrative, descriptive, definitional, persuasive, transitional, or summary and concluding. The skilled reader recognizes how paragraphs function within the total context of the selection.

Specific relationships also exist within narratives (i.e., stories) and expository material (i.e., nonfiction). Stemming from the work of Bartlett (1932), several studies have attempted to specify the logical relations existing within stories (Mandler & Johnson, 1977; Rumelhart, 1975; Stein & Glenn, 1979; Thorndyke, 1977). Stories are usually organized in consistent, predictable patterns. The reader expects relations that specify themes, setting, characters, goals, and resolutions. Thorndyke (1977) states that some story structures (e.g., fairy tales and fables) become more familiar with experience and that stories with several cause-effect relations are easier to comprehend than those without causal relations. (Chapter 11 provides more information specific to the comprehension of narrative material.) Similarly, expository material also uses the writing patterns of problem-solution and cause-effect, but includes as major patterns time order, compare-contrast, listing of facts, and enumeration as well. (Chapter 12 presents information specific to the comprehension of expository material.)

In summary, recognizing organization is key to understanding written material. The reader must identify who or what the material is about, discover the relationship between actors or agents and actions, and determine the function or purpose of the material. This "process of synthesizing and organizing individual idea units into a summary or organized series of related general ideas is called **macroprocessing**" (Irwin, 1991, p. 4).

Environmental Factors

Essentially two environments affect reading comprehension—the home and the school. The preceding emphasis on prior knowledge and experience explains the important role of the home environment in providing the language base necessary for reading comprehension. The student with an extensive language base comes to school better equipped for the comprehension process than a student who has not been spoken to frequently, read to, taken on trips, or involved in other concept-developing activities.

The school environment refers, for the most part, to the student's classroom, teacher, and peers. However, the atmosphere of the entire school and the attitude of administrators and other teachers also affect reading comprehension, even if only in a general, indirect sense.

While the classroom teacher has the most direct influence on reading comprehension, classmates provide a source of competition or approval or a standard for comparison. Unfortunately, classmates may also have an emotionally negative influence as sources of ridicule or harassment.

Teachers can do much to affect comprehension both instructionally and emotionally. Teachers influence comprehension in a positive way through the following practices:

1. *Establishing a comfortable, risk-free atmosphere in which students do not fear ridicule or penalty for failure.* Teachers should provide the kind of feedback that encourages curiosity, risk-taking, and creativity.

2. *Providing a model for their students.* Reading is perceived as a valuable, enjoyable, and relevant activity when students see their teachers reading and are read to by their teachers.

3. *Providing direct instruction.* This includes preparing students for reading by discussing backgrounds and essential vocabulary of text, and by helping students establish purposes for reading with appropriate follow-up activities.

4. *Choosing appropriate materials for instruction.* Teachers must know their students' strengths, needs, and reading levels. Frustrating material does nothing to help comprehension.

5. *Planning the type of questions they will ask.* Teachers' questions are often poorly planned with respect to the objectives of the lesson (Bartolome, 1969) and do not demand much thinking beyond a literal level (Bartolome, 1969; Cecil, 1995; Dantonio, 1990; Durkin, 1981; Guszak, 1967). Instructional techniques in this chapter and those that follow emphasize this important aspect of comprehension instruction.

6. *Providing ample opportunities and time to read.* Students need large blocks of time to just read, at least twenty minutes each day. The benefits go beyond enhancing reading comprehension to improving writing, self-esteem, and attitude toward school (Block & Cavanaugh, 1998; Elley, 1991; Krashen, 1993). Block (1999) refers to this type of comprehension instruction as "Type 1 lessons," whose purpose "is to provide enough time for students to not merely read but to live within a book. . . students select their own books and reading goals. . . and have time to read without having to perform a task about what they comprehended" (pp. 101–102). Students, especially those who are struggling with reading, need more practice reading whole text, not less. Classroom organizational patterns that include activities such as book clubs or literature circles and DEAR time (see Chapter 11) are desirable.

THEORIES AND MODELS OF THE COMPREHENSION PROCESS

Schema Theory

Linguists, cognitive psychologists, and psycholinguists have used the concept of **schema** (pl. *schemata*) to understand the interaction of key factors affecting the comprehension process. The term *schema* itself is not new (Bartlett, 1932; Kant, 1787/1963), but the recognition of its importance to reading is more recent (Rumelhart, 1975, 1980, 1994). Simply put, schema theory states that all knowledge is organized into units. Within these units of knowledge, or schemata, is stored information. A *schema,* then, is a generalized description or a conceptual system for understanding knowledge—how knowledge is represented and how it is used.

According to this theory, schemata represent knowledge about concepts: objects and the relationships they have with other objects, situations, events, sequences of events, actions, and sequences of actions. A simple example is to think of your schema for *dog.* Within that schema you most likely have knowledge about dogs in general (bark, four legs, teeth, hair, tails) and probably information about specific dogs, such as collies (long hair, large, Lassie) or springer spaniels (English, docked tails, liver and white or black and white, Millie). You may also think of dogs within the greater context of animals and other living things; that is, dogs breathe, need food, and reproduce. Your knowledge of dogs might also include the fact that they are mammals and thus are warm-blooded and bear their young as opposed to laying eggs. Depending upon your personal experience, the knowledge of a dog as a pet (domesticated and loyal) or as an animal to fear (likely to bite or attack) may be a part of your schema. And so it goes with the development of a schema. Each new experience incorporates more information into one's schema.

What does all this have to do with reading comprehension? Individuals have schemata for everything. Long before students come to school, they develop schemata (units of knowledge) about everything they experience. Schemata become theories about reality. These theories not only affect the way information is interpreted, thus affecting comprehension, but also continue to change as new information is received. As stated by Rumelhart (1980),

> schemata can represent knowledge at all levels—from ideologies and cultural truths to knowledge about the meaning of a particular word, to knowledge about what patterns of excitations are associated with what letters of the alphabet. We have schemata to represent all levels of our experience, at all levels of abstraction. Finally, our schemata *are* our knowledge. All of our generic knowledge is embedded in schemata. (p. 41)

Schema theory has great importance to a discussion of corrective reading. According to Carver (1992), "ideas from schema theory are likely to have direct relevance to reading situations involving relatively hard materials that require studying" (p. 173). Carver bases this statement on his **rauding theory** (1977, 1990), which purports five basic reading processes: skimming, scanning, rauding, learning, and memorizing. Rauding, simply stated, means normal, typical, ordinary reading. In short, rauding theory holds that when individuals are using the reading process they operate with for ordinary narrative-type reading, schema theory is not directly relevant. Schema theory *is* relevant for the other processes, however, especially learning and memorizing. Whenever readers have to shift out of their normal reading process (rauding), schema theory and its derived variables of predicting, prior knowledge, and text type (i.e., narrative vs. expository) become quite important. Such may often be the case for corrective readers, because they may not have developed a "normal reading process." In other words, for corrective readers rauding may not exist at all or may be more likely when reading narrative-type text (e.g., stories). However, these same readers will likely need much assistance in building or activating schemata before reading expository (e.g., informational) text (see Chapter 12), or text they find difficult.

The importance of schema theory to reading comprehension also lies in how the reader uses schemata. This issue has not yet been resolved by research, although investigators agree that some mechanism activates just those schemata most relevant to the reader's task. While theories try to explain the comprehension process, related models have been developed that "serve as metaphors to explain and represent the theory" (Ruddell & Ruddell, 1994, p. 812). Five categories of models have been derived to explain literacy processes. These five classifications are termed cognitive-based, sociocognitive, transactional, transactional-sociopsycholinguistic, and attitude-influence.

Reading Comprehension as Cognitive-Based Processing

There are several models based on cognitive processing (see Ruddell & Ruddell, 1994, p. 813). For example, the LaBerge-Samuels Model of Automatic Information Processing (Samuels, 1994) emphasizes internal aspects of attention as crucial to comprehension. Samuels (1994, pp. 818–819) defines three characteristics of internal attention. The first, *alertness,* is the reader's active attempt to access relevant schemata involving letter-sound relationships, syntactic knowledge, and word meanings. *Selectivity,* the second characteristic, refers to the reader's ability to attend selectively to only that information requiring processing. The third characteristic, *limited capacity,* refers to the fact that the human brain has a limited amount of cognitive energy available for use in processing information. In other words, if a reader's cognitive energy is focused on decoding and attention cannot be directed at integrating, relating, and combining the meanings of the words decoded, then comprehension will suffer. "Automaticity in information processing, then, simply means that information is processed with little attention" (Samuels, 1994, p. 823). Comprehension difficulties occur when the reader cannot rapidly and automatically access the concepts and knowledge stored in the schemata.

One other example of a cognitive-based model is Rumelhart's (1994) Interactive Model. Information from several knowledge sources (schemata for letter-sound relationships, word meanings, syntactic relationships, event sequences, and so forth) are considered *simultaneously.* The implication is that when information from one source, such as word recognition, is deficient, the reader will rely on information from another source, for example, contextual clues or previous experience. Stanovich (1980) terms the latter kind of processing *interactive-compensatory* because the reader *(any reader)* compensates for deficiencies in one or more of the knowledge sources by using information from remaining knowledge sources. Those sources that are more concerned with concepts and semantic relationships are termed *higher-level stimuli;* sources dealing with the print itself—that is, phonics, sight words, and other word-attack skills—are termed *lower-level stimuli.* The interactive-compensatory model implies that the reader will rely on higher-level processes when lower-level processes are inadequate, and vice versa. Stanovich (1980) extensively reviews research demonstrating such compensation in both good and poor readers.

Reading Comprehension as Sociocognitive Processing

A sociocognitive processing model takes a constructivist view of reading comprehension; that is, the reader, the text, the teacher, and the classroom community are all involved in the construction of meaning. Ruddell and Ruddell (1994, p. 813) state, "The role of the classroom's social context and the influence of the teacher on the reader's meaning negotiation and construction are central to this model [developed by R. B. Ruddell and N. J. Unrau, 1994] as it explores the notion that participants in literacy events form and reform meanings in a hermeneutic [interpretation] circle." In other words, this model views comprehension as a process that involves meaning negotiation among text, readers, teachers, and other members of the classroom community. Schema for text meanings, academic tasks, sources of authority (i.e., residing within the text, the reader, the teacher, the classroom community, or some interaction of these), and sociocultural settings are all brought to the negotiation task. The teacher's role is one of orchestration of the instructional setting, and being knowledgeable about teaching/learning strategies and about the world.

Reading Comprehension as Transactional

The **transactional model** takes into account the dynamic nature of language and both aesthetic and cognitive aspects of reading. According to Rosenblatt (1994, p. 1063), "Every reading act is an event, or a transaction involving a particular reader and a particular pattern of signs, a text, and occurring at a particular time in a particular context. Instead of two fixed entities acting on one another, the reader and the text are two aspects of a total dynamic situation. The 'meaning' does not reside ready-made 'in' the text or 'in' the reader but happens or comes into being during the transaction between reader and text." Thus, text without a reader is merely a set of marks capable of being interpreted as written language. However, when a reader transacts with the text, meaning happens.

Schemata are not viewed as static but rather as active, developing, and ever changing. As readers transact with text they are changed or transformed, as is the text. Similarly, "the same text takes on different meanings in transactions with different readers or even with the same reader in different contexts or times" (Rosenblatt, 1994, p. 1078).

Reading Comprehension as Transactional-Sociopsycholinguistic

Building on Rosenblatt's transactional model, K. S. Goodman (1994) conceptualizes literacy processing as including reading, writing, and written texts. He states,

> Texts are constructed by authors to be comprehended by readers. The meaning is in the author and the reader. The text has a potential to evoke meaning but has no meaning in itself; meaning is not a characteristic of texts. This does not mean the characteristics of the text are unimportant or that either writer or reader are independent of them. How well the writer constructs the text and how well the reader reconstructs it and constructs meaning will influence comprehension. But meaning does not pass between writer and reader. It is represented by a writer in a text and constructed from a text by a reader. Characteristics of writer, text, and reader will all influence the resultant meaning. (p. 1103)

In a transactional-sociopsycholinguistic view, the reader has a highly active role. It is the individual transactions between a reader and the text characteristics that result in meaning. These characteristics include physical characteristics such as orthography—the alphabetic system, spelling, punctuation; format characteristics such as paragraphing, lists, schedules, bibliographies; macrostructure or text grammar such as that found in telephone books, recipe books, newspapers, and letters; and wording of texts such as the differences found in narrative and expository text.

Understanding is limited, however, by the reader's schemata, making what the reader brings to the text as important as the text itself. The writer also plays an important role in comprehension. Additionally, readers' and writers' schemata are changed through transactions with the text as meaning is constructed. Readers' schemata are changed as new knowledge is assimilated and accommodated. Writers' schemata are changed as new ways of organizing text to express meaning are developed. According to K. S. Goodman (1994):

> How well the writer knows the audience and has built the text to suit that audience makes a major difference in text predictability and comprehension. However, since comprehension results from reader-text transactions, what the reader knows, who the reader is, what values guide the reader, and what purposes or interests the reader has will play vital roles in the reading process. It follows that what is comprehended from a given text varies among readers. Meaning is ultimately created by each reader. (p. 1127)

Reading Comprehension as Influenced by Attitude

Mathewson's (1994) Model of Attitude Influence upon Reading and Learning to Read is derived from the area of social psychology. This model attempts to explain the roles of affect and cognition in reading comprehension. The core of the attitude-influence model explains that a reader's whole attitude toward reading (i.e., prevailing feelings and evaluative beliefs about reading and action readiness for reading) will influence the intention to read, in turn influencing reading behavior. *Intention to read* is proposed as the primary mediator between attitude and reading. *Intention* is defined as "commitment to a plan for achieving one or more reading purposes at a more or less specified time in the future" (Mathewson, 1994, p. 1135). All other moderator variables (e.g., extrinsic motivation, involvement, prior knowledge, and purpose) are viewed as affecting the attitude-reading relationship by influencing the intention to read. Therefore, classroom environments that include well-stocked libraries, magazines, reading tables, and areas with comfortable chairs will enhance students' intentions to read. Mathewson (1994, p. 1148) states, "Favorable attitudes toward reading thus sustain intention to read and reading as long as readers continue to be satisfied with reading outcomes."

SKILLED VERSUS LESS SKILLED COMPREHENDERS

An early review of the literature on good and poor comprehenders by Golinkoff (1975/1976) reveals that good comprehenders are adaptable and flexible. They seem to be aware that reading is a process for gaining information or expanding one's knowledge about the world. More specifically, in terms of three comprehension subskills that Golinkoff uses to compare good and poor comprehenders, the skilled comprehender is a master at decoding, accessing single word meanings, and extracting relationships between words in sentences and larger units of text.

Poor comprehenders, on the other hand, are less adaptive and flexible in their reading style. They make more decoding errors and take more time to decode. They tend to read word-by-word, which implies one of three things: they are unfamiliar with the printed words (decoding), they are unaware of the clues to proper phrasing (syntactic aspects), or they are unaware that reading involves using what they already know about the concepts and contextual constraints found in the text to construct meaning. This last characteristic is also supported by McKeown's (1985) research on the acquisition of word meanings from context (semantic aspects).

While such characterizations have led to the conclusion that poor comprehenders are more concerned with pronouncing words correctly than with getting meaning from the printed page, this is not necessarily the case. Stanovich (1980) gives evidence that in some situations poor readers rely *more* on contextual information than good readers. To cope with a large number of visually unfamiliar words, some poor readers depend too much on the syntactic and semantic clues available. This phenomenon is referred to as the interactive-compensatory hypothesis, and has been tested and supported by (Yoon) Kim and Goetz (1994).

Kolers (1975) presents evidence that such dependence on syntactic and semantic clues to avoid decoding may be a common source of reading difficulty. Kolers's subjects, good and poor readers ages 10–14, read sentences in normal and reversed type. The poor readers made ten times as many substitution errors as the good readers. Also, the reading speed of the poor readers was less affected by the reversed type than that of the good readers. The poor readers guessed frequently and paid relatively little attention to the typographical (graphemic) aspects of the print. These results were interpreted as indicating an overreliance on syntactic and semantic clues.

Stanovich (1980) distinguishes between two types of contextual processing when discussing differences between good and poor comprehenders. The first type involves relating new information to known information and imposing structure on the text (text organization). The second type is the contextual hypothesis-testing strategy that allows previously understood material to help with ongoing word recognition. Good readers use both types of contextual processing, whereas poor readers are more adept at the second type. In itself this is not a problem; however, if processing is being used to aid word recognition, the reader is depleting valuable cognitive resources that could otherwise be employed for making inferences or relating new information to old. Stanovich views the comprehension problem as a direct result of slow and nonautomatic word recognition skills that require the poor reader to draw on the wrong kinds of knowledge sources. As stated by Stanovich (1980):

> Given that the ability to use prior context to facilitate word recognition is not a skill that differentiates good from poor readers, there appear to be two general types of processes that good readers perform more efficiently than poor readers. Good readers appear to have superior strategies for comprehending and remembering large units of text. In addition, good readers are superior at context-free word recognition. There is some evidence indicating that good readers have automatized the recognition of word and subword units to a greater extent than poor readers. However, good readers recognize even fully automated words faster than poor readers. . . . In short, the good reader identifies words automatically and rapidly. . . . The existence of this rapid context-free recognition ability means that the word recognition of good readers is less reliant on conscious expectancies generated from the prior sentence context. The result is that more attentional capacity is left over for integrative comprehension processes. (p. 64)

A study by Kletzien (1991) looked at the comprehension strategies used by good and poor comprehenders with expository material at the secondary level. Results support earlier findings (see Golinkoff, 1975/1976) that good comprehenders are more flexible in their use of strategies. By means of student self-reports Kletzien found that both good and poor comprehenders are aware of a variety of strategies, but attention to vocabulary, rereading, making inferences, and using prior knowledge were the most frequently used strategies for both groups. More strategies were used with easier material. Poor comprehenders used fewer strategies as the difficulty of the material increased. Kletzien concluded that poor comprehenders need to know when, how, and why to use a particular strategy.

Poor comprehenders apparently do not effectively use the strategies that good comprehenders do. Research by Olshavsky (1976/1977) reveals that poor readers are not proficient in using context to aid reading fluency, or in using their knowledge of the language to add information that is not in the text but would help in understanding of the material (making inferences). Olshavsky concluded that, in general, poor readers use fewer strategies than good readers, but Kletzien's research indicates that this may be due to uncertainty as to when to use a strategy rather than a lack of awareness of the strategies themselves.

Rumelhart (1980, p. 48) offers additional explanations of failure to comprehend a selection, assuming that the words are automatically recognized.

1. The reader does not have the appropriate schemata necessary (lack of conceptual background).
2. The reader has the appropriate schemata, but clues provided by the author are insufficient to suggest them.
3. The reader interprets the text but not in the way intended by the author.

These breakdowns are likely when reading something in a new field of study or something abstract, vague, technical, or too difficult.

In conclusion, comprehension demands that the reader be active, attentive, and selective while reading. As Tierney and Pearson (1994, p. 497) advocate, "teaching procedures that encourage students to monitor their own processing strategies—how they allocate attention to text versus prior knowledge, how they can tell *what* and *that* they know (i.e., metacognition), and how to apply fix-up strategies when comprehension is difficult" should be adopted.

ASSESSMENT AND INSTRUCTION FOR GENERAL COMPREHENSION

Reading comprehension, as discussed in this text, includes three major areas: comprehension of individual word meanings (vocabulary); comprehension of stories (narrative); and comprehension of informational text (expository). And because there are strategies that are particularly well-suited for each of these areas, the three chapters that follow will address each of them, respectively. The following reading comprehension strategies are effective for any type of text, whether it be narrative or expository. I am calling these general comprehension strategies, and they are appropriately used with either narrative or expository material.

Reading comprehension requires a number of thinking and reasoning skills. No longer is it sufficient to consider material "comprehended" if the reader can recall elements of the text. As Pearson (1985) has stated, "no longer do we regard text as a fixed object that the reader is supposed to 'approximate' as closely as possible as s/he reads. Instead we now view text as a sort of blueprint for meaning, a set of tracks or clues that the reader uses as s/he builds a model of what the text means" (p. 726). It is only when readers actively construct logical connections among their own prior knowledge, ideas in the text, the specific task at hand, and the situation they are in, and can express these ideas in their own words, that the text is considered comprehended.

Teachers also need to recognize the importance of prior knowledge and writing to reading comprehension. "Writing is one of the most powerful tools for developing comprehension because it can actively involve the reader in constructing a set of meanings that are useful to the individual reader" (Irwin, 1991, p. 24). Because writing activities help develop reading comprehension, many of the assessment and instruction techniques discussed in Chapter 7 are also relevant here.

In addition, **listening,** or oral language comprehension, is an area in which much assumptive teaching occurs. Many teachers associate listening with hearing and assume listening is simply a matter of either paying attention or not paying attention. Not true. After extensive study, Lundsteen (1979, p. 15) concluded that listening is "the process by which spoken language is converted to meaning in the mind," and as such, involves the same processes as reading comprehension.

Briefly, listening comprehension involves both **attentive listening** (i.e., attending to the message) and **auditory comprehension** (i.e., constructing meaning from an oral message). Auditory comprehension includes literal understanding of the message and also critical evaluation of what is heard. Both auditory comprehension and attentive listening are prerequisites to academic success because as much as 60 percent of a student's time in school requires following oral directions and listening to teachers or guest speakers (Wilt, 1958). Because of their prerequisite connection to abilities associated with academic learning, such as note taking, techniques for assessment and instruction of attentive listening and auditory comprehension are presented in Chapter 13.

In summary, instruction in reading comprehension involves helping learners with such processes as predicting, visualizing, inferring, self-questioning, monitoring, summarizing, and synthesizing.

Assessing the Ability to Organize Text

Reading comprehension requires that readers make connections between their own prior knowledge and the organization of the text. **Text organization** refers to the relationships between words, sentences, paragraphs, and longer units. As such, it is key to reading comprehension. In constructing relations between words, the reader must be able to construct meaning at (1) a sentence level, (2) a paragraph level, and (3) a level involving longer passages or series of paragraphs (Irwin, 1991; Pennock, 1979). For example, using a single sentence, can the student tell who or what the sentence is about (subject), what the action is (verb or predicate), and where or when the action is taking place? Does the student understand pronoun referents? Does the student appreciate how punctuation can affect meaning? Can the student recognize that different sentences can have the same meaning?

These same questions can be asked about paragraphs, and are best asked directly during reading. For example, assume the following paragraph is being read.

Andrew was being very selfish. He did not want to share his toys. Because of this, he played alone.

The teacher can ask:

- Who is the first sentence (or paragraph) about? (Response: Andrew)
- What is Andrew doing in this sentence (in this paragraph)? (Response: being selfish, playing alone)
- Who is the "he" in the second sentence? (Response: Andrew)

- Why did Andrew play alone? (Response: he wouldn't share his toys)
- What does "this" refer to in the last sentence? (Response: he didn't share his toys)
- What is another way to say the last sentence (or "Is this another way . . ." depending on child's response). (Response: Andrew played alone because he would not share his toys.)

This last question is really asking for a main idea. Determining the main idea of a paragraph is analogous to determining a category title for a set of words. Pearson and Johnson (1978) discuss several types of main idea organizations that are useful for both assessing and teaching. Knowledge of each of these organizations can be observed by asking the student to locate the sentence that best expresses the main idea of the paragraph. The material used should correspond to the student's instructional level.

1. *Explicit main idea is stated at the beginning of a paragraph.*
   Polar bears are well adapted to life in the Arctic. Their color makes them hard to see against a snowy background. A jacket of fat keeps them warm and helps them float in the water. Hair on the soles of their paws gives them good footing on ice.

2. *Explicit main idea is stated at the end of the paragraph.*
   The color of polar bears makes them hard to see against a snowy background. A jacket of fat keeps them warm and helps them float in the water. Hair on the soles of their paws gives them good footing on ice. Polar bears are well adapted to life in the Arctic.

3. *Main idea is implicit—that is, not stated.*
   The color of polar bears makes them hard to see against a snowy background. A jacket of fat keeps them warm and helps them float in the water. Hair on the soles of their paws gives them good footing on ice.

Recognizing explicit main ideas is easier than determining implicit main ideas. Both tasks are simplified by providing multiple-choice responses. Example choices should include the four types of distractors shown in the following example:

Polar bears are fat, hairy, and white. *(too specific)*

Polar bears are good swimmers. *(not mentioned)*

Life in the Arctic. *(too general)*

Polar bears are well adapted to life in the Arctic. *(right level of generality)*

For assessing text longer than a sentence or a single paragraph, the student can be asked about cause-and-effect relationships, enumeration, and sequence, as well as compare-and-contrast, question-and-answer, and generalization organizational frameworks. This does not mean the reader is required to label the function or purpose of a series of paragraphs, but should be able to recognize the characteristics, or key words, for each type. One effective way of assessing comprehension of these organizational frameworks is with paragraph frames (see also Chapter 12). A paragraph frame will make use of common key words to signal the relationships among paragraphs. For instance, cause-and-effect relationships are signaled by key words such as *because, since, for, hence, so, therefore, if . . . then,* and *as a result.* Look for key signal words in the following series of paragraphs.

In the early years of our country the Mississippi River was important for both trading and travel. First it was used by the Indians, then by the Spanish explorers. Finally French fur traders used the river.

Later, the river helped many settlements get started. But *because* the railroads came, river traffic almost disappeared. Then came World War I.

As a result the United States was shipping so many goods to help fight the war, river traffic once again became important. The railroads could not carry all the goods. Today the river remains busy.

Ask: What caused Mississippi River traffic to almost disappear? Why did river traffic once again become important? (Important key words are in italics.)

A paragraph frame for assessment of cause-and-effect relationships would ask readers to supply, in their own words, the missing information. For example,

In the early years of our country the Mississippi River was important for both trading and travel. First it was used by the Indians, then by the Spanish explorers. Finally French fur traders used the river.

But because _____.

As a result, _____.

Today, _____.

Common key words for other paragraph relationships are:

Enumeration: one, two, three, another, more, also, most important, to begin with

Sequence: first, second, third, last, before, after, while, then, later, finally

Compare-and-contrast: but, however, although, yet, even though, on the other hand

Question-and-answer: why, how, when, where, what

Generalization: for example, for instance, characteristics are, in fact

Instruction for General Comprehension

No single, easy way has been found to improve comprehension skills. Because of the complex interrelationship between the many factors operating during comprehension, better understanding cannot be assured by having a student experience a certain activity. However, if the teacher is aware of the factors within the reader, the text, and the learning environment and tries to account for these factors in instruction, the chances for improvement appear greater.

Instructional techniques especially relevant for the struggling comprehender follow and are organized according to the three major text organization categories: sentence level, paragraph level, and longer units. Underlying all comprehension instruction is the assumption that the teacher is aware of and uses good questioning techniques. Facilitating questions must be asked at the right times to help both the teacher and the student further understand the comprehension process. A good questioning technique models appropriate strategies and teaches students to ask themselves questions while reading; this ensures active participation and helps students realize that the material being read should and must make sense.

Instructional Techniques Using Sentences

The main purpose of instruction at the sentence level is to teach students how to note the important details of a sentence, how to use word order and punctuation to indicate the meaning of the sentence, and to realize that the same thing can be said more than one way. According to Kamm (1979), focusing on the details of a sentence is an analysis task that should begin with simple sentences such as: *The dog ran.* (Language experience and students' creative stories provide an excellent source for such sentences.) This sentence is read aloud, and the student is asked to identify the action. If the response is "running" or "ran," the sentence is shown to the student and the specific word representing the action underlined. The next question asks who or what is running, and if the student responds "the dog," the word dog is underlined twice. The student then sees "The <u>dog</u> <u>ran</u>."

Through sentence expansion (see also "Add a Word/Stretch the Sentence" in Chapter 7), the student is shown that the action and agent do not change even if words are added. For example, the sentence may be expanded to *The brown dog ran down the street*. The following sequence then applies:

- What is the action? *(ran)* Underline once.
- Who or what ran? *(dog)* Underline twice.
- What color is the dog? *(brown)*
- Where did the dog run? *(down the street)*
- How else could you describe the dog? *(black, spotted, lost, frightened)*
- Where else could the dog have run? *(away, into the house, across the street)*

A follow-up activity for this type of instruction is to transform sentences into telegrams, teaching the reader that recognition of just the important words still gives the meaning of the sentence.

Sentence expansion also allows instruction in word order. Using just the form *The brown dog ran down the street,* the student is asked, "Why might the dog run down the street?" In most responses a prepositional phrase will be added. All forms of open-ended sentences or sentence fragments aid teaching word order. For example:

The brown dog _____.

The brown dog ran _____.

Down the street _____.

The writing technique of sentence combining and collecting (Speaker & Speaker, 1991) can help students gain knowledge of more complicated syntactic structures—an ability that transfers to reading. For example, the sentences *The dog ran down the street* and *The dog is brown* can be combined as *The brown dog ran down the street*. (See Chapter 7 for additional ideas.) Hughes (1975) observed that training in sentence combining was most effective for lower- and middle-ability students. Similarly, Neville and Searls (1991) report that sentence combining has more impact on reading comprehension for elementary students.

Another aspect of sentence comprehension is synthesis (Kamm, 1979). At this stage the learner is involved in paraphrasing sentences (see "Rephrasing" in Chapter 7). This paraphrasing takes two forms: rearranging the words in the sentence, or substituting appropriate synonyms.

One way to begin teaching paraphrasing is to give students a set of four to seven sight words. These words are taken from students' personal word banks. The students are then shown how to form as many different sentences as possible. Each word is used only once. For example, *Bob-what-Mary-does-says* can become:

1. Bob does what Mary says.
2. Mary does what Bob says.
3. What Mary says Bob does.

4. Mary says what Bob does.

5. Bob says what Mary does.

6. What Bob says Mary does.

Once the sentences are developed, the teacher instructs the student to find those that mean the same thing and asks questions as follows. "What action goes with *Bob* in sentence 1?" Response: *does.* "What action goes with *Mary* in sentence 1?" Response: *says.* "Find any other sentences where *Bob does* and *Mary says* are together." Response: *sentences 3 and 4.* The conclusion to be drawn is that sentences 1, 3, and 4 mean the same thing even though the word order is different. "What about sentences 2, 5, and 6?" Response: *They have the same meaning because in all three Mary does and Bob says.*

bodily-kinesthetic

After this kind of explicit instruction, students practice with a new set of sentences or sentence pairs. This practice can consist of role playing or dramatizing the action in the sentences to especially help those whose strengths are bodily-kinesthetic.

Instruction in comprehension should also provide the student a strategy for unlocking meaning. Therefore, the teacher must ask questions that the students should ask of themselves when the time comes to work independently: Who or what is this sentence about? What is happening in this sentence? When? Is there missing information? What seems to be missing? Incorrect responses must be discussed as well as correct responses so that the students understand which features are important.

Comprehension instruction that focuses on deriving meaning from single sentences or pairs of sentences is also discussed by Durkin (1978/1979). She suggests providing a sentence and asking students to name everything it tells. Her example, *The little kindergarten boy was crying,* elicits the responses that tell about the boy. All the facts of the sentence are written on the board. If a student speculates on why the boy was crying, this response leads into a list of what the sentence does not tell. This latter step is an application of "negative type questions" (Willford, 1968). Such questions represent an attempt to move away from the "right answer syndrome" (Caskey, 1970) to more speculation and predicting. As an example, Willford (1968) relates:

> Watch a five or six year old. You put a picture up and say, "Okay, what can you do with a horse?" Out of a group of 10, five of them have had an experience. The others don't know what you can do with a horse. We turn it completely around and say, "What can't you do with a horse?" You ought to see the different responses we get. Every child can tell you what you can't do with a horse. "What can't you do?" "Well you can't take a horse to bed with you." Someone else might say, "You can too if you live in a barn." This kid never thought about this. So now we find, what can you do with a horse? You can take a horse to bed with you if you live in a barn. You can flip the thing over by using a negative question as a stimulus to get a variety of answers. Kids love to do this. You may get more conversation from a single picture than any single thing you can do. (p. 103)

Sentence-level instruction should move from a literal level of understanding to an implied or inferred level. Heilman and Holmes (1978), in *Smuggling Language into the Teaching of Reading,* give two excellent activities for this level of instruction. To help students understand the reasoning involved, the directions and questions here have been modified.

logical - mathematical

1. *Choose the best meaning for the following sentence:* The moving van stopped in front of the empty house.
   a. The truck was probably empty.
   b. The truck was there to pick up furniture.

   c. The truck contained furniture for the people moving into the house. (p. 68)
   Questions: Why did you make the choice you made?
   What clues were in the sentence?

2. *Fill in the blank.* Only one word makes sense. Put two lines under any words that helped you decide what the *one* word had to be.
   a. The score was <u>tied</u> <u>seven</u> to <u>(seven)</u>.
   b. The <u>right</u>-hand <u>glove</u> will <u>not fit</u> on your <u>(left)</u> hand.
   c. The <u>umpire</u> said, " <u>(Strike)</u>   <u>three</u>, you're <u>out</u>!"

(Note how important background knowledge is at the implied or inferred level.)

At all levels of comprehension instruction, students should be directed to form mental pictures of what they are reading, and to attend to text illustrations if they are present (Gambrell & Jawitz, 1993). While an imagery strategy may not benefit all readers having comprehension difficulty, imagery instruction may help readers whose reading vocabulary is adequate but whose comprehension is poor (Gambrell & Bales, 1986; Wilhelm, 1997).

Imagery instruction begins by having students "make a picture in their heads" for specific things, such as a favorite animal or a place they have visited. These pictures are then shared so that each student can respond and listen to others' descriptions. The students are now ready to form mental pictures about the reading material. For example, if the reading contained the phrase, *As I was walking alone on that cold winter afternoon,* appropriate questions would be: "Where are you walking?" "What does the sky look like?" "How do you feel?" "How are you dressed?" Selections used for imagery instruction should not have overly elaborate descriptions. Material already rich in imagery leaves nothing for the student to visualize. Some students may wish to draw their images either as a pre-reading activity or as a follow-up activity (Whitin, 1996).

spatial

Instructional Techniques Using Paragraphs

Instruction in comprehension must include helping the reader see the relationships between ideas in a paragraph. As with sentences, however, the corrective student must be helped to construct literal meanings of paragraphs before implicit meanings. Marvin Cohn (1969) developed **structured comprehension,** a technique that moves quite well from the sentence level to the paragraph level. Cohn suggests that material selected for this technique be somewhat difficult for the students to read in their usual fashion. Passages from content-area materials are recommended. Only a selection of two or three sentences is needed for this technique, as instruction proceeds sentence by sentence and can become tedious if the selection is overly long.

Once the sentences are selected, the background is given to the students to put the sentences into their appropriate context. The next step is for the students (or the teacher) to read just the first sentence aloud. Any decoding errors are simply corrected. The students are then directed to ask themselves, "Do I know what this sentence means?" They may ask the teacher as many questions as necessary to understand the sentence. Once the students' questions have been answered, the teacher asks several questions about each sentence. These questions must be prepared in advance, because Cohn recommends that certain questions always be asked if the opportunity presents itself (see the following text). Students may look back to the text for answers, but the answers must be written. The questions asked should require only two or three words to answer; questions requiring longer answers are put in a multiple-choice format.

Questions always to be asked seek the following information:

1. Clarification of the referent for a pronoun

2. Clarification of meaning when a word has multiple or unusual meanings

3. The meaning of figurative expressions

4. Definition of causal or other relationships left implicit

Answers for each question are discussed. For incorrect answers, the teacher demonstrates why they are incorrect and explains the reasoning behind the correct answer. Correct answers, when put back into the text, make sense; incorrect answers do not. This cross-checking procedure also helps students *demand* that material read be meaningful.

Initially Cohn recommends that literal meanings be stressed more than relationships or implied information. Beginning with emphasis on the literal meaning provides more success for students and also allows them the opportunity to develop appropriate questioning techniques. The passive reader may become more actively involved through this process. Possible teacher questions can be seen in the "Andrew" paragraph discussed earlier in this chapter. For an example of a structured comprehension lesson used with expository material, see Figure 12.6.

A useful strategy for helping the reader identify who or what a paragraph is about uses the concepts of repeated and replaced words. **Repeated words** are those found in almost every sentence of the paragraph. Given the following paragraph, the student should be able to recognize the repeated word and tell what (or who) the paragraph is about.

> The city of Bern, Switzerland, starts its holiday season each year with *onions*. The fourth Monday in November is *Onion* Market Day. On this day farmers display *onions* in the public square. Red, yellow, and white *onions* are piled in colorful mounds. Wreaths and garlands of *onions* are on view. Visitors can sample free *onion* cake and hot *onion* soup.

Replaced words are substitutes for words that would normally be repeated. The pronoun is the most common substitute. Given the following paragraph, the student should be able to mentally substitute each replaced word with its referent and thus recognize who (or what) the paragraph is about.

> Two *scientists* "camped" for a week at the bottom of the sea. *Their* underwater home was a cabin shaped like a barrel. The *men* did not spend all *their* time in *their* underwater bubble. *They* went out to explore the sea bottom.

In addition to recognizing who or what a paragraph is about, the reader also must be able to identify significant details. Newspaper articles are a ready source of material that lends itself to the kind of questioning involved in teaching students to look for details. The following questions may be asked regarding the article in Figure 9.1.

1. Who was involved in this event? *(residents of the nursing home, police officers, firefighters)*

2. What took place? *(a fire)*

3. Where did it take place? *(Bryn Mawr Nursing Home in Minneapolis, Minnesota)*

4. When did it take place? *(Saturday, September 22)*

5. How or why did it take place? *(Police believe the fire was caused by arson.)*

Menus, recipes, and directions are additional sources of written materials rich in details for one main idea.

Main-idea instruction easily follows from here. Instruction in main ideas begins by using material with a topic sentence that explicitly states the main idea. Using the

Figure 9.1   Example of Newspaper Article that Helps Students Look for Details

The Times-Picayune   **Sunday, September 23**

Nursing Home Hit in Arson?

By JOHN LUNDQUIST

MINNEAPOLIS (AP)—Police said they believe the nursing home fire which claimed the life of one elderly resident and injured three others Saturday was the work of an arsonist.

A 38-year-old female resident of the Bryn Mawr Nursing Home, who was not identified, was taken into custody about 3½ hours after the blaze broke out, police said.

Charges were not filed immediately, police said.

Teams of firemen who responded to the three-alarm blaze helped many of the elderly at the home to safety from second floor windows. The residents were carried down ladders in rescue baskets or down stairways in their wheelchairs.

One fireman, Jeff Bartholomew, about 30, suffered smoke inhalation when he took off his mask and put it over the face of a woman he helped out of the two-story building, said Capt. Cecil Klingbile, one of the station fire chiefs on the scene.

"He took a lot of smoke when he did that," said Klingbile, who aided in the rescue.

Bartholomew was treated and released.

The Hennepin County medical examiner identified the dead woman as Fanny Anttila, 85.

Two elderly women in serious condition suffering from smoke inhalation were identified as Rose Seiger, 80, and Esther Cotter, 79.

A 75-year-old man, whose identification was being withheld until relatives had been notified, was in critical condition with second-degree burns.

Twenty-five other people were taken to hospitals but they were not admitted. David Lesperance, associate administrator, said they were "disposition cases," meaning the hospital was arranging accommodations for them.

One of the displaced residents was Richard Fobes, 71, who sat in a waiting room with his two sons.

"I was sitting in the recreation room on the first floor when the fire broke out," he said. "They (nursing home workers) told us to get in our rooms, and pretty soon they came and got us outside."

Fire Capt. Ronald Knoke said 44 firefighters from nine engine and four hook-and-ladder companies answered the alarm.

He said the fire was discovered at 9:54 a.m. (CDT) in the closet of a resident room, then spread down the hall to other parts of the second floor. Firefighters had the blaze under control at 10:28 a.m.

Knoke said most of the danger was from smoke, because of the age of the residents.

From *New Orleans Times-Picayune*. Used with permission of AP Newsfeatures, New York.

paragraph about polar bears discussed earlier, the student is first directed to find the key words or significant details, words that occur more than once, and a sentence that summarizes these details. The following questions might be asked:

What do most of the key words seem to point out?

What key words occur more than once?

What do these words relate to?

Is there a sentence that summarizes these ideas?

Polar bears are well adapted to life in the Arctic. Their color makes them hard to see against a snowy background. A jacket of fat keeps them warm and helps them float in the water. Hair on the soles of their paws gives them good footing on ice.

Figure 9.2   Diagram for Denoting Main Ideas and Supporting Details in the Polar Bear Paragraph

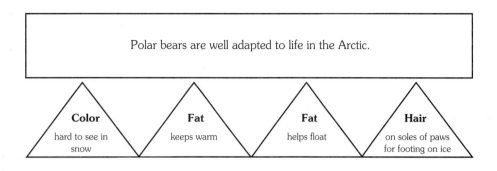

The first step is to underline key words, as shown in the paragraph. These key words aid in determining the significant details. In searching for recurring words, students are first led to discover the pronoun referents. Ask: "Who or what is the first sentence about?" Response: *polar bears.* Ask: "Who or what does the word *their* refer to in the second sentence?" Response: *polar bears.* "In the same sentence you see the word *them.* What does *them* refer to?" Response: *polar bears.* In actuality then, the term *polar bears* occurs quite frequently in this paragraph, which is a clue to the main topic of the paragraph. Significant details about polar bears should then be discussed by asking, "What does this paragraph tell us about polar bears?" A diagram may be used, such as that shown in Figure 9.2, and compared to students' maps used for pre-writing to demonstrate **spatial** how reading and writing are connected.

Going back to the paragraph, ask, "Can you choose one sentence that includes all of the supporting details or summarizes those details?" Elicit the response that the first sentence does this. Explain why this sentence summarizes the others if students have difficulty (1) recognizing that the first sentence describes the main idea of the paragraph or (2) determining why polar bears are well adapted to life in the Arctic.

The usefulness of activities such as the structured comprehension lesson for teaching paragraph understanding should now be apparent. Instruction in this area helps the student know what to look for in a paragraph to determine its meaning. After instruction, the following activities should be easier for students.

1. *In this activity, the student must find the sentence that does not belong in this paragraph.*

   Tommy was baking a cake for Mother's birthday. He sifted flour, added two eggs, and put it in the oven to bake. It seemed to take forever to be done. At last the potatoes were ready. The frosting was chocolate with marshmallows. (Heilman & Holmes, 1978, p. 65)

   Possible questions to ask regarding this paragraph are:
   • What is this paragraph about?
   • Which sentence doesn't seem to belong? Why?

2. *In this activity, the student attempts to determine implied information.*

   Tomorrow is the big day. John has been practicing ever since school started. Now is his chance to show all his friends his special tricks. This is the time of year when spooky things are really popular. He doesn't even need to wear a costume to scare people. After the parade the older kids get to put on a show for the little ones. Gee! It will be great fun to see their faces turn white. It's a good thing it will be on the last day of the school week. They will have the weekend to recover from their fright (Heilman & Holmes, 1978, p. 70).

Possible questions to ask regarding this paragraph are:
• What day of the week will something important take place?
   a. Saturday   b. Sunday   c. Friday

To help students answer this question, the teacher directs their attention to the appropriate sentences. "What sentences in the paragraph mention the word *day?*" Response: *first and eighth sentences.* "Does the first sentence help us to know what day it is?" Response: *no, only tomorrow.* "What about the eighth sentence?" Response: *yes, the last day of the school week is Friday.*
• What holiday do you think it is?
   a. Halloween   b. Fourth of July   c. Easter

Once again the relevant sentences are discussed. First, the teacher elicits key words associated with Halloween, Fourth of July, and Easter. Next, the students look for key words in the paragraph. Once the words *spooky, costume, trick, scare,* and *fright,* elicited for Halloween, are also found in the paragraph, the holiday becomes apparent.
• How long has John been practicing?
   a. about two weeks   b. about two months   c. about two hours

Ask: "What sentence mentions practicing?" Response: *the second sentence.* "When does school start?" Response: *late August or early September.* "When is Halloween?" Response: *late October.* "How much time is between late August or early September and late October?" Response: *about two months.*

As noted before, prior knowledge and experience are important for success in implied-information activities. Most of the guiding questions require the readers to think about something they already know or have experienced. Additional activities and discussion of implicit main ideas can be found in Pearson and Johnson's (1978) *Teaching Reading Comprehension,* Chapter 5.

The questions in the foregoing examples represent the direction that instruction in paragraph comprehension should take. Students must be shown explicitly how to deal with paragraph information. Teachers instruct best by modeling or thinking out loud with their students to reveal the strategies they themselves use. Once shown the strategy, students can practice and apply this type of thinking to material read independently. They can write their own paragraphs and plan a lesson for transmitting the main idea to other students. This gives students the opportunity to practice the question-asking strategies involved.

Sometimes the problem of not understanding material can be attributed to inappropriate phrasing. Even material used in a structured comprehension lesson can be rewritten into phrase units to aid the reader. This technique, referred to as *chunking* (Walker, 2000), "facilitates comprehension and fluency by using thought units rather than word-by-word reading" (p. 200). An example from Heilman and Holmes (1978, p. 127) follows.

> This material
> is written
> in short phrases
> so that you
> can practice

seeing words
in thought units.
This helps you
read faster.
However,
remember also
that reading
in phrases
or thought units
helps the reader
get the meaning.

Some commercial materials intended for use with readers with special language needs or with learning disabilities use chunking, or phrasing, in their printed books. One example page of text from *Reading Milestones* (Quigley, King, McAnally, & Rose, 1998) is printed as:

The bus	stopped	near the woods.	
The boys	looked	at the trees.	
The girls	looked	at the trees,	too.

Echo reading (discussed in Chapter 8) can also be used to model appropriate phrasing.

Instructional Techniques Using Longer Units

When teaching reading comprehension for units of discourse longer than a single paragraph, it is useful to think of a comprehension framework for strategic reading (Dowhower, 1999). This framework consists of three phases: pre-reading, active reading, and post-reading. During the pre-reading phase, students engage in accessing their prior knowledge, or building background knowledge for the upcoming reading, and focusing on the intent of the strategy being taught or used by the teacher. In other words, students should be informed of the purpose of the strategy, what it is, and why it is being used. During the active reading phase, students set purposes for reading, monitor their reading, and interact with the text in some way. During the post-reading phase, the student responds to the reading either independently or within a group. This might include a retelling activity, a written response, or some other extension activity such as a presentation or a self-assessment. The strategies that follow are all applicable to this comprehension framework.

Stauffer's (1975, 1981) **directed reading-thinking activity (DRTA)** incorporates all three aspects of the comprehension framework. It also can be easily modified to suit the particular needs of students having difficulty in comprehension. The goal of the DRTA strategy is to enhance reading (or listening) comprehension through a cycle of prediction making on the part of the reader. This prediction cycle ensures active reading as the reader (listener) is checking to see whether the predictions made are confirmed. The sample lesson (see Figure 9.3) focuses on helping students learn to use both their prior knowledge and the context of the material to make predictions throughout the text, and ultimately to understand the value of the common earthworm (a content goal). This strategy is equally effective with both narrative and expository material, and with very young students or nonreaders if modified to a directed listening-thinking activity (DLTA). The only difference between the DRTA and the DLTA is who does the actual reading of the material. When the student reads, it is a DRTA; when the teacher reads, it is a DLTA, as the student will be listening while thinking.

Visual structures, including graphic organizers, maps, charts, webs, grids, matrices, and diagrams, provide a visual representation of the material read. These visual structures

A Focus on SLL: The Experience-Text-Relationship Method

Because reading integrates information in the text with the student's previous experience, teachers must expand the background knowledge of the student especially if there are cultural variations in background knowledge affecting comprehension.

The *experience-text-relationship method* (Au, 1979) allows the teacher to motivate students to talk about their experiences relevant to the central focus of a story or content chapter (the *experience* step); read natural segments of text (the *text* step); and relate the content of a story with the prior experiences discussed in the story (the *relationship* step). The sample lesson transcript from Au (1979) that follows illustrates the teacher-student interaction in developing reading of culturally diverse students. Techniques like this one allow the teacher and students to bridge the knowledge gap between learners' experiences and the text. Likewise, the experience-text-relationship method allows students to become actively involved with the text and permits culturally compatible styles of interaction between teacher and students. Au and Kawakami (1985) found that a focus on comprehension, rather than on word identification, and a culturally compatible style of interaction greatly improve the quality of reading by sociolinguistically diverse students. Teachers need to recognize that students from various cultures possess culturally unique communication routines that often contrast with the verbal discourse routines of the school (Au, 1993a; Barnitz, 1994; Cazden, John, & Hymes, 1972; Heath, 1983; Hiebert, 1991; Tharp & Gallimore, 1988).

Sample Lesson

Experience Step

Teacher:	. . . Okay, let's think if we could do anything else with a frog. What would you do, Shirley?
Ann:	I wouldn't touch the legs. Yuck.
Shirley:	I would put it in a bucket.
Teacher:	You would put it in a bucket. Okay, that's something different. What would you do with it?
Shirley:	*(Inaudible)*
Ann:	Yeah, you eat the legs?

Teacher:	Okay, Shirley might even eat it. Good, you can eat frog, can't you?

Text Step

Teacher:	. . . Shirley, why did you say Freddy laughed? Okay, read the part that you said—when Freddy laughed.
Shirley:	*(Reading)* "I would take it fishing. Freddy laughed."
Teacher:	Okay, who says, "I would take it fishing"?
Nathan:	Mr. Mays.
Teacher:	Mr. Mays. And why did Freddy laugh?
Ann:	Because maybe he didn't—maybe he didn't know that he was going to use the frog.
Teacher:	No, he laughed for another reason, Ellie? Who can read that?
Ellie:	Because—'cause Mr. Mays didn't know what to do with the frog. That's all he could think was—he didn't know that he could use frogs was—was a bait. That's why Freddy laughed.
Teacher:	Okay, wait a minute. That's not the reason Freddy laughed.
Nathan:	Frogs can't fish.
Teacher:	Right. Okay, Mr. Mays says, "I don't have a frog, but if I did, I'd take it fishing," and Freddy thinks, hah, going fishing with the frog sitting down with the fishing pole?

Relationship Step

Teacher:	. . . Did you know before this that fish like to eat frogs?
Group:	Nooo.
Teacher:	I didn't—I never heard of using frogs for bait. Do you think they really do?
Nathan:	Yeah.
Teacher:	You think so.
Ann:	My daddy—my daddy—use bread.
Teacher:	Yeah, some people use bread. What else do you use for bait?
Shirley:	Fish.
Teacher:	Sometimes you use smaller fishes.

From "Using the Experience–Text–Relationship Method with Minority Children," by Kathryn Hu-Pei Au, *Reading Teacher,* March 1979. Reprinted with permission of Kathryn Hu-Pei Au and the International Reading Association.

Figure 9.3   Example Lesson Using Directed Reading-Thinking Activity (DRTA)

A DRTA lesson usually contains the following components, which will be highlighted in the example presented.
  I. Building Background for the Reading Selection
 II. The DRTA Cycle
      a. Students set purposes, make predictions
      b. Silent reading (or listening if a DLTA)
      c. Students verify predictions, satisfy purposes
III. Comprehension Check
IV. Rereading Parts of the Selection for Specific Purposes
 V. Enrichment, or Follow-Up, Activities

DRTA Lesson
Teacher Goals:
1. To help students discover how to use the clues in text to anticipate upcoming text using both prior knowledge and context clues
2. To expose students to a more expository (informational) writing style

Student Objectives:
1. Each student will participate in the lesson by:
      a. offering answers to the opening riddle
      b. making predictions about what (who) the text will be about
      c. verifying their predictions by citing evidence in the text
      d. answering comprehension questions following the silent reading and verification of predictions
      e. writing their own "first person" riddle

Materials:
Text: *A Not So Ugly Friend* by Stan Applebaum and Victoria Cox. This text is from *The Satellite Books* published by Holt, Rinehart, and Winston and is a Level 10 book, meaning it is intended for use with second-semester second-grade readers. The text begins by using a riddle format, each page providing clues for the reader about what is being described—in other words, who is the "not so ugly friend." For example, from the first page: "I can't see you. I have no eyes, but I can feel you walking. I have no nose, but I have a mouth and I can taste. Do you know what I am?" Midway through the book the answer to the riddle is revealed, and then the book becomes informational about the earthworm and how valuable earthworms are to us—why we should consider them friends.

Procedures:
To develop *background* for this lesson, introduce the idea of "first person" riddles, as the text is written in this format. It may be an unusual format for the students. These "practice" riddles will relate to people and things very familiar in the students' lives. In teaching new concepts it is much better to relate the unfamiliar to the familiar. For example, one practice riddle is: "I am something you drink. I come from a cow, and I'm white. Babies really like me a lot. Do you know what I am?" The riddles will be on individual index cards so that students can take turns reading them. After each riddle is solved, students must tell what the important clues were in the riddle that helped them solve it. At this point, students should be eager to solve yet one more riddle, the one in the text.

The *DRTA Cycle* will begin by introducing the title of the selection. Students will be told that this text is written like the riddles they just solved. The cover of the text may also be used if desired. Predictions will be made based on the key question, "What or who do you think is the not so ugly friend?" Students' predictions will be written on the chalkboard. Once all predictions are made, each student is asked to choose one they think is correct. Their purpose for reading then is to verify whether their prediction is accurate. With this text, proceed one page at a time, reading silently.

continued

Figure 9.3 *continued*

After each page, students will reevaluate their predictions and make changes, although they must be able to use the clues to justify their changes or new predictions. Once the answer is revealed in the text, discuss the clues as a group. At this point a new key question is introduced: "What does the earthworm do for us?" Again, write their ideas on the board. Students again read the rest of the selection silently to verify their predictions. Discuss their predictions and which ones were supported and what new information they discovered.

The questions for the *comprehension check* include vocabulary items that may be new or are important to the understanding of the text. Sample questions are:

1. Who is this book about? (earthworm) *textually explicit*
2. Who is telling the story? (earthworm) *textually implicit*
3. Can earthworms *really* talk? (no) *scriptally implicit*
4. What is soil? (dirt, earth) *scriptally implicit; possibly textually implicit*
5. What does it mean to make the soil richer? (better for plants, helps plants grow better, provides nutrients) *scriptally implicit*
6. Why does the earthworm come out of the ground when it rains? (because the water fills the earthworm's underground hole) *textually implicit*
7. Why doesn't the earthworm like to be out in the sun? (because the sun dries out its skin) *textually implicit*
8. Where do earthworms come from (or how are they born)? (eggs) *textually explicit*
9. What did you learn about earthworms that you did not know before? (answers will vary) *textually explicit, textually implicit*
10. Can we think of earthworms as our friends? (yes, no, give reasons) *scriptally implicit, textually implicit, textually explicit*

Following the questions, students will be asked to *reread for the specific purpose* of completing a semantic map of the selection to help them organize what they have read. The core question of the map is, "What does an earthworm do?" The students are allowed to look back to the text since this is a rereading activity. Each idea can then be read aloud if desired.

The *enrichment* activity for this lesson should be done individually. The students are to write three "first person" riddles that ask "Who Am I?" or "What Am I?" as their last line. These can then be posted later for other students to solve.

---

spatial

are especially appealing to second-language learners as they summarize text in fewer words. Different visual structures suit a variety of purposes. **Semantic webbing** (also called **mapping**) specifically aids readers in organizing what they read, thus improving comprehension (Freedman & Reynolds, 1980; Reutzel, 1985; Sinatra, Stahl-Gemake, & Berg, 1984). With semantic webbing a visual display is constructed representing relationships in the content of a story or expository selection (Davidson, 1982; Freedman & Reynolds, 1980). The technique is especially helpful for readers who struggle but have a strong spatial intelligence, because it visually demonstrates how main ideas are logically related to subordinate ideas (Sinatra, Stahl-Gemake, & Berg, 1984).

Four steps are basic in constructing a web, or map.

1. Answer the *core question*.

2. Use the answers to the core question as *web strands*.

3. Provide *strand supports*—facts, events, inferences, and generalizations taken from the text that distinguish one web strand from another.

4. Decide what *strand ties* exist—that is, how strands are related to each other. (Dotted lines may be used to indicate strand ties, or locations on the map itself, such as grouping.)

Before using a semantic web with students, the teacher must organize the content of the selection conceptually. For instance, in step 1, the core question, the focus of the web for *The Three Little Pigs,* is chosen by the teacher (Figure 9.4) and placed in a central position. Answers to the core question elicited through discussion (i.e., the eight characters) become the web strands. The strand supports are facts, events, inferences, and generalizations that distinguish the characters from one another. Strand ties in this example are represented by placing the man with straw beside Pig #1, the man with twigs beside Pig #2, and so forth. Placement in sequential order also indicates the repetitive pattern in

Figure 9.4   Semantic Web for *The Three Little Pigs*

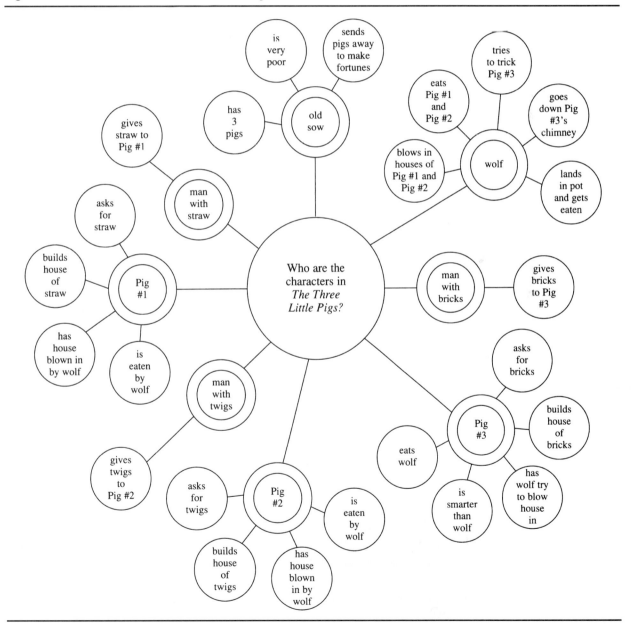

Figure 9.5   Using Semantic Webs as Advance Organizers

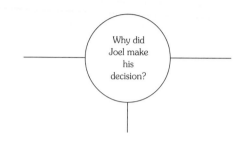

this story. The relationship between Pig #3 and the wolf is actually more complex than the strand supports in the figure indicate, however. The story contains a series of episodes in which the wolf tries to trick the pig and the pig outsmarts the wolf. If the teacher thinks further exploration of a part of the web would be beneficial, a section such as the relationship between the wolf and Pig #3 may be enlarged to examine the more complex relationships.

Semantic webs may also be introduced in incomplete form as organizers in advance of reading or writing. In an example suggested by Cleland (1981) and seen in Figure 9.5, three distinct responses are indicated; students reading the selection will know to look for three major reasons for Joel's decision. A similar approach but one that provides more detail from the story is the cloze story map (Reutzel, 1986).

The real benefit from using semantic webs and charts comes from the discussion that the teacher directs. The teacher guides the students in constructing the web or chart by pointing out relationships between ideas and characters and events in the material read. Such techniques are *not* reserved for stories, but like DRTAs, work as well with expository material. In using content area material, Davidson (1982) observed that "as students interact with one another by sharing maps and asking questions about various elements in each other's maps, they gain insights about the various reasoning processes used by others" (p. 56). For detailed examples of a wide variety of mapping ideas, refer to Heimlich and Pittelman's (1986) *Semantic Mapping: Classroom Applications*.

Reutzel (1985) summarizes the ways maps, webs, and charts help teachers and students to

- plan and execute more purposeful, focused reading lessons;
- organize readers' efforts toward specific comprehension objectives;
- focus questions and discussion on the important aspects of the text;
- create a workable structure for storage and retrieval of important information learned from the text;
- provide a visually coherent summary of the text;
- furnish a structure for guiding prereading experiences;
- supply students with a model for organizing and integrating text information in the content areas;
- present events and concepts in divergent visual patterns designed to emphasize specific types of relationships;

- experience a visual representation of text arrangements to encourage sensitivity to varying text patterns;

- summon the correct collection of background experiences and knowledge to facilitate comprehension of the text; and

- encourage students to think about and monitor their reading (p. 403). (See Chapter 12.)

Additional types of visual structures for aiding comprehension appear in subsequent chapters.

The goal of all comprehension instructional techniques is to help students become more actively involved with text. Instruction focuses on encouraging flexibility, risk taking, and depth of thinking. Questions mold the student's thinking, rather than test for right and wrong answers. As Schwartz and Sheff (1975, pp. 151–152) state, "Instruction should provide a type of questioning that consciously directs the reader to become involved in understanding what he reads."

However, the ultimate goal of all reading instruction is to develop independent readers. Comprehension instruction must bring the corrective reader to the point of active communication with the text. The teacher must focus on encouraging students to *ask themselves* questions about what they are reading. The teacher-posed questions of a structured comprehension lesson or a DRTA provide models for students. However, a gradual transfer from teacher-posed to student-posed questions is desirable in developing independent readers (Gillespie, 1990/1991). This transfer, referred to by Singer (1978) as the **phase-out/phase-in strategy,** promotes active comprehension.

The most important procedure in promoting active comprehension is to *ask a question that requires another question as the response.* Using "The Hare and the Fox" seen in Figure 9.6, a lesson may proceed as follows, with the teacher asking questions to elicit initial student questions. (Even though the example is for narrative text, this strategy is equally effective with expository text.)

Figure 9.6   Teaching Active Comprehension

The Hare and the Fox

A small, brown hare was sitting near a creek sunning himself, when he saw a fox. The fox was getting a drink in the small stream.

The hare ran from his nest, but the fox saw him hopping in the grass. Quick as a wink, the fox was running to catch the hare.

The brown hare ran into a hole in an old log. The hole was too small for a fox.

As the hare ran from the hole, he saw the fox digging to get into it.

When the fox got inside the old log, he did not find a hare. All he saw was a hole as long as the log.

"The Hare and the Fox." From *Basic Reading,* Book C. © J. B. Lippincott Company, 1975, p. 37. Used by permission.

Teacher: "Look at the title. What questions could you ask about this story after reading just the title?"

Possible student questions:

"What will the hare and the fox be doing?"

"What is a hare?"

"What will happen to the hare?"

"What will happen to the fox?"

"Will the fox chase the hare?"

"Will the fox catch and eat the hare?"

"Will the hare get away?"

The teacher then asks questions paragraph by paragraph.

Teacher, paragraph 1: "What else would you like to know about the hare? What else about the fox?"

Possible student questions:

"Is it a baby hare?"

"Is the hare a fast runner?"

"Is the fox a fast runner?"

"Is the fox hungry?"

Teacher, paragraph 2: "What would you like to know more about when the fox starts running to catch the hare?"

Possible student questions:

"Will the fox catch the hare?"

"Will the hare get away?"

Teacher, paragraph 3: "Is there anything you'd like to know when the hare runs into the log?"

Possible student questions:

"Will the hare be safe?"

"Will the fox get into the log?"

"Will the fox wait for the hare to come out of the log?"

Teacher, paragraph 4: "What would you like to ask when the hare runs from the log?"

Possible student questions:

"Why did the hare run from the log?"

"Is the fox waiting outside to catch the hare?"

"Where will the hare run to next?"

"Will the fox be able to catch the hare?"

Teacher, paragraph 5: "After you read the last paragraph, what questions about the hare and the fox do you still have?"

Possible student questions:

"Did the fox run out of the log to chase the hare some more?"

"Where did the hare go?"

"Did the hare get away from the fox?"

"What happened to the fox and the hare next?"

This lesson sequence supplies example questions for each paragraph in order to provide more explicit practice for the corrective reader. This procedure is not necessary for every lesson, however. The teacher may receive such a variety of questions at the initial stage that the students will be motivated enough to read the rest of the story or expository text material. When students are able to find answers to their own questions, they become active comprehenders. In this particular example, the reader is not told in the text what happens to the characters. Answers to the last set of questions could be used as the basis for creative writing or a language experience story. In any case, the students become involved in reading; situations or problems are identified and further understandings are sought while reading. Comprehension is the result.

Corrective readers also benefit from direct instruction in how to answer questions. They need to know about the different sources of information available for answering questions (Raphael & Pearson, 1985). As Raphael (1982) has pointed out, many poor comprehenders do not realize that it is both acceptable and necessary to use one's prior knowledge about the world to answer some types of comprehension questions. Thus instruction in **question-answer relationships (QARs)** is especially helpful.

Raphael's classification scheme for QARs is based on Pearson and Johnson's (1978) question taxonomy of **textually explicit** (the answer to the question is directly stated in one sentence in the text), **textually implicit** (the answer to the question is in the text but requires some integration of text material, as the answer might span several sentences or paragraphs), and **scriptally implicit** (the answer must come from the reader's prior knowledge).

In Raphael's original scheme, the first QAR was termed *right there* because the answer is directly stated in a single sentence. The second QAR was termed *think and search* because the answer requires information that spans several sentences or paragraphs. The third QAR was termed *on my own* because readers must rely totally on their own background knowledge for the answer.

After conducting several research studies, Raphael (1986) revised her classifications to include a fourth QAR, *author and me,* which recognizes that for some questions the answer comes from the reader's background knowledge, but only in connection with information provided by the author. The revised classification scheme now consists of two main categories, *in the book* and *in my head; right there* and *putting it together* (formerly *think and search*) falling under *in the book;* and *author and me* and *on my own* falling under *in my head.*

An introductory lesson in QARs must first define all the question types. Using the nursery rhyme *Little Miss Muffet,* consider the following questions as examples of each type.

> Little Miss Muffet sat on a tuffet,
> Eating her curds and whey.
> Along came a spider that sat down beside her,
> And frightened Miss Muffet away.

1. What did Miss Muffet sit on?
   Response: A tuffet
   QAR: Right there

2. Why did Miss Muffet get up from the tuffet?
   Response: A spider sat beside her and scared her away
   QAR: Putting it together

3. What are curds and whey?
   Response 1: Something to eat
   QAR: Right there
   Response 2: In making cheese, the milk is allowed to sour. The curds are the thick part that separates from the watery part, the whey (something like cottage cheese).
   QAR: On my own

4. What do you think Miss Muffet did when she first saw the spider?
   Response: She probably threw her curds and whey up in the air, screamed, and jumped up as fast as she could to get away.
   QAR: Author and me

Depending on the age and ability of the students, follow-up lessons will be needed for practice in recognizing the category types and using this knowledge in answering comprehension questions. Raphael (1986) suggests beginning QAR instruction with first- and second-grade students by introducing only the two-category distinction: *in the book* and *in my head.* Middle-grade students can learn all four QARs in one lesson, although the types can still be distinguished by the two headings *in the book* (*right there* and *putting it together*) and *in my head* (*author and me* and *on my own*). Sample text is presented with the questions, responses, and QAR provided, and the *reasons for each classification are discussed.* Once students understand category differences, other samples of text, questions, and responses can be provided so they can identify the QAR. Finally, students, when provided text and questions only, will have learned to recognize the key words in questions that cue them as to whether the answer lies in the text or in their heads. At this point, students are well on their way in using text organization as an aid to comprehension.

Helfeldt and Henk (1990) suggest a combination of ReQuest Procedure (Manzo, 1969, 1985) and QAR instruction in a technique they term **reciprocal question-answer relationships (ReQARs).** Intended for middle- and upper-grade students, particularly those with word recognition difficulties, the technique helps these readers anticipate the nature of teachers' questions, focus on informative parts of text, and learn how to construct appropriate responses to questions. Essentially, the goal of ReQAR is to assist students in viewing comprehension as the goal of reading. The instructional sequence is outlined in the original source, and the reader is encouraged to consult that source.

Teachers should not overlook the value of group discussion. Goldenberg (1992/1993) discusses "instructional conversations" as discussion-based lessons intended to support and enhance students' conceptual and linguistic development. The teacher's responsibility becomes one of weaving students' prior knowledge, experiences, and discussion comments and contributions into the conversation. Interested readers are referred to the original source for an example exchange in an instructional conversation. Similar ideas include "grand conversations," or dialogue among readers about their interpretations of a book or story they have read in common in order to co-construct meaning (Peterson & Eeds, 1990), and the student-led small group discussions and closing "Community Shares" that are part of book club programs (McMahon & Raphael, 1997).

interpersonal

Other recommended comprehension instructional techniques are Hennings's (1991) *essential reading,* in which students survey text, similar to a **picture walk,** to predict the main idea of the selection before reading; Gillespie's (1990/1991), Helfeldt and Henk's (1990), Manzo's (1969), and Singer's (1978) emphasis on student involvement in questioning for comprehension; and Manzo's (1975, 1985) *guided reading procedure (GRP).* Some types of cloze training (Aulls, 1978; Carr, Dewitz, & Patberg, 1989) also aid comprehension of longer selections.

In summary, students struggling with comprehension are most likely to improve if their special needs are considered. The results of a study by Taylor (1979) suggest that ineffective readers' comprehension, more so than that of good readers, suffers when their use of prior knowledge is restricted. But when provided with easy, familiar material, ineffective readers comprehend adequately. Thus the best way to begin instruction in comprehension for students needing help in this area is to use short, easy, familiar (in terms of background) material. Also, when students read their own writing to others, those listening might indicate they don't understand who the piece is about or how one section leads to another. Writing-group discussions help clarify these points. The modeling that such discussions provide can effectively transfer to similar situations in reading (refer to Chapter 7 for more on the reading/writing connection).

SUMMARY

Poor comprehenders generally do not approach reading as a meaning-making task; therefore, comprehension instruction for the corrective reader must emphasize understanding as the paramount purpose of reading. Direct instruction includes use of short selections, concrete words and examples, and appropriate questions. It must be explicit—that is, involve teacher-student interaction. Teachers should verbalize for their students the strategies they themselves use while trying to comprehend text. These strategies might include finding the main idea or predicting an outcome. Comprehension instruction is not limited to intermediate grades and beyond; it *must* be taught from the first grade. Many techniques presented in this chapter can be adapted as listening activities. To be good comprehenders, students must first realize that written materials should make sense. Until this realization has been internalized by the student, no instruction in comprehension is likely to help.

Suggested Readings

Gambrell, L., & Almasi, J. (Eds.). (1996). *Lively discussions! Fostering engaged reading*. Newark, DE: International Reading Association.

> *A variety of techniques for using discussion in primary and elementary classrooms are presented in this book. These practical, classroom-based strategies focus on the interpretation and comprehension of both narrative and expository text. Specific assessment techniques are also addressed.*

Hoyt, L. (1999). *Revisit, reflect, retell: Strategies for improving reading comprehension*. Portsmouth, NH: Heinemann.

> *Complete with reproducibles, this highly practical collection of comprehension strategies supports a focus on thoughtful reflection and retelling by the reader as key to comprehension. This book provides a detailed look at why to respond to text, when to respond and how readers can be encouraged to respond.*

Keene, E., & Zimmermann, S. (1997). *Mosaic of thought: Teaching comprehension in a reader's workshop*. Portsmouth, NH: Heinemann.

> *A friendly, personal book that shows how to help students become thoughtful, independent readers who understand deeply what they read. The focus is on helping students connect their reading to their background knowledge, create sensory images, ask questions, draw inferences, synthesize ideas, and solve problems.*

Rasinski, T., Padak, N., Church, B., Fawcett, G., Hendershot, J., Henry, J., Moss, B., Peck, J., Pryor, E., & Roskos, K. (Eds.). (2000). *Teaching comprehension and exploring multiple literacies: Strategies from* The Reading Teacher. Newark, DE: International Reading Association.

> *This compilation of articles from previous issues of* The Reading Teacher *presents the "best of the best" classroom-tested ideas for comprehension instruction. Included are strategies that help students comprehend different types of texts and different forms of literacy, from technology-related literacy to visual, theater, and music literacy.*

Taylor, B., Graves, M., & Van Den Broek, P. (2000). *Reading for meaning: Fostering comprehension in the middle grades*. New York: Teachers College Press, and Newark, DE: International Reading Association.

> *This is a collection of some of the best thinking for improving reading comprehension. The text provides a broad overview of effective strategies for teaching reading comprehension to middle school students.*

10 Meaning Vocabulary

Objectives

After you have read this chapter, you should be able to:
1. develop assessment activities for word meanings;
2. devise an instructional program in vocabulary development for a student with a limited meaning vocabulary.

Key Concepts and Terms

associative words	homophones	specialized vocabulary
homographs	List-Group-Label	structured overview
homonyms		

INTRODUCTION

There is a reciprocal relationship between meaning vocabulary and comprehension; as one grows it enhances the other, and a cycle of growth in both areas is the result. Competent readers know many words, while students with limited vocabularies often struggle with reading. But "reading instruction that focuses on the growth of children's vocabulary results in enhancing their abilities to infer meanings and [in turn] to better comprehend what they read" (Rupley, Logan, & Nichols, 1998/1999, p. 336).

The importance of having a large meaning vocabulary also increases as the learner approaches the upper and middle grades. The emphasis on content-area learning and more sophisticated works of literature requires a rich vocabulary base. Students will be learning new words for already familiar concepts as well as new words for entirely new concepts almost on a daily basis.

Vocabulary growth is not an area that should be left to chance. While it is true that many new words are learned incidentally through wide reading, direct instruction has an important role in vocabulary acquisition. In addition to teaching new words and concepts explicitly, direct instruction can also provide strategies that will assist readers, even capable decoders, in figuring out new word meanings as they are encountered during independent reading. Instruction for meaning vocabulary is an important and sometimes neglected area of focus in literacy education. Therefore, this chapter serves to inform classroom teachers of assessment and instructional strategies for word meanings.

ASSESSING KNOWLEDGE OF WORD MEANINGS

When assessing knowledge of word meanings, the degree of word knowledge should be considered. According to Dale, O'Rourke, and Bamman (1971), levels of familiarity with a word proceed from total ignorance ("I never saw it before"), to an awareness ("I've heard of it, but I don't know what it means"), to a general knowledge ("I recognize it in context—it has something to do with . . ."), and finally to accurate knowledge ("I know it").

Dale and colleagues (1971) suggest that in a vocabulary program, it is probably best to move the *almost known* words into the category of *known* words. Therefore, in testing students' vocabulary knowledge for the purpose of discovering their vocabulary needs, identifying words that are at least at an awareness level is recommended.

Dale and colleagues (1971, p. 20) propose four methods of testing awareness vocabulary that are easily adaptable by classroom teachers for direct assessment.

1. *Identification.* In this simple, most direct method, the student is asked to indicate orally or in writing whether the meaning of a word is known as it is used in specific text. The meaning is identified according to its definition or use, or by an associated word.

2. *Multiple choice.* The student selects the correct meaning of the tested word from three or four definitions or examples.

3. *Matching.* The tested words are presented in one column and the matching definitions are presented, out of order, in another column.

4. *Checking.* The student checks the words that are known or not known.

Within these four methods are a variety of techniques teachers can use to test vocabulary. Some examples follow.

Identification

A list of words, preferably related to material the student will be asked to read, is constructed in an easy-to-read sequence. The students are later asked to define (orally or in written form) only checked words. In preparation for a selection on skydiving, the following list might be used:

_____ sport	_____ hover	
_____ speed	_____ harness	
_____ target	_____ daredevil	
_____ parachute	_____ coordination	
_____ ripcord	_____ plummet	

Multiple Choice

Words are presented in context, and several answers are provided. The student selects the best response. For example:

A. Mary was <u>hungry.</u> She wanted her _____.
   (flower, coat, snack)
B. He bought an <u>expensive</u> gift.
   1. very beautiful
   2. did not cost too much
   3. cost a lot

Matching

Several types of matching exercises evaluate vocabulary development. Examples of three useful types follow.

A. Matching words with definitions

1. _____ census
2. _____ suburb
3. _____ urban

   a. A town near a large city
   b. Areas where people live close together in towns and cities
   c. Where people live on the surface of the earth
   d. A count of people
   e. The study of where people live and carry on their activities

B. Matching affixes with definitions

1. _____ pre
2. _____ es
3. _____ er
4. _____ bi
5. _____ un

   a. three
   b. someone who
   c. not
   d. against
   e. two
   f. more than one
   g. before

C. Matching words with related words or phrases. These are matches of associations and not definitions. Lines are drawn to the matches. (The first match is done for you.)

1. owl   flies high
   eagle   called wise
2. canine   puppy
   feline   kitten
3. lions   pride
   geese   gaggle
4. carat   diamond
   caret   editing

Checking

intrapersonal

The fourth method involves checking by the student. This alerts both the student and the teacher to vocabulary strengths and needs. Two types of self-checking tests follow.

A. If the underlined word in the sentence is used correctly, the student puts a check beside it. If both sentences in the unit are incorrect, the student checks "neither" (Gipe, 1977).

1. a. _____ The gooey <u>bramble</u> stuck to the roof of his mouth.
   b. _____ The <u>bramble</u> caught on Mary's coat.
   c. _____ Neither
2. a. _____ <u>Graphite</u> will erase the mark Jim made with his pencil.
   b. _____ <u>Graphite</u> will leave a mark on the paper.
   c. _____ Neither
3. a. _____ The cat's cries were <u>luminous</u> in the night.
   b. _____ The cat's eyes were <u>luminous</u> in the night.
   c. _____ Neither
4. a. _____ Our friend brought good <u>tidings.</u>
   b. _____ We bought some <u>tidings</u> from our friend.
   c. _____ Neither

B. The student indicates on a chosen list of words how well each word is known. The code to use might be:

+   means "I know it well."
√   means "I know it somewhat."
0   means "I've seen it or heard of it."
—   means "I don't know it at all."

For example, the following type of list, drawn from a science book, is best used analytically before new material or a unit of study is introduced.

_____ hypothesis

_____ experiment

_____ interact

_____ substance

_____ element

These assessment methods are primarily intended to help the teacher determine strengths and gaps in students' vocabularies. They should also serve as a source of motivation for students. Once students are sensitized to words and recognize that they can expand their vocabularies, they develop a sense of excitement about words. A teacher who is enthusiastic about developing vocabulary will, in turn, enhance the students' enthusiasm. Many exercises on word meanings are found in workbooks and teachers' manuals accompanying basal readers. These exercises also serve as informal tests for vocabulary at an awareness level.

For assessment of full conceptual knowledge of vocabulary, the tasks required must be more sensitive to the specific dimensions of the vocabulary items than those used for assessing an awareness level. Simpson (1987) suggests a hierarchy of four processes that, in turn, suggest formats for assessing full conceptual knowledge. The four processes are as follows:

1. Students should be able to recognize and generate the critical attributes, examples, and nonexamples of a concept. . . .

2. Students should be able to sense and infer relationships between concepts and their own background information. . . .

3. Students should be able to recognize and apply the concept to a variety of contexts. . . .

4. Students should be able to generate novel contexts for the targeted concept. (p. 22)

Simpson also provides examples of alternative formats for these four processes.

INSTRUCTION FOR WORD MEANINGS

General Instructional Procedures

While meaning vocabulary is certainly learned incidentally through experience and reading (Nagy, Anderson, & Herman, 1987), this way of learning vocabulary is slow and not at all predictable (Dale, O'Rourke, & Barbe, 1986), especially for students who do not read well or often. Readers with limited meaning vocabularies, to include many second-language learners, must receive direct and intense instruction focused on vocabulary expansion. Planned lessons for vocabulary development might include firsthand experience, such as field trips, in-class demonstrations, or laboratory experiences in math or science. Related discussions before, during, and after the experience use the key vocabulary words.

Vocabulary is usually taught by other than firsthand experiences, however. Words should be taught that help readers comprehend material at their instructional reading levels and understand content-area class discussions. These words are found in the books and content-area materials being used in the classroom.

Most effective methods of teaching new vocabulary involve the use of context (Gipe, 1977; Nagy, 1988; Sternberg, 1987). Typically, teachers present new vocabulary words by writing sentences on the board. Meanings are discussed and the material is then read. For corrective readers this kind of vocabulary instruction may not be appropriate. According to Goodman (1994),

> it is a mistake to think that vocabulary-building exercises [alone] can produce improved comprehension. Language is learned in the context of its use. Word meanings are built in relationship to concepts; language facilitates learning, but it is the conceptual development that creates the need for the language. Without that, words are empty forms. So vocabulary is built in the course of language use including reading. It is probably more accurate to say that people have big vocabularies because they read a lot than that they read well because they have big vocabularies. (p. 1127)

It makes more sense, then, to discuss most new vocabulary *after* material is read so the reader has access to the word's appropriate use. Or, if a new word is especially crucial to the understanding of the material to be read, introduce it before reading, and discuss it further after the reading. It would not be wise to try to introduce too many words before reading, however, as interest in the material may wane.

As noted earlier in the discussion of schema theory and comprehension, schemata relevant to the reader's task (in this case, learning the meaning of a new word) must be activated. Vocabulary instruction that encourages this activation is most effective. Students learn and retain many new vocabulary words when the words are introduced in familiar, meaningful sentences and stories. Therefore, vocabulary instruction is desirable that helps students (1) relate new vocabulary to what they already know, (2) develop broader understanding of word knowledge in a variety of contexts, (3) become actively involved in learning new words, and (4) develop strategies for independent vocabulary acquisition (Carr & Wixson, 1986; Kibby, 1995). Marzano and Marzano (1988) provide four clear principles for vocabulary instruction:

1. Wide reading and language-rich activities should be the primary vehicles for vocabulary learning. Given the large number of words students encounter in written and oral language, general language development must be encouraged as one of the most important vocabulary development strategies.

2. Direct vocabulary instruction should focus on words considered important to a given content area or to general background knowledge. Since effective direct vocabulary instruction requires a fair amount of time and complexity, teachers should select words for instruction that promise a high yield in student learning of general knowledge or of knowledge of a particular topic of instructional importance.

3. Direct vocabulary instruction should include many ways of knowing a word and provide for the development of a complex level of word knowledge. Since word knowledge is stored in many forms (mental pictures, kinesthetic associations, smells, tastes, semantic distinctions, linguistic references), direct vocabulary instruction should take advantage of many of these forms and not emphasize one to the exclusion of others. [This particular principle is consistent with multiple intelligences theory suggesting the linking of learning new concepts, skills, and tasks to as many different intelligences as possible

spatial
bodily-kinesthetic
musical
intrapersonal

(Armstrong, 1993). For example, to learn a new word: spell the word aloud; visualize the word and then write the word; form the word, or a representation of its meaning, in clay or with paints; create a song that explains the word and its meaning; relate the word and its meaning to a personal experience; think about the word's origin or the spelling rules it might follow; and have another person "test" you on the word by asking questions that require you to explain the new word.]

4. Direct vocabulary instruction should include a structure by which new words not taught directly can be learned readily. Again, given the large number of words students encounter and the limited utility of direct instruction, some structure must be developed to allow the benefits of direct vocabulary instruction to go beyond the words actually taught (pp. 11–12).

Research by Gipe (1978/1979, 1980) indicates that new word meanings are effectively taught by providing appropriate and familiar context. A four-step procedure is recommended. Students are given a passage in which the first sentence uses the new word appropriately, thereby providing valuable syntactic and semantic information. The context is composed of familiar words and situations. The second sentence of the passage describes some of the attributes of the new word. As with the first sentence, terms are already familiar to the students. The third sentence defines the new word, with care being taken to use familiar concepts. The last sentence gives students an opportunity to relate the new word to their own lives by asking them to write an answer to a question about the word's meaning or to complete an open-ended statement that requires application of the word's meaning. An example of a complete passage follows:

> The boys who wanted to sing together formed a *quintet*. There were five boys singing in the *quintet*. *Quintet* means a group of five, and this group usually sings or plays music. If you were in a *quintet,* what instrument would you want to play?

Talk Through (Piercey, 1982) is another technique that recognizes the importance of helping students relate what they already know to a word that is unfamiliar or has multiple meanings. In Talk Through, the teacher identifies key concept words, perhaps prior to a content-area reading selection, that students are likely to find difficult. These words may be totally new, may have been introduced previously, or may possess a different meaning from the common meaning.

The teacher begins by using the word in a sentence on the chalkboard:

> The frog has gone through a complete *metamorphosis* from its days as a tadpole.

At this point the teacher helps relate the meaning of the new word to students' own lives and personal experiences. The teacher *asks* students for input, as opposed to telling them what the word means. For example,

> *Teacher:* "James, remember when you brought in a tree branch that had a cocoon attached to it? What made that cocoon?"
>
> *James:* "The caterpillars in the trees in my backyard made that cocoon."
>
> *Teacher:* "Class, does anyone remember what happened to the cocoon? Lisa?"
>
> *Lisa:* "One day a butterfly came out of it."
>
> *Teacher:* "Yes, and right after that happened, remember I read you the story of *The Very Hungry Caterpillar* by Eric Carle. What happened to *that* caterpillar? Tony?"
>
> *Tony:* "The caterpillar ate one bite out of lots of different things, leaves, apples, tomatoes, and then it went to sleep inside a cocoon. Then one day it became a butterfly."

The next step the teacher takes is to write the word of interest in isolation:

metamorphosis

Then the teacher writes

meta + morphe
(over) (shape or form)

and says, "*Metamorphosis* comes from two Greek words—*over* or *beyond* and *shape* or *form*—combined to mean that the shape or form of something changes over to a different shape or form. Our experience with the cocoon and the story of *The Very Hungry Caterpillar* showed us that the *shape* or *form* of a caterpillar changed *over* to the shape or form of a butterfly. That is what *metamorphosis* means."

At this point the teacher seeks to further relate the new word to students' lives.

Teacher: "What else goes through a metamorphosis that you are familiar with?"
Possible responses:
   "We had some mealworms once to feed our pet chameleon. They changed into beetles."
   "I think some caterpillars change into moths."
   "My mom told me that flies lay eggs that hatch out little white worms. And then later on those worms turn back into flies."
   "I saw a movie once where a man turned into a wolf."
   "Frogs must change—it's in the sentence on the board."

And so it goes! The concept of metamorphosis is more meaningful now than if the students were simply told what it meant and then told to read the text containing the subject matter.

Corrective readers also must be taught how to use context clues as well as structural analysis clues (see Chapter 8) to help them determine the meanings of unknown words. But first, as Blachowicz and Zabroske (1990) point out, students need to be aware of the kinds of clues provided by context. "Context can clue you to—what a word is (what it's like); what a word isn't (what it's different from); what it looks like; something about its location or setting; something about what it's used for; what kind of thing or action it is; how something is done; a general topic or idea related to the word; other words related to the word; and so forth" (p. 506).

Buikema and Graves (1993) field-tested a vocabulary instructional unit with seventh- and eighth-grade students for the purpose of helping them learn to use descriptive context cues to infer word meanings. After beginning instruction using "What am I?" word riddles to introduce the idea of *descriptive* context cues, students were introduced to this same notion in text passages. Students could refer to a posted definition of descriptive context cues that read, "Descriptive cues give us clues as to the *sensual* aspects of an unknown word (its appearance, smell, taste, feel, or sound) or the *action* the word indicates or the *purpose* the word has" (p. 452). Following modeling and group work with sample passages for several days (instruction lasted for five consecutive fifty-minute periods), students learned the strategy.

Students were then given many opportunities to use the strategy with their reading materials. A sample practice worksheet to accompany this strategy is presented in Figure 10.1. The worksheet was modified to show this strategy as an adaptation of Gipe's (1978/1979) strategy discussed earlier.

Any vocabulary instruction can include the hypothesis/test strategy steps used by Blachowicz and Zabroske (1990). The steps should be modeled in stages for students. They are as follows:

Look—before, at, after the word

Reason—to connect what you know with what the author tells you

Predict—a possible meaning

Resolve or redo—decide whether you know enough, should try again, or should consult an expert or reference (p. 506)

Figure 10.1   Inferring Word Meanings from Context

PRACTICE WORKSHEET

Name: _____ Date: _____

Strategy Practice: Using the descriptive cues strategy, do all the following for the short paragraph below.

1. Underline the unknown word(s).
2. List in the space the descriptive cues that give hints for the word's meaning.
3. List any thoughts, experiences, or statements that helped you decide on the word's meaning.
4. Using your cue list, write a possible definition for the word.

The boys who wanted to sing together formed a <u>quintet</u>. There were five boys singing in the <u>quintet</u>. This group of five boys often sings and plays music together. If you were in a <u>quintet</u> would you want to sing or play a musical instrument?

1.   quintet

2.   to sing together
     five boys
     sings and plays music together

3.   I heard my dad talk about a barbershop quintet
     being at the mall on Saturday.

4.   I think a quintet is five people singing or
     playing musical instruments together.

---

interpersonal

These steps can then be applied during literature circle discussions or literature study groups by using the "vocabulary enricher" job sheet (Daniels, 1994). The role of the vocabulary enricher is to select new, important, or interesting words from the assigned reading, determine a definition for these words, and teach these words to the other group members. There are a variety of ways the words can be shared with group members (see Harmon, 1998).

Vocabulary Exercises

The easiest vocabulary exercises employ simple associations. Students use knowledge already in their schemata to work with synonyms, antonyms, homophones, and **associative words** that often occur together (e.g., green/grass, bacon/eggs), and to classify (e.g., animal: dog, cat, horse). The following activities can be used as the core of lessons, as practice activities, or as learning games designed to promote vocabulary development. For these activities to be considered instructional, student and teacher must interact. If they are done independently, they become practice activities.

Synonyms

Students are often taught that synonyms are words that have the same meaning. This is not exactly true, however. Synonyms have *similar* meaning, which allows us to express the same idea in a variety of ways.

The study of synonyms is probably the easiest and most efficient place to start expanding students' vocabularies because it starts with a familiar word. The student already has a schema for the known word; by comparing synonyms the student sees the relationships between words and is able to further generalize and classify words, thus enhancing the current schema. Some characteristic synonym activities follow.

1. Underline the word that means about the same as the word underlined in the sentence. (Note that this activity encourages the use of context clues.)
   We almost missed Sue's name because she wrote so <u>tiny</u>.
   large   small   big   hot

2. Match the words with about the same meaning. (Note how the structural clue, the prefix *un-,* can help with this task.)
   a. _____ large   (1) unhappy
   b. _____ tiny   (2) big
   c. _____ hen   (3) chicken
   d. _____ sad   (4) small

3. Circle the two words that could complete each sentence.
   a. The clown did a _____ right in front of us.
      treat   stunt   trick
   b. The neighborhood kids play baseball in the _____ lot.
      empty   vacant   full
   c. A large tree _____ blew down in the storm.
      branch   leaf   limb

4. Use the words in the box to complete the paragraph. Each word will be used twice, and it will have a different meaning each time. A synonym has been provided in parentheses for each space.

keen   slim   serious

   The hikers were (eager) _____ to reach the cabin. The approaching storm could be (dangerous) _____. Already, a (sharp) _____ wind was blowing, and the possibility of finding a cave to shelter in was (unlikely) _____. "Come on," said the guide, a tall, (thin) _____ woman. Her expression was (solemn) _____.

These formats are easily adapted to language experience stories or other creative writings with the use of a thesaurus (see Chapter 7 for additional ideas).

Comparing synonyms helps students see the relationships between words of similar meaning and also recognize that fine distinctions often should be made. Before these fine discriminations are possible, however, gross discriminations, as in the first three exercises, must be mastered. For example, the word *tiny* from the first set of exercises has many synonyms (*little, small, minute, diminutive, miniature, microscopic,* and so on), but not all of these terms are interchangeable. The use of contextual clues, a dictionary, and discussion will help the student determine the most appropriate shade of meaning for the following sentences.

1. We all agreed that Mary's feet were _____ but smaller yet were
   Sue's _____ feet.   small   tiny
      small   tiny

2. The doll was an exact _____ of a real British soldier.
                      miniature   diminutive

The meanings of synonyms, while similar, are not exactly the same. Choosing a synonym depends on how the word is used. Dale, O'Rourke, and Barbe (1986) provide an excellent example for synonyms of the word *get*. The student is directed to write the best word to use in place of *get*. *Buy, catch,* and *win* are the synonyms.

1. I will *get* the ball you throw.
2. The fastest runner will *get* a prize.
3. Will you *get* a new sweater at the store? (p. 85)

This type of activity is especially valuable during editing of students' written compositions. Laframboise (2000) suggests the use of webs for "tired" words as a way to expand vocabulary growth toward ownership of new words with the side effect of enhancing written compositions. Termed a "Said Web" because of the greatly overused word "said" in children's written stories, a group of students is asked to brainstorm words that are related to the "tired" word. These words do not have to be restricted to synonyms, as synonyms often trigger antonyms as responses as well. All these words can be accepted during brainstorming, as their relationships will become part of the follow-up discussion. The words that are listed are then categorized according to relationships, and charts are created. These charts can then be posted in the writing center for reference.

interpersonal   A group cloze activity (Jacobson, 1990) can be used to help students fine-tune their knowledge of synonyms and language use in general. The cooperative completion of a cloze passage can enhance each student's understanding and retention of the material read in addition to providing practice with the vocabulary and language patterns used by skilled writers. Basically the steps are as follows:

1. Each student individually completes the cloze passage (see Chapter 6 for construction of cloze passages).
2. In groups of three (triads), students discuss the reasons for each other's supplied words. Each student tries to convince the others that her choice is best, but if the others are convinced of another word there is no problem (or penalty) for changing words.
3. One triad then meets with a second triad to discuss word choices. Changes can again be made if reasons are clear.
4. Results are shared with the whole class. The teacher might have the original passage on an overhead transparency to allow for whole-class discussion.

Certain authors of children's literature are very aware of the opportunity they have to increase vocabulary through the use of synonyms (e.g., Franklyn Branley, Vicki Cobb, Joanna Cole, Ron and Nancy Goor, Kathryn Lasky, Patricia Lauber, Bianca Lavies, Molly McLaughlin, Hershell and Joan Nixon, Dorothy Patent, Laurence Pringle, Helen Roney Sattler, Jack Denton Scott, Millicent Selsam, and Seymour Simon). A good example is Molly McLaughlin's *Dragonflies* (1989). Numerous synonyms are used to help readers understand vocabulary related to dragonflies:

"This larva, or nymph, is quite different from its colorful flying parents." (p. 16)
"This remarkable lip, or labium, is one of the tools that make the 'pond monster' such a fearsome hunter." (p. 19)
"As the time for the big change, or metamorphosis, comes closer, the nymph's behavior changes, too." (p. 22)

Antonyms

Just as no two synonyms are exactly alike in meaning, no two antonyms are exact opposites. To develop the concept of opposites, however, antonyms can be grouped according to their general meaning. Most activities suggested for synonyms can be modified for antonyms:

1. The student is instructed to change the underlined word so the sentence will have almost the opposite meaning.
   Jack <u>hates</u> to read.
   Spot is a <u>fat</u> dog.
   It is a <u>hot</u> morning.

   The study of antonyms is readily adapted to the use of structural analysis clues. The teacher can purposely present pairs of words to illustrate how opposites result from the addition of certain prefixes and suffixes (e.g., happy/unhappy; fear/fearless).

spatial

2. Antonym trees are useful to help study the formation of antonyms (Figure 10.2). Given a root word at the base of the tree, students prepare "leaves" for the tree by writing words that mean the opposite of the root word. Students soon discover the use of prefixes and suffixes in forming antonyms. Some antonyms formed from prefixes and suffixes are listed here (Dale, O'Rourke, & Bamman, 1971, p. 57).

Prefixes Forming Antonyms

*in*doors	vs. *out*doors	*in*hale	vs. *ex*hale
*pre*paid	vs. *post*paid	*sub*ordinate	vs. *super*ordinate
*in*flate	vs. *de*flate	*under*fed	vs. *over*fed
*post*test	vs. *pre*test	*pro*gress	vs. *re*gress

Figure 10.2   Antonym Tree. Students Make "Leaves" with Words Opposite in Meaning to the "Root" Word at the Base of the Tree

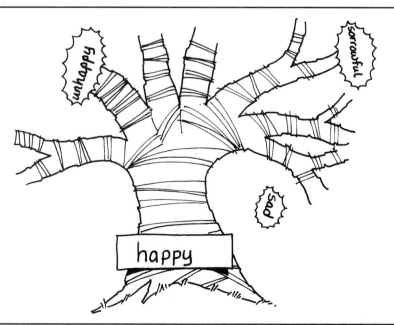

Suffixes Forming Antonyms

worthy	vs.	worth*less*	widow	vs. widow*er*
lion	vs.	lion*ess*	use*less*	vs. use*ful*
beard*less*	vs.	beard*ed*	hero	vs. hero*ine*

3. The student is told to read the sentence and choose the word that best completes the sentence.

Cowardly means the opposite of a person who is _____.
   timid   courageous   fearful

Was the bread fresh, or had it become _____?
   burned   stale   delicious

Homophones

Words that sound alike but are different in spelling and meaning are called **homophones** (e.g., *dear* versus *deer*). Related terms are **homonyms,** words that sound alike and are spelled alike, but have different meanings, e.g., *row* (a line) versus *row* (move a boat); and **homographs,** words that are spelled alike, but do not sound alike and have different meanings, e.g., *bow* (and arrow) versus *bow* (as in curtsy). Homophones may confuse encoding and decoding tasks (e.g., distinguishing between *reed* and *read*) but may help the comprehension task (e.g., the reader knows *reed* refers to a tall grass), as opposed to homonyms and homographs, which are words spelled alike. With homonyms and homographs, context *must* be used to infer the appropriate meaning. As with synonyms and antonyms, the student needs much practice discriminating between one homophone and another. In the activities that follow, several approaches are presented. Many **bodily-kinesthetic** of these activities can be performed as pantomimes using body language and signs for "sounds like."

1. Students practice exercises in which they are given a word and asked to supply its homophone. This task begins simply by giving letter-space clues.
   bear, b a r e   stare, s t a i r
   cite, s i g h t   hour, o u r

2. The student is directed to choose the correct homophone using context clues.
   a. They met on the *(stairs, stares)*.
   b. They spent a *(weak, week)* at the beach.
   c. We stayed for the *(hole, whole)* game.
   d. *(Meet, Meat)* me at six o'clock.

3. The student is directed to supply the correct homophone using definition clues.
   a. It stops a bike. It sounds like *break*. __ __ __ __ __
   b. It's an animal skin. It sounds like *fir*. __ __ __
   c. Boats stop here. It sounds like *peer*. __ __ __ __
   d. It's taking what doesn't belong to you. It sounds like *steel*. __ __ __ __

Associative Words

Unexpected responses for associative activities are not uncommon. The teacher must be flexible regarding acceptable responses for association activities.

A. The student is directed to underline the word that best fits the sentence. Responses should be discussed as to why one choice is better than another.
   The sky is so _____ it looks like the ocean.
   blue   orange   red

A Focus on SLL: Homophones, Homographs, and Idioms

Many young second-language learners have trouble understanding common English expressions, and they take many idioms literally. For example, "It's raining cats and dogs!" would bring looks of amazement at the thought of cats and dogs falling from the sky. In the Spanish language, for instance, there aren't any words that have multiple meanings and there are no homonyms. Therefore, the following books are especially helpful for the young learner whose first language is Spanish.

Cox, James. (1980). *Put Your Foot in Your Mouth and other Silly Sayings.* New York: Random.

Gwynne, Fred. (1970). *The King Who Rained.* New York: Prentice-Hall (also *A Chocolate Moose for Dinner,* 1976).

Hunt, Bernice Kohn. (1975). *Your Ant Is a Which.* New York: Harcourt Brace Jovanovich.

Terban, Marvin. (1990). *Punching the Clock: Funny Action Idioms.* New York: Clarion (also *Eight Ate: A Feast of Homonym Riddles,* 1982; *In a Pickle and Other Funny Idioms,* 1983; *Mad as a Wet Hen and Other Funny Idioms,* 1987).

In addition, it would be helpful for second-language learners to participate in vocabulary role play (Herrell, 1998). Vocabulary role play encourage learners to connect their past experiences with the content being studied and the vocabulary that is new within that content. Students and the teacher discuss the vocabulary and then students are asked to create a skit that uses the new vocabulary.

Dave's ESL Café is a useful Web site for teachers of second-language learners. The address is http://www.eslcafe.com/. See also the Web site for the online TESL Journal at http://www.aitech.ac.jp/~iteslj.

B. The student matches the word in the first column with one from the second column that is usually associated with it.

1. _____ tall   a. tiger
2. _____ electric   b. buildings
3. _____ green   c. energy
4. _____ ferocious   d. sky
5. _____ blue   e. fields

Classifying or Categorizing Activities

Instruction in classifying and categorizing develops an understanding of word relationships. Once a new word is identified as belonging to an already familiar category, all attributes of the known category can be assigned to the new word, and the new word becomes known. This is also an example of how schemata are expanded. Consider the familiar category of colors, and *azure* as the unfamiliar word. Once azure is identified as a color, it receives all the attributes that may be associated with color (e.g., hue, shade, brilliance). Further, once azure is identified as the color of the blue sky, it will take on the additional attributes of the already familiar word *blue*.

A teacher can present classification or categorization activities in many ways. The following general formats can be modified to accommodate many categorizing needs. The same formats provide the basis for classification games.

logical-mathematical

1. *Direct categorization.* The student is given a worksheet with category titles and a set of words to be categorized. The student lists the words under the appropriate category title. A higher level of difficulty would be a **List-Group-Label** (Taba, 1967) activity. Given a list of words (25 is sufficient) such as those found on the word wall in Figure 8.6, students examine the list for ways to group words that have something in common with one another. Each group should have at least three words in it. Words can be used in more than one group. The list is then re-sorted and the groupings labeled in a way that indicates the relationship of the words contained in that grouping. The teacher will record the categorized listings on the board, on an overhead transparency, or on poster paper.

naturalist

Students are asked to verbally explain why they have grouped the words in these ways. For example, the words *lava, ash, rocks, dust,* and *smoke* were grouped together and students explained that these words are all things emitted from a volcano. Groupings developed by students using the words from Figure 8.6 included: Things That Float on Top of the Water *(schooners, raft, oil tankers, sailboats);* Kinds of Sea Shells *(cowrie, whelk, conch, five-hole sand dollar, arrowhead sand dollar, sand dollar, common sand dollar);* and Plants That Live in the Sea *(plankton, seaweed, kelp).*

Word sorting is also used to involve students in categorizing. For example, a group (or individual) may be given a set of words that represent several different common elements:

ray	tangent	rhombus
triangle	octagon	dodecagon
hexagon	pentagon	trapezoid

interpersonal

The group sorts the words (e.g., *rhombus, trapezoid; ray, tangent; rhombus, trapezoid, triangle, pentagon, octagon, hexagon, dodecagon*) and reads out the words in one group to the rest of the class. Those listening must determine the category title (e.g., quadrilaterals; lines; polygons). Discussion follows that focuses on essential characteristics of the categories.

2. *Categorizing by omission.* The student is given a set of words (e.g., *four, too, six, eight*) and asked to indicate the word that does *not* fit the category represented by the majority of the words. Subsequent discussion reveals the category title.

spatial
naturalist

3. *Structured vocabulary overview.* In preparation for, or in review of, a unit of study it is helpful to fit words into categories. For example, a unit on algae might call for the categories of *microscopic* and *nonmicroscopic.* The specialized vocabulary items to be classified might be desmids, Irish moss, brown kelp, and diatoms. *Fresh water* and *sea water* are two additional categories for classifying these same words.

4. *Looking for common elements.* The student is given a group of words that all have something in common. The student decides what the words have in common. For example, given the words *buffalo, prairie dog,* and *eagle,* the student may conclude that all these make their habitat in the Great Plains.

spatial

5. *Word maps.* The Frayer model of concept attainment (Frayer, Frederick, & Klausmeier, 1969) provides a basis for word map activities. This model offers a structure that encourages the independent learning of new word meanings. Briefly, concepts are presented in relation to relevant and irrelevant attributes; examples and nonexamples; and superordinate, coordinate, and subordinate aspects of the concept. Using the Frayer model leads readily to thinking about new words in relation to known, related words. Following discussion, a new concept can be *mapped* using the structures illustrated in Figure 10.3.

Similarly, Schwartz (1988) presents a concept definition word map that describes four types of relationships: (1) the general class to which the concept belongs (what is it?), (2) the primary properties of the concept and those that distinguish it from other members of the class (what is it like?), (3) examples of the concept (what are some examples?), and (4) comparison of the new concept with an additional concept that belongs to the same *general* class but differs from the target concept (comparisons). An example of a concept definition word map is displayed in Figure 10.4.

spatial

One additional example is the *concept circle* or *concept wheel* (Rupley, Logan, & Nichols, 1998/1999). In this technique, students use their background knowledge to

Figure 10.3   The Frayer Model of Concept Attainment Encourages Thinking About New Concepts in Relation to Known, Related Concepts

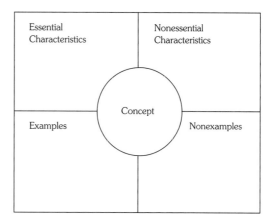

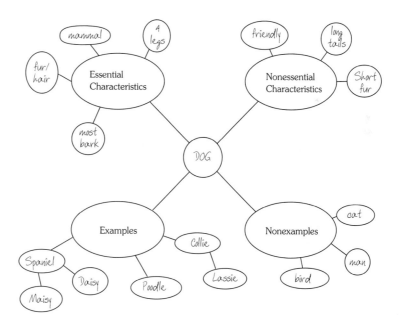

suggest words that they associate with the target word. Consider the previous example of the new word *polygon*. Students are asked for words they think of when they hear the word *polygon,* and to explain why they thought of that word. Some suggestions might include *hexagon,* because it has the same ending sound; *triangle,* because it is a geometric figure; and *rectangle,* because it is a geometric figure that has four sides. Students continue

Figure 10.4   Concept Definition Word Map

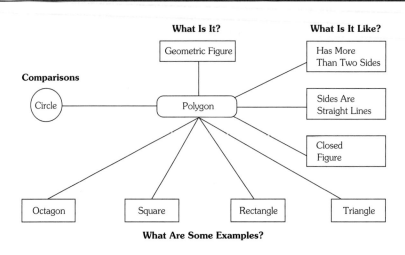

to make suggestions until it is apparent that no new information is forthcoming, or that the students are moving off track. The teacher then produces a list of words that appropriately reflects the word *polygon,* including as many of the students' suggestions as possible. At this point, the definition of the new word is read to the students. The list is then compared to the definition. Finally, the teacher asks the students to narrow the list down to three words that will help them remember the new word (see Figure 10.5).

Figure 10.5   Concept Circle for *Polygon*

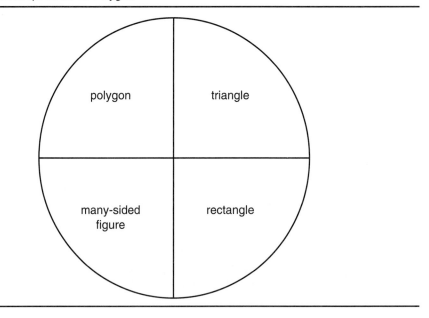

Instruction for Specialized Vocabulary

The **specialized vocabulary** of content areas must also be addressed directly. Content-area materials may introduce ten or more technical (a meaning of a common word form specific to a content field) or unfamiliar words on a page. These words are not usually repeated often, nor are they unimportant words to the understanding of the subject matter. They are usually labels for important concepts being discussed. For example, in the area of social studies, abstract words such as *culture, technology,* and *adaptation* may be unfamiliar but extremely important to understanding the material. Not all words in content-area materials are new in terms of pronunciation, however. Common words such as *mouth, matter, suit,* or *recess* may be confusing if a specialized meaning is attached to them. While most students associate the word *recess* with time out to play, a different meaning is presented in the following sentence: "When it was time to do his homework, Bob hid in the *recess* hoping that his mother would not find him." *Mouth* may refer to the facial cavity, to a part of a musical instrument, or to the place where a stream enters a larger body of water. Content-area materials abound with words that have multiple meanings.

Under most circumstances, assessment of specialized vocabulary for a content area is not necessary. Instead the teacher may safely assume that the specialized words are unknown and proceed with teaching procedures.

Most teachers at all levels agree that specialized vocabulary representing a *crucial* concept is best introduced before the lesson, although research by Memory (1990) indicates no superior time of presentation (before, during, or after) for technical vocabulary. Before reading, the teacher may (1) give the students a sentence using the new word and show how the context implies the meaning, or (2) give students a brief list of words (perhaps as part of a study guide or simply to copy from the board) and direct them to look up each word's meaning in the book's glossary and copy it down for later reference while they are reading. After reading, the teacher can discuss new word meanings using the context of the material read, along with glossary definitions.

Vocabulary techniques are essentially useless without discussion. New words can be discussed in many ways that greatly enhance understanding of their meaning and, in turn, understanding of the material read. The new concept should be related to something already familiar to the students (Gipe, 1980). For example, the students may be studying history and about to confront the word *tariff,* which is unfamiliar. While *tariff* is new, the word *tax* is probably not. Thus, any discussion about the new word should include mention of taxes and experiences students have had with them, such as having a dollar but not being able to buy a 99-cent item unless they have more money for the tax.

New terms are probably best taught as new concepts. In addition to relating the new word to familiar concepts, the specific characteristics of the new concept must become part of the students' understanding as well. Eventually the students must be able to distinguish examples and nonexamples of the particular concept. The technique of the concept circle, discussed earlier, would be appropriately used for relating new words to familiar concepts. The concept ladder (Figure 10.6) is another technique for thinking of the meaning of one word in relationship to the meaning of other words. For instance, meanings of words often have hierarchical relationships with other words. A dog is not just a four-legged animal that barks and has fur, but is also a kind of mammal. And there are different kinds (breeds) of dogs as well as stages (puppies grow up to be dogs). Upton (1973) proposes a set of questions to be asked when pursuing more depth in understanding a word's meaning: What is it a kind of/what are the kinds of it? What is it a part of/what are the parts of it? What is it a stage of/what are the stages of it? What is it a product or a result of/what are the products or results of it? At least three of these four pairs of questions should be asked as part of the concept ladder activity. Sometimes both parts of the question are not relevant. In those cases, just answer the parts that are relevant. Figure 10.6 shows how one student completed a concept ladder for the concept of *cetacean*.

interpersonal

It is also important to provide students opportunities to identify and discuss words new to them that may not have been selected by the teacher for discussion. Haggard (1986) suggests the *Vocabulary Self-Collection Strategy* (VSS) to help students learn to identify important words and concepts, and to use passage context to determine meaning. Following the reading of a content-area selection, teams of two to five students select a word they feel is important to understanding that content. A spokesperson then nominates the word before the entire class and states where the word occurred in the text, the team's definition for the word, and why the team feels it is important for the class to learn. Classmates discuss the word's value and definition. Finally, with teacher guidance, words are narrowed to only those that the class wishes to learn. These words and their final agreed-upon definitions are written in learning logs or vocabulary notebooks and used in follow-up activities. This strategy can be readily adapted to any content area. Chase and Duffelmeyer (1990) developed a modification for use in English literature called *VOCAB-LIT,* and found it an effective tool for helping students recognize that knowledge of literary elements is essential to understanding and appreciating novels.

spatial

A specific technique developed not only for introducing new vocabulary but also for introducing overall organization of a selection, including important concepts, is the **structured overview.** This particular technique, developed by Richard Barron (1969), uses a graphic representation of terms that are indispensable to the essence of the selection to be read. The graphic representation makes this technique doubly attractive for the corrective reader. The steps for developing and using a structured overview are as follows:

1. List the vocabulary words that are important to understanding the selection. (This analysis could include both familiar and new words.)

Figure 10.6   Concept Ladders for Vocabulary Development

Concept Ladder for *Cetacean**

What kinds of cetaceans are there?	What is a cetacean a part of?	What is a cetacean a product of?
toothed whale	marine mammals	other male and
baleen whale		female cetaceans

What are the kinds of cetaceans?	What are the parts of a cetacean?	What are the products of a cetacean?
whales	flippers	oil
dolphins	flukes	whale blubber
porpoises	dorsal fins	waste products

POSSIBLE ANSWERS:

whales	flippers	calves	baleen whale	waste products	the sea
dolphins	food	oil	whale blubber	humpback whale	flukes
blowhole	blue whale	manatees	toothed whale	porpoises	dorsal fins
	marine mammals		other male and female cetaceans		

*Any one of an order of aquatic (mostly marine) mammals including the whales, dolphins, porpoises, and related forms with large head; fishlike, nearly hairless body; and paddle-shaped forelimbs.

2. Arrange these words so they show the interrelationships among the concepts represented.

3. Add to the diagram vocabulary that the students understand and that further helps to show relationships.

4. Evaluate the diagram. Does it clearly depict the major relationships? Can it be simplified and still communicate the important ideas?

5. Introduce the lesson by displaying the diagram (perhaps as a transparency for an overhead projector). Explain why you arranged the terms the way you did. Encourage the students to contribute any information they have. Give each student familiar vocabulary terms on slips of paper. As you discuss the overview, the students then help construct it by placing their vocabulary terms in logical positions.

6. As the selection is read, continue to relate the new information to the structured overview.

An example of a structured overview was developed for a section of a social studies text dealing with explorers coming to the New World (Figure 10.7). Students had previously studied the Incan, Aztec, and Mayan cultures.

Figure 10.7   Example of a Structured Overview for Social Studies

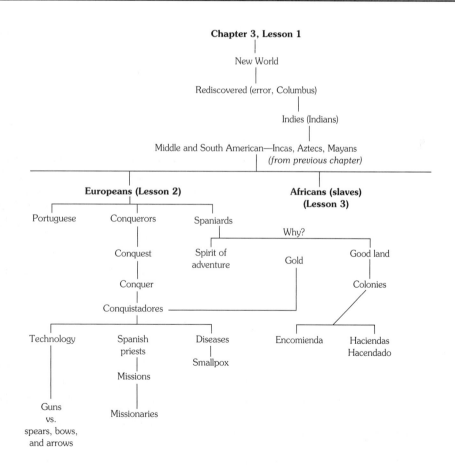

Other examples of content area structured overviews can be found in *Improving Reading in Science* (Thelan, 1976), *Reading in the Mathematics Classroom* (Smith & Kepner, 1981), *Reading in the Science Classroom* (Bechtel & Franzblau, 1980), *Reading in the Social Studies Classroom* (Bullock & Hesse, 1981), and *Teaching Reading and Mathematics* (Earle, 1976), as well as in journal articles ("Structured Overviews for Teaching Science Concepts and Terms," Wolfe & Lopez, 1992/1993).

Burmeister (1978) presents teaching techniques for words that have both common and specialized meanings. She suggests a two-part activity: part 1 demonstrates the common meanings and part 2 uses sentences with blanks for the unique meanings. The students must fill in the blanks in part 2. Burmeister provides examples for several content areas; a few items follow for clarification.

Mathematics

Part 1

Term	Common Use
1. difference	You know the *difference* between right and wrong.
2. root	The tree *root* was growing through the sidewalk.
3. base	Jim made it to first *base*.

Part 2

1. The subtraction operation finds the (difference) between two numbers.
2. Find the square (root) of 9.
3. The (base) of the triangle is 10 cm long.

Activities that reinforce the idea that words may have several meanings are worthwhile and easily developed for any lesson; simply use a dictionary and put together a list of sentences directly from the material of interest.

Some excellent general formats for specialized vocabulary instruction and practice follow. Each activity is easily modified to fit the needs of the teacher in any content area.

Word Pairs (Stevenson & Baumann, 1979)

Use a table that allows students to show the relationship of various word pairs. Students may add word pairs to the list. The word relationships should be discussed.

Word Pair	Almost the Same	Opposite	Go Together	Not Related
land/sea		X		
ship/galleon	X			
merchant/commerce			X	
pirate/bread				X

spatial

Semantic Mapping (Heimlich & Pittelman, 1986; Johnson & Pearson, 1984)

1. Select a word central to the material to be read (e.g., *transportation*) or from any other source of classroom interest. Write it on the chalkboard.

2. Ask the class to think of as many words as they can that are related in some way to the word you have written. Jot them on paper.

3. Have individuals share the words they have written. As they do, write the words on the board and attempt to put them into categories.

4. Number the categories and have the students name them:
   a. Kinds of transportation
   b. Places we can travel to
   c. Reasons for transportation

5. Discuss the words. This is crucial to the success of semantic mapping. Students then learn meanings of new words, new meanings for known words, and see relationships between words.

6. If time permits, select one word from the existing semantic map and begin to develop a new one (e.g., start a new map with the word *exploration*).

Constrained Categorization (Stevenson & Baumann, 1979)

Give students a chart with relevant category titles listed across the top and various letters listed along the side. Have students fill in the chart using a word that fits the category and also begins with a certain letter. Some of the words should be available in the material read. Others can be researched by groups or individuals.

	Solids	*Liquids*	*Gases*
S	salt		
C		coffee	carbon dioxide
I	ice		
E		ether	ethylene
N			neon
C		cleaning fluid	
E	earth		

Semantic Feature Analysis (Pittelman, Heimlich, Berglund, & French, 1991)

1. Select a category *(vehicles)*.

2. List, in a column, some words within the category *(car, train)*.

3. List, in a row, some features shared by some of the words *(engine, wheels)*.

4. Put pluses or minuses beside each word, beneath each feature *(? is used when uncertain)*.

5. Add additional words.

6. Add additional features.

7. Complete the expanded matrix with pluses and minuses.

8. Discover and discuss the uniqueness of each word. *(Try to eliminate ?s through research.)*

9. Repeat the process with another category.

	engine	*4 wheels*	*steering wheel*	*handlebars*	*runners*	*carries many people*
car	+	+	+	–	–	–
train	+	–	?	–	–	+
bus	+	?	+	–	–	+
truck (semi)	+	–	+	–	–	–
bicycle	–	–	–	+	–	–
sled	–	–	–	?	+	–

Some beginning categories:

games	vegetables	pets
occupations	food	clothing
tools	buildings	animals
plants	transportation	

Later categories:

moods	sizes	entertainment
feelings	shapes	modes of communication
commands	musical instruments	

spatial

Do You Know Your Sports? (Chant & Pelow, 1979)

Note to the teacher: Many words may be categorized under two headings. For instance, *center* refers to a position played in football or basketball. *Yards* relates to the number of yards on a golf drive or the number gained or lost on a particular play in football. Simply color-code the answer key to include more than one answer. In addition, many compound words are found among sports terms (Figure 10.8). Why not use these terms to study compound words?

Figure 10.8   Sport Terms Include Compound Words and Can Be Used to Study the Latter

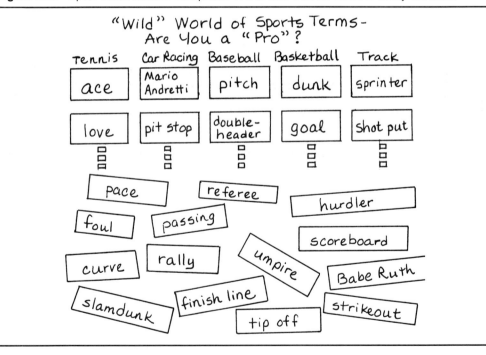

SUMMARY

A student who is successful with these basic vocabulary activities will be ready for instruction in some of the more difficult aspects of vocabulary development (e.g., analogies, connotative and denotative meanings, figures of speech, and word origins). Because these aspects of vocabulary are not easily learned, a firm vocabulary base is essential for effective reading comprehension.

Suggested Readings

Dale, E., O'Rourke, J., & Bamman, H. A. (1971). *Techniques of Teaching Vocabulary.* Palo Alto, CA: Field Educational Publications.

This classic work contains myriad examples of vocabulary activities. The authors support a systematic approach to vocabulary development and one that occurs within the context of communication. It is truly a work that was ahead of its time.

Heimlich, J. E., & Pittelman, S. D. (1986). *Semantic mapping: Classroom applications.* Newark, DE: International Reading Association.

This monograph is devoted entirely to the instructional technique of semantic mapping. Examples for a variety of purposes and content areas are included as well as procedures for implementation.

Johnson, D. D. (1986). Journal of Reading: A themed issue on vocabulary instruction. *Journal of Reading, 29,* 580.

For a view of the issues surrounding vocabulary instruction, this themed issue is must reading. Johnson's piece in particular provides a succinct overview of the status of vocabulary instruction.

Johnson, D. D. (2001). *Vocabulary in the elementary and middle school.* Boston: Allyn & Bacon.

This book contains numerous explanations, examples, and classroom applications for stimulating and expanding meaning vocabulary. One of the chapters presents word games and language play that students will find motivating.

Pittelman, S. D., Heimlich, J. E., Berglund, R. L., & French, M. P. (1991). *Semantic feature analysis: Classroom applications.* Newark, DE: International Reading Association.

This monograph is devoted solely to the instructional technique of semantic feature analysis. Examples for a variety of content areas are provided as well as applications that support integrated reading and writing.

11 Reading Comprehension and Strategic Reading for Narrative Text

Objectives

After you have read this chapter, you should be able to:
1. assess comprehension of narrative material using retellings;
2. provide instruction for story retellings;
3. use graphic organizers for teaching story structure;
4. recognize the relationship between writing and reading comprehension of narrative text.

Key Concepts and Terms

book club	literature circles	story grammar
Goldilocks Strategy	story frames	story impressions

A s noted in Chapter 9, reading comprehension is a complex ability affected by many factors. It was pointed out that knowledge of word meanings is a critical subskill of reading comprehension. In addition to vocabulary knowledge, reading comprehension requires the use of thinking and reasoning skills. Different types of text (e.g., narrative, expository) require different kinds of thinking and reasoning. As mature readers, we approach narrative and expository text differently because their internal structures are different. We need to also teach our students about these differences. This chapter and the next present strategies best suited for narrative and expository text, respectively. Taken together, Chapters 9, 11, and 12 provide a large repertoire of strategies for comprehension.

ASSESSMENT FOR NARRATIVE TEXT: RETELLINGS

Reading comprehension requires that readers make connections between their own prior knowledge and the organization of the text. *Text organization* for narrative text includes a setting or settings, characters, and a goal, followed by some problem(s), events, and a resolution. These elements, essential to any well-formed story, result in a structure referred to as **story grammar.** In general, narrative text is easier for children to recall and comprehend than expository text (Leslie & Cooper, 1993). This could be due simply to greater familiarity and exposure at early ages to narrative text, or it could be due to the fact that narratives are about people engaged in goal-oriented action, thought to be the building blocks of cognition (Mandler, 1984; Nelson, 1986). Another factor relates to the consistent structure of the narrative as opposed to expository structures (e.g., compare-contrast, description, enumeration, sequence) (see Chapters 9 and 12). Even though narrative text is generally easier to comprehend doesn't mean that all readers find narrative text easy. Many readers can decode words easily yet do not make the connections to the text that are necessary for comprehension. One of the critical connections is between the reader's prior knowledge and the content of the story. The more prior knowledge, the better the comprehension. One easy way to assess prior knowledge for narrative text is through a free-association task (Leslie & Cooper, 1993). Simply ask readers to tell what they think of, or are reminded of, or what is meant by either several well-chosen words from the story, or the title, or the cover of the book before it is read. Another way to assess prior knowledge is to ask for a prediction about the story based solely on the title or book cover.

The use of a story-retelling rubric is a commonly used tool for assessing the extent of a reader's awareness or understanding of the structure or features found in a particular narrative text. The generic form found in Chapter 6 was used to assess Matt's retelling of Aesop's "The Lion and the Mouse" (see Figure 11.1). Teachers should note that this scoring rubric provides a percentage score that can be loosely interpreted using the same criteria for reading comprehension scores from an IRI administration (see Table 6.1). In the scoring rubric, point values out of 100 are determined by the total number of items to be recalled. In this example, there were 17 items; therefore $100/17 = 5.88$. Rounding off meant each item recalled was worth 6 points. The student received two scores: one for

Figure 11.1   Story Retelling Scoring Rubric for Matt's Retelling of an Aesop Fable

Name: _Matt_ _____ Grade: _4_ Date: _9/16_

Story Title (and Author): _The Lion and the Mouse   (Aesop)_

Context: Story Read by Child _✓_ Silently ____ Orally _✓_ Story Read to Child ____

Main Points for Retelling		Unprompted	Prompted
CHARACTERS (_6_ points each)	(12)		
1. _lion_		✓	
2. _mouse_		✓	
3. _hunters_			
4.			
5.			
SETTING (_6_ points each)			
1. _lion's den_	(6)		(6) ✓
2. _forest_		✓	
3.			
4.			
EVENTS/PLOT (_6_ points each)			
1. _lion asleep in den_	(30)		(12) ✓
2. _mouse wakes lion_			✓
3. _lion catches mouse to kill_		✓	
4. _mouse begs for life_		✓	
5. _mouse promises to repay lion_		✓	
6. _lion lets mouse go free_		✓	
7. _lion caught in hunters' net_		✓	
8. _lion roars loudly_			
9. _mouse recognizes lion's roar_			
10.			
RESOLUTION/THEME (_6_ points each)			
1. _mouse chews through rope_	(12)	✓	
2. _lion freed by mouse_		✓	
3. _Moral: Even small acts of kindness are important_			

TOTAL POINTS: _78_/100 = _78_ %   _60_/100   +   _18_/100

Evaluative Comments: _Matt read the story fluently and seemed comfortable during the retelling. He recalls major points of the plot. His overall comprehension of 78% is adequate — this material is at his instructional reading level. He demonstrated understanding of the moral. Matt said, "Just because you're small doesn't mean you can't help somebody." Maybe compare to silent reading recall._

Figure 11.2   A Story Frame

Title: *Goldilocks and the Three Bears*
In this story, the problems start when _____
_____

After that, _____
_____

Next, _____
_____

Then, _____
_____

This was a problem because _____
_____

After that, _____
_____

Next, _____
_____

Then, _____
_____

The problem was solved when _____
_____

In the end, _____
_____

---

unprompted and one for prompted recall. These scores can be interpreted separately, or combined for a total percentage recall score.

Retellings can be either oral or written. In the case of oral retellings, a tape recorder should be used to capture the retelling for later analysis. It is difficult to listen to a retelling and at the same time make notations of all points recalled. Use of a tape recorder also allows students to record their own retellings while the teacher works with other students. Written retellings can take a variety of forms. One form, **story frames,** is useful for assessing knowledge of story structure and also the degree to which the story is recalled (Cudd & Roberts, 1987; Fowler, 1982). Story frames provide the key words or phrases representing the organizational pattern of the text. See Figure 11.2 for an example.

INSTRUCTION FOR NARRATIVE TEXT

Questions and activities based on story grammar (see also Chapter 7) may improve students' comprehension by enhancing their schemata for narrative material (Fitzgerald & Spiegel, 1983) and their level of involvement during reading (Dimino, Gersten, Carnine, & Blake, 1990). In Mandler and Johnson's (1977) story grammar, the story elements are described as a setting (who, where, and when); a beginning or initiating event (the problem for the hero); a reaction (what the hero says or does in response to the problem); a goal (what the hero decides to do about the problem); an attempt (the effort or efforts to solve the problem); an outcome (the consequence or result of what the hero does); and an ending (a brief wrap-up of the whole story).

Dimino, Gersten, Carnine, and Blake (1990) investigated the use of story grammar as a framework for improving at-risk high school students' comprehension and recall of short stories. Four categories of story grammar components were modeled, explained, and practiced: conflict/problem, character information, attempts/resolution/twist, and reaction/theme. Student engagement in lessons approached in this way was high. As a result these researchers conclude that "it is unfair to deprive low-track students of the potentially rich and stimulating experiences of analyzing and discussing works by authors such as Nathaniel Hawthorne, Dorothy Parker, Toni Morrison, or Guy de Maupassant simply because their reading ability is not as high as their peers" (p. 19).

Sadow (1982, p. 520) suggests five generic questions to be asked about stories:

1. Where and when did the events in the story take place and who was involved in them? *(setting)*

2. What started the chain of events in the story? *(initiating event)*

3. What was the main character's reaction to this event? *(reaction)*

4. What did the main character do about it? *(action: goals and attempts)*

5. What happened as a result of what the main character did? *(consequence, outcome)*

spatial   A format such as the story map seen in Figure 11.3 can help students see the structure of stories. A story feature chart can also be provided, as shown in Figure 11.4. These activities can help prepare a student for either oral or written retelling assessments. Gambrell, Pfeiffer, and Wilson (1985); Gambrell, Koskinen, and Kapinus (1991); and Morrow (1988) have found that retellings significantly improve comprehension and sense of story structure. But retelling is a skill in and of itself that needs to be practiced (see Hoyt, 1999, p. 42). The prompting that the story map, story feature chart, and checklists containing questions such as those suggested by Sadow (1982), seen previously, provide effective scaffolds for developing the skill of retelling for struggling readers and second language learners alike.

Semantic webbing, also called *mapping* (discussed in Chapter 9), constructs a visual display representing relationships in the content of a story. Questions based on story grammar and asked in conjunction with developing story maps help students see the underlying organization of ideas and relationships in a story (Beck & McKeown, 1981). For instance, in *The Three Little Pigs* (refer to Figure 9.4), once the web strands (characters) are identified, the initiating event is asked about in order to begin eliciting information about each strand: "What caused the three pigs to go out on their own?" The responses provide strand supports for the old sow. Likewise, the reaction (in this example, three separate reactions for each pig) is elicited by asking: "What does each pig decide to do?" The goals, attempts, and outcomes follow by asking: "What does Pig #1 (Pig #2, Pig #3) decide to build?" "What is the first problem for the pigs?" "What happens to Pig #1?" "What is the next problem for the pigs?" "What happens to Pig #2?" "What is the problem for Pig #3?" "What happens to Pig #3?" "How is Pig #3 different from Pig #1 and Pig #2?" The ending is addressed by a question regarding a theme or a moral, such as, "Which pig is the hero, and why?" These questions develop the story map; however, questioning in the form of extension or enrichment can continue once the map (web) is completed.

A strategy that shows students how story features relate to each other is *find the features and connect them* (Richards, Gipe, & Necaise, 1994). The teacher first familiarizes students with the basic story features of character, setting, problem, and solution. Then the connection strategy is introduced by using a familiar story and discussing the way two elements are connected. Figure 11.4 shows one way in which this discussion might be recorded for students to examine. Students can also use such a chart for prewriting or planning their creative stories.

Unfortunately, many young readers and readers with difficulties have trouble relating to the human element in stories. While they may be able to name the characters in a

Figure 11.3   Story Map for *Goldilocks and the Three Bears*

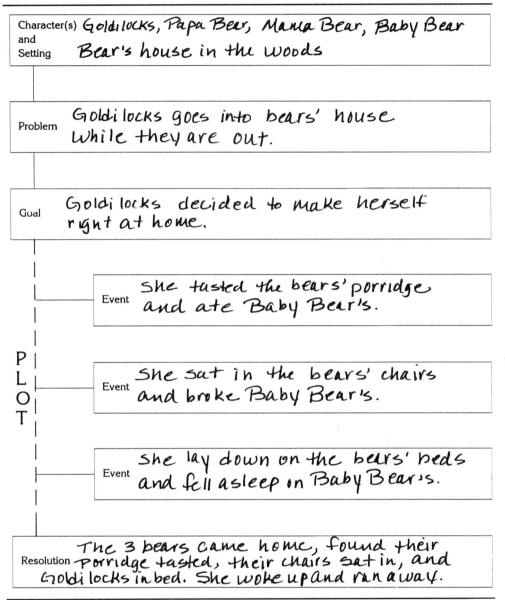

Character(s) and Setting	Goldilocks, Papa Bear, Mama Bear, Baby Bear Bear's house in the woods
Problem	Goldilocks goes into bears' house while they are out.
Goal	Goldilocks decided to make herself right at home.

P L O T

Event	She tasted the bears' porridge and ate Baby Bear's.
Event	She sat in the bears' chairs and broke Baby Bear's.
Event	She lay down on the bears' beds and fell asleep in Baby Bear's.
Resolution	The 3 bears came home, found their porridge tasted, their chairs sat in, and Goldilocks in bed. She woke up and ran away.

story, these students cannot identify with the characters or understand their feelings, goals, or motives. Comprehension is certainly affected in these cases. Developing a *getting to know my character* map (Richards & Gipe, 1993; Tompkins & Hoskisson, 1991) may help students better understand stories they read, as well as develop broader social understanding in general. Through modeling and explanation of the teacher's own thinking, both descriptive and inferred information about a main character is discussed and placed on a map (see Figure 11.5).

logical-mathematical   Several other useful graphic organizers help students focus on story features. Some of these include the *story structure chart* (Worthy & Bloodgood, 1992/1993), used for

Figure 11.4   Example of a Story Feature Chart

Student's Name _David_		Story Title _Goldilocks and the Three Bears_
FIND THE FEATURES AND CONNECT THEM		
Story Feature: Characters	**Story Feature: Setting**	**The Connection**
Mama Bear Papa Bear Baby Bear Goldilocks	the woods	The bears lived <u>in</u> the woods. Goldilocks lived <u>near</u> the woods. Goldilocks walked <u>in</u> the woods.
Story Feature: Problem	**Story Feature: Solution**	**The Connection**
The porridge was too hot to eat.	The bears went for a walk.	Some of the porridge got cool while the bears were gone.

spatial

charting similarities and differences among story features for several versions of the same story (e.g., Figure 11.6), and *Venn diagrams* to compare and contrast story elements (see Figure 11.7). When only contrasts are of interest, a *T-chart* works better than a Venn diagram (see Figure 11.8). Worthy and Bloodgood (1992/1993) present an interesting version of the traditional Venn diagram for comparing story plots. This technique is called a *circle graph* and allows students to draw representative sketches for important plot elements as well as list the elements (see Figure 11.9). Finally, the Somebody/Wanted/But/So *plot relationships chart* helps students look at each story feature from the perspective of the characters in the story. The column headings, in order, each relate to the characters, goals, problems, and solutions found in the story. See Figure 11.10 for a completed chart.

Dramatizing material read can also enhance comprehension. In addition to the reading and re-reading required to prepare a Readers' Theater script and drama production, activities that accompany these productions—such as preparing backdrops, deciding

intrapersonal

Figure 11.5   Example of a Character Map

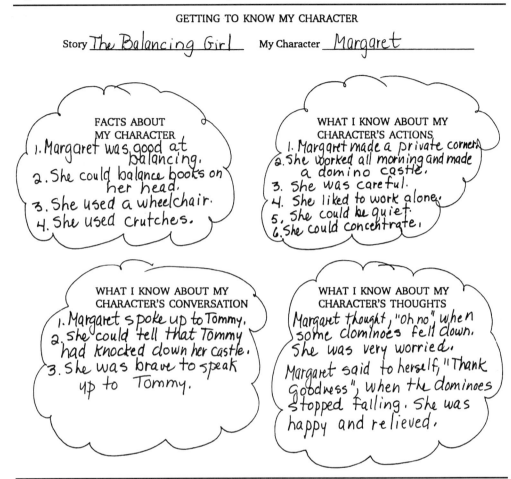

From Janet C. Richards and Joan P. Gipe, "Recognizing Information about Story Characters: A Strategy for Young and At-Risk Readers," *The Reading Teacher,* 47, Copyright © 1993 by the International Reading Association. All rights reserved. Reprinted with permission of Janet C. Richards and Joan P. Gipe and the International Reading Association.

intrapersonal
interpersonal
spatial
bodily-kinesthetic

on props, and conducting library research to verify content—help comprehension (see Chapter 14 for examples). Bidwell (1990) lists several ideas and ways to use drama in the classroom for the purposes of increasing motivation, comprehension, and fluency. The reading/writing connection is also made clear in preparing these productions, through writing the plot, developing characters, and revising and editing the final script.

Writing stories will also help reading comprehension. Reluctant writers are greatly assisted by **story impressions** (McGinley & Denner, 1987), a strategy that introduces a list of words or phrases (no more than three words) to be used in their written story, with order of use indicated by arrows.

Stories can be written by individuals or by groups. The words and phrases are selected to designate characters, setting, and key elements of the plot. Depending on the age of the student, limit the number of words and phrases listed to ten to fifteen. Figure 11.11 shows the word list followed by a group story.

A Focus on SLL: Generating Stories

Teachers can assist learners to use culturally relevant children's literature to motivate both reading and writing. For example, Cynthia Rylant's (1982) book *When I Was Young in the Mountains* can be used to help students learn about mountain culture as well as to motivate reflection on students' own lives while writing their own memoirs: *When I Was Young in* _____. In doing so, the students can make their own individual books or a class book with one page written and illustrated by each student. The students will be integrating their writing with their reading in a social context so that all learners (from various cultures and neighborhoods) can share stories about themselves and their self-generated language with each other. Moreover, in the context of this activity, the students are developing their awareness of complex sentence structure (e.g., subordinated adverbial clauses) and story structure while using the language of the author and themselves for a real audience.

In a culturally diverse classroom, children's literature about various ethnic cultures can enhance cross-cultural understanding as well as empower learners to read books that relate to their own cultures. (See Appendix D for a list of a variety of books recommended for students from various cultural backgrounds.) Further, teachers can encourage parents to use literature activities as part of their children's lives in family and community contexts (Barnitz & Barnitz, 1996). In recent years, family literacy programs and parenting programs have been established to facilitate literacy development in the community (Morrow, 1995; Rasinski, 1995; Thomas, Fazio, & Stiefelmeyer, 1999 a, 1999 b).

Use of wordless picture books is also of special benefit to linguistically different readers because they can easily provide a successful interaction with text (Cassady, 1998). Such books can be used to develop prediction strategies, plot story maps, develop vocabulary, and make connections between written and spoken language. Second language learners can initially "read" the book in their native language to stimulate oral communication and a sense of accomplishment. Then, working with a partner, they can create a story to accompany the book and share the story with the class. Variations in either or both languages can be prepared. Partners could be directed to work together as follows:

"Read" the story silently first.

Discuss interpretations with your partner.

"Read" the story into a tape recorder (to be typed later).

Cut apart the typed sentences and paper clip them to the appropriate pages in the picture book.

Read the story to another person.

A strategy related to phase-out/phase-in for active comprehension (see Chapter 9), but one better suited to narrative text, and one very simple for students to grasp, is called *I Wonder . . . ?* (Richards & Gipe, 1996). Beginning with the title and cover of a book, students are encouraged to ask "I wonder" questions. For example, using the book *Fox Song* by Joseph Bruchac (1993), some questions might be:

"I wonder if the fox will sing?"

"I wonder where the fox is?"

"I wonder why the fox is alone?"

"I wonder what the fox is looking at?"

This process can occur at other points in the story as well. Students then read (or listen) to satisfy their own purposes, a process that facilitates comprehension.

Perhaps the most effective way to increase readers' abilities to comprehend narrative text is to allow them large blocks of time to read. As introduced in Chapter 9, a minimum of twenty minutes each day for silent reading should be a goal; more time would be even better. A **book club** program (McMahon & Raphael, 1997) in which students choose the books they wish to read, discuss them with others in a small group, and later come together in a "Community Share" to share and hear about other books that other clubs have read, or the use of **literature circles,** similar to book clubs with the added

Figure 11.6 Story Structure Chart for Several Versions of a Story

TITLE	Little Red Riding Hood	Lon Po Po	Little Red Riding Hood	Little Red Riding Hood
COUNTRY	France	China	USA	Canada
AUTHOR	Perrault	Young	Hyman	Lang (Editor)
ILLUSTRATOR	Holmes	Young	Hyman	?
CHARACTERS (with a one word description)	Mother (loving) Little Red (naive) Wolf (shrewd) Grandma (kindly)	Mother (trusting) Shang (clever) Tao (plump) Paotze (sweet) Wolf (stupid)	Mother (prim) Little Red (free-spirited) Wolf (shrewd) Grandma (sickly) huntsman (brave)	Mother (loving) Little Red (pretty) Grandma (sickly) Wolf (tricky)
SETTING	village	country house	forest, Grandma's house	forest
EVENTS (list the major (events)	1. LRRH goes to Grandma's 2. Meets wolf 3. Wolf pretends to be Grandma	1. Mother leaves to go to Po Po's house 2. Wolf comes to house as Po Po 3. Children trick wolf to come to the gingko tree 4. Wolf is killed	1. LRRH takes food to Grandma 2. Meets wolf 3. LRRH picks flowers 4. Wolf eats Grandma 5. LRRH arrives 6. Wolf eats LRRH 7. Huntsman comes	1. LRRH goes to Grandma's 2. Meets wolf 3. Wolf races to get to Grandma's house first 4. Wolf eats Grandma 5. Wolf eats LRRH
ENDING	Wolf eats both	Children go back inside and to bed	Wolf is killed and the huntsman frees Grandma and LRRH	Wolf eats both
THEME	Deception	Symbolism	Magic	Deception

Figure 11.7 Venn Diagram Comparing and Contrasting *Little Red Riding Hood* and *Lon Po Po*

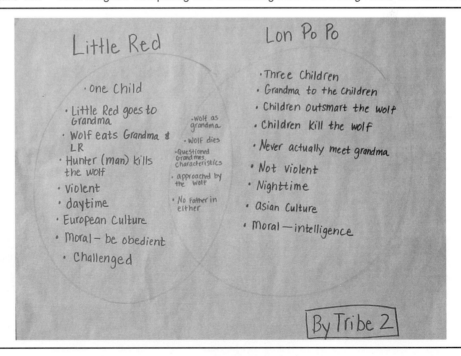

285

Figure 11.8   Reader Response Example: T-Chart for Contrasting Two Versions of *Little Red Riding Hood*

Little Red Riding Hood	*Lon Po Po*
Mother stays home and sends Red Riding Hood to Grandma's house	3 children, Shang, Paotze, and Tao, stay home and Mother goes to Grandma's house
Red Riding Hood is trusting of Wolf	Oldest child, Chang, is clever and discovers Wolf is a wolf
Wolf is clever	Wolf is easily tricked
Grandma and Red Riding Hood are eaten by Wolf (violent death)	children kill Wolf (subtle death)
Huntsman is the hero and saves Grandma and Little Red Riding Hood	children are the heroes who outsmart the wolf
Grandma is a main character	Grandma, Lon Po Po, is only a name in the story, as well as the title
Foods mentioned are bread, wine, sweet butter	Food mentioned is gingko nuts

Figure 11.9   Circle Graph Summarizing the Stories *Little Red Riding Hood* (Outer Circle) and *Lon Po Po* (Inner Circle)

Figure 11.10 Plot Relationships Chart for *Goldilocks and the Three Bears*

SOMEBODY	WANTED	BUT	SO
Goldilocks	to sit	chair was too soft	tried another chair
Goldilocks	to sit	chair was too hard and big	tried another chair
Goldilocks	to sit	chair was too small	chair broke
Goldilocks	to eat	food was too hot	tried another bowl
Goldilocks	to eat	food was too cold	tried another bowl
Goldilocks	to eat	food was just right	ate all the food
Goldilocks	to sleep	bed was too hard	tried another bed
Goldilocks	to sleep	bed was too soft	tried another bed
Goldilocks	to sleep	bed was just right	She fell asleep until the bears came home and they woke her up. Then she ran away.

Figure 11.11 Example of a Story Impressions Group Story

Story Impressions

Directions: Use these words in your story in the order listed.

Grandma and me

↓

beach

↓

windy

↓

hot dogs

↓

seashell

↓

deep water

↓

fins and mask

↓

sand castle

↓

home

continued

Figure 11.11   *continued*

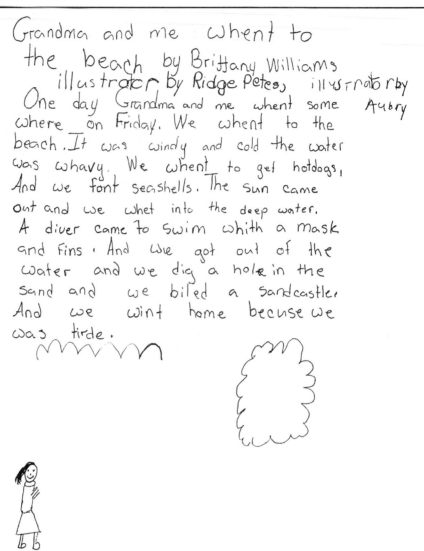

Grandma and me whent to
the beach by Brittany Williams
    illustrator by Ridge Petes, illustrator by
One day Grandma and me whent some   Aubry
where on Friday. We whent to the
beach. It was windy and cold the water
was whavy. We whent to get hotdogs,
And we font seashells. The sun came
out and we whet into the deep water.
A diver came to swim whith a mask
and fins. And we got out of the
water and we dig a hole in the
sand and we biled a sandcastle,
And we wint home becuse we
was tirde.

feature of students fulfilling specific job responsibilities such as "Vocabulary Enricher," "Passage Master," and "Summarizer" (Daniels, 1994), will ensure that students get a large amount of silent reading time. For students in transition who need direct support during reading, a buddy system or paired reading can be implemented. Because students will be selecting their own books to read, they also need to know how to select an appropriate book for their ability level. Recall that a high interest level can sometimes allow readers to stretch and read beyond their actual ability. But how to select a book needs to be discussed, especially with younger students. In addition to the five-finger method described in Chapter 9, the **Goldilocks strategy** (Ohlhausen & Jepsen, 1992) is an effective way of helping young readers select an appropriate book. Relating to the story sequence in *Goldilocks and the Three Bears,* students together with their teacher describe what might make a book "too easy," "too hard," or "just right." These characteristics can then be listed and posted in the library section of the classroom. "Just right" books might have the following characteristics.

- I want to read this book; it looks interesting.
- I can decode most of the words.
- My teacher, or someone I know, has read this book to me before.
- I have read other books by this author before.
- I already know something about this topic.
- My reading buddy can help me if I need it.

SUMMARY

Poor comprehenders generally do not approach reading as a meaning-making task; therefore, comprehension instruction for struggling readers must constantly emphasize understanding as the paramount purpose of reading. Direct instruction includes use of short selections, concrete words and examples, and appropriate questions. It must be explicit, that is, involve teacher-student interaction. Teachers should verbalize for their students the strategies they themselves use while trying to comprehend narrative text. These strategies might include predicting an outcome or charting the story features. Comprehension instruction is not limited to students who have mastered decoding; it *must* be taught from the very beginning to everyone. Many techniques presented in this chapter can be adapted as art activities so that a reader who is not yet fluent with responding to text in writing can respond through visual representations. To be good comprehenders, students must first realize that written materials should make sense. Until this realization has been internalized by the student, no instruction in comprehension is likely to help.

Suggested Readings

Glazer, S. M. (1992). *Reading comprehension: Self-monitoring strategies to develop independent readers*. New York: Scholastic.

A most readable monograph presenting an explanation of the comprehension process and strategies that help children monitor and make decisions about their own reading. Ways to create classroom environments conducive to supporting independence in reading and writing are also discussed.

Hill, B., Johnson, N., & Schlick Noe, K. (Eds.). (1995). *Literature circles and response*. Norwood, MA: Christopher-Gordon.

The editors have compiled a set of chapters that provide practical suggestions about implementing literature circles, but they also provide an example of how to support continued professional growth. This book makes it clear that inquiry-based classrooms are the perfect setting for literature circles.

McNeil, J. D. (1992). *Reading comprehension: New directions for classroom practice* (3rd ed.). New York: Harper-Collins.

This book attempts to address what should be taught as an aid to comprehension and how comprehension instruction should be delivered. Chapter 10 provides excellent ideas for enhancing comprehension through writing.

Palincsar, A. S., & Brown, A. L. (1984). Reciprocal teaching of comprehension-fostering and comprehension-monitoring activities. *Cognition and Instruction, 1* (2), 117–175.

One of the most successful techniques for helping students develop a self-questioning attitude while reading is reciprocal teaching. This original source provides actual discussion scenarios so the process can be more readily understood by teachers.

After you have read this chapter, you should be able to:
1. identify ways to determine whether students know about and are able to use strategies for reading expository text;
2. describe the three stages of studying;
3. give examples of skimming versus scanning;
4. explain what happens in comprehension monitoring;
5. describe techniques for teaching self-questioning skills and postreading organizational skills.

Assignment Mastery
comprehension
    monitoring
during-reading stage
guided reading strategy
    (GRS)
K–W–L
metacognition

PORPE
postreading stage
prereading stage
reciprocal teaching
ReQuest Procedure
    (*Re*ciprocal
    *Quest*ioning)

scanning
skimming
SQ3R strategy
studying
think-links
understanding questions

Study Outline

   I. Assessing awareness of strategic reading and study habits

  II. Instructional techniques for developing strategic reading habits

     A. Stages of studying

       1. Prereading

         a. Direct instruction for skimming and scanning

         b. Accessing prior knowledge

       2. During reading

         a. Comprehension monitoring

         b. Self-questioning

       3. Postreading

         a. Mapping

         b. Think-links

         c. Paragraph frames

         d. Dramatization

     B. General study strategies

       1. SQ3R

       2. GRS

       3. PORPE

       4. Additional acronyms for study strategies

 III. Summary

 IV. Suggested readings

How do you intend to read this chapter? The steps you follow make up your plan, or strategy. If you are a good strategic reader you might proceed in the following manner.

1. *Look through the entire chapter and ask questions.* How long is this chapter? How much time will I need to read it? Do the headings refer to familiar ideas, or does this material seem difficult? Do the figures (tables or graphs) appear helpful?

2. *Decide upon purposes for reading.* I want to know more about some of the terms used. The figures appear interesting. I want to know more about the techniques they represent.

3. *Read the material.* At the same time try to paraphrase sections (note taking) and continue asking questions. Do I know what this means? Do I see how I can apply this with students? Also decide what needs further clarification from the instructor.

4. *Question yourself after reading the material.* Can you go to the objectives listed at the beginning of the chapter and honestly say you have met them? Can you outline, from memory mostly, the important points? (Your outline should resemble the study outline already provided.) Can you explain the meaning of the terms listed at the beginning of the chapter?

If you have never tried to read expository text, such as this textbook chapter, strategically, why not try it now, using the preceding list if you like. See whether employing a strategy helps you remember more. If you are convinced that using some kind of strategy helps you remember more of what you read, you will be more likely to teach expository reading strategies to your students.

Strategic readers understand that for the purpose of learning or remembering specific information, a different set of strategies is needed from that which they might use when reading for enjoyment. When the purpose of reading includes study, readers process text material with the expectation of learning or remembering something specific. Good strategic readers (1) think about what they already know about the topic; (2) clarify their purpose for reading; (3) focus their attention on the content; (4) monitor whether they are understanding what they read; (5) use fix-up strategies (e.g., look back, reread, read ahead, consult a dictionary) when they do not understand; (6) fit new material into what they already know; (7) take notes; (8) think aloud to be sure of their understanding; (9) create mental images to aid understanding of difficult concepts; (10) summarize what they have read by mapping or using some other form of graphic organizer; (11) evaluate their understanding of what they read, whether or not their purpose was achieved; and, if necessary, (12) seek outside sources for additional information (Orange County Public Schools, 1985, 1986). Thus, an important characteristic of **studying** is that it is student-directed instruction. In other words, a teacher is *not* available to ask guiding questions, point out or clarify important concepts, or help with decisions about what to do next when material is not understood. (Additional information about specific study skills can be found in Chapter 13.)

Nevertheless, teachers need to demonstrate, or model, the variety of strategies available for the purpose of studying so that students can become independent learners. Garner (1987) proposes six guidelines for effective strategy instruction.

1. Teachers must care about the processes involved in reading and studying, and must be willing to devote instructional time to them.

2. Teachers must do task analyses of strategies to be taught.

3. Teachers must present strategies as applicable to texts and tasks in more than one content domain.

4. Teachers must teach strategies over an entire year, not in just a single lesson or unit.

5. Teachers must provide students opportunities to practice strategies they have been taught.

6. Teachers must be prepared to let students teach each other about reading and studying processes. (pp. 131–138)

ASSESSING AWARENESS OF STRATEGIC READING AND STUDY HABITS

One quick way to determine whether students are aware of and use study strategies is to administer a questionnaire similar to the one found in Figure 12.1. If you worry about students answering honestly, you can give the questionnaire on an anonymous basis to the entire group. A tally of the responses to each item indicates areas in which students need instruction.

Another way to assess students' strategic reading abilities is through observation. After directing a group of students to study some reading materials for a test, observe their behavior. Some type of survey of the material should be apparent, such as a quick perusal of the title and headings or looking at pictures, charts, or graphs. Often in a survey of the material, a reader quickly reads the first and last paragraph in the various sections of the material or the introductory and summary passages.

After a survey of the material, most students start reading from the beginning. Observable behaviors, such as note taking, underlining, looking back at previously read text, or rereading, indicate that the reader is actively studying the material.

Figure 12.1   Questionnaire to Determine Study Strategies and Habits

Appendix Item 69
Skill Test for Study Skills and Habits

Name _____

Directions:
Put a check mark (√) in the column that describes how often you do the following. Be honest. I shall help you learn to study if needed.

	Never	Sometimes	Usually
1. Do you look over what you are going to read before you read it?			
2. Do you form questions about the selection before you read it?			
3. Do you use a slower rate when you are reading your textbooks?			
4. Do you try to pronounce and define words that are in bold print or italics?			
5. Do you read the tables, graphs, and diagrams in your textbooks?			
6. Do you answer questions as you go along?			
7. Do you outline the important ideas and facts as you read?			
8. Do you reread the materials you do not understand?			
9. Do you review what you have read when you have finished?			
10. Do you set a time for study?			
11. Do you have a place to study at home or near your home? Are your supplies ready?			
12. Are you able to concentrate when studying?			
13. If you are doing math problems, do you read them carefully and then reread them to see if your answer is correct?			
14. If you must turn work in to your teacher, are you proud of it? Is it neat and well organized?			

From *The Reading Corner* by Harry W. Forgan, Jr. Reproduced by permission of Scott, Foresman and Company. © 1977.

A number of behaviors are possible when readers complete their reading. Some readers go back and try to outline the material. Others choose to go back and take notes or underline certain information.

Both the questionnaire and the observable behaviors indicate three phases in the process of studying. A student may consistently exhibit behavior for one of the phases but not for all three. These phases will be discussed in detail in the next section.

INSTRUCTIONAL TECHNIQUES FOR DEVELOPING STRATEGIC READING HABITS

Stages of Studying

Behaviors observed in skilled readers' studying text reveal three stages. These stages are prereading, during reading, and postreading.

Briefly, the **prereading stage** is characterized by attention to the overall theme of a selection. The student prepares to read the selection by considering what is already known about the topic. Headings, subheadings, graphs, tables, and new vocabulary words are typical items of concern at this stage. The student also clarifies a specific purpose for reading that helps in focusing attention on the content to be read.

The **during-reading stage** is more difficult to describe because of the wide variety of possible behaviors. Ideally, this stage is characterized by active involvement with the print. Recently, the term *comprehension monitoring* has been used to describe what should be happening at this stage (this will be discussed in a later section). Readers who monitor their comprehension continuously ask themselves, "Do I understand this material?" (Baker, 1979). If material is not understood, fix-up strategies must be used. The reader also tries to relate any new information to what is already known, and to recognize the organizational structure of the text (see Chapter 9).

In the **postreading stage,** students engage in activities that help them retain information. The most commonly used activities are organizational (outlines, maps), translational (paraphrases, annotations, formulating of questions), and repetitional (recitations, rehearsals). Instructional techniques for each stage will now be presented.

Prereading

Throughout this text I have emphasized trying to understand the processes involved in the various reading domains. Even for the domain of strategic reading for expository text, task requirements, or underlying processes, are important considerations. When the purpose is to learn and remember information, students must look over the material: titles, headings, illustrations, tables, introductions, summaries, and topic sentences. The prereading stage thus demands that students be proficient in **skimming** and **scanning.** "*Skimming* and *scanning* both refer to rapid reading during which the reader does not direct attention to all of the information on the page. *Scanning* is fast reading to obtain answers to specific questions. . . . while *skimming* is rapid reading to find out what something is about or a general idea" (Schachter, 1978, p. 149).

Flexibility in rate of reading is a skill that every student can and should practice. Even young children can be asked to skim or scan pictures for particular objects or colors. They can scan magazines or newspaper articles for a specific letter of the alphabet, or catalogs for objects beginning with a specific sound. Just about any type of printed material can be used to teach skimming and scanning, including telephone books (both yellow and white pages), menus, catalogs, newspapers, or textbooks.

Direct Instruction for Skimming and Scanning. Corrective readers often demonstrate a tendency to read every word. As students progress through the grades, teaching them when and how to vary their reading rate takes on increasing importance. An introduction to skimming and scanning uses a technique that shows the student what is meant by flexible reading rate, or skimming and scanning. For example, ask a student to look up a classmate's phone number in the telephone book (father's name: William Jenkins). Point out that the student would not start at the beginning and read the whole book or even start at the beginning of the *J*s and read through all of the names beginning with *J*. Instead, using alphabetizing skills, the student finds the general location and then scans to locate *Jenkins, William*. If asked, students are usually able to identify other situations from real life in which they skim or scan material, for example, scanning the TV schedule to decide what channel to watch or a recipe to see if the needed ingredients are available.

In direct instruction, students are taught to skim and scan for a variety of purposes. Initially, directions are simple, with activities chosen specifically to teach the concepts of skimming and scanning. Eventually, activities are more directly related to what students will be expected to do on their own as strategic readers of expository material. Some specific activities follow.

1. Direct the students to scan a passage that is easy to read and underline ten verbs. The teacher might set time limits on this task and gradually decrease the time allowed.

2. Direct the students to locate five items on a menu that sell for less than three dollars.

3. With the librarian's help, give students copies of brand-new book arrivals. Have each student skim a book (consider a time limit) and briefly share the general idea of the book.

4. Give students a list of questions to answer from the classified ads: How much does the 1997 Mustang cost? What breed of cat was lost? Where can you call to buy a used dishwasher? How much does a thirty-foot sailboat cost?

5. Questions similar to those in activity 4 can be used with content-area material. Tables of contents and indexes are ready sources for similar questions. Here are some sample question starters: Find the place at which. . . . Locate the page on which. . . . List the chapters that. . . .

6. More directly related to studying is an activity that uses a content-area textbook and question guide. Students are told to look specifically for the answers to the questions and *not* to read every word. Sample directions include the following:

   • Look at the paragraph headings for pages 17 through 24. After reading *just the headings,* write a sentence or two that tells what this section is about.

   • List the steps that tell how a bill is passed.

   • Read the section "The President Wears Many Hats" to find out how many different jobs the president has.

Accessing Prior Knowledge. Ineffective readers often start reading without first thinking about the subject of what they are reading. They fail to realize that they may already know something about the material, and that this knowledge can help them during their reading. There are several useful strategies teachers can demonstrate that will help these readers focus on what they already know about a subject.

An uncomplicated procedure discussed by Ogle (1986) that can be used with any content or grade level, individually or with groups, is the **K–W–L** strategy. The K step requires that students identify what is already *known* about the subject. If a group is applying the strategy, this step involves brainstorming information the group already knows about the subject. (This information is then categorized.) The W step requires students to reflect on what is already known and determine what they still *want* to learn. Thus, the W becomes a question: "What do I want to find out?" The L step actually occurs *after* the material is read. Each student writes down what was *learned.* Students should make sure that any questions they identified at the W stage have been answered. A chart similar to that found in Figure 12.2 can be used to provide a graphic structure for the reader.

spatial

Modifications of the K–W–L strategy have also been developed. The *What Do You. . . .* chart (International Reading Association, 1988, p. 15) seen in Figure 12.3 combines aspects of K–W–L and DRTA (see Chapter 9) formats. Such a chart encourages the student to focus on the subject, the title, or the cover of a book, and distinguish between what is known for certain and what is predicted to be covered.

Depending on the age and ability of the students, a simplified version of such organizational charts might focus only on accessing prior knowledge and making predictions. Such a version is *What do you know/What do you think* (J. Richards, personal communication, Oct., 1988). Given a topic, title, or book cover, the student states what is known ("just the facts") before stating what is predicted. When introducing any new strategy,

Figure 12.2   Chart for the K–W–L Strategy

K	W	L
What Do I **KNOW?**	What Do I **WANT** to Learn?	What Did I **LEARN?**
Categories of information I expect to use: A. B. C. D.		

such as What do you know/What do you think, begin by keeping all other aspects of the lesson familiar. For example, since the strategy is new, a well-known familiar narrative will be used to introduce the strategy. Thus, given the title and cover of the story *Goldilocks and the Three Bears,* the stated facts might include the following:

This is a story about a girl, Goldilocks, and three bears.

The bears have a house in the woods (based on cover illustration).

The girl has yellow hair (based on cover illustration).

There are two big bears and one small bear (based on cover illustration).

Predictions are then based on the known facts, and also on the reader's familiarity with other stories of a similar nature. Responses to the question "What do you think?" might include the following:

I think this story will tell about what happens to Goldilocks and the bears.

I think the bears will scare the girl.

Figure 12.3   What Do You . . .

Know You Know?	Think You Know?	Think You Will Learn?	Know You Learned?

I think Goldilocks visits the bears in their house in the woods.

I think that Goldilocks will make friends with the little bear.

I think that the bears will help Goldilocks.

When a book cover or illustration is used, the first question can be changed to "What do you see?" and a three-column map can be prepared for written responses, as seen in Figure 12.4. In this way, even very young students can learn to be strategic readers by beginning with familiar narrative material and moving into more difficult, expository material. Additional modifications of the K–W–L include the K–W–W (where I can learn this)–L (Bryan, 1998), the K–W–L–Q (more questions) (Schmidt, 1999), and the K–W–L–S (what I still need to learn) (Sippola, 1995).

A variation of the DRTA that focuses on accessing prior knowledge is discussed by Richek (1987). The variation DRTA SOURCE helps students recognize that readers use both the text and their prior knowledge when making DRTA predictions. In DRTA SOURCE, students stop after making predictions and identify which part of each prediction was based on something in the text and which part on prior knowledge. The value of this strategy is that it helps students become aware of how important their own prior knowledge is to reading.

During Reading

A wide variety of behavior is seen in the second stage of studying. After previewing the material, good strategic readers generally start at the beginning and read through the material, engaging in what is termed **comprehension monitoring.** Through this process, students constantly evaluate their level of understanding of what is being read. The ability to monitor one's own comprehension is so critical to studying that this topic deserves further elaboration.

Comprehension Monitoring. Research in the area of comprehension monitoring is fairly recent and is part of a larger area of study called **metacognition.** Instruction in metacognitive strategies can be very effective for readers having difficulty (Nolan, 1991).

Metacognition refers to one's knowledge concerning one's own cognitive processes and products or anything related to them, e.g., the learning-relevant properties of information or data. For example, I am engaging in metacognition (metamemory, metalearning, metaattention, metalanguage, or whatever) if I notice that I am having more trouble learning A than B; if it strikes me that I should double-check C before accepting it as a fact; if it occurs to me that I had better scrutinize each and every

Figure 12.4   Three-Column Map for *Goldilocks and the Three Bears*

What Do You See?	What Do You Know?	What Do You Think?
a girl with yellow hair	Goldilocks is a girl	The bears will scare Goldilocks
two big bears, one little bear	There are three bears	Goldilocks will hide from the bears
house in the woods	This is a fairy tale	The story will begin "Once upon a time . . ."

alternative in any multiple-choice type task situation before deciding which is the best one; if I sense that I had better make a note of D because I may forget. (Flavell, 1976, p. 232)

Metacognitive activities of interest for the during-reading stage include keeping track of the success with which one's comprehension is proceeding and, if comprehension breaks down, taking action to remedy the failure (Baker, 1979; Baker & Brown, 1984; Brown, 1980; Garner, 1987; Markman, 1979, 1981; Wagoner, 1983). Research in this area yields ample evidence that poor comprehension-monitoring ability is characteristic of ineffective readers. Additionally, comprehension-monitoring ability is not likely to develop simply with maturity; it depends on knowledge, experience, and instruction (Brown & DeLoache, 1978).

Beginning readers and less able readers are generally deficient in evaluating their understanding of text (Baker & Brown, 1984; Garner, 1980; Markman, 1979; Paris & Myers, 1981; Winograd & Johnston, 1980). If the reader does not know whether the text has been understood, the teaching of techniques for correcting comprehension breakdowns could be premature. Thus, the first step is to help students develop their own comprehension awareness.

For readers to be able to monitor their own comprehension, they need to be actively involved with what they are reading. Very young readers and those having difficulty demonstrating monitoring behaviors would benefit from the *Yes/No . . . Why?* and *It Reminds Me Of . . .* strategies (Richards & Gipe, 1992). These two strategies easily involve students by encouraging them to use their background knowledge to make decisions about their understanding of the material read. In the *Yes/No . . . Why?* strategy, the teacher and students both read silently (or orally if desired) an agreed-upon portion of the text. This might be a page or a paragraph. Following the silent reading, the teacher models a *yes* and a *no*. A *yes* is something that the reader liked or understood about the passage. A *no* is something not liked or not understood about the passage. A reason for the *yes* or *no* is also provided. Then a student shares a *yes* and a *no* with reasons. For example, the teacher might introduce and model the strategy by reading the familiar nursery rhyme *Jack and Jill,* and then say, "My *yes* is that I like the way Jack and Jill were doing their chores because it tells me they are helpful to their mother. My *no* is that I didn't like that they fell because they got hurt." Then a student might respond with, "My *yes* is that I like the name Jill because my cousin's named Jill. My *no* is that I don't know what Jack broke. I never heard that word before." After a period of sharing *yes/no*s, with the teacher modeling a variety of responses to text, the students will become more involved with the material and will become better able to summarize, clarify, predict, and identify main ideas about the material.

To be able to say what a passage "reminds them of," students have to make a connection between the material and their own background, especially when the material being read needs to be learned or remembered, as with informational text (Carver, 1992). Again with teacher modeling, students can tell or write their responses about what they are reminded of following the reading of a brief portion of text. For example, after reading a paragraph in a newspaper article that talks about flooding along the Mississippi River, the teacher might say, "This reminds me of the story of Noah's ark." The teacher may choose to further elaborate, depending on the needs of the students. Then students are given the opportunity to respond to the same paragraph. As students become more comfortable with these techniques they will be better able to identify points at which they are not understanding what they read, and will then be receptive to learning what to do to improve that situation (i.e., strategic reading behaviors).

Teaching strategic reading behaviors to corrective readers is especially important because it puts them in control of their own learning. Instruction in strategic reading behaviors for expository text requires that students learn and use comprehension-monitoring skills. Because one of the first steps in comprehension-monitoring is recognizing whether the text has been understood (Baker, 1979), that seems a logical place to begin instruction. Therefore, when students are comfortable with strategies such as *yes/no . . . Why?* and *It Reminds Me Of. . . ,* they are ready to develop strategies to use during reading.

intrapersonal

Glazer (1992) presents a *Thinkalong* strategy accompanied by a self-monitoring checklist (see Figure 12.5) for use during reading. The types of strategic behaviors that are individually modeled for students are listed here.

1. Making a picture in one's mind about the text;
2. Predicting from pictures, subtitles, and words during reading;
3. Asking oneself questions about the text;
4. Going back and rereading when the text doesn't make sense;
5. Personalizing the text based on one's own experiences;
6. Guessing the meanings of words during reading. (p. 64)

Self-Questioning. Research examining self-interrogation ability reveals that this is a promising area of instruction for improving comprehension-monitoring skills (Andre & Anderson, 1978/1979; Frase & Schwartz, 1975; Schmelzer, 1975). Results from these studies

Figure 12.5   Thinkalong Self-Monitoring Checklist of Strategic Reading Behaviors

SELF-MONITORING SHEET—THINKALONGS

Thinkalong	Always	Sometimes	Never
I know when I don't understand something.			
I ask myself questions to understand the text.			
I make a picture in my mind to help me understand the text.			
I reread to help myself understand.			
I personalize the ideas and relate them to my own experiences. I think about something I know that fits into the new information.			
I reread when I don't know what a word means.			
Sometimes I predict what I will read about next in the text.			

Name: _____

Date: _____

From Susan M. Glazer, *Reading Comprehension: Self-Monitoring Strategies to Develop Independent Readers.* Copyright © 1992 by Scholastic, New York, NY. Reprinted with permission.

indicate that students remember more when they formulate questions during studying by either writing them down or verbalizing them to a friend. Nolan (1991) found that a "self-questioning with prediction-making" strategy was more effective than self-questioning alone, since readers then must monitor not only whether questions are answered but also whether predictions are correct. The following steps are learned in this strategy:

1. Identify the main idea.
2. Write down the main idea.
3. Think of a question based on the main idea and write it down.
4. Answer your question.
5. Predict what will happen next. (p. 135)

Anderson (1980) recommends the use of **understanding questions** to help students monitor their comprehension. Because obstacles to comprehension may occur at the word, sentence, or paragraph level, understanding questions check all three. Some examples are: Does this sentence have any new words? Is a word I know being used in a new way? Did this sentence make sense? Does this sentence fit with what I already know about the topic? What was this section about? Can I explain this in my own words? What were the important facts? Have I read something similar to this before?

Self-generation of questions may be an effective strategy because the student is forced to pause frequently, deal with the effort to understand, determine whether comprehension exists, and finally, become concerned about what to do if comprehension has not been achieved.

Instructional techniques for explicitly teaching students how to use understanding questions and read expository text strategically are not taught directly or modeled often enough. Nevertheless, it is clear that "helping poor readers become strategic readers demands modeling of mental processes" (Duffy, Roehler, & Herrmann, 1988, p. 766). Duffy, Roehler, and Herrmann (1988) emphasize the importance of the teacher modeling the mental processes (as opposed to procedural steps) that would otherwise be invisible to the students. In this way, the students will have heard examples of appropriate reasoning they can then use to read strategically for themselves.

A few promising techniques for training self-questioning behaviors can be found in the literature. Collins and Smith (1980) recommend a modeling technique in which the teacher demonstrates the various types of understanding questions the students could ask themselves. The teacher tries to think aloud for the students, showing them where and when they would appropriately ask questions. The actual instructional method suggested by Collins and Smith (1980) proceeds in three stages similar to Singer's (1978) active comprehension lesson (see Chapter 9). Initially, the teacher models by reading a passage aloud, pausing, and asking relevant understanding questions along the way. The second stage includes the students by asking them to pose the understanding questions, gradually lessening the teacher's involvement. The third stage is silent reading by the students with teacher input only if difficulties are encountered.

Recall structured comprehension (Cohn, 1969), introduced in Chapter 9, as a sentence-by-sentence technique that uses a particular set of questions to help students clarify their understanding of what they are reading. See Figure 12.6 for an example of a structured comprehension lesson used with a social studies selection.

Another technique, similar to structured comprehension, is called the **ReQuest Procedure (*Reciprocal Questi*oning)** developed by Anthony Manzo (1969, 1985). This procedure, which is used with individuals or small groups, aids students in setting their own purposes for reading. The teacher guides the students through the silent reading of

Figure 12.6   Structured Comprehension Lesson

Background: The student is told that the Constitution is a list of the rights that the American people have. Soon after the Constitution was written, the people wanted to add more rights. These additional rights are called the Bill of Rights.

Passage: "The Bill of Rights says that every person can speak freely. A person can criticize the government or its officials if he believes that they are not doing a good job. We call this freedom of speech.

—Herbert H. Gross et al., *Exploring Regions of the Western Hemisphere*

Questions

Sentence 1
1. Does "speak freely" mean you won't have to pay before speaking?
2. Is the Bill of Rights a person?
3. How can the Bill of Rights "say" anything?
4. This sentence means:
   a. the Bill of Rights think no one should have to pay to speak
   b. an important right of all people is to be able to say whatever they think is important to say
   c. a new law was passed that has cured people who couldn't speak, so that now they can speak

Sentence 2
1. What does "criticize" mean?
2. What does "its" refer to?
3. Who does "he" refer to?
4. Who does "they" refer to?
5. This sentence means:
   a. if the government or the people who are leaders in the government are not doing a good job, anybody can say that they aren't
   b. when the government does not do a good job, the people must believe that they are doing a good job anyway
   c. it is impossible for the government to do a bad job

Sentence 3
1. Who does "we" refer to?
2. What does "this" refer to?
3. "Freedom of speech" means no one can charge to hear a speech. True or false?
4. This sentence means:
   a. all people have the right to speak out if the government does not do what it's supposed to do
   b. the Bill of Rights is also called freedom of speech
   c. the government can say anything it wants to for free

---

as many sentences of a selection as are necessary to enable them to complete the passage independently. Once again, as in structured comprehension, questions are exchanged by student and teacher, sentence by sentence. Every question asked by a student or teacher must be answered from recall, or an explanation must be given for why it cannot be answered. The teacher's questions serve as models for the kinds of questions students should ask of themselves while reading. Also, when responding to students' questions, the teacher gives reinforcement, such as "That was an excellent question" or "You might want to reword the question in this way . . ." or "I think your questions are really improving." When the teacher thinks students are ready to proceed independently (no more than three paragraphs should be handled reciprocally), a general purpose-setting

A Focus on SLL: GIST—Generating Interaction between Schemata and Text

GIST (Cunningham, 1982) is a particularly effective strategy for second-language learners because the participants have a chance to discuss and clarify meaning with the help of a strong English language user as they decide on the best summary sentence for a selection from an expository text. Once the teacher has identified a section of text that is likely to cause difficulty for the second-language learner, a decision is made to summarize this text paragraph by paragraph (or other logical stopping points). The class is divided into groups so that there is at least one strong English language speaker/reader in each group, as well as other students of the same language background as the second-language learner who may be able to provide language support if needed. The goal of GIST is to facilitate understanding of expository text material through discussion and negotiation of a best summary sentence consisting of no more then twenty-five words. This summary can be completed first in the student's native language and then translated to English. However, if the teacher's purpose includes facilitating English communication, then the discussion and summary sentence generated should be done in English solely. As each group completes their "twenty-five words or less" summary sentence, these can be shared with the whole group and further discussion can occur. The teacher acts as a facilitator, making sure the summary sentences do indeed capture the "gist" of the material read, by asking appropriate questions or further supporting students' understanding of the material. Once the entire text selection has been read, the groups read and compare all of their summary sentences, maintaining a twenty-five-word maximum as additional material is read and summarized. By the end of the paragraph, all students should have an effective and concise summary of the material, and clarification of previous misconceptions.

question is asked: "Did we raise the best question or purpose for which to read this selection?" (Manzo, 1985). At this point, the rest of the selection is read silently.

A technique born of Manzo's original ReQuest Procedure, and which proceeds paragraph by paragraph, is called **reciprocal teaching** (Palincsar & Brown, 1984, 1986). In this interactive procedure, students are taught to summarize sections of text, anticipate questions that a teacher may ask, make predictions about upcoming text, and clarify unclear sections of text. Initially, the teacher plays a major instructional role by modeling these behaviors and helping students in a collaborative effort with the wording of summaries and questions. Working with seventh-graders who were described as adequate decoders but poor comprehenders,[1] Palincsar and Brown were able to train the students to use comprehension-monitoring behaviors after only fifteen to twenty sessions. They also trained classroom teachers to use the technique with similar success.

interpersonal

Reciprocal teaching can be used with either individuals or small groups. (For best results with poor comprehenders, use small groups of two or three students.) In any case, the adult teacher takes turns with each student participant role-playing "teacher" and leading a dialogue on a section of text read, usually a paragraph. After each section, the "teacher" asks a main idea question. If this is difficult, a summary is attempted. A clarification of some aspect of the text may be asked for, or a prediction about upcoming text may be given. Feedback and praise are given by the adult teacher whenever appropriate. In group sessions, feedback also comes from other students.

Early training sessions require much guidance from the teacher. As students become better able to summarize and ask main idea questions, the teacher's level of participation decreases. Sessions should last about thirty minutes. Although Palincsar and Brown worked with expository passages of about 1,500 words, any type or length of reading material can be used.

---

[1] The students decoded at least 80 words per minute with a maximum of 2 words per minute incorrect and were two grades or more behind on a standardized reading comprehension test.

Another way to help students develop their self-questioning ability is to provide study guides that list the kinds of questions students should ask themselves. The Revised Extended Anticipation Guide (Duffelmeyer & Baum, 1992) is a good example (see Figure 12.7). Part 1 is a prereading activity in which students activate their schema for the topic by reflecting on their beliefs and/or perceptions and agreeing or disagreeing with teacher-developed statements about the topic. Class discussion following Part 1 will reveal student differences and provide further motivation for reading the selection, in addition to reading to verify choices made in Part 1. Part 2 is completed *during* reading. Here students are constantly asked to question their choices in Part 1. If a choice is supported by the reading, the *yes* column is checked and evidence or justification is written in the space provided. Likewise, if a choice is *not* supported, the *no* column is checked and a paraphrasing of what was stated in the material to refute the choice is written.

Paris and Lipson (1982) describe a program of instruction that relies on bulletin boards and related worksheets to teach students to use what they term *focal questions,* which are similar to the understanding questions already discussed. Their research indicates that metacognitive skills can be taught.

Once students have reached a level of awareness regarding comprehension, they can deal with the question of "what to do next" (Anderson, 1980). Anderson provides the following guidelines:

1. If a reader reads something that he or she does not understand, the reader may decide to take some strategic action immediately or may store the information in memory as a pending question.
2. If the reader stores it as a pending question, he or she may formulate a possible meaning (usually one) that is stored as a tentative hypothesis.
3. If the reader forms a pending question, he or she usually continues to read.
4. If a triggering event occurs after the reader forms the pending question (i.e., too many pending questions or repetitions of the same pending question), the reader may take some strategic action.
5. If the reader takes some strategic action, he or she may:
   a. *reread* some portion of the text in order to collect more information that will either answer a pending question or form a tentative hypothesis related to a pending question;
   b. *jump ahead* in the text to see if there are headings or paragraphs that refer to the pending question and might answer the pending question;
   c. *consult* an outside source (e.g., dictionary, glossary, encyclopedia, expert) for an answer to some pending question;
   d. make a *written record* of a pending question;
   e. *think/reflect* about the pending question and related information that the reader has in memory;
   f. *quit* reading the text.
6. If the strategic action is successful, the reader usually continues to read from the point at which the comprehension failure was last encountered.
7. If the strategic action is not successful, the reader usually continues to read by taking some other strategic action. (pp. 498–499)

An instructional technique described by Babbs (1984) is appropriate for this area. Using a reading plan sheet and comprehension monitoring cards, readers are first taught to be aware that they may have a comprehension problem while reading (the plan sheet) and then are taught strategies for dealing with comprehension failure (the cards).

Figure 12.7   Example of a Revised Extended Anticipation Guide

Part 1: Before Reading

Directions: Before you begin your reading assignment, *Understanding Autism*, read each of the sentences below. If you think the sentence is true, put a check in the Agree column. If you think the sentence is false, put a check in the Disagree column. You will be asked to explain your choices.

Autism	Agree	Disagree
1. People with autism lack normal language ability.	✓	
2. Mental retardation is a characteristic of autism.		✓
3. Autism is a more common disorder than Down syndrome.		✓
4. Autism is believed to be the result of poor parenting.		✓
5. Hans Asperger is close to finding a cure for autism.	✓	
6. The essential characteristic of autism is mindblindness, or an inability to understand what other people are thinking/feeling.	✓	

Part 2: During Reading

Directions: If the information you read supports our choices in Part 1, put a check in the Yes column, below. Then write what the text says in your own words in Column A under "Why is my choice correct?" If what you read does NOT support your choices, put a check in the No column. Then write what the text says in your own words in Column B under "Why is my choice incorrect?"

Support? Yes	No	A Why is my choice correct?	B Why is my choice incorrect?
1. ☐	✓		True only for "classic" autism. Mild versions still have high language function.
2. ✓	☐	Many with autism test in the normal range for intelligence.	
3. ☐	✓		Autism affects 1 in 500, more common than Down syndrome or childhood cancer.
4. ✓	☐	Autism is brain-based; suspected causes are: genetic mutations, viruses, toxic chemicals.	
5. ☐	✓		H.A. is the pediatrician who identified a mild version of autism (called Asperger Syndrome).
6. ✓	☐	Research suggests mind-blindness is the core of all autism. Even those with mild forms cannot interpret facial expressions or emotions.	

The reading plan sheet asks five questions: "(1) What is reading? (2) What is my goal? (3) How difficult is the text? (4) How can I accomplish my goal? (5) How can I check on whether or not I accomplished my goal?" (Babbs, 1984, p. 201). The questions presented on this plan sheet represent a study strategy, and you may see similarities between these questions and the strategy presented earlier in this chapter. Students should practice using the plan sheet so that these questions are automatically asked before beginning to read expository material.

**logical-
mathematical**

The comprehension monitoring cards encourage readers, in a step-by-step fashion, to evaluate their own understanding of the text read, and also aid readers in knowing what to do when a comprehension problem occurs. The nine cards and their identifying numbers, are as follows: (1) Click—I understand. (2) Clunk—I don't understand. (3) Read on. (4) Reread the sentence. (5) Go back and reread the paragraph. (6) Look in the glossary. (7) Ask someone. (8) What did it say? (to check comprehension at the paragraph level) (9) What do I remember? (to check comprehension at the page level) (Babbs, 1984, pp. 201–202).

A modeling procedure is recommended to teach students to use the cards. The teacher reads a sentence of text, then asks, "Did I understand that?" If the answer is yes, the Click card is raised and the teacher goes on to the next sentence. If the answer is no, the Clunk card is raised and cards 3 through 7 are selected. If the problem is with a word, the order of the strategy cards is 4–3–6–7. If the problem is with the whole sentence or with a pronoun referent, the order of the strategy cards is 4–5–3–7. The teacher models all of these possibilities, using a variety of several sentences.

After a complete paragraph has been modeled, the teacher looks away from the page, holds up card 8, and answers that question. If the question cannot be answered, the paragraph is reread without further use of the strategy cards. Likewise, after a complete page has been modeled, the teacher again looks away from the text, holds up card 9, and answers the question. If the question cannot be answered, the page is reread using card 8 after each paragraph.

Once the teacher has modeled the process, Babbs (1984) recommends that each student have a turn modeling before going on to individual practice. She also states that fifteen sessions of twenty-two minutes each were allowed for learning both the reading plan sheet questions and the use of the comprehension monitoring cards. At that point the students could describe details of both of these elements from memory.

interpersonal

A similar format is described by Klingner and Vaughn (1999) and is called Collaborative Strategic Reading (CSR). Rather than individual students working with a set of Click-Clunk cards, CSR involves group members helping each other with new vocabulary and textbook "clunks." Found to be especially helpful for second-language learners, the four Clunk cards direct students as follows: (1) "Reread the sentence with the clunk and look for key ideas to help you figure out the unknown word. Think about what makes sense." (2) "Reread the sentences before and after the clunk looking for clues." (3) "Look for a prefix or suffix in the word that might help." (4) "Break the word apart and look for smaller words that you know" (Klingner & Vaughn, 1999, p. 742).

Such activities will help students form habits of (1) thinking about what they know and believe about a topic *before* reading, (2) questioning their understanding of material *during* reading, and (3) focusing on clarifying new information *after* reading.

Postreading

In the final stage of studying, activities that help the student organize and remember important information are appropriate. Outlining, paraphrasing, and reciting or rehearsal of information are common activities for this last stage. These activities are usually difficult for students to master, however.

spatial

Mapping. *Mapping* (also called *semantic webbing*) aids the learner in linking ideas together (see also Chapters 9, 10, and 11). As discussed here, mapping is intended as a substitute for the organizational activity of outlining. Hanf (1971) discusses three basic steps for designing a map: (1) identify the main idea, (2) identify principal parts that support the main idea (called secondary categories), and (3) identify supporting details. The skeleton of a map may be completed during the prereading stage (i.e., the title of the selection becoming the main idea or central theme and the headings becoming secondary categories that support the main idea). However, the map itself should be completed from memory during the postreading stage. The student must add the supporting details. If the map cannot be completed, the student knows to go back and reread the material. Thus there is a built-in feedback device. If the student can complete some parts of the map but not others, the map has provided feedback on categories needing further study. An example of a map for the study of a science chapter entitled "Power for Work"[2] is found in Figure 12.8.

logical-mathematical

When the K–W–L strategy discussed earlier is combined with mapping and summarization, the technique helps students construct meaning from the text in an independent fashion. This modification of K–W–L, called *K–W–L Plus* (Carr & Ogle, 1987), has been used successfully with secondary readers having reading and writing difficulty. Basically, students must think critically about what they have read in order to organize, restructure, and apply what they have learned to the formation of a map and a written summary. Figure 12.9 shows how a ninth-grader went from the K–W–L listings to a concept map. The map can then be used as an aid for preparing a written summary and also preparing for exams.

Think-Links. Wilson (1981) refers to another organizational strategy called **think-links.** Upon completion of the during-reading stage of study, the teacher directs the students to think about what they have read. The following steps are then taken (Figure 12.10).

1. Write the name of the person the chapter is about (Lincoln) and some words that describe his early life.
2. Ask students for examples that show that Lincoln's early life was hard, and record them.
3. Step 2 is repeated using other descriptive words.

spatial

After all of the words have been used, the students have actually reconstructed, graphically, the important parts of the material read.

Once the teacher has helped students develop several think-links, they can start to develop them on their own. Think-links are used to summarize any type of reading material; during the instructional process, different types are constructed with the students so they can see a variety of types.

Paragraph Frames. As discussed in Chapter 9, paragraph frames provide a useful instructional tool for helping students write about what they learn in content areas (Cudd & Roberts, 1989). A cloze format provides sentence starters focusing on the organizational pattern of the text. Intended for students of all grade levels, the introduction of paragraph frames is easiest with sequentially ordered material. The teacher might write a brief paragraph based on a content-area topic just read, using such key words as *first, next, then, now, finally,* and *after this.* The individual sentences are put on sentence strips, and as a group of students are asked first to review the topic read and then to arrange the sentence strips in the logical sequence of events. The resulting paragraph is read for "correctness."

---

[2] From *In Your Neighborhood* (pp. 91–96) by A. O. Baker, G. C. Maddox, and H. B. Warrin, 1955, New York: Rand McNally.

Figure 12.8   Example of a Map for a Science Chapter, "Power for Work"

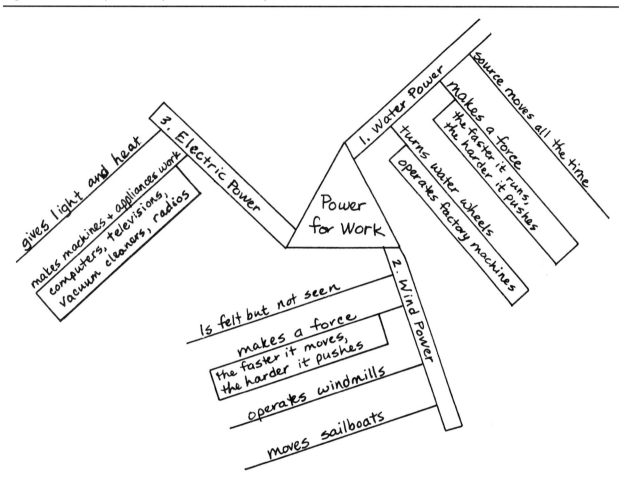

Mapping is thinking: constructing and creating the organizational design of ideas, selecting the information that is relevant, sorting this into its proper place, relating all facts to the whole and relating facts to other facts, and finally responding with personal reaction to the material. (Hanf, 1971, p. 229)

Following the group work, individual students reorder the sentences on their own, write the paragraph, and illustrate the important parts. Figure 12.11 provides an example of a completed paragraph frame.

Dramatization. As presented for narrative text, dramatization can enhance comprehension. A similar response can be made to expository material. Fennessey (1995) describes how to integrate literature, drama, music, and dance to make history more meaningful for her fifth-grade students. Cooter and Chilcoat (1990) focus on the use of melodramas to build understanding of expository text. "Melodrama, as applied to historical instruction, is an expository text response activity that uses sensational action, exuberant emotions, and somewhat stereotyped characterization to present a message about history" (p. 274).

bodily-kinesthetic

interpersonal   A *Jeopardy*-type skit could be developed to correspond with a particular content-area unit of study. To prepare the skit, students work with a partner to produce a set of

Figure 12.9   Example of a Ninth-Grader's K–W–L Worksheet and Resulting Concept Map

A ninth-grade disabled reader's K–W–L worksheet on killer whales		
K (Know)	**W** (Want to know)	**L** (Learned)
They live in oceans.	Why do they attack people?	D — They are the biggest member of the dolphin family.
They are vicious.	How fast can they swim?	D — They weigh 10,000 pounds and get 30 feet long.
They eat each other.	What kind of fish do they eat?	F — They eat squids, seals, and other dolphins.
They are mammals.	What is their description?	A — They have good vision underwater.
	How long do they live?	F — They are carnivorous (meat eaters).
	How do they breathe?	A — They are the second smartest animal on earth.
		D — They breathe through blowholes.
		A — They do not attack unless they are hungry.
Description		D — They are warm-blooded.
Food		A — They have echo-location (sonar).
Location		L — They are found in the oceans.

Final category designations developed for column L, information learned about killer whales:
A = abilities, D = description, F = food, L = location

The ninth-grader's concept map

Abilities (2)
kill for food
detect pebble-sized aspirin
  tablet in 30 feet of water
find food in cloudy water
echo-location

Description (1)
warm-blooded
dolphin family
second smartest animal next to man
born alive
10,000 lbs.
30 feet long
blow holes

Killer whales

Location (4)
all oceans
sea worlds

Food (3)
small dolphins
carnivorous (meat eaters)
400 lbs. salmon daily

(1) through (4) indicate the order of categories the student chose later for writing a summary.

Adapted from Carr, Eileen M., & Ogle, Dorna M. (1987, April), "K–W–L Plus: A Strategy for Comprehension and Summarization." *Journal of Reading, 30* (7), 626–631. Reprinted wth permission of Eileen Carr and the International Reading Association.

questions and answers, as well as appropriate categories and point values. Or, the teacher may provide the answers and categories based on curriculum goals, and the student partners may generate corresponding questions for a selected category, as well as point values. The entire class can take turns participating as contestants and as audience.

Figure 12.10   Think-Links are Used to Summarize Grapically the Important Parts of Any Type of Reading Matter

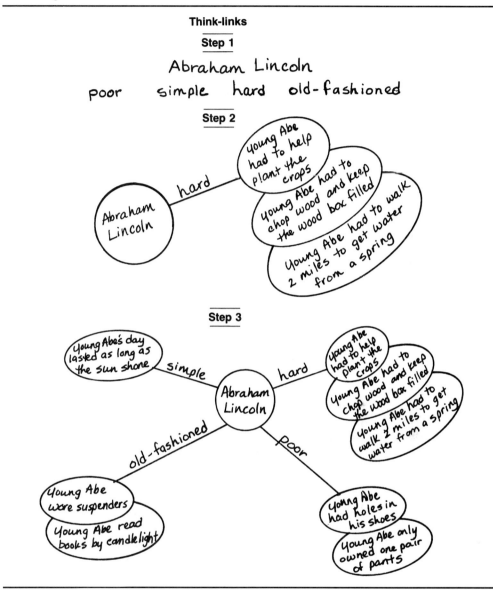

General Study Strategies

SQ3R

The best-known study strategy recommended for helping students make optimum use of study time is Robinson's (1961) **SQ3R** (survey, question, read, recite, review) **strategy.** This strategy is designed to (1) provide specific purposes for reading, (2) provide self-comprehension checks, and (3) fix information in memory (Tadlock, 1978). Briefly, in the *survey* step, the student reads the title, introductory statement, and main headings; surveys the illustrations; reads the chapter summary; and tries to mentally construct an outline of the chapter. In the *question* step, the student again looks at the main headings and

Figure 12.11   Example of a Completed Paragraph Frame, Including Illustrations

Example 3 (Rob, grade 1)

Mother box turtles prepare for their babies in a very interesting way. First, she looks for a safe place to burry her eggs. Next, she digs a hole so it will be moist for her eggs. Finally, she lays her eggs, burrys the hole, and then tamps it down. After this, the mother turtle leaves her babies on their own.

From Cudd, Evelyn T., & Roberts, Leslie L. (1989, February). "Using Writing to Enhance Content Area Learning in the Primary Grades." *The Reading Teacher, 42* (6), 392–404. Reprinted with permission of Evelyn Cudd and the International Reading Association.

uses them to formulate questions to be answered in the next step. The *read* step has the main purpose of finding answers to the questions formed in the question step. In the *recite* step, the student literally recites the answers aloud to the questions. At this point the student should also be concerned about the quality of the answers; for example, does the author provide answers that satisfy the question? The last step, *review,* is done from memory, with the entire chapter or selection being reviewed in survey fashion. The mental outline is reconstructed. The author's main ideas are recalled, and new ways to use these ideas are considered. A second and even a third review should take place over as many days.

However, several investigations of SQ3R have shown it not to be as effective as expected for students with reading difficulties (McCormick & Cooper, 1991). Instructional adaptations to SQ3R suggested by these studies are as follows:

- Providing shorter selections (300 words), as students did better when reading passages of this length. This presents students with an easier task.
- Having frequent discussion sessions to allow for direct teacher input if reading longer selections.

- Integrating discussion questions at short intervals throughout the selection, rather than asking all questions at the end of a reading.

A technique developed by Edward Strickland (1975) is called **Assignment Mastery.** The steps themselves closely parallel those in SQ3R: scanning, preparation for reading, reading, recitation and review, and reading review. The biggest difference from SQ3R is that specific questions are developed for students to ask themselves during the scanning, preparation, and reading stages:

Scanning

- How difficult does the work appear to be?
- Is it a relatively large amount of work?
- Will I have to alter my schedule to get it done?
- Are the terms generally familiar?
- What is the main theme of the assignment?
- What main headings and subheadings are there?
- What words are stressed (in italics or bold print)?

Preparation for Reading (with the help of a dictionary or glossary)

- Are there related terms that I use?
- Have I learned something that changes the meaning of the term from what I thought it was?
- Does the theme of the material appear to challenge or support my ideas?

Reading

- What is the meaning of what I am reading?
- What illustrations of that meaning are given?
- Can I recall any examples from my own experience that would clarify the meaning of the material?
- What questions should I ask my instructor that will help clarify the meaning of this material?

Strickland also stresses the underlining or outlining of main themes and illustrative examples while reading. (For a detailed description of how to teach the SQ3R strategy, see Forgan and Mangrum's (1985) *Teaching Content Area Reading Skills,* pp. 180–182.)

GRS

The **guided reading strategy (GRS)** (Bean & Pardi, 1979), developed specifically for corrective readers, is a modification of the guided reading procedure (Manzo, 1975). Briefly, the steps of a GRS are as follows:

1. Survey the chapter or chapter sections, reading only the chapter title, subtitles, vocabulary lists, graphs, maps, and chapter questions.
2. Close the book and orally state everything remembered from the survey. The teacher records what is remembered on the board.
3. Students recheck the chapter for any missing information; this is added to the board.

4. A crucial step, the teacher and students discuss the results of the chapter survey and organize this information into a topical outline on the board. This organizing highlights the structure of the information and enhances the ability to remember it later.

5. Students read the chapter or selection silently.

6. Students complete a ten-item true/false quiz.

7. About a week later, students take a ten-item pop quiz.

Of the general study strategies, the teacher may find that using the GRS as an introduction to the other strategies is most helpful.

PORPE

A strategy developed by Simpson (1986) for secondary- and college-level students as a less teacher-directed strategy uses writing as the main learning strategy for planning, monitoring, and evaluating the reading of any content-area material. **PORPE** (*P*redict, *O*rganize, *R*ehearse, *P*ractice, *E*valuate) is especially useful for students preparing to take essay examinations. Once the five steps of PORPE are modeled and mastered, it becomes a learning strategy that gives the student complete independence and control. The five steps are briefly presented here, but interested readers are urged to refer to Simpson's (1986) detailed description of the steps, and how to teach them to students.

1. *Predict*. Students are asked to generate possible essay questions on the material read.

2. *Organize*. Students summarize and synthesize the important ideas in the material. Charts, maps, or outlines are all possible ways for organizing the material.

3. *Rehearse*. Students recite the overall organizational structure of the chart, map, or outline, eventually adding important ideas and examples to this recitation. The purpose is to place these important ideas and organizational structure into long-term memory.

4. *Practice*. Students actually practice writing answers to the predicted essay questions from recall.

5. *Evaluate*. Students judge the quality of their responses from the perspective of the instructor. An evaluative checklist might be developed to aid in this process.

Two validation studies (Simpson, Stahl, & Hayes, 1989) show PORPE to be a practical and robust strategy for long-lasting learning and student independence.

Additional Acronyms for Study Strategies

There are many other valuable study strategies, but space constraints do not allow for their thorough explanation. The following listing is intended to alert you to several of these other possibilities, some of which are content-area specific. Interested readers are referred to the sources cited for more information.

AIM (Author's Intended Message)—a metacognitive strategy for constructing the main idea of text (Jacobowitz, 1990).

FLIP (Friendliness, Language, Interest, Prior knowledge)—a framework for helping middle school and secondary students estimate the difficulty of their content-area reading assignments (Schumm & Mangrum, 1991).

PLAE (Preplan, List, Activate, Evaluate)—emphasizes the self-regulatory processes involved in planning, monitoring, and evaluating; field-tested with college developmental reading students (Nist & Simpson, 1989; Simpson & Nist, 1984). Three validation studies conclude that (1) planning is significantly related to performance on tests (Nist, Simpson, Olejnik, & Mealey, 1989), (2) PLAE positively affects both test performance and metacognitive abilities (Nist & Simpson, 1989), and (3) students using PLAE outperformed those using traditional time management on four content-area examinations (Nist & Simpson, 1990).

PLAN (Predict, Locate, Add, Note)—a study-reading strategy, involving mapping before, during, and after reading, that helps students from middle school through college develop an active role in comprehension (Caverly, Mandeville & Nicholson, 1995).

PQRST (Preview, Question, Read, Summarize, Test)—developed to help students read physical science texts (Spache, 1963).

REAP (Read, Encode, Annotate, Ponder)—intended to help readers synthesize an author's ideas and use writing as an aid for future recall and study of ideas (Eanet & Manzo, 1976).

SCAIT (Select key words; Complete sentences; Accept final statements; Infer; Think)—intended for high school students; uses cooperative learning to help students learn how to select important information from text and develop higher-level thinking skills (Wiesendanger & Bader, 1992).

SQRQCQ (Survey, Question, Read, Question, Compute, Question)—developed to help students solve mathematical reading/reasoning problems (Fay, 1965).

SUMMARY

The techniques presented here have been chosen because they stress student involvement with text and appear in the literature as effective techniques. Teachers must be concerned with developing study strategies, or strategic reading of expository text, even for the young reader. At the early stages this may simply involve scanning printed material for a specific word or being taught to question material while reading it; that is, asking "Do I understand this?" Teacher modeling of the types of questions to ask while reading is one direct way of providing instruction in the area of self-questioning. Also, students at all levels, when given appropriate materials, can be taught to organize what they have read to aid them in remembering that material. Because of their graphic form, mapping and think-links are especially promising techniques for students who demonstrate spatial intelligence.

The general study strategies discussed are most easily learned if the students have previously received instruction in the three stages of studying, because these strategies include all three phases. Study strategies do not simply develop—they must be modeled, explained, and practiced.

Suggested Readings

Freeman, E. B., and Person, D. G. (1992). *Using nonfiction trade books in the elementary classroom: From ants to zeppelins.* Urbana, IL: National Council of Teachers of English.
This resource will help teachers provide interesting content-area material for their students. Students may be more willing to try the strategies presented in this chapter with

the materials discussed in this text. Teachers who wish to use thematic units will find this book especially valuable.

Leu, D. J., & Leu, D. D. (1997). *Teaching with the Internet: Lessons from the classroom.* Norwood, MA: Christopher-Gordon.

This book presents a wealth of lesson ideas and appropriate Web sites for integrating Internet use in the classroom. All the content areas are represented with projects for all grade levels.

Moore, D., Moore, S., Cunningham, P., & Cunningham, J. (1994). *Developing readers and writers in the content areas K–12* (2nd ed.). New York: Longman.

The second part of this text contains narrative accounts of how teachers in grades 2 and 5, secondary social studies and English, and secondary science and math imple- *ment the kinds of techniques described not only in this chapter but earlier chapters as well. The narratives are organized in a month-by-month format for an entire school year.*

Duthie, C. (1996). *True stories: Nonfiction literacy in the primary classroom.* York, ME: Stenhouse.

This book is the story of how a first grade teacher incorporated more nonfiction into her teaching. She found that nonfiction material was welcomed by her students because it satisfied their "inborn sense of wonder."

13 Study Skills

Objectives

After you have read this chapter, you should be able to:
1. list and describe the major study skills;
2. identify prerequisite skills for a given study skill;
3. identify sources of material other than stories for teaching study skills;
4. develop assessment activities for any study skill;
5. develop instructional activities for any study skill.

Key Concepts and Terms

arrays
Collaborative Listening-
   Viewing Guide
content words
equal-status relationships
expository material
GRASP (Guided Reading
   and Summarizing
   Procedure)

herringbone technique
locational skills
main ideas
NOTES
paraphrase
study skills
subordinate
   relationships
summarizing

superordinate
   relationships
synthesizing
thought units
topic

315

Study Outline

Study skills refers to the tool aspects of reading that allow a reader to extend and expand knowledge as well as literacy abilities. Any discussion of study skills assumes that the reader has some basic word recognition and comprehension ability—one cannot "extend and expand" something that is not present. Only minimum reading ability is necessary, however, as word recognition, comprehension, and study skills are all interrelated. Growth in one area aids growth in another. Instruction in study skills, like strategic reading for expository text, should *not* be delayed until a reader demonstrates well-developed word recognition and comprehension abilities.

The material used to teach study skills is distinctly different from that used to teach word recognition and comprehension strategies. The narrative material of the basal reader, fiction book, or language experience story does not provide an opportunity to learn and apply study skills. For example, the various uses of book parts to locate information cannot be taught when a book's table of contents lists only titles of stories. Being able to use a table of contents is an important study skill, although other book parts typically found in content-area textbooks (e.g., title page, index, glossary) more readily help students realize that specific parts of books can help them locate specific kinds of information. Other study skills, such as using the card catalog or computer system in the library, or interpreting a bar graph, simply cannot be learned most effectively by relying on narrative material. Likewise, the internal structure of expository material is different from that of narrative material.

An increasing number of secondary teachers complain that "students can't read the textbook" or that "students don't know how to find information for their term project." A student who may otherwise be a good reader, or one who was thought *not* to have reading difficulties in elementary school, often cannot deal independently with secondary-level textbooks and assignments. At present, direct teaching of study skills seems to be overlooked or ignored during the elementary school years. Part of the problem may be that the elementary-level teacher judges a reader's progress in the areas of comprehension and word recognition only with narrative material. The teacher then assumes that the reader can apply this ability with narrative material to the material found in content-area textbooks. Thus, an otherwise good reader suddenly has difficulties upon entering the intermediate grades, in which content-area reading increases.

In summary, study skills are tools that enhance the reader's understanding of content-area textbooks and other informative materials. Basic study skills are found in Figure 13.1. The rest of this chapter presents specific assessment and instructional techniques for the first three of the four major categories listed previously. Strategic reading for expository text was discussed in Chapter 12.

STUDY SKILLS AND THE STRUGGLING READER

Study skills differ from other areas of reading in that there are identifiable prerequisite skills, or underlying abilities, that will assist the learner in the effective use of a particular study skill. For example, Rosa must have certain prerequisite abilities to use an index. The study skills checklist in Figure 13.1 arranges the subskills within each category according to an underlying hierarchy so that these prerequisite abilities can be easily identified. Thus, for Rosa to use an index effectively, she must be able to alphabetize by first, second, and third letters.

To provide appropriate help then, not only must the area of difficulty be identified but also any gaps in prerequisite abilities. If Jackie cannot use the encyclopedia and other reference materials, she may not be able to alphabetize properly or know how to use the various book parts. Being asked to use reference materials without first learning these prerequisite abilities will likely be frustrating.

In summary, this chapter stresses the need to consider underlying abilities. This emphasis is especially relevant for the struggling reader, who typically have experienced gaps in their learning.

Figure 13.1   Study Skills Checklist*

Student's Name:

Study Skill	Knows	In Progress	Does Not Know	Not Assessed
I. Locating information				
A. Alphabetizes by first letter				
B. Alphabetizes by second letter				
C. Alphabetizes by third letter				
D. Knows and uses book parts (e.g., table of contents, index, glossary)				
E. Knows and uses reference materials (e.g., dictionary, thesaurus, encyclopedia, directories)				
F. Uses the library (card catalog or computer system, Dewey Decimal System)				
II. Organizing information				
A. Knows and uses specialized vocabulary				
B. Categorizes information				
C. Recognizes main ideas/supporting details				
D. Sequences events				
E. Summarizes/synthesizes information				
F. Takes effective notes				
G. Outlines effectively				
III. Interpreting graphic and pictorial materials				
A. Uses pictures				
B. Uses graphs				
C. Uses tables				
D. Uses maps				
IV. Has and uses a study strategy (Chapter 12)				

*Note to teacher: Place dates rather than checkmarks in boxes to provide a chronology of skill development.

ASSESSING LOCATIONAL SKILLS

Most standardized achievement tests include subtests on a limited range of **locational skills,** usually termed *work-study skills*. The most common skills tested are interpretation of tables and graphs and use of reference materials (e.g., *Iowa Test of Basic Skills; Comprehensive Test of Basic Skills*). Because the range of skills tested is small and the yield is simply a percentile, stanine, or other standard score reflecting a general level of achievement only, information obtained by the teacher for instructional purposes is minimal. The standardized test may indicate low achievement, but direct assessment will be needed to pinpoint specific teachable units.

Teacher-made tests, if constructed with some thought, are a valuable source of information for instructional decision making. In the checklist (Figure 13.1), the ability to locate information has the prerequisite knowledge of being able to alphabetize by first, second, and third letters and beyond. Most teachers will have no difficulty devising an instrument to determine whether students have these prerequisite subskills.

Alphabetizing

Some sample exercises for assessing the ability to alphabetize follow. They are presented in an order of increasing difficulty.

1. Present letters and have students provide the letter that comes immediately before and after.

    ___(q)___ r ___(s)___   _____ f _____

    _____ c _____   _____ v _____

2. Present a random listing of letters to students and have them arrange the list in alphabetical order.

    x, c, r, j, d, s, u, t, a, m

3. Provide students a random listing of familiar words that begin with different letters. Ask them to arrange the list alphabetically, or place words alphabetically in their word banks or personal dictionaries.

    the, dog, cat, me, house, baby

4. Provide students a random listing of words that begin with the same letter but have different second letters. Ask them to arrange the list alphabetically.

    cat, come, cup, city, cent

5. Provide students a random listing of words that are sometimes different in the first or second letter. Ask them to arrange the list alphabetically.

    give, bed, foot, jump, gave, bad

6. Provide students a random listing of words that are alike in the first and second letters, but differ in the third. Ask them to arrange the list alphabetically.

    bowl, boat, boy, bottle

7. Provide students a list of words that vary to any extent. Ask them to arrange the list alphabetically.

    such, as, to, try, come, camp, look, like, boy, road, read

Book Parts

Knowledge of book parts can be checked simply by asking the student to locate a particular part and then describe its purpose or how it might be used. Figure 13.2 shows an example of a skills test for assessing knowledge of book parts in a written format. Book parts that students should be tested on are the title page; date of publication page; table

Figure 13.2 Skills Test for Parts of a Book

Name: ____________________________

KNOW YOUR BOOK

Directions:

Use your ________________________________ book to answer these questions.

1. What is the title of this book?
2. Who are the authors?
3. When was the book copyrighted?
4. What is a copyright?
5. What company published the book?
6. What edition is this book?
7. What kind of information is in the preface?
8. Why do some books have more than one edition?
9. Give an example of how the table of contents can help you.
10. Is there a list of tables, maps, or diagrams?
11. How can this help you?
12. How are new words shown?
13. Is there a glossary?
14. How can the glossary help you?
15. Where is the index located?
16. When will you use the index?
17. Is there an appendix?
18. What information is presented in the appendix?

From *The Reading Corner,* by Harry W. Forgan, Jr. Reproduced by permission of Scott, Foresman and Company. © 1977.

of contents; lists of tables, graphs, maps, illustrations, and so on; preface or foreword; glossary; index; appendix; and bibliography or references.

Reference Materials

The ability to recognize and use a variety of reference materials needs to be assessed. Activities for assessing the more common information sources should come first. For example, use of a text-based dictionary and/or encyclopedia can be assessed by the following activities.

Dictionary

1. Students must be able to alphabetize and interpret diacritical marks to use a dictionary or glossary. An exercise similar to the following, containing words that the students already know how to pronounce, is recommended.

   Directions to students: Use the following pronunciation key and circle the correct dictionary respelling of the numbered words. The first one has been done for you.

   Pronunciation Key

fat	āpe	cär	ten	ēven
hit	bīte	gō	yü as in few	to͞ol
book	up	für	ə = a in ago	

   1. dad

      dād   (dad)   däd   dEd

   2. look

      lo͞ok   look   lōk   lŏk

   3. main

      man   män   mān   mǎin

   4. cute

      cute   kute   kut   kyüt

   About ten items should be given.

2. Provide students sets of guide words from the dictionary (e.g., *mill/mind*). Ask questions about the sets: Which word will be found at the bottom of the page? Why is *mill* written before *mind?* Where will you find *mill* on this page?

3. Provide students guide words from two pages of the dictionary. Then give them other words and ask them to identify the page on which the word will be found, or whether it cannot be found on either page. For example:

domain/door	*downcast/drain*
dragon	double
doze	doorway
donkey	downstairs
dog	dome

4. Have students write in the guide words for the pages in their personal dictionaries.

5. Provide students a list of words and have them write the guide words of the page on which they found each word.

6. Provide the students several dictionary entries. The students should study each entry and be able to answer the following questions. Try to include a variety of parts of speech, accents, syllables, and diacritical marks. Note that dictionary activities assume knowledge that is typically taught as a decoding skill. For example, students must be able to recognize syllables, accents, and diacritical markings before a task like the following can be assigned.

Example:

freight (frāt), *n.* 1. a load of goods shipped by train, ship, truck, airplane, etc. 2. the cost of shipping such goods. *v.* 1. to load with freight. 2. to send by freight.

    a. What is the vowel sound heard to this word? __(long a)__

    b. How many syllables does this word have? __(one)__ If more than one, on what syllable is the accent? _____

    c. The letter *n* means __(noun)__.

    d. The letter *v* means __(verb)__.

    e. If the guide words on a page of the dictionary were *framework* and *free,* would *freight* be on that page, on a page before, or on a page after? __(after)__

    f. Which definition and part of speech for *freight* is being used in the following sentence? The *freight* for the package was $2.75. __(second; noun)__

Encyclopedia

Today students have access to a wide variety of CD-ROM-based encyclopedias. In order to use these CD encyclopedias effectively, students need to know the types of categories and classifications used for storing information (see the section in this chapter on classifying words).

In order to use information from a text-based encyclopedia effectively, a reader must be able to use the encyclopedia index, information on the spine of each volume, guide words, cross-references, and bibliographies at the end of articles. Each of these items needs assessing. An example skills test for assessing encyclopedia knowledge might proceed as follows:

Students are provided a set of encyclopedias. Questions are then asked about the set.

1. How many volumes are in this set of encyclopedias? _____
2. To find out more about the climate in Alaska, which volume would you use? _____
    a. How would you proceed? _____
    b. What would you look for in the index? _____
    c. On what page is the information you need? _____
3. What number and letter(s) are on the volume you would use to find information about each topic in the following list? Which pages give you information about each topic?

Topic	Number	Letter(s)	Pages
climate			
polar			
bees			
Eskimos			
whales			
zebras			

In addition to the dictionary and encyclopedia, students should be able to use the thesaurus, directories (e.g., the Yellow Pages), almanacs, and periodicals. Assessment tasks are just as easily constructed for these materials as for the dictionary and encyclopedia.

Reference Skills

This major area dealing with locational skills includes use of the library—helping students go beyond the dictionary and encyclopedia as reference materials and recognize that information can be found in many other resources. To use the library effectively the student must be able to use its card catalog or computer reference system, its particular classification scheme (most likely the Dewey Decimal System or Library of Congress classification), and its special collections (e.g., periodicals; records, tapes, and CDs; filmstrips and videos; trade books).

An effective way to help students learn reference skills and, in turn, identify those needing assistance, is to create an authentic need for information to be found in the library. Providing students opportunities to research topics of their own choice is recommended by Greenlaw (1992). She suggests the use of a "curiosity" sheet at the beginning of a new unit of study (see thematic units in Chapter 14). On this sheet students list topics they are curious about, related to the subject of the unit. Once topics are identified and shared with the whole class, there are sure to be several students interested in the same topic. These students can work together on a collaborative research report—

interpersonal

logical-mathematical

although the following steps work for individual students as well (Tompkins, 1994). At this point, students working together can brainstorm questions they would like to have answered and identify possible sources of information for answers to those questions (see Figure 13.3). A map or a data chart (see Figure 13.4) can then be developed to aid in the gathering and organizing of information. Such a chart lends itself to the paraphrasing of information since space is limited. By using several sources, students also learn to synthesize information.

When students have their questions ready, a need to visit the library or explore the Internet has been created. If the school library is not well equipped, a field trip to the local public library should be arranged. The librarian, advised earlier of the nature of the trip, will give a thorough tour to include use of the card catalog or computer system, location of the various materials that will be helpful, and assistance when students

Figure 13.3   Possible Sources of Information for a Research Project

Student Name(s): _____

Project Title: _____

Information sources we might be able to use for this research project are indicated with a check.

_____ almanac	_____ Internet	_____ photographs
_____ art	_____ interviews	_____ posters
_____ atlas	_____ magazines	_____ records, tapes, or CDs
_____ biographies	_____ maps	_____ slides
_____ dictionary	_____ microscopic slides	_____ television programs
_____ encyclopedia	_____ museum exhibits	_____ thesaurus
_____ filmstrips	_____ newspapers	_____ video, video disks
_____ history books	_____ nonfiction books	

Others: _____

Figure 13.4   Research Map and Data Chart for Organizing Research Information

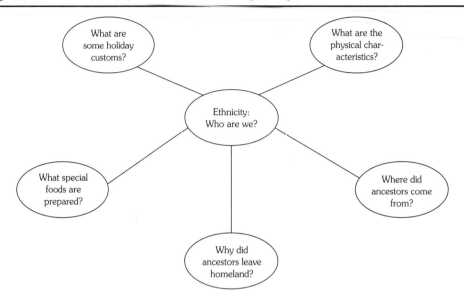

Source	What are the physical characteristics?	Where did ancestors come from?	Why did ancestors leave homeland?	What special foods are prepared?	What are some holiday customs?
1					
2					
3					

are attempting to locate the information for their data charts. Once the information is obtained, a report is written. In this way students also learn about and practice expository writing.

As the teacher observes all stages of this process, those students having difficulty will become apparent. Once again, the study skills checklist (Figure 13.1) serves as a record of observations for the teacher. As checklists are marked, the teacher can consider ad hoc groupings of students needing explicit instruction in related locational skills.

INSTRUCTION FOR DEVELOPING LOCATIONAL SKILLS

An attempt should be made to provide corrective readers lessons that are motivating and relevant to their experiences. Rather than using the students' textbooks and workbooks, more unusual materials are employed. Following are some items that are atypical, yet make good sources for work in the entire area of study skills.

catalogs	newspapers
TV program guides	globes
diaries	*Guinness Book of World Records*
job applications	how-to-make-it books
maps	ingredient labels
menus	advertisements
travel brochures	driver's manual
thesauruses	insurance forms
encyclopedias	weather maps and reports
magazines	police reports

General Teaching Procedures for Direct Instruction

With some modifications, the exercises used for assessment can also serve as the basis for a lesson. The student is first made aware of the purpose for learning locational skills. For alphabetizing, students are shown that being able to alphabetize allows them to use such valuable resources as the dictionary, telephone directory, and encyclopedia. Once the purpose of the lesson is established, some motivation for pursuing the lesson may be necessary. For example, in order to play a new game, such as an alphabetizing relay, participants must know how to alphabetize.

The teacher is now ready to teach a mini-lesson to the students directly. Usually this means demonstrating how a random list of words can be arranged alphabetically. After explaining the actual process used to alphabetize, the teacher invites student feedback to see if the explanation was clear. This may mean simply asking a student to re-explain the procedure just described.

Once the students demonstrate that they understand the explanation, the teacher gives them a chance to practice the new skill with no penalties for errors. This practice stage also allows the teacher to clarify any misunderstandings. When the teacher is satisfied that the students understand the process, they are redirected to the immediate purpose, in this case the alphabetizing relay. After the relay, the teacher may evaluate each student with a worksheet exercise on the same material.

An important part of direct instruction is to give the students many opportunities to apply the newly learned skill in appropriate situations. For example, soon after the alphabetizing mini-lesson, perhaps later in the day or week, a new science term may be introduced. The teacher asks the students how they can find out what the word means and also check on its pronunciation. If no one says the dictionary, the teacher simply suggests using the dictionary and reemphasizes the skill taught in the alphabetizing mini-lesson (in this case, how the word would be found in the dictionary using the first letter as a guide).

Another planned application is development of a classroom directory. The students first list their names, last names first, on the chalkboard one at a time. Then, using the skills taught in the initial alphabetizing mini-lesson, they alphabetize the list. The directory is completed by looking up the names in the telephone directory and copying the address and telephone information. Periodic checks with similar activities should be planned to ensure that the skill is being maintained.

Thus, the steps of the mini-lesson are as follows:

1. Establish the purpose of the lesson.
2. Provide motivation for the lesson.
3. Teach the skill directly.
   a. Demonstrate and explain the process.
   b. Check students' understanding of the explanation.
   c. Allow opportunities for students to practice the new skill.
   d. Review the purpose and complete the original task (motivation).
4. Allow independent practice (e.g., a follow-up worksheet).
5. Provide application opportunities.
6. Plan for distributed practice (periodic checks).

Specific Activities

This general format can be used in planning lessons to develop the locational skills and many other study skills. Following are some especially worthwhile activities for readers having difficulty with locational skills.

Alphabetical Order

As students place new words in personal dictionaries or vocabulary notebooks (see Chapter 7), they will need to decide where to write each new word in relation to the words already written. This need provides an opportunity for activities such as the following.

1. *Directions:* Fill in the blanks using the words *before* and *after.* The first one has been done as an example.

   g is ___(after)___ **e** and ___(before)___ **h**   **re** is _____ **ra** and _____ **ro**
   t is _____ **u** and _____ **s**   **se** is _____ **sc** and _____ **sl**
   p is _____ **o** and _____ **q**   **br** is _____ **bu** and _____ **bl**

2. *Directions:* Circle "Yes" or "No" to answer the following questions.

   Would *margin* come before *marker?*   Yes   No
   Would *alligator* come after *allow?*   Yes   No
   Would *picnic* come before *pickles?*   Yes   No

3. *Directions:* Circle the word on the right that would come between the two words on the left.

   beam–beauty   beaver   bean   beak
   disk–display   disappear   distance   dislike
   drift–drip   drink   driveway   dried

4. *Directions:* Look at each row of words. For each row, circle the word that would come first in the dictionary. Underline the word that comes last in the dictionary.

   Example: <u>grew</u>   grade   go   (gasp)
   1. boy   down   city   over
   2. little   lot   lake   letter
   3. dance   date   days   dark

Parts of Books

Have the students locate the table of contents in any content-area textbook.[1] Ask questions such as the following:

1. On what pages do you find the chapter called "The Founding of our Nation?" _(173–202)_

2. On what page does the chapter called "The Civil War Divides the Nation" begin? _(263)_

3. Does this book include a chapter on what the United States is like today? _(yes, chapter 13)_

4. If you wanted to read about the settlers moving westward across the Appalachian Mountains, which chapter would you go to? _(chapter 8, "Exploring the North Central States")_

5. How many pages are in the chapter called "Exploring the New World"? _(24)_

6. Does this book have an index? _(yes, begins on page 463)_

Using an Index

Have the students locate the index in any content-area textbook and use the index to find answers to questions. Students write the answer, the page on which they found it, and any heading from the index that helped them.

Choosing Resources

Give the students a variety of resource books. Ask them to decide which resource would be most appropriate for locating information to answer questions the teacher either asks or has written for them to answer independently. For example, ask whether a dictionary, telephone book, thesaurus, almanac, atlas, or encyclopedia would be used to find the following:

1. Address of a friend

2. Words that mean the same

3. Information about a certain animal

4. Population of the United States

5. Winner of the World Series in 1980

ASSESSING FOR ORGANIZING INFORMATION

The study skill area of organizing information is closely related to comprehension ability, as discussed in Chapters 9, 11, and 12. However, while such skills as finding main ideas, sequencing, summarizing, and synthesizing are end products in the reading of story material, they are prerequisite to the more commonly recognized study skills of note taking and outlining. Thus, to be able to take effective notes and develop good outlines, the student must be able to apply the notions of main ideas, sequence, and supporting details to content-related material, through listening, viewing, reading, speaking, visually representing, and writing.

The best and most direct way to assess the ability to organize information is simply to ask students to make an outline (or map) or to take notes from a short written

---

[1]Used for this example was the table of contents from H. H. Gross et al., *Exploring Regions of the Western Hemisphere*. Chicago: Follett, 1966.

selection or video. The written selection should be easy for the students with regard to word identification and comprehension to ensure that the study skill itself is actually being assessed.

If a student has difficulty in outlining or note taking, additional practice may not necessarily be the solution. The student may be having difficulty with prerequisite knowledge: attentive listening; classifying words, phrases, or sentences; main ideas; sequencing; summarizing or synthesizing; listening, or auditory comprehension; or knowledge of specialized vocabulary (see Chapter 10). This prerequisite knowledge should therefore be assessed before providing instruction that the student may not be ready for.

Attentive Listening

Assessing the ability to pay attention is complicated; a student may be attending to the speaker without being able to understand the speaker (Norton, 1993). Therefore, Otto and Smith (1980) suggest that procedures designed to assess attention should *not* stress the student's ability to process ideas.

According to Norton (1993, p. 129), "ability to follow oral directions explicitly demands attentive listening." Because idea processing is not being evaluated, directions must be simple. For example, a young child may be told: "Take out your blue crayon, your green crayon, and your red crayon. Pick up the red crayon and show it to me." Or for older students: "Take out a piece of paper and a pencil. Put the point of your pencil on the top center of the paper and draw a circle the size of a quarter. Draw a larger circle below the first circle. Draw a smaller circle inside the first circle." The older the student, the more complicated the oral directions might be.

Classifying Words, Phrases, and Sentences

Being able to distinguish main ideas from supporting details is a prerequisite to summarizing, outlining, or drawing inferences from **expository** (explanatory, content-area) **material.** However, before students can identify main ideas in paragraphs, they must be able to distinguish **superordinate** (general or main idea), **subordinate** (specific or supporting details), and **equal-status** (equally general or equally specific) **relationships** between words, phrases, and sentences. For instance, if Othell has trouble categorizing *hammer, axe,* and *lathe* as specific examples of tools, he will have difficulty identifying the main idea and supporting details in paragraphs discussing the role of tools within a social studies technology unit.

Some assessment techniques for classifying words, phrases, and sentences follow.

1. In one format, students are given a list of category titles such as *birds, mammals, planets,* and *reptiles.* Test items group the members (specific, subordinate relationships) of each category title (general, superordinate relationships), and the student must identify the correct category for the series of items. For example:
   a. deer, whale, dog   (mammals)
   b. Mars, Saturn, Venus _____
   c. robin, oriole, blue jay _____
   d. alligator, chameleon, salamander _____

2. Another format combines the specific examples with the general topic. Students are directed to circle the word that represents the general topic. For example:
   a. deer   mammal   whale   dog

   b. Mars   Saturn   planets   Venus
   c. birds   robin   oriole   blue jay
   d. alligator   chameleon   salamander   reptiles

3. A third format provides the specific items at the top of the page, followed by the skeleton of an outline format. Students must place the specific items under appropriate general headings to complete the outline. For example:

butterfly   dog   beetle   sandpiper   sparrow
Mrs. Jones   firefly   iguana   mouse   haddock
trout   frog   terrapin   swallow   herring

   I. Insects   II. Reptiles
      A. butterfly   A.
      B.   B.
      C.   C.
   III. Mammals   IV. Fish.   V. Birds
      A.   A.   A.
      B.   B.   B.
      C.   C.   C.

Phrases and sentences are assessed in much the same way. Some examples follow.

4. Students are instructed to circle the phrase or sentence that describes all the other items in the list.
   a. cows and pigs   farm animals
      ducks and chickens   sheep and goats
   b. Streets fell apart.   Cars were lost.
      Windows rattled.   An earthquake occurred.
   c. Scientists dig up fossils.
      Scientists learn about dinosaurs.
      Scientists look at the size and shape of bones.
      Scientists study where the bones were found.
   d. They wanted to have their own church.
      They were Separatists.
      They were Englishmen.
      They had secret church meetings.

Main Ideas and Supporting Details

When the student is able to classify words, phrases, and sentences, the next area to be assessed is that of locating the main idea (superordinate topic) and supporting details (subordinate topics) in a single expository paragraph (Aulls, 1978). As discussed in Chapter 9, **main ideas** may be explicit or implicit, and some paragraphs have no main idea at all. For assessment, paragraphs with stated main ideas should be used, as students must be able to recognize stated main ideas before being asked to determine an implicit main idea. Recall from Chapter 9 that main ideas may be stated in the first or last sentences of a paragraph or somewhere in between. Students should be given paragraphs with the main idea stated in each of the three positions and asked to underline the appropriate sentence. Teachers might use the content-area materials adopted in their schools as a source for assessment paragraphs; however, the students should be assessed with material at their instructional or independent reading level. To achieve this, the teacher might have to use a content-area text from a different grade level than the one the student is in currently.

Sequencing

Sequencing is important prerequisite knowledge for outlining because outlines reflect a chronological, forward-moving summary of material read. Sequencing is especially important in studying history and conducting science experiments, because time order (first, second, third, and so on) may be critical to understanding the material. The easiest way to assess this ability is to give the student pictures, phrases, or sentences that relate a sequence of events. The items are out of order, and the student must sequence the items. For example:

> *Directions:* Put a 1 in front of the event that would come first, a 2 for second, and a 3 for third.
>
> a. _____ The air becomes warm.
>
> _____ Ice and snow cover the ground.
>
> _____ Green leaves appear on the plants.
>
> b. _____ Put the pan on the burner.
>
> _____ The water boils.
>
> _____ Pour the water into the pan.

Paragraph frames can be readily adapted for use in sequencing (see earlier discussion in Chapter 9 and see Chapter 12 for examples).

Summarizing and Synthesizing

The primary difference between **summarizing** and **synthesizing** is that a summary usually contains the essential ideas of *one* selection, while synthesizing summarizes information from *several* sources. Thus, students must be able to summarize before they can synthesize. The most obvious application of these skills is in writing a report or term paper. Summarizing and synthesizing relate to the ability to paraphrase material read. Specifically, readers must be able to locate the main idea and supporting details, apply literal and inferential thinking skills, and interpret the information in their own words.

Methods that involve *retelling* of material read (not to be confused with *recall*) are appropriate for assessment. In a retelling, the reader's ability to interact with, interpret, and draw conclusions from the text are assessed. Other assessment procedures are likely to include questions that ask about main ideas and inferred information. These questions may take the following general form:

> What is this section about?
>
> What was learned from this experiment?
>
> What was the purpose of the article?
>
> How would you describe this period of history?
>
> Could this poem mean something else?
>
> Explain that in your own words.

Most teacher's manuals contain questions that ask students to summarize or synthesize information at the end of chapters or units. When some students consistently have difficulty with these questions, an analysis should be made in the areas of main ideas, supporting details, and paraphrasing (Chapter 9).

Listening, or Auditory Comprehension

Classroom teachers are likely to rely on observation and the use of checklists or anecdotal records to make listening assessments. One additional technique that is commonly used is the informal reading inventory (see Chapter 6). Instead of the student reading the graded passages, the passages are read to the student and comprehension questions asked, or a retelling requested. The listening comprehension level is attained when the student can correctly answer at least 75 percent of the questions or recall about 80 percent of the material. Activities used to teach more specific listening skills, such as listening for main ideas, sequence, details, and so forth, can also be used for assessment.

INSTRUCTION FOR ORGANIZING INFORMATION

The techniques suggested here demonstrate how teachers can provide both instruction and practice in using materials that require students to apply these study skills independently. Many of the instructional techniques presented in Chapter 9 can be adapted for use in content-areas. I attempt to suggest techniques for the most commonly taught content areas, in which reading difficulty may be the prime cause of poor achievement. The most valuable instructional methods employ the concepts and specialized vocabulary found in the content-area material the students are or will be using.

Attentive Listening

Students are not naturally good or poor listeners. Listening skills can, and should, be taught. It is all too common that students ask for directions to be repeated or are scolded for not following directions. Oftentimes, the teacher may have to take some responsibility for this inattentiveness. Otto and Smith (1980) suggest four factors of inattentiveness: "(1) poor motivation to hear the speaker's message, (2) too much teacher talk, (3) excessive noise and other distractions, and (4) lack of a mental set for anticipating the speaker's message. By careful attention to these four factors, a teacher can help students become more attentive listeners" (p. 307).

bodily-kinesthetic

Specific activities and methods help students develop attentive listening. Simon Says involves careful listening to directions. A leader gives an oral command, and the group must do as told *if* the "magic" words *Simon says* precede the command. If the command is not preceded by *Simon says,* those students who obey the command are eliminated from the game.

To encourage students to listen, give oral directions only once. When a student requests a repetition, ask other students to recall and restate the directions. Learning centers for listening can easily be developed. Listening center supplies may include commercial audiobooks or teacher-made tapes, records, cassettes, CDs, radios, and accompanying printed materials (Baskin & Harris, 1995). Furness (1971) claims that it is especially appropriate for students with listening comprehension difficulties and learning difficulties in general to number the steps of the oral directions, repeat the number of steps involved, and relate each step to its number.

Classifying

Aulls (1978) suggests that teaching the classification skills of superordinate, subordinate, and equality relationships, which are so important to main ideas and supporting details, involves

> (1) an introductory teacher directed lesson; (2) a teacher directed reinforcement lesson which reviews the introductory lesson but uses different examples; (3) a pupil directed review activity where pupils work individually, in pairs or in small groups using worksheets, games, or learning centers; (4) an application to one of the weekly content area reading assignments; and, (5) a post test of ten to twenty test items. . . . Approximately 80 percent accuracy is suggested as a criterion. (p. 95)

The introductory lesson concentrates on the meaning of general (superordinate), specific (subordinate), and equal word, phrase, and sentence relationships. The discussion involves the students in making decisions first about pairs of items. For example, the teacher might ask:

> "Is *beetle* the general or specific word in the pair 'beetle–insect'?" *(response)*

> "How can you tell? Use the rule: Is the *(specific)* a type of *(general)?* If *beetle* fits the first blank, it is the specific word. The word that fits the second blank is the general word."

Responses should compare "beetle, a type of insect" and "insect, a type of beetle" to conclude that *beetle* is the specific word. Many examples should follow. For phrases or sentences the rule may vary:

> Does *(specific)* describe *(general)?*

For example, the teacher might ask:

> "Does *Englishmen* describe *Separatists* or does *Separatists* describe *Englishmen?*"

Gradually introduce the equal relationship concept by comparing three items instead of pairs. For example:

> "Wanted to have their own church" *(specific)* describes "Separatists" *(general).*

> "Secret church meetings" *(specific)* describes "Separatists" *(general).*

These two sentences demonstrate that "wanted to have their own church" and "secret church meetings" both describe "Separatists," so they are *equally specific.* Continue these lessons until students achieve 80 percent accuracy with four items.

Categorization activities similar to those found in Chapter 10 and the activities included in the assessment section in this chapter for classifying words, phrases, and sentences can also be used as bases for lessons. In addition, with corrective readers especially, some "real life" application is needed to show these students how skills that help them read better can also help them *outside* the classroom in their daily lives. An example of one such activity follows.

The Yellow Pages lists, alphabetically, categories of services available in the area. The companies providing those services are in turn listed alphabetically under their particular heading; for example, Ed's Moving Company would be found under "Movers," along with a telephone number and possibly additional information. As in a dictionary, guide words give the first and last service listed on a page. Students are given hypothetical situations and asked to determine what service is needed; this is a classification task.

Similar activities can be devised using mail-order catalogs, tables of contents, indexes, almanacs, and newspapers (Cheyney, 1992; Olivares, 1993; Short & Dickerson, 1980).

Main Ideas and Supporting Details

Students who can distinguish general, specific, and equal word, phrase, and sentence relationships are ready to learn how to identify main ideas and supporting details. Aulls (1978) suggests moving from lessons in classifying to identifying the general topic of a picture. A **topic** differs from a main idea in that it is usually a word or phrase that represents the major subject of a picture, paragraph, or article. *Main ideas* are statements that give the most important ideas regarding the topic. Thus, the topic must be identified before an important idea about it can be identified.

Direct teaching is essential before students are asked to practice a new skill. The teaching sequence suggested for classifying skills also applies here. Initial lessons involve pictures and paragraphs with one topic and several details supporting that topic. For example:

naturalist

There are many kinds of seeds. There are small seeds and large seeds. There are seeds with wings that can fly through the air. There are seeds with stickers that catch on your clothes. There are seeds that can float on the water.

After reading the paragraph, students are asked to identify the topic of the paragraph from some listed words.

| wind | wings |
| seeds | stickers |

Based on the previous discussion about classifying words, phrases, and sentences as general, specific, and equal, the students are often helped with the rule, "Does _____ describe _____?" Specific to the example are the questions: "Are (small seeds) specific kinds of seeds?" "Are (seeds with wings) specific kinds of seeds?" Practice should follow with more paragraphs of the same simple structure.

Finally, students who can identify the topic of a paragraph are ready for instruction in main ideas. Students learn that the main idea is the most important thing that the author wants the reader to understand about the topic (Aulls, 1978).

Instruction proceeds from the writer's point of view. The teacher may suggest a topic and one important piece of information about it. For example, the teacher writes *Water is moving all the time* on the board and says that this statement is the main idea the writer wishes to make in a paragraph. Students are then invited to supply some specific statements that describe the main idea. Some possible responses might include:

Water moves in the ocean.

It runs over rocks in streams.

It falls over waterfalls.

It ripples on the lake.

If students can understand main ideas from the writer's point of view, they may better understand main ideas from the reader's point of view.

Instruction proceeds to paragraphs with the main idea stated in the first sentence, followed by paragraphs with the main idea stated last, and finally to paragraphs with the main idea stated somewhere in between.

Content-area textbooks can be used to help students apply what they have learned. The teacher may use an illustration that summarizes one of the written sections particularly well. Science and social studies textbooks lend themselves best to this type of activity. For example, a section may discuss the concept of the water cycle, while an accompanying illustration clearly shows the whole process. Students are asked to think of a sentence that explains the main idea of the picture and thus the concept of the water cycle. Supporting, or specific, details are then found in the text and listed as brief items below the sentence (Figure 13.5).

Sequencing

Many activities are suitable as bases for sequencing lessons other than the more common exercises that ask the student to put comic strip frames in the proper sequence. The teacher wants to encourage students to think logically. By first relating sequencing to events in their daily lives, the teacher helps students realize that events usually occur in a sensible step-by-step fashion. Initially, activities take a very simple form.

Example: What would you do first?
1. Put the cake in the oven to bake, or combine eggs and water with the mix?
2. Put on your shoes or put on your socks?
3. Get dressed or get out of bed?

Figure 13.5 Example of Illustration that Helps Students Identify Main Idea and Supporting Details

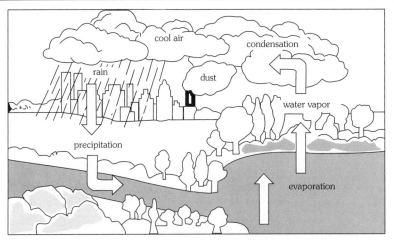

Main Idea: The evaporation and condensation of water over and over again is called the water cycle.
Supporting Details: When water evaporates, it changes into a gas called water vapor. Water vapor is cooled as it is carried up by warm, rising air. The cooling changes it back into a liquid. The vapor condenses into a cloud. Clouds bring precipitation.

From Joseph Abruscato et al., *Holt Elementary Science,* p. 126. Copyright © 1980 by Holt, Rinehart and Winston, Publishers. Used with permission.

Having students follow simple written directions to make or cook something also reinforces the idea that certain steps precede others. Remind students to look for key words (e.g., *first, second, third, next, then, finally, last*) and other hints of sequence, or enumeration. For example, if a science selection deals with the growth stages of insects, the word *stages* is a hint that a sequence of events is going to be related. Students must be made aware of these hints. Many times the stages are listed, giving a numerical hint of what comes first, second, and so forth. (Be careful, though; not all listings are sequential.) Having students write directions for making something so that other students can follow them also reinforces the importance of proper sequencing.

logical-mathematical

Students can also be invited to create meaningful sentences to help them remember otherwise difficult sequences, such as the order of historical events, or a particularly long and troublesome spelling word. For example, one commonly known sentence for remembering the order of the planets is "Mankind's verdant earth must journey (as a) star unites nine planets." *Mankind's* stands for Mercury (planet no. 1); *verdant* stands for Venus (planet no. 2); *earth* stands for earth (planet no. 3); *must* stands for Mars (planet no. 4); *journey* stands for Jupiter (planet no. 5); (as a) *star* stands for Saturn (planet no. 6); *unites* stands for Uranus (planet no. 7); *nine* stands for Neptune (planet no. 8); and *planets* stands for Pluto (planet no. 9). Since there are two planets that start with M, just note that *mankind* has the same number of letters as *Mercury* and *must* has the same number of letters as *Mars*. One of my own memories for help with spelling the word *arithmetic* is the sentence "A rat in the house might eat the ice cream." in which the first letter in each word represents the spelling of the word. These activities may appeal to students with a strong logical-mathematical intelligence.

Summarizing and Synthesizing

Often techniques used to teach summarizing skills do not differ very much on the surface from activities requesting identification of main ideas. However, in summarizing, instead of the main idea being explicitly stated, the reader is asked to infer a main idea or draw a conclusion about what has been read.

One method to help students learn to summarize is teaching them to **paraphrase,** or restate text in their own words. Instruction in paraphrasing begins at a sentence level. Initially, two sentences are compared for meaning. For example:

"Do the following sentence pairs have the same meaning?"
The harbor was safe for small boats.
Small boats were protected in the harbor.

In order to get to the New World, the Pilgrims needed a ship.
The Pilgrims needed a ship to take them to the New World.

Most of the Pilgrims were farmers, weavers, or shopkeepers.
The Pilgrims were farmers.

At this initial level of instruction, the student must simply recognize one sentence as a paraphrase of another sentence.

The next stage in the instructional sequence moves from recognition of paraphrased sentences to production of paraphrased sentences. One method is to have students give synonyms for the **content words** (nouns, verbs, adjectives, adverbs) in a sentence, as in the following examples.

Automobiles, airplanes, and dirigibles are operated by gasoline engines.
Cars, planes, and blimps are run by gasoline engines.

When students can paraphrase sentences with ease, instruction proceeds to short paragraphs. Synonyms again are used. However, instead of trying to substitute one word for another, with paragraphs one thought unit is substituted for another. The following word problem demonstrates this procedure.

"Oranges are priced at three for 90¢. How much would you pay for four oranges?"

The first step is to divide the paragraph into **thought units,** or short phrases that contain only one idea. The thought units for this example might be listed as:

oranges are priced
three for 90¢
how much (would you pay)
for four oranges

The next step is to paraphrase each thought unit. One student might suggest:

oranges cost
30¢ each
How much will four oranges cost?

The paraphrases may vary; the concern is that all the thought units in the original paragraph are represented in the paraphrase.

The last step is to compare various paraphrases for meaning changes. If the meaning is the same, the paraphrase is acceptable. No personal translation is incorrect as long as the meaning is the same. For example:

"Oranges cost 90¢ for three. How much will I have to pay for four?"

"Three oranges cost 90¢. Four oranges will cost how much?"

In paraphrasing, other skills, such as sentence combining (Chapters 7 and 9), can be applied. In fact, many comprehension skills are involved in paraphrasing: vocabulary knowledge (synonyms), literal understanding of words and sentences, sentence combining, and sentence expansion. The following example demonstrates the use of sentence combining to paraphrase.

naturalist

Original: There is a plant that helps people tell the time. The plant has flowers that may be white, red, yellow, or pink. These flowers open in the late afternoon. The flowers close in the morning. The plant is named the "four-o'clock." (From *Specific Skill Series, Primary Overview, Drawing Conclusions—Booklet C* [level 3] by Richard Boning, 1985, Baldwin, NY: Barnell Loft.)

Paraphrase: There is a plant, called the "four-o'clock," that helps people tell time. Its flowers, which can be white, yellow, red, or pink, open at about four o'clock in the afternoon, and close in the morning.

logical-mathematical

As noted previously, synthesizing paraphrases and combines information from more than one source. To teach synthesizing, at least two different sources must be used. The easiest way to introduce the concept of synthesizing is to give the students two different versions of the same story and have them look for similarities and differences. Children's stories, such as *Goldilocks and the Three Bears, Jack and the Beanstalk,* and *Cinderella,* are usually available in different versions. Summaries that use topics and specific details for each version can be listed on the board and then compared (see Story Structure Chart in Figure 11.6).

The next step is to apply this idea to content-area material. Choose a topic that is presented in different ways (usually different texts or different levels of the same textbook series). As an example, here are two versions of difficulties the Pilgrims faced.

Version 1

Sickness. There was terrible sickness in Plymouth that first winter. There were some days in February when only six or seven people were well enough to take care of the ones who were sick.

By spring, about half of the Pilgrims and sailors were dead. Three whole families died during this terrible time. (From *. . . if you sailed on the Mayflower* [p. 48] by Ann McGovern, 1969, New York: Scholastic Book Services.)

Version 2

Hard times. New England winters are long and cold. Icy winds blow across the land. The Pilgrims were not used to such cold weather, nor did they have proper clothing. They got wet going to and from the *Mayflower.* So many became sick that at one time only six or seven settlers were well enough to look after the others. They moved the sick to the Common House and used it as a hospital. By the end of the winter, half the Pilgrims had died. (From *Exploring Regions of the Western Hemisphere* [pp. 120–121] by H. H. Gross et al., 1966, Chicago: Follett.)

Guide the students to summarize each version, using topics and specific details. Paraphrasing should be encouraged. Example summaries follow for each version.

Version 1

Sickness in Plymouth *(topic)*
terrible sickness *(detail)*
first winter *(detail)*
February—only six or seven people well enough to care for others *(detail)*
by end of winter, half the Pilgrims and sailors died *(detail)*
three whole families died *(detail)*

Version 2

Hard times for Pilgrims *(topic)*
long, cold New England winters *(detail)*
icy winds *(detail)*
Pilgrims not used to such winters *(detail)*
Pilgrims didn't have the right clothes *(detail)*
they got wet *(detail)*
so many became sick *(detail)*
at one time only six or seven settlers well enough to care for others *(detail)*
moved sick to Common House *(detail)*
Common House used as hospital *(detail)*
by end of winter, half the Pilgrims died *(detail)*

Students then compare the summaries and put a check mark by the details that occur in both versions. The teacher may wish to point out that details found in both versions are probably important and should be included in any written synthesis of the information.

Depending on the teacher's purpose and the needs of the students, the teaching sequence may proceed to a written synthesis of the two versions. Sentence-combining strategies (Chapters 7 and 9) are useful at this stage. For example, the Pilgrims' "first winter" from version 1 can be described with details from version 2 such as "long, cold, New England, icy winds" and result in the following sentence:

The Pilgrims' first New England winter was long and cold with icy winds.

Instruction in summarizing and synthesizing also helps prepare students for writing reports that reflect more understanding of a subject than copying information from an encyclopedia. Hayes (1989) developed an extension of the Guided Reading Procedure (Manzo, 1975) to show students how to group details into a prose summary. His strategy is referred to as **GRASP (Guided Reading and Summarizing Procedure).** Briefly, students read for information and are directed to remember all they can. After reading, students tell all they remember and the teacher lists *all* recollections, no matter how trivial or inaccurate. Following this listing students reread the material to add to, delete, or correct information on the list. At this point the teacher shows students how to organize the information by grouping details that belong together. Discussion about how information in each group relates to other information leads to an outline or map (see also Hill, 1991, for use of concept maps in summarizing). Once the relatedness of the information is displayed, a prose summary is developed, revised, and refined into a final summary.

Jeanne Day (1980) suggests the following basic rules of summarizing.

1. Delete trivial or unnecessary details. (For instance, a detail found in only one version in the previous example—the Pilgrims got wet—could be omitted.)
2. Delete redundant material.
3. Use a category heading for items mentioned within a single category. (For example, if the text mentions *roses, lilies,* and *petunias,* substitute the word *flowers*.)
4. Combine component actions into one encompassing action. (For example, instead of noting that James ate five doughnuts on Monday, ten doughnuts on Tuesday, ten more doughnuts on Wednesday, and so on, say James ate fifty doughnuts in one week.)
5. Identify a topic sentence, or what seems to be the author's summary.
6. If a topic sentence is not apparent, make up your own.

Any summarization strategy involves teacher modeling and discussion of students' ideas and responses. In teaching the strategy, material that students find easy (independent level) should be used initially.

Listening, or Auditory Comprehension

Students with listening, or auditory, comprehension difficulties need help in defining the purposes for their listening. For example, to help students listen to oral directions, key words such as *first, second,* and *finally* may be stressed. Have students close their eyes and visualize themselves carrying out each step of the directions as they hear it. Then ask them to describe each step. Finally, have them physically perform the activity.

Some activities for developing listening follow.

bodily-kinesthetic

- Using *Pin the Tail on the Donkey,* direct the blindfolded student to move to the right, to the left, and so on.
- Using a cassette tape, provide a series of numbers *once,* such as 8-5-2-6-9. Ask which number is closest to the sum of two plus two.

- Have each student prepare a two-minute talk on "How to Make a Peanut Butter Sandwich." As the directions are spoken, ask the listeners to first visualize themselves following the directions, and next, ask some volunteers to do *exactly* as the speaker directed. (This activity can be just as valuable for the speaker.)
- To help students listen attentively and for details, play simple listening games with increasingly difficult instructions given to one student and then another. For example, "Jim, take the book from the second shelf and carry it to the windowsill." "Bill, you take it from the windowsill to the library corner and then to my desk." "Janet, you take it from the desk and walk around the desk twice with it, then carry it to the library corner and then to the windowsill, and finally back to the second shelf." And so forth.

An effective listener must be able to follow a sequence of ideas, perceive their organization, recognize the main ideas and important details, predict outcomes, and critically evaluate what is heard. The same can be said for an effective comprehender. Thus, most comprehension activities can be used, with only slight modifications, for instruction in auditory comprehension. The following techniques and activities are recommended.

1. *Listening for main ideas and supporting details.* The teacher selects paragraphs in which the main idea is stated (easiest) or inferred (more difficult). These paragraphs should also state several supporting details. The difficulty level of the paragraphs conforms to the students' ability level. One easy example follows.

I have a new puppy. It is little. It can run and jump. My puppy can do tricks. The puppy is funny.

The teacher reads the paragraph and asks the students to listen carefully for the main idea. After they have suggested a main idea, they should tell why. A request for a good title might be substituted for the phrase *main idea* in case students are unfamiliar with this term. In either circumstance, the students are told that the main idea, or title, can be turned into a question in order to find the supporting details. For example:

What is a new puppy like?
Why is the puppy funny?

After students hear the paragraph read once more, they are asked to identify supporting details. The "main idea" question will be answered by the supporting details. In other words, of the two questions suggested, one will be answered by the supporting details. For example:

It is little.
It can run and jump.
It can do tricks.
It is funny.

These details best answer the first question, so the first sentence, "I have a new puppy," represents the main idea. If working with titles, "A New Puppy" or "My Puppy" is an appropriate suggestion. Descriptive paragraphs are especially helpful for this activity.

2. *Listening for details that do and do not support the main idea.* Further development of listening skills includes a weighing of information for its importance to the topic. The teacher may read a paragraph in which one detail does not relate to the rest of the

paragraph or to the main idea. The students are then asked to state the main idea, the supporting details, and the nonsupporting detail. For example:

> Bob and Mary do not know what to do. They don't want to watch TV. They looked for a game to play, but could not find one they liked. Mother went to visit her friend.

3. *Listening for sequence.* Activities to develop this skill first stress listening for key words that signify sequences, such as *first, second,* and *finally.* Once the students have been alerted to these key words, they listen to an oral presentation that emphasizes the usefulness of such words. For example:

> I have a picture of three monkeys. The first monkey is covering his eyes. The next one is covering his ears. The third one is covering his mouth with his hands. On the bottom a sign says, "See no evil, hear no evil, speak no evil."

Point out to students how the key words signal a certain sequence. This can be demonstrated by rearranging the order of the paragraph to make less sense. Also help students discover the usefulness of the introductory statement, "I have a picture of three monkeys," and show how each of the monkeys is then identified by a signal word: *first, next, third.* This type of activity can be easily adapted to develop understanding of paragraph structure in preparation for writing paragraphs.

Other activities include cutting up comic strips into their individual frames, whiting out the words, mixing up the frames, and then reading the original comic strip aloud while the students put the strip back in order. A flannel board provides the opportunity for students to listen to a story, hear its sequential organization, then retell it via pictures or main idea statements in proper sequence.

4. *Listening to predict outcomes.* The procedure is much like that of a directed reading-thinking activity (Stauffer, 1981). The title of a story is read to the students and they are asked to write a prediction, or suggest to the teacher, what they think they will hear about in the story. The teacher discusses the reasons for these predictions with the students and then reads the story. Some stories lend themselves to breaks where repredicting can occur. This activity motivates students to listen carefully to see if their individual predictions are correct. Films can also be used in this manner, or a talk or lecture can be stopped at certain points to have students predict what the speaker will say next. The level can be very easy (predicting the next word in a sentence) or more difficult (predicting the possible content or conclusion).

5. *Listening to evaluate.* Students are aided in this area by learning to develop questions to be answered by listening and to listen for cause-and-effect relationships, propaganda, or persuasive statements. As for any lesson, students must be prepared, in this case by being given something to anticipate. For example, after the topic of the talk or lecture is previewed, the students are asked to list three questions they would like to hear answered. A planned study guide helps students use what they already know and alerts them to information particularly important to understanding what they will hear. Devine (1981) suggests that an effective listening guide should include the following:

a. A preview of the talk, including a statement of its purpose and perhaps even an outline

b. A list of new words and concepts

c. Questions for students to think about as they listen

d. Space for students to write questions *they* want answered as they listen

e. Provision for *anticipation* (that is, some problem, question, or student concern that students can look forward to learning about as they listen)

f. Questions to help the student-listener personalize what is being said—for example, "Have you ever had an experience like this?" or "In what way does this affect your own life?"

g. Space for students to write such things as main ideas and supporting details

h. Appropriate visuals that can be duplicated in the guide (e.g., graphs, tables)

i. Follow-up activities (e.g., possible test questions, related readings) (pp. 24–25)

Activities for evaluative listening may include (1) identifying cause and effect and (2) discriminating information from propaganda.

For *identifying cause and effect,* a cause is stated, followed by the reading of a series of consequences, some of which are results of the cause and others that are not. Students are to identify any matching cause-effect relationships. For example:

logical-mathematical

Cause

It was the hottest summer that had ever been recorded.

Effects

The greatest danger was the possibility of frostbite. *(No match)*
The hospital reported large numbers of cases of heatstroke. *(Match)*
After a while, a bad water shortage developed. *(Match)*
Most people dressed carefully, wearing many layers of clothes. *(No match)*
It was uncomfortable to leave your home to go outdoors. *(Match)*

For *discriminating information from propaganda,* television commercials provide a never-ending source of material. Tapes are prepared to be analyzed and later placed in listening centers to give practice in listening for persuasive statements. A speaker whose purpose is to persuade also provides information while trying to convince the listener of something. Listeners are constantly exposed to such situations. Examples other than the TV commercial include the campaigning politician at all levels of government, the salesperson (e.g., cars, magazines, appliances), and very often our friends. The listener must be able to distinguish statements that inform from those that are intended to persuade. The listener then examines and evaluates only the information before deciding what to do. Students are first instructed in the differences between informative and persuasive statements. For example:

Information tells you about the item being sold.

1. This bicycle comes with a headlight and a rear light.
2. This bicycle is lightweight (twenty pounds) and has hand brakes.

Persuasion tries to make you think you want to buy what is being sold.

1. This bicycle is only for people who want the best.
2. Famous stars prefer this bicycle.

A list of statements is then read to students and they determine which inform and which persuade. For example:

- These knives are made of stainless steel. *(Information)*
- Our gum contains no sugar. *(Information)*
- Why not use what the pros use? *(Persuasion)*
- The jackets come in three sizes. *(Information)*
- Just what you've been waiting for! *(Persuasion)*

- The rubber sole will keep you from slipping. *(Information)*
- This is a nonalkaline-pH shampoo. *(Information)*
- This is a special gift for that special person. *(Persuasion)*
- This dish will not chip or crack. *(Information)*
- Everyone thinks _____ is the best. *(Persuasion)*

Listening must be considered a vital aspect of comprehension ability, although it is often overlooked. It may be mistakenly assumed that a student who hears well also listens well. Instruction in listening must begin in the early grades to help students prepare and develop independence for such tasks as note taking and class discussions.

The lack of listening materials places even greater responsibility for the development of instructional practices on the classroom teacher. The following questions (Burns, 1980) alert teachers to their responsibilities:

1. Do I provide a classroom environment (emotional and physical) that encourages good listening?
2. Am I a good listener and do I really listen to the pupils?
3. Do I use appropriate tone, pitch, volume, and speed in my speaking?
4. Do I vary the classroom program to provide listening experiences (films, discussions, debates, reports) that are of interest to the students?
5. Am I aware of opportunities for teaching listening throughout the day?
6. Do I help pupils see the purpose of listening in each activity?
7. Do I help students see the importance and value of being good listeners?
8. Do I build a program in which listening skills are consistently taught and practiced? (p. 113)

Other listening strategies may be found in the professional literature. One of the most complete collections is *Listening Aids through the Grades* (Russell & Russell, 1979), which includes almost 200 teaching ideas ranging from general to specific and from simple to complex.

Note Taking

Instruction in the previous skills of summarizing and synthesizing leads directly to instruction in note taking. In essence, when taking notes on printed material, the student is summarizing the material. If notes are being taken on material presented orally, the process assumes the additional skill of auditory comprehension; if notes are taken on material that is both oral and visual, additional kinds of processing skills may be needed. In any case, the ability to summarize and translate information into one's own language is imperative.

Note taking is a complex skill, as evidenced by the prerequisite skills already discussed. Research by Dunkeld (1978) on taking notes while reading offers some helpful suggestions. First, students are introduced to note taking while reading or listening to a familiar story (e.g., *Goldilocks and the Three Bears*). Second, in the early stages of note taking, a textbook with subheadings is used. Third, the teacher demonstrates the format of good notes on the chalkboard or overhead using students' own examples. Fourth, students are encouraged to use their notes during class discussions.

Simpson and Nist (1990) suggest a textbook annotation strategy as a way to study and take notes from texts. They conclude from their research that it is the special elements of the strategy—that actively involve students in constructing ideas and monitoring their own learning—that makes this strategy effective. Additional support for an annotation strategy is provided by Strode (1993) in her adaptation of the REAP strategy (see Chapter 12). She notes the following major benefits:

- There is more active involvement in reading, since writing will occur afterward.
- Information is processed more thoroughly and has more meaning as a result of the writing component.
- Students write more succinct summaries as a result of learning to write annotations.
- Students attend to often overlooked aspects of text.

This adaptation of REAP is an effective strategy for note taking as well as for enhancing comprehension, specifically for main ideas, and for clearer writing.

Stahl, King, and Henk (1991) present "a four-stage instructional sequence of modeling, practicing, evaluating, and reinforcing activities for developing student-directed note-taking strategies" (p. 614). Teachers first model and provide opportunity to practice any one of a number of suggested note-taking procedures, some of which follow:

- Draw a margin and keep all running lecture notes to one side; use the other side for organization, summarizing, and labeling
- Skip lines to show change of ideas
- Use numbers, letters, and marks to indicate details
- Paraphrase
- Use underlining, circling, and different colors of ink to show importance

The unique aspect of the four-stage sequence lies in the last two stages, evaluating and reinforcing. These two stages occur simultaneously when **NOTES** (Notetaking

A Focus on SLL: Dictogloss

Originally developed for use with high school students by Ruth Wajnryb (1990), *dictogloss* is a particularly valuable strategy for teachers of second-language learners of any age because it involves and integrates the four skills of listening, speaking, reading, and writing along with collaboration. It is intended to help students develop a knowledge base in a specific content area such as science or social studies, but more important for the second-language learner, to have an opportunity to use the language modeled in textbooks.

To start, students are directed to "just listen carefully" as the teacher reads a text passage two or three times at normal reading speed. The passage is then read again, but this time students are asked to write down key words or key phrases they recall. The passage is read once again and students asked to again write down additional key words or phrases they recall. Next, students work in pairs to discuss their notes and to recreate as much of the text as they can by expanding on their notes. Each pair then joins with another pair to form a foursome. The group of four then works together to recreate as much of the text as they can from their combined notes. This should lead to a fairly accurate version of the original text. Finally, the group attempts to produce a coherent written text that is as close to the original as possible. Follow-up discussion can include analyzing the sections in the text that were especially difficult to recreate. The use of dictogloss with various content-area texts can help the second-language learner begin to appreciate the ways in which the choices of words and phrasing in English are influenced by the purpose of the writing and the audience for which the writing is intended.

Observation, Training and Evaluation Scales) is applied. "With NOTES, students receive both instructor feedback and peer review of the quality of their notes. They also receive reinforcement as they measure their progress with a record chart in the NOTES packet" (Stahl et al. [1991], p. 616). NOTES evaluation criteria, or scoring rubrics, and accompanying record sheets, progress charts, and evaluation directions can be found in Stahl et al. (1991).

With the increased use of video presentations and locating information on the Internet, students need to be able to take notes while processing all types of information: written, oral, and visual. Flood & Wood (1998) offer a format for guiding students in their note-taking efforts when the information presented is on a videotape. Figure 13.6 provides an example of the **Collaborative Listening-Viewing Guide** as used with a group of university students viewing a video on differentiating instruction.

Effective note-taking instruction provides students many short practice sessions with the clear purpose of improving their skills. At the end of each session students share their notes, so that the variety of note-taking styles (use of key words, phrases, full sentences) can be discussed.

Figure 13.6 Example of a Collaborative Listening-Viewing Guide

Collaborative Listening-Viewing Guide (CLVG)

Course: ED 309 Date: 9/18/00 Topic: Differentiated Instruction

Name: Linda M Group Members: Karen K, Cheryl S, Joanne R.

We know that: the intent is to meet individual student needs, concepts taught are the same but children learn them in different ways.

My notes	Our group notes
1. 2, 3, 4 learning options, not 20 _content (concepts, skills to learn) match with readiness concrete vs abstract simple to complex few directions to many _activities (the way they explore) alternate ways to manipulate ideas multiple paths _products (demonstrate what is learned) modified grading, rubrics 2. grouping-flexible _readiness (except-change) _learning profile (multiple intelligences) _student interest (relevance)	Key is flexibility and dynamic grouping. Teacher role is redefined—be open minded, a facilitator. Be careful not to just give brighter students more work—make all levels seem the same in terms of work load. Lots of hands-on, not just lecture, or reading.

We learned that: The teacher is not the center of the classroom when differentiated instruction is used. Groups change often. DI is valuable at <u>any</u> grade level. Teaching is more effective.

We will find out:

How challenging it will be to implement DI.

If the politics of education today (e.g, the emphasis on standardized testing) will interfere with a teacher's ability/desire to differentiate instruction.

Outlining

The underlying abilities needed for note taking and outlining are similar. As with note taking, outlining involves identification of main ideas and specific details. With outlining, however, these elements must be properly related. Outlines use any of the following formats: phrases or topics; sentences; paragraphs; or graphic representations. Instruction in outlining begins with easy material and much teacher guidance, discussion, and practice.

The first sessions in outlining should provide a completed outline of the material for the students on a worksheet, chalkboard, or overhead transparency. The assumption here is that the students will better understand the function of outlining if they can see how the writer organized the selection. After students have read the material, the reasons for selecting certain topics as main ideas and others as supporting details for the outline are discussed. For example, if the selection being read is about bees and how they communicate, the outline may appear as follows:

I. Bees communicate with each other.
   A. One bee discovers honey.
   B. Other bees soon appear.
II. Bee gives message.
   A. Scout bee returns to hive.
   B. Scout bee begins to dance.
   C. Dance tells story.

The discussion emphasizes that the major headings represent the main ideas in the selection. The subheadings provide more specific details that explain the major headings. The outline could be used before the actual reading to help students anticipate the selection's content. Through these activities, students eventually recognize the ways in which written material follows an outline. The teacher is responsible for choosing material that is simple and well-organized.

A later stage may provide students with the supporting details and instruction for filling in the main headings. Then a complete skeleton outline can be provided with a few random topics filled in and instruction for completing the outline. Eventually only the structure of the outline is given. Finally, after much practice at each stage, students will be able to formulate outlines without assistance. Examples of outlines for early instruction can be found in Figures 13.7 and 13.8.

spatial   In addition to the preceding techniques, the strategies of mapping (Hanf, 1971), semantic webbing (Freedman & Reynolds, 1980), and the herringbone technique (Tierney, Readence, & Dishner, 1990) are useful for developing outlining skill. Semantic webbing (mapping) and *the herringbone technique* are graphic representations of the relationships of ideas in a selection. The visual result clearly reveals the major topic, main idea, and supporting details. Such graphic representations have also been called **arrays** (Hansell, 1978). Hansell provides a definition: "An array is essentially a free form outline which requires that students decide how to arrange key words and phrases to show how the author fit them together" (p. 248). Therefore, in maps, webs, and arrays, the student constructs an organizational design of ideas by selecting relevant information, sorting this into its proper place, and relating all facts to the whole and to the other facts. Figure 13.9 shows an example of an array for the African folktale *Anansi the Spider* (McDermott, 1972). In this folktale, Anansi buys all the stories in the world from the Sky God. To pay for the stories, Anansi captures and gives to the Sky God a hive of hornets, a jaguar, and a great python. The diagram shows how these events fit together by the arrangement of key words and arrows designating direct relationships.

Figure 13.7   Selecting Main Headings for an Outline

Paris

Many people think of Paris as one of the most beautiful cities in the world. It has been called the City of Light because of the beauty of its lights at night.   Colorful flower beds and famous statues line paths through lovely public gardens throughout the city.   Children in Paris go to the parks to enjoy puppet shows and to sail their toy boats in the ponds.

Over the years Paris fashions have been famous throughout the world. When women want to know the latest in fashion, they look to the fashion shows in Paris.   Many well-known designers of women's clothes live and work in Paris.

The city of Paris is also famous for its art. Priceless art treasures are on display in several museums. Paintings and statues are among the most popular kinds of art seen in Paris.   Many people from all over the world come to Paris each year to study in the outstanding schools of art.

Put the main headings where they belong.

City of fashion
City of art
City of beauty

I. City of beauty
   A. Lights
   B. Gardens
   C. Parks

II. City of fashion
   A. Worldwide fame
   B. Fashion shows
   C. Fashion designers

III. City of art
   A. Museums of art
   B. Kinds of art
   C. Schools of art

Plan 17, Pages 127-130

Comprehension: Selecting main headings for an outline

Directions: Have pupils read the selection and complete the outline.

Exploration: On the board write cleaning a cut, treating with medicine, and bandaging. Have pupils list the materials needed under each heading.

From *Mysterious Wisteria Activity Book,* p. 56. Copyright © 1972 by The Economy Company, Oklahoma City. Reprinted with permission.

Hansell's research suggests certain steps in teaching students how to prepare arrays. First, the teacher selects ten to twenty key words or phrases (assuming passages of 400 to 800 words) from the material. Next, the teacher develops questions that require students to organize what they already know about the passage—for example, "How would you capture a jaguar?"

logical-mathematical

Next, the students are assigned to small groups. Each group receives several strips of paper that contain the key words and phrases from the passage. This step allows the teacher to pronounce and explain any of the key words or phrases if necessary. After the

interpersonal

paper strips have been distributed, the teacher asks the organizing questions. At this point the students actually read the passage, but they are now reading for two very definite purposes: (1) to check their answers to the organizing questions against what is stated in the passage and (2) to find out how the key words and phrases are related.

The students, still in groups, compare the strips of paper to select the most important idea. This strip is placed at the top or the center to stress its importance. The other strips are positioned around it in a way that reflects the relationships in the material. This positioning must be done with teacher guidance; the teacher asks appropriate questions,

Figure 13.8   Outlining by Relating Subheadings to the Main Heading

Make an Outline

	The Ocean
If you wanted to use the following ideas in a report about the ocean, how would you set up an outline?	I. Bottom of the ocean
	A. Shelves
Use these words for the main headings in the outline.	B. Slopes
	C. Floor
Bottom of the ocean Movement of the ocean Life in the ocean	II. Movement of the ocean
	A. Tides
	B. Waves
Put these words under the main headings in the outline.	C. Currents
Seaweeds Tides Shelves Waves Slopes Fish Floor Shellfish Whales Currents	III. Life in the ocean
	A. Seaweeds
	B. Fish
	C. Shellfish
	D. Whales

(Arrangements under each heading may vary.)

Plan 31, Pages 230-234	Directions: Have pupils read the instructions and complete the page independently.	Exploration: Have pupils write an article with content based on these headings and subheadings.
Study Skills: Outlining by relating subheadings to main headings		

encourages, and makes suggestions while moving from group to group. When the group is satisfied with the position of all the paper strips, one member copies the array onto a piece of paper, drawing arrows to show connected ideas and the direction of relationships.

The last step is for each group to share their arrays and discuss reasons for the arrangement and placement of arrows. The teacher asks extending questions at this time.

Hansell recommends that at least four teacher-guided arrays be constructed before expecting students to do an unguided array. In an unguided array, students select the key words and phrases themselves. Eventually, by moving from free-form arrays to skeletal outlines, students are ready to prepare individual outlines. The array approach is useful because it focuses on the primary reason for outlining in the first place, that is, to identify relevant ideas and fit them into a meaningful pattern. Unfortunately, the focus of most instruction in outlining is on the format, which assumes that students understand the relationships presented in the material—a "cart before the horse" approach. Instruction in array formation puts the horse back in front of the cart. In addition, the Inspiration software (see Chapter 7) has the potential to lead students to a better conceptual understanding of outlining.

Figure 13.9   Example Array Showing Interrelationship of Character and Events

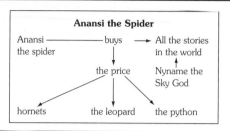

From Hansell, T. Stevenson, (1978). "Stepping up to outlining." *Journal of Reading, 22*: 248–252. Reprinted with permission of T. Stevenson Hansell and the International Reading Association.

The **herringbone technique** (Tierney, Readence, & Dishner, 1990, pp. 312–316) is a structured outlining procedure useful for helping students organize information from text. This strategy uses six basic comprehension questions to obtain the important information: who, what, where, when, how, and why.

As with arrays, the teacher must make some specific preparations for teaching the herringbone technique. Important preparation questions for the teacher to ask include the following:

1. What are the major concepts my students should understand from this material?

2. What are the important vocabulary items?

3. How will my students learn this information?

4. Which concepts do I expect *all* my students to master and which do I expect only my better students to achieve?

The teacher introduces the lesson as usual, with concern for developing motivation and conceptual background. Then the herringbone technique is introduced. The herringbone form (Figure 13.10) can be easily provided to students as a photocopied handout. Students are told they will be seeking answers to the questions that appear on the form. The answers themselves can also be written right on the form. The first few lessons that involve the herringbone technique are walked through with teacher guidance, using an overhead transparency.

Figure 13.10   The Herringbone Form

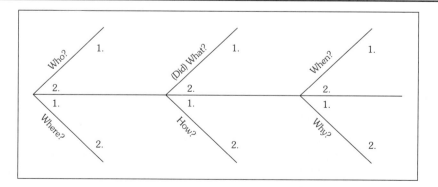

As students read the assigned material they will be noting answers to the following questions:

1. Who (person or group) was involved?
2. What did this person or group do?
3. When was it (the event from question 2) done?
4. Where was it done?
5. How was it done?
6. Why did it happen?

**logical-
mathematical**

The answers to these questions help the student recognize the important relationships in the material. For example:

For a chapter in a social studies textbook entitled "Europeans Rediscover the Western Lands," the students were instructed to read the topic, "Columbus Tries to Get Help from Portugal," and to answer the six key questions. The answers to be recorded on the herringbone form were as follows:

Who?   Columbus, king of Portugal, king's experts
What?   Columbus went to the king to ask for ships and supplies to sail west to reach the Indies. King's experts thought Columbus was wrong.
When?   _____
Where?   Portugal
How?   _____
Why?   Columbus wanted to prove (1) that it was possible to sail straight west to reach the Indies because the earth is round and (2) that this route was shorter than going around Africa. King's experts knew the earth was round but thought the distance was much greater than Columbus thought.

As seen in this example, texts do not always contain all the information needed to answer the six key questions. The teacher must decide whether the missing information is important enough to look for elsewhere. The herringbone technique readily reveals these information gaps. The teacher can also use the textual answers as springboards for further discussion and research. Figure 13.11 shows the information recorded on the herringbone form.

Mapping, webbing, array tasks, and the herringbone technique use processes employed in both note taking and outlining. More important, they give students a structure for observing relationships in text that further enhance comprehension and retention of information. When these techniques are used as prewriting strategies as well, students will quickly begin to understand text organization. Once students are familiar and comfortable with mapping activities, it would be appropriate to introduce the software program Inspiration (Inspiration Software, Inc, 1998–1999). This software provides a powerful electronic tool for mapping alternatives (referred to as the Diagram view) and also allows these maps to be converted to outlines (referred to as the Outline view).

ASSESSING FOR INTERPRETATION OF GRAPHIC AND PICTORIAL MATERIALS

The skills to be discussed in this section differ considerably from those discussed in the previous sections. While the previous skills overlapped with the comprehension skills discussed in Chapters 9, 11, and 12, the reading of graphic and pictorial materials requires a unique set of skills.

Figure 13.11   Herringbone Outline Showing Gaps in Information

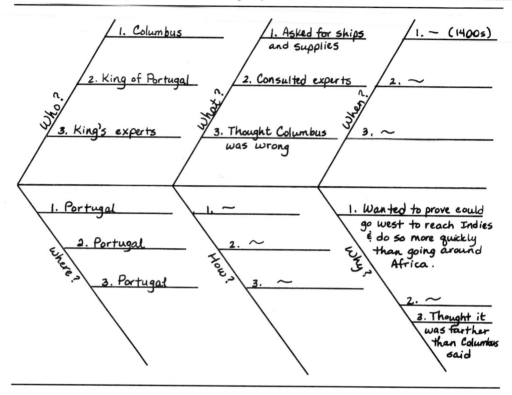

As stated early in this chapter, the interpretation of tables and graphs is a subtest commonly found on standardized achievement tests. However, if the information from such a test is not readily available to the teacher (i.e., tests are machine scored), the instructional benefits are minimal. Informal measurements developed by the teacher will provide a readily available source of information.

Graphic and pictorial materials help readers understand text by explaining, clarifying, or providing additional information. A reader must have skill with the following materials.

1. *Pictures.* Students must be able to use pictures that present or clarify concepts, afford new experiences vicariously, or stimulate discussion. Political cartoons are included in this category.

2. *Timelines.* Students should be able to recognize timelines as graphic presentations of events in chronological order. Both the time and the event are presented on a timeline.

3. *Tables and charts.* Students must be able to read the variety of facts presented in a table or chart. These may be in single-column or multicolumn formats.

4. *Graphs.* Many types of graphs clarify and illustrate comparisons. Students should be able to read and interpret circle graphs, line graphs, bar graphs, and picture graphs.

5. *Maps and globes.* Students must be able to interpret a legend and its symbols; the scale indicated; the directions of north, south, east, and west; and the lines of latitude and longitude to read maps and globes effectively.

To assess whether students can use these five types of materials, the teacher simply has to develop a set of questions that can be answered only if the picture, timeline, table, chart, graph, map, or globe has been read properly. These measures are quite easily constructed.

INSTRUCTION FOR INTERPRETING GRAPHIC AND PICTORIAL MATERIALS

General Teaching Procedure

Interpretation of pictorial and graphic material, an important aspect of visual literacy, is best taught according to a five-step procedure (Cooper, Warncke, Ramstad, & Shipman, 1979):

1. Explanation of the use or purpose of the material being taught.

2. An understanding of the meanings of the words used to describe the material being learned.

3. The teaching of the specific skills needed for use of the material.

4. A demonstration of the use of the material.

5. The guidance of the students through the initial usage of the material. (p. 259)

spatial

The activities described in the remainder of this section point out how the teacher can follow each of the five steps. Because a large amount of visual information is available through multimedia resources as well as textbooks, teachers soon discover that readers who master interpretation of pictorial and graphic materials greatly enhance their understanding of content-area materials.

1. When explaining the use and purpose of pictures, examples must be available for students to view during the lesson. For instance, to explain the purpose of arrows, dotted lines, or other directional markers in diagrams found in texts, some actual text pages should be shown. Then, for follow-up practice, students might be directed to produce a similar diagram. The explanation may begin by giving students a sentence describing a scene that can be easily sketched. For example, the students may be asked to draw a picture to correspond to the following sentence:

The ball rolled down the street and hit a big tree.

The resulting drawings are shared, with a discussion of the techniques used to indicate "rolled" and "hit" (refer to step 3). Students should experience a need to indicate the passage of time in their drawings. Some may resolve this problem by showing several pictures that indicate the ball getting closer to the tree; others may use dotted lines to show the ball moving toward the tree (Figure 13.12). Both solutions are found in content-area material.

2. An example from a textbook is appropriate for demonstrating how important it is to understand the key words used. The following sentence was taken from a science text:

The paramecium pinched in the middle and split in two.

First, this sentence may be difficult to visualize if the important words are unfamiliar (e.g., *paramecium, pinched, split*). Therefore, step 2, understanding or at least recognition of the key words, is important. The picture itself attempts to clarify concepts in the text that would otherwise be difficult to understand, as the picture associated with the example sentence clearly demonstrates (Figure 13.13). In this case, the picture provides the

Figure 13.12 Pictures Drawn by a 7-Year-Old Boy *(Left)* and an 8-Year-Old Girl *(Right)* Showing a Rolling Ball Hitting a Tree

reader with a better understanding of the sentence than the words themselves. The whole illustration shows how a paramecium reproduces itself. This kind of concept is best illustrated by a series of pictures (recall the "rolling ball" sentence). Other concepts are better described using arrows, or dotted lines if direction or distance is involved (Figure 13.14).

3. Some illustrations have legends that the reader must use to understand the concepts involved. Students must be taught how to use these legends for pictures, maps, and titles and column headings in tables, and how to relate the pictorial or graphic information back to the text. Show students where to find the legend on a map and how to interpret the symbols for state roads versus interstate highways, for example. Then have students develop a map of their neighborhood, including symbols for houses, stores, mailboxes, traffic lights, stop signs, and other features unique to their neighborhood. These maps can be posted in the classroom for other students to interpret.

4. The *TV Guide* provides a real-world example to demonstrate the use of legends. In the early part of the guide there is a key to the symbols used within. Programs are rated as to appropriateness for age groups. A *Y* is used for programs appropriate for all children; *Y7* for children age 7 and older; *G* for general audience; *PG* for parental guidance; *14* for programs unsuitable for children under age 14; and *MA* for mature audiences

Figure 13.13 Illustration Clarifying the Concept of a Paramecium Splitting in Two

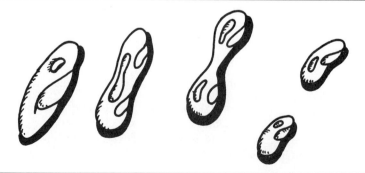

Figure 13.14   Use of Arrows to Aid the Reader in Understanding the Concepts Involved

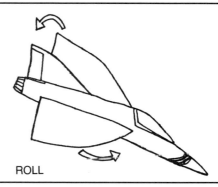

ROLL

only. Other symbols are used as well. Students can be shown how to locate these symbols by certain programs and determine the appropriateness for viewing.

5. Guidance is essential initially and can be given only by direct instruction. A variety of pictorial and graphic materials with questions relevant to interpretation is the basis of such instruction. Figure 13.15 is a familiar example. The following questions would be appropriate to use with this graph.

1. What kind of graph is this? Circle one.

   bar graph   circle graph   picture graph

2. This graph shows that 30 fifth-graders like (hamburgers) best.

3. Two foods are liked the same. What are these two foods? (french fries) (hot dogs)

4. How many fifth-graders like pizza best? (60)

5. How many fifth-graders were asked what their favorite food was? (120)

To maintain their competence in this area, students must have many opportunities to use and apply these skills.

Figure 13.15   Students Can Be Instructed in Interpreting Graphic Materials by Being Asked a Series of Relevant Questions that Relate the Graphic Information to the Question Responses

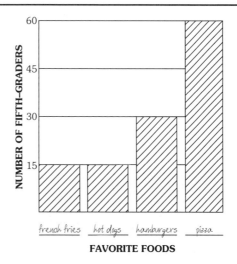

Real-World Usage

logical-mathematical

The best support for developing graphic and pictorial skills is real-world usage. For instance, to learn about the bar graph, the class could collect its own data and construct its own graph. The teacher will be enhancing not only graph skills but math skills as well.

Teachers must be alert to the many opportunities in daily life that help students appreciate the need for learning graphic and pictorial skills. Bus schedules, newspaper weather maps, TV guides, and city street maps are obvious items that can be brought into the classroom. Students who have been taught to graph their own progress on spelling tests could also use this skill to graph progress in a weight-loss program. Who hasn't been asked to draw a map giving directions from "my house" to "your house"? Students can help make maps "from classroom to cafeteria" or "from school to the ice-skating rink." Most large shopping malls have maps that locate the stores. In the Southeast and on the East Coast, hurricane tracking maps are free to teachers in large quantities during the hurricane season.

Knowing the students and the community in which they live broadens the opportunity to practice graphic and pictorial skills. The least we can do for our students is to give them skills needed for daily life.

SUMMARY

Students considered to be successful readers are often at a loss when given an assignment to "report on one of the following topics" or to "take notes on Chapter 6 in your history book for homework." Such assignments assume the student can locate and organize information and interpret graphic or pictorial information. In short, the student must be an independent reader *and learner*—not just a reader who can recognize words in print and understand the message.

Knowing *how* to learn is what study skill instruction is all about. Study skills must be taught directly. Teachers must "extend and expand" reading to include a variety of material. Also, study skills must be taught from the beginning. If students are to be independent learners and readers, they must know how to find information they need, how to organize information, and how to interpret the visual aids accompanying information ("reading to learn"). Teachers therefore must provide reading instruction within content-area classes in which students can see the application of the study skills.

Suggested Readings

Cheyney, A. B. (1992). *Teaching reading skills through the newspaper* (3rd ed.). Newark, DE: International Reading Association.
  This brief (59-page) monograph is a valuable resource for using the newspaper across the curriculum. As a readily available resource for teachers and a motivation source for students, the newspaper can help students gain control over their own learning. Informational reading can be readily practiced within an authentic context.

Peresich, M. L., Meadows, J. D., & Sinatra, R. (1990). Content-area cognitive mapping for reading and writing proficiency. *Journal of Reading, 33,* 424–432.

  This article shows mapping to be a practical, visual way to apply schema theory in the classroom while teaching students about text structure. Several examples of content applications are presented in the article.

Vacca, R. T., & Vacca, J. L. (1998). *Content area reading* (6th ed.). New York: Harper-Collins.
  Chapter 10, "Study Strategies," is particularly relevant to a discussion of study skills. Teachers working with upper elementary, middle school, or secondary students will find the suggestions in this text chapter clearly explained, with examples for many of the ideas presented.

14 Arts at Every Opportunity
Weaving It All Together

Janet C. Richards,
University of Southern Mississippi–Gulf Park

Objectives

After reading this chapter, you should be able to:
1. understand how to nurture and develop your own and your students' abilities to link reading and writing events with the visual arts, dramatic arts, music, and dance at every opportunity.
2. recognize how integrating literacy lessons with the visual and performing arts extends and strengthens students' literacy abilities and motivations for reading and writing.
3. understand how creative expressions and communication, supported by multiple intelligences theory (Gardner, 1983, 1999), and national standards benefit all students—including students from nonmainstream backgrounds; dialect speakers; and those with special learning requirements, diverse aptitudes, and varying instructional needs.

Key Concepts and Terms

dioramas
drama improvisations
dramatic play
genre
literacy-based
multi-literacies

multimedia materials
scaffolding
sign systems
symbol systems
text set

thematic units of
    instruction
visual arts
visual arts media
visuals

Overview
    II. Meeting the needs of all learners
        A. Multiple intelligences
        B. Empowering students from diverse backgrounds
  III. Support for integrating the arts
  IV. Using creativity, imagination, and professional expertise to plan lessons
        A. Arts at every opportunity in a corrective reading program
        B. Developing proficiency in weaving literacy lessons with the arts
        C. Carefully studying student responses
        D. Complementing literature with creative visuals
    V. Linking literacy lessons with the visual arts
        A. Beginning in modest ways
        B. Combining creative writing with the visual arts
        C. Creating visual representations of Snow White and the poison apples
        D. Mural constructions of *Gregory Cool*
        E. K–W–L and *The Very Hungry Caterpillar*
  VI. Linking literacy lessons with drama enactments
        A. Choral reading
        B. A more formal drama enactment
        C. A scripted, rehearsed puppet show
 VII. Linking literacy lessons with music
        A. Infusing music into every teaching session
        B. Enjoyment and informality
        C. A chant with rhyming words
        D. Content reading and music
        E. A Native American song with "talking hands"
VIII. Linking literacy with dance
        A. Spontaneous dance
        B. Envisioning the solar system through dance
        C. Dance of the birds, reptiles, and mammals
  IX. Summary
   X. Suggested readings

OVERVIEW

In our after school corrective reading program,[1] preservice teachers integrate the arts at every opportunity. We believe the arts are not extras to be addressed if there are a few minutes left to spare in instructional sessions (Blecher & Jaffee, 1998). Rather, artistic pursuits serve to unify our instructional program into a cohesive community of learners where students are prized for their unique aptitudes, talents, and opinions.

---

[1] In the after school "Arts at Every Opportunity" corrective reading program referred to in this chapter, each preservice teacher works with a group of three or four students for an hour and a half twice weekly throughout a semester. We believe that working in collaborative learning teams provides opportunities for students to enhance their thinking, oral language, and background knowledge by sharing personal opinions and responding to peers' ideas. Collaborative interactions also help students learn to respect and appreciate others' language, heritage, and special multiple intelligences.

MEETING THE NEEDS OF ALL LEARNERS

Since the arts "have the potential to communicate ideas and feelings [with and] without words" (Cornett, 1999, p. 3), we have found that visual and performing arts activities especially meet the needs of emergent readers and writers who are learning about language and literacy. For example, as a prelude to journal writing with a partner, young students can draw and sketch their thoughts and opinions. After listening to a story, emergent readers can use puppets or dress in costumes to help make story characters come to life (see Figure 14.1 for students' characterizations of *The Grouchy Ladybug* [Carle, 1977]).

The arts also support students who struggle with reading and writing—for example, students who have had limited exposure to literacy events in their homes and those with learning disabilities in language and literacy. Art activities such as painting, singing, dancing, and engaging in spontaneous or scripted drama enactments offer opportunities for students to share their ideas about story characters' goals and actions and portray their thinking about what might happen next in a story. In addition, students can become authors and visual artists by writing and illustrating their own stories and books and reading them aloud for peers' and younger students' enjoyment (see Figure 14.2 and Appendix K for an example of a student-created book).

Certainly, the arts also enhance students' comprehension and recall of informational text. By adopting both an efferent and aesthetic stance,[2] students can identify important

Figure 14.1   Students' Characterization of *The Grouchy Ladybug*

---

[2] An efferent stance occurs when readers concentrate on retaining facts and details commonly presented in informational text. A predominately aesthetic role is generally adopted when readers interact with fiction. This stance stirs up feelings, and generates strong personal perceptions, opinions, and attitudes (Rosenblatt, 1993).

Figure 14.2 Example of a Student-Created Book

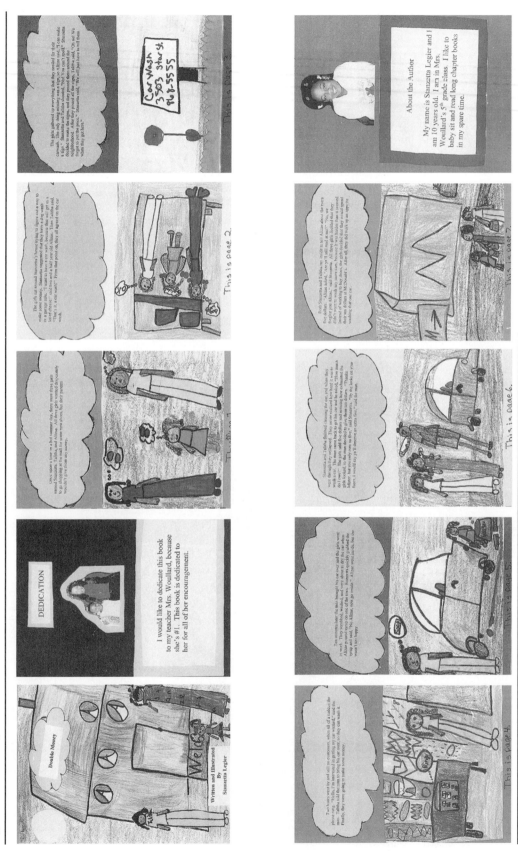

ideas in their textbooks or nonfiction books, and then create murals, scripts, **dioramas, drama improvisations,** or skillfully illustrated concept maps that portray their opinions and thinking about what they have read (see Figure 14.3 for an example of a concept map).

Multiple Intelligences

Artistic engagements also provide opportunities for students with special literacy learning requirements to use their distinctive multiple intelligences (Gardner, 1983, 1999). Students who are encouraged to augment the literacies of reading and writing with their MI strengths (e.g., spatial, musical, bodily-kinesthetic) can more easily solve problems creatively, explore their reasoning, and extend and express their points of view.

Empowering Students from Diverse Backgrounds

The arts clearly empower students who come from diverse ethnic and linguistic backgrounds. Students can use the arts along with their varied cultural experiences, values, identities, beliefs, and languages to convey their thinking. Blending literacy events with artistic pursuits also creates possibilities for students from nonmainstream backgrounds

Figure 14.3   Example of a Concept Map

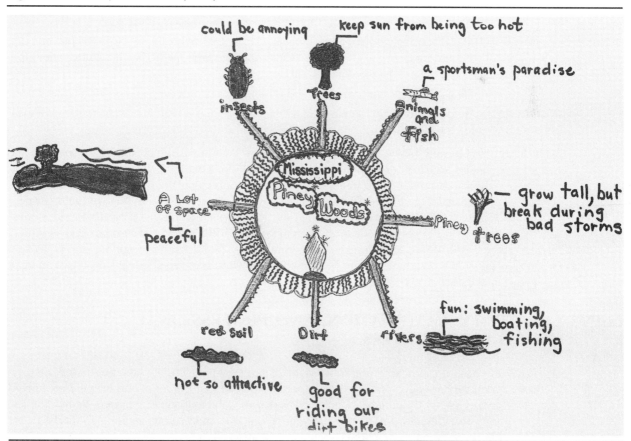

or nonstandard-English-speaking families or second-language learners to increase their oral and written language by constructing, extending, and sharing meaning from the texts they read and to generate new and novel texts (Graves, Juel, & Graves, 1998). Most important, the arts provide cultural opportunities that are not related to social class, academic ranking, or standard English proficiency (Pankratz & Mulcahy, 1989).

SUPPORT FOR INTEGRATING THE ARTS

Integrating literacy events with the arts unequivocally is supported by twenty-first-century visions of literacy that extend definitions of language far beyond reading and writing. This broadened concept of literacy (i.e., **multi-literacies**) informs new dimensions for literacy learning and teaching by considering pursuits such as dance, music, the visual arts, poetry, and drama as legitimate expressions of understanding and communication (see Blecher & Jaffee, 1998; Flood, Heath, & Lapp, 1997; Wolf & Balick, 1999).

Acknowledging this new, expanded perspective of literacy, and recognizing the power and benefits of a strong, integrated language arts curriculum for all students, the *Standards for the Arts* (*Standards of Arts Education,* 1994), adopted by 47 states (U.S. Department of Education, Office of Statistics, 1995), and the *Standards for the English Language Arts* (International Reading Association/National Council for the Teachers of English Language Arts, 1996) reflect the current transformation and extension of the term *literacy* beyond reading and writing. Listings of communicative standards in these two documents that particularly apply to literacy and arts linkages include the following:

1. making connections between the visual arts, music, dance, and other disciplines;
2. comparing and incorporating art forms by analyzing methods of presentation and audience response for theater and dramatic media (such as films, television, and electronic media) and other art forms;
3. listening to, analyzing, and describing music; and
4. developing a wide range of strategies for comprehending, interpreting, and evaluating texts.

Literacy-based arts programs also are validated by numerous, well-respected, and scholarly sources of research and practice (Morado, Koenig, & Wilson, 1999). These foundational sources include trailblazing research concerning brain development (Goleman, 1995; Sternberg, 1999); Erickson's classic work about eight Life Stages (1950); Piaget's Stages of Cognitive Development (1980); Maslow's conceptions of Needs-Based Motivation (1970); Vygotsky's ideas about **scaffolding** and the Zone of Proximal Development (see Moll, 1993); sociodramatic play (Smilansky, 1968); Reader Response theory (Rosenblatt, 1993); Readers' Theater (see Buehl, 2001); and Howard Gardner's theory of multiple intelligences (1983, 1999).

USING CREATIVITY, IMAGINATION, AND PROFESSIONAL EXPERTISE TO PLAN LESSONS

The rest of this chapter describes our Arts at Every Opportunity literature-based arts program for corrective readers. It is important to note that the ideas and activities portrayed are not meant to serve as model lessons that must be explicitly replicated. Rather, the lessons are offered to broaden your awareness and stimulate your thinking about the possibilities of literacy/arts connections that will arise often as you work with students. Using your own innate creativity, imagination, and expanding professional expertise, you will want to go beyond the ideas presented in this chapter to collaborate with your outstandingly imaginative and talented students in planning literacy lessons that transcend traditional reading/writing "skill and drill" instruction. You will discover that weaving literacy with the arts will enable your students to achieve remarkable success and also "recognize the bread'n and depth of their learning" (Gallas, 1992, p. 31).

Arts at Every Opportunity in a Corrective Reading Program

At the start of every semester, many preservice teachers who enroll in our Arts at Every Opportunity corrective reading methods course initially believe they cannot effectively link literacy instruction with the arts. "I'm not artistic," some confide. "I never had a class in music or the visual arts." Other preservice teachers confess, "I'm not creative. I can't think of any arts activities to do except let my students color pictures." A few preservice teachers emphatically claim, "I can't sing, create poetry, or dance. I'm not comfortable in front of an audience. I don't have any imagination."

As the semester progresses, however, all of the preservice teachers become confident and adept in combining literacy instruction with the arts at every teaching session. For example, following Vygotsky's Zone of Proximal Development (see Moll, 1993; Vygotsky, 1978), the preservice teachers collaborate with their students in presenting student-authored puppet shows, Readers' Theater, and drama productions. They work side-by-side with their students, scaffolding, modeling, and creating text-based murals, story quilts, and songs; as co-constructors of knowledge along with their students, they improvise dances and create songs and poetry.

Developing Proficiency in Weaving Literacy Lessons with the Arts

Our preservice teachers begin to discover their proficiencies for weaving literacy lessons with the arts during the very first week of class. They collaborate, plan together, and craft original, three-dimensional interest inventories containing approximately ten questions designed to help them determine their new students' interests. The questions also provide opportunities for the preservice teachers and their students to become acquainted with one another. For example, a preservice teacher recently initiated her first teaching session by showing her students a giant yellow cardboard school bus she had created. In keeping with our Vygotskian framework, the preservice teacher first modeled the interest inventory activity for her students by opening the school bus door and pulling out a question printed on a card designed like a bus tire. "If you could be anywhere in the world right now, where would you like to be?" she read aloud. Continuing to model her thinking for her students, she answered the question by saying, "I'd like to be swimming and sunbathing at the beach." Then, each of her students took turns answering this first question as the preservice teacher recorded their responses. Next, a student chose a second question to read aloud. "What books do you like to read?" he asked. The interest inventory activity continued until all the questions were read. The preservice teachers read the inventory questions aloud for emergent readers. (See Chapter 6 for representative interest inventory questions.)

Carefully Studying Student Responses

The preservice teachers carefully take notes about all of the student responses generated during the interest inventory activity. The dated notes serve as the first entry in each student's anecdotal record profile kept by the preservice teachers throughout the semester. The students and preservice teachers also study the interest inventory responses together in order to determine small-group, broadly-based themes or **thematic units of instruction** that allow for all types of explorations (e.g., Celebrations; Magic and Mystery; Going Places and Doing Things). Theme teaching allows for continuity of instruction and serves as a strong foundation for selecting quality fiction and nonfiction across a variety of **genre** in our literature-based, integrated arts program.

Complementing Literature with Creative Visuals

As the semester progresses, our preservice teachers continue to uncover and discover their artistic aptitudes by creating original, appealing, book-specific **visuals** to accompany each story their students read or hear. Visuals pique students' interests for literature and serve to enhance their imaginations. In addition, visuals help students remember how the story elements of characters, settings, problems, and solutions relate to one another. Equally important, attractive visuals that represent various facets of stories provide opportunities for our tutorial students to experience a language-based activity (i.e., reading), through a different **sign** or **symbol system** (i.e., the visual arts).[3] For example, when a preservice teacher read the story *Goldilocks and the Three Bears* (a Brothers Grimm fairy tale retold by Brett, 1987) to her first-grade students, she assembled small, medium, and large-sized bowls, spoons, chairs, and toy beds. As she read the story, her students took turns manipulating the visuals when the bowls, spoons, chairs, and beds were mentioned in the story. At the end of the fairy tale, the students used the visuals to offer an informal drama improvisation for other students and preservice teachers in our program.

spatial

Other preservice teachers create inexpensive, engaging visuals by constructing masks, mobiles, and three-dimensional dioramas. They use the Internet to obtain color illustrations of story characters and settings, sew and stuff large dolls dressed like story characters, craft papier-mâché lily pads with frog princes, create trees from authentic bark and palm leaves, bring in stuffed animals to hold and cuddle, make pigs' ears and noses, and construct pigs' houses out of straw, wood, and brick (see Figure 14.4 for visuals that complement the story of *The Three Little Pigs*).

LINKING LITERACY LESSONS WITH THE VISUAL ARTS

Children of all ages instinctively use the **visual arts** as a natural means of expression. For example, toddlers spontaneously scribble their ideas on all available surfaces. Kindergarten students enjoy using large pieces of colored chalk to decorate sidewalks. Primary students "come into the classroom drawing pictures" (Blecher & Jaffee, 1998, p. 70).

---

[3] Gardner maintains that authentic constructions of knowledge occur only when a learner can transform ideas, information, and skills from one domain to another (e.g., the transformation of oral or written language to the languages of music, dance, or the visual arts). Such a view is an important rationale for weaving the arts with literacy instruction (see Blyth & Gardner, 1990).

Figure 14.4 Visuals to Accompany *The Three Little Pigs*

Urban youths seek empowerment and recognition by spray-painting representations of their emotions and social, cultural, and political experiences on bridges, buildings, and highway exit ramps.

The visual arts allow students to convey meaning without oral or written language. Therefore, visual arts activities are ideal for students who struggle with reading and writing. They offer opportunities for students to think in pictures and see ideas. Further, the visual arts provide all sorts of options for personal expression because they can be combined with other forms of the language arts, such as reading, creative writing, and drama (Piazza, 1999).

Beginning in Modest Ways

Understandably, most of our preservice teachers initially link reading and writing lessons with the visual arts in modest ways. Like their students in the corrective reading program, few preservice teachers have had opportunities to work with **visual arts media** (e.g., tempera paint, pastels, fine and broad markers, crayons, glue, glitter). They also have not combined **multimedia materials,** such as strands of wool, leaves, bark, sand, cotton, paint, markers, feathers, glue, tongue depressors, computer-generated icons, cardboard, aluminum foil, and glitter to create text-based murals (see Figures 14.5 and 14.6 for examples of text-based murals).

Combining Creative Writing with the Visual Arts

After a few teaching sessions, our preservice teachers discover their innate imaginations and creative identities. For instance, wearing a sunbonnet, a fluffy apron, and a pair of "old-timey," black lace-up shoes, a preservice teacher played the part of Great Aunt

Figure 14.5   Example of a Text-Based Mural

Arizona as she read *My Great Aunt Arizona* (Houston, 1992) to her fourth-graders. Because the story depicts Aunt Arizona's imaginary travels, following the reading, the fourth-graders used watercolors, crayons, and fine-line markers to create individual illustrations showing where they wished they could travel. Combining creative writing with the visual arts, they printed the book's title and author on their paintings, included information about the story ("Great Aunt Arizona dreamed about traveling to wonderful

Figure 14.6   Close-Up of Part of a Text-Based Mural

places"), and composed short paragraphs about their imaginary travel wishes (e.g., "I want to travel to Disneyland because I have never been there and all my friends say it is cool. They have scary rides and Mickey and Minnie Mouse"). The preservice teacher then helped her students mount the drawings and paragraphs on sturdy cardboard. Finally, she bound their work into a large collaborative book. To continue explorations about travels, the students used the Internet to discover places they would like to visit (e.g., Australia to see marsupials and the Great Barrier Reef, and the Amazon Basin to see reptiles and rain forests). The students also read fiction and content text (i.e., multiple texts, formats, and genres), that pertained to their dream travels, such as *Verdi* (Cannon, 1997), a story about a young green python, and *The Great Kapok Tree: A Tale of the Amazon Rain Forest* (Cherry, 1990).

Creating Visual Representations of Snow White and the Poison Apples

Another preservice teacher read *Snow White and the Seven Dwarfs* (a Brothers Grimm fairy tale retold by Gag, 1938) to his first-grade students. Recognizing that 6- and 7-year-olds cannot sit still for long periods of time, the preservice teacher stopped at appropriate places in the book and used visuals (e.g., an apple, a computer-generated illustration of Snow White, and small ceramic figures of the seven dwarfs), to help his students predict what might happen next in the story, an important element of the DLTA strategy being taught (see Chapter 9). As the story progressed, the preservice teacher and his students created clay and tempera paint representations of Snow White. Further on in the story, they used large pieces of colored chalk to illustrate their ideas about how the story might end. As a culminating, postreading activity, the students created large papier-mâché "poison" apples. Then they wrote to Snow White, offering advice about being careful when eating strange foods and not to eat food offered by strangers.

spatial

Mural Constructions of *Gregory Cool*

A preservice teacher working with fifth-graders read the story *Gregory Cool* (Binch, 1994) to coincide with their theme of "Going Places and Doing Things." In the story, Gregory, who lives in a large U.S. city, visits his grandparents on the small island of Tobago. Gregory initially has great difficulty adjusting to island life and pretends he is so "cool" that he isn't interested in joining his cousin in island activities such as fishing, eating unusual food like *bake* and *buljol* (bread and saltfish), and climbing coconut trees. Following the story, the fifth-graders created a large mural that included their letters of advice and solace to Gregory (see Figures 14.7, 14.8, 14.9 and 14.10 for examples of letters to Gregory Cool).

**spatial
interpersonal**

K–W–L and *The Very Hungry Caterpillar*

In another impressive lesson, prior to reading *The Very Hungry Caterpillar* (Carle, 1987) to a group of first-graders, a preservice teacher linked the K–W–L reading comprehension strategy (Ogle, 1986) with the visual arts by creating a large drawing of the hungry caterpillar. The first-graders listed their Ks (what I already *know*) on one caterpillar body segment and their Ws (what I *want* to know) on another caterpillar body segment. After completing the story, they listed their Ls (What I *learned*) on a third caterpillar body segment (see Figure 14.11 for the K–W–L caterpillar). Then, with their preservice teacher's

**spatial
naturalist**

Figure 14.7 Letter to Gregory Cool

Dear Gregory, November 10, 1998
Try to express your feelings. And speak out.
Don't be embarassed to tell anybody your feelings.
Let Lennox help you learn new things.
Care about what you have to eat, drink, and
where to sleep. Eat your food. Dont be afraid
to try new things. Be yourself. Give new
things a chance. Don't hide from your real
feelings. Gregory don't be afraid to stay
with your grandparents. Let Lennox teach you
how to climb a tree a get a coconut. Give
new things a chance and don't be afraid.
PS. Don't be afraid.

truely yours
Megan L.

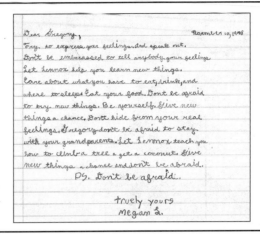

help, the students created their own very hungry caterpillar (see Figure 14.12). The first-graders also contacted Eric Carle through his e-mail address: fanclub@eric-carle.com.

LINKING LITERACY LESSONS WITH DRAMA ENACTMENTS

We recognize that drama activities "support every aspect of [students' language and] literacy development" (McMaster, 1998, p. 575). Because the benefits of dramatizations are so wide-ranging, it is not surprising that some scholars consider drama the nucleus of oral

Figure 14.8 Letter to Gregory Cool

Dear Gregory,

I like when you say the word cool, I have been whondering if you are real, like alive thats what I mean and also I have been whondering if you can help me whith my problems like, well really I want my mom to get a man, because I want a dad but she dose not want a man and you can try to not hide your feelings. Can you help me with my ather problems? O.K. now my ather problem is my two best friends well really three of my friends are some times they are mean to me. One of my friends is Brittany and I am, Chelsea and today this boy he gave me me christed me and then he asked Chelsea if she wanted it and she said yes. you have a good story!

from: Ashley Ladner
to: Gregory

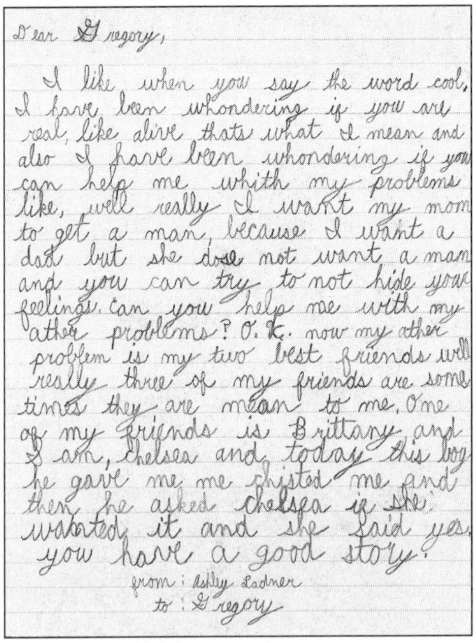

Figure 14.9 Letter to Gregory Cool

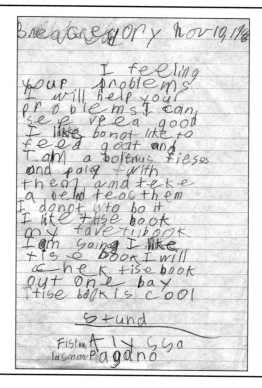

and written language expansion for all students, including those who struggle with reading and writing and those who are linguistically and culturally diverse (Edminston, Encisco, & King, 1987). For example, drama encourages a variety of meaningful communication skills, including oral language, listening abilities, creative writing, and interpretations of authors' works. Drama enactments also provide a venue for students to experience and understand how characters feel and think and to participate in imaginary, desired adventures. In addition, dramatizations increase students' motivation for learning because

Figure 14.10 Letter to Gregory Cool

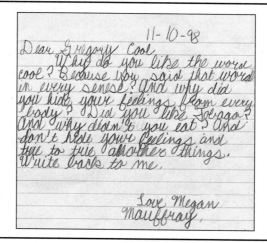

Figure 14.11   K–W–L Caterpillar

they get to experience the social aspects of language (Gardner, 1983). Further, peers, teachers, and parents recognize, appreciate, and applaud their efforts and talents. Because of the wide-ranging benefits of drama activities, our preservice teachers strive to integrate reading and writing lessons with Readers Theatre (see the SLL box), choral reading, puppet shows, scripted plays, improvisational scenes, and videotaped "television shows"

Figure 14.12   One Student's Caterpillar

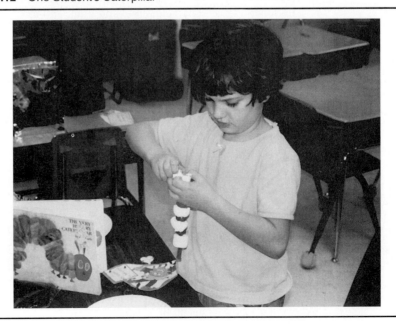

A Focus on SLL: Choral Reading and Readers Theatre

Children's literature books are very useful in reinforcing standard English word patterns. For example, with Gag's *Millions of Cats* (1928), students can perform a choral reading of "Hundreds of cats, thousands of cats, millions and billions and trillions of cats" (practicing plural suffixes) while experiencing an interesting parable that also teaches values. Our students can practice *-ed* and *-er* suffixes while doing choral readings of parts of *Drummer Hoff* (Emberly, 1967) as part of a thematic unit on military history. While teachers should focus on the aesthetic, meaningful experience that literature allows, the acquisition of standard structures can be an important by-product of an authentic literary experience. Students who use only workbooks are deprived of the richness of language, culture, and thinking that literature provides. Choral reading activities with various predictable plot books or books with rhymes are useful for facilitating the literacy development of second language learners especially.

The following stories contain repetitive lines and/or predictable patterns. Choral reading allows students to read within the safety of a group; thus, they are more likely to take risks. Students who cannot read independently can participate successfully by orally "reading" the lines of repetition they recall from memory.

dePaola, Tomie. (1975). *Strega Nona*. Upper Saddle River, NJ: Prentice-Hall.

Martin, Bill Jr. (1983). *Brown Bear, Brown Bear, What Do You See?* New York: Holt.

Martin, Bill Jr. (1991). *Polar Bear, What Do You Hear?* New York: Holt.

Peek, Merle. (1985). *Mary Wore Her Red Dress (and Henry Wore His Green Sneakers)*. New York: Ticknor & Fields.

Soule, Jean Conder. (1964). *Never Tease a Weasel*. New York: Parents Magazine Press.

In addition, the use of Readers Theatre can be of special benefit to second language learners. Readers Theatre has been defined as the oral presentation of drama, prose, or poetry by two or more readers. Students begin by reading a story, then transform the story into a script, formulate and refine their interpretations, and finally, perform their reading for an audience.

The steps for preparing a Readers Theatre production follow.

1. Select a story or part of a story. Good sources of materials are children's books with lots of dialog or plays that can be used without the proscribed stage directions. Other sources include folk tales, myths, fantasy or fairy tales, and even poetry. Also see Aaron Shepards' website at http://www.aaronshep.com/rt/ for prepared scripts in a variety of languages.

2. Script writing begins once the selection has been read. Students are able to include their own ideas about the characters and events as they begin to write the dialog.

3. Rehearsal of the script includes repeated readings to help the students use techniques such as intonation and characterization to bring their reading roles to life. A good technique is to ask them to "become" the character and use their imaginations to answer questions not only about the character's personality, but also about what is happening to the character in the story. These "who," "what," "when," and "where" questions help to develop thoughts, intentions, and feelings for what is happening and where the action is occurring.

4. Performance is the fun part. It can be as simple as a brief presentation for the class, or as elaborate as a stage production for other classes and parents. Parts are always read, not memorized.

5. Evaluation of the experience and follow-up commentary often reveals greater understanding of the characters, setting, and plot development because the students have not only read the material, but have also experienced it.

whenever possible. We stress early in the semester that drama activities do not have to entail complex extravaganzas. They can range from simple, spontaneous story enactments and **dramatic play** to formal productions that require scripts, rehearsals, and costumes.

Choral Reading

interpersonal

One spontaneous whole-group choral reading occurred when three preservice teachers and their second- and third-grade students collaborated in reading the story of *The Three Billy Goats Gruff* (a Brothers Grimm tale retold by Southgate, 1968). The irritated troll's repetitive question, "Who's that trip-trapping over my bridge?," especially appealed to the students, who began to chime in whenever the troll repeated the line in the story. Soon, all of our tutorial students and preservice teachers gathered around the group to add their "troll" voices to the troll's question. When the students asked to do the story again, preservice teachers and sixth-graders served as narrators; kindergarten and first-grade students took the first billy goat's part; second-graders took the second billy goat's part; and third-graders took the third billy goat's part. Fourth- and fifth-graders played the part of the grumpy troll.

A More Formal Drama Enactment

bodily-kinesthetic

A more formal drama enactment materialized when sixth-graders followed their theme of "Space and Spaces" and decided to create a television newsroom, complete with a weather forecaster, two news anchors, and three news reporters reporting "live" from outer space assignments. To add authenticity to the newsroom, the preservice teachers decided to tape the production over several weeks. Then they invited all of the students and preservice teachers in the program to view the edited tape that ended with scenes of the numerous, humorous "bloopers" that occurred during the taping. The newsroom student "crew" enjoyed the drama activity so much that the preservice teachers bought each student a copy of the tape to keep as a memento. In addition, the preservice teachers arranged for newscasters from the local television news channel to visit the after-school program and share information about how the daily news is produced and directed.

A Scripted, Rehearsed Puppet Show

spatial
bodily-kinesthetic

The idea for a scripted and rehearsed puppet show emerged from the book *Saint George and the Dragon* (Hodges, 1990). Two preservice teachers and their fifth-grade students constructed the puppet stage from a large discarded board they found behind a local grocery store. After covering the board with dark green paper, and sketching a castle scene on the paper with chalk and tempera paint, the preservice teachers drilled holes at various places in the board so that students could simultaneously use the top of the board and the drilled holes to enable their sock puppet characters to interact. The dragon puppet was especially striking. It was created from a bright electric-green-and-black striped sock. Black buttons formed the dragon's eyes and a red triangular piece of felt served as the dragon's glistening tongue. Since the students became fascinated with dragons, the preservice teachers extended the story reading and drama production into a three-week unit of instruction about dragons. Teachers and students used the Internet to obtain photographs and facts about Komodo dragons. They visited the library to get *National Geographic* photos and maps about Komodo dragons, and wrote in their dialogue journals from the points of view of dragons, dragon slayers, people chased by dragons, and friendly dragon families.

LINKING LITERACY LESSONS WITH MUSIC

Many teachers recognize that "the melodic and rhythmical features of language are a valuable means of creative thinking" (Piazza, 1999, p. 63; see also Gardner, 1983; Jackendoff, 1995; Lerdah, 1996). Music enhances students' creativity by activating forgotten ideas and experiences and generating novel adventures, thoughts, and visual images.

Music reminds students of special trips they have taken; favorite friends and relatives; cherished pets; and memorable films, video, and story characters. Music also provides opportunities for students who experience difficulty with reading and writing to think and learn through another language that is repetitive, melodious, and emotional.

Infusing Music into Every Teaching Session

musical

Preservice teachers in our program infuse music into every teaching session by taking turns bringing in tapes and compact discs of classical music. Played as soft background music, the sonatas, etudes, concertos, and symphonies add an ambience of peacefulness, unity, and creativity to our workplace. Our students and preservice teachers also learn to appreciate a broad spectrum of classical music. As the semester progresses, they request their favorite pieces to be played and tell us which sections of the music they particularly enjoy.

Enjoyment and Informality

As is the case with most literacy/arts initiatives, enjoyment and informality are important ingredients when linking literacy lessons with music. Teachers who are reluctant to sing aloud in front of an audience can use taped instrumental or vocal music selections to set the mood for students' storytelling or to provide background music as students personally respond to literature read or heard. Famous pop vocalists such as Little Richard and Ella Fitzgerald offer "movement-oriented song collections on tape and CD for children" (Cornett, 1999, p. 389). In addition, many fine compact discs combine music with dancing, such as the Hokey Pokey (Knapp & Knapp, 1976) and the Twist. Teachers and students also can use rhythm instruments to provide atmosphere and sound effects as students create or recreate stories (e.g., finger cymbals, tambourines, bells, sticks, small

musical

drums, and xylophones). Song lyrics can be made available so students can read along as they sing.

A Chant with Rhyming Words

Three preservice teachers and their fourth-grade students linked the dramatic arts with music when they performed a skit based upon the story *Double Trouble in Walla Walla* (Clements, 1997). Modeling the characters in the book who speak in rhymes, the preservice teachers and student actors also used rhyming words (e.g., *nit-wit, okey-dokey, wowie-zowie, jeepers-creepers*). Then, as the book explains, without warning, hundreds of

musical

rhyming words began to fill the air. Rather than merely repeating all of these rhyming words, the students had fun and played with language. Beating small drums, stamping their feet, and snapping their fingers faster and faster, they chanted,[4] "Fuzzy-wuzzy, fuddy-duddy, loosey-goosey, lovey-dovey, kissy-kissy, huggy-huggy, rink-a-dink-a-doo, ga-ga, rah-rah, go-go, so-so, frou-frou, goo-goo, pooh-pooh, wooh-wooh, rinky-dinky, arf-arf, argy-bargy, woof-woof, boogie-woogie, bow-wow, rinky-dinky, clippity-cloppity,

---

[4] Extending across cultures and traditions, "a chant is a type of verbal performance, half speech, half song" (Piazza, 1999, p. 81).

hippity-hoppity, clickity-clackety, rickety-rackety, blah-blah-blah, baa-baa-baa, ha-ha-ha, clip-clop, drip-drop, click-clack, rick-rack, eager-beaver, lucky-ducky, comfy-dumfy, fat-cat, hee-haw, tweet-tweet, chirp-chirp, cheep-cheep, cluck-cluck, quack-quack, rick-rack, eager-beaver, hee-haw, yuk, yuk, yuk!"

Content Reading and Music

As part of theme-based activities centered on a specific period in U.S. history, four pre-service teachers united their groups of fifth-grade students to read about the Revolutionary War. Determined to culminate the reading lesson with a music activity, prior to the lesson, the preservice teachers and their students accessed the Internet to locate a song that was popular during that time period. To ensure the lesson's success, the preservice teachers carefully planned what each of their responsibilities would be during the actual teaching session. One preservice teacher introduced the lesson by modeling the PreP pre-reading strategy (Langer, 1981), and then having the students participate. A second preservice teacher modeled the SQ3R reading comprehension strategy (Robinson, 1970) and then helped the students survey, question, read, recite, and review during the reading assignment. A third preservice teacher served as the scribe, writing the students' questions and responses on an overhead projector. The fourth preservice teacher was responsible for the post-reading music activity. She prepared copies of the song "Yankee Doodle" and served as song leader. After singing "Yankee Doodle" through once, the students spontaneously decided to add their own choreographed[5] movements to the music. They held hands and circled left and right, moved into the center of their circle, marched, bowed, jumped, and stamped their feet. Then they performed the song with their original choreographed actions for all of our program participants to enjoy.

musical bodily-kinesthetic

A Native American Song with "Talking Hands"

After reading a social studies chapter entitled "The First People in Mississippi," another group of preservice teachers and their fourth-grade students were inspired to weave literacy with music by connecting the ideas in the chapter about Native Americans with the contemporary folk song "Go My Son" (as performed by Rainer, 1994). The lyrics depict a Native American mother who encourages her son to get an education. The students and preservice teachers agreed to use a taped version of the song to accompany and help reinforce their singing. They discovered that the publishers of the compact disc had included drawings and directions showing how to use hand movements (i.e., talking hands) similar to authentic Native American "signs." The signs portrayed the ideas in the song. The students voted to learn the authentic Native American hand signs to accompany their singing. They were so pleased with their efforts that they decided to present their work in a formal setting. They wrote letters inviting friends and family to the presentation, designed and constructed Native American costumes and scenery, and created programs with Native American scenes as focal points (also see *Indian Signals and Sign Language,* Fronval & Dubois, 1994).

musical bodily-kinesthetic

---

[5] Originally created by Raoul Fuillet in 1701, choreography is the detailed planning and "writing down" or coding of a dance. "The word *choreography* comes from the Greek *khoros,* meaning dancing, and *graphia,* meaning writing" (Piazza, 1999, p. 133).

LINKING LITERACY WITH DANCE

Dancers use their bodies to communicate nonverbally. Therefore, harmonizing literacy events with dance improvisations and more structured dance enactments are ideal alternatives for inspiring and liberating corrective reading students who may struggle with oral and written language. Dancing provides freedom for students to take risks, use their imaginations, and express themselves with confidence and joy. Dancing offers a way for students to internalize and convey complex ideas, emotions, and thinking through movement. In fact, "the expression of personal thoughts and feelings is central to creative dance" (Drewe, 1998, p. 41).

interpersonal

In addition to facilitating personal expressions and confidence, dance as an alternative language provides students with a venue for portraying complicated ideas about literature. For example, accompanied by appropriate music, students can communicate encompassing moods depicted in stories, such as Jamie's deep sadness about her grandmother's death in the Native American story *Fox Song* (Bruchac, 1993), or the feistiness and gumption of Margaret, the physically challenged primary student in *The Balancing Girl* (Rabe, 1981). Dance also provides opportunities for students to portray characters' goals and actions, and to use their imaginations and bodily-kinesthetic intelligence to communicate alternative resolutions and endings to fairytales, fables, folktales, and chapter books.

Unfortunately, dance is excluded from educational curricula in many schools (Drewe, 1998). Yet a significant amount of research indicates that kinesthetic movement, such as dance, is central to language development (Bruner, 1966; Piaget & Inhelder, 1969; Vygotsky, 1978). In addition, dance and movement enhance students' problem-solving abilities, concentration, memory, and imagination (Eisner, 1981; Gardner, 1983; Greene, 1988; Jensen, 1998; Montessori, 1967; Vygotsky, 1978). Dancing also can serve to unite students' motor and cognitive understanding (Cecil & Lauritzen, 1994). Further, as a distinctive mode of expressing knowledge and feelings, dance provides an alternative way for students from diverse cultures and heritages to successfully contribute to class projects and group collaborations.

Spontaneous Dance

bodily-kinesthetic

Soft background music plays continually during our after-school corrective reading program. As a result, students often dance spontaneously as they enter our workplace, engage in visual arts activities, or move from one learning group to another. It is also quite common for preservice teachers to express their joyful feelings through dance as they set up their teaching supplies prior to lessons. Good music, freedom of expression, and the program's positive, creative climate serve as a stimulus for all types of spontaneous dance enactments.

Envisioning the Solar System through Dance

More structured dance opportunities also are intentionally integrated into our literacy lessons whenever applicable. However, we are not interested in students practicing and performing formal dance routines. Rather, we are committed to enriching students' literacy development through personal, uninhibited dance expressions. For example, a group of preservice teachers decided that dance would serve as the perfect vehicle for enhancing fourth-grade students' background knowledge prior to reading informational text about the solar system. Combining the visual arts with writing and dance, the preservice teachers created and labeled cardboard models of the planets, sun, and moon (e.g., "This is Venus"; "Here is Mars"; "Jupiter has 16 moons"). Then, with assistance from the preservice teachers, the students held up their models and moved according to their particular sun, moon, or planet positions in the solar system. After a few practice sessions, **musical** the group added "outer space"-type music to the prereading activity which helped to optimize the lesson. The students began to move gracefully in time to the music. They became so captivated by the activity that they created their individual interpretations of a **bodily-kinesthetic** planet, sun, and moon dance. Some students twirled slowly in circles. Others moved their outstretched arms high and low. A few soared dramatically into "outer space." Of course, all of our program participants enjoyed viewing the novel solar system dance. At the same time, all our corrective reading students enhanced their background knowledge about the movements and positions of the sun, moon, and planets.

Dance of the Birds, Reptiles, and Mammals

Another very successful dance exploration served to culminate a thematic unit that focused on how animals grow and change. To initiate the unit, three preservice teachers and their sixth-grade students collaborated in assembling a very extensive fiction and in**naturalist** formational **text set** about all types of animals. They also used the Internet to research answers to questions: How are animals classified? How do animals grow and change? How do individual animals move? What are the differences among birds, reptiles, and mammals?

As the students read, discovered, and discussed information, they also generated and recorded questions that arose during their study: How can you tell if turtles have backbones? If birds' feathers keep birds warm, why do tropical birds have so many feathers and why don't birds lose their feathers in the summer? If reptiles are cold-blooded, why don't they freeze in the winter in cold climates?

After locating the answers to their questions through considerable inquiry and exploration, the students created murals that depicted how animals could be classified. They also produced a student newspaper as a venue for sharing their knowledge about animals. As a culminating activity, the sixth-graders voted to present a "Dance of the Birds, Reptiles, and Mammals" for all program participants. The students each chose an **musical** animal they wished to represent. Then they brought in tapes of music that sparked their imaginations and helped them formulate ideas for their individual mammal, bird, or reptile dance. Soaring, free music represented birds. Mysterious, slow music exemplified **bodily-kinesthetic** cold-blooded animals. Happy, graceful music portrayed dolphins and whales. During the dance presentation, students wore costumes they created from crepe paper and cardboard. Following the performance, as a special treat, they served "animal" food to the audience, such as animal crackers, "spiders" made of chocolate-covered marshmallows with licorice legs, jellied candy "worms" and "fish" suspended in green Jello, and a "dolphin" cake made from blue icing.

SUMMARY

This chapter explains how artistic pursuits can meet the needs of all literacy learners, including emergent readers, students of all ages who struggle with reading and writing, those with well-developed multiple intelligences, and students who come from diverse ethnic and linguistic backgrounds. The chapter also discusses how integrating literacy events with the arts is supported by newer conceptions of literacy (i.e., multiple literacies), and is validated by numerous areas of research (e.g., brain development, Zone of Proximal Development, MI Theory, Reader Response Theory). In addition, the chapter describes introductory activities that help nurture and develop preservice teachers' and corrective reading students' abilities to link literacy events with artistic pursuits. The core of the chapter explains the benefits of the visual arts, dramatic arts, music, and dance in a corrective reading program, and presents authentic lessons that weave literacy instruction with the arts.

It is important to remember that literacy is more than reading and writing. In the twenty-first century, we recognize many forms of literacy, to include all types of media. The communicative arts now includes print, technology, and the visual and performing arts. To deny students access to all forms of literacy will limit the ways students can construct meaning, learn, think, and demonstrate their knowledge and abilities. It is time we endorse the view that there are many paths to literacy, especially for students who have been devalued due to their lack of success with the printed word. It is up to knowledgeable educators to find a way for these students to succeed. The arts may very well provide the path to success for many of our struggling readers.

Suggested Readings

Blecher, S., & Jaffee, K. (1998). *Weaving in the arts: Widening the learning circle.* Portsmouth, NH: Heinemann.
> *This most readable book offers new ways for classroom teachers to include music, dance, poetry, and the visual arts in their literacy instruction. The fine arts are viewed as a methodology for helping students interpret what they know and understand.*

Morado, C., Koenig, R., & Wilson, A. (1999). Miniperformances, many stars! Playing with stories. *The Reading Teacher, 53,* 116–123.
> *This article describes a program for at-risk students that integrates literature, drama, music, and movement to support literacy development. Examples are provided, as is a list of children's literature appropriate for such miniperformances.*

Piazza, C. (1999). *Multiple forms of literacy: Teaching literacy and the arts.* Columbus, OH: Merrill.
> *This book creates a bridge between arts specialists and classroom teachers responsible for teaching literacy. It serves as a great resource for ideas that link literacy and the arts.*

Richards, J., & Gipe, J. (2000). "First we read a great book": Interfacing literacy instruction with the arts in two urban elementary schools: Preservice teachers' case quandaries and accomplishments. *Research in the Schools, 7* (2), 11–20.
> *This article provides a glimpse of the successes and dilemmas expressed by preservice teachers trying to integrate the arts into their literacy instruction. Several actual cases are presented so readers can anticipate the kinds of problems they might experience in trying to incorporate the arts into their teaching.*

 Weekly Progress Report

Come to school on time	4	3	2	1	Gets to school on time	4	3	2	1
Stay on task/pay attention	4	3	2	1	On task/pays attention	4	3	2	1
Do my best	4	3	2	1	Does his/her best	4	3	2	1
Read and write each day	4	3	2	1	Reads/writes each day	4	3	2	1
Use new strategies	4	3	2	1	Applies new strategies	4	3	2	1
Cooperate with my teacher	4	3	2	1	Cooperates with me	4	3	2	1

Student comments: _____

_____

_____

_____

Teacher's comments: _____

_____

_____

_____

Parent comments:_____

_____

_____

_____

Date: _____   Signatures: _____   _____   _____

                              (student)   (teacher)   (parent/guardian)

B Useful Websites Related to Literacy Development

Web sites on the Internet are a rapidly changing phenomenon. Therefore, the following sites have been chosen because they: (1) appear to be relatively stable, (2) offer a wealth of information and links for additional related sites, and (3) can serve both teacher and students well. Well-known directories and search engines such as Google, Yahoo!, Alta Vista, and Yahooligans are recommended.

Aaron Shepard's RT Page
http://www.aaronshep.com/rt/
Resource for Readers Theater scripts for young readers as well as college and professional readers.

American Library Association (ALA)
http://www.ala.org/parents/index.html
Provides Web resources for parents, teens, and young children.

Children's Literature Web Guide
http://www.acs.ucalgary.ca/~dkbrown
A comprehensive Internet resource related to books for children and young adult readers. Also includes links to stories written by children and Readers Theatre scripts, as well as authors' and illustrators' Web pages.

Cyberkids
http://www.cyberkids.com/
Cyberkids is a magazine for kids that solicits children's writing, art, and even musical compositions, making it a wonderful outlet for teachers who try to accommodate students' multiple intelligences. This is also a great location for student free-reading time. Click on Creative Works and check out Stories.

DiscoverySchool.com
http://www.school.discovery.com/
Offers education links for teachers, students, and parents as well as guides to channel offerings.

Global Schoolhouse
http://www.gsh.org/
Sponsored by Lightspan.com, this site is a great source for online collaboration projects.

Helping Your Child Learn to Read
http://www.ed.gov/pubs/parents/Reading/index.html
Useful information for teachers to print out for parents or to have available for parent-teacher conferences. The site also contains information about writing.

International Reading Association
http://www.reading.org/
The most important source of information about the largest professional group devoted to literacy.

The JASON Project

http://www.jasonproject.org/

This site provides a year-long electronic field trip, giving students the opportunity to participate in science, history, and anthropological activities. Each year the project explores a new location. This past year JASON XII: Hawaii—A Living Laboratory fit nicely with our "At the Beach" theme, as did several previous JASON projects. The site offers access to information obtained from the previous projects.

Kathy Schrock's Guide for Educators

http://www.school.discovery.com/schrockguide

A well-known site that helps teachers use search engines and directories for finding valuable educational information on the Internet.

KidLink

http://www.kidlink.org/

This international Web site is designed for K–12 students as a place to communicate with students around the world. Students can also find an electronic pen pal through this site.

Library of Congress

http://lcweb.loc.gov/

Library exhibits, indexes, historic collections, and congressional information are readily available. One literacy example: Locate Abraham Lincoln's "rough draft" of the Gettysburg Address to demonstrate how all writers go through the revision process (http://www.loc.gov/exhibits/gadd/gadrft.html).

Little Explorers

http://www.enchantedlearning.com/dictionary.html

This site makes it easy for young students to find Web sites that have been screened for appropriate content. The format is that of a picture dictionary, with new picture entries continuously being added. The picture provides the link to related Web sites. Dictionaries for French, German, Portuguese, and Spanish are also available.

National Gallery of Art

http://www.nga.gov/education/education.htm

This site provides a complete listing of the museum's programs and resources for teachers as well as links to other areas of the museum.

Scholastic Publishing

http://scholastic.com/

Extensive site for teachers, kids, and parents. Visit each category.

Smithsonian Institution

http://www.si.edu

Electronic exhibits and information on activities throughout the Smithsonian museum complex.

Stone Soup

http://www.stonesoup.com/

Stone Soup is an international magazine for children up to age 13. Students visiting this site can read stories and poems written by other children. Directions are provided for students who wish to submit their own work. This site is definitely worth visiting.

T.H.E. Journal Educator's Road Map to the Internet
http://www.thejournal.com/features/rdmap/
This site provides hundreds of links organized by categories of interest to educators.

WebMuseum Network
http://sunsite.unc.edu/wm/
Access to worldwide art museums, exhibits, artist profiles, and an online tour of Paris.

APPENDIX

C IRA/NCTE Standards for the English Language Arts

The vision guiding these standards is that all students must have the opportunities and resources to develop the language skills they need to pursue life's goals and to participate fully as informed, productive members of society. These standards assume that literacy growth begins before children enter school as they experience and experiment with literacy activities—reading and writing and associating spoken words with their graphic representations. Recognizing this fact, these standards encourage the development of curriculum and instruction and make productive use of the emerging literacy abilities that children bring to school. Furthermore, the standards provide ample room for the innovation and creativity essential to teaching and learning. They are not prescriptions for particular curriculum or instruction.

Although we present these standards as a list, we want to emphasize that they are not distinct and separable; they are in fact, interrelated and should be considered as a whole.

1. Students read a wide range of print and nonprint texts to build an understanding of texts, of themselves, and of the cultures of the United States and the world; to acquire new information; to respond to the needs and demands of society and the workplace; and for personal fulfillment. Among these texts are fiction and nonfiction, classic and contemporary works.

2. Students read a wide range of literature from many periods in many genres to build an understanding of the many dimensions (e.g., philosophical, ethical, aesthetic) of human experience.

3. Students apply a wide range of strategies to comprehend, interpret, evaluate, and appreciate texts. They draw on their prior experience, their interactions with other readers and writers, their knowledge of word meaning and of other texts, their word identification strategies, and their understanding of textual features (e.g., sound-letter correspondence, sentence structure, context, graphics).

4. Students adjust their use of spoken, written, and visual language (e.g., conventions, style, vocabulary) to communicate effectively with a variety of audiences and for different purposes.

5. Students employ a wide range of strategies as they write and use different writing process elements appropriately to communicate with different audiences for a variety of purposes.

6. Students apply knowledge of language structure, language conventions (e.g., spelling and punctuation), media techniques, figurative language, and genre to create, critique, and discuss print and nonprint texts.

7. Students conduct research on issues and interests by generating ideas and questions, and by posing problems. They gather, evaluate, and synthesize data from a variety of sources (e.g., print and nonprint texts, artifacts, people) to communicate their discoveries in ways that suit their purpose and audience.

8. Students use a variety of technological and informational resources (e.g., libraries, databases, computer networks, video) to gather and synthesize information and to create and communicate knowledge.

9. Students develop an understanding of and respect for diversity in language use, patterns, and dialects across cultures, ethnic groups, geographic regions, and social roles.

10. Students whose first language is not English make use of their first language to develop competency in the English language arts and to develop understanding of content across the curriculum.

11. Students participate as knowledgeable, reflective, creative, and critical members of a variety of literacy communities.

12. Students use spoken, written, and visual language to accomplish their own purposes (e.g., for learning, enjoyment, persuasion, and the exchange of information).

D Books to Build the Self-Esteem of Students in Multiethnic Settings

A disproportionate number of ethnic students, a large number of whom are African Americans, do not learn to read and write successfully (Hoover & Fabian, 2000; Ogbu, 1987). The reasons are complex. But part of the reason may involve a historical lack of role models within the cultural group who have improved their lot in life as a result of academic success (Ogbu, 1987). Literacy instruction for African American and other ethnic groups needs to assist them in meeting both personal and societal goals (Parks, 1987). Schools can change this condition; "multiethnic literature can be used in [classrooms] to affirm the cultural identity of students of diverse backgrounds, and to develop all students' understanding and appreciation of other cultures" (Au, 1993a, p. 176). Au (1993a) summarizes the benefits of using multiethnic literature:

- Students of diverse backgrounds feel pride in their own identity and heritage.
- Both mainstream students and students of diverse backgrounds learn about diversity and the complexity of American society.
- All students gain more complete and balanced views of the historical forces that shaped American society.
- All students can explore issues of social justice. (p. 178)

Teachers and school librarians must seek out "literature that accurately reflects a group's culture, language, history, and values" (Au, 1993a, p. 176). The following bibliography is intended to help teachers of all grade levels in their search for quality children's literature. The books mentioned can be read either *by* students or *to* students.

Following is a partial list from a more extensive bibliography[1] available in the Instructor's Manual that accompanies this text. The author gives course instructors prior permission to duplicate this bibliography for their students.

African American Literature

Picture Books

Pickney, Sandra. (2000). *Shades of black*. New York: Scholastic.

Altman, Linda, (2000). *The legend of Freedom Hill*. New York: Lee & Low.

Easy Fiction

Cameron, Ann. (2000). *Gloria's way*. New York: Farrar Strauss.

Greenfield, Eloise. (1993). *Talk about a family*. New York: Harper.

---

[1] This bibliography was prepared by Coleen C. Salley, professor emeritus at the University of New Orleans and respected children's literature expert.

Fiction, Middle School

Bolden, Tonya. (1996). *Just family*. New York: Penguin.

Pinkney, Andrea. (1996). *Hold fast to dreams*. New York: Simon & Schuster.

Folktales

Medearis, Angela. (1996). *Tailpo*. New York: Holiday.

San Souci, Robert. (1996). *The house in the sky*. New York: Dial.

Poetry

Greenfield, Eloise. (1996). *For the love of the game, Michael Jackson and me*. New York: Harper.

Grimes, Nikki. (1994). *Meet Danitra Brown*. New York: Lothrop.

Nonfiction

Cooper, Floyd. (1996). *Mandela*. NY: Putnam.

Parks, Rosa. (1996). *Dear Mrs. Parks: A dialogue with today's youth*. New York: Lee & Low.

Asian-Pacific American Literature

Picture Books

Wahl, Jan. (2000). *Three pandas*. Honesdale, PA: Boyds Mill.

Wong, Janet. (2000). *The trip back home*. New York: Harcourt Brace.

Fiction

Dalkey, Kara. (1996). *Little sister*. New York: Harcourt.

Yep, Laurence. (1995). *The ghost fox*. New York: Scholastic.

Folklore

Lee, Jeanne. (2000). *I once was a monkey*. New York: Farrar Strauss.

Sierra, Judy. (2000). *The gift of the crocodile: A Cinderella story*. New York: Simon & Schuster.

Nonfiction

Cha, Dia. (1996). *Dia's story cloth: The Hmong people's journey of freedom*. New York: Lee & Low.

Kuklin, Susan. (1995). *Kodomo*. New York: Putnam.

Poetry

Ho, Minfong. (1996). *Maples in the mist*. New York: Lothrop.

Myers, Walter Dean. (1995). *Glorious angels*. New York: Harper.

Latin American/Mexican American Literature

Picture Books

Anaya, Rudolfo. (2000). *Favorite's for Abuelo*. New York: Hyperion.

Freschet, Gina. (2000). *Naty's parade*. New York: Farrar Strauss.

Nonfiction

Ancona, George. (1996). *Fiesta U.S.A*. New York: Penguin.

Patent, Dorothy. (1996). *Quetzal*. New York: Morrow.

Folklore

Dclacrc, Lulu. (1996). *Golden tales: Myths, legends, and folktales from Latin America*. New York: Scholastic.

Montes, Marisa. (2000). *Juan Bobo goes to work*. New York: HarperCollins.

Easy Fiction

Hurwitz, Johanna. (1990). *Class president*. New York: Morrow.

Stanley, Diane. (1996). *Elena*. New York: Hyperion.

Holiday

Cowley, Joy. (1996). *Gracias*. New York: Scholastic. (Thanksgiving)

Winter, Jeanette. (1996). *Josefina*. New York: Harcourt. (Christmas)

Poetry

Delacre, Lulu. (1989). *Arroz con Leche: Popular songs and rhymes for Latin America*. New York: Scholastic.

Medina, Jane. (2000). *My name is Jorge*. Honesdale, PA: Boyds Mill.

Native American Literature

Picture Books

Schick, Eleanor. (1996). *My Navajo sister*. New York: Simon & Schuster.

Wood, Douglas. (1996). *Northwoods cradle song*. New York: Simon & Schuster.

Folklore

Bruchac, Joseph. (1985). *Iroquois stories: Heroes and heroines, monsters and magic*. Freedom, CA: The Crossing. (Also: cassette tape, 1988)

Goble, Paul. (1996). *Remaking the earth*. New York: Orchard.

Poetry

Bruchac, Joseph. (1995). *The earth under Sky Bear's feet*. New York: Putnam.

Philip, Neil. (1996). *Earth always endures*. New York: Viking.

Fiction

Sneve, Virginia Driving Hawk. (1995). *High Elk's treasure*. New York: Holiday.

Whelan, Gloria. (1996). *The Indian school*. New York: Harper.

Nonfiction

Freedman, Russell. (1996). *The life and death of Crazy Horse*. New York: Holiday.

Hucko, Bruce. (1996). *A rainbow at night: The world in words and pictures by Navajo children*. San Francisco: Chronicle Books.

APPENDIX

E Text Readability

Readability refers to the difficulty level of printed material. Low readability means the material is difficult to read; however, an index for such material will be a high number often given in terms of grade level. Likewise, material with high readability (easy to read) will be reflected by a low index.

Several factors affect the readability of material: the number of difficult or new words, the length and complexity of sentences, the number of new or unfamiliar concepts, the organization and cohesion of the material, the reader's background knowledge for reading the material, and even the material's appearance.

Thus, the use of any readability index as the sole determinant of a book's appropriateness is not advised. However, if the teacher uses the index in conjunction with other factors affecting readability, determining the readability index of a material can be a valuable and valid exercise (Fry, 1989).

Several methods can be used to determine readability. You will be provided with directions for using three methods: Fry's Graph for Estimating Readability (Figure E.1), the Raygor Readability Estimate (Figure E.2), and the cloze procedure (Figure E.3).

FRY'S GRAPH

When using Fry's graph, be aware that grade-level scores are most valid near the center line on the graph. Scores falling in the gray areas are invalid, and additional samples may be needed. Fry's estimates are considered accurate to within plus or minus one year of the true estimate of readability.

For material that is shorter than 100 words, Forgan and Mangrum (1985, pp. 31–32) provide the following directions for using the Fry graph.

1. Count the total number of words in the selection and round down to the nearest ten. For example, if there are forty-four words in your selection, use only the first forty to count the number of syllables and sentences.

2. Count the number of syllables and sentences in the selected words.

3. Multiply the total number of sentences and syllables by the number in the conversion chart that corresponds with the number of words in your selection.

4. Refer to Fry's graph, as shown in Figure E.1, to find the grade-level band that indicates the readability level.

Conversion chart for Fry's Graph for Selections of Fewer than 100 Words

If the number of words in the selection is:	Multiply the number of syllables and sentences by:
30	3.3
40	2.5
50	2.0
60	1.67
70	1.43
80	1.25
90	1.1

RAYGOR RADABILITY ESTIMATE

For those who have a difficult time counting syllables, the Raygor graph is often preferred. With this graph, words of six or more letters are counted as long words. The other procedures used are identical to those of Fry, except numerals are *not* counted when using Raygor.

CLOZE PROCEDURE FOR READABILTY/SUITABILITY

The difficulty or ease with which material can be read can also be determined by means of the cloze procedure (Bormuth, 1968; Taylor, 1953). Use of the cloze procedure doesn't yield a readability estimate for the material; rather, it indicates the suitability of material for the student completing the cloze passage. Following the same guidelines for construction and scoring presented in Chapter 6, the example seen in Figure E.3 reveals a score of 70 percent accuracy. This material then would be suitable for this student even if teacher guidance is not available (i.e., a score above 50 percent indicates suitability at an independent level). A score of 30 to 50 percent indicates an instructional level that requires teacher guidance, and a score of less than 30 percent indicates that the material is unsuitable.

Figure E.1 Fry's Readability Graph

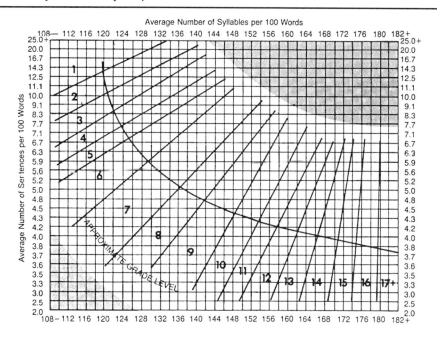

1. Randomly select three (3) sample passages and count out exactly 100 words each, beginning with the beginning of a sentence. *Do* count proper nouns, initializations, and numerals.
2. Count the number of sentences in the 100 words, estimating length of the fraction of the last sentence to the nearest one-tenth.
3. Count the total number of syllables in the 100-word passage. If you don't have a hand counter available, an easy way is to simply put a mark above every syllable over one in each word; then when you get to the end of the passage, count the number of marks and add 100. Small calculators can also be used as counters by pushing numeral 1, the + sign; then push the = sign for each word or syllable when counting.
4. Enter graph with *average* sentence length and *average* number of syllables: plot a dot where the two lines intersect. The area where the dot is plotted will give you the approximate grade level.
5. If a great deal of variability is found in syllable count or sentence count, putting more samples into the average is desirable.
6. A word is defined as a group of symbols with a space on either side; thus, *Joe, IRA, 1945,* and *&* are each one word.
7. A syllable is defined as a phonetic syllable. Generally, there are as many syllables as vowel sounds. For example, *stopped* is one syllable and *wanted* is two syllables. When counting syllables for numerals and initializations, count one syllable for each symbol. For example, *1945* is four syllables, *IRA* is three syllables, and *&* is one syllable.

Note: This "extended graph" does not outmode the earlier (1968) version or render it inoperative or inaccurate; it is an extension.

Figure E.2   The Raygor Graph

These are the directions for using the Raygor graph:

1. Count out three 100-word passages at the beginning, middle, and end of a book. Be sure to include proper nouns in your word count, but *do not* count numerals.

2. Count the number of sentences in each passage, estimating to the nearest tenth.

3. Circle and count the words having six or more letters. Words having six or more letters are defined as *long* (hard) words.

4. Average the sentence length and the number of long (hard) words over the three samples, and plot the average on the graph.

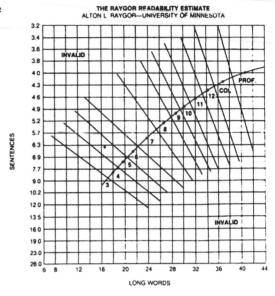

Figure E.3   Example of a Completed Cloze Passage for Readability

Directions: Skim through the entire passage *before* you begin to fill in the missing words Then go back and fill in as many words as you can.

According to Raths, one responsibility of a good teacher is preparing materials. All teachers recognize the _importance_ of available materials for _meeting_ individual needs of each _student_, so they prepare supplemental _materials_—handouts, review sheets, test _papers_, directions for assignments and _projects_, and summaries from magazines and _newspaper_ articles. Since students must _be_ able to read these _materials_, it is imperative that _teachers_ be able to write _them_ at appropriate reading levels.

Teachers often cannot understand why _their_ students fail an examination _after_ hours of teaching and reviewing. _These_ teachers claim the students _knew_ the answers the day _before_ the test, but on _the_ day of the test _they_ do not seem to _remember_ a thing! When one _examines_ the test items, it is relatively easy to understand _why_ students failed.

The same _problem_ arises if assignment sheets, _study_ outlines, summaries, or other _materials_ are too difficult for _students_. Both teachers and students _are_ frustrated because they are _not_ communicating. Teachers are often _confused_ about talking above the _heads_ of their students, and _must_ take equal caution with _written_ communication.

We are not _suggesting_ that content tea chers should _lower_ their course standards; rather _they_ should do a more _careful_ job of communicating so _their_ students can achieve high _grades_. Just as students do _not_ like teachers to talk _down_ to them, neither do _they_ enjoy materials that insult _their_ reading capabilities, nor do _they_ want to be confused // _by_ materials that are too _difficult_ to understand. Somewhere between these two extremes clear communication is possible (52 total deletions. // indicates the point at which 50 deletions have occurred.)

Actual words for items missed (in order of occurrence from left to right):
inadequacies   items   activities   some   knew   know
course   handouts   become   warned   levels
should   effective   the   standards

Source: Forgan, H. W., & Mangrum, C. T. (1985). *Teaching Content Area Reading Skills.* (3rd ed.) (p. 46). Columbus, OH: Prentice-Hall/Merrill.

Instructional Environment Survey

The following checklist is a compilation of several others previously developed for helping teachers critically examine their classroom environment (Glazer, 1992; Glazer & Brown, 1993; Vacca, Vacca, & Gove, 1991).

Directions: Check *Yes* if the item is currently true; check *Maybe* if you are interested in pursuing this item further; check *No* if the item is not true. Reflect upon the results of the survey after it is completed.

	Yes	*Maybe*	*No*
1. I know my students' interests.	_____	_____	_____
2. I know my students' attitudes and perceptions about reading and writing.	_____	_____	_____
3. My classroom has its own library including:			
a. trade books	_____	_____	_____
b. reference books	_____	_____	_____
c. student-authored books	_____	_____	_____
d. alternate text books	_____	_____	_____
4. I encourage my students to read and write recreationally by providing time for them to do so.	_____	_____	_____
5. There are places for small groups to work on reading and writing activities.	_____	_____	_____
6. There are places for individuals to work quietly.	_____	_____	_____
7. I share what I am reading and writing with my students.	_____	_____	_____
8. I encourage students to share their reading through:			
a. art	_____	_____	_____
b. drama	_____	_____	_____
c. speaking	_____	_____	_____
d. writing	_____	_____	_____
9. I tell students what I like about their work.	_____	_____	_____
10. I do not use reading as a punishment.	_____	_____	_____
11. I do not use writing as a punishment.	_____	_____	_____

12. I know some ways to integrate literature with reading and writing. _____ _____ _____

13. I know some ways to use trade books with pupils who have special needs or are from a culture diverse from my own. _____ _____ _____

14. My classroom contains:
   a. typewriters and/or computers _____ _____ _____
   b. chalkboard space for group writing _____ _____ _____
   c. large sheets of paper on wall for composing _____ _____ _____
   d. transparencies/overhead projector _____ _____ _____
   e. videotaping equipment (VCR & camera) _____ _____ _____
   f. Internet access _____ _____ _____
   g. Scanner or digital camera _____ _____ _____

15. My classroom has a listening center with tape recorders and headsets. _____ _____ _____

16. A variety of writing instruments are available to students, including:
   a. pencils/pens _____ _____ _____
   b. crayons/colored markers _____ _____ _____
   c. chalk/erasers _____ _____ _____
   d. computers/color printer

17. A variety of supplies are available to students, including:
   a. lined paper _____ _____ _____
   b. construction paper _____ _____ _____
   c. tissue paper _____ _____ _____
   d. crepe paper _____ _____ _____
   e. yarn/fabric _____ _____ _____
   f. scissors _____ _____ _____
   g. glue/paste _____ _____ _____
   h. tape, all types _____ _____ _____
   i. stapler/hole punch _____ _____ _____
   j. needle/thread _____ _____ _____

Levels of Analysis and Correlative Diagnostic Questions: A Summary

Level 1: Determining Lack of Success in Reading

- Is the learner experiencing a lack of success in reading?

Under what conditions or in what situations?
(This question should be asked after *every* diagnostic question that follows.)

Level 2: Determining the Domain(s) in Which Difficulty Occurs

- Does the learner demonstrate underdeveloped oral and/or written language ability?
- Does the learner have difficulty with word recognition?
- Does the learner have difficulty with comprehension of narrative text?
- Does the learner have difficulty with strategic reading of expository text or with study skills?

Level 3: Determining the Area(s) within the Domain(s)

Oral and Written Language Ability

- Does the learner demonstrate underdeveloped oral (i.e., speaking and/or listening) and/or written language ability?

Word Recognition

- Does the learner have a word recognition strategy?
- Does the learner have a limited sight vocabulary?
- Does the learner have difficulty in the area of word analysis, or decoding?
- Does the learner have difficulty using context clues?

Reading Comprehension and Strategic Reading for Narrative Text

- Does the learner have a limited meaning vocabulary?
- Does the learner have difficulty with thinking or problem-solving skills associated with comprehension of narrative text, such as identifying story features, predicting events, or evaluating a character's actions?
- Does the learner have difficulty recognizing his or her own inability to understand what was read?
- Does this apparent comprehension problem result from difficulty with word recognition?

---

[1]This appendix was designed and recommended by Dr. Ramona C. Moore, Western Washington University.

- Does the learner's apparent comprehension problem result from difficulty in strategic reading for expository text and/or study skills?

Strategic Reading for Expository Text and Study Skills

- Does the learner have difficulty with content-specific vocabulary?
- Does the learner have difficulty with content-specific skills, such as reading visual displays, formulas, or other unique symbols?
- Does the learner have difficulty recognizing whether the text is meaningful to him or her?
- Does the learner have difficulty locating information?
- Does the learner have difficulty organizing information?

Components Outside the Major Domains: Reading-Related Factors

- Does the learner demonstrate the influence of a factor related to reading?
- Has the learner had opportunities for reading and writing related to his or her needs and interests?
- Does the learner have a negative attitude toward reading?
- Does the learner lack interest in reading?
- If someone asked my students, "What is reading?" what would they say?
- Is my curriculum so skills-oriented that students never have the opportunity to read for their own purposes?
- Have I examined my own beliefs and attitudes about the way this learner might need to learn?
- Have I explored alternative instructional approaches that might benefit this learner?

 Gathering Affective Information

The corrective reading program must develop learners who read and who feel good about themselves and their reading ability. To promote positive reading attitudes, a teacher gathers information about students' attitudes and self-concepts. Efforts to change negative attitudes or reinforce positive attitudes proceed once a student's attitudes toward reading are known. A teacher gleans some of this information from observing students for such behaviors as (1) choosing to read a book during free time, (2) requesting that a book be read aloud, (3) checking out books from the library, (4) finishing books started, and (5) talking about books read. In addition, paper-and-pencil techniques provide more detailed information as well as a record of this information for interpretation.

The Incomplete Sentence Projective Test (Boning & Boning, 1957) presented here allows each student to write (or provide orally) information regarding how they feel about the item in question (Figure H.1). Responses may be more honest if the teacher tells students the information will be used to provide materials they will enjoy. Any interpretation should be modified and verified by observations over time.

Before administering the incomplete sentences, decide whether oral or written responses are most appropriate. Directions for an oral administration might be: "I will begin a sentence with a few words and then stop. When I stop, you tell me the very first thing that you think of to finish the sentence. I will write down just what you say. Let's do a practice sentence. I think pizza tastes _____ . Are you ready to begin?" Directions for a written administration might be: "Finish each sentence with the first idea that comes to your mind. Let's try the first one together."

In order to interpret the results, the following areas have been identified by item number.

Overall attitudes and self-concept: 1, 3, 4, 5, 8, 9, 14, 16, 19, 20, 22, 25, 27, 29, 30, 33, 35, 36, 38, 42

Family relations: 6, 11, 26, 31

School attitudes: 7, 10, 12, 18, 21, 24

Reading process: 2, 28, 32, 34, 37, 40, 41 (Boning and Boning [1957] found that the most revealing responses were to item 40.)

Reading interest: 13, 15, 17, 23 (Use item 17 to get clues for helping direct children toward increased recreational reading.)

Responses to the overall attitudes and self-concept area are very important to evaluate. They often provide insight into a student's academic problems. Some supplementary questions for the reading process and reading interest areas follow.

1. *Supplementary reading process questions:*
   a. Reading is . . .
   b. I cannot read when . . .
   c. When reading new words I . . .

Figure H.1   Incomplete Sentence Projective Test

1. Today I feel . . . .
2. When I have to read, I . . . .
3. I get angry when . . . .
4. To be grown up . . . .
5. My idea of a good time is . . . .
6. I wish my parents knew . . . .
7. School is . . . .
8. I can't understand why . . . .
9. I feel bad when . . . .
10. I wish teachers . . . .
11. I wish my mother . . . .
12. Going to college . . . .
13. To me, books . . . .
14. People think I . . . .
15. I like to read about . . . .
16. On weekends I . . . .
17. I'd rather read than . . . .
18. To me, homework . . . .
19. I hope I'll never . . . .
20. I wish people wouldn't . . . .
21. When I finish high school . . . .
22. I'm afraid . . . .
23. Comic books . . . .
24. When I take my report card home . . . .
25. I am at my best when . . . .
26. Most brothers and sisters . . . .
27. I don't know how . . . .
28. When I read math . . . .
29. I feel proud when . . . .
30. The future looks . . . .
31. I wish my father . . . .
32. I like to read when . . . .
33. I would like to be . . . .
34. For me, studying . . . .
35. I often worry about . . . .
36. I wish I could . . . .
37. Reading science . . . .
38. I look forward to . . . .
39. I wish . . . .
40. I'd read more if . . . .
41. When I read out loud . . . .

Source: From Boning, T., and Boning, R. "I'd Rather Read Than . . ." *Reading Teacher,* April 1957, p. 196. Reprinted with permission of the International Reading Association.

   d. Reading out loud . . .
   e. I read better when . . .
2. *Supplementary reading interest questions:*
   a. I like reading about . . .
   b. I don't want to read about . . .
   c. The best thing about reading . . .
   d. I laugh when I read about . . .
   e. The best book I know about . . .

APPENDIX

I Stages in Spelling Development

The stages represented here should be viewed from a developmental perspective; that is, a student's spelling is likely to change over time so that it resembles the examples seen at each stage. The following stages are those proposed by J. Richard Gentry (1982, 1987, 1996).

Stage 1: Precommunicative Spelling

Typical of children ages 3 through 5, the learner at this stage uses scribbles, letterlike forms, and letters, showing a preference for uppercase letters. There is no match between letters and phonemes.

Examples: candy SCOZ]

went ƎNᵒC

(strings of letters) Crtog Dok

Stage 2: Semiphonetic Spelling

Representative of the spelling of 5- and 6-year-olds, the learner has discovered the phonetic principle—that is, awareness that letters are used to represent sounds. However, letters for only one or two sounds in a word are generally written down.

Examples: My brother was crying all night.

MBRW KLN+

I like to go to the zoo.

I LK to G++Z

Stage 3: Phonetic Spelling

Six-year-old children are typically phonetic spellers. At this stage the learner represents all essential sounds in spelling a word and chooses letters that show a relationship to the sound heard in the word (e.g., *AT* for *eight; PEKT* for *peeked*).

Examples: Jackie
I had a apel For lungsh
(I had an apple for lunch.)

bob —
a boy so The man run Awa
(A boy saw the man run away.)

397

Stage 4: Transitional Spelling

Once a student begins reading, typically around age 7, spelling begins to change as the learner visually notices the spelling of words and relies less on spelling words according to the way they sound. Transitional spelling looks more like standard or conventional spelling as the learner uses silent letters such as e-markers (e.g., *clime* for *climb*) and vowel letter combinations (e.g., digraphs such as *whair* for *where;* diphthongs such as *zoo*), demonstrating more reliance on how the words look rather than how they sound. Transitional spellers also use a vowel in every syllable and spell many words correctly.

Examples:

> Can I go see a movee wif
> My fren Susi sed her mom
> sed oka win we go
>
> (Can I go see a movie with my friend Susie? She said
> her Mom said OK. When can we go?)
>
> goin To The zoo is fun I
> lik The linz and The big
> burdz wit blue feters
>
> (Going to the zoo is fun. I like the lions and
> the big birds with blue feathers.)

Stage 5: Correct Or Mature Spelling

With more exposure to print and more opportunities to write, learners reach this stage around age 8 or 9. The student recognizes when words look misspelled and can consider alternative spellings. Most basic rules of English orthography are applied to include use of silent letters and double consonants, and many irregular words are spelled correctly. Occasionally, spellings may still be constructed for some words.

ASSESSING SPELLING DEVELOPMENT

In order to accurately assess spelling development, students must write words they have *not* been taught or memorized. If a student is willing to write freely, then those words can be assessed for spelling development. However, some students are unwilling to write freely because they are not confident of their spelling ability. For these students a more structured approach is needed. Following are recommended word lists for spelling assessment. Direction, scoring, and a scored example for the K–2 list are provided.

Directions:

1. Explain to students that they are not expected to know how to spell all of these words. You want to know how they *think* the words should be spelled. They should do their best, but this exercise will not be graded.

2. If they are stumped by a word, they should first try the beginning of the word, then the middle, then the end.

3. The teacher will read the word, then the sentence, then read the word again, twice. (Do not exaggerate any of the parts—just say the word normally.)

Spelling List (Grades K–2)

1. late — Kathy was *late* to school again today.
2. wind — The *wind* was loud last night.
3. shed — The wind blew down our *shed*.
4. geese — The *geese* fly over Texas every fall.
5. jumped — The frog *jumped* into the river.
6. yell — We can *yell* all we want on the playground.
7. chirped — The bird *chirped* when it saw a worm.
8. once — Jim rode his bike into a creek *once*.
9. learned — I *learned* to count in school.
10. shove — Don't *shove* your neighbor when you line up.
11. trained — I *trained* my dog to lie down and roll over.
12. year — Next *year* you'll have a new teacher.
13. shock — Electricity can *shock* you if you aren't careful.
14. stained — The ice cream spilled and *stained* my shirt.
15. chick — The egg cracked open and a baby *chick* climbed out.
16. drive — Bob's sister is learning how to *drive*.

Spelling List (Grades 3 and Up)

1. setter — Her dog is an Irish *setter*.
2. shove — Don't *shove* when you line up.
3. grocery — I'm going to the *grocery* store.
4. button — Did you lose a *button* from your shirt?
5. sailor — My cousin is a good *sailor*.
6. prison — The robber will go to *prison*.
7. nature — We walked on the *nature* trail.
8. peeked — He *peeked* at the answers to the test.
9. special — Tomorrow is a *special* day.
10. preacher — The *preacher* talked for over an hour.
11. slowed — We *slowed* down on the bumpy road.
12. sail — The boat had a torn *sail*.
13. feature — We saw a double *feature* at the movies.
14. batter — The first *batter* struck out.

Scoring

The words are scored according to the stage of spelling they reflect. The word is scored:

0 if it is *precommunicative*.

1 if it is *semiphonetic*.

2 if it is *phonetic*.

3 if it is *transitional*.

4 if it is *correct*.

For example, from spelling list (Grades K–2):

1.	Lat	2
2.	wnd	2
3.	sead	3
4.	Gees	3
5.	Bout	2
6.	uL	2
7.	cutp	2
8.	Los	2
9.	Lud	2
10.	suf	2
11.	trad	2
12.	ter	2
13.	sock	3
14.	sad	2
15.	cek	2
16.	drif	2

The mode should be determined. The mode is the single score that occurred most often. (The average can be distorted by the possibility that the student had memorized some of the spellings.) In the preceding example, the mode is 2, meaning that most of the student's spellings were in the phonetic stage (Temple, Nathan, Burris, & Temple, 1988, pp. 105–107).

Laminack and Wood (1996) suggest the "index of control" as a numerical measure indicating the degree of control a writer has over his or her spelling. They provide a formula to be used periodically over the course of a school year as a way of showing growth in spelling, especially in classrooms that use writer's workshop or where there are many opportunities for students to write in their own voice. Because of the time-consuming nature of the formula and the reservations that the authors express over the results being misused to give grades, interested readers are referred to their text, *Spelling in Use: Looking Closely at Spelling in Whole Language Classrooms,* pp. 47–52.

INSTRUCTION FOR SPELLING DEVELOPMENT

The goal of spelling instruction is to increase knowledge about how words are spelled and the range of spelling strategies, as opposed to moving students to the next spelling stage. Spelling stages are just a way to organize discussion about spelling growth.

Strategies for Spelling

1. Look at word spelled. Does it look correct? Circle if not.
2. Does it sound like another word I know?
3. Is it written anywhere nearby? In a book?

4. Ask somebody.

5. Mark it and check later.

Instruction for Precommunicative (or Prephonemic) Spellers

Learn to represent *some* sounds.

1. LEA (connection between voice and print).

2. Individual help listening for sounds and writing them down.

3. Dialog journaling—to provide a written model.

Instruction for Semiphonetic (or Phonemic) Spellers

Learn to represent *more* sounds and spell some words conventionally.

1. Model listening to one syllable at a time and ignore some "off" spellings.

2. Mini-lessons during LEA.

3. Say, "That is how you could spell it in your writing, but it is actually written this way."

Instruction for Phonetic (or Letter Name) Spellers

Moving away from spelling what you hear.

1. Reading environment rich in print and opportunities to read.

2. Students, uncomfortable with "invented" letter name spellings are showing growth and will benefit from introduction to several spelling strategies.

3. Instruction should draw attention to visual information contained in conventional spellings. Say, "Think about what the word looks like in books" (as opposed to "Write what you hear," as in earlier stages).

4. Word sort lessons on visual patterns directed to specific needs.

Instruction for Transitional Spellers

Increase expanding knowledge of the regularities in English language orthography.

1. Say, write and say, check, trace and say, write from memory, check.

2. 5–6 words of personal interest.

3. Word games (e.g., Hangman, Boggle, Spill and Spell, Scrabble).

4. Word derivations and words with similar meanings tend to have similar spellings (e.g., *sign, signal*).

5. Plurals, past tense markers–spelled same although sound different (*pigs, cups, raked, purred, traded*).

6. Categorize spelling errors over time; infer the rule (inductive learning) *(their, there, they're)*.

J Scoring Systems for Writing

Regardless of how writing instruction is provided, there comes a time when student writing must be evaluated. Traditionally, all samples of student writing were graded intensively and negatively with every error being marked. This procedure of correcting, tallying errors, and assigning grades, however, did not produce a noticeable improvement in subsequent writing. It drained time and energies without contributing to improved writing or to accurate assessment. It also was threatening to students, and it caused many of them to write only because they feared failure.

Ideally, writing would not be graded; unfortunately, most school systems still require that teachers assign grades or scores. Fortunately, teachers and school districts no longer believe that *all* writing must be scored. When students are writing exploratively, there is no need to formally mark or score their work. However, when the decision is made to score students' writing (e.g., end of a marking period; portfolio assessment; student-selected best work; draft stages), the criteria used to score the writing should get to the heart of writing and should not focus just on mechanical errors.

No one scoring system or approach is ideal. By far the best scoring guides are those that the teacher and students construct together. These guides can be content-specific, focusing the evaluation on those aspects that the teacher and students together have identified as important. If this procedure is not feasible, the teacher should explore other scoring systems and combine the most desirable qualities of each major approach of evaluating and grading students' written products to devise an approach based on students' needs and the instructional writing program. Regardless of the scoring system used, however, the goal of assessment and evaluation should be to help students improve as writers and feel successful (Tompkins, 1990).

HOLISTIC SCORING

Holistic scoring initially labeled a variety of approaches to rank-ordering pieces of writing. It involves judging a piece of writing in terms of the whole instead of its individual parts. Rather than evaluating a piece of writing word for word, marking all errors, pointing out weaknesses, and suggesting changes, the teacher reads the piece as a whole, considers certain features, and immediately assigns a score or grade. The grade may be a single rating for the entire piece of writing, or a set of ratings for different features being considered (Cooper & Odell, 1977). While every aspect of the student writing—content and mechanics—affects the teacher's response, none of them are specifically identified. This system, which is similar to methods used by the National Assessment of Education Progress and the Educational Testing Service, is often used in conjunction with student conferences or peer response groups.

This appendix was prepared by Ramona C. Moore, Ph.D. at Western Washington University, Everett Education Center; and English teacher at Kamiak High School, Mukilteo, Washington.

Using holistic scoring, teachers can evaluate quickly because they do not circle errors or make comments in the margins. They are also able to evaluate more consistently because the same carefully developed criteria are used for all pieces of writing. This approach, however, is not an appropriate choice for a teacher who wants to assess how well students have used a particular writing form or applied specific writing skills. According to Tompkins (1990), research studies have indicated that the major drawback to this approach in elementary schools is that teachers may bias their assessments by unknowingly placing too much emphasis on mechanics, especially spelling, grammar and usage, and handwriting (Rafoth & Rubin, 1984; Searle & Dillon, 1980). In recent years, holistic scoring has been interpreted more narrowly and includes both impressionistic and focused approaches.

Impressionistic Holistic Scoring

As the name implies, the impressionistic holistic approach involves reading a student's paper quickly and marking it (e.g., 1, 2, 3, or 4; A, B, C, or D) based on some general feeling or impression of the overall quality of the paper. The teacher must read quickly and carefully to arrive at a "feel" for the piece and a score. The paper is then placed in one of three or four piles without any marking. When all of the papers have been read, the teacher goes back to the piles to verify the relative value of the papers, and assigns scores. This approach is efficient and reliable, particularly if the criteria have been shared and illustrated with the writers as well as the readers (raters). This approach has its limitations. Students only know that, when compared to other students' papers, their paper received a 1, a 2, a 3, or a 4. While this overall rating does not give students advice on how to revise the writing, these limitations can be addressed by focusing on developing fluency in first drafting and fine-tuning during revision stages.

Focused Holistic Scoring

In focused holistic scoring, the teacher decides upon a number of specific features of the writing to attend to while reading students' papers. The next step is developing a scoring guide with a list of the specific features and distributing it to students before they begin writing. This step ensures that the students know the criteria the teacher will use to assess their writing. An example of a focused holistic approach to scoring students' stories might include *story features* (e.g., setting, characters, problem, and resolution), as a criterion. The teacher would develop a guide listing these features. The reading of the paper would then be focused on how these features contribute to the quality of the whole piece of writing. After this focused reading of the students' papers, the teacher would again place a 1, a 2, a 3, or a 4 on the piece, and would end up with three or four stacks of papers ranked as to worth according to the selected criteria.

Roundtable Holistic Scoring

Roundtable holistic scoring is a way of getting students involved in the evaluation process. Students read papers, establish criteria, and evaluate the papers. This process helps students become better judges of their own work and get a clearer idea of their own performance on a particular paper. Then, based on the teacher's input and markings by peers, the student assigns a grade. Since the students established the criteria for evaluation (rubric), they have a clearer idea of what they can or should do to improve their own writing. Kirby, Liner, and Vinz (1988) recommend that this peer scoring system, which was adapted from the one used by Educational Testing Services to rate student writing samples, be "thoroughly structured and patiently implemented" (p. 222).

A Holistic Guide for Evaluating Student Writings

Many holistic guides are available for evaluating student writings. The following guide is recommended by Kirby, Liner, and Vinz (1988) as a reminder of important characteristics of good writing and not as a scale of criteria:

1. *Impact:* The paper engages the reader; the writer has something to say and is imaginatively involved; the idea is conveyed with fluency or intensity; the writing is convincing.

2. *Inventiveness:* The paper surprises the reader; new and unexpected elements, such as a clever title, expressive language, or unusual ending, are introduced.

3. *Individuality:* The paper has a voice or a flavor of its own.

OTHER APPROACHES TO SCORING

Anthony, Johnson, Mickelson, and Preece (1991, p. 141) developed the following procedure from a suggestion by Williams (1989). The teacher should respond to the content and not the form. The teacher should also find something honestly complimentary to say and should indicate how the piece might be further developed. If a formal score or mark must be given, the teacher should ensure that all students are doing the same task and that all students are aware of the criteria that will be used in judging/evaluating their work. If students are all working on different tasks, uniform criteria for marking are impossible. Given this situation, the teacher might choose to use the following method:

- Read through all of the papers quickly without a pencil in hand. Place each paper into one of three stacks: above expectation, at expectation, below expectation.

- Reread each paper more carefully. Use the negotiated criteria to determine compliments and criticisms to write in marginal notes. Be sure that the comments indicate how the paper might be improved.

- Add a positive summary comment. Briefly explain how the grade was earned.

- Return the papers to the students and ask them to check your comments and the grade against the negotiated criteria. Schedule individual conferences to deal with students' concerns.

Analytic Scoring

Another approach to scoring student writing is analytic scoring. Whereas holistic scoring focused on an overall assessment of the worth of an entire piece of student writing, analytic scoring focuses on assessing the writing in terms of its individual parts. Tompkins (1990, p. 391) includes an analytic scoring system adapted from Paul Diederich's (1974) scale for high school and college students. This adapted system (Figure J.1), which can be used to assess the quality of elementary students' writing, divides the traits of good writing into four categories: ideas, organization, style, and mechanics. This approach places less emphasis on mechanics than do other analytic scoring systems, such as Diederich's.

Figure J.1   An Analytic Scoring System

	STRONG	AVERAGE	WEAK
Ideas			
1. Ideas are creative.	———	———	———
2. Ideas are well developed.	———	———	———
3. Audience and purpose are considered.	———	———	———
Organization			
1. An organizational pattern is used.	———	———	———
2. Ideas are presented in logical order.	———	———	———
3. Topic sentences are clear.	———	———	———
Style			
1. A good choice of words is displayed.	———	———	———
2. Figurative language is used.	———	———	———
3. A variety of sentence patterns is used.	———	———	———
Mechanics			
1. Most words are spelled correctly.	———	———	———
2. Punctuation and capitalization are used correctly.	———	———	———
3. Standard language is used.	———	———	———

Comments:

Evaluation/scoring should be integrated with the other elements of the writing program and not considered as separate from it. Writing should be a positive learning experience, not a threatening one. One way to ensure that evaluation is as open as possible and not done "over the heads or behind the backs" of students is to involve the students during instruction in negotiating or jointly developing the criteria for assessment and evaluation (Anthony et al., 1991, p. 90) and to stop looking for errors.

EXAMPLES OF SCORING USING TWO DIFFERENT APPROACHES

Focused Holistic Scoring Using Story Features

Prior to having her students write, a teacher identified the features that she would attend to while reading the papers (i.e., setting, characters, problem, resolution). Along with her students, she developed the following list as a guide:

Setting: Does the paper include an appropriate setting?
Characters: Are the characters listed and developed?
Problem: Is the problem obvious?
Resolution: Does the story end with the problem being resolved convincingly and appropriately?

She told her students that while reading each paper, she would focus on the following question: How do these features contribute to the quality of the whole piece of writing? She explained to her students that since she had been trained to use holistic scoring and since she had scored many papers, she did not need a numbered scale. Her purpose in developing the example, however, was to give them a better understanding of how their papers were scored. She also wanted to help them learn how to evaluate and score one another's papers and eventually to evaluate their own writing. Her example was as follows:

4—All of the story features are included; they contribute to the development of an interesting and original story.

3—All of the story features are included, but they are not appropriately developed. There is some evidence of originality/believability/imagination.

2—At least three of the story features are included; the story lacks structure/believability/originality/imagination.

1—There is little evidence of how story features contribute to the development of a story; there appears to be no story line; the story lacks structure/believability/originality/imagination.

Using the following student-written edited version placed on the overhead, the teacher talked through her focused scoring procedure.

The People in the Sea[1]

One day Eric saw Ariel swimming. He wanted to swim with her so he did. Then they saw a big whale. Then they started to swim fais (fast) and they went to Ariels (Ariel's) father to speack (speak) to him. They said that a whale was chaising (chasing) them all the way her (here). Then Ariel and Eric went swimming again. They saw the whale again and the whale had take (to take) a reast (rest) and forgeat (forget) about them. And they all lived hapily (happily) ever after.

Teacher: I'm going to read this paper quickly, but I have to tell myself to think of my focus. For this paper I want to know how the story features that we have identified contribute to the quality of the whole piece of writing. (She reads orally.) I notice the setting is in the sea; the characters are Eric, Ariel, the whale, and Ariel's father; the problem is that the whale is chasing them; and the resolution is that the whale forgets about them during his rest so they all lived happily ever after. Now that I have finished reading, I think that this is a pretty good story. All of the features contributed to its development. But I don't think the whale would have to rest, and I don't think he would forget about them. Let's see. I think I will place this paper in this stack because it is similar to the other papers. (She stops her thinking aloud.) My next steps would be to read and sort all of the papers, and then to decide if the papers are in the right stack. This might mean that I have to quickly look over some of the papers again. Once I feel sure that all of the papers in each stack have similar overall qualities, I decide on scores or grades. Going back to "The People in the Sea," I would give this paper (and the other similar ones) a score of 2.

The Anthony et al. Approach to Scoring

Using the procedure developed by Anthony, Johnson, Mickelson, and Preece (1991), the teacher placed "The People in the Sea" in the stack identified as *below expectation*. Using the same negotiated criteria as in the focused scoring, she wrote the following comments on the student's paper:

> I like how you have included all of the story features. It also seemed like the wise thing to do to go to Ariel's father for help. I think you could improve your paper by answering some of these questions: What did Eric and Ariel tell her father? What did he tell them? Why would they go back into the water? What could have happened to the whale that would make him take a rest and forget about the swimmers? Do you think they ever thought about the whale again? Your score was a C− because you still need to place yourself as a writer in your reader's mind as well as in your characters' shoes (or should I say flippers?). The ideas in your paper appear to be flowing in with the tide—keep them coming!

K James McCarthy's "Our Visit to the Farm"

Our Visit to the Farm

written and illustrated by
James McCarthy

This book was completed by James McCarthy with the help and support of Daun Calvert, his tutor and a preservice teacher at the University of New Orleans, and Dr. Janet C. Richards, course instructor.

Our Visit to the Farm

written and illustrated by
James McCarthy

This book is dedicated to my mother.

Once upon a time, Trinity, Ariena, and I went to visit a farm.

Page
1

When we arrived we saw a cow.

Page
2

Then we saw some chickens, roosters, and hens.

Page 3

Finally, we saw a pig. I asked Trinity and Ariena, "Why is that pig sleeping?"

Page 4

Trinity and Ariena said, "Maybe the pig is sick."

Page 5

Just then a veterinarian began to examine the pig. "The pig is sick," said the veterinarian. "I will take him to town."

Page 6

We went home very sad about the pig. However, a few days later, we went back to the farm to see if the pig was feeling better.

Page 7

We went to the pig's pen and saw the pig eating and making a funny noise. Trinity, Ariena, and I were very happy.

THE END.

Page 8

ABOUT THE AUTHOR

1996

James McCarthy is a second grader at Haley Elementary School located in an urban area in New Orleans. James has three sisters. His favorite subject is math, his favorite book is *The Mask*, and James wants to be a policeman when he grows up.

L Useful Phonics Generalizations

1. The *c* rule. When *c* comes just before *a, o,* or *u,* it usually has the *hard* sound heard in *cat, cot,* and *cut.* Otherwise, it usually has the *soft* sound heard in *cent, city,* and *bicycle.*

2. The *g* rule. When *g* comes at the end of words or just before *a, o,* or *u,* it usually has the *hard* sound heard in *tag, game, go,* and *gush.* Otherwise, it usually has the *soft* sound heard in *gem, giant,* and *gym.*

3. The *VC* pattern. This pattern is seen in words such as *an, can, candy,* and *dinner.* As a verbal generalization it might be stated as follows: In either a word or syllable, a single vowel letter followed by a consonant letter, digraph, or blend usually represents a short vowel sound. (Note that *C* stands for either a letter, digraph, or blend, e.g., *bat, bath, bask.*)

4. The *VV* pattern. This pattern is seen in words such as *eat, beater, peach, see, bait, float,* and *play.* As a verbal generalization it might be stated like this: In a word or syllable containing a vowel digraph, the first letter in the digraph usually represents the long vowel sound and the second letter is usually silent. According to Clymer (1963/1996), this generalization is quite reliable for *ee, oa,* and *ay* (e.g., *fee, coat, tray*) and works about two-thirds of the time for *ea* and *ai* (e.g., *seat, bait*), but is not reliable for other vowel digraphs such as *ei, ie,* or *oo,* or diphthongs, such as *oi, oy, ou,* and *ow.*

5. The *VCE* (final *e*) pattern. This pattern is seen in words such as *ice, nice, ate, plate, paste, flute, vote,* and *clothe.* As a generalization it might be stated this way: In one-syllable words containing two vowel letters, one of which is a final *e,* the first vowel letter usually represents a long vowel sound, and the *e* is silent. If the vowel is not long, try the short sound.

6. The *CV* pattern. This pattern is seen in one-syllable words such as *he, she, go, my, cry, hotel, going,* and *flying.* As a generalization, it might be stated this way: When there is only one vowel letter in a word or syllable and it comes at the end of the word or syllable, it usually represents the long vowel sound.

7. The *r* rule. This rule applies to words such as *far, fare, fair, girl, fur, her,* and *here.* As a generalization it might be stated as follows: The letter *r* usually modifies the short or long sound of the preceding vowel letter.

8. The *VCCV, VCV,* and the *Cle* patterns are three syllabication rules worth knowing. For the *VCCV* pattern, the rule is to divide between the two consonants. This pattern is represented in words such as *blanket, happy,* and *represent.* For the *VCV* pattern, the rule is to divide before or after the consonant. Words representing this pattern are *robot, robin, divide,* and *before.* For the last pattern, *Cle,* the rule is to divide before the consonant. Words representing this pattern are *Bible, uncle, table,* and *example.*

(*Note:* Phonics generalizations should be taught inductively. Known words in a meaningful context should be used to illustrate a letter-sound relationship. When teaching something new, use words familiar to children. To learn whether children can apply what has been taught, use words they cannot read. Practice phonics in context whenever possible. Once a generalization has been taught inductively, concentrate on unknown words in the context of a sentence or brief passage.)

Glossary

abstract referent The concept behind words that do not evoke a clear visual image (*way, there, democracy*, and so forth).

academic reading Instructional reading; reading to gain knowledge or information.

ADD/ADHD A biological disorder with primary symptoms of hyperactivity, impulsivity and distractibility, effectively treated with medication and behavior modification.

affect The psychological domain of the brain that is connected with feelings.

African American Vernacular English (AAVE) A variation of standard English dialect spoken by the people in many African American communities across the United States; based on its own set of phonological patterns and rules.

aliterates People with the ability to read who choose not to do so due to a lack of positive attitudes, habits, and interests.

alphabetic principle A principle by which each sound or phoneme in our language has its own distinctive graphic representation.

analytic process In reading, a methodical system designed to assist teachers in their observation and assessment of students' engagement of the reading process, allowing them to identify strengths and weaknesses and plan appropriate instruction no matter what the involved domain, method of teaching, or curriculum.

analytic teaching A way of observing and assessing students' literacy development that recognizes, respects, and appreciates students' abilities.

analytical vocabulary Words that students identify correctly in reading, but only after careful examination of the word's graphic image.

anecdotal records Carefully prepared short notes that objectively describe student behavior and aid in the recollection of observations over time.

arrays Outlines of relationships between topics, ideas, and details in graphic form; examples include semantic webs, mapping, and the herringbone technique.

artifacts Items chosen for inclusion in a portfolio.

assessment The process of gathering information (data) about students' strengths, abilities, and need for further instruction.

Assignment Mastery A reading strategy developed by Strickland designed to teach readers self-monitoring techniques through the asking of specific questions during each of the various phases of reading (i.e., scanning, preparation for reading, recitation and review, and reading review).

associative words Words that often occur together in reading (e.g., happy birthday, bacon and eggs).

assumptive teaching Instruction resulting from teachers' improper assumptions about what students can and cannot do, which leads to a disharmony between the instructional program and the learner.

at-level testing A survey reading test using a single level of test for each specific grade level so that the same level of test is given to all students in a specified grade.

at risk The state of a student for whom two or more non-reading factors (such as low SES level, health considerations) are believed to threaten the student's chances for success in reading.

attentive listening The act of attending to sounds in spoken language and concentrating on acquiring the message being transmitted.

attributional retraining The act of instructing students to accept responsibility for their own learning in the case of both their failures and their successes; includes teaching students that failure can often be defeated through diligent attempts and perseverance.

auditory acuity The degree of one's ability to distinctly hear sounds.

auditory blending The sounding process, usually employed by emerging readers, by which the student says the word parts and blends them together to cue a meaningful response; the blending of phonemes to form a word.

auditory comprehension The ability to make meaning from oral language, ranging from very literal comprehension to the ability to critically evaluate the spoken message.

auditory discrimination The ability to differentiate sounds.

auditory memory The ability to recall a series of sounds.

auditory perception The ability to determine, combined with auditory memory and the ability to blend, sounds.

The author is forever grateful to Susan Glynn Mulé for preparing this glossary. Thank you, Susan!

author's chair   A chair of "distinction" that students sit in to share their writing with classmates.

automaticity   The act of perceiving and comprehending units of print so thoroughly that almost no effort is needed to recognize new words or parts of words.

balanced reading   Instruction that provides the proportion of skills, strategies, materials, and social and emotional support that learners need.

basic story features   Those parts essential to the making of a real story (i.e., characters, setting, problem, and solution).

best practices   Recommendations from research that provide a knowledge base for improving literacy instruction.

bibliotherapy   A process by which students are matched with books containing a character or situation with which they can identify, allowing them to better understand themselves through the reading event.

book club   An instructional framework developed by Susan McMahon and Taffy Raphael that relies on students choosing books they wish to read, discussing them in small groups, and learning and sharing with the entire group.

brain-based learning   Instructional environment created to make the brain more receptive to learning.

cloze procedure   A method for determining a student's instructional reading level; requires the student to fill in a series of blanks that have been systematically deleted from a passage; often used to determine the suitability of a particular text.

cognition   Thinking; the ability to design concepts and to organize acquired information; the nature of knowing and of intellectual development.

Collaborative Listening Viewing Guide   A type of study guide useful when information is obtained from a video, TV program, or web-based video clip.

collaborative writing   Facilitated instruction allowing students to experience writing within a social context, which includes a partner or partners and a university tutor serving as role models.

communicative competence   The ability to use language proficiently within a wide variety of social situations.

comprehension monitoring   The act of continuously evaluating and monitoring one's understanding while engaged in the act of reading.

concrete referent   The clear visual image evoked by certain words (*dog, table, blue,* and so forth).

construct validity   The degree to which a test measures a particular trait or ability, usually by measuring the behaviors believed to reflect the trait or ability involved.

constructed spelling   The developmentally appropriate form of spelling a word (precommunicative, semiphonetic, phonetic, or transitional). Also called *invented* or *temporary spelling.*

content validity   The degree to which a test measures what it is supposed to be measuring; how well it matches the teacher's instructional objectives.

content words   Words holding the meaning in a particular passage or text.

context   A cue system for decoding unknown words in which the student uses the words surrounding an unknown target word to trigger recognition or meaning.

conventional spelling   Correct spelling.

corrective reading   A type of instruction designed to ameliorate the obstacles to growth in literacy that have been prohibiting students from reaching their full potential.

correlation coefficients   The number indicating how strongly two variables are related; the higher the number, the stronger the relationship.

creative writing   Writing that stems from the writer's experiences; includes fiction, drama, and poetry.

criterion-referenced tests   Tests that measure how well a learner performs a particular task as compared to a specified desired level of competence.

decodable text   Text using sequenced sound-spelling correspondences based on both frequency and phonic principles.

deductive teaching   A didactic style of teaching in which a teacher presents a generalization or rule to students and expects them to apply the rule to specific examples.

diagnosis   Identification of reading difficulties based on gathering and evaluating information about student reading behaviors.

dialects   Surface variations in the way that a particular language is spoken in different parts of a country or among different ethnic groups, but still completely rule-governed, fully developed systems of speaking.

dialogue journals   Collections of daily written conversations over time between students and teachers wherein students are free to express their opinions and feelings about topics of their choosing without fear of judgment or reprisal.

didactic teaching   A transmission style of teaching by which a teacher presents certain material to students and expects them to learn it.

diorama   Visual art created within a box (e.g., a shoe box), usually depicting the major elements of a story.

direct assessment   Assessment measures are used within classrooms and by individual teachers, as opposed to the prepared, standardized type of test given to large groups of students.

direct instruction   A highly structured, teacher-directed style of teaching whereby teachers share planned "strategy lessons."

directed reading-thinking activity   An instructional strategy developed by Russell G. Stauffer to enhance reading comprehension through a prediction-making cycle.

discourse   Meaningful language units larger than a sentence; also, a component of communication relating ideas to a particular subject for a specified purpose.

discovery teaching   Also called *inductive teaching,* a style of teaching in which students are provided with an appropriate environment and encouraged to seek generalizations for themselves.

drama improvisation An informal or scripted and rehearsed stage presentation.

dramatic play Informal, spontaneous drama among young children.

during-reading stage The second stage of reading, characterized by a reader's direct interaction with print.

dyslexia A persistent, hereditary neurological disorder manifested by difficulty in reading at the word level.

early reader A reader just beginning to use word recognition and comprehension strategies.

emergent literacy The belief that reading and writing begin at birth and gradually emerge over time through frequent interactions with literacy events.

emergent writers Beginning writers; young children in the process of experimenting with written language through scribbling in the attempt to communicate a written message.

emotional maltreatment Inappropriate parenting that may include, but is not restricted to, neglect, constant belittling, or verbal abuse.

end-of-unit tests Tests in the teacher's manual or student workbooks of many basal reading systems; may contain useful information regarding student accomplishments on small segments of material.

entry point An activity chosen specifically to engage and connect a learner with a desired literacy task.

equal-status relationship The relationship of words or sentences that describe equal associations between concepts.

ESL (English as a second language) students Students whose first language is not English.

evaluation The process of judging student growth and making decisions regarding student achievement through the analysis of collected student data.

evaluation activity The direct assessment of a lesson's effectiveness and the accuracy of the teacher's hypothesis through teacher-made activities directly related to the tasks involved in the lesson; used to determine whether additional practice is needed by the student or whether a new hypothesis should be formed by the teacher.

expectancy clues The concepts, and the words that go with them, that rise to mind when a topic is introduced; the schema that is activated from memory storage when new material is encountered.

experience-text-relationship method A reading strategy designed to help students relate personal experiences to the central events in a story through a cycle of discussing experiences (experience step), reading the text (text step), and relating the experiences to the story (relationship step).

expository material Material that is explanatory, such as that found in content-area reading.

facilitating questions Questions designed to encourage continued thinking on the part of the learner, to make the discovery of the solution to a particular problem easier.

fluency Smooth, expressive, and rhythmic reading or writing.

fluent reader A reader who reads easily with both accuracy and comprehension at levels beyond normal expectations.

formal tests Also called *standardized tests,* tests that have been administered in the same way to a large group of students for the purpose of establishing a reference (also called *norm*) group to which all future groups of students can be compared.

frustration reading level The level at which a student's reading deteriorates to the point whereby continuation is impossible because the material is too difficult even with the guidance of an instructor.

genre Written works with similar characteristics, such as fairy tales, historical fiction, nonfiction, poetry, mystery.

Goldilocks strategy A method used to help young readers select material at an appropriate level of difficulty.

grade-equivalent scores A type of standardized test score, usually stated in terms of years and tenths of a year, that uses as its reference point a grade in school; is often misinterpreted.

grapheme A written or printed symbol for a phoneme (speech sound). Some examples are *f* for /f/ or *ph* for /f/ and *oy* for /oi/ as in *boy.*

graphophonic cue system The reading cue system pertaining to sounds and symbol clues and letter/sound relationships.

GRASP (Guided Reading and Summarizing Procedure) A reading strategy in which students under teacher guidance read for information and are instructed to remember as much as they can; list all recollections following reading; reread to add, delete, and correct information; and then organize information by grouping details.

Guided Reading Strategy (GRS) A modification of the GRASP strategy, developed specifically for corrective readers, that contains the following steps: survey of the chapter or section, orally stating everything remembered from the survey; rechecking the chapter for missing information; discussion between teacher and student about the results of the survey and organizing the information into a topical outline; careful silent reading of the chapter or selection; immediate ten-item true/false quiz; and, finally, about one week later, an additional ten-item pop quiz on the material.

guided practice An activity that allows students to apply recently learned information while teacher assistance is still available.

herringbone technique A strategy designed to help students organize information from text in the form of a structured outline, using six basic comprehension questions to obtain the important information: who, what, where, when, how, and why.

high-stakes testing Reliance on a single test score to make important and substantial educational decisions.

holistic view   A viewpoint that holds that literacy instruction should encourage experimentation and approximation, as in learning to talk, but using whole text; also called *top-down*.

homographs   Words that are spelled alike, but do not sound alike and do not have the same meaning (e.g., *sow* seeds versus *sow* as a female pig).

homonyms   Words that sound alike and are spelled alike, but have different meanings (e.g., *run* a race, a dog *run*, *run* in your stocking, etc.).

homophones   Words that sound alike but have different origins and meanings and are often spelled differently.

independent practice   An opportunity for students to apply what they have learned without teacher assistance, which gives the teacher further information regarding the accuracy of the hypothesis and effectiveness of the given lesson.

independent reading level   The level at which a learner can read and comprehend comfortably, without teacher assistance.

indirect assessment   Assessment obtained from standardized, norm-referenced testing.

inductive teaching   Also called *discovery teaching*, a style of teaching in which students are provided with an appropriate environment and encouraged to seek generalizations for themselves.

informal reading inventory (IRI)   A nonstandard, direct measure, consisting of a series of graded passages that students read and answer questions about in order to help the teacher (1) observe students' reading tactics, (2) choose appropriate reading material, (3) identify students' three levels of reading, and (4) learn more about students' strengths and needs.

instructional reading level   The level of reading that is challenging, but not frustrating, for students to successfully read during normal classroom instruction.

integrative processing   Comprehension of a unit of sentences, as within a paragraph; the process of understanding and or making inferences about the relationships between sentences and/or individual clauses.

interactive assessment   The action by which a teacher attempts to determine situations under which students will have the most successful reading experiences.

interactive view   Viewpoint that reading comprehension results from the interaction between the reader and the text, with cognitive processing using both whole text and parts of text as necessary.

invented spelling   The developmentally appropriate form of spelling a word (precommunicative, semiphonetic, phonetic, or transitional).

key word   A familiar word used to represent a particular phonic element.

kidwatching   Conscious observation of students by teachers; includes use of field notes.

K–W–L   A reading strategy designed by Donna Ogle to assess students' prior knowledge and help them to set purposes for reading; in the K step, students list everything they *know* about a topic; in the W step, students generate questions about what they *want* to know about the topic; in the L step, students list what they have *learned* about the topic and what they still want to learn.

language   The system through which meaning is expressed; communication in either oral, written, or visual form.

language comprehension   The act of receiving or decoding a written or oral message.

language conventions   The rules governing written and oral language.

language experience approach (LEA)   An approach to reading instruction by which the teacher makes use of the children's experiences through the children's dictation of stories to the teacher, who then analyzes the material and follows up with the students by helping them expand upon the language through discussion and questioning; as students read and reread their own words, sight vocabulary, language knowledge, and graphophonemic awareness are increased and developed.

language functions   The purposes for communication in oral or written language.

language production   The act of sending an oral or written message.

learning centers   An actual location within a classroom, or simply a manila folder, that contains clearly defined objectives and instructions; is equipped with appropriate instructional materials for meeting the learning objectives.

learning disability   A severe discrepancy between achievement and intellectual ability in one or more academic areas that is not the result of vision, hearing, motor handicaps; mental retardation; emotional disturbance; or environmental, cultural, or economic disadvantage.

learning style   A preferred modality for learning (e.g., visual, auditory, or kinesthetic).

lexicon   The total vocabulary of a language, speaker, or subject.

linguistic competence   Knowledge that a reader has about language; proficiency in the standard system of language.

list-group-label   A categorizing strategy developed by Hilda Taba intended to enhance vocabulary and concept development.

listening   The action by which oral language is mentally transformed into meaning.

listening capacity   Also known as *listening comprehension level*; the highest level at which a student can understand 75 percent of the material read aloud; sometimes used as an indication of a reader's ability to understand oral language or as an estimate of reading expectancy.

listening vocabulary   Words understood at the level of oral language.

literacy-based Any activity that requires the learner to communicate through reading, writing, speaking, listening, viewing, or visually representing.

literature circle A group of students who choose to read and discuss the same book; usually employs guidelines for fulfilling a particular "job," such as summarizer or discussion director.

literature genre A classification of literature surrounding a particular topic (e.g., adventure, animal, detective, fairy tales, fantasy, mystery, romance).

locational skills Also known as *work-study skills;* the small areas of proficiency tested on many standardized achievement tests.

macroprocessing The method of instituting and systematizing components of ideas into a synopsis or orderly sequence of prevailing connected concepts.

main ideas The statements in a passage that provide the most significant ideas concerning the topic.

mapping Also called *semantic webbing;* a visual display of the relationships in the composition of a story or expository selection.

mastery tests Criterion-referenced tests or skills management systems that attempt to assess or instruct through focus on reading subskills.

maze technique A variation of the cloze procedure that offers several possible selections in place of the missing word; a multiple-choice item.

meaning clues The meaning in the context that allows students to decipher unknown words through recognition where only a limited number of word choices can sensibly be used without altering the intended meaning of a passage.

meaning vocabulary The words that a person understands, whether in written or oral language.

metacognition Self-knowledge regarding one's ability to think; in reading, the ability to self-monitor for comprehension and the ability to recognize when difficulty occurs.

microprocessing The task of grouping and selectively recalling individual units of ideas; the ability to relate ideas among isolated sentences in reading.

miscue Any deviation by a reader from what is written in print.

miscue analysis An examination of deviations from print made by a reader; gives the teacher insight into whether a reader is reading for meaning, as well as into the reader's use of graphophonemic, semantic, and syntactic cues.

morphemes The smallest meaningful structures in language.

morphology The study of meaningful word structures in language.

multi-literacies Communication beyond traditional reading and writing, including the literacies of music, dance, visual art, drama, and computer technology.

multiple intelligences A theory proposed by Howard Gardner that there are at least eight relatively autonomous intelligences (intellectual competencies or talents) indicating a need to expand our framework for thinking about intelligence; the intelligences are linguistic, spatial, musical, logical-mathematical, bodily-kinesthetic, interpersonal, intrapersonal, and naturalist.

narrative ability A set of sociolinguistic competencies that includes linguistic competence, sociolinguistic competence, fluency of expression, and the ability to sequence ideas.

normal curve equivalent (NCE) scores A type of standard score based on the normal bell curve with scores ranging from 1 to 99 with a mean of 50, differing from percentiles in that the scores are in equal units rather than piling up around the mean.

nondirective teaching A teaching model designed to help students set personal goals through facilitated teaching.

nonreading factors Also called *reading-related factors;* elements not directly relating to reading but affecting learning, such as physical factors, visual acuity and perception, auditory acuity, neurological factors, poverty, and so forth.

nonstructured writing Student-centered writing activities that allow students to write about whatever interests them as a natural, purposeful activity whereby students learn about written language without direct instruction.

norm-referenced tests Standardized tests; standardization requires the preparation of a standard set of directions, a specified amount of time, and sample administration to a large group of students to establish a reference to which subsequent administrations of the test can be compared.

norms The scores obtained from a large group of students to whom a standardized test is administered, which establish the reference that is then used for comparison in subsequent administrations of the test.

NOTES As part of a four-stage sequence for learning note-taking skills, NOTES (Notetaking, Observation, Training, and Evaluation Scales) provides both instructor and peer feedback on the quality of notes taken.

onsets Single consonants, consonant blends, and consonant digraphs coming before the first vowel in a word.

oral interaction A fundamental societal skill that consists of such competencies as initiating discourse, changing the topic of a conversation, taking turns, using tact, and basic pragmatic abilities such as knowing what to say (or what not to say), pertinence, directness, and so forth.

orthography The conventional use of written symbols in a given language; the writing system, or correct spelling, for a given language.

out-of-level testing An indirect measure of assessment used when the average achievement of a class is either high or low; allows the teacher to select the test level best suited to the class in order to increase the reliability of the test.

outlaw word   A word that does not conform to rules of pronunciation (e.g., *to, come, have*).

paradigm   A pattern or process.

paraphrase   To summarize or restate in one's own words by using synonyms in place of the existing words, rearranging existing words, or a combination of the two measures.

passage dependent   The state of questions that can be answered either literally or inferred by reading a particular passage.

percentile scores   Scores obtained by converting the raw scores of a standardized test into numbers from 1 to 99 in order to compare students with others of the same age or grade either through a norm group or directly with others in the same classroom or school.

perceptual unit   Unit of analysis; the size of the visual stimuli used for analysis in reading instruction (i.e. letter, syllable, word, sentence, or whole passage).

performance assessments   Methods of assessing student knowledge by having students read, write, and solve problems under circumstances like those in the instructional environment.

personal dictionary   A place where each student can record interesting new words from stories, LEAs, journals, or other learning experiences by writing down the word under the appropriate letter of the alphabet, writing a sentence with the word, and drawing a picture to further reinforce the meaning.

phase-out/phase-in strategy   The gradual transfer from teacher-posed to student-posed questions in order to promote independent reading.

phonemes   The sound structures of language.

phonemic awareness   Awareness of sounds that make up spoken words; the capacity to distinguish and manipulate sounds in words.

phonics   Letter-sound relationships; the sounds of phonemes and corresponding letters.

phonological awareness   Awareness of words: that words are made up of syllables, word parts such as onsets and rimes, and individual sounds.

phonological system   An understanding of individual sounds in language, an understanding of how these sounds are combined to make words, and an understanding of the effects of stress, pitch, and juncture on language.

phonology   The sounds and sound processes of a language.

physical abuse   Deliberate injury of a child that results in bruises, burns, broken bones, or internal injuries.

physical neglect   Abandonment or a lack of provisions such as clothing, shelter, food, or supervision.

picture clues   The pictures in a book that provide clues to the text by bringing certain words to mind.

picture walk   A technique used to survey the pictures in a text prior to reading for the purpose of clarifying concepts and/or predicting storyline.

PORPE   A student-directed learning strategy designed by Simpson for secondary- and college-level students to help them plan, monitor, and evaluate their reading by proceeding through the following five steps: predict, organize, rehearse, practice, and evaluate.

postreading stage   The final stage of studying, characterized by the use of any number of organizational, translational, or repetitive activities for reinforcing learned information (e.g., graphic organizers, paragraph frames, annotations, recitations, K–W–L charts, think links).

pragmatic cue system   Rules connecting the interpretation of language within the social context.

predictable text   Text that contains rhythmical, repetitive, or cumulative patterns that assist emergent and early readers to easily predict what the author will say.

prereading stage   The first stage of reading, characterized by scanning or skimming text and previewing such information as titles, headings, summaries, illustrations, and topic sentences in preparation for reading in order to activate schema and increase comprehension.

problem-solving questions   Questions designed to assist students in dynamic thinking by (1) making them aware that not knowing an answer is acceptable to the teacher and (2) prompting the students to figure out the strategies necessary to come up with the answer.

process of comprehension   The thinking and integration of information sources used by the reader in constructing meaning while reading.

productive language   The process by which students generate or identify possible words in the prereading period that may appear in the text, in order to improve their use of expectancy cues.

proficient reader   A reader who demonstrates skills, strategies, and reading achievement appropriate for age and grade level.

protocol   In the administration of IRIs, the list of main points expected for free recall, and questions based on the passages that are typed in advance on separate sheets of paper and duplicated to serve as the record sheet.

psychological set   The ideas, and the words associated with them, that are retrieved from memory storage upon the introduction to a topic; the activated schemata.

qualitative analysis   In IRIs, the analysis of the kinds of miscues made by a reader to determine a pattern and to discover whether the miscues affect the meaning of the text.

quantitative analysis   Determination of the number of errors a reader makes without regard to kind or effect on meaning.

question-answer relationships (QARs) A reading strategy designed to assist students in determining the difference between questions whose answers are textually explicit ("right there"), which can be found directly in the text; textually implicit ("putting it together"), which can be found in the text but require some synthesis of the text material; and scriptally implicit ("on my own" and "author and me"), which require the reader to use prior knowledge.

quickwrite A writing activity that requires students to write nonstop for five to ten minutes, usually focused on a topic, also used as a prewriting activity to generate ideas or to clarify thoughts about a topic.

randing theory The idea that schema theory is not directly relevant for ordinary narrative-type reading.

reading-related factors Also called *nonreading factors;* elements not directly relating to reading but affecting learning, such as physical factors, visual acuity and perception, auditory acuity, neurological factors, poverty, and so forth.

reading vocabulary Words in meaning vocabulary that are read and understood in print.

reciprocal question-answer relationships (ReQARs) A reading strategy that combines the elements of the ReQuest and QAR strategies to assist middle- and upper-grade students in word recognition, anticipate the nature of teachers' questions, focus on informative portions of text material, and construct appropriate responses to questions.

reciprocal teaching An interactive learning strategy designed to teach children to summarize sections of text, anticipate possible questions, predict, and clarify difficult portions of text; students initially observe the teacher model the target behaviors and then gradually take the instructional role from the teacher.

recreational reading Independent reading to foster positive attitudes and interests as well as good reading habits.

recursive nature of writing The back-and-forth nature of writing: as writers think of changes they wish to make in their work while they are writing, they often go back to reword or add new information to previously written material.

reflective thinking The act of continuous questioning about past events in a purposeful attempt to solve educational problems and improve one's approach to teaching.

regional dialects A thoroughly developed linguistic system identifiable to a particular geographic location.

reliability In standardized testing, the level of consistency of scores when the same test is given to a group of students more than once within a short frame of time.

repeated words Content words found in almost every sentence of a paragraph.

replaced words Substitutes for content words that would normally be repeated in a passage (e.g., pronouns).

ReQuest Procedure (*Reciprocal Questioning*) A procedure used with individuals or small groups to aid students in setting their own purposes for reading; the teacher guides the students as they silently read as many sentences of a selection as it takes for them to be able to read the selection independently, with the teacher and student exchanging questions sentence by sentence as they go along, until finally a general-purpose question is asked and the students begin reading alone.

resiliency The capacity to bounce back from adversity.

rimes Phonograms; the parts of rhyming words that are the same; the vowel and any consonants after it in a syllable.

running records A way of coding passages for miscue analysis using a combination of proofreading symbols and check marks without need for a preprinted copy of the material being read by the student.

scaffolding Supporting learning through teacher modeling and assistance as needed.

scanning A type of fast reading used when a reader is seeking answers to specific questions.

schema A general description for background knowledge; a conceptual system for understanding knowledge.

schematic cue system The use of information from a reader's prior knowledge or personal association with the content or structure of the text.

scoring rubric A set of evaluation criteria used for rating a student's performance on a specific task.

scriptal information Background information.

scriptally implicit In QARs, the state of answers to questions from which the knowledge must come from the student's own background knowledge.

semantic system What a reader knows about meaning in language, including the meanings of words, the underlying concepts of words, and how those concepts are related, thus allowing a reader to organize concepts and make determinations about the importance of various concepts.

semantic webbing Also called *mapping;* a visual display of the relationships in the composition of a story or expository selection.

semantics Meaning in language.

sexual abuse The sexual exploitation, molestation, or prostitution of another individual.

showcase portfolio A portfolio displaying evidence concerning a student's literacy development that contains examples of writing chosen by the student with an attached statement as to why that sample has been selected.

sight vocabulary Those words that students encounter in print, which are instantly and effortlessly recognized.

sight words The small set of words in our language that do not conform to traditional analysis methods, which must be learned by sight (e.g., *are, to, of, have, come*)

sign systems Any and all forms of communication.

skills-based view   Viewpoint that important subskills related to reading and writing must be learned before proficiency can be achieved.

skimming   A type of fast reading used when a reader is attempting to obtain a general idea as to what a passage might be about.

social dialects   Surface variations of standard English among cultural groups or social classes.

sociolinguistic competence   The use of language to accomplish some goal.

specialized vocabulary   Common word forms specific to a content field.

SQ3R strategy   A reading strategy designed by Robinson to help students make the best use of their study time by using the steps of *survey, question, read, recite,* and *review* to set purposes for reading, provide self-comprehension checks, and fix information into memory.

standard deviation   In standardized testing, the measure of distribution that indicates variability; the higher the standard deviation, the greater the variation in the scores.

standard dialect   The variety of a language accepted as formal and used in commerce; the variety of language used by the well educated or by people in higher income brackets.

standard error of measurement   In standardized testing, also referred to as *SEmeas* or *SEM,* the statistic that denotes the degree to which a person's score can be predicted to fluctuate each time the test is taken.

standard scores   In standardized testing, uniformly spaced scores derived from the raw scores; indicate how far an individual score is from the mean, in terms of the variability of the distribution.

standardized tests   Also called *formal tests,* tests that have been administered in the same way to a large group of students for the purpose of establishing a reference (also called *norm*) group to which all future groups of students can be compared.

stanine scores   In standardized testing, equally spaced scores derived from the raw scores such that the lowest score is 1 and the highest 9, with a stanine of 5 representing the mean, and having a standard deviation of 2.

story frames   A listing of key words used to guide students' organization of written story retellings by providing a structure through enumeration, generalization, comparison or contrast, sequencing, or question and answer, allowing students to express their awareness of story structure.

story grammar   The arrangement that outlines the essential elements of a complete story, including the setting, initiating event, a reaction, a goal, an attempt, an outcome, and a solution.

story impressions   A prewriting strategy that introduces a list of words to be used in a story along with the order in which they should be used.

structural analysis   An instructional unit dealing with meaningful word parts such as variants (word endings), compounds, and derivatives (affixes).

structured comprehension   A reading strategy developed by Cohn that moves from the sentence level to the paragraph level, assisting students by (1) providing students with the proper context, (2) reading the sentence and decoding any miscues, (3) clarifying student questions about the sentence, and (4) asking students a series of predetermined questions to further clarify the information.

structured overview   A learning strategy designed to introduce new vocabulary as well as the overall organization of a selection that uses a graphic representation of terms essential to the selection through the use of the following steps: (1) listing the essential vocabulary; (2) arranging the words to show relationships between concepts: (3) adding vocabulary familiar to the students that assists in developing the relationships; (4) evaluating the diagram; (5) introducing the lesson by displaying the diagram and explaining the reason for the arrangement; and (6) continuing to relate information as the selection is read.

structured practice   An opportunity for students to practice what has been demonstrated by the teacher while the teacher is still involved.

study skills   Perspectives of reading that permit readers to expand on and build their knowledge through literacy.

studying   Student-directed instruction that expands and reinforces the knowledge gained in the classroom through various comprehension strategies.

stuttering   A speech disorder whose basis is neurological.

style shifting   The ability to adapt and adjust oral and written language to meet the needs and styles of various listeners and readers.

subordinate relationship   The relationship of specific or supporting details in a passage to the overall text.

summarizing   Condensing text by paraphrasing to include only the most important ideas.

superordinate relationship   The relationship of general or main idea of a passage to the overall text.

symbol system   Any arbitrary conventional written or printed mark intended to communicate, such as letters, numerals, ideographs, etc.

syndrome   A set of overt signs or observable behaviors occurring together.

syntactic system   The system of language concerned with the word order of sentences, the placement of punctuation, and the use of capital letters to help a reader determine the grammatical sense of a selection.

syntax   The component of language concerned with the order of words and their placement in phrases and sentences.

synthesizing   Summarizing text by combining relationships between the ideas of several different selections through students' interpretation of the material.

teachable units Parcels of information small enough to be learned through direct instruction; a specific learning segment.

teacher-guided writing lessons Writing lessons based on students' specific needs that concentrate on discrete aspects of written language that are new to the learners, such as spelling, punctuation, and so forth, as well as more global aspects of language, such as prewriting, paraphrasing, and editing.

teaching hypothesis The instructional plan determined by the teacher to be most beneficial to a particular student's instructional needs following the collection and analysis of educational data,

text organization The establishment of relationships between words, sentences, paragraphs, and larger units, which is the key to reading comprehension.

text-related tests Tests that measure the content, skills, and subskills learned by a reader from recently completed text material.

text set A collection of books, both fiction and nonfiction, that center around a particular topic; a book display with a theme.

textually explicit In QARs, the state of answers to questions that are stated literally and directly in the text material.

textually implicit In QARs, the state of answers to questions that are in the text, but which require the student to synthesize material spanning several sentences or paragraphs.

thematic units of instruction Particular topics of instruction upon which much of the instruction in a particular classroom is based, usually incorporating multiple disciplines and often arising naturally within the context of the school day.

think-links An instructional strategy developed by Wilson to help teachers guide their students into thinking about what they have read by having the students write down key words about a selection, then connect the key words first with specific examples and then with descriptive words, thereby reconstructing the important elements of the material.

thought units Short phrases, selected from text, that contain only one idea.

topic A word or phrase that represents the major subject of a text selection or picture.

transactional model A model of the reading process that takes into account the dynamic nature of language and both the cognitive and aesthetic aspects of reading by maintaining the concept that meaning exists in reading only through the interaction between the author's words and the reader's background knowledge.

transactive Relating to the construction of meaning by the active interchange of ideas between reader and text or between speaker and listener.

transfer of training The ability to generalize the specific process involved in the recognition of certain unknown words to other unknown words encountered in the future.

understanding questions A type of question recommended by Anderson to help students monitor their comprehension at the word, sentence, and paragraph levels by homing in on possible barriers to meaning such as new words, unfamiliar facts, and the relationship between the text material and existing knowledge.

validity In standardized testing, the extent to which a test measures what it claims to measure and does what it claims to do.

variables The factors being compared in a correlational study.

vernacular dialects The language varieties commonly used in informal circumstances; prevalent among lower socioeconomic groups.

viewing A receptive language art related to visual literacy and the unique visual symbols found with the use of videotapes, certain CD-ROM software, and other visual media.

visual A representation of important characters or settings in a piece of literature, such as a teddy bear, a sail boat, or a frog.

visual acuity The degree of one's ability to see with clarity and sharpness.

visual art Any form of art that provides meaning when viewed, such as dioramas, murals, or paintings.

visual arts media Crayons, tempera paint, chalk, colored pencils, water colors, and the like.

visual perception The skills of visual awareness, such as the ability to discriminate visually, the concept of constancy in spatial orientation, and the ability to remember visual sequences.

visual synthesizing The process in reading that follows auditory blending and allows readers to analyze words mentally without having to sound them out.

visually impaired Unable to see with appropriate keenness and acumen even with corrective lenses, thus requiring large-print accommodations for reading.

visually representing A language art related to the production of visual representations for the comprehension of text, such as graphs, charts, maps, clusters, drawings, and murals.

voices of composing The points of view taken by an author in writing, including the expressive, the poetic or imaginative, and the expository.

word wall A large surface for posting words being learned, studied, or used often in reading or writing.

working portfolio A portfolio that contains various works in progress, including a student's current project, works that may never be completed, work generated during various writing activities, ideas for future projects, copies of postwriting questionnaires, and anything else not selected for the showcase portfolio.

References

Aardema, V. (1981). *Bringing the rain to Kapiti Plain.* New York: Dial.

Adams, M. J. (1990). *Beginning to read: Thinking and learning about print.* Cambridge, MA: The MIT Press.

Adger, C. T. , Christian, D., & Taylor, O. (1999). *Making the connection: Language and academic achievement among African American students.* Champaign, IL: Center for Applied Linguistics and Delta Systems Co., Inc.

Alexander, F. (1993). National standards: A new conventional wisdom. *Educational Leadership, 50,* 9–10.

Alexander, J. E., & Cobb, J. (1992). Assessing attitudes in middle and secondary schools and community colleges. *Journal of Reading, 36,* 146–149.

Allen, R., Brown, K., & Yatvin, J. (1986). *Learning language through communication: A functional perspective.* Belmont, CA: Wadsworth.

Allington, R. (1994). The schools we have, the schools we need. *The Reading Teacher, 48,* 14–29.

Allington, R. (1995). Literacy lessons in the elementary schools: Yesterday, today, and tomorrow. In R. Allington and S. Walmsley (Eds.), *No quick fix: Rethinking literacy programs in America's elementary schools* (pp. 1–15). Columbia University, NY: Teachers College Press, and Newark, DE: International Reading Association.

Allington, R., & Walmsley, S. (Eds.). (1995). *No quick fix: Rethinking literacy programs in America's elementary schools.* Columbia University, NY: Teachers College Press, and Newark, DE: International Reading Association.

Almasi, J. (1996). A new view of discussion. In L. Gambrell and J. Almasi (Eds.). *Lively discussions! Fostering engaged reading* (pp. 2–24). Newark, DE: International Reading Association.

Alvarez, L., & Kolker, A. (Producers) (1987). *American tongues* [film]. (Available from New York: Center for New American Media).

Anderson, L., Raphael, T., Englert, C., & Stevens, D. (1992). *Teaching writing with a new instructional model: Variations in teachers' beliefs, instructional practices, and their students' performance.* East Lansing, MI: National Center for Research on Teacher Learning, Michigan State University.

Anderson, R. C., & Freebody, P. (1981). Vocabulary knowledge. In J. Guthrie (Ed.), *Comprehension and teaching: Research reviews* (pp. 77–117). Newark, DE: International Reading Association.

Anderson, T. H. (1980). Study strategies and adjunct aids. In R. J. Spiro, B. C. Bruce, & W. F. Brewer (Eds.), *Theoretical issues in reading comprehension.* Hillsdale, NJ: Erlbaum.

Andersson, B., & Gipe, J. (1983). Creativity as a mediating variable in inferential reading comprehension. *Reading Psychology, 4,* 313–325.

Andre, M. E. D. A., & Anderson, T. H. (1978/1979). The development and evaluation of a self-questioning study technique. *Reading Research Quarterly, 14,* 605–623.

Anthony, R., Johnson, T., Mickelson, N., & Preece, A. (1991). *Evaluating literacy: A perspective for change.* Portsmouth, NH: Heinemann.

Armstrong, T. (1993). *7 kinds of smart.* New York: Plume/Penguin.

Armstrong, T. (1999). *ADD/ADHD alternatives in the classroom.* Alexandria, VA: Association for Supervision and Curriculum Development.

Armstrong, T. (2000). *Multiple intelligences in the classroom* (2nd ed.). Alexandria, VA: Association for Supervision and Curriculum Development.

Arnold, R. D., & Sherry, N. (1975). A comparison of reading levels of disabled readers with assigned textbooks. *Reading Improvement, 12,* 207–211.

Atwell, N. (1987). *In the middle: Writing, reading, and learning with adolescents.* Portsmouth, NH: Heinemann.

Au, K. (1993a). *Literacy instruction in multicultural settings.* Fort Worth, TX: Harcourt Brace Jovanovich.

Au, K. (1993b, April). *New perspectives on assessment: Portfolios and ownership.* Featured speaker for the Organization of Teacher Educators in Reading at the annual meeting of the International Reading Association, San Antonio, TX.

Au, K. H. (1979). Using the experience-text-relationship method with minority children. *The Reading Teacher, 32,* 677–679.

Au, K. H., & Kawakami, A. J. (1985). Research currents: Talk story and learning to read. *Language Arts, 62,* 406–411.

Aulls, M. W. (1978). *Developmental and remedial reading in the middle grades* (Abridged ed.). Boston: Allyn & Bacon.

Babbs, P. J. (1984). Monitoring cards help improve comprehension. *The Reading Teacher, 38,* 200–204.

Baker, L. (1979). *Comprehension monitoring: Identifying and coping with text confusions* (Tech. Rep. No. 145). Champaign: University of Illinois, Center for the Study of Reading.

Baker, L., & Brown, A. L. (1984). Metacognitive skills and reading. In P. D. Pearson (Ed.), *Handbook of reading research*. New York: Longman.

Barnitz, J. G. (1985). *Reading development of nonnative speakers of English: Research and instruction* (Language in Education: Theory and Practice series, Monograph No. 63). ERIC Clearinghouse on Languages and Linguistics. Washington, DC: Center for Applied Linguistics, and Orlando, FL: Harcourt Brace Jovanovich. (ERIC Document Reproduction Service No. ED 256 182)

Barnitz, J. G. (1986). Toward understanding the effects of cross-cultural schemata and discourse structure on second language reading comprehension. *Journal of Reading Behavior, 18,* 95–116.

Barnitz, J. G. (1994). Discourse diversity: Principles for authentic talk and literacy instruction. *Journal of Reading, 37,* 586–591.

Barnitz, J. G. (1997). Linguistic perspectives in literacy education: Emerging awareness of linguistic diversity for literacy instruction. *The Reading Teacher, 51,* 264–266.

Barnitz, J. G. (1998). Linguistic perspectives in literacy education: Revising grammar instruction for authentic composing and comprehending. *The Reading Teacher, 51,* 608–611.

Barnitz, J. G., & Barnitz, C. G. (1996). Celebrating with language and literature at birthday parties and other childhood events. *The Reading Teacher, 50,* 110–117.

Barnitz, J. G., Gipe, J. P., & Richards, J. C. (1999). Linguistic perspectives in literacy education: Exploring linguistic benefits of literature for children's language performance in teacher education contexts. *The Reading Teacher, 52,* 528–531.

Barone, D. (1995). "Be very careful not to let the facts get mixed up with the truth": Children prenatally exposed to crack/cocaine. *Urban Education, 30* (1), 40–55.

Barone, D. (1996). Children prenatally exposed to crack or cocaine: Looking behind the label. *The Reading Teacher, 49,* 278–289.

Barrie, B. (1994). *Adam Zigzag.* New York: Delacourt Press.

Barron, R. F. (1969). The use of vocabulary as an advance organizer. In H. Herber and P. Sanders (Eds.), *Research in reading in the content areas: First year report.* Syracuse, NY: Syracuse University Press.

Bartch, J. (1992). An alternative to spelling: An integrated approach. *Language Arts, 69,* 404–408.

Bartlett, F. C. (1932). *Remembering: A study in experimental and social psychology.* New York: Cambridge University Press.

Bartolome, P. I. (1969). Teachers' objectives and questions in primary reading. *The Reading Teacher, 23,* 27–33.

Base, G. (1986). *Animalia.* New York: Abrams.

Baskin, B., & Harris, K. (1995). Heard any good books lately? The case for audiobooks in the secondary classroom. *Journal of Reading, 38,* 372–376.

Batey, C. (1996). *Parents are lifesavers: A handbook for parent involvement in schools.* Thousand Oaks, CA: Corwin Press.

Baugh, J. (1983). *Black street speech.* Austin: University of Texas Press.

Bean, T. W., & Pardi, R. (1979). A field test of a guided reading strategy. *Journal of Reading, 23,* 144–147.

Bear, T., Schenk, S., & Buckner, L. (1992/1993). Supporting victims of child abuse. *Educational Leadership, 50,* 42–47.

Bechtel, J., & Franzblau, B. (1980). *Reading in the science classroom.* Washington, DC: National Education Association.

Beck, I. L. (1981). Reading problems and instructional practices. In G. E. Mackinnon & T. G. Waller (Eds.), *Reading research: Advances in theory and practice* (Vol. 2) (pp. 53–95). New York: Academic Press.

Beck, I. L., & McKeown, M. B. (1981). Developing questions that promote comprehension of the story map. *Language Arts, 58,* 913–917.

Bedsworth, B. (1991). The Neurological Impress Method with middle school poor readers. *Journal of Reading, 34,* 564–565.

Benedict, S., & Carlisle, L. (1992). *Beyond words: Picture books for older readers and writers.* Portsmouth, NH: Heinemann.

Berglund, R. L. (1987). Reading assessment: An interactive process. *Reading Today, 5,* 3, 21.

Berlin, I. (1949). Give me your tired, your poor. Words and music in *Miss Liberty,* Sherwood, L. & Berlin, I. New York: Broadway Musical.

Berliner, D. C. (1981). Academic learning time and reading achievement. In J. T. Guthrie (Ed.), *Comprehension and teaching: Research reviews.* Newark, DE: International Reading Association.

Bernhardt, E. B. (1991). *Reading development in a second language: Theoretical, empirical, and classroom perspectives.* Norwood, NJ: Ablex.

Bernhardt, E. B. (2000). Second language reading as a case study of reading scholarship in the twentieth century. In M. L. Kamil, P. B. Mosenthal, D. Pearson, & R. Barr (Eds.), *Handbook of reading research* (Vol. 3) (p. 791). Mahwah, NJ: Erlbaum.

Betancourt, J. (1993). *My name is Brain/Brian.* New York: Scholastic.

Betts, E. (1946). *Foundations of reading instruction.* New York: American Book.

Bidwell, S. M. (1990). Using drama to increase motivation, comprehension, and fluency. *Journal of Reading, 34,* 38–41.

Biemiller, A. (1993). Students differ: So address differences effectively. *Educational Researcher, 22* (9), 14–15.

Binch, C. (1994). *Gregory Cool.* New York: Dial Books for Young Readers.

Blachowicz, C. L. Z., & Zabroske, B. (1990). Context instruction: A metacognitive approach for at-risk readers. *Journal of Reading, 33,* 504–508.

Blair-Larsen, S., & Williams, K. E. (Eds.). (1999). *The balanced reading program: Helping all students achieve success*. Newark, DE: International Reading Association.

Blecher, S., & Jaffee, K. (1998). *Weaving in the arts: Widening the learning circle*. Portsmouth, NH: Heinemann.

Block, C. C. (1999). Comprehension: Crafting understanding. In L. Gambrell, L. Morrow, S. Neuman, and M. Pressley (Eds.), *Best practices in literacy instruction* (pp. 98–118). New York: Guilford Press.

Block, C., & Cavanaugh, C. (1998). Teaching thinking: How can we and why should we? In R. Bernhardt, C. Hedley, G. Cattaro, & V. Svolopoulous (Eds.), *Curriculum leadership: Rethinking schools for the 21st century* (pp. 301–320). Alexandria, VA: Association for Supervision and Curriculum Development.

Bloem, P. L., & Padak, N. D. (1996). Picture books, young adult books, and adult literacy learners. *Journal of Adolescent and Adult Literacy, 40,* 48–53.

Bloome, D. (1991). Anthropology and research on teaching the English language arts. In J. Flood, J. M. Jensen, D. Lapp, and J. R. Squire (Eds.). *Handbook of research on teaching the English language arts* (pp. 46–56). New York: Macmillan.

Bloome, D., & Egan-Robertson, A. (1993). The social construction of intertextuality in classroom reading and writing lessons. *Reading Research Quarterly, 25,* 305–333.

Blyth, T., & Gardner, H. (1990). A school for all intelligences. *Educational Leadership, 47,* 33–37.

Bolton, F., & Snowball, D. (1996). *Teaching spelling: A practical resource*. Portsmouth, NH: Heinemann.

Boning, R. (1985). *Specific Skill Series, Primary Overview, Drawing Conclusions—Booklet C*. Baldwin, NY: Barnell Loft.

Boning, T., & Boning, R. (1957). I'd rather read than. . . . *The Reading Teacher* (April), 196–200.

Borkowski, J. G., Wehing, R. S., & Turner, L. A. (1986). Attributional retraining and the teaching of strategies. *Exceptional Children, 53,* 130–137.

Bormuth, J. R. (1967). Comparable cloze and multiple-choice comprehension test score. *Journal of Reading, 10,* 291–299.

Bormuth, J. R. (1968a). The cloze readability procedure. *Elementary English, 45,* 429–436.

Bormuth, J. R. (1968b). Cloze test readability: Criterion reference scores. *Journal of Educational Measurement, 5,* 189–196.

Bormuth, J. R. (1975). The cloze procedure: Literacy in the classroom. In W. D. Page (Ed.), *Help for the reading teacher: New directions in research* (pp. 60–90). Urbana, IL: ERIC Clearinghouse on Reading and Communication Skills.

Bottomley, D., Henk, W., & Melnick, S. (1997–1998). Assessing children's views about themselves as writers using the Writer Self-Perception Scale. *The Reading Teacher, 51,* 286–296.

Brett, J. (1987). *Goldilocks and the three bears*. Boston: Houghton-Mifflin.

Bridges, L. (1995). *Assessment: Continuous learning*. York, ME: Stenhouse.

Britton, J., Burgess, T., Martin, N., McLeod, A., & Rosen, H. (1975). *The development of writing abilities* (pp. 11–18). Schools Council Research Studies. London: Macmillan.

Bromley, K. (1989). Buddy journals make the reading-writing connection. *The Reading Teacher, 43,* 122–129.

Brown, A. L. (1980). Metacognitive development and reading. In R. J. Spiro, B. C. Bruce, & W. F. Brewer (Eds.), *Theoretical issues in reading comprehension* (pp. 453–481). Hillsdale, NJ: Erlbaum.

Brown, A. L., & DeLoache, J. (1978). Skills, plans, and self-regulation. In R. Siegler (Ed.), *Children's thinking: What develops?* Hillsdale, NJ: Erlbaum.

Brown, C. S. (1985, April). *Assessing perceptions of language and learning: Alternative diagnostic approaches*. Paper presented at the International Reading Association Convention, New Orleans, LA.

Brown, D. A. (1982). *Reading diagnosis and remediation*. Upper Saddle River, NJ: Prentice-Hall.

Brown, J. I., Fishco, V. V., & Hanna, G. S. (1993). Nelson-Denny Reading Test, Forms G & H. Itasca, IL: Riverside.

Brozo, W. G. (1990). Learning how at-risk readers learn best: A case for interactive assessment. *Journal of Reading, 33,* 522–527.

Bruchac, J. (1993). *Fox song*. New York: Putnam.

Bruner, J. (1966). *Toward a theory of instruction*. Cambridge, MA: Harvard University Press.

Bryan, J. (1998). K–W–W–L: Questioning the known. *The Reading Teacher, 51,* 618–620.

Bryson, M., & Scardamalia, M. (1991). Teaching writing to students at risk for academic failure. In B. Means, C. Chelmer, & M. Knapp (Eds.), *Teaching advanced skills to at-risk students: Views from research and practice* (pp. 141–167). San Francisco: Jossey-Bass.

Buehl, D. (2001). *Classroom strategies for interactive learning*, 2nd edition (pp. 118–120 for Readers theatre). Newark, DE: International Reading Association.

Buikema, J. L., & Graves, M. F. (1993). Teaching students to use context to infer word meanings. *Journal of Reading, 36,* 450–457.

Burling, R. (1973). *English in black and white*. New York: Holt, Rinehart, & Winston.

Burmeister, L. E. (1978). *Reading strategies for middle and secondary school teachers*. Reading, MA: Addison-Wesley.

Burns, P. C. (1980). *Assessment and correction of language arts difficulties*. Columbus, OH: Merrill.

Burns, P. C. (1998). *Informal reading inventory: Preprimer to twelfth grade*. St. Charles, IL: Houghton Mifflin.

Byars, B. (1975). *The lace snail*. New York: Viking.

Calkins, L. (1986). *The art of teaching writing*. Portsmouth, NH: Heinemann.

Cambourne, B. (1988). *The whole story: Natural learning and the acquisition of literacy.* Auckland, New Zealand: Ashton-Scholastic.

Cambourne, B. (1995). Toward an educationally relevant theory of literacy learning: Twenty years of inquiry. *The Reading Teacher, 49,* (3), 182–190.

Campbell, L., Campbell, B., & Dickinson, D. (1999). *Teaching and learning through multiple intelligences.* Needham Heights, MA: Allyn & Bacon.

Cantrell, S. (1998/1999). Effective teaching and literacy learning: A look inside primary classrooms. *The Reading Teacher, 52,* 370–378.

Cardarelli, A. F. (1988). The influence of reinspection on students' IRI results. *The Reading Teacher, 41,* 664–667.

Carle, E. (1987). *The very hungry caterpillar.* New York: Scholastic.

Carle, E. (1996). *The grouchy ladybug.* New York: Harper-Collins.

Carr, E., Dewitz, P., & Patberg, J. (1989). Using cloze for inference training with expository text. *The Reading Teacher, 42,* 380–385.

Carr, E., & Ogle, D. (1987). K–W–L plus: A strategy for comprehension and summarization. *Journal of Reading, 30,* (7), 626–631.

Carr, E., & Wixson, K. K. (1986). Guidelines for evaluating vocabulary instruction. *Journal of Reading, 29,* 588–595.

Carrell, P. L., Devine, J., & Eskey, D. E. (Eds.). (1988). *Interactive approaches to second language reading.* Cambridge, England: Cambridge University Press.

Carver, R. P. (1977). Toward a theory of reading comprehension and rauding. *Reading Research Quarterly, 13,* 6–63.

Carver, R. P. (1990). *Reading rate: A review of research and theory.* New York: Academic Press.

Carver, R. P. (1992). Commentary: Effect of prediction activities, prior knowledge, and text type upon amount comprehended: Using rauding theory to critique schema theory research. *Reading Research Quarterly, 27,* 164–174.

Cary, S. (2000). *Working with second language learners: Answers to teachers' top ten questions.* Portsmouth, NH.: Heinemann.

Caskey, H. J. (1970). Guidelines for teaching comprehension. *The Reading Teacher, 23,* 649–654, 669.

Cassady, J. K. (1998). Wordless books: No-risk tools for inclusive middle-grade classrooms. *Journal of Adolescent & Adult Literacy, 41,* 428–432.

Caverly, D., Mandeville, T., & Nicholson, S. (1995). PLAN: A study-reading strategy for informational text. *Journal of Adolescent & Adult Literacy, 39,* 190–199.

Cazden, C. B., John, V. P., & Hymes, D. (Eds.). (1972). *Functions of language in the classroom.* New York: Teachers College Press.

Cecil N. L. (1995). *The art of inquiry: Questioning strategies for K–6 classrooms.* Winnipeg, Canada: Peguin.

Cecil, N., & Lauritzen, P. (1994). *Literacy and the arts for the integrated classroom: Alternative ways of knowing.* White Plains, NY: Longman.

Chant, S. A., & Pelow, R. A. (1979, May). *Activities for functional reading and language: Preschool through middle school.* Paper presented at the annual meeting of the International Reading Association, Atlanta, GA.

Chase, A. C., & Duffelmeyer, F. A. (1990). VOCAB-LIT: Integrating vocabulary study and literature study. *Journal of Reading, 34,* 188–193.

Chasnoff, I. (1991). Drugs, alcohol, pregnancy, and the neonate. *JAMA, 266* (11), 1567–1568.

Chasnoff, I. (1992). President's message. *Perinatal Addiction Research and Education Update,* 2–3.

Cherry, L. (1990). *The great kapok tree: A tale of the Amazon rain forest.* New York: Harcourt Brace and Co.

Cheyney, A. B. (1992). *Teaching reading through the newspaper,* 3rd edition. Newark, DE: International Reading Association.

Clay, M. M. (2000). *Running records for classroom teachers.* Portsmouth, NH: Heinemann.

Cleland, C. J. (1981). Highlighting issues in children's literature through semantic webbing. *The Reading Teacher, 34,* 642–646.

Clements, A. (1997). *Double trouble in Walla Walla.* Brookfield, CT: Millbrook Press.

Clemmons, J., Laase, L., Cooper, D., Areglado, N., & Dill, M. (1993). *Portfolios in the classroom: A teacher's sourcebook.* New York: Scholastic.

Clymer, T. L. (1963). The utility of phonic generalizations in the primary grades. *The Reading Teacher, 16,* 252–258. (Reprinted 1996, *The Reading Teacher, 50,* 182–187.)

Cochran-Smith, M. (1991). Learning to teach against the grain. *Harvard Educational Review, 61,* 279–310.

Cohen, D., & Rudolph, M. (1984). *Kindergarten and early schooling.* Upper Saddle River, NJ: Prentice-Hall.

Cohn, M. L. (1969). Structured comprehension. *The Reading Teacher, 22,* 440–444, 489.

Collier, V. P. (1987). Age and rate of acquisition of second language for academic purposes. *TESOL Quarterly, 21,* 617–641.

Collier, V. P. (1989). How long? A synthesis of research on academic achievement in a second language. *TESOL Quarterly, 23,* 509–631.

Collins, A., & Smith, E. E. (1980). *Teaching the process of reading comprehension* (Tech. Rep. No. 182). Champaign: University of Illinois, Center for the Study of Reading.

Collinson, V. (1995). Making the most of portfolios. *Learning, 24* (1), 43–46.

Comrie, B. (Ed.). (1990). *The world's major languages.* New York: Oxford University Press.

Conner, U. (1996). *Contrastive rhetoric: Cross-cultural aspects of second-language writing.* New York: Cambridge University Press.

Cook-Gumperz, J. (Ed.). (1986). *The social construction of literacy*. Cambridge, England: Cambridge University Press.

Cooper, C., & Odell, L. (Eds.). (1977). *Evaluating writing: Describing, measuring, judging*. Urbana, IL: National Council of Teachers of English.

Cooper, J. D., Warncke, E. W., Ramstad, P., & Shipman, D. A. (1979). *The what and how of reading instruction*. Upper Saddle River, NJ: Prentice-Hall/Merrill.

Cooper, L. J. (1952). *The effect of adjustment of basal reading materials on achievement*. Unpublished doctoral dissertation, Boston University.

Cooter, R. B., & Chilcoat, G. W. (1990). Content-focused melodrama: Dramatic renderings of historical text. *Journal of Reading, 34,* 274–277.

Cornett, C. (1999). *The arts as meaning makers: Integrating literature and the arts throughout the curriculum*. Upper Saddle River, NJ: Merrill/Prentice-Hall.

Coulmas, F. (1989). *The writing systems of the world*. Oxford, England: Blackwell Publishers.

Cowan, J. R., & Sarmad, Z. (1976). Reading performance of bilingual children according to the type of school and home environment. *Language Learning, 26,* 353–376.

Cudd, E. T., & Roberts, L. L. (1987). Using story frames to develop reading comprehension in a first grade classroom. *The Reading Teacher, 41,* 74–79.

Cudd, E. T., & Roberts, L. L. (1989). Using writing to enhance content area learning in the primary grades. *The Reading Teacher, 42* (6), 392–404.

Cummins, J. (1994). The acquisition of English as a second language. In K. Spangenberg-Urbschat & R. Pritchard (Eds.), *Kids come in all languages: Reading instruction for ESL students* (pp. 36–62). Newark, DE: International Reading Association.

Cunningham, J. (1982). Generating interactions between schemata and text. In J. Niles & L. Harris (Eds.), *New inquiries in reading research and instruction* (pp. 42–47). Washington, DC: National Reading Conference.

Cunningham, P. (1991). *Phonics they use: Words for reading and writing*. New York: HarperCollins.

Cunningham, P. (1999). What should we do about phonics? In L. Gambrell, L. Morrow, S. Neuman, & M. Pressley (Eds.) *Best practices in literacy instruction* (pp. 68–89). New York: Guilford Press.

Curtis, M. E., & McCart, L. (1992). Fun ways to promote poor readers' word recognition. *Journal of Reading, 35,* 398–399.

Dale, E., O'Rourke, J., & Bamman, H. A. (1971). *Techniques of teaching vocabulary*. Palo Alto, CA: Field Educational Publications.

Dale, E., O'Rourke, J., & Barbe, W. (1986). *Vocabulary building: A process approach*. Columbus, OH: Zaner-Bloser.

D'Alessandro, M. (1990). Accommodating emotionally handicapped children through a literature-based reading program. *The Reading Teacher, 44,* 288–293.

Daniels, H. (1991). Commentary on chapter 5 (Teaching writing to students at-risk for academic failure). In B. Means, C. Chalmers, & M. Knapp (Eds.), *Teaching advanced skills to at-risk students: Views from research and practice* (pp. 168–175). San Francisco: Jossey-Bass.

Daniels, H. (1994). *Literature circles: Voice and choice in the student-centered classroom*. York, ME: Stenhouse.

Danielson, K. E. (1992). Picture books to use with older students. *Journal of Reading, 35,* 652–654.

Dantonio, M. (1990). *How can we create thinkers? Questioning strategies that work for teachers*. Bloomington, IN: National Education Services.

Davidson, J. L. (1982). The group mapping activity for instruction in reading and thinking. *Journal of Reading, 26,* 52–56.

Davis, A. L. (1972). English problems of Spanish speakers. In D. L. Shores (Ed.), *Contemporary English: Change and variation* (pp. 123–133), New York: Lippincott.

Davis, C. (1978). The effectiveness of informal assessment questions constructed by secondary teachers. In P. D. Pearson & J. Hansen (Eds.), *Reading: Disciplined inquiry in process and practice* (pp. 13–15). 27th Yearbook of the National Reading Conference, Clemson, SC.

Davis, F. B. (1944). Fundamental factors of comprehension in reading. *Psychometrika, 9,* 185–197.

Day, J. D. (1980). *Training summarization skills: A comparison of teaching methods*. Unpublished doctoral dissertation, University of Illinois, Urbana.

DeFina, A. A. (1992). *Portfolio assessment: Getting started*. New York: Scholastic.

Degen, B. (1983). *Jamberry*. New York: Harper & Row.

DeSylvia, D. A., & Klug, C. D. (1992). Drugs and children: Taking care of the victims. *Journal of the American Optometric Association, 63* (1), 59–62.

Devine, T. G. (1981). *Teaching study skills: A guide for teachers*. Boston: Allyn & Bacon.

Dewey, J. (1933). *How we think: A restatement of the relation of reflective thinking to the educational process*. Boston: Heath.

Diederich, P. B. (1974). *Measuring growth in English*. Urbana, IL: National Council of Teachers of English.

Diller, D. (1999). Opening the dialogue: Using culture as a tool in teaching young African American children. *The Reading Teacher, 52,* 820–827.

Dimino, J., Gersten, R., Carnine, D., & Blake, G. (1990). Story grammar: An approach for promoting at-risk secondary students' comprehension of literature. *Elementary School Journal, 91,* 19–32.

Dionisio, M. (1989). Write? Isn't this reading class? *The Reading Teacher, 36,* 746–749.

Doake, D. B. (1988). *Reading begins at birth*. New York: Scholastic.

Dolch, E. (1953). *Dolch basic sight vocabulary*. Champaign, IL: Garrard.

Dowhower, S. (1999). Supporting a strategic stance in the classroom: A comprehension framework for helping teachers help students to be strategic. *The Reading Teacher, 52,* 672–688.

Dowhower, S. L. (1989). Repeated reading: Research into practice. *The Reading Teacher, 42,* 502–507.

Drewe, S. B. (1998). *Creative dance inspirations: Facilitating expression.* Calgary, Alberta, Canada: Detselig Enterprises LTD.

Dreyer, S. (1987). *The bookfinder: Guide to children's literature about the needs and problems of youth aged 2–15.* Circle Pines, MN: American Guidance Services.

Drummond, M. J. (1994). *Learning to see: Assessment through observation.* York, ME: Stenhouse Publishers.

Duffelmeyer, F. A., & Baum, D. D. (1992). The extended anticipation guide revisited. *Journal of Reading, 35,* 654–656.

Duffelmeyer, F. A., & Black, J. (1996). The Names Test: A domain-specific validation study. *The Reading Teacher, 50,* 148–150.

Duffelmeyer, F. A., & Duffelmeyer, B. B. (1989). Are IRI passages suitable for assessing main idea comprehension? *The Reading Teacher, 42,* 358–363.

Duffelmeyer, F. A., Kruse, A., Merkley, D., & Fyfe, S. (1994). Further validation and enhancement of the Names Test. *The Reading Teacher, 48,* 118–128.

Duffelmeyer, F. A., Robinson, S. S., & Squier, S. E. (1989). Vocabulary questions on informal reading inventories. *The Reading Teacher, 43,* 142–148.

Duffy, G. (1997). Powerful models or powerful teachers? An argument for teacher-as-entrepreneur. In S. A. Stahl & D. A. Hayes (Eds.), *Instructional models in reading* (pp. 351–365). Mahwah, NJ: Erlbaum.

Duffy, G. G., Roehler, L. R., & Herrmann, B. A. (1988). Modeling mental processes helps poor readers become strategic readers. *The Reading Teacher, 41,* 762–767.

Duffy-Hester, A. (1999). Teaching struggling readers in elementary school classrooms: A review of classroom reading programs and principles for instruction. *The Reading Teacher, 52,* 480–495.

Dunkeld, C. (1978). Students' notetaking and teachers' expectations. *Journal of Reading, 21,* 542–546.

Durkin, D. (1978). *Teaching them to read* (3rd ed.). Boston: Allyn & Bacon.

Durkin, D. (1978/1979). What classroom observations reveal about reading comprehension instruction. *Reading Research Quarterly, 14,* 481–533.

Durkin, D. (1981). Reading comprehension instruction in five basal reading series. *Reading Research Quarterly, 14,* 515–544.

Durrell, D. D. (1963). *Phonograms in primary grade words.* Boston: Boston University.

Dyer, H. S. (1968). Research issues on equality of educational opportunity: School factors. *Harvard Educational Review, 38,* 38–56.

Eanet, M. G., & Manzo, A. V. (1976). REAP—a strategy for improving reading/writing study skills. *Journal of Reading, 19,* 647–652.

Earle, R. A. (1976). *Teaching reading and mathematics.* Newark, DE: International Reading Association.

Echols, L., West, R., & Stanovich, K. (1996). Using children's literacy activities to predict growth in verbal cognitive skills: A longitudinal investigation. *Journal of Educational Psychology, 88,* 296–304.

Edminston, B., Enciso, P., & King, M. (1987). Empowering readers and writers through drama: Narrative theater. *Language Arts, 64,* 219–229.

Eeds, M., & Wells, D. (1989). Grand conversations: An exploration of meaning construction in literature study groups. *Research in the Teaching of English, 23* (10), 4–29.

Ehri, L. (1992). Reconceptualizing the development of sight word reading and its relationship to reading. In P. Gough, L. Ehri, and R. Treiman (Eds.), *Reading acquisition* (107–143). Hillsdale, NJ: Erlbaum.

Eisner, E. (1981). The role of the arts in cognition and curriculum. *Phi Delta Kappan, 63,* 48–52.

Ekwall, E. E., & Shanker, J. L. (1988). *Diagnosis and remediation of the disabled reader* (3rd ed.). Boston: Allyn & Bacon.

Ekwall, E. E., & Shanker, J. L. (1999). *Ekwall/Shanker reading inventory,* Boston: Allyn & Bacon.

Elbow, P. (2000). *Everyone can write: Essays toward a hopeful theory of writing and teaching.* New York: Oxford University Press.

Elley, W. (1991). Acquiring literacy in a second language: The effect of book-based programs. *Language Learning, 41* (3), 375–411.

Emberly, B. (Adapted by). (1967). *Drummer Hoff.* New York: Prentice-Hall.

Emig, J. (1983). *The web of meaning: Essays on writing, teaching, learning, and thinking.* Portsmouth, NH: Heinemann.

Englert, C. S., & Thomas, C. C. (1987). Sensitivity to text structure in reading and writing: A comparison between learning disabled and non–learning disabled students. *Learning Disabilities Quarterly, 10,* 93–105.

Enright, D. S., & McCloskey, M. L. (1988). *Integrating English: Developing English language and literacy in the multilingual classroom.* Reading, MA: Addison-Wesley.

Erickson, E. (1950). *Childhood and society.* New York: Norton.

Ericson, L., & Juliebo, M. F. (1998). *The phonological awareness handbook for kindergarten and primary teachers.* Newark, DE: International Reading Association.

ESA Word List. (1977). In E. C. Kennedy, *Classroom approaches to remedial reading.* Itasca, IL: Peacock.

Estes, T. H., Estes, J. J., Richards, H. C., & Roettger, D. (1981). *Estes attitude scales: Measures of attitude toward school subjects.* Austin, TX: Pro-Ed.

Farr, R. (1992). Putting it all together: Solving the reading assessment puzzle. *The Reading Teacher, 46,* 26–37.

Fay, L. (1965). Reading study skills: Math and science. In J. A. Figurel (Ed.), *Reading and inquiry*. Newark, DE: International Reading Association.

Fennessey, S. (1995). Living history through drama and literature. *The Reading Teacher, 49,* 16–19.

Fennimore, F. (1980). Attaining sentence verve with sentence extension. In G. Stanford (Ed.), *Dealing with differences*. Urbana, IL: National Council of Teachers of English.

Ferdman, B. M., Weber, R. M., & Ramirez, A. G. (Eds.). (1994). *Literacy across languages and cultures*. Albany: SUNY Press.

Fernald, G. M. (1943). *Remedial techniques in basic school subjects*. New York: McGraw-Hill.

Fisher, D., Gallego, M., Lapp, D., & Flood, J. (2000, April). Children's use of community libraries: Access, fluency, and reading performance. Paper presented at the Annual Meeting of the American Educational Research Association, New Orleans, LA.

Fitzgerald, J. (1999). What is this thing called "balance"? *The Reading Teacher, 53* (2), 100–107.

Fitzgerald, J., & Spiegel, D. L. (1983). Enhancing children's reading comprehension through instruction in narrative structure. *Journal of Reading Behavior, 15,* 1–17.

Flavell, J. H. (1976). Metacognitive aspects of problem solving. In L. B. Resnick (Ed.), *The nature of intelligence*. Hillsdale, NJ: Erlbaum.

Flood, J., Heath, S. B., & Lapp, D. (1997). *Handbook of research on teaching literacy through the communicative and visual arts*. New York: Simon & Schuster.

Flood, J., & Wood, K. (1998). Viewing: The neglected communication process or "When what you see isn't what you get." *The Reading Teacher, 52,* 300–304.

Flores, B. M. (1984). *Language interference or influence: Toward a theory for Hispanic bilingualism*. Doctoral dissertation, University of Arizona, Tucson.

Flynt, E. S., & Cooter, R. B. (1998). *Flynt-Cooter reading inventory for the classroom*. Columbus, OH: Prentice-Hall/Merrill.

Forgan, H. W., & Mangrum, C. T. (1985). *Teaching content area reading skills* (3rd ed.). Columbus, OH: Prentice-Hall/Merrill.

Fowler, G. L. (1982). Developing comprehension skills in primary students through the use of story frames. *The Reading Teacher, 37,* 176–179.

Fox, B. J. (2000). *Word identification strategies: Phonics from a new perspective* (2nd ed.). Upper Saddle River, NJ: Merrill/Prentice-Hall.

Fox, S. E., & Allen, V. G. (1983). *The language arts: An integrated approach*. New York: Holt, Rinehart & Winston.

Frase, L. T., & Schwartz, B. J. (1975). Effect of question production on prose recall. *Journal of Educational Psychology, 67,* 628–635.

Frayer, D. A., Frederick, W. C., & Klausmeier, H. J. (1969). *A schema for testing the level of concept mastery*. (Tech. Rep.

No. 16). Madison: University of Wisconsin, R & D Center for Cognitive Learning.

Frazee, B. (1993). Core knowledge: How to get started. *Educational Leadership, 50,* 28–29.

Freedman, G., & Reynolds, E. G. (1980). Enriching basal reader lessons with semantic webbing. *The Reading Teacher, 33,* 677–684.

Freeman, Y. S., & Freeman, D. E. (1992). *Whole language for second language learners*. Portsmouth, NH: Heinemann.

Freire, P. (1992). *Pedagogy of the oppressed*. New York: Continuum Press.

Fronval, G., & Dubois, D. (1994). *Indian signals and sign language*. New York: Wing Books.

Fry, E. B. (1980). Test review: Metropolitan Achievement Tests. *The Reading Teacher, 34,* 196–201.

Fry, E. B. (1989). Reading formulas—Maligned but valid. *Journal of Reading, 32,* 292–297.

Fry, E. B., Kress, J., & Fountoukidis, D. (1993). *The reading teacher's book of lists*. Upper Saddle River, NJ: Prentice-Hall.

Furness, E. L. (1971). Proportion, purpose, and process in listening. In S. Duker (Ed.), *Teaching listening in the elementary school* (pp. 53–57). Metuchen, NJ: Scarecrow Press.

Gag, W. (1928). *Millions of cats*. New York: Coward, McCann & Geoghegan.

Gag, W. (1938). *Snow White and the seven dwarfs* (original story by Jacob Grimm freely translated and illustrated). Eau Claire, WI: E. M. Hale and Company.

Gallant, R. (1964). *An investigation of the use of cloze tests as a measure of readability of materials for the primary grades*. Unpublished doctoral dissertation, Indiana University, Bloomington.

Gallas, K. (1992). Arts as epistemology: Enabling children to know what they know. In M. Goldberg & R. Phillips (Eds.), *Arts as education*. Boston: Harvard Educational Review.

Gambrell, L. B., & Bales, R. (1986). Mental imagery and the comprehension monitoring performance of fourth- and fifth-grade poor readers. *Reading Research Quarterly, 11,* 454–464.

Gambrell, L. B., & Jawitz, P. B. (1993). Mental imagery, text illustrations, and children's story comprehension and recall. *Reading Research Quarterly, 28,* 264–276.

Gambrell, L. B., Koskinen, P. S., & Kapinus, B. A. (1991). Retelling and the reading comprehension of proficient and less-proficient readers. *Journal of Educational Research, 84,* 356–362.

Gambrell, L. B., & Mazzoni, S. (1999). Principles of best practice: Finding the common ground. In L. Gambrell, L. Morrow, S. Neuman, & M. Pressley (Eds.) *Best practices in literacy instruction* (pp. 11–21). New York: Guilford Press.

Gambrell, L. B., Morrow, L., Neuman, S., & Pressley, M. (Eds.). (1999). *Best practices in literacy instruction*. New York: Guilford Press.

Gambrell, L. B., Wilson, R. M., & Gantt, W. N. (1981). Class-room observations of task-attending behaviors of good and poor readers. *Journal of Educational Research, 24,* 400–404.

Gambrell, L. B., Pfeiffer, W., & Wilson, R. (1985). The effects of retelling upon reading comprehension and recall of text information. *Journal of Educational Research, 7,* 216–220.

Garcia, G. E. (2000). Bilingual children's reading. In M. L. Kamil, P. B. Mosenthal, P. D. Pearson, & R. Barr (Eds.), *Handbook of reading research, volume III.* (pp. 813–834). Mahwah, NJ: Erlbaum.

Garcia, G., & Pearson, P. D. (1991). *Literacy assessment in a diverse society.* (Tech. Rep. No. 525). Champaign: University of Illinois, Center for the Study of Reading. (Also in E. H. Hiebert [Ed.], *Literacy for a diverse society* [pp. 253–278], New York: Teachers College Press.)

Gardner, H. (1983). *Frames of mind: The theory of multiple intelligences.* New York: Basic Books.

Gardner, H. (1991). *The unschooled mind: How children think and how schools should teach.* New York: Basic Books.

Gardner, H. (1995). Reflections on multiple intelligences. *Phi Delta Kappan, 77,* 200–209.

Gardner, H. (1999). *Intelligence reframed: Multiple intelligences for the 21st century.* New York: Basic Books.

Garner, R. (1980). Monitoring of understanding: An investigation of good and poor readers' awareness of induced miscomprehension of text. *Journal of Reading Behavior, 12,* 55–64.

Garner, R. (1987). *Metacognition and reading comprehension.* Norwood, NJ: Ablex.

Gaskins, I., Ehri, L., Cress, C., O'Hara, C., & Donnelly, K. (1996/1997). Procedures for word learning: Making discoveries about words. *The Reading Teacher, 50,* 312–327.

Geissal, M. A., & Knafle, J. D. (1977). A linguistic view of auditory discrimination tests and exercises. *The Reading Teacher, 31,* 624–644.

Gentry, J. R. (1982). An analysis of developmental spellings in *Gnys at wrk. The Reading Teacher, 36,* 192–200.

Gentry, J. R. (1987). *Spel . . . is a four-letter word.* New York: Scholastic.

Gentry, J. R. (1996). *My kid can't spell! Understanding and assisting your child's literacy development.* Portsmouth, NH: Heinemann.

Gentry, J. R. (2000). A retrospective on invented spelling and a look forward. *The Reading Teacher, 54,* 318–333.

Gillespie, C. (1990/1991). Questions about student-generated questions. *Journal of Reading, 34,* 250–257.

Gipe, J. P. (1977). *An investigation of the effectiveness of four techniques for teaching word meanings with third- and fifth-grade students.* Unpublished doctoral dissertation, Purdue University.

Gipe, J. P. (1978/1979). Investigating techniques for teaching word meanings. *Reading Research Quarterly, 14,* 624–644.

Gipe, J. P. (1980). Use of a relevant context helps kids learn new word meanings. *The Reading Teacher, 33,* 398–402.

Glasgow, J. (1996). It's my turn!: Motivating young readers. *Learning & Leading with Technology, 24* (3), 20–23.

Glasser, W. (1969). *Schools without failure.* New York: Harper & Row.

Glazer, S. M. (1992). *Reading comprehension: Self-monitoring strategies to develop independent readers.* New York: Scholastic.

Glazer, S. M. (1993). Children and self-assessment: A "risky" experience. *Teaching PreK–8, 23* (8), 106–108.

Glazer, S. M., & Brown, C. S. (1993). *Portfolios and beyond: Collaborative assessment in reading and writing.* Norwood, MA: Christopher-Gordon.

Goldenberg, C. (1992/1993). Instructional conversations: Promoting comprehension through discussion. *The Reading Teacher, 46,* 316–326.

Goleman, D. (1995). *Emotional intelligence: Why it can matter more than IQ.* New York: Bantam.

Golinkoff, R. M. (1975/1976). A comparison of reading comprehension processes in good and poor comprehenders. *Reading Research Quarterly, 11,* 623–659.

Goodman, K. S. (1968). The psycholinguistic nature of the reading process. In K. S. Goodman (Ed.), *The psycholinguistic nature of the reading process.* Detroit, MI: Wayne State Press.

Goodman, K. S. (1973). *Theoretically based studies of patterns of miscues in oral reading performance.* Washington, DC: U.S. Department of Health, Education and Welfare, Office of Education, Bureau of Research.

Goodman, K. S. (1979). *Miscue analysis: Applications to reading instruction.* Urbana, IL: National Council of Teachers of English.

Goodman, K. S. (1982). Revaluing readers and reading. *Topics in Learning and Learning Disabilities, 1,* 87–93.

Goodman, K. S. (1986). *What's whole in whole language?* Portsmouth, NH: Heinemann.

Goodman, K. S. (1994). Reading, writing, and written texts: A transactional sociopsycholinguistic view. In R. B. Ruddell, M. R. Ruddell, & H. Singer (Eds.), *Theoretical models and processes of reading* (4th ed.) (pp. 1093–1130). Newark, DE: International Reading Association.

Goodman, K. S. (1996). *On reading.* Portsmouth, NH: Heinemann.

Goodman, K. S., & Buck, S. (1973). Dialect barriers to reading comprehension revisited. *The Reading Teacher, 27,* 6–12. [Reprinted 1997, *The Reading Teacher, 50,* 454–459.]

Goodman, K. S., & Goodman, Y. (1978). *Reading of American children whose language is a stable rural dialect of English or a language other than English.* University of Arizona, Final Report, Project NIE-C-00-3-0087. (ERIC Document Reproduction Service No. ED 173 754)

Goodman, K. S., Goodman, Y. M., & Hood, W. J. (1989). *The whole language evaluation book*. Portsmouth, NH: Heinemann.

Goodman, Y. M. (1996). Revaluing readers while readers revalue themselves: Retrospective miscue analysis. *The Reading Teacher, 49,* 600–609.

Goodman, Y., & Burke, C. (1972). *Reading miscue inventory manual: Procedure for diagnosis and evaluation.* New York: Macmillan.

Goodman, Y. M., & Burke, C. (1980). *Reading strategies: Focus on comprehension.* New York: Holt, Rinehart & Winston.

Goodman, Y., & Marek, A. (1996). *Retrospective miscue analysis: Revaluing readers and reading.* Katonah, NY: Owen.

Goodman, Y. M., Watson, D. J., & Burke, C. L. (1987). *Reading miscue inventory: Alternative procedures.* New York: Owen.

Goswami, U., & Mead, F. (1992). Onset and rime awareness and analogies in reading. *Reading Research Quarterly, 27,* 152–162.

Gough, P. B. (1984). Word recognition. In P. D. Pearson (Ed.), *Handbook of reading research* (pp. 225–253). New York: Longman.

Gould, M. (1982). *Golden daffodils.* Reading, MA: Addison-Wesley.

Grady, E. (1992). *The portfolio approach to assessment.* Bloomington, IN: Phi Delta Kappa Educational Foundation.

Graves, D. (1983). *Writing: Teachers and children at work.* Portsmouth, NH: Heinemann.

Graves, D. (1992). Help students learn to read their portfolios. In D. Graves & B. Sunstein (Eds.), *Portfolio portraits* (pp. 85–95). Portsmouth, NH: Heinemann.

Graves, D., & Murray, D. (1980). Revision in the writer's workshop and in the classroom. *Journal of Education, 162,* 38–56.

Graves, M., Juel, C., & Graves, B. (1998). *Teaching reading in the 21st century.* Boston: Allyn & Bacon.

Great Atlantic and Pacific Word List. (1972). From W. Otto & R. Chester, Sight words for beginning readers. *Journal of Educational Research, 65,* 436–443.

Greene, M. (1988). *The dialectic of freedom.* New York: Teachers College Press.

Greene, M. (1995). *Releasing the imagination: Essays on education, the arts, and social change.* San Francisco: Jossey-Bass.

Greene, P. J. (1981). *The morpheme conceptualization barrier: Adult non-inflected language speakers' acquisition of English morpheme structures.* Unpublished doctoral dissertation, University of New Orleans.

Greenlaw, M. J. (1992). Using informational books to develop reference skills. In E. B. Freeman & D. G. Person (Eds.), *Using nonfiction trade books in the elementary classroom* (pp. 131–145). Urbana, IL: National Council of Teachers of English.

Griffith, P. L., & Olson, M. W. (1992). Phonemic awareness helps beginning readers break the code. *The Reading Teacher, 45,* 516–523.

Grognet, A. G., Pfannkuche, A., Quang, N. H., Robson, B., Convery, A., Holdzkom, D., Quynh-Hao, H. T., & Vu, T. N. (1976). *A manual for Indochinese refugee education.* Arlington, VA: The National Indochinese Clearinghouse, Center for Applied Linguistics.

Gross, H. H. (1966). *Exploring regions of the western hemisphere.* Chicago: Follett.

Grossman, P. (1992). Why models matter: An alternate view on professional growth in teaching. *Review of Educational Research, 62,* 171–179.

Gunning, T. (1995). Word building: A strategic approach to the teaching of phonics. *The Reading Teacher, 48,* 484–488.

Gunning, T. (2001). *Building words: A resource manual for teaching word analysis and spelling strategies.* Boston: Allyn & Bacon.

Guszak, F. J. (1967). Teachers' questions and levels of reading comprehension. In T. C. Barrett (Ed.), *The evaluation of children's reading achievement.* Newark, DE: International Reading Association.

Guthrie, J. T., Seifert, M., Burnham, N. A., & Caplan, R. I. (1974). The maze technique to assess, monitor reading comprehension. *The Reading Teacher, 28,* 161–168.

Haberman, M. (1991). The pedagogy of poverty versus good teaching. *Phi Delta Kappan, 73,* 290–294.

Hadaway, N., & Mundy, J. (1999). Children's informational picture books visit a secondary ESL classroom. *Journal of Adolescent & Adult Literacy, 42,* 464–475.

Haggard, M. (1986). The vocabulary self-collection strategy: Using student interest and world knowledge to enhance vocabulary growth. *Journal of Reading, 29,* 634–642.

Hall, W. S., & Freedle, R. (1975). *Culture and language.* New York: Halstead Press.

Hallcom, F. (1995). *A guide to linguistics for ESL teachers.* Dubuque, IA: Kendall/Hunt.

Haller, E. J., & Waterman, M. (1985). The criteria of reading group assignments. *The Reading Teacher, 38,* 772–781.

Halliday, M. A. K. (1978). *Language as a social semiotic.* Baltimore: University Park Press.

Hanf, M. B. (1971). Mapping: A technique for translating reading into thinking. *Journal of Reading, 14,* 225–230, 270.

Hansell, T. S. (1978). Stepping up to outlining. *Journal of Reading, 22,* 248–252.

Hansen, J. (1987). *When writers read.* Portsmouth, NH: Heinemann.

Harmon, J. M. (1998). Vocabulary teaching and learning in a seventh-grade literature-based classroom. *Journal of Adolescent and Adult Literacy, 41,* 518–529.

Harris, A. J., & Jacobson, M. D. (1972). *Basic elementary reading vocabularies.* New York: Macmillan.

Harris, A. J., & Sipay, E. R. (1990). *How to increase reading ability* (9th ed.). New York: Longman.

Harris, V. J. (Ed.). (1993). *Teaching multicultural literature in grades K–8*. Norwood, MA: Christopher-Gordon.

Harste, J., Woodward, V., & Burke, C. (1984). *Language stories and literacy lessons*. Portsmouth, NH: Heinemann.

Hart, D. (1994). *Authentic assessment: A handbook for educators*. Reading, MA: Addison-Wesley.

Hayes, D. A. (1989). Helping students GRASP the knack of writing summaries. *Journal of Reading, 33,* 96–101.

Heath, S. (1983). *Ways with words: Language, life and work in communities and classrooms*. Cambridge, England: Cambridge University Press.

Heckelman, R. G. (1969). A neurological-impress method of remedial reading instruction. *Academic Therapy, 4,* 277–282.

Heilman, A. W., & Holmes, E. A. (1978). *Smuggling language into the teaching of reading*. Columbus, OH: Prentice-Hall/Merrill.

Heimlich, J. E., & Pittelman, S. D. (1986). *Semantic mapping: Classroom applications*. Newark, DE: International Reading Association.

Helfeldt, J. P., & Henk, W. A. (1990). Reciprocal question-answer relationships: An instructional technique for at-risk readers. *Journal of Reading, 33,* 509–515.

Henderson, E. H., & Beers, J. (Eds.). (1980). *Developmental and cognitive aspects of learning to spell*. Newark, DE: International Reading Association.

Henk, W. A., & Melnick, S. A., (1995). The Reader Self-Perception Scale (RSPS): A new tool for measuring how children feel about themselves as readers. *The Reading Teacher, 48,* 470–482.

Henk, W. A., & Selders, M. L. (1984). A test of synonymic scoring of cloze passages. *The Reading Teacher, 38,* 282–287.

Hennings, D. G. (1991). Essential reading: Targeting, tracking, and thinking about main ideas. *Journal of Reading, 34,* 346–353.

Herber, H. L. (1970). *Teaching reading in content areas*. Upper Saddle River, NJ: Prentice-Hall.

Herrell, A. (1998). *Exemplary practices in teaching English language learners*. Fresno: California State University, Fresno.

Herrmann, B. A. (1988). Two approaches for helping poor readers become more strategic. *The Reading Teacher, 42,* 24–28.

Hiebert, E. H. (Ed.). (1991). *Literacy for a diverse society: Perspectives, practices and policies*. New York: Teachers College Press.

Hill, M. (1991). Writing summaries promotes thinking and learning across the curriculum—but why are they so difficult to write? *Journal of Reading, 34,* 536–539.

Hodges, M. (1990). *St. George and the dragon*. Boston: Little Brown and Co.

Hoover, M. R., & Fabian, E. M. (2000). A successful program for struggling readers. *The Reading Teacher, 53,* 474–476.

Hopkins, L. B. (1987). *Click, rumble, roar: Poems about machines*. New York: Crowell.

Hoyt, L. (1999). *Revisit, reflect, retell: Strategies for improving reading comprehension*. Portsmouth, NH: Heinemann.

Huey, F. B. (1977). *The psychology and pedagogy of reading*. Cambridge, MA: MIT Press. (Original work published 1908.)

Hughes, T. O. (1975). *Sentence combining: A means of increasing reading comprehension*. Bloomington, IN: ERIC Clearinghouse on Reading. (ERIC Document Reproduction Service No. ED 11 2421)

Hunt, J. (1989). *Illuminations*. New York: Bradbury Press.

Hutchins, P. (1976). *Don't forget the bacon!* New York: Morrow.

Hymes, D., (with Chafin, A., & Gonder, P.). (1991). *The changing face of testing and assessment: Problems and solutions*. Arlington, VA: American Association of School Administrators.

Inspiration Software, Inc. (1998–1999). *Inspiration*. Portland, OR: Inspiration Software, Inc.

International Dyslexia Association (2000). *About dyslexia* [On-line]. Available: *http://www.interdys.org/about_dy.htm*.

International Reading Association. (1988). *New directions in reading instruction*. Newark, DE.

International Reading Association & National Council of Teachers of English (1996). *Standards for the English Language arts*. Newark, DE: International Reading Association; Urbana, IL: National Council of Teachers of English.

IRI/Skylight Publishing. (1995). *Integrating curricula with multiple intelligences: Teams, themes, and threads*. Palatine, IL: IRI/Skylight Publishing.

Irwin, J. W. (1991). *Teaching reading comprehension processes* (2nd ed.). Upper Saddle River, NJ: Prentice-Hall.

Irwin, P. A., & Mitchell, J. N. (1983). A procedure for assessing the richness of retellings. *Journal of Reading, 26,* 391–396.

Jackendoff, R. (1995). *Languages of the mind: Essays on mental representation*. Cambridge, MA: MIT Press.

Jackson, L. A. (1981). Whose skills system? Mine or Penny's? *The Reading Teacher, 35,* 260–262.

Jacobowitz, T. (1990). AIM: A metacognitive strategy for constructing the main idea of text. *Journal of Reading, 33,* 620–624.

Jacobson, J. M. (1990). Group vs. individual completion of a cloze passage. *Journal of Reading, 33,* 244–251.

Jensen, E. (1998). *Teaching with the brain in mind*. Alexandria, VA: Association for Supervision and Curriculum Development.

Jewell, M. G., & Zintz, M. V. (1986). *Learning to read naturally*. Dubuque, IA: Kendall/Hunt.

Johns, J. (1997). *Basic reading inventory: Preprimer through grade twelve & early literacy assessments*. Dubuque, IA: Kendall/Hunt.

Johnson, D. D. (2001). *Vocabulary in the elementary and middle school*. Boston: Allyn & Bacon.

Johnson, N. J., & Rose, L. M. (1997). *Portfolios: Clarifying, constructing, and enhancing*. Lancaster, PA: Technomic Publishing Company.

Johnson, D. D., & Pearson, P. D. (1984). *Teaching reading vocabulary*. New York: Holt, Rinehart, & Winston.

Johnson-Weber, M. (1989). Picture books for junior high. *Journal of Reading, 33,* 219–220.

Johnston, P. (1984). Prior knowledge and reading comprehension test bias. *Reading Research Quarterly, 19,* 219–239.

Johnston, P. (1992). Nontechnical assessment. *The Reading Teacher, 46,* 60–62.

Johnston, P., & Winograd, P. (1985). Passive failure in reading. *Journal of Reading Behavior, 17,* 279–301.

Jorgenson, G. W. (1977). Relationship of classroom behavior to the accuracy of the match between material difficulty and student ability. *Journal of Educational Psychology, 69,* 24–32.

Jorm, A. (1977). Effect of word imagery on reading performance as a function of reader ability. *Journal of Educational Psychology, 69,* 46–54.

Joyce, B., Weil, M., & Calhoun, E. (2000). *Models of teaching* (6th ed.). Needham Heights, MA: Allyn & Bacon.

Juel, C. (1988). Learning to read and write: A longitudinal study of 54 children from first through fourth grades. *Journal of Educational Psychology, 78,* 243–255.

Juel, C. (1991). Cross-age tutoring between student athletes and at-risk children. *The Reading Teacher, 45,* 178–186.

Juliebö, M., & Edwards, J. (1989). Encouraging meaning-making in young writers. *Young Children, 44* (2), 22–25.

Kamil, M. L., Mosenthal, P. B., Pearson, P. D., & Barr, R. (Eds.). (2000). *Handbook of reading research, volume III.* Mahwah, NH: Erlbaum.

Kamm, K. (1979). Focusing reading comprehension instruction: Sentence meaning skills. In C. Pennock (Ed.), *Reading comprehension at four linguistic levels.* Newark, DE: International Reading Association.

Kant, I. (1963). *Critique of pure reason* (2nd ed.). (N. Kemp Smith, Trans.). London: Macmillan. (Original work published 1787.)

Kaplan, R. B. (1966). Cultural thought patterns in intercultural education. *Language Learning, 16,* 1–20.

Karlsen, B., & Gardner, E. F. (1995). *Stanford diagnostic reading tests* (4th ed.). San Antonio, TX: Harcourt. (Also available online at *http://www.hemweb.com/trophy/readtest/sdrt4.htm.*)

Karnowski, L. (1989). Using LEA with process writing. *The Reading Teacher, 42,* 462–465.

Kastler, L. A., Roser, N. L., & Hoffman, J. V. (1987). Understanding of the forms and functions of written language: Insights from children and parents. In J. E. Readance & R. S. Baldwin (Eds.), *Research in literacy: Merging perspectives* (pp. 85–92). Rochester, NY: National Reading Conference.

Kavale, K. (1979). Selecting and evaluating reading tests. In R. Schreiner (Ed.), *Reading tests and teachers: A practical guide* (pp. 9–34). Newark, DE: International Reading Association.

Kavale, K., & Schreiner, R. (1979). The reading processes of above average readers: A comparison of the use of reasoning strategies in responding to standardized comprehension measures. *Reading Research Quarterly, 15,* 102–128.

Kear, D. J., Coffman, G. A., McKenna, M. C., & Ambrosio, A. L. (2000). Measuring attitude toward writing: A new tool for teachers. *The Reading Teacher, 54,* 10–23.

Kennedy, E. C. (1977). *Classroom approaches to remedial reading* (2nd ed.). Itasca, IL: Peacock.

Kibby, M. (1995). The organization and teaching of things and the words that signify them. *Journal of Adolescent and Adult Literacy, 39,* 208–223.

Kirby, D., Liner, T., & Vinz, R. (1988). *Inside out: Developmental strategies for teaching writing.* Portsmouth, NH: Boynton/Cook.

Kletzien, S. B. (1991). Strategy use by good and poor comprehenders reading expository text of differing levels. *Reading Research Quarterly, 26,* 67–86.

Kletzien, S. B., & Bednar, M. R. (1990). Dynamic assessment for at-risk readers. *Journal of Reading, 33,* 528–533.

Klingner, J., & Vaughn, S. (1999). Promoting reading comprehension, content learning, and English acquisition through Collaborative Strategic Reading (CSR). *The Reading Teacher, 52,* 738–747.

Knapp, M., & Knapp, H. (1976). *One potato, two potato: The folklore of American children.* New York: Norton.

Kolers, P. A. (1975). Pattern-analyzing disability in poor readers. *Developmental Psychology, 11,* 282–290.

Kornhaber, M., & Gardner, H. (1993). *Varieties of excellence: Identifying and assessing children's talents: A series on authentic assessment and accountability.* (ERIC Document No. ED 363 396)

Koskinen, P. A., & Blum, I. H. (1986). Paired repeated reading: A classroom strategy for developing fluent reading. *The Reading Teacher, 40,* 70–75.

Kozol, J. (1991). *Savage inequalities: Children in America's schools.* New York: Crown.

Krashen, S. D. (1987). *Principles and practice in second language acquisition.* Upper Saddle River, NJ: Prentice Hall.

Krashen, S. (1993). *The power of reading.* Englewood, CO: Libraries Unlimited.

Kress, J. E. (1993). *The ESL teacher's book of lists.* West Nyack, NY: The Center for Applied Research in Education.

Labbo, L. (2000). 12 things young children can do with a talking book in a classroom computer center. *The Reading Teacher, 53,* 542–546.

Labbo, L. D., & Teale, W. H. (1990). Crossage reading: A strategy for helping poor readers. *The Reading Teacher, 43,* 362–369.

LaBerge, D., & Samuels, S. J. (1974). Toward a theory of automatic information processing in reading. *Cognitive Psychology, 6,* 293–323.

Labov, W. (1975). *The study of nonstandard English*. Urbana, IL. National Council of Teachers of English.

Laframboise, K. (2000). Said webs: Remedy for tired words. *The Reading Teacher, 53,* 540–542.

Laminack, L., & Wood, K. (1996). *Spelling in use: Looking closely at spelling in whole language classrooms*. Urbana, IL: National Council of Teachers of English.

Langer, J. (1981). From theory to practice: A prereading plan. *Journal of Reading, 25,* 152–156.

Lazarus, E. (1883). (1993). The new colossus. In W. J. Bennett (Ed.), *The book of virtues: A treasury of great moral stories*. New York: Simon & Schuster.

Lazear, D. (1994). *Multiple intelligence approaches to assessment: Solving the assessment conundrum*. Tucson, AZ: Zephyr Press.

Lerdah, F. (1996). *A generative theory of tonal music*. Cambridge, MA: MIT Press.

Leslie, L., & Caldwell, J. (2000). *Qualitative reading inventory*. New York: HarperCollins College.

Leslie, L., & Cooper, J., (1993). Assessing the predictive validity of prior-knowledge assessment. In D. J. Leu and C. K. Kinzer (Eds.), *Examining central issues in literacy research, theory and practice* (pp. 93–100). Chicago, IL: National Reading Conference.

Lindamood, C. H., & Lindamood, P. C. (1979). *Lindamood Auditory Conceptualization Test (LAC)*. Evanston, IL: Cognitive Concepts Inc.

Lindfors, J. W. (1989). The classroom: A good environment for language learning. In P. Rigg & V. G. Allen (Eds.), *When they don't all speak English: Integrating the ESL student into the regular classroom* (pp. 39–54). Urbana, IL: National Council of Teachers of English.

Lipson, M., & Wixson, K. (1991). *Assessment and instruction of reading disability: An interactive approach*. New York: HarperCollins.

Lowenfeld, V. (1970). *Creative and mental growth* (5th ed.). New York: Macmillan.

Lundsteen, S. (1979). *Listening: Its impact on reading and other language arts* (Rev. ed.). Urbana, IL: National Council of Teachers of English.

MacGinitie, W., MacGinitie, R., Maria, K., & Dreyer, L. (2000). *Gates-MacGinitie reading tests (GMRT)* (4th ed.). Forms S & T. Itasca, IL: Riverside.

Mandler, J. (1984). *Stories, scripts and scenes: Aspects of schema theory*. Hillsdale, NJ: Erlbaum.

Mandler, J. M., & Johnson, N. S. (1977). Remembrance of things parsed: Story structure and recall. *Cognitive Psychology, 9,* 111–151.

Manzo, A. V. (1969). The ReQuest procedure. *Journal of Reading, 13,* 123–126.

Manzo, A. V. (1975). Guided reading procedure. *Journal of Reading, 18,* 287–291.

Manzo, A. V. (1985). Expansion modules for the ReQuest, CAT, GRP, and REAP reading/study procedures. *Journal of Reading, 28,* 498–502.

Markman, E. M. (1979). Realizing that you don't understand: Elementary school children's awareness of inconsistencies. *Child Development, 50,* 643–655.

Markman, E. M. (1981). Comprehension monitoring. In W. P. Dickson (Ed.), *Children's oral communication skills*. New York: Academic Press.

Marshmallow. (1971). *Childcraft: The how and why library* (Vol. 6, *How things change*, p. 177). Chicago: Field Enterprises Educational Corporation.

Martin, B. (1970). *The haunted house*. New York: Holt, Rinhart & Winston.

Martin, B. (1983). *Brown bear, brown bear, what do you see?* New York: Holt.

Martinez, M., Roser, N., & Strecker, S. (1998/1999). "I never thought I could be a star.": A Readers Theatre ticket to fluency. *The Reading Teacher, 52,* 326–334.

Marzano, R. J., & Marzano, J. S. (1988). *A cluster approach to elementary vocabulary instruction*. Newark, DE: International Reading Association.

Maslow, A. (1970). *Motivation and personality*. New York: Harper & Row.

Mathewson, G. C. (1994). Model of attitude influence upon reading and learning to read. In R. B. Ruddell, M. R. Ruddell, & H. Singer (Eds.), *Theoretical models and processes of reading* (4th ed.) (pp. 1131–1161). Newark, DE: International Reading Association.

McAuliffe, S. (1993). A study of the differences between instructional practice and test preparation. *Journal of Reading, 36,* 524–530.

McCormick, S., & Cooper, J. O. (1991). Can SQ3R facilitate secondary learning disabled students' literal comprehension of expository text? *Reading Psychology, 12,* 239–271.

McDermott, G. (1972). *Anansi the spider*. New York: Holt.

McGinley, W., & Denner, P. (1987). Story impressions: A prereading/writing activity. *Journal of Reading, 31,* 248–253.

McGovern, A. (1969). . . . *if you sailed on the Mayflower*. New York: Scholastic.

McKenna, M. C. (1976). Synonymic versus verbatim scoring of the cloze procedure. *Journal of Reading, 20,* 141–143.

McKeown, M. (1985). The acquisition of word meaning from context by children of high and low ability. *Reading Research Quarterly, 20,* 482–496.

McLaughlin, M. (1989). *Dragonflies*. New York: Walker and Company.

McMahon, S., & Raphael, T. (Eds.). (1997). *The book club connection: Literacy learning and classroom talk*. New York: Teachers College Press, and Newark, DE: International Reading Association.

McMaster, J. (1998). "Doing" literature: Using drama to build literacy. *The Reading Teacher, 51* (7), 575–583.

McNeil, J. D. (1974). False prerequisites in the teaching of reading. *Journal of Reading Behavior, 6,* 421–427.

McNinch, G. H. (1981). A method for teaching sight words to disabled readers. *The Reading Teacher, 35,* 269–272.

McWhorter, J. (2000). *Spreading the word: Language and dialect in America*. Portsmouth, NH: Heinemann.

Memory, D. M. (1990). Teaching technical vocabulary: Before, during, or after the reading assignment? *Journal of Reading Behavior, 22,* 39-53.

Menges, R. (1994). Promoting inquiry into one's own teaching. In K. Howey & N. Zimpher (Eds.), *Informing faculty development for teacher educators* (pp. 51–97). Norwood, NJ: Ablex.

Mercer, C. (1997). *Students with learning disabilities* (5th ed.). Upper Saddle River, NJ: Prentice-Hall.

Merwin, J. C. (1973). Educational measurement of what characteristic, of whom (or what), by whom, and why. *Journal of Educational Measurement, 10,* 1–6.

Meyer, B. F. (1984). Organizational aspects of text: Effects on reading comprehension and applications for the classroom. In J. Flood (Ed.), *Promoting reading comprehension* (pp. 113–138). Newark, DE: International Reading Association.

Miller, G. R., & Coleman, E. B. (1967). A set of 36 prose passages calibrated for complexity. *Journal of Verbal Learning and Verbal Behavior, 6,* 851–854.

Miller, T. (1998). The place of picture books in middle-level classrooms. *Journal of Adolescent & Adult Literacy, 41,* 376–381.

Mills, H., O'Keefe, T., & Stephens, D. (1992). *Looking closely: Exploring the role of phonics in one whole language classroom*. Urbana, IL: National Council of Teachers of English.

Mitchell, J. V. (Ed.). (1985). *The ninth mental measurements yearbook*. Lincoln, NE: University of Nebraska Press.

Moe, A. J. (1972a). *High frequency nouns*. St. Paul, MN: Ambassador.

Moe, A. J. (1972b). *High frequency words*. St. Paul, MN: Ambassador.

Moe, A. J., & Manning, J. C. (1984). Developing intensive word practice exercises. In J. F. Baumann & D. D. Johnson (Eds.), *Reading instruction for the beginning teacher: A practical guide* (pp. 16–27). Minneapolis, MN: Burgess.

Moll, L. (1993). *Vygotsky and education: Instructional implications and applications of sociohistorical psychology*. New York: Cambridge University Press.

Monroe, M. (1932). *Children who cannot read*. Chicago: University of Chicago Press.

Montessori, M. (1967). *The absorbent mind*. New York: Dell.

Morado, C, Koenig, R., & Wilson, A. (1999). Miniperformances. Many stars! Playing with stories. *The Reading Teacher, 53,* 116–123.

Morningstar, J. (1999). Home response journals: Parents as informed contributers in the understanding of their child's literacy development. *The Reading Teacher, 5,* 690–697.

Morrice, C., & Simmons, M. (1991). Beyond reading buddies: A whole language crossage program. *The Reading Teacher, 44,* 572–577.

Morrow, L. M. (1985a). Reading and retelling stories: Strategies for emergent readers. *The Reading Teacher, 38,* 870–875.

Morrow, L. M. (1985b, April). *Story retelling: A diagnostic approach for evaluating story structure, language and comprehension*. Paper presented at the International Reading Association Convention, New Orleans, LA.

Morrow, L. M. (1988). Retelling as a diagnostic tool. In S. Glazer, L. Searfoss, & L. Gentile (Eds.), *Re-examining reading diagnosis: New trends and procedures in classrooms and clinics* (pp. 128–149). Newark, DE: International Reading Association.

Morrow, L. M. (Ed.). (1995). *Family literacy: Connections in schools and communities*. Newark, DE: International Reading Association.

Morrow, L. M., & Gambrell, L. B. (2000). Literature based reading instruction. In. M. L. Kamil, P. B. Mosenthal, P. D. Pearson, & R. Barr (Eds.), *Handbook of reading research, volume III* (pp. 563–586). Mahwah, NJ: Erlbaum.

Morrow, L. M., & Smith, J. (1990). The effects of group size on interactive storybook reading. *Reading Research Quarterly, 25,* 213–231.

Morrow, L. M., Tracey, D. H., Woo, D. G. & Pressley, M. (1999). Characteristics of exemplary first-grade literacy instruction. *The Reading Teacher, 52,* 462–476.

Moustafa, M., & Maldonado-Colon, E. (1999). Whole-to-parts phonics instruction: Building on what children know to help them know more. *The Reading Teacher, 52,* 448–458.

Murray, D. (1984). *Write to learn*. New York: Holt, Rinehart and Winston.

Nagy, W. E. (1988). *Teaching vocabulary to improve reading comprehension*. Newark, DE: International Reading Association.

Nagy, W. E., Anderson, R. C., & Herman, P. (1987). Learning word meanings from context during normal reading. *American Educational Research Journal, 24,* 237–270.

Nathan, R., Temple, C., Juntunen, K., & Temple, F. (1989). *Classroom strategies that work: An elementary teacher's guide to process writing*. Portsmouth, NH: Heinemann.

National Reading Panel. (2000). *National Reading Panel Report*. [On-line]. Available: *http://www.nationalreadingpanel. org/Publications/publications.htm.*

National Standards of Arts Education (1994). *Standards for the Arts*. Reston, VA: Music Educators National Conference.

Neal, J. C., & Moore, K. (1991/1992). The very hungry caterpillar meets Beowulf in secondary classrooms. *Journal of Reading, 35,* 290–296.

Nelson, K. (1986). *Event knowledge: Structure and function in development*. Hillsdale, NJ: Erlbaum.

Neville, D. D., & Searls, E. F. (1991). A meta-analytic review of the effect of sentence-combining on reading comprehension. *Reading Research and Instruction, 31,* 63–76.

Newkirk, T. (1982). Young writers as critical readers. *Language Arts, 59,* 451–457.

Newman, J. (1985). *Whole language theory and use*. Portsmouth, NH: Heinemann.

Newmann, F. M., & Wehlage, G. G. (1993). Five standards of authentic instruction. *Educational Leadership, 50,* 8–12.

Nicholson, T., Lillas, C., & Rzoska, M. A. (1988). Have we been misled by miscues? *The Reading Teacher, 42,* 6–10.

Nieto, S. (1999). *The light in their eyes: Creating multicultural learning communities.* New York: Teachers College Press.

Nikkel, S. (1996, December). *The effects of interactive computer software on literacy acquisition.* Paper presented at the annual meeting of the National Reading Conference, Charleston, SC.

Nist, S. L., & Simpson, M. L. (1989). PLAE, a validated study strategy. *Journal of Reading, 33,* 182–186.

Nist, S. L., & Simpson, M. L. (1990). The effects of PLAE upon students' test performance and metacognitive awareness. In J. Zutell & S. McCormick (Eds.), *Literacy theory and research: Analyses from multiple paradigms* (pp. 321–327). Chicago: National Reading Conference.

Nist, S. L., Simpson, M. L., Olejnik, S., & Mealey, D. L. (1989). *The relation between self-selected text learning variables and test performance.* Unpublished manuscript.

Nolan, T. E. (1991). Self-questioning and prediction: Combining metacognitive strategies. *Journal of Reading, 35,* 132–138.

Norton, D. (1992). Assessing the processes students use as writers. *Journal of Reading, 36,* 244–246.

Norton, D. (1993). *The effective teaching of language arts* (4th ed.). New York: Merrill.

Noyce, R. M., & Christie, J. F. (1989). *Integrating reading and writing instruction in grades K–8.* Boston: Allyn & Bacon.

O'Flahavan, J., & Blassberg, R. (1992). Toward an embedded model of spelling instruction for emergent literates. *Language Arts, 69,* 409–417.

Ogbu, J. U. (1987). Opportunity structure, cultural boundaries, and literacy. In J. A. Langer (Ed.), *Language, literacy, and culture: Issues of society and schooling* (pp. 149–177). Norwood, NJ: Ablex.

Ogle, D. M. (1986). K–W–L: A teaching model that develops active reading of expository text. *The Reading Teacher, 39,* 564–570.

Ohlhausen, M., & Jepsen, M. (1992). Lessons from Goldilocks: "Someone has been choosing my books but I can make my own choices now!" *The New Advocate, 5,* 31–46.

Olivares, R. A. (1993). *Using the newspaper to teach ESL learners.* Newark, DE: International Reading Association.

Olshavsky, J. E. (1976/1977). Reading as problem solving: An investigation of strategies. *Reading Research Quarterly, 12,* 654–674.

Opitz, M. (Ed.). (1998). *Literacy instruction for culturally and linguistically diverse students: A collection of articles and commentaries.* Newark, DE: International Reading Association.

Opitz, M. (2000). *Rhymes & reasons: Literature and language play for phonological awareness.* Portsmouth, NH: Heinemann.

Opitz, M., & Rasinski, T. (1998). *Good-bye round robin: 25 effective oral reading strategies.* Portsmouth, NH: Heinemann.

Orange County Public Schools. (1985). *Reading resource specialist handbook.* 445 W. Amelia St., Orlando, FL 32801.

Orange County Public Schools. (1986). *Middle school curriculum planning guide for reading.* 445 W. Amellia St., Orlando, FL 32801.

Otto, W., & Smith, R. J. (1980). *Corrective and remedial teaching* (3rd ed.). Boston: Houghton Mifflin.

Palincsar, A. (1987, January). Reciprocal teaching: Can student discussions boost comprehension? *Instructor,* 56–60.

Palincsar, A. S., & Brown, A. L. (1984). Reciprocal teaching of comprehension-fostering and comprehension-monitoring activities. *Cognition and Instruction, 1* (2), 117–175.

Palincsar, A. S., & Brown, A. L. (1986). Interactive teaching to promote independent learning from text. *The Reading Teacher, 39,* 771–777.

Pallotta, J. (1986). *The icky bug alphabet book.* New York: Trumpet Club.

Pankratz, D., & Mulcahy, K. (Eds.). (1989). *The challenge to reform arts education: What role can research play?* ACA Arts Research Seminar Series. New York: American Council for the Arts.

Pappas, C., Kiefer, B., & Levstik, L. (1999). *An integrated language perspective in the elementary school: An action approach,* 3rd edition. New York: Longman.

Paris, S., & Myers, M. (1981). Comprehension monitoring, memory, and study strategies of good and poor readers. *Journal of Reading Behavior, 13,* 7–22.

Paris, S. G., & Lipson, M. Y. (1982, April). *Metacognition and reading comprehension.* Research colloquium presented at the annual meeting of the International Reading Association, Chicago, IL.

Parks, R. J. (1987). Three approaches to improving literacy levels. *Educational Horizons, 66* (1), 38–41.

Pearson, P. D. (1985). Changing the face of reading comprehension instruction. *The Reading Teacher, 38,* 724–738.

Pearson, P. D., & Johnson, D. D. (1978). *Teaching reading comprehension.* New York: Holt, Rinehart, & Winston.

Pennock, C. (Ed.). (1979). *Reading comprehension at four linguistic levels.* Newark, DE: International Reading Association.

Peregoy, S. F., & Boyle, O. F. (1997). *Reading, writing and learning in ESL: A resource book for K–12 teachers.* New York: Longman.

Perfetti, C. A. (1991). Representations and awareness in the acquisition of reading competence. In L. Rieben & C. A. Perfetti (Eds.), *Learning to read: Basic research and its implications* (pp. 33–44). Hillsdale, NJ: Erlbaum.

Peterson, R., & Eeds, M. (1990). *Grand conversations: Literature groups in action.* New York: Scholastic.

Piaget, J. (1980). *To understand is to invent.* New York: Penguin Books.

Piaget, J., & Inhelder, B. (1969). *The psychology of the child.* New York: Basic Books.

Piazza, C. (1999). *Multiple forms of literacy: Teaching literacy and the arts.* Upper Saddle River, NJ: Merrill/Prentice-Hall.

Piercey, D. (1982). *Reading activities in content areas.* Boston: Allyn & Bacon.

Pikulski, J. J., & Tobin, A. W. (1982). The cloze procedure as an informal assessment technique. In J. J. Pikulski & T. Shanahan (Eds.), *Approaches to the informal evaluation of reading* (pp. 42–62). Newark, DE: International Reading Association.

Piper, T. (1998). *Language and learning: The home school years,* 2nd edition. Columbus, OH: Prentice Hall.

Pittelman, S. D., Heimlich, J. E., Berglund, R. L., & French, M. P. (1991). *Semantic feature analysis: Classroom applications.* Newark, DE: International Reading Association.

Polette, K. (1989). Using ABC books for vocabulary development in the secondary school. *English Journal, 78,* 78–80.

Powell, W. R. (1970). Reappraising the criteria for interpreting informal inventories. In D. DeBoer (Ed.), *Reading diagnosis and evaluation.* Newark, DE: International Reading Association.

Powell, W., & Dunkeld, C. (1971). Validity of the IRI reading levels. *Elementary English, 48,* 637–642.

Puma, M., Karweit, N., Price, C., Ricciuti, A., Thompson, W., & Vaden-Kiernan, M. (1997). *Prospects: Student outcomes, final report.* Washington, DC: U.S. Department of Education, Office of Educational Research and Improvement.

Quigley, S., King, C., McAnally, P., & Rose, S. (Eds.). (1998). *Reading Milestones: An alternative reading program* (2nd ed.). Austin, TX: Pro-Ed.

Rabe, B. (1981). *The balancing girl.* New York: Dutton.

Rafoth, B. A., & Rubin, D. L. (1984). The impact of content and mechanics on judgments of writing quality. *Written Communication, 1,* 446–458.

Rainer, J.(1994). Go My Son (Compact Disk). Provo, UT.

Raines, S. (2000). Educators influencing legislators: Commentary and the Kentucky case. *The Reading Teacher, 53,* 642–643.

Rankin, E. F., & Culhane, J. W. (1969). Comparable cloze and multiple-choice comprehension scores. *Journal of Reading, 13,* 193–198.

Raphael, T. E. (1982). Question-answering strategies for children. *The Reading Teacher, 36,* 186–190.

Raphael, T. E. (1986). Teaching question-answer relationships, revisited. *The Reading Teacher, 39,* 516–522.

Raphael, T. E., & Pearson, P. D. (1985). Increasing students' awareness of sources of information for answering questions. *American Educational Research Journal, 22,* 217–235.

Rasinski, T. (Ed.). (1995). *Parents and teachers: Helping children learn to read and write.* Fort Worth, TX: Harcourt Brace.

Region 1 Goals 2000 Preservice Consortium. (1996). *Communicating with parents: A resource guide for preservice teachers.* (Available from Region 1 Service Center, 8348 Hwy 23, Belle Chasse, LA 70037.

Reutzel, D. R. (1985). Story maps improve comprehension. *The Reading Teacher, 38,* 400–404.

Reutzel, D. R. (1986). Clozing in on comprehension: The cloze story map. *The Reading Teacher, 39,* 524–528.

Reynolds, R. E., Taylor, M. A., Steffensen, M. S., Shirey, L. L., & Anderson, R. C. (1981). *Cultural schemata and reading comprehension* (Tech. Rep. No. 201). Champaign: University of Illinois, Center for the Study of Reading.

Rhodes, L. K., & Dudley-Marling, C. (1988). *Readers and writers with a difference: A holistic approach to teaching learning disabled and remedial students.* Portsmouth, NH: Heinemann.

Rhodes, L. K., & Dudley-Marling, C. (1996). *Readers and writers with a difference: A holistic approach to teaching struggling readers and writers.* Portsmouth, NH: Heinemann.

Rhodes, L. K., & Shanklin, N. (1993). *Windows into literacy: Assessing learners K–8.* Portsmouth, NH: Heinemann.

Richards, J. C. (1985). *Theoretical orientation and first- and third-grade teachers' reading instruction.* Unpublished doctoral dissertation, University of New Orleans.

Richards, J. C., & Gipe, J. (1996). I wonder . . . ? A strategy to help children listen actively to stories. *The Whole Idea, 7*(1), 10–11.

Richards, J. C., & Gipe, J. P. (1992). Activating background knowledge: Strategies for beginning and poor readers. *The Reading Teacher, 45,* 474–476.

Richards, J. C., & Gipe, J. P. (1993). Recognizing information about story characters: A strategy for young and at-risk readers. *The Reading Teacher, 47,* 78–79.

Richards, J. C., Gipe, J. P., & Necaise, M. A. (1994). Find the features and connect them. *The Reading Teacher, 48,* 187–188.

Richards, J., Goldberg, M., McKenna, M. (In press). *Teaching for multiple literacies: K–8 Cases and commentaries.* Mahwah, NJ: Erlbaum.

Richards, M. (2000). Be a good detective: Solve the case of oral fluency. *The Reading Teacher, 53,* 534–539.

Richek, M. A. (1987). DRTA: 5 variations that facilitate independence in reading narratives. *Journal of Reading, 30,* 632–636.

Rigg, P. (1989). Language Experience Approach: Reading naturally. In P. Rigg & V. G. Allen (Eds.), *When they don't all speak English: Integrating the ESL student into the regular classroom* (pp. 65–76). Urbana, IL: National Council of Teachers of English.

Rigg, P., & Allen, V. G. (Eds.). (1989). *When they don't all speak English: Integrating the ESL student into the regular classroom.* Urbana, IL: National Council of Teachers of English.

Rinsky, L. A. (1993). *Teaching word recognition skills* (5th ed.). Scottsdale, AZ: Gorsuch Scarisbrick.

Roberts, T. (1976). "Frustration level" reading in the infant school. *Educational Research, 19,* 41–44.

Robinson, F. P. (1970). *Effective study* (4th ed.). New York: Harper & Row.

Robinson, H. A. (1983). *Teaching reading, writing and study strategies: The content areas.* Boston: Allyn & Bacon.

Robinson, H. M. (1946). *Why pupils fail in reading.* Chicago: University of Chicago Press.

Rogers, L. K. (1999). Spelling cheerleading. *The Reading Teacher, 53,* 110–111.

Roller, C. (1998). *So . . . What's a tutor to do?* Newark, DE: International Reading Association.

Rosenblatt, L. (1983). *Literature as exploration,* 4th edition. New York: The Modern Languages Association of America.

Rosenblatt, L. M. (1994). The transactional theory of reading and writing. In R. B. Ruddell, M. R. Ruddell, & H. Singer (Eds.), *Theoretical models and processes of reading* (4th ed.) (pp. 1057–1092). Newark, DE: International Reading Association.

Rosenshine, B. V. (1980). Skill hierarchies in reading comprehension. In R. J. Spiro, B. C. Bruce, & W. F. Brewer (Eds.), *Theoretical issues in reading comprehension.* Hillsdale, NJ: Erlbaum.

Ross, E., & Roe, B. (1990). *An introduction to teaching the language arts.* Chicago: Holt, Rinehart, & Winston.

Roswell, F., & Chall, J. (1997). *Roswell-Chall auditory blending test.* La Jolla, CA: Essay Press.

Routman, R. (1991). *Invitations: Changing as teachers and learners K–12.* Portsmouth, NH: Heinemann.

Routman, R. (2000). *Conversations: Strategies for teaching, learning, and evaluating.* Portsmouth, NH: Heinemann.

Ruddell, R. B. (1964). A study of the cloze comprehension technique in relation to structurally controlled reading material. In J. A. Figurel (Ed.), *Improvement of reading through classroom practice* (pp. 298–303). Newark, DE: International Reading Association.

Ruddell, R. B., & Ruddell, M. R. (1994). Models of reading and literacy processes: Introduction. In R. B. Ruddell, M. R. Ruddell, & H. Singer (Eds.), *Theoretical models and processes of reading* (4th ed.) (pp. 811–815). Newark, DE: International Reading Association.

Ruddell, R. B., & Unrau, N. J. (1994). Reading as a meaning-construction process: The reader, the text, and the teacher. In R. B. Ruddell, M. R. Ruddell, & H. Singer (Eds.), *Theoretical models and processes of reading* (4th ed.) (pp. 996–1056). Newark, DE: International Reading Association.

Rumelhart, D. E. (1975). Notes on a schema for stories. In D. G. Bobrow & A. M. Collins (Eds.), *Representation and understanding: Studies in cognitive science.* New York: Academic Press.

Rumelhart, D. E. (1980). Schemata: The building blocks of cognition. In R. J. Spiro, B. C. Bruce, & W. F. Brewer (Eds.), *Theoretical issues in reading comprehension* (pp. 33–58). Hillsdale, NJ: Erlbaum.

Rumelhart, D. E. (1994). Toward an interactive model of reading. In R. B. Ruddell, M. R. Ruddell, & H. Singer (Eds.), *Theoretical models and processes of reading* (pp. 864–894). Newark, DE: International Reading Association.

Rupley, W., Logan, J., & Nichols, W. (1998/1999). Vocabulary instruction in a balanced reading program. *The Reading Teacher, 52,* 336–346.

Russell, D. H., & Russell, E. (1979). *Listening aids through the grades* (2nd ed.). New York: Teachers College Press.

Rutland, A. D. (1987). Using wordless picture books in social studies. *History and Social Science Teacher, 22,* 193–196.

Rylant, C. (1982). *When I was young in the mountains.* New York: Dutton.

Sadow, M. W. (1982). The use of story grammar in the design of questions. *The Reading Teacher, 35,* 518–522.

Samuels, S. J. (1979). The method of repeated readings. *The Reading Teacher, 32,* 403–408. (Reprinted 1997, *The Reading Teacher, 50,* 376–381.)

Samuels, S. J. (1988). Decoding and automaticity: Helping poor readers become automatic at word recognition. *The Reading Teacher, 41,* 756–761.

Samuels, S. J. (1994). Toward a theory of automatic information processing in reading, revisited. In R. B. Ruddell, M. R. Ruddell, & H. Singer (Eds.), *Theoretical models and processes of reading* (4th ed.) (pp. 816–837). Newark, DE: International Reading Association.

Sautter, R. (1994). An arts education school reform strategy. *Phi Delta Kappan, 75,* 432–437.

Sax, G. (1980). *Principles of educational and psychological measurement and evaluation* (2nd ed.). Belmont, CA: Wadsworth.

Schachter, S. W. (1978). Developing flexible reading habits. *Journal of Reading, 22,* 149–152.

Schell, L. M., & Hanna, G. S. (1981). Can informal reading inventories reveal strengths and weaknesses in comprehension subskills? *The Reading Teacher, 35,* 263–268.

Schirduan, V., & Case, K. (2000). Focusing on the positive: The self-concept of students with ADHD in schools using MI theory. *Multiple Intelligences: Theory and Practice, 1* (1), 3–5.

Schmelzer, R. V. (1975). *The effect of college student constructed questions on the comprehension of a passage of expository prose* (Doctoral dissertation, University of Minnesota, 1975). *Dissertation Abstracts International, 36,* 2162A.

Schmidt, P. R. (1999). KWLQ: Inquiry and literacy learning in science. *The Reading Teacher, 52,* 789–792.

Schön, D. A. (1987). *Educating the reflective practitioner.* San Francisco: Jossey-Bass.

Schumm, J. S., & Mangrum, C. T. (1991). FLIP: A framework for content area reading. *Journal of Reading, 35,* 120–124.

Schwartz, E., & Sheff, A. (1975). Student involvement in questioning for comprehension. *The Reading Teacher, 29,* 150–154.

Schwartz, R. M. (1988). Learning to learn: Vocabulary in content area textbooks. *Journal of Reading, 32,* 108–117.

Seaborg, M., & Sturtevant, E. (1996, December). *E-mail keypals: Multiple dimensions of an e-mail penpal program.* Paper presented at the National Reading Conference, Charleston, SC.

Search Institute. (1997). 40 developmental assets. Available from the Search Institute, 700 S. Third Street, Suite 210, Minneapolis, MN 55415; 800-888-7828; *http://www.search-institute.org/assets/).*

Scarfoss, L. (1993). Assessing classroom environments. In S. Glazer & C. Brown (Eds.), *Portfolios and beyond: Collaborative assessment in reading and writing* (pp. 11–26). Norwood, MA: Christopher-Gordon.

Searle, D., & Dillon, D. (1980). Responding to student writing: What is said or how it is said. *Language Arts, 57,* 773–781.

Seuss, Dr. (1960). *Green eggs and ham.* New York: Beginner Books.

Shafer, R. E., Staab, C., & Smith, K. (1983). *Language functions and school success.* Glenview, IL: Scott, Foresman.

Shannon, P. (1989). *Broken promises: Reading instruction in twentieth-century America.* Granby, MA: Bergin & Garvey.

Shannon, P. (1990). *The struggle to continue: Progressive reading instruction in the United States.* Portsmouth, NH: Heinemann.

Shaw, N. (1989). *Sheep on a ship.* Boston: Houghton Mifflin.

Shefelbine, J. (1998). *Fun with Zip and Zap.* New York: Scholastic.

Sherwood, L., & Berlin, I. (1949). *Miss Liberty.* New York: Broadway Musical (Compact Disc, Original Broadway Cast), (1991). Lieberman, G. [Producer] Sony Broadway Services, (p. 179).

Shnayer, S. W. (1969). Relationships between reading interest and comprehension. In J. A. Figurel (Ed.), *Reading and realism.* Newark, DE: International Reading Association.

Shores, E. (1995). Howard Gardner on the eighth intelligence: Seeing the natural world. *Dimensions of Early Childhood, 23* (4), 5–7.

Short, K. (1993). Teacher research for teacher educators. In L. Patterson, C. Santa, K. Short, & K. Smith (Eds.), *Teachers are researchers: Reflection and action* (pp. 155–159). Newark, DE: International Reading Association.

Short, J. R., & Dickerson, B. (1980). *The newspaper: An alternative textbook.* Carthage, IL: Fearon Teacher Aids.

Shuy, R. W. (1981a). A holistic view of language. *Research in the Teaching of English, 15,* 101–111.

Shuy, R. W. (1981b). Learning to talk like teachers. *Language Arts, 58,* 168–174.

Shuy, R. W. (1988). Sentence level language functions. In J. R. Staton, R. W. Shuy, J. K. Peyton, & L. Reed (Eds.), *Dialogue journal communication.* Norwood, NJ: Ablex.

Sidelnick, M. & Svoboda, M. (2000). The bridge between drawing and writing: Hannah's story. *The Reading Teacher, 54,* 174–184.

Silva, C., & Yarborough, B. (1990). Help for young writers with spelling difficulties. *Journal of Reading, 34,* 48–53.

Simpson, M. L. (1986). PORPE: A writing strategy for studying and learning in the content areas. *Journal of Reading, 29,* 407–414.

Simpson, M. L. (1987). Alternative formats for evaluating content area vocabulary understanding. *Journal of Reading, 31,* 20–27.

Simpson, M. L., & Nist, S. L. (1984). PLAE: A model for planning successful independent learning. *Journal of Reading, 29,* 218–223.

Simpson, M. L., & Nist, S. L. (1990). Textbook annotation: An effective and efficient study strategy for college students. *Journal of Reading, 34,* 122–129.

Simpson, M. L., Stahl, N. A., & Hayes, C. G. (1989). PORPE: A research validation. *Journal of Reading, 33,* 22–28.

Sinatra, R. (1991). Integrating whole language with the earning of text structure. *Journal of Reading, 34,* 424–433.

Sinatra, R. C., Stahl-Gemake, J., & Berg, D. N. (1984). Improving reading comprehension of disabled readers through semantic mapping. *The Reading Teacher, 38,* 22–29.

Singer, H. (1978). Active comprehension: From answering to asking questions. *The Reading Teacher, 31,* 901–908.

Sippola, A. E. (1975). K–W–L–S. In T. Rasinski, et al. (Eds.), *Teaching comprehension and exploring multiple literacies: Strategies from The Reading Teacher* (pp 37–38). Newark, DE: International Reading Association.

Slaughter, H. B. (1988). Indirect and direct teaching in a whole language program. *The Reading Teacher, 42,* 30–34.

Sleeter, C. E. (Ed.). (1991). *Empowerment through multicultural education.* Albany, NY: SUNY Press.

Sloyer, S. (1982). *Readers theatre: Story dramatization in the classroom.* Urbana, IL: National Council of Teachers of English.

Smilansky, S. (1968). *The effects of socio-dramatic play in disadvantaged preschool children.* New York: Wiley.

Smith, C. F., & Kepner, H. S. (1981). *Reading in the mathematics classroom.* Washington, DC: National Education Association.

Smith, F. (1986). *Insult to intelligence: The bureaucratic invasion of our classrooms.* Portsmouth, NH: Heinemann.

Smith, F. (1988). *Understanding reading* (4th ed.). Hillsdale, NJ: Erlbaum.

Smith, R. J., & Johnson, D. D. (1980). *Teaching children to read.* Reading, MA: Addison-Wesley.

Smith, S. P., & Jackson, F. H. (1985). Assessing reading/learning skills with written retellings. *Journal of Reading, 28,* 622–630.

Smitherman, G. (1985). What go round come round: King in perspective. In C. K. Brooks (Ed.), *Tapping potential: English and language arts for the black learner.* Urbana, IL: National Council of Teachers of English.

Smitherman, G. (1991). "What is Africa to me?": Language, ideology, and African American. *American Speech, 66,* 115–132.

Snider, M., Lima, S., & DeVito, P. (1994). Rhode Island's literacy portfolio assessment project. In S. Valencia, E. Hiebert, & P. Afflerbach (Eds.), *Authentic reading assessment: Practices and possibilities* (pp. 71–88). Newark, DE: International Reading Association.

Solley, B. (2000). *Writers' workshop: Reflections of elementary and middle school teachers.* Boston: Allyn and Bacon.

Soto, G. (1993). *Too many tamales.* New York: Putnam.

Southgate, V. (1968). *The three billy goats gruff.* Leicestershire Learning Systems.

Spache, G. (1963). *Toward better reading.* Champaign, IL: Garrard.

Spache, G. (1976). *Diagnosing and correcting reading disabilities.* Boston: Allyn & Bacon.

Spangenberg-Urbschat, K., & Pritchard, R. (Eds.). (1994). *Kids come in all languages: Reading instruction for ESL students.* Newark, DE: International Reading Association.

Speaker, R. B., Jr., & Barnitz, J. G. (1999). Linguistic perspectives in literacy education: Electronic and linguistic connections in one diverse twenty-first century classroom. *The Reading Teacher, 52,* 874–877.

Speaker, R., & Speaker, P. (1991). Sentence collecting: Authentic literacy events in the classroom. *Journal of Reading, 35,* 92–95.

Spiegel, D. (1999). The perspective of the balanced approach. In S. Blair-Larsen, and K. Williams (Eds.), *The balanced reading program: Helping all students achieve success* (pp. 8–23). Newark, DE: International Reading Association.

Stahl, N. A., King, J. R., & Henk, W. A. (1991). Enhancing students' notetaking through training and evaluation. *Journal of Reading, 34,* 614–622.

Standards for the Arts. (1994). *Standards for the Arts.* Reston, VA: Music Educators National Conference.

Stanovich, K. E. (1980). Toward an interactive-compensatory model of individual differences in the development of reading fluency. *Reading Research Quarterly, 16,* 32–71.

Staton, J. (1987). The power of responding in journals. In T. Fulwiler (Ed.), *The journal book* (pp. 47–63). Portsmouth, NH: Heinemann.

Staton, J. (1988). Discussing problems. In J. Staton, R. W. Shuy, J. K. Peyton, & L. Reed (Eds.), *Dialogue journal communication: Classroom, linguistic, social and cognitive views* (pp. 202–244). Norwood, NJ: Ablex.

Staton, J., Shuy, R. W., Peyton, J. K., & Reed, L. (Eds.) (1988). *Dialogue journal communication: Classroom, linguistic, social and cognitive views.* Norwood, NJ: Ablex.

Stauffer, R. G. (1975). *Directing the reading-thinking process.* New York: Harper & Row.

Stauffer, R. G. (1981). Strategies for reading instruction. In M. Douglas (Ed.), *45th Yearbook of the Claremont Reading Conference.* Claremont, CA: Claremont Graduate School Curriculum Laboratory.

Steffensen, M. S. (1987). The effect of context and culture on children's L2 reading: A review. In J. Devine, P. L. Carrell, & D. E. Eskey (Eds.), *Research in reading in English as a second language* (pp. 41–54). Washington, DC: Teachers of English to Speakers of Other Languages.

Stein, N., & Glenn, C. (1979). An analysis of story comprehension in elementary school children. In R. Freedle (Ed.), *New directions in discourse processing.* Norwood, NJ: Ablex.

Sternberg, R. (1987). Most vocabulary is learned from context. In M. McKeown & M. Curtis (Eds.). *The nature of vocabulary acquisition* (pp. 89–105). Hillsdale, NJ: Erlbaum.

Sternberg, R. (1999). *Handbook of creativity.* Cambridge: University Press.

Sternberg, R. J. (1991). Are we reading too much into reading comprehension tests? *Journal of Reading, 34,* 540–545.

Stevenson, J., & Baumann, J. (1979, May). *Vocabulary development: Semantic feature analysis and semantic mapping.* Microworkshop presented at the 24th annual meeting of the International Reading Association, Atlanta, CA.

Sticht, T. G., & Beck, L. J. (1976, August). *Experimental literacy assessment battery (LAB)* (Final Rep. No. AFHRL-TR-76-51). Lowry Air Force Base, CO: Air Force Human Resources Laboratory, Technical Training Division.

Sticht, T. G., & James, J. H. (1984). Listening and reading. In P. D. Pearson (Ed.), *Handbook of reading research* (pp. 293–317). New York: Longman.

Stieglitz, E. (1997). *The Stieglitz informal reading inventory: Assessing reading behaviors from emergent to advanced levels.* Boston: Allyn & Bacon.

Stowe, C. M. (2000). *How to reach and teach students with dyslexia.* West Nyack, NY: The Center for Applied Research in Education.

Strickland, D. (2000). Classroom intervention strategies: Supporting the literacy development of young learners at risk. In D. Strickland and L. Morrow (Eds.), *Beginning reading and writing* (pp. 99–110). New York: Teachers College Press and Newark, DE: International Reading Association.

Strickland, E. (1975, October). Assignment mastery. *Reading World,* 25–31.

Strickland, K. (1995). *Literacy NOT labels: Celebrating students' strengths through whole language.* Portsmouth, NH: Boynton/Cook.

Strode, S. L. (1993). An adaptation of REAP for the developmental reader. *Journal of Reading, 36,* 568–569.

Suhor, C., & Suhor, B. (1992). *Teaching values in the literature classroom: A debate in print.* Bloomington, IN: ERIC Clearinghouse on Reading and Communication Skills, and Urbana, IL: National Council of Teachers of English.

Sulzby, E. (1985). Kindergartners as writers and readers. In M. Farr (Ed.), *Advances in writing research: Vol. 1. Children's early writing development* (pp. 127–199). Norwood, NJ: Ablex.

Sunstein, B., & Lovell, J. (2000). *The portfolio standard: How students can show us what they know and are able to do.* Portsmouth, NH: Heinemann.

Swearingen, R., & Allen, D. (1997). *Classroom assessment of reading processes.* Boston: Houghton Mifflin.

Taba, H. (1967). *Teacher's handbook for elementary social studies.* Reading, MA: Addison-Wesley.

Tadlock, D. F. (1978). SQ3R—Why it works, based on an information processing theory of learning. *Journal of Reading, 22,* 110–112.

Taylor, B. H. (1979, May). *Good and poor readers, recall of familiar and unfamiliar text.* Paper presented at the 24th annual meeting of the International Reading Association, Atlanta, GA.

Taylor, B. H., Harris, L. A., & Pearson, P. D. (1988). *Reading difficulties: Instruction and assessment.* New York: Random.

Taylor, D., & Dorsey-Gaines, C. (1988). *Growing up literate: Learning from inner-city families.* Portsmouth, NH: Heinemann.

Taylor, W. L. (1953). Cloze procedure: A new tool for measuring readability. *Journalism Quarterly, 30,* 415–433.

Teale, W. H., & Sulzby, E. (1986). (Eds.). *Emergent literacy: Writing and reading.* Norwood, NJ: Ablex.

Teale, W. H., & Sulzby, E. (1989). Emergent literacy: New perspectives. In D. S. Strickland & L. M. Morrow (Eds.), *Emerging literacy: Young children learn to read and write* (pp. 1–15). Newark, DE: International Reading Association.

Temple, C., Nathan, R., Burris, N., & Temple, F. (1988). *The beginning of writing* (2nd ed.). Boston: Allyn & Bacon.

Templeton, S. (1991). *Teaching the integrated language arts.* Boston: Houghton Mifflin.

Tharp, R., & Gallimore, R. (1988). *Rousing minds to life: Teaching, learning, and schooling in social context.* New York: Cambridge University Press.

Thelan, J. (1976). *Improving reading in science.* Newark, DE: International Reading Association.

Thomas, A., Fazio, L., & Stiefelmeyer, B. (1999a). *Families at school: A guide for educators.* Newark, DE: International Reading Association.

Thomas, A., Fazio, L., & Stiefelmeyer, B. (1999b). *Families at school: A handbook for parents.* Newark, DE: International Reading Association.

Thonis, E. W. (1976). *Literacy for America's Spanish speaking children.* Newark, DE: International Reading Association.

Thorndike, E. L. (1917). Reading as reasoning: A study of mistakes in paragraph meaning. *Journal of Educational Psychology, 8,* 323–332. (Reprinted 1971, *Reading Research Quarterly, 6,* 425–434.)

Thorndyke, P. (1977). Cognitive structures in comprehension and memory of narrative discourse. *Cognitive Psychology, 9,* 77–110.

Tiedt, I. (2000). *Teaching with picture books in the middle school.* Newark, DE: International Reading Association.

Tierney, R. J., Carter, M. A., & Desai, L. E. (1991). *Portfolio assessment in the reading-writing classroom.* Norwood, MA: Christopher-Gordon.

Tierney, R. J., & Pearson, P. D. (1994). Learning to learn from text: A framework for improving classroom practice. In R. B. Ruddell, M. R. Ruddell, & H. Singer (Eds.), *Theoretical models and processes of reading* (4th ed.) (pp. 496–513). Newark, DE: International Reading Association.

Tierney, R. J., Readence, J. E., & Dishner, E. K. (1990). *Reading strategies and practices: A compendium* (3rd ed.). Boston: Allyn & Bacon.

Tompkins, G. (1990). *Teaching writing: Balancing process and product.* New York: Macmillan.

Tompkins, G. (1994). *Teaching writing: Balancing process and product* (2nd ed.). New York: Merrill/Macmillan.

Tompkins, G., & Hoskisson, K. (1991). *The language arts curriculum: Content and teaching strategies.* New York: Merrill.

Topping, K. (1995). Cued spelling: A powerful technique for parent and peer tutoring. *The Reading Teacher, 48,* 374–383.

Trachtenburg, P. (1990). Using children's literature to enhance phonics instruction. *The Reading Teacher, 43,* 648–654.

Troike, R. C. (1972). English and the bilingual child. In D. L. Shores (Ed.), *Contemporary English: Change and variation.* Philadelphia: Lippincott.

Upton, A. (1973). *Design for thinking: A first book on semantics.* Palo Alto: Pacific Press.

U.S. Department of Health and Human Services. (2000). *Child maltreatment 1998: Reports from the states to the National Child Abuse and Neglect Data System.* Washington, DC: U.S. Government Printing Office.

Vacca, J. L., Vacca, R. T., & Gove, M. K. (1991). *Reading and learning to read* (2nd ed.). New York: HarperCollins.

Valencia, S., Hiebert, E., & Afflerbach, P. (Eds.). (1994). *Authentic reading assessment: Practices and possibilities.* Newark, DE: International Reading Association.

Valmont, W. (1972). Creating questions for informal reading inventories. *The Reading Teacher, 25,* 509–512.

Valmont, W. J. (1983). Cloze and maze instructional techniques: Differences and definitions. *Reading Psychology, 4,* 163–167.

Van Allsburg, C. (1981). *Jumanji.* New York: Houghton Mifflin.

Venezky, R. L. (1999). *The American way of spelling: The structure and origins of American English orthography.* New York: The Guilford Press.

Villaume, S , & Hopkins, L. (1995). A transactional and socio-cultural view of response in a fourth-grade literature discussion group. *Reading Research and Instruction, 34,* 190–203.

Vygotsky, L. S. (1978). *Mind in society: The development of higher psychological processes.* Cambridge, MA: Harvard University Press.

Wagoner, S. A. (1983). Comprehension monitoring: What it is and what we know about it. *Reading Research Quarterly, 17,* 328–346.

Wagner, R. K., Torgesen, J. K., & Rashotte, C. A. (1999). *Comprehensive Test of Phonological Processes.* Austin, TX: PRO-ED Publishers.

Wajnryb, R. (1990). *Grammar dictation.* Oxford, England: Oxford University Press.

Walker, B. J. (2000). *Diagnostic teaching of reading: Techniques for instruction and assessment* (4th ed.). Upper Saddle River, NJ: Merrill/Prentice-Hall.

Waller, M. B. (1992/1993). Helping crack-affected children succeed. *Educational Leadership, 50,* 57–60.

Weaver, C. (1994). *Reading process and practice: From socio-psycholinguistics to whole language.* Portsmouth, NH: Heinemann.

Weaver, C. (1998). *Teaching grammar in context.* Portsmouth, NH: Heinemann.

Whitin, P. (1996). *Sketching stories, stretching minds: Responding visually to literature.* Portsmouth, NH: Heinemann.

Whitmore, K., & Goodman, Y. (Eds.) (1996). *Whole language voices in teacher education.* York, ME: Stenhouse.

Wiesendanger, K. D., & Bader, L. (1992). SCAIT: A study technique to develop students' higher comprehension skills when reading content area material. *Journal of Reading, 35,* 399–400.

Wilde, S. (1996). Foreword. In L. Laminack & K. Wood, *Spelling in use: Looking closely in whole language classrooms* (pp. x–xi). Urbana, IL: National Council of Teachers of English.

Wilde, S. (1997). *What's a schwa sound anyway? A holistic guide to phonetics, phonics, and spelling.* Portsmouth, NH: Heinemann.

Wilhelm, J. D. (1997). *"You Gotta BE the Book.": Teaching engaged and reflective reading with adolescents.* New York: Teachers College Press.

Willford, R. (1968). Comprehension: What reading's all about. *Grade Teacher, 85,* 99–103.

Williams, J. D. (1989). *Preparing to teach writing.* Belmont, CA: Wadsworth.

Wilson, R. M. (1981). *Diagnostic and remedial reading for classroom and clinic* (4th ed.). Columbus, OH: Prentice-Hall/Merrill.

Wilt, M. (1958). A study of teacher awareness of listening as a factor in elementary education. *Journal of Educational Research, 43,* 626–636.

Winograd, P., & Johnston, P. (1980). *Comprehension monitoring and the error detection paradigm* (Tech. Rep. No. 153). Champaign: University of Illinois, Center for the Study of Reading.

Wiseman, D. (1992). *Learning to read with literature.* Boston: Allyn & Bacon.

Wolf, K. P. (1993). From informal to informed assessment: Recognizing the role of the classroom teacher. *Journal of Reading, 36,* 518–523.

Wolf, D., & Balick, D. (Eds.) (1999). *Art works! Interdisciplinary learning powered by the arts.* Portsmouth, NH: Heinemann.

Wolfe, R., & Lopez, A. (1992/1993). Structured overviews for teaching science concepts and terms. *Journal of Reading, 36,* 315–317.

Wolfram, W. (1991). *Dialects and American English.* Upper Saddle River, NJ: Prentice-Hall, Inc. and Center for Applied Linguistics.

Wolfram, W., Adger, C., & Christian, D. (1999). *Dialects in schools and communities.* Mahwah, NJ: Erlbaum.

Woods, M. L., & Moe, A. J. (1999). *Analytical reading inventory.* Columbus, OH: Prentice-Hall/Merrill.

Worthy, M. J., & Bloodgood, J. (1992/1993). Enhancing reading instruction through Cinderella tales. *The Reading Teacher, 46,* 290–301.

Wylie, R. E., & Durrell, D. D. (1970). Teaching vowels through phonograms. *Elementary English, 47,* 787–791.

(Yoon) Kim, Y. H., & Goetz, E. (1994). Context effects on word recognition and reading comprehension of poor and good readers: A test of the interactive-compensatory hypothesis. *Reading Research Quarterly, 29,* 179–187.

Yopp, H. (1995). A test for assessing phonemic awareness in young children. *The Reading Teacher, 49,* 20–29.

Yopp, H. K., & Yopp, R. H. (1996). *Oo-pples and Boo-Noo Noos: Songs and activities for phonemic awareness.* San Diego: Harcourt Brace.

Young, T., & Crow, M. (1992). Using dialogue journals to help students deal with their problems. *The Clearing House, 65,* (May/June), 307–310.

Zutell, J. (1996). The Directed Spelling Thinking Activity (DSTA): Providing an effective balance in word study instruction. *The Reading Teacher, 50,* 98–108.

Index